797,885 Books
are available to read at

www.ForgottenBooks.com

Forgotten Books' App
Available for mobile, tablet & eReader

ISBN 978-1-334-45028-0
PIBN 10664909

This book is a reproduction of an important historical work. Forgotten Books uses state-of-the-art technology to digitally reconstruct the work, preserving the original format whilst repairing imperfections present in the aged copy. In rare cases, an imperfection in the original, such as a blemish or missing page, may be replicated in our edition. We do, however, repair the vast majority of imperfections successfully; any imperfections that remain are intentionally left to preserve the state of such historical works.

Forgotten Books is a registered trademark of FB &c Ltd.
Copyright © 2015 FB &c Ltd.
FB &c Ltd, Dalton House, 60 Windsor Avenue, London, SW19 2RR.
Company number 08720141. Registered in England and Wales.

For support please visit www.forgottenbooks.com

1 MONTH OF FREE READING

at

www.ForgottenBooks.com

By purchasing this book you are eligible for one month membership to ForgottenBooks.com, giving you unlimited access to our entire collection of over 700,000 titles via our web site and mobile apps.

To claim your free month visit: www.forgottenbooks.com/free664909

* Offer is valid for 45 days from date of purchase. Terms and conditions apply.

English
Français
Deutsche
Italiano
Español
Português

www.forgottenbooks.com

Mythology Photography **Fiction** Fishing Christianity **Art** Cooking Essays Buddhism Freemasonry Medicine **Biology** Music **Ancient Egypt** Evolution Carpentry Physics Dance Geology **Mathematics** Fitness Shakespeare **Folklore** Yoga Marketing **Confidence** Immortality Biographies Poetry **Psychology** Witchcraft Electronics Chemistry History **Law** Accounting **Philosophy** Anthropology Alchemy Drama Quantum Mechanics Atheism Sexual Health **Ancient History Entrepreneurship** Languages Sport Paleontology Needlework Islam **Metaphysics** Investment Archaeology Parenting Statistics Criminology **Motivational**

Prohibition in Canada

A Memorial to
FRANCIS STEPHENS SPENCE

By
RUTH ELIZABETH SPENCE

Published by
THE ONTARIO BRANCH OF THE DOMINION ALLIANCE
TORONTO, CANADA

COPYRIGHT, CANADA, 1919
By
THE ONTARIO BRANCH OF THE DOMINION ALLIANCE

Printed and bound by
WILLIAM BRIGGS

TO
FRANCIS STEPHENS SPENCE

LOVED COMRADE, HONORED LEADER,
THIS MEMORIAL HISTORY OF THE PROHIBITION
MOVEMENT IN CANADA IS DEDICATED AS
A TRIBUTE OF RESPECT BY THE
ONTARIO BRANCH OF THE
DOMINION ALLIANCE

EDITOR'S PREFACE.

ON the eve of victory of the prohibition movement in Canada, it was felt by many that a history of that movement would form the most appropriate tribute to one whose life was spent in the service of the cause, and whose efforts contributed so largely to its triumph. The time is a fitting one for the production of such a history. Our country faces the tremendous issue of whether she shall attack her post-war problems in the full strength of a sober citizenship, or handicapped by the liquor traffic. To review the experiences of the past, to appreciate the struggles of those through whose labors we have been enabled to reach this pinnacle of opportunity, will surely strengthen our purpose and steady our hands to seize the victory now.

The purpose of the volume explains its plan. All the way through the narrative, the man to whom the book is dedicated has naturally been given prominence. In the brief philosophy of the movement presented at the outset, it is he who is speaking, and the quotations at the beginning of the sections are his. Moreover, a very large part of the uncredited narrative is from his writings in *The Canada Citizen*, *The Vanguard*, *The Camp-Fire*, *The Pioneer*, Alliance reports, and other publications, so that he who was pre-eminently the authority on the temperance movement in Canada is the virtual author of this history.

The book deals chiefly with the march of events. If too little place has been given to the men and women who made the events, it is only because, confronted by an overwhelming aggregate of happenings, one is unable to deal at all adequately with the individual contributions. There is little reference, except incidentally, to the growth of opinion. There is no attempt to argue the case for prohibition, except in so far as the presenting of the facts themselves constitutes

EDITOR'S PREFACE.

an argument. The desire has been to make the book, as far as possible, a reliable and impartial record of historical incidents; but the editor has had a keen appreciation of the historian's problem in chronicling events of recent or contemporary interest, from which the dust of controversy has not entirely blown away.

My thanks are due to the many friends who have generously helped me with information and advice. I wish specially to thank the Dominion Alliance for giving me the opportunity of sharing in this tribute to my father.

RUTH ELIZABETH SPENCE.

April 18, 1919.

CONTENTS.

	PAGE
Frontispiece.	
DEDICATION	iii
FOREWORD—J. R. DOUGALL	xi
F. S. SPENCE AT LAKE WINONA	xii
I. THE MOVEMENT AND THE MAN	1–15
II. EARLY HISTORY	17–33
1. French Régime	19
2. Early Legislation Under British Rule	27
III. ORGANIZATIONS	35–74
1. The Pledge-Signing Crusade	37
2. Fraternal Temperance Societies	46
Sons of Temperance	46
Independent Order of Good Templars	49
British American Order of Good Templars	53
Royal Templars of Temperance	54
3. Various Societies	56
4. The W.C.T.U.	61
5. The Dominion Alliance	72
Ontario Branch of the Dominion Alliance	73
IV. MAINE LAW PERIOD	75–101
1. New Brunswick	77
2. Nova Scotia	82
3. Canada	85
The Dunkin Act	91
The Ontario License Law	100

CONTENTS.

V. SCOTT ACT PERIOD . . . . . . 10.	
1. Ontario Temperance and Prohibitory League	
2. Royal Commission of 1874 . .	107
3. Formation of the Dominion Alliance	115
4. Jurisdiction Difficulty	119
5. Canada Temperance Act	122
6. The Act Established	125
7. The Act in Operation	127
8. The Issue in Parliament	133
VI. POLITICAL ACTION	139–158
1. Canada's New Party	141
2. Nova Scotia Prohibition Party	148
3. Montreal Convention, 1888	150
VII. ROYAL COMMISSION OF 1892	159–179
1. Parliamentary Action	161
2. The Commission at Work	166
3. Report of Commission	175
VIII. PROVINCIAL PLEBISCITE PERIOD	181–228
1. The North-West Experiment in Prohibition Law	183
2. Manitoba Plebiscite . . .	190
3. New Brunswick	192
4. Prince Edward Island Plebiscite	192
5. Ontario Plebiscite . .	193
The Bill	199
The Campaign . .	207
Sir Oliver Mowat's Pledge .	211
6. Nova Scotia Plebiscite	216
7. Privy Council Decision	219
8. Premier Hardy and the Harcourt Bill	222
IX. DOMINION PLEBISCITE	229–258
1. Liberal Convention of 1893 .	231
2. Dominion Election, 1896	236
3. Dominion Plebiscite Campaign .	240
4. Parliamentary Inaction	252

CONTENTS.

	PAGE
X. PROVINCIAL ACTION	259–320
1. Manitoba Referendum	261
Testing the Act	266
Referendum Campaign	268
The Vote	274
2. The Ontario Referendum	278
The Bill	284
The Campaign	292
After the Vote	300
Parliamentary Inaction	304
Election Campaign	313
The Alliance Manifesto	318
XI. PROVINCIAL PROHIBITION	321–478
1. Prince Edward Island	323
2. Nova Scotia	331
3. New Brunswick	343
The Prohibition Act	349
4. Quebec	353
Franciscan Crusade	357
License Law Amendments	363
Prohibition Bill	371
5. Ontario	381
The Three-Fifths Clause	385
License Reduction	390
License Law Amendments	391
Party Platforms	394
License Commission	397
Ontario Temperance Act	400
6. Manitoba	408
7. Saskatchewan	427
Pictures of Prohibition Progress	444
8. Alberta	446
9. British Columbia	459
10. Yukon Territory	475
XII. DOMINION PROHIBITION	479–492

CONTENTS.

		PAGE
XIII. WORLD PROGRESS	. . . . . .	493–566
America	. . . .	496

        Newfoundland—United States—Mexico Central America—South America.

    Europe 514

        Great Britain — Scotland — Ireland France—Spain and Portgual—Belgium—Holland—Denmark—Iceland—Greenland—Faroe Islands—Norway—Sweden—Russia—Finland—Greece—Serbia—Bulgaria — Roumania — Turkey — Germany—Austria-Hungary— Switzerland Italy.

    Asia 549

        India — China — Japan — Other Asiatic Countries.

    Africa 555

    Australasia 558

        Australia—New Zealand.

    International Co-operation 564

APPENDICES 567–612

INDEX 613

FOREWORD.

No nobler memorial could be erected to a man wholly devoted to his generation, and particularly to one great reform, than to link his name with a history of the cause in which he spent himself. He was worthy for whom this is here done. The movement for the deliverance of society from its most destructive foe had had an exuberant springtime before the day of Frank Spence. He was indeed one of the robust fruits of that copious flowering.

The apostolates of Father Matthew in Ireland, of Father Chiniquy in Canada, of the Washingtonians in the United States, are examples of movements that might well be called national; and though the fire of them may later have burned low, they left the world with a new conscience—a knowledge of good and evil to which its eyes had not been open before. The movement to express this new conscience in law had to follow hard upon the effort at persuasion. Those fighting a public curse could not be parties to its formal sanction by the governments for which, as free citizens, they were responsible. Even for the continuance of indoctrination it was psychologically necessary to have a goal toward which to strive. The prohibition movement that had its beginning in the State of Maine spread rapidly. The neighboring states and provinces declared for prohibition, including the Province of New Brunswick, which actually passed a prohibitory law, and the Province of Canada, whose Parliament only passed a resolution. Had it been possible to drive evil from the world, either by declaring it to be evil, or by forbidding it, the end would have been gained long ago. The discovery was soon made that men are prone to evil, and that to save them from it they must be saved from themselves.

It was at the time when this long conflict between good and evil had become a chronic condition that the hero to

FOREWORD.

whom this work is dedicated took the field as a chosen leader. He was the man to put a stout heart to a stiff hill, and to find in all rebuffs an incentive to new devotion and to more trained and experienced leadership. He was the Greatheart of the war—knightly in his stern repelling, as a public man, of every appeal to his personal interest with a "Get thee behind me, Satan"; knightly in his self-forgetfulness and meekness in the presence of detraction, not only from quarters where he might well look for it, but also from quarters where he might have looked for loyal sympathy, if not in all things for agreement. With one high purpose, he determinedly ignored injuries and readily effaced himself whenever he imagined the need for unity of effort bade him or the organization which bore the grime of battle and of hard knocks, stand aside. But as the tides rose and fell, the Dominion Alliance with its chieftain was still there, sound and unshaken. His mantle is on other shoulders; his good lance is in trusty hands; and the victory whose light shone unwavering in his face is still beckoning.

J. R. DOUGALL.

Montreal, May 1, 1919.

F. S. SPENCE AT LAKE WINONA.

The story of the fight against the liquor power is the same in Canada as it is in the United States, and as it is throughout all Christendom. It is a story of *stern* effort and steady progress, to which there can be only one result. The temperance cause is winning; the temperance cause will win. Lack of confidence in this certainty is the result of a failure to understand the end of the movement. That movement is not a mere human invention or fake, created by some novelty-seeking cranks. It is the inevitable result of great universal conditions and forces. Wherever you find an evil of any kind, something that curses and hurts humanity, and into contact with that evil you bring men and women of Christian character, unselfish thought, and earnest purpose, there you have the elements of a moral reform. That reform will spring from those conditions, and will inevitably and irresistibly go on, until either the moral purpose dies out or the evil is overthrown. This is the origin of this great reform; the awful curse of intemperance and the God-given desire to be rid of it. Therefore if you could wipe the whole movement out of existence, with all its literature, its agencies, its methods and forms, but leave the curse and the God-inspired purpose, you would have the whole history over again. Progressing through all the stages it has passed, that movement would come to exactly the same position in which it stands to-day, and go on to the future victory that lies ahead, and we trust not very far away. Just as surely as to-morrow will follow to-day, so surely will the suppression of the liquor traffic follow the *unholy* system of encouraging, of protecting and licensing that traffic by *so-called*—and shamefully miscalled—*Christian legislation*.

The progress of this great reform has been almost unparalleled in the world's history. Even the supreme reform of

F. S. SPENCE AT LAKE WINONA.

Christianity did not make, in the same period of time, as much advance as the temperance cause has made. Think of the fact that one hundred years ago to-day there did not exist a temperance society as we understand the term. Uncensured and uncriticized, the liquor traffic was dominant everywhere. Drunkenness was so common as to call forth little comment and to involve practically no disgrace. Incredible vice and degradation prevailed. The idea of legislating to remedy the curse had no advocates. Look at our position now. Every Church inculcates temperance. Every corner of Christendom has its temperance society. Inebriety is a disgrace and is looked upon as a disqualification in any applicant for employment or any candidate for public position or favor. The statute books of every civilized nation are filled with laws for the regulation of the traffic and for the restraint and punishment of the vice. To-day there are living under prohibitory laws more people than were in the whole British Empire when the temperance movement was inaugurated. No one claims that this progress has been unvarying or unmarked by defects and weaknesses. Although it is God's cause, and therefore certain to triumph, it is promoted and carried on by human instrumentalities; therefore mistakes will certainly occur, but these are not always disasters. Men learn by blundering. Up the ladder of failure they climb to the platform of success. To a certain extent we are wise to-day because of our ignorance of yesterday. We were guilty of folly which brought its own penalties, from which we gathered knowledge. This is the experience of every man, every movement, every community. Every institution and appliance of our modern civilization has come from some experiment that resulted in failure out of which grew knowledge that led to success.

The temperance movement is no exception. Earnest men who never dreamed of total abstinence, deplored the evils of drunkenness, and set out to remedy them by advocating a moderate use of intoxicating liquors. To their minds drunkenness was the evil with which they had to deal. It did not cross their

F. S. SPENCE AT LAKE WINONA.

minds that there was anything wrong in drinking. More is known to-day of the nature and effects of alcoholic liquors. We know that lives may be shortened, health impaired, money wasted, moral character lowered, by the drinking of men who are never seen drunk. The early temperance reformers started out to remedy the evil of drunkenness by promoting what they considered to be wise kinds of drinking. Sometimes they tried pledges against anything but moderate indulgence in intoxicants. Sometimes they tried abstinence from ardent spirits, and encouragement of lighter beverages. They failed, but in their efforts they learned that drunkenness grew out of liquor drinking, and that if lager beer and light wines were tolerated the worst forms of drink would be sold under false names. Driven by the logic of the effects that they could not ignore, they boldly struck all permissions out of their pledges and came up to the position of total abstinence in which all consistent, well-informed temperance men stand to-day.

When this point was reached, they thought that they had solved the problem, but they found themselves still facing failure. The evil they opposed had a two-fold character; it was popular and legal. Wrong customs and ideas can only be met by moral suasion and total abstinence practices. The law protecting the liquor traffic can only be opposed by political action. The law provided temptation, and lured the reformed drunkard back to the abyss from which he had been rescued. Legalized liquor-selling trained the youth to believe that alcoholic indulgence was proper and safe. Driven again by stern necessity, the temperance reformers broadened their plans, enlarged their programme, and hoisted the battle flag of " total abstinence for the individual and total prohibition for the community."

That flag floats over the fighting line to-day. We are told to remedy intemperance by moral suasion. What use is moral suasion, while the forces of law and government are arrayed in defence of the liquor evil? Some people believe that prohibitory legislation alone will be effective. This is another blunder. Prohibitory law is the embodiment of public

F. S. SPENCE AT LAKE WINONA.

opinion, without which that law cannot be secured, and would not be of any value if secured. Law is the machinery that, operated and wisely guided, will accomplish results. Public opinion is the motive power that drives the machinery. Without both, success is impossible.

Further experience has taught us that the law, the effective machinery, impelled by public opinion, the motive power, must be wisely and honestly directed if good work is to be done. We have seen prohibitory laws backed by strong expressions of popular sentiment, administered by unsympathetic or dishonest officials; and again we have had to acknowledge failure because of human weakness and lack of previous knowledge to guide preparation for the emergency.

Thus, after years of study, experience, failure, knowledge, success, we stand to-day in a position logically and practically far ahead of any we occupied before. We know that to win in this great struggle we must have, firstly, sound sentiment in the community, and secondly, wise laws on the statute books, and thirdly, honest administration of the law when it is enacted. When these three essentials are secured, the temperance reform will be a success. It never will be while any of them is lacking.

—*Address by F. S. Spence at Lake Winona, Ind., July 17, 1908.*

SECTION I.

THE MOVEMENT AND THE MAN.

HIS LAST "COPY."

NOTE.—Uppermost on a batch of copy left by Mr. F. S. Spence, prepared for the printer, was the following:—

" *When I am dead, if men can say*
'He helped the world upon its way'—
If they can say—if they but can—
'He did his best; he played the man;
His way was straight; his soul was clean;
His failings not unkind, nor mean;
He loved his fellow men, and tried
To help them,' I'll be satisfied."

—WHITTIER.

Prohibition in Canada.

THE MOVEMENT AND THE MAN

THE prohibition movement, which is affecting to-day all parts of the social structure, has employed the energies of very many men and women interested in diverse features of public weal: legislators concerned with social and economic matters; ministers of the Gospel, confronted with the moral aspect; scientists, absorbed in both medical and industrial problems; business men, with commercial interests. The flood which is sweeping on to ocean in its mighty strength has gathered to itself many tributaries of individual effort. It is so with every reform; the movement is mightier than the man. A leader, while he may do much to inspire, is powerless to achieve until he has at last behind him an overwhelming popular conviction.

Yet in almost every historic line of progress there is some person who, because of circumstances, social, geographical, or chronological, has a particular part to play. In the history of the temperance reform in Canada a place of special prominence is held by F. S. Spence. While he worked among the people, even more at his death, they called him leader; they could erect to his memory no more eloquent memorial. Many devoted men gave themselves to the cause before he was born; he did not see with mortal vision the consummation of national prohibition; and to others it is left to consolidate the victory and to ensure that the salvation dearly bought be not lost again. But to F. S. Spence was given a peculiar task, a unique place in the movement.

He entered the field of action as a young man, with the glorious daring of youth, just at a time when impetus and ardor and faith and fiery zeal were all-important. The Dunkin Act period was drawing to a close. That first attempt at prohibitory legislation was revealing weaknesses and suggesting failure. Something new was being started in the Scott Act, which was yet to be tried out. Through the days when the temperance movement needed above all things contagious enthusiasm, F. S. Spence had it to give. He never lost that, but he acquired other things in their season. During the long period of delay, litigation, plodding, promise of victory, and hope deferred, he brought to the cause the strength and courage and patience of maturity. When the ship was entering the harbor of provincial prohibition, he was a pilot with the wisdom of the years to steer it through the intricate channels of the port. And to-day his influence surely lives, giving the inspiration that must not now be allowed to fail. The history of this movement that had a hundred heroes is not the place for a story of his life. Neither would his biography, written exclusively from the viewpoint of the temperance reform, be a well-balanced estimate of the man himself. In one sense it is true that his life synchronized remarkably with the temperance movement during its most important period, and that the record of his activities would give a comparatively accurate outline of the march of events. For from the time when he gave himself to the work, until his passing, there was scarcely a detail of significance, certainly not a happening of national importance, with which he was not connected; and in many local conflicts, apart from his own particular place in the battle-line, he lent a hand.

But the temperance movement did not comprise the whole life of F. S. Spence. While there was an essential unity in his interests, they had a breadth and scope not to be comprehended in any one phase. He was a social reformer. His heart was set on the bringing in of the kingdom of righteousness upon earth. He agreed with Richard Cobden that " the temperance reform lies at the basis of all other reforms." That accomplished, the way would be cleared for many another that demands the consecrated service of a highly

THE MOVEMENT AND THE MAN.

developed and ennobled humanity for its realization. Therefore he gave himself first of all to the cause of temperance; the best he had was laid upon that altar. In many fields of activity, however, he found opportunity of working out his ideal of civic righteousness. For instance, his interest in municipal reform was second only to advocacy of the temperance cause. He first began to serve Toronto's civic life on the School Board in 1887. In 1896 he took a place in the City Council, where he sat as alderman or controller almost continuously until 1915. He was at various times president, vice-president and secretary of the Ontario and Canadian Municipal Associations and vice-president of the Union of American Municipalities. Systematically, thoroughly, he studied to make himself a wise, broad-minded and efficient civic administrator, until he was acknowledged, not only throughout this land but internationally, as an outstanding authority on municipal affairs.

Without any attempt, then, at biography, it may not be inopportune to suggest some of the outstanding characteristics which gave the man his recognized position in Canada during thirty-five years of the fight for national prohibition.

The primary source of his strength lay in whole-souled consecration to his work. Very early in life he saw a vision of God's plan for working righteousness through human instrumentality. That purpose inspired his ideals; for its service his gifts of heart and head were developed; to its accomplishment his span of mortality was offered. The force that sustained that consecration was faith in God and His power and in man and his potentialities, the faith that is the substance of things hoped for, the element of which are born the souls of prophets. And closely connected with his faith was the quality by which, probably, he was the most commonly known and the one for which he was best loved, old-fashioned, scriptural Christian charity. It was a vital article of his creed.

I remember well his discussing on one occasion the American revised version of the thirteenth chapter of First

PROHIBITION IN CANADA.

Corinthians, with its rendering of faith, hope, and love. He thought the translation not a good one. Love, he said, is less than charity. Love is subjective; it is limited to its own; it elicits a return; it has received its reward. Charity which extends to all men, which as often as not is absolutely unreciprocated, rises above every suggestion of self, and hence is the highest expression of the Spirit of Christ.

"Frank Spence was kind." It was because he looked beyond trivialities in people and circumstances and saw the great issues, that he never felt antagonism to individuals, even when he had to oppose vehemently the things for which they stood. His bitterest opponents had to acknowledge his chivalry, and they were often among his most sincere admirers.

These three fundamentals, then—consecration, faith, and Christian charity—were the warp on which the pattern of his life was woven. They cannot be dissociated.

Service was the unalterable standard by which he measured all things—to work for the good of humanity the purpose of his existence. In taking civic office, for instance, he sought to serve the people; but it was his faith that they could be truly served only by fidelity to the highest ideals of righteousness. Thus his sole election promise was that he would do what he believed to be right. In the municipal elections of 1905, the question of reducing the number of licenses in Toronto was to be submitted to the people's vote, and during the campaign Mr. Spence, who was a mayoralty candidate, was asked—somewhat superfluously—what would be his attitude on the question in council. If the vote of the people should be against the reduction, would he try to carry out the will of the majority? "You ask me, if the people do wrong, will I do wrong?" was the measure of his democracy.

"Our characters need in these days the element of the stern iron of an intolerant hatred of wrong. We should be more fearful of compromising with evil than of antagonizing iniquity and its sympathizers." This was the standard he set for himself.

THE MOVEMENT AND THE MAN.

If a matter received his support in council it was because he believed in the intrinsic merit of the case. He considered as an insult any suggestion that he take a certain course for the sake of the popular support it would command. On one occasion a group of city employees waited upon him in his office to seek his help in a certain project. He gave their case the careful, courteous consideration which he always showed, when in the course of the conversation one of the men hinted that the group represented a considerable number of municipal votes, and election day was approaching. "Gentlemen, good afternoon," he said, and closed the interview.

He carried that refusal to seek popularity to the extreme of a refusal to defend himself at the expense of others. Here is a personal letter written the day after a municipal election:

"Dear Sir,—

"You wrote me a note during the recent election about action which you thought I had taken in council.

"I did not reply at the time, as I am always averse to anything that would look like favoring or opposing any proposition for the sake of votes on any ground except that of my own judgment and convictions. It is fair, however, after the election to say that you were mistaken in your criticism, as the alderman whose voting you referred to was another person whose name was the same as mine. I was not in the council at the time the matter you mentioned was dealt with."

He believed in fair play, fair play for those handicapped by circumstances of birth or nationality or education; fair play for little children born to the sordidness of the city streets—and he worked to have playgrounds established; fair play for women, and he advocated woman suffrage; fair play for the policemen, and he insisted upon their having a day of rest; fair play for the soldiers' wives, and he worked out the scheme of municipal insurance of soldiers. Because he was known to be the champion of the needy, he was beset with requests for assistance, and his position for many years in civic life gave him numerous opportunities of helping, for which he was never too busy. Sometimes it required considerable tact to make his position clear to those who had not been trained to such absolute disinterestedness of motive. A Chinaman, for whom he had helped to secure a laundry license, in sincere gratitude sent Mr. Spence a rather handsome gift in token of appreciation, which was forthwith returned with a kind note. Evidently Mr. Spence succeeded in making himself understood in that case, for he received the next day the following reply:

"Dear Sir,—

"We think send a little thing for present to my Friend. You return the goods to me on yesterday. You very justice."

His tenacity of principle and his readiness to fight for it are well illustrated by the occasion of the issue of the widening of Strachan Avenue. He favored the project and supported it vigorously in council, but it was defeated and an agreement was made with a certain firm upon the basis of the narrower street. Then a new council saw that it would be an advantage to the city to have the street widened, albeit to the detriment of the firm which had received the city's bond. The question was fought out in council again, F. S. Spence this time opposing the widening as vigorously as before he had favored it. "Inconsistent," jeered his critics, but he was keeping the pledge of the city. There was no differentiation with him between personal and civic morality.

The oneness of his purpose and the singleness of his aim might perhaps have been expected to bias his judgment. He had indeed all the zeal of a fanatic, but he had the clear-headedness, the coolness and the equipoise that are not usually associated with the term. The explanation lies in the fact that not only was he an enthusiast but he was a student of the problems with which he dealt. Thoroughness and accuracy to a degree marked his methods of study in little things and big. Thus with his knowledge of detail and his grasp of the whole, he was frequently compelled to check

THE MOVEMENT AND THE MAN.

the precipitancy of those who had looked at a question from only one side or who had failed to weigh and ponder all the considerations. As some one put it, he was the balance-wheel, steadying the machinery and keeping it nicely adjusted.

Liberal by training and conviction, he was sometimes accused by those who opposed his temperance policy of being politically biassed and of sacrificing the temperance cause to the Liberal party. He did identify himself with that party, because he believed it best represented many things for which he worked, but no one had a greater scorn than he for party servility or insisted more stringently upon the necessity for independent thinking. The Alliance manifesto of 1904, one of the mightiest denunciations ever hurled against a political party in Canada, when the Ontario Liberal Government was held up to condemnation for its breach of faith, was prepared and signed by F. S. Spence. Moreover, as a matter of fact, in spite of his liberal principles, all his life he acted as the conservative force in the prohibition ranks, restraining impulses toward unwise radicalism. Every break made in the line was by those who wanted to go faster, who lost patience with the steady, methodical progress, and who were continually finding new schemes which they believed would accomplish results over-night. To such he was an obstructionist.

In 1883, in the early days of the strenuous Scott Act fights, he wrote:

"Good and evil are so continually found together that the utmost care is needed to distinguish between them. The good is overlooked in reckless condemnation of the connected evil, and we pull up the tares and the wheat together. Herein is the weakest point of moral enterprise. We crusade with iconoclastic zeal against prejudices without appreciating the solidity of the foundations upon which they rest, and waste our strength on making them broader and stronger. We vainly and foolishly fight the flood when we might seek out the source and close the sluice-gates.

"Herein is an important lesson for would-be radicals. To be a good reformer you must first be a staunch conservative, and when you would assail some citadel of wrong, first inquire of what right it is a perversion, for a misstated truth is the stronghold of every lie."

It took discernment to detect the fallacies of enthusiastic revolutionaries and skill to guide without quenching enthusiasm. It took patience to be calm and await the orderly development of things, but it was the calmness of power under a mighty control, not the quiescence of inertia. There was nothing of indifference in the man who breathed this spirit:

"Procrastination is the curse of our temperance reform. It is the besetting sin of the workers of this generation. It is the great enemy to human progress. Difficulties will never disappear by non-resistance. Battles will never be won by passivity. A courageous commencement will tremendously tell in all battles of right."

He had the sanity of the "long view." That was the secret of his undaunted optimism. He wrote:

"To measure progress rightly, it is necessary to take an adequate period of time and compare the conditions at the beginning of that period with the conditions at its termination. A man's lifetime is a little part of the world's history, yet the lifetime of many a man has seen changes in the habits of the people, advance in legislation, and other features of temperance progress that are little short of marvelous.

"Were we to be brought face to face with the conditions that existed in this country one-half a century ago, we would be full of gratitude for the great improvement that has been achieved. The progress has been steady. It is still going on. In the facts that surround us, we have multiplied reasons to 'thank God and take courage.'

"All these ought to give us an inspiration to continued and earnest activity. We have experience that 'worketh hope.' That assurance of result of our labors is in itself sufficient reward for all the sacrifices that we make. Better things than we have dreamed of are coming. The liquor traffic will be overthrown. Righteous laws for the suppression of intemperance will be well enforced. Public opinion will be so overwhelmingly in favor of

THE MOVEMENT AND THE MAN.

right customs and right legislation that men and women will be ashamed to drink and afraid to sell.

"This is no fanatical vision. The attainment of such a result during the next fifty years would be no more miraculous than the attainment of the results of the last fifty years.

"Apart from all this, we have sufficient encouragement to beget confidence in the manifest nature of our cause. Even if the efforts made had not produced such splendid fruits, they would have certainty of success in the fact of their motive and object. What an ennobling aim is that of true Christian philanthropy. The temperance reform is rooted and grounded in hatred of evil and earnest desire for the welfare of humanity. From such a source can come only good."

The sense of proportion that came with breadth of vision was one of his most useful qualities as a leader. It was said of him: "When he spoke as a practical man his utterances were surcharged with idealism, and when he spoke as an idealist he stood upon a firm basis of practical experience."

Again, mastery of his subject, added to the heritage of a logical brain, made him of service as a public exponent of the temperance cause on the platform and in the press.

A student by birth, probably the individual effort and discipline necessitated by self-instruction gave to natural ability a peculiar power of memory capacity and a system and orderliness of thinking that were invaluable. He had the debater's power of analysis, and he was often charged with being a destructive critic. But those who saw him only in that light had not caught the glow of his passion to achieve, to make of his faith a reality. Such zeal as his is essentially positive. Apart from the temperance movement, the Hydro-Electric System of Ontario to-day bears witness to his constructive ability, and Toronto's new water-front, which he helped largely to plan, will be a lasting testimony to a power of vision that was strong to create.

With the eloquence of the orator, he had the ability of the executive officer, and that genius which consists in an infinite capacity for hard work. His labors were literally unceasing from the time that he took up the burden. A cursory outline

PROHIBITION IN CANADA.

of the positions he held may give some idea of the magnitude of his work.

In 1883 he officially entered temperance work as manager and editor of the *Canada Citizen,* a weekly newspaper that had been published since 1880 and was being reorganized. He edited it until 1889. This was the Scott Act period. In the voting campaigns he did yeoman service, particularly in public debates with the liquor champions.

In January, 1884, Mr. Spence was made Secretary of the Council of the Dominion Alliance, and in March of the same year was also elected Secretary of the Ontario Branch. When the reaction against the Scott Act set in during the years 1886-8, he was one of the bravest defenders of the measure; and when county after county repealed the act, instead of accepting this verdict as final defeat, with characteristic Irish pugnacity he planned for further fighting

Through his efforts, in 1890 the Ontario Legislature re-enacted local option, and a campaign was started to secure the passing of that measure by municipalities throughout the province.

In 1892, when the Dominion Parliament appointed a Royal Commission to investigate the whole prohibition situation, the united temperance organizations chose Mr. Spence to represent them before the Commission, and the great volume of testimony favorable to prohibition that was presented to the Commission was largely due to his untiring effort. When the report of the Commission was presented he prepared a summary of the evidence, at the request of the temperance people, and this book, "The Facts of the Case," has since been the standard reference work of the temperance forces in Canada.

In 1894, when the Ontario Government took a provincial plebiscite upon the prohibition question, Mr. Spence was chosen secretary and general manager of the union committee of temperance workers formed to carry on the campaign. In 1898, at the time of the Dominion plebiscite, a campaign committee was formed to co-ordinate the work in the various

THE MOVEMENT AND THE MAN.

provinces, and again the choice for campaign manager fell upon him.

In 1902 he led the Ontario referendum campaign. Since 1895 he had edited a small weekly, *The Camp Fire*. In 1902, feeling the need for a bigger and more influential publication, he undertook *The Pioneer*. There was not money at the time in the Alliance treasury to finance the enterprise, but some friends were interested and saw that the funds were raised to pay the printer for two years, when the Alliance felt able to take over the paper as its official organ.

In the years following 1903 came the local option period of temperance history in the Province of Ontario, and each year from that time until 1916 fights were carried on in various municipalities. The outstanding figure during this entire period, the man who was naturally looked to for guidance, who furnished the ammunition for the men on the firing line, was F. S. Spence. Nearly every Sunday of those years, following a week of steady grind at the office, he was in the pulpit two or three times. Many times he travelled the length and breadth of the land, and even crossed the sea, in the service of the cause. His energy and vitality were marvellous. They were only one evidence of that iron self-control that increased a thousandfold the usefulness of all his consecrated powers.

He was always one of the spokesmen for the multitudinous deputations to Provincial Legislature and Dominion Parliament when the temperance people, with unfailing importunity, repeated their request for prohibitory legislation; and when the Ontario Temperance Act finally passed the Legislature he was present and was one of the first to offer his congratulations to the Government.

In 1907 he gave up the secretaryship of the Ontario Branch of the Dominion Alliance and was made honorary president, and later honorary president of the Dominion Council. With the carrying of the provincial measure there came the growing need for emphasis upon Dominion prohibition, and the moving spirit in the "On to Ottawa" campaign

PROHIBITION IN CANADA.

was Mr. F. S. Spence. He took part in the formation of the Dominion Prohibition Committee, of which he was a member, and he was also a member of the sub-executive. He it was who prepared the manifesto sent out by this committee, and upon his death-bed he revised the proofs of that magnificent document.

He had set out with an ideal of serving other people, and he very soon acquired the habit of simply ignoring himself. That explained a great deal. His humility, for instance, was not the humility which shrinks from undertaking in the dread of failure and is only another name for coddled self-esteem, but the humility which values personal talents simply at their worth to the cause and offers them willingly. His consideration for others may be well illustrated perhaps by an incident of his last municipal election campaign.

During the campaign, a not unusual series of roorbacks had appeared in a section of the press that was unsympathetic with Mr. Spence, and the attack was so peculiarly virulent that a group of representative ministers of the city felt impelled to take up the question. They prepared a circular containing extracts from the objectionable editorial, extracts from Mr. Spence's public utterances which had been distorted, and an open letter over their signatures to electors explaining the situation. The letter read as follows:

"Toronto, December 23, 1916.

"Dear Sir and Brother,—

"Permit us to call your attention to a particularly offensive and unfair editorial in last night's ———, and to set before you some facts in connection with the matter discussed.

"One of the accompanying sheets gives extracts from the editorial referred to, the other quotations from public utterances of Mr. F. S. Spence. These speak for themselves.

"No man in Canada commands in a greater degree the confidence and esteem of temperance citizens, regardless of their party preferences, than does Frank Spence. His life and singular talents have been unselfishly devoted to the temperance reform.

"For years Mr. Spence battled heroically against tremendous

THE MOVEMENT AND THE MAN.

difficulties, yet never flinched and never trimmed. In the fight he earned the enmity of unscrupulous politicians in both party camps, and at the same time the gratitude and respect of the thousands who to-day rejoice in victory won.

"We strongly resent this uncalled-for attack and brand it as unworthy of the consideration of right-loving citizens, and cannot help observing the significant fact that it comes from the only 'daily' in Toronto that now accepts liquor advertising.

"Personally we propose to take occasion to refer to the matter publicly in a suitable way, and feel it our duty to place the facts before our fellow citizens."

Before the circulars were sent out, however, Mr. Spence learned of the plan and, deeply grateful for the solicitation of his friends, he refused to allow them to proceed, lest on account of their public and official positions they might be injured by complication in the affair.

One quality of the man which perhaps should have been mentioned first because of the way it gleamed and glinted through every other, or again one which scarcely need be mentioned at all, so surely is its presence tacitly implied by the nature of the rest, was his humor. This Celtic birthright was connected with keenness of intellect and proved invaluable to him on the platform. But there were in it such qualities of the heart as sympathy and sensitiveness, so that it was never bitter and never unkind. Proof of its genuineness lay in his ability to laugh with others and at himself. It was a humor born of optimism, and often it cleared a murky atmosphere or helped over a rocky road. To many, the most vivid memory of F. S. Spence will be of the winning smile lighting up the earnest eyes and speaking a message of kindliness, confidence and brave good cheer.

To him, and to all those, his comrades in the battle, we may pass on the triumphant word of John Oxenham to the soldiers of another war:

"Here or hereafter, you shall see it ended,
  This purpose high to which your souls are set·
If from beyond—then, with the vision splendid,
  You shall smile back, and never know regret."

SECTION II.

EARLY HISTORY

The history of civil government and governmental methods, records no more complete failure than that which has invariably attended all efforts to regulate admitted evils. Slavery, gambling, social vice, the liquor traffic, have all developed their worst features and produced their worst results under legislation enacted with the avowed object of controlling them and making them revenue productive.

I. THE FRENCH REGIME.

FROM the early days of French rule, the liquor traffic has created one of the most serious problems of government in Canada. The story of the white man's relations with the Indians of North America, how he took a fair land and gave in exchange the blessings of a Christian civilization, has many sad chapters of selfish exploitation, not the least sad of which is that of the introduction of intemperance.

Père de Rochemontaix, in a history of "The Jesuits and New France in the Seventeenth Century," is authority for the statement that prior to the taking of Quebec by the English, in 1629, drunken disorders amongst the Indians were never heard of. The English, he says, introduced fire-water in exchange for furs, and the French traders, on coming back to Quebec in 1632, continued a practice which they found already established. But whether or not the French are justified in thus disclaiming initial responsibility for the introduction of the evil, at any rate brandy was very early made the chief source of profit in the French and Indian fur trade, in spite of the express prohibition of the governors and the strong opposition of the Church.

Bishop Laval and the Jesuit missionaries from the start set themselves with untiring vigor and determination to save the newly-discovered country from the curse of intoxication brought in the wake of the Europeans. Honor must be given, in a history of Canada's temperance reform, to those first temperance workers, although, in the face of the heartless cupidity of fur-traders and royal ministers, their efforts for the time being did not avail. But their labors bore fruit at a later date, for the Indians were the first people of Canada to receive protection by law from the ravages of the liquor traffic.

The Indians showed a peculiar susceptibility to the dangers of intemperance. They drank for the express purpose of

PROHIBITION IN CANADA.

becoming completely intoxicated; and if the supply of brandy in a council or friendly gathering was insufficient for all present to attain this desired end, they would apportion the liquor to the few of the number for whom it would suffice, so that all, at one time or another, might be granted the privilege of making themselves madly drunk. In that condition an Indian was like a wild beast and was held as irresponsible as one, and absolved by his countrymen from all guilt. Early records are filled with descriptions of the crime and violence resulting from the Indians' inordinate passion for liquor.

"Pagans and converts give themselves up to the most deplorable excesses of immorality and barbarism. Songs of joy are always followed by most shameful excesses—cries, howls, quarrels, bloody fights. Blood flows at the feast. The women get drunk like the men and resemble veritable furies. Nothing more horrible can be imagined than a wigwam of braves, awakening the day after the carousal to find themselves disfigured, crushed, surrounded sometimes by the dead bodies of their relatives or of their friends." (Rochemontaix.)

These debauches occurred not only in the St. Lawrence trading posts, but in the forests, where liquor was carried by the *coureurs de bois* and where the evil was beyond all regulation, and even around the outposts of the Algonquin missions on the Northern Lakes, where the soldiers of the garrisons sent out by the Governor were granted special trading privileges in part payment for their services.

At the beginning of the French period, while New France was pre-eminently a mission field and the supremacy of the Church's authority was as yet unchallenged, the opposition of the Jesuits to the sale of liquor produced considerable results. Parkman, in "The Old Régime in Canada," gives an account of a temperance meeting held at the mission of Sillery in the summer of 1648—" the first in all probability on this continent."

"The drum beat after mass, and the Indians gathered at the summons. Then an Algonquin chief, a zealous convert of the

EARLY HISTORY.

Jesuits, proclaimed to the crowd a late edict of the Governor, imposing penalties for drunkenness, and in his own name and that of the other chiefs exhorted them to abstinence, declaring that all drunkards should be handed over to the French for punishment. Father Jérome Lalemant looked on delighted. 'It was,' he says, 'the finest public act of jurisdiction exercised among the Indians since I have been in this country. From the beginning of the world they have all thought themselves as great lords, the one as the other, and never before submitted to their chiefs any further than they chose to do so.'"

On March 7, 1657, an edict was issued by Louis XIV, prohibiting all sale of liquor to the Indians, the prohibition to extend "to all ranks and classes in the community, whether high or low." The penalty for violation of the law was, for the first offence, three hundred livres, one-third of which went to the informer, one-third to the *Hôtel Dieu,* and one-third to the royal treasury. Furthermore, the law-breakers were to be subjected to corporal punishment and placed under the censures of the Church.

"The Jesuits entered with a high hand on the work of reform. It fared hard with the culprit caught in the act of selling brandy to the Indians. They led him after the sermon to the door of the church where, kneeling on the pavement, partially stript and bearing in his hand the penitential torch, he underwent a vigorous flagellation laid on by Father le Mercier himself, after the fashion formerly practised in the case of refractory schoolboys." (Parkman.)

But neither fines nor chastisement sufficed to bridle the avarice of the liquor dealers, and in **1660** Bishop Laval resorted to a supreme method of punishment. After consultation with the Jesuits on February 24, 1660, he issued the sentence of excommunication against those who indulged in the traffic, and besides the spiritual penalty for law-breakers the sentence of death was decreed. Moreover, to insure the rigid enforcement of the decree, the Bishop made of the offence *un cas reservé*—that is to say, the right of absolution in a case of this kind rested with him alone.

PROHIBITION IN CANADA.

This action was taken by Laval just before a change of governors, and the new governor, Baron d'Avaugour, anxious to conciliate the influential Jesuits at the outset of his administration, at first enforced the law. Shortly after his arrival, it is recorded, two men were shot and one whipped for selling brandy to the Indians. For a time these methods proved efficacious. Father Lalemant wrote some months later, "The disorders have no more appeared since the excommunication, so great has been the blessing of Heaven upon it." The law met with the approval of earnest Indian converts, as well as of a good many right-minded settlers at Quebec; but it was generally unpopular, for the majority in the settlement were in some way or other interested in the liquor trade, and thus liable to the most severe penalties. After a short period of vigorous enforcement, an occasion arose which gave to Governor d'Avaugour the opportunity, apparently long desired, of opposing the Jesuits and annulling the law.

A woman at Quebec was convicted of selling brandy to the Indians and sent to prison by the Governor. When Father Lalemant, moved by the prayers of her relatives and friends, interceded for her, d'Avaugour, in a fit of ill-temper, replied

"You and your brethren were the first to cry out against the trade, and now you want to save the traders from punishment. I will no longer be the sport for your contradiction. Since the traffic in fire-water is not a punishable offence for this woman, it shall henceforth not be such for anyone."

There was an immediate and violent reaction. Liberty became license; the neophytes over whom the missionaries had labored became apostates; the most terrible conditions of vice and violence prevailed. Laval, in great sorrow and indignation, launched excommunications against the offenders. Bishop, Jesuits, and lay priests appealed to the Governor to rescind his order. But d'Avaugour made it a point of honor not to retract, and so intense was the popular fury against the Church that Laval was forced to yield and

EARLY HISTORY.

to revoke his sentence of excommunication just two years after it had been issued.

The Governor persistently ignored the fearful disorders that followed his action, and Laval, discouraged, went to France to report the situation and to secure the recall of d'Avaugour. He found Louis XIV not altogether sympathetic. Complaints had been sent from liquor dealers in Canada that the ecclesiastical authority was encroaching upon the civil jurisdiction. Moreover, Colbert, the keen Finance Minister of the King, was convinced that it was necessary to allow the sale of fire-water to the Indians in order to retain their allegiance. However, in 1663 Laval persuaded the monarch to forbid once again the sale of brandy to the Indians and to recall the troublesome d'Avaugour.

Upon his return, the bishop found a temporary and interesting reformation of his flock, due to the thorough fright sustained by the colony over a severe earthquake and landslide. The marvellous occurrences of blazing serpents—a globe of flame—fiery figures in the air—of which vivid accounts are given in contemporary documents, were regarded by the terrified sinners as the direct warning of Heaven against their misdeeds, and there was a sudden and intense, though short-lived, religious revival.

The new Governor, Mézy, began bravely by announcing a penalty of £300 for the first offence and chastisement or banishment for repeated occurrences of sale to Indians; but this order was rescinded the next year. The fact is that there was beginning to be felt a serious rivalry between the Crown and the Church, and the influential liquor interests were thrown into the scale against the prohibition policy of the missionaries. The military authorities, too, clung jealously to their special trade privileges. "Always," says Rochemontaix, "the traffic in fire-water was the real battlefield between the authorities, civil and religious."

The king was appealed to on the question. In some embarrassment between the dictates of conscience, or perhaps the severe censure of a powerful Church on the one hand, and

PROHIBITION IN CANADA.

the lure of a revenue-producing trade on the other, he shifted responsibility by referring the matter to the Fathers of the Sorbonne, who pronounced solemnly against the liquor traffic as a mortal sin. This was not altogether satisfactory. The question was next referred to an assembly of chief merchants and inhabitants of Canada held in the Château St. Louis—men who were themselves largely interested in the business. As might have been expected, the majority favored an unrestricted trade in brandy, a few supported a policy of restriction, while only two or three declared for total prohibition. The king himself was only too glad of the singular argument produced for him by the traders, that the sale of brandy by Frenchmen saved the Indians from the dangers of contact with heresy, into which they would certainly come if they were driven by a prohibitory policy on the part of the French to deal with the Protestant Dutch traders to the south.

Various prohibitory decrees were issued from time to time, and as often revoked. Without the sympathy of the military authorities for their enforcement they were worse than useless.

In 1664 a royal ordinance was passed charging *cent pour cent* on all liquors imported into Canada. Even this heavy duty did not lessen importation to any great extent; and Intendant Talon, alarmed by the great consumption of wine and brandy by the settlers, built a brewery in order to substitute beer-drinking for the use of ardent spirits. Colbert approved the Intendant's plan because "the vice of drunkenness would thereafter cause no more scandal by reason of the cold nature of beer, the vapors whereof rarely deprive men of the use of judgment," a theory which has found supporters since his day.

Talon at first resolutely opposed the liquor traffic and supported Bishop Laval in his temperance campaign. But later on, driven probably by political exigencies, he changed his attitude. Matters were complicated by the Dutch traders, who, being under no restraint from the Catholic prelates, freely sold liquor to the Indians, especially around the mission

EARLY HISTORY.

of Michilimackinac, and this seriously interfered with French trade. Under accumulated pressure, Talon at length yielded, and in 1666 issued an order removing all restrictions from the sale of spirits. The results of this order were disastrous. Father Carheil writes from Michilimackinac:

"Our missions are reduced to such extremity that we can no longer maintain them against the infirmity of disorder, brutality, violence, injustice, impiety, insolence, scorn and insult, that the deplorable and infamous traffic in brandy has spread universally among the Indians of these parts. . . . In the despair in which we are plunged nothing remains for us but to abandon them to the brandy sellers as a domain of drunkenness and debauchery. .
All our Indian villages are so many taverns for drunkenness and Sodoms of iniquity, which we shall be forced to leave to the just wrath and vengeance of God."

Parkman quotes a Frenchman visiting Canada about 1670-1690 regarding the results of Talon's order:

"All the rascals and idlers in the country are attracted into the business of tavern-keeping. They never dream of tilling the soil, but on the contrary they deter other inhabitants from it, and end with ruining them. I knew seigniories where there were but twenty houses, and more than half of them were dram-shops. At Three Rivers there are twenty-five houses, and liquor may be had at eighteen or twenty of them. Ville Marie and Quebec are on the same footing."

Charlevoix, who visited Canada in 1705, wrote in one of his published letters regarding the situation after the repeal of prohibition:

"Husbands, wives, fathers, mothers, brothers, and sisters were frequently seen in the streets of Montreal in a state of intoxication, worrying one another with their teeth like so many enraged wolves."

From this time on, measures involving more or less restriction of the traffic were enacted, but no steps were taken that effectively combated the evil. Frontenac, who came out as

PROHIBITION IN CANADA.

governor in 1673, was openly hostile to the temperance policy of the Church. He considered the liquor traffic necessary for the maintenance of the treasury, the development of industry and prosperity, and the maintaining of friendly relations with the Indians. Moreover, he declared that the Jesuits were guilty of great exaggeration in their denunciations of the evils of brandy, and he even went so far as to accuse them of "interested motives" in their agitation for the suppression of the traders, a desire to carry on by themselves an illicit trade. In return, Frontenac himself is accused of not being entirely disinterested in his motives, "his private fortune," says Rochemontaix significantly, "being nothing."

In 1669 an edict forbade, under severe penalties, the sale of drink to Indians in the woods, while permitting it in French habitations. Later, another edict prohibited, on pain of confiscation, the importation of impure compounded extracts from France or any other country. The same edict further enacted that no brewery, either for domestic or public use, should be permitted to exist without first obtaining the direct permission of the king—the first foreshadowing of the license system.

Coming down to a somewhat later period, in 1705 an ordinance was issued from Paris, requiring that all duties on wine, spirits and tobacco should be paid in French money. In the following year a very extraordinary piece of legislation was enacted, which applied only to the Island of Montreal. It was to the effect that in any contract for the sale of real estate, the title deeds should have in them the following clause: "That if at any time intoxicating liquor should be sold to the Indians on that property, the title deeds should be cancelled and the property forfeited." The provisions of this law were after a while considered too severe, and they were disallowed by the Imperial Government. A few years after this a further law was passed making special regulations to be observed by hotel-keepers, in which it was enjoined "that they should never sell liquor to the Indians on truck."

EARLY HISTORY.

The penalty for breaking this law was five hundred livres, to be equally divided between the informer and the *Hôtel Dieu.*

Thus when the policy of prohibition was abandoned, an endless series of regulating acts filled the pages of the French statute books. But they did not cure the evils of intemperance. This baneful product of the French régime, the legalized liquor traffic in Canada, though not specifically mentioned in the Treaty of Paris, was an indisputable part of the acquisitions of Great Britain in 1763.

II. EARLY LEGISLATION UNDER BRITISH RULE.

The first step in dealing with the liquor traffic under British administration was to establish it as a recognized revenue-producer by the inauguration of a license system.

The Quebec Revenue Act was passed by the Imperial Parliament in 1774, and was entitled "An Act to establish a fund towards defraying the charges of the Administration of Justice and support of the Civil Government within the Province of Quebec in America." Except that the act was not to make void French revenues reserved to the sovereign at the conquest, all regulations which had existed under French rule were abolished, and in their stead provision was made for the granting by the Governor, Lieutenant-Governor, or Commander-in-Chief of the Province of a license for the keeping of houses or places of entertainment, or for retailing wine, brandy, rum or any other spirituous liquors. The license fee was £1 16s.; the penalty for selling without a license was £10. Also the import duties were raised on all kinds of ardent spirits and an incipient preferential tariff was adopted. The rate of three per cent. levied by French law on the value of all liquors was abolished, and a new one imposed as follows:

3d. per gallon on brandy and rum manufactured in Great Britain.

PROHIBITION IN CANADA.

6d. per gallon if imported from sugar colonies in the West Indies.

9d. per gallon if imported from any other British Dominions or colonies in America.

1s. per gallon of foreign manufacture, regardless of the place from which it was imported.

It was further provided that spirits were not to be admitted at any port except St. John's near the River Sorel, on pain of confiscation. The revenue from this law was to be applied first of all in defraying expenses of administration of justice and in support of the civil government; the surplus was to go to the treasury.

In 1777 an ordinance was issued to prevent the selling of strong liquors to the Indians in the Province of Quebec.

It would be a formidable task, and a comparatively unprofitable one, to give an abstract of the complicated and diversified pieces of liquor legislation which have accumulated upon the statute books of Canada for the last hundred and twenty-five years. Some of these were favorable to the liquor dealers, but the general trend was towards increased restriction of the traffic. A few of the most outstanding features of these measures may be mentioned in very brief, to give an idea of the character of the legislation enacted:

Upper Canada.

1792—It was provided that no license be given to retail liquor in the jails or prisons.

1793—An additional fee of 20s. currency was added to the license fee.

1794—A duty was levied upon stills. The license for the still permitted the sale of liquors in more than three-gallon quantities. A person might not be licensed at the same time both to distil and to sell retail.

1794—Power was given to magistrates to limit the number of licenses. Thus a considerable time of each Quarter Session was taken up with the consideration of applications for licenses.

EARLY HISTORY.

1796—A penalty of £20 was imposed on a keeper of a public house for selling without a license, one-half of which was to go to the informer and one-half to the public treasury.

1797—No person, whether keeper of a public house or not, was allowed to sell liquor in quantities of less than three gallons without a license.

1800—Provision was made for the summary conviction of persons selling without a license.—An act was passed which forbade the sale by licensed retailers of smaller quantity than one quart.

1801—An act was passed which prohibited the sale or barter of rum in the tract of land occupied by the Indians on the river Thames in the West District. This measure was the result of a petition presented to the Governor, Council, and Representatives on June 18, 1801, by G. S. Oddell, C. J. Denkey, and Michael Young, missionaries to the Indians, sent by the Episcopal Church of Moravians, who prayed for permission to introduce religion among the Indians of that district and also for the prohibition of the sale of liquor among the Indians.

1803—An act was passed providing for appointment of inspectors to issue licenses and collect the revenues derived therefrom.

1813—An act permitted the Provincial Government to prohibit the exportation of grain and other provisions, and also to restrain the distilling of spirituous liquors from grain.

1814—The license fees were increased for stills, shops, and taverns.

1818—Magistrates were empowered to make regulations for the conduct of tavern-keepers. They were directed to inquire into the life and character of the applicants for licenses, and to grant them to "such persons as are sober, honest, diligent, and good subjects of our Lord, the King."

PROHIBITION IN CANADA.

The *Queen's Quarterly*, Kingston, in October, 1901, printed an account of the Quarter Session from March, 1815, to December, 1818. It is here recorded that among the first regulations made under the law of 1818 were the following:

1. Unlawful games were prevented.
2. Good order and rule were to be kept in the houses.
3. Innkeepers were forbidden to sell liquors, except for the use of travellers, after ten o'clock at night in the winter and nine o'clock in the summer.
4. They were not to sell on Sundays except to sick persons and travellers.
5. They were to prohibit any tradesman, laborers, or others abiding in their homes longer than an hour in the daytime, in order to drink and tipple.
6. Every innkeeper was to possess an enclosed yard and shed for the accommodation of travellers and their carriages.

1818—An additional duty of £5 was added to the fee for shop licenses. Distillers who had taken out licenses to distil might sell without further license.

1821—Licensed tavern-keepers were permitted without further license to retail liquor to be consumed outside their houses.

1823—An act required that licenses should be taken out for the sale in the villages of beer, ale and cider, and other liquors not spirituous.

1824—After June 1, 1824, and after January 5 in every ensuing year, every shop-keeper selling spirituous liquors by wholesale was required to take out a license and pay £5 therefor.

1832—An act required that licenses should be taken out for selling liquor on steamboats, the revenue therefrom to be applied to the improvement of public highways and bridges. £2 was added to the license fee.

1834—The consumption of spirituous liquors was forbidden in shops or buildings of which the shops were a part.

1836—Proceeds of fines were to be expended on the highways. No part of the fine was to go to the informer.

EARLY HISTORY.

1840—One-half of the fine was to go to the informer.—The Indians at the Grand River, Credit, Muncey, and other places petitioned that the sale of liquor to the Indians be prohibited. Thus, in 1840, an act was passed prohibiting the sale, barter, exchange, or giving to any Indian, man, woman, child, of any spirituous liquor in any shape, manner, or way.

A fine of £5 or one month's imprisonment was imposed upon any person supplying spirits to a prisoner in jail. An act appropriated all moneys arising from the granting of licenses and fines, for the general use of the province.

Lower Canada.

1795—Licenses for keeping houses of public entertainment, or for retailing liquors in quantities of less than three gallons at a time, were to be taken out and renewed annually. The fee was to be £2.

1799—Keepers of public houses within cities and parishes of Quebec and Montreal were required to pay £2 to road treasurers for keeping the streets in repair.

1805—The sale of wine and spirits was prohibited on Sunday, except for sick persons or to travellers with meals.

1839-1840—Licensed tavern-keepers were required to post a notice conspicuously in their houses; licenses were to be forfeited on conviction for keeping a disorderly house; and persons selling malt liquors without a license were made subject to a penalty

1840-1841—An act forbade grocers to retail spirits in quantities less than three half-pints, under penalty.

Another act gave the Governor of the Province power to grant licenses to persons who had failed to obtain the required certificates.

United Canada.

1842—An act imposed duties on distilleries in that part of the province which had been Lower Canada.

PROHIBITION IN CANADA.

1845—The Legislature of United Canada enacted that the revenues derived from liquor licenses should belong to the municipalities.

1847—The municipalities were empowered to increase the license duties.

1849—The municipalities in that part formerly known as Upper Canada were empowered to make liquor laws for regulating houses of public entertainment, or sale of liquor, to limit their number, and to provide for licensing them where there is no other provision for such. The proceeds were to go to the public fund of the corporation.

1850—Tavern-keepers were subject to fine and imprisonment in case accidents happened to intoxicated people to whom they sold liquor. Also the Legislature placed local licensing power in the hands of the church warden, the senior magistrate and the senior militia officer, thus providing a sort of local option.

Another act provided that no spirituous liquors should be furnished to Indians.

There was passed "An Act for the more effective suppression of intemperance." Its provisions were:

1. The license certificates for the sale of intoxicating liquors were granted by the senior magistrate of the locality, the senior officer of the militia of the battalion of the place where the hotel was to be kept, and the church warden in the office. In case of disagreement, the signatures of any two of them were sufficient.

2. No certificate for tavern licenses might be granted unless the applicant proved, by a requisition signed by the magistrate of the municipal electors, that a tavern was necessary at that place.

3. The applicant must hold real or personal property and must provide two sureties of £50 each and his own at £100. He must have certificates from two justices of the peace or from ten municipal electors that he was of unblemished reputation. If all these conditions were filled, the Governor would grant the license at a fee of £10 currency.

EARLY HISTORY.

4. The penalty for intoxication was arrest, with fine or imprisonment.

5. For a license in a town or city, it was necessary to secure a petition signed by six magistrates or by twenty-five electors, stating that the tavern or shop was necessary. Gambling was strictly prohibited under penalty of £10.

1851—The second license law of Quebec was passed, entitled "An Act to make better provisions for granting licenses to keepers of taverns and dealers in spirituous liquors in Lower Canada, and for the more effectual repression of intemperance." This act forms the real basis of the present license law of Quebec Province, all the main provisions of which are to be found in it. It fixed the license fee, specified the qualifications of license holders, and regulated the hours and conditions of sale.

1853—The law was amended with regard to Quebec and Montreal. In these cities the consent of fifty municipal electors of the ward was necessary for the issuing of the license.

License laws did not solve the liquor problem; the very number of them is in itself a witness to their inefficacy. The legal sanction and authorization given to the traffic by the system of taxation and regulation served to make it respectable, to establish it as an apparent source of profit, and altogether to perpetuate an institution founded on the greed and selfishness of the few and tolerated by the ignorance and indifference of the many.

SECTION III.

ORGANIZATIONS.

Is it not a weakness in our present methods that we fail to carry on the campaign of education by which former generations were convinced of the danger and folly of drinking and the wisdom of teetotalism? The great intelligent temperance revival in the middle of the last century naturally led to a sweep of prohibitory legislation that was repealed mainly because of its crudity and imperfection. To-day we have carefully devised and developed law that proves effective, but the public conscience and knowledge concerning the nature and results of drink and drinking are not what they ought to be. In other words, we need a renewal in some form of the work that fifty years ago was being done by Bands of Hope, Blue Ribbon Clubs, and Temperance Orders, and that also took the form of temperance sermons and church temperance societies.

I. THE PLEDGE-SIGNING CRUSADE.

THE temperance movement in Canada has had a phenomenally rapid development. To appreciate the truth of that it is necessary only to see the facts in perspective, to take an adequate period of time in which to measure the progress made. Less than one hundred years ago temperance public opinion did not exist; the supremacy of the liquor traffic was unquestioned.

In " Old Time Records of Upper Canada," collected by Mr. Casey in the *Beaver*, we read of the reminiscences of William Gibbard, born at Wilton, Lennox County, 1810. " He remembered when there were more distilleries than grist mills in the country and more taverns than schools. Whiskey was considered almost as indispensable as flour. Farmers took their rye to the distillery and brought back whiskey, and their wheat to the grist mill and brought back flour. In many families whiskey was served to each member of the household in the morning. It was considered to be a precaution against colds and to enable one to do hardy work."

Organized temperance reform, which reached Canada from the United States early in the nineteenth century, began with a few individuals who, realizing that ardent spirits used as a beverage had a baneful effect, took the eccentric step of voluntarily renouncing them. Those who pledged themselves to that course formed little groups or temperance societies for mutual encouragement and the propagation of their ideas. There was at first no suggestion of abstinence from wine, ale or beer; in fact, the use of these was encouraged, in the supposed interests of true temperance. Those who before long became convinced that the use of light liquor in moderation was a fatal cause of backsliding, met with bitter hostility from the moderates, and were accused of promulgating a dangerous doctrine. There are men living to-day who can

PROHIBITION IN CANADA.

boast of having been refused by insurance companies because as total abstainers they were considered to be subnormal. As late as March 16, 1840, there was published in the *Canada Temperance Advocate* a letter from the Wesleyan Methodist Leaders' Meeting, Montreal (now St. James Methodist Church), which contained the following statement:

"We deem it necessary to decide that no member of this meeting shall be allowed to agitate the question of temperance, especially in the extreme view of it called teetotalism or total abstinence, with the view of making it a church question or a test or condition of membership in our society."

A comparatively brief period, scarcely exceeding the span of a man's lifetime, has seen revolutionary changes in the habits of people and in legislation, the promotion of the temperance idea from being scoffed at or ignored as the fanatical delusion of a handful of dreamers to a position where it is supported by the most modern findings of science and has become the established policy of nations.

There is some uncertainty as to what spot should be honored as the home of the temperance movement in Canada. The inspiration in this case, as in the case of so many other reforms, seems to have been felt in several localities practically simultaneously. For many years it was generally believed that the first Canadian temperance society was that formed at Beaver River, in Nova Scotia, on April 25, 1828. But when a statement to that effect was published in the *Canadian Voice,* Halifax, on May 3, 1890, it was challenged by Senator Billa Flint, a most faithful advocate of temperance from the day he signed the pledge on June 19, 1827, and one of Canada's strongest prohibition legislators. Senator Flint declared that in June or July, 1827, the Rev. Mr. Christmas, pastor of the American Presbyterian Church, formed in Montreal the first society. "After that," said Mr. Flint, "he came to Brockville, Upper Canada, and formed a society on the old pledge of three members, Luther Houghton, Stephen Skinner, and myself. We got two others to join

ORGANIZATIONS.

us, Stephen Richards and Adriel Sherwood, who were in business together. An election came on in 1828, and as the last two differed in politics they withdrew to be able to treat those who agreed with them politically, and the original three were then all the society."

Rev. Wm. Scott, editor for some years of *The Canada Temperance Advocate,* Montreal, differs with Mr. Flint as to dates. In an article on the "Rise and Progress of Temperance Societies in Canada," published on January 1, 1851, he states that the Montreal Society for the Promotion of Temperance was formed by Mr. Christmas on June 9, 1828, with twenty-nine members—which would give the Beaver River society first place. Further, the *Advocate* says that in Canada West (Upper Canada) the first temperance society was formed at Bastard by Doctor Schofield on June 10, 1828, only one day later than the Montreal society

But the Beaver River society, whether or not it was first in historical order, was pre-eminent for its continuity of existence. Until 1908 it held meetings in Memorial Hall, built over the spot where the first pledge was signed. In the original minutes book of the society can be plainly traced the growth of the teetotalism idea. The original pledge of 1828 reads as follows:

"We, the undersigned, firmly believing and most assuredly gathering that the use of spirituous liquor is prejudicial to the body and soul of mankind in general, both spiritual and temporal, and to remedy this great and spreading evil.

"We, therefore, whose names are hereunto annexed, do forever renounce the use of ardent or distilled spirituous liquors of any kind except what may be taken as a medicine in case of sickness.

"And we pray Almighty God to establish our hearts and strengthen our serious resolutions.

"John Whetmore, Sen., Recording Secretary.

"Beaver River, April 25th, 1828."

PROHIBITION IN CANADA.

This pledge was subsequently amended as follows:

"January, 1830.

"Resolved, that the Society consider the use of wine, except in the administration of the Lord's Supper or sickness, a violation of the rules of the Society.

"William C. Williams, Corresponding Secretary."

And again:

"March, 1851.

"Resolved, that this Society consider the use of any kind of spirituous liquors or wines as a medicine in case of sickness, except when prescribed by a physician, a violation of the rules of the Society.

"Reuben Perry, Secretary."

Evidently the influence of this parent society spread throughout Nova Scotia, and was quickly manifested in the organization of other societies, for we read the announcement of two temperance conventions, one at Halifax in 1834, and the other at Annapolis for the west of the province in 1835, to which Beaver River society was invited to send delegates. At the Halifax convention the following resolution was adopted:

"Resolved, that the Legislature should be applied to to give up giving regard to the amount of revenue derived from the duty on ardent spirits, or from their sale, and should raise revenue from a more worthy source than the vices of the people."

The Montreal Temperance Society, organized in 1827 or 1828, was for many years the centre of activity in Lower Canada, and from it the work spread rapidly through the province.* In 1834 the first provincial temperance convention

---

* CONSTITUTION OF THE MONTREAL TEMPERANCE SOCIETY.

Article 1.—That this society shall be called the Montreal Temperance Society.
Article 2.—That the requisites of membership shall be conformity to the rules of the society and signing the following pledge:

ORGANIZATIONS.

was held in the Baptist Church of Montreal, at which were represented twenty-seven societies with an aggregate membership of 4,250. In May, 1835, the society took an important step in publishing the *Canada Temperance Advocate,* a monthly periodical, "devoted to temperance, agriculture and education." In 1841 it was doubled in size and published fortnightly. This paper ran for a great many years, and was finally amalgamated with the *Canada Casket,* published by Mr. T. W. Casey at Napanee. On October 22, 1835, the society strengthened itself by adopting the teetotal principle, conjointly with the moderate system. The latter was entirely dropped in 1837.

A district convention was held in Montreal on February 23, 1836. The following condensed review of the various reports made at that convention, which is quoted by Mr. Scott in the "Teetotalers' Hand Book," is an indication of the state of the temperance cause at that period:

No. of Societies reported	30
Ordinary members	4,751
Total abstainers	764
Expelled	205
Withdrawn or removed	272
Taverns	358
Stores selling liquor	207
Temperance inns and stores	34
Distilleries or breweries at date of formation	43
Distilleries or breweries now	21

"We, the undersigned, do agree that we will not use intoxicating liquors as a beverage, nor traffic in them, that we will not provide them as an article of entertainment, nor for persons in our employment, and that in all suitable ways we will discountenance their use throughout the community."

Article 3.—The officers of this society shall consist of a president, vice-presidents, treasurer, secretaries, and committee.

Article 4.—That the officers shall be chosen at an annual meeting at which a report of the proceedings of the committee and the treasurer's account shall be presented.

Article 5.—That any member may withdraw from the society on notifying the secretary of his intention.

Article 6.—That no alteration in this constitution shall be made but at the annual meeting and with the sanction of two-thirds of the members present.

PROHIBITION IN CANADA.

A pioneer worker whose name was prominent in the records of those early days was John Dougall, who with his brother was engaged in general business in Amherstburg, under the firm of J. & J. Dougall. In an old book of the Montreal Temperance Society, under the date 1834, the name of John Dougall stands the first subscribed to a pledge of total abstinence. His was one of the first extensive mercantile houses to give up selling liquor. In 1842 he wrote:

" So far from having to suffer from doing right, our business increased rapidly and our losses from bad debts diminished (perhaps because our best liquor customers left us, and they are not generally the best pay.) We also did our business with much greater ease and comfort, and we would not on any account deal in intoxicating drinks again, although no considerations were involved except pecuniary interest."

One of the most devoted workers of this period was Father Chiniquy, the missionary priest, who labored among the Roman Catholics of the Lower Province. He began his temperance crusade in 1838, when, as Abbé of Beauport, he was brought into close touch with the havoc wrought by drunkenness amongst his flock. In order to make himself a more efficient teacher on the subject of temperance, he completed in 1840 a regular course in anatomy at Quebec. He was remarkably successful in Beauport in pledging his parishioners to total abstinence, so much so that in 1841 his work was recognized and blessed by the Bishop of Nancy, who on his arrival in Canada was immediately impressed with the immense good the humble priest had accomplished. The formal consecration of his work aided Father Chiniquy not a little. He was soon called to extend his labors along the Beaupré shore and in a number of parishes to the south of the St. Lawrence River, and finally was invited to preach by the Bishop of Montreal. With headquarters at Kamouraska, his native place, in four years he converted to sobriety more than twenty of the surrounding parishes. In 1844 he published the first edition of the " Manuel de Tempérance,"

ORGANIZATIONS.

an exhortation to total abstinence, dedicated to the youth of Canada, four thousand copies of which were sold in six months, and which ran through a second edition of six thousand in eighteen months. A little later, in order to be more free for his temperance work, Father Chiniquy resigned from his position as curé and, after a period of rest, study and contemplation in the Novitiate of the Pères Oblats at Longueuil, he gave himself up to the wandering, laborious life of a missionary. In eighteen months of the years 1848 and 1849 he visited one hundred and twenty parishes and won more than two hundred thousand converts to total abstinence. In 1851 he broke with the Roman Catholic Church and went to Illinois. At Beauport, where he began his mission, there stands a memorial column in recognition of the work of this apostle of temperance. A more enduring monument is to be found, however, in the temperance sentiment which he was able to create amongst the French population of Lower Canada.

At the same time the work was being carried on in Upper Canada. William Lyon Mackenzie has given the following account of an early organization in that province:

"The first temperance society in Toronto was formed in the old Methodist Chapel on King Street in 1831. Mr. Jesse Ketchum was its warmest advocate. I was present, and remember that the attendance was not large. Mr. Vaux, of the Assembly, acted as secretary. In March, 1832, first anniversary, the number of members had increased to 252, and Dr. Rolph succeeded Dr. Stoyell as president, and made a very effective appeal to the people. In February, 1833 a Young Men's Temperance Society was formed at the same place, at the organization of which Rev. James Richardson and Messrs. William Lawson, W. P. and A. Patrick, G. and L. Bostwick, John Doel, R. Emery, A. Hamilton, and R. Brewer took an active part. In June that year the constitution of the original society was changed at a meeting in the Primitive Methodist Chapel, Mr. Receiver-General Dunn in the chair. Messrs. Jesse Ketchum and Rev. W. Rintoul were elected vice-presidents and Rev. J. Harris, secretary."

PROHIBITION IN CANADA.

On June 15, 1835, the first total abstinence society in Upper Canada was formed at St. Catharines, with forty names on the roll. In 1836 delegates from thirteen societies met in convention at Toronto. In 1840, upon the union of the provinces, a convention was held, to which the societies of both Upper and Lower Canada were asked to send delegates. Ninety-one societies responded, reporting 13,618 members. In 1841 travelling agents were sent out by the Montreal Temperance Society to organize Canada West. The journals of these missionaries are rich with the romance that attaches to all pioneer effort. Here are a few typical extracts which indicate some methods employed and results obtained:

"18th of November, 1841, *Dawn Mills.*—At the hour appointed about sixty persons assembled in the school house. Rev. T. Williams delivered a short address, after which I spoke two hours, and concluded amidst the cry of 'Go on.' This was the first temperance address in this place.

"19th, *Zone Mills.*—Held a meeting in the schoolhouse close by a distillery and whiskey shop; the gentlemen belonging to both were present, as also about forty others. I did not know till afterwards that the two individuals above named were present. I, however, spoke particularly on the iniquity of the traffic. The distiller made an attempt to leave the place, but the other seizing his hat, he went away without it. In a little time the retailer made an attempt to go, but a lady snatched his hat and kept him in through the whole meeting. Five gave in their names to the pledge.

"23rd, *Raleigh.*—Not many present. Mr. Dolson, president of the Society, in the chair. Ten names were added; one drunkard present. One local preacher refused to sign, the only one I have met with in my tour. A few other influential Methodists in the neighborhood also refused. Cider is in the way.

"24th, *Windsor.*—On the steamboat I found a brewer from Chatham who knew well who I was and what was my business. He commenced an attack on the teetotallers, and expatiated on the excellent qualities of his beer. This I took as a fair challenge and a favorable opportunity to expose the beer system. I went through the whole process of malting and brewing, and then dissected a pint of his beer and showed the whole company what

ORGANIZATIONS.

it contained, after which the brewer was completely crestfallen. One cried out, ' Oh, sir, you are taken aback '; another, ' You have got into the wrong shop.' The brewer said to me afterwards that he would as soon as possible turn his distillery into a tannery.

"7th of December, *Oxford*.—The schoolhouse was crowded. The Rev. J. Harris, Wesleyan minister, and the writer addressed this meeting. Four or five signed the pledge and ten subscribed for the *Advocate*. Many moderate drinkers not willing yet to give up wine, beer, and cider. This society has two pledges.

"8th, *Aldborough*.—The president of the society here entreated me to stop and hold a meeting, to which I consented. Four joined. An elder attempted to defend wine-drinking by quoting Scripture. I answered his objections, at which several were well pleased."

Thus the pledge-signing movement made rapid progress from the time of its inception, and for fifty years its influence spread throughout the length and breadth of the land. There was a temperance society in every hamlet. Temperance was taught in Bands of Hope, unions, lodges, leagues, and clubs. It was a veritable revival, a campaign of education, in which the fundamentals of sound prohibition doctrine took root in the public conscience, in preparation for the later growth of prohibitory legislation. This order of development from the personal to the social, from abstinence by the individual to prohibition by the state, was essential under democratic institutions. As Mr. F. S. Spence once pointed out when making an appeal for greater activity in temperance education:

'The advocacy of prohibition legislation by anyone who does not favor abstinence from drinking is inconsistent and absurd. . Not only historically, but logically, the temperance movement in its personal aspect lies behind the prohibition propaganda."

PROHIBITION IN CANADA.

II. FRATERNAL TEMPERANCE SOCIETIES.

The temperance reform, like all other movements for bettering the conditions of society, has been evolutionary in its character. Step by step the public conscience has been educated in its apprehension of the evils of the alcohol habit, and the methods of dealing with these evils have advanced with growing intelligence.

THE SONS OF TEMPERANCE.

The organization of fraternal societies, on a total abstinence basis, followed very naturally Father Matthew's movement in Ireland, the Washingtonian movement in the United States, and the pledge-signing campaign in Canada. The Sons of Temperance were the first to adopt plans to conserve the results of these wonderful teetotal movements and crystallize the great emotional waves of sentiment into permanent rescue and educational agencies. Ten men in the city of New York were seized with the conviction that something must be done to assist the multitudes of reformed men to keep the pledge of total abstinence and to educate a generation of total abstainers. They issued the following call:

"SONS OF TEMPERANCE.

"New York Division No. 1.

"*Sir*,—You are invited to attend a select meeting at Teetotalers Hall, No. 71 Division Street, on Thursday evening, September 29, 1842, at half-past seven o'clock.

"The object of the meeting is to organize a beneficial society based on total abstinence, bearing the above title.

"A constitution will be submitted on the above evening, and if the principles adopted meet your approbation you are invited to become a member of the division.

"The enclosed ticket will procure your admittance."

The records of the organization declare its objects to be "To shield its members from the evils of intemperance; to

ORGANIZATIONS.

afford mutual assistance in case of sickness; and to elevate their characters as men."

The two men who, more than any others, were responsible for the early success of the movement were Daniel H. Sands, a reformed tippler, and John W. Oliver, a reformed drunkard. Mr. Sands was the first Grand Worthy Patriarch.

The early years presented a series of triumphs for the Order. At the close of 1845, three years after its first establishment, it numbered 14 Grand Divisions, 640 Subordinate Divisions, and 40,000 members. At the close of the next year the membership reached 100,000, an increase of 60,000 in a single year.

The Order is composed of Subordinate, Grand, and National Divisions. Subordinate Divisions are the local branches, which as a rule have weekly meetings. Grand Divisions are constituted of all presiding officers (Worthy Patriarchs) and Acting Past Worthy Patriarchs of the Subordinate Divisions. The National Division is constituted of Acting and Past Grand Worthy Patriarchs, Associates and Scribes of the Grand Divisions. The National Division of North America, being the parent body, reserves to itself the right and power to charter other National Divisions in other countries. This it has done in Great Britain, South Africa, Australia, New Zealand and India.

In 1847 the Order was planted in Quebec, New Brunswick and Nova Scotia. The growth in the eastern provinces was phenomenal. Grand Divisions were early instituted in each of these and also in Quebec. The Order has remained the mainstay of temperance propaganda in those provinces. Brockville has the honor of having instituted the first Division in Ontario, the date being June 21, 1848. By April of the following year, six divisions had been instituted in Eastern Ontario, and the Grand Division of Ontario was then organized. A new Subordinate Division each week, on the average, was instituted during the next five years.

It is impossible to exaggerate the benefits that have come to Canada from these seventy years of social service and

PROHIBITION IN CANADA.

education. Tens of thousands of homes have been saved from the curse of drink. Members of the Order have been helped in sickness by the benefit fund they themselves have sustained, young men have been trained in parliamentary practice and have learned the first lessons in public speaking and debate. Some of Canada's most distinguished public men have graduated from the Temperance Division and Lodge.

A decade after the organization of the first Division of the Order, the question of prohibition as the ultimate and logical method of dealing with the liquor traffic came to the front. In 1852 the National Division, on the motion of General S. F. Carey, adopted a resolution affirming the desirability of entirely suppressing the manufacture and traffic in intoxicating liquors. From that day to the present the Order has been committed to the legal extermination of the traffic, demonstrating that those who have done most by the moral suasion method for the individual are leaders in seeking prohibition for the state.

Among illustrious members of the Order in the United States may be mentioned: Presidents Abraham Lincoln and Rutherford B. Hayes, Horace Greeley, Theodore L. Cuyler, Bishop Mallelieu, General Wagner, Hiram Price, John Stearns, J. B. Gough, the great temperance lecturer of worldwide reputation, and Neal Dow, the unconquerable idealist, who led the teetotal Israel into the promised land of constitutional prohibition. In Canada the outstanding names are those of Sir Leonard Tilley, Sir Geo. W. Ross, Sir Geo. E. Foster, Hon. E. J. Davis, Edward Carswell, the Canadian Gough; W. H. Orr, Thomas Caswell, D. L. Brethour, and Dr. Anson Buck, M.R.C.S. (Eng.).

Of Ontario men who have passed through the Grand Worthy Patriarch's chair and are still active leaders of the Order may be mentioned: J. M. Walton, Theo. N. Wilmott, J. O. McCarthy, Samuel Holland, F. C. Ward, Rev. A. P. Brace, and Rev. J. R. Wilkinson. The officers of the Grand Division of Ontario for 1919 are: G.W.P., J. M. Walton, Aurora; G.W.A., S. Draper, Toronto; G.S., Theo. N. Wilmott,

ORGANIZATIONS.

Orillia; Grand Treas., Rev. Jas. A. Miller, Toronto; G. Chap., Rev. A. P. Brace, Toronto; G. Con., G. B. Stevens, Solina; G. Sen. S., Jarvis Tansley; G. Patron of Cadets, W. A. Tice, Toronto.

Others just as worthy as those whose names have been mentioned have done yeoman service in Grand and Subordinate Divisions, and will have an honored place at the last roll call as having taken their part faithfully in the great work of social reconstruction.

The time may come when the mission of the fraternal temperance societies shall have been accomplished, though that time is not yet. But of this we may be assured, temperance reform will go forward and not backward, and, as suggested by a choice bit of familiar ritual, when the star of the Sons of Temperance sets, it will not set as sets the evening star, which goeth down behind the darkened west, but as sets the morning star, which fades into the glory of heaven.

THE INDEPENDENT ORDER OF GOOD TEMPLARS.

The Independent Order of Good Templars for sixty years has been the largest temperance organization in the world. Like the Sons of Temperance, it originated in the United States, but about ten years later.

In 1850 there was organized in Oneida County, New York, a society known as "The Knights of Jericho." In the following year the name was changed to "Good Templars." At that time there were thirteen lodges in the county, but there was no Grand Lodge. In July, 1852, a convention was held in Utica for the purpose of organizing a Grand Lodge. At that convention leaders clashed and L. C. Coon withdrew and organized two other lodges, and these, with the Syracuse Lodge, on August 17 of the same year, organized the first Grand Lodge of the Independent Order of Good Templars. Nathaniel Curtis was elected Grand Worthy Chief Templar and L. C. Coon, Past Grand. Mr. Coon, the father of the Order, removed to Canada and dropped out of sight. Mr.

PROHIBITION IN CANADA.

Curtis threw himself vigorously into the work of organizing lodges, and before the end of the year twelve were in healthy operation. Other active co-workers with Mr. Curtis were Rev. H. P. Barnes, Dr. S. C. Miles, Garey Chambers and the Rev. D. W. Bristol. The latter was the author of the ritual for the several degrees.

In two years and a half, lodges were planted in New York, Pennsylvania, Canada, Iowa, Kentucky, Indiana, Michigan, Missouri, Illinois, and Ohio. In May, 1855, representatives of the Grand Lodges of the states mentioned met and organized the International Grand Lodge, which has since been the supreme governing body of the Order throughout the world.

Up to the time of the Civil War the growth of the Order was slow compared with that of the Sons of Temperance, but the Good Templars suffered less from the war for the reason that their membership was almost wholly in the Northern States. In the ten years following the war, the Order had a wonderful growth. By 1875 it had spread all over the civilized world and had a total membership of 735,000; in Great Britain alone the membership was 200,000.

The Good Templars differs from the Sons of Temperance in being a temperance organization without insurance or sick benefit features. It also has to its credit the honor of being the first society of any importance to recognize the equality of women with the men both as to membership and eligibility to office. The Sons of Temperance gave the sisters tardy recognition, and during some years of agitation with regard to this question lost thousands of members from their Order, most of whom went to the Good Templars.

The Good Templars, however, had their troubles growing out of the "color" problem. The constitution of the Order distinctly affirmed the equality of colored men with white. The Grand Lodges of the Southern States commonly refused charters to colored men, and subordinate lodges often blackballed such candidates when offered for membership. The Supreme Lodge, while recognizing constitutional "equality," held that the Grand Lodge is the sole judge of the persons to

ORGANIZATIONS.

whom it shall issue a charter, and that the International Lodge had no power to coerce the Southern brethren. The British Lodges held the opposite view, and on this issue withdrew from the Supreme Lodge held in Louisville in 1876. The British seceders were joined by delegates from Nova Scotia and Newfoundland and from three of the states. They at once met and organized another Right Worthy Grand Lodge. The work of the seceding organization was largely confined to Great Britain, Canada, and Australia. Eleven years later the breach was healed and the Orders united at Saratoga Springs.

The British American Order of Good Templars was an offshoot from the Grand Lodge of Canada, the separation taking place in 1858. Eight years later the word "American" was dropped from the name, and the Order spread extensively through the British dominions.

The Independent Order, in the early fifties, made very substantial progress in Canada, especially in Ontario. Grand Lodges were early formed in Nova Scotia and New Brunswick. Upper and Lower Canada had a single Grand Lodge, organized in Hamilton in 1854. In 1877 Ontario and Quebec were erected into separate jurisdictions.

Among the more prominent members of the Order who were elected to attend the sessions of the Right Worthy Grand Lodge during the first twenty years of its history we find the names of the following: John Ormiston, W. S. Williams, Dr. J. W. Ferguson, Alex. Henry, Doctor Oronhyatekha, Marvin Knowlton, Rev. I. B. Aylesworth, Rev. W. Scott, Rev. M. L. Pearson, J. B. Nixon, G. E. Henderson, Daniel Able, W. I. Case, Rev. Alex. Campbell, H. A. Craine, W. A. Ferguson, Samuel Morrell, J. McWhinney, J. Russel, J. W. Stone, Rev. A. Tolmie, A. D. Wadsworth, and E. B. Reed.

Representatives during this period from the Maritime Provinces were: J. J. Hingley, W. J. Cutton, John Meahan, David Churchill, R. M. Taylor, Rev. J. O. Banyoun, J. T. Bulmer, P. J. Chisholm, and W. S. Troop, M.P.P.

PROHIBITION IN CANADA.

As a prophecy of the change in woman's social status that has followed the world war, Mrs. E. E. Miller, Mrs. W. S. Williams, and Mrs. M. A. Perry were elected to the International Grand Lodge.

Since the year 1876 the following have filled the office of Grand Chief Templar in Canada, most of whom have been delegates to the International Grand Lodge: Rev. John Shaw, J. H. Flagg, F. S. Spence, Doctor Oronhyatekha, E. Botterill, Wm. Munroe, E. S. Cummer, J. L. Robertson, J. C. Madill, J. D. Andrews, W. F. Brockenshire, Geo. Spence, M. Nasmith, E. Storr, J. H. McMullen, James Graham, James Armstrong, John Eagleson, J. H. Day, F. S. Morrison, J. T. Dyson, and M. Brown.

Mr. F. S. Spence was elected Grand Chief Templar for Canada in the year 1885 and again in 1892; he was Grand Secretary for three years beginning with 1894. During these periods he was several times elected to represent Canada at the sessions of the International Grand Lodge. He was also for a number of years District Deputy for the city of Toronto, and was succeeded in this position by Mr. W. C. Wilkinson, who held it for many years.

Among the Grand Secretaries, upon whom the success of the Order has so largely depended, have been Thos. Lawless, A. R. Scoby, Duncan Marshall, T. W. Casey, and A. H. Lyle. Alex. Stewart placed the Order under obligation by launching the *Good Templar*.

Other members of the Order eminently worthy of mention are: J. S. Robertson, Rev. Jas. Kines, Rev. J. J. Noble, Rev. Geo. Browne, Rev. Wm. McDonagh, Prof. J. J. Bowman, J. E. Wilson, J. J. Mahony, W. F. McIntyre, J. B. Hay, James Graham, Horace Wallis, Frank Metcalf, and A. Burnett.

Among the sisters that have played an important part may be mentioned: Mesdames David Smellie, Kate Watson, R. W. Williams, Geo. Spence, J. H. Day, R. McDonnell, S. A. Mitchell, W. L. Scott, R. Morrison, J. H. Irwin, M. L. Ferguson, and Esther Kerr.

ORGANIZATIONS.

It is a matter of extreme regret that the necessary limitations of this article do not permit more adequate recognition of the magnificent band of men and women who, in Grand Lodge and Subordinate, have ungrudgingly given their time and strength to the work of the Order, and to whom its success is so largely due.

BRITISH AMERICAN ORDER OF GOOD TEMPLARS.

The British American Order of Good Templars was organized in the city of London, Ontario, in November, 1858. It rapidly extended through Canada. In 1865, in order to facilitate the extension of its operations beyond Canada, the name was changed to "The British Order of Good Templars." At a convention held at St. John, N.B., August, 1866, the constitution was materially amended and the name changed to "British Templars." At this time there were forty thousand members in the Order, which was soon after extended to Great Britain, Australia, and New Zealand. In 1872 the Most Worthy Grand Lodge made overtures for union with the Free Templars of St. John in Scotland, the Independent Order of Free Templars in England, and the United Order of Great Britain and Ireland. A basis of union was drawn up and accepted by each, which resulted in the formation of the "United Temperance Association," the National Lodge of Canada being organized in London, Ont., August, 1876. At the formation of the National Lodge, a simplified system of working was adopted with the understanding that a degree system should be instituted and affiliated with the primary lodge to provide a mutual relief system of sick and death benefits. Before this supplementary system could be established, the Order of Royal Templars of Temperance, a society that insisted upon all members holding insurance benefits, was introduced into Canada from the United States. The society was making very rapid growth in Ontario, and it occurred to United Temperance Association leaders that, provided the Canadian work of the Royal Templars could be

PROHIBITION IN CANADA.

made independent of the Supreme body in the United States, a union of the two societies for Canada would make a strong and ideal combination for social reform work and mutual protection. Negotiations were satisfactory, and the union became effective in the year 1884.

ROYAL TEMPLARS OF TEMPERANCE.

The Order of Royal Templars of Temperance was organized in the city of Buffalo in January, 1887. At the close of that year there were twenty Subordinate Councils in the State of New York, and a Grand Council was organized. In October, 1878, the Order was introduced into Canada by the institution of Pioneer Council No. 1, in the City of Toronto. At the close of 1881 there were thirty Councils in Ontario, and in April of the following year a Grand Council for Ontario was organized.

About this time correspondence was initiated by the Rev. A. M. Phillips with a view to the fusion of the United Temperance Association, of which he was the presiding officer, with the Royal Templars. The Association had a large total abstaining membership, but it provided no benefits; the R. T. of T., a total abstaining membership, all carrying insurance benefits. The union was consummated and proved an ideal one for temperance work and mutual protection in case of sickness or death.

In 1884 the united Order in Canada was set free by the Supreme body in the United States to work out its own destiny under the name of "The Royal Templars of Canada and Newfoundland."

Grand Councils were at once organized in Manitoba, Quebec, and the Maritime Provinces, the Dominion retaining jurisdiction over such Councils and having exclusive charge of the insurance department. Sick and funeral benefits are under Grand Council administration.

At the institution of the Dominion Council, the Rev. A. M. Phillips, B.D., was elected Past Dominion Councilor. The following have, in the order named, filled the presiding

ORGANIZATIONS.

officer's chair, each serving two or more terms: Rev. W. Kettlewell, W. W. Buchanan, A. M. Featherston, Geo. H. Lees, J. H. Flagg, James Hales, LL.B., J. A. Austin, and Rev. W. P. Fletcher. The Secretaries have been J. H. Land and Dr. C. V. Emory. Dr. B. E. McKenzie, until his recent demise, filled the office of Dominion Referee. Dr. Wm. Crawford, of Hamilton, has succeeded Doctor McKenzie.

The presiding officers of the Ontario Grand Council have been in the order named: Rev. John Kay, J. H. Flagg, A. C. Steele, Rev. T. A. McNair, Rev. W. Kettlewell, Geo. H. Lees, Frank Buchanan, J. A. Austin, W. J. Armstrong, Rev. W. P. Fletcher, A. B. Spencer, Thos. S. Morris, and John Buchanan. The Grand Secretaries have been Dr. C. V. Emory and W. M. McMillan.

Other outstanding members of the Order: The Revs. J. R. Gundy, Geo. Mitchell, M.A., Wm. Burns, D. L. Brethour, Alfred Andrews, H. S. Matthews, C. W. Watch, Geo. A. Cropp; also F. S. Spence, P. H. Stewart, L. C. Peake, Captain R. Holton, Lyman Lee, B.A., A. C. Neff, F.C.A., W. A. Holliday, Geo. M. Henry, and Sister Annie J. Gray.

In common with other temperance orders, the Society is not as large to-day as it was twenty years ago. The young people's societies of the churches are largely doing the work done by the lodges in years past, and temperance effort has been directed, perhaps too exclusively, to the political and legislative aspects of the reform, to the neglect of educational work. The Royal Templars, however, have found their system of insurance and sick benefits a wholesome check on the tendency to drift away from the lodge room when the novelty is past. Their sick benefit department has been very successful, and has amply demonstrated that total abstinence reduces the amount and periods of sickness. The life insurance department, like all of the older fraternal societies, commenced its business with inadequate monthly assessments; nevertheless, its death-rate has been much lower than that called for by the standard tables, and having recently adopted the government rates for members, old and new, the department would seem to have before it a useful career.

The Royal Templars for thirty-five years have done a valuable work in the education of the young in temperance principles, have been in the van of active prohibition propaganda, and are praying and working for "a bone-dry" Dominion.

III. VARIOUS SOCIETIES.

An organization typical of organizations throughout the province, was the Toronto Temperance Reformation Society; but, strangely enough, considerable difficulty has been experienced in obtaining detailed information concerning its history. The following manuscript was found, the authorship of which has not been traced, yet which bears an evident stamp of authenticity, and dates probably from about 1886.

"Many visitors to our Queen City have been struck by finding in the very heart of Toronto a large 'Temperance' Hall, situated on a 'Temperance' Street. Our temperance mayor and temperance council and perfect archipelago of temperance societies are but in keeping with the present aggressive sentiment in this premier province, that naturally finds its apex in the capital city; but these old landmarks speak emphatically of a high standard, and a practical one, in temperance reform. Away back in the old days when Toronto was just crystallizing about its historic Yonge Street, temperance work at that time was almost entirely in the hands of the evangelical churches; and some time between 1840 and 1845, Mr. Jesse Ketchum, a big-hearted, thoroughly in earnest laborer in temperance, conceived the idea of erecting a hall that should be the nucleus of all effort along that line. To materialize this thought, he offered to donate a lot provided other temperance men would erect a suitable building, and gave a choice between the site where Temperance Hall now stands and a similar one at the corner of Elm and Yonge Streets. For the purpose of meeting this generous offer the Toronto Temperance Reformation Society was formed, which undertook to raise funds and erect upon the

ORGANIZATIONS.

lot a creditable structure. The earliest minute book of this society available dates its first meeting of the executive committee on June 1st, 1847, when Mr. A. T. McCord occupied the chair, and John Boyd subscribed himself as recording secretary; the collectors were admonished to rapidly finish the raising of subscriptions for the hall, and it was likewise resolved to plaster and furnish the building as soon as possible that it might be given, gratis, to the Free Church for use while rebuilding their place of worship that had just been burned down. Indeed, this 'gratis' spirit seems to have permeated their entire course, as very frequently are found entries of granting the hall free to some worthy organization or other.

"The annual meeting for 1847 was held on October 11th, when Hon. R. B. Sullivan occupied the chair. The following officers were elected for the year: President, Rev. John Roof; Corresponding Secretary, Doctor Richardson; Recording Secretary, John Boyd; Treasurer, R. H. Brett. The following names were added to the previous list of vice-presidents: Jas. Leslie, P. Freeland, J. S. Howard, A. Christie, and Rev. Wm. Cowel. The committee consisted of Messrs. R. Wightman, J. Stevenson, J. Rowell, J. White, J. Withrow, T. W. Anderson, H. Parry, A. McGlashan, Thos. Hennings, J. Wightman, R. H. Brett, E. F. Whitterune, T. Burgess, J. H. Lawrence, Jos. Leslie, T. Ewart, J. Macara, J. W. Ross, J. McBean, Mr. Williard, Mr. Willoughby, and Jos. Farquhem.

"An Act of Incorporation was passed on the 30th of August, 1851, which gave the society all the rights and privileges of a corporate body.

"The property of the society was limited to £1,000, and a pledge of total abstinence made the *sine qua non* for membership. The records show that the eloquent Gough was twice employed by the society: once during October, 1850, when he so pleased the members that they voluntarily gave him £25 over and above his charge, and again during the Provincial Exhibition in 1852, where the tickets were put at 7½d. a head.

"On June 11, 1857, through the exertions of Messrs. Morphy and Sweatman, the deed for the lot on which the hall stands was duly registered in the York office, and at frequent intervals improvements were added to the building. Passing over a few years replete with good and faithful work, we find that at the fourth annual meeting under incorporation, held January 16, 1860, Hon. Robt. Spence was elected president; James Withrow and Edward Childs, vice-presidents; Samuel Rogers, treasurer; and J. J. Withrow and Thos. H. Carroll, secretaries.

"Through the years that followed regular meetings were held and the routine work of the society carried on successfully and with patient persistence. At one time the chair was occupied by Rev. Bishop Richardson; and, indeed, well-nigh every name prominent in the annals of Toronto temperance work is found at some time or other subscribed to the minutes either as president or secretary. As the finances of the order permitted, various inforcements were added to the building: now a coat of paint, then the refitting of the basement, until finally the entire hall was rebuilt. By generous subscriptions from friends and members the building was lifted another story, several commodious and convenient rooms added that now make a home for the many city organizations, the hall itself vastly improved, while over the platform was hung a portrait of Mr. Jos. French, who had donated $1,000 to the fund for rebuilding.

"If any are of the opinion that old age is necessarily synonymous with weakness, let them visit Temperance Hall any Sunday afternoon during the working season of the winter, and they will find that the pioneer temperance society of Toronto, cradled nearly a half century ago, is still vigorous and aggressive and carrying on, under President Wardell and his coterie of workers, a hot and successful battle against the crumbling power of the drink traffic."

The last big improvements made in Temperance Hall were covered by a heavy mortgage, held by the Toronto Police Benefit Fund. As expenses increased and the revenue of the society was reduced, it was found impossible to maintain the building, which passed into the hands of the mortgagee. With the loss of their property the society went out of existence.

On October 28, 1886, the Toronto Young Men's Prohibition Club was organized at a meeting held in Richmond Hall, at which Mayor W. H. Howland presided. The object of the organization, as set out in the constitution adopted, was:

ORGANIZATIONS.

(*a*) Its objects shall be the securing of the total prohibition of the traffic in intoxicating beverages, and with this end in view, the nomination and election to municipal and parliamentary positions of candidates who are known prohibitionists, and who will vote and work for the enacting, sustaining and enforcing of prohibitory legislation, and also the systematic opposition to candidates interested in, or in sympathy with, the liquor traffic.

(*b*) Its work shall be to disseminate its principles by means of public meetings, the spread of prohibition literature and personal intercourse; to aid in campaign work; to harmonize, combine, and direct the energies of young men with a view to attaining national prohibition.

For years it filled an important place. It inaugurated a series of Sunday afternoon Gospel temperance meetings on a large scale. They were held in the Horticultural Pavilion for some years, then in Association Hall, and were a potent factor in the success of the reform at that time. The club took an especially active part in municipal elections, and the backing it gave to various candidates for civic honors helped in materially bettering the city council from a temperance standpoint.

One of the most recent of the pledge-signing societies was the Canadian Temperance League, organized in November, 1889, with headquarters at Toronto, and incorporated in 1890.

The work of the League was mainly along educational lines. Meetings were held every Friday evening at which part of the time was regularly devoted to the study of temperance problems. Also Gospel temperance mass meetings were held every Sunday afternoon from November to May, for a number of years in the old Horticultural Pavilion in the Allan Gardens, and later in Massey Hall until 1912. During twenty-three consecutive years of Sunday meetings, about forty thousand signatures were obtained to the total abstinence pledge. Outstanding platform talent was secured, and these gatherings were pronounced by eminent authorities as the largest continuous Sunday temperance meetings in the world.

PROHIBITION IN CANADA.

In addition to the regular meetings, special series of revival services were held from time to time, one of the most famous being that conducted for a period of thirteen or fourteen months by Joe Hess, a converted saloon-keeper and prize-fighter. The League also carried on work in the Mercer Reformatory, the Central Prison, the Asylum, the Haven, the Girls' and Boys' Reformatory Schools at Mimico, and in the city slums.

Another department was the Coffee House movement, an undertaking to supply cheap coffee and sandwiches for working men. A house on the corner of Edward and Terauley Streets, specially built for the purpose by League members, was opened on New Year's night, 1890, and this work was carried on for some years.

At one time entrance was gained by the League into the public schools, the School Board being induced to permit the writing of temperance essays by the pupils, for which prizes were given by the League. Another popular feature that will be remembered by many was the mock trial, "John and Jane Temperance," a dramatic performance that was presented many times and in many places.

The Canadian Temperance League is still in existence, the officers for 1919 being: President, J. S. Robertson; Secretary, Miss Smith; Treasurer, R. S. Shenstone.

During the progress of the temperance movement many other organizations came and went, a number of which will be referred to in the narrative. Some were created for emergencies, some by disagreements, others to give expression or emphasis to a particular phase of the work. All filled a place in the movement and added their contribution to the final result.

ORGANIZATIONS.

IV. THE WOMAN'S CHRISTIAN TEMPERANCE UNION.

It is on record that in 1847 the "Ladies' Total Abstinence Society" of St. John, N.B., petitioned the House of Assembly to prohibit the importation of intoxicating liquors into the province. But it was not until a quarter of a century later that women's temperance work was effectively organized in the W.C.T.U., which has been, since its inception, one of the main factors in temperance advance in this country.

The first union in America was formed at Chautauqua, N.Y., in 1874, as an outgrowth of the Ohio women's temperance prayer crusade. The movement did not take long to reach Canada. It was introduced into the Dominion by Mrs. Doyle, of Owen Sound. When the crusade began in Ohio, Owen Sound was a lake port town of between three and four thousand population, noted from Halifax to Vancouver for drunkenness and gambling. From the beginning of the women's crusade in the United States, Mrs. Doyle was deeply interested in watching its progress and results. For years she had been much concerned about conditions in Owen Sound. The example of the crusaders was evidently the means of inspiring her with that faith in God and that fine enthusiasm for which many Woman's Christian Temperance Union women have since been noted. In May of 1874, Mrs. Doyle called a meeting of the Christian temperance women of the town, with the result that a Woman's Prohibition League was formed with forty members, every woman present joining.

This organization lost little time in getting to work. One of the first things they accomplished was the closing of all the billiard rooms for five years. They were instrumental in having temperance men elected to the council, in reducing the number of liquor licenses, and in procuring a better enforcement of the liquor license law. Educational work was carried on by the distribution of literature and through the columns of the local press. When Mrs. Mary J. Hunt, of Boston, first visited Ontario, Mrs. R. J. Doyle engaged her to address a meeting in Owen Sound, with the result of

PROHIBITION IN CANADA.

reorganizing the women under the name of the Woman's Christian Temperance Union.

From that day to this Owen Sound has been kept in the foreground in the temperance fight. When local option was revived in 1905-1906, Owen Sound stepped into the fray and almost immediately pased a local option by-law, which at that time required only a majority vote. Owen Sound had many a stormy battle for repeal, but it held its own, and the members of Canada's premier Woman's Christian Temperance Union materially aided in every fight.

The leader of women's work in the early days was Mrs. Letitia Youmans, of Picton, Ontario. It was at Chautauqua that Mrs. Youmans received the inspiration to enter on the work of temperance organization, and at Picton in 1874 she formed the second union of Canada, shortly after that of Owen Sound was started. The first effort of the Picton union was directed against the licensed grocery stores, and this menace to the family was one of the first strongholds of the traffic to yield in the greater part of Canada to the attacks of the W.C.T.U.

On the invitation of the Temperance Reformation Society, Mrs. Youmans visited Toronto, and on October 25, 1875, in Shaftesbury Hall organized the Central Union, the mother union of Toronto's forty societies. The work spread rapidly to Hamilton, Dundas, London, Brantford, and elsewhere, until there was a network of local unions throughout the province, which in time were grouped into county organizations. In 1877, they became strong enough to form a provincial union. By 1887, the membership of Toronto alone had become so numerous that the city dropped out of the York County group and formed the Toronto District Woman's Christian Temperance Union. In October, 1891, the Toronto District Woman's Christian Temperance Union opened up headquarters at 56 Elm Street, the first function held in the building being a banquet to the Provincial W.C.T.U. Convention then in session. " Headquarters " became the centre of

ORGANIZATIONS.

woman's temperance work in the city. This building was, after years of useful service, superseded by Willard Hall, on Gerrard Street East, the corner-stone of which was laid by the Duchess of Connaught on November 30, 1911. The new headquarters in Toronto is one of the finest Woman's Christian Temperance Union buildings in the world. It has office and lecture-rooms, gymnasium, dining-hall and boarding-house for girls, and additional ground has been secured on which to erect an extension to the present building.

The brief records now obtainable indicate that the Maritime Provinces early fell into line. The first local organization of the East was started at Moncton, N.B., in 1875, and at Fredericton in 1879, through the efforts of Mrs. R. H. Phillips, five local unions affiliated to form the Woman's Christian Temperance Union of New Brunswick. Four years later, this was merged into the Maritime Woman's Christian Temperance Union, which included Prince Edward Island and Nova Scotia. In 1895, the Maritime Union was dissolved and three provincial organizations were formed. In 1906 New Brunswick and Prince Edward Island combined, an arrangement that obtains until the present.

The first union in Quebec Province was formed at Stanstead, in 1877, by Mrs. Pierce, of Boston. Early in 1883, Mrs. Youmans, on the invitation of the Rev. T. W. Gale, Secretary of the Quebec Branch of the Dominion Alliance, visited Montreal, and on October 17th organized a union there. She also started societies in a number of other places in the province, and in the autumn of the same year a provincial union was established. The work in Quebec was subject to peculiar difficulties owing to racial and religious differences.

During the same year Mrs. Youmans travelled west as far as Alberta, and formed unions in Brandon, Portage la Prairie, and Winnipeg. She also organized Morley and Calgary in the territory of Alberta, and Regina in Saskatchewan. On returning from a visit to California, in 1886, she was met at Victoria, B.C., by members of a Woman's Christian Temperance Union that had been started there a year previously

PROHIBITION IN CANADA.

by Frances Willard. There is no known gauge for measuring spiritual forces, but it is safe to say that if it had not been for the Woman's Christian Temperance Union these western provinces, representing so much of Canada's actual and potential wealth, might not now be under prohibition.

The Dominion Woman's Christian Temperance Union, organized at Montreal in October, 1883, was incorporated by Act of Parliament on July 21, 1894. The Incorporation Act carries the names of the following women: Mrs. Letitia Youmans, Toronto, Ont.; Mrs. Ella F. M. Williams, Montreal, Que.; Mrs. Harriet Todd, St. Stephen, N.B.; Miss Julia Tilley, Toronto, Ont.; Mrs. Annie O. Rutherford, Toronto, Ont.; Mrs. Roberta E. Tilton, Ottawa, Ont.; Mrs. Edith J. Archibald, Cow Bay, Cape Breton, N.S.; Mrs. Myrtle Blakeley, Winnipeg, Man.; Mrs. Elizabeth Middleton, Quebec City, Que.; Mrs. C. Spofford, Victoria, B.C.; and Mrs. C. W. Strong, Summerside, P.E.I. There have been seven Dominion presidents:

    Mrs. Letitia Youmans, Toronto, Ont., 1883–1889.
    Mrs. Ellen G. Foster, Knowlton, Que., 1889–1890.
    Mrs. Michael Fawcett, Toronto, Ont., 1890–1891.
    Mrs. E. J. Steadman, Fredericton, N.B., 1891–1892.
    Mrs. Ella F. M. Williams, Montreal, Que., 1892–1894.
    Mrs. A. O. Rutherford, Toronto, Ont., 1895–1905.
    Mrs. Gordon Wright, London, Ont., 1905–1919.

The purpose of the Dominion organization, which meets biennially, is to unite more closely the women of the provincial unions and to devise plans for the general good, to be carried out in detail by the provinces.

Speaking broadly, the principles for which the Woman's Christian Temperance Union stands are the uniting of women of all countries and the educating of public opinion to oppose the making, sale, or use of intoxicating liquors as beverages. As set forth at length in the constitution of the Ontario Provincial Union, the aim of the organization is:

To unitedly array the Christian women of Ontario against the manufacture, sale, and use of intoxicating liquor as a beverage

ORGANIZATIONS.

To educate and influence society in favor of sobriety and virtue.

To impress upon the youth of our province the awful responsibility resting upon those either supporting or engaged in the liquor traffic, and the folly as well as guilt of partaking of intoxicants of any kind.

To gather statistics, facts, and incidents relating to the traffic in intoxicating liquors, and make use of them in such a way as will best promote the interests of temperance.

To labor individually for the inebriate, the liquor-seller, the fallen of our sex, and for the neglected masses in our cities and towns, hitherto unreached and uncared for.

To give active expression to our sympathy with the family of the inebriate, and to endeavor to elevate his children from the debasing influences with which they are surrounded.

To heartily co-operate with other temperance societies in combating the evils of intemperance, and to unite with any other society or association which is endeavoring, justly, appropriately, and guided by Christian principles, to procure total prohibition of the liquor traffic.

To strive by every means in our power to secure the thorough enforcement of the temperance laws we already possess.

For the accomplishment of these objects we shall faithfully and conscientiously employ all the means God has placed within our reach, and we shall continuously seek His direction and blessing on our work.

The Canadian Woman's Christian Temperance Union pledge has a noteworthy feature. It specifically mentions within brackets "wine, beer and cider" as explanatory of the general term "fermented and malt" beverages that are to be abstained from. The prohibition of cider is particularly striking when it is taken into consideration that this drink, made out of waste apples, was in general use at the time that the pledge was formulated, especially in rural districts.

The unions work through departments, such as: Evangelistic; Prison Reform and Police; Unfermented Wine; Anti-Narcotics; Legislation and Law Enforcement; Work among Lumbermen, Railroad Employees, Soldiers, Sailors and Indians; Temperance in Sabbath Schools. From time to time

PROHIBITION IN CANADA.

other departments are added as new fields of opportunity are opened up. A comparatively recent undertaking is the Little White Ribboners Department, which works amongst mothers for the safeguarding of infants.

The Press Department is concerned with the important work of publicity. The first official organ of the Woman's Christian Temperance Union was the *Woman's Journal*, a monthly publication started in 1884 by Mrs. Addie Chisholm, and adopted in 1889 by the Dominion Woman's Christian Temperance Union under the management of Miss Mary Scott, of Ottawa. From the beginning, urgent need was felt for distinctly Canadian temperance publications. In 1895 the Dominion Union purchased from the Ontario Union its stock of pamphlets and started a literature depository at Toronto under the management of Mrs. A. M. Bascom.

Scientific temperance instruction in the public schools has from the first been part of the policy of the Woman's Christian Temperance Union. Their desiderata are:

1. Scientific temperance instruction made compulsory in all classes in our public schools.
2. A graded series of textbooks on the subject, which shall be placed in the hands of the scholars.
3. Instruction given regularly in this study, as in other studies of the course, and similar examinations required of the pupils.

This department of work is undertaken by every provincial union in Canada. The Maritime Provinces early won out in the fight. There the teaching begins with oral instruction for small children, followed up with authorized textbooks adapted to the grades. The work is continued in the high schools, and student teachers in normal and model schools are given special methods in the subject. Scientific temperance ranks as an examination subject, and the law is observed. The temperance instruction thus given had not a little to do with limiting the sale of liquor years ago to small areas in New Brunswick and Nova Scotia, and with making Prince Edward Island the first prohibition province in the Dominion in 1901.

ORGANIZATIONS.

A vigorous campaign was undertaken in Ontario in 1887, when Mrs. A. O. Rutherford was superintendent of the Scientific Temperance Department. An investigation was made, revealing that in only six schools was temperance being systematically taught. A petition was circulated, to which thousands of signatures were secured of parents, clergymen, teachers and members of temperance societies. Mrs. Chisholm and Mrs. Rutherford waited upon the Minister of Education, Hon. G. W. Ross, and found that a bill for compulsory scientific temperance education was being introduced. They interviewed and presented the petitions to members of Parliament, and undoubtedly had much influence in securing the passage of the bill. Physiology and temperance were thus made compulsory. They were not, however, subjects for departmental examination, and so did not receive the prominence desired, and the Woman's Christian Temperance Union continued its efforts. These subjects were later put on the entrance examination as optional, and in 1893 were ruled by the Educational Department to be compulsory and equal with other subjects for entrance examination.

The following description of the endeavor to secure an adequate textbook, subsequent to the securing of compulsory teaching of the subject, was written by Mrs. S. G. E. McKee, one-time president of the provincial union, and is illustrative of Woman's Christian Temperance Union efforts in various departments·

"Then began the earnest effort for a suitable book or books, for we found that while our friends over the line were fully equipped with a graded set, thanks to the untiring diligence of Mrs. Mary J. Hunt, we had only one textbook, and that not of the kind to make the study attractive, the result being that only those teachers interested produced results in this branch of knowledge so important to the physical and moral well-being of Ontario children.

"In process of time a new book was introduced which, while similar in style and not so scientific, was more adapted to the study of physiology, and had a very small share of the theme of temperance, as we call it. As yet we were not pleased, and we verified the well-known adage that women are hard to please, but it was because we knew that no difficulty is settled until it is settled right. Our interviews, memorials and petitions have kept the Department of Education in waste-basket literature, trying to reach the condition and position of the schools in the United States, where every state in the Union has state legislation on the question of compulsory scientific temperance education.

"In 1901 our provincial sub-executive was made aware of a plan to make a vigorous onslaught on the public school curriculum by the so-called leaders of educational matters in this province, and at the Provincial Teachers' Association resolutions asking for the cutting off of the temperance and hygiene subjects were introduced, and while the teachers' section and inspectors' section turned them down, the public meeting in the evening, where only those determined on the change were present, carried them. The provincial executive had brought Mrs. Mary J. Hunt from Boston to speak on the subject, but by vote she was allowed only fifteen minutes, and during that time the confusion of noise and disorder was shameful.

"In 1902 or 1903 a book was planned by Professor Knight, of Queen's University, which was of immense value to students and teachers, being lectures given to adults, but was too technical for young children. More recently a later work by the same author has been adopted by the Minister of Education, and is a very suitable book.* Temperance is required to be taught in grades 2, 3 and 4, but is not made an examinational test subject for entrance to the high schools.

"And now we are still agitating. This time it is for the re-establishment of the subject of scientific temperance as an examinational test, for be it understood that while the Government paid no attention to the resolution of the Toronto educationalists at the time, later it did. One of the last acts of that Ontario Government was the dropping of scientific temperance, with some other studies, from entrance examinations."

The Woman's Christian Temperance Union also pioneered the road that led to the enfranchisement of women in Dominion and province, and nowhere has its influence been

---

* This text-book is now out of date and is being revised.

ORGANIZATIONS.

more felt. The Canadian unions were more conservative about adopting this policy than were those of the United States, where Miss Willard, always an earnest suffragist, early led the way. It was not until October, 1889, that the first Franchise Department was organized in Canada, at the Ontario Provincial Convention held in Galt. The convention expressed the belief that the extension of the vote to women would be the surest and speediest way to obtain the prohibitory legislation desired by the temperance organizations. The first superintendent was Mrs. Jacob Spence, mother of F. S. Spence. In her address to the members, Mrs. Spence explained the purpose of the women in taking up this line of work. She said:

"It is not the clamor of ambition, ignorance, or frivolity trying to gain position. It is the prayer of earnest, thoughtful Christian women in behalf of their children and their children's children. It is in the interest of our homes, our divinely-appointed place, to protect the home against the licensed evil which is the enemy of the home, and also to aid in our efforts to advance God's Kingdom beyond the bounds of our homes.

"It is only by legislation that the roots of great evils can be touched, and for want of the ballot we stand powerless in face of our most terrible foe, the legalized liquor traffic. The liquor sellers are not afraid of our unions, they are not afraid of our conventions, but they are afraid of our ballots. Witness the following resolution which was passed by the National Association of Brewers in Chicago·

"'Resolved, That we oppose always and everywhere the ballot in the hands of women, for woman's vote is the last hope of the prohibitionists.'

"Surely this utterance ought to inspire the heart and nerve the hand of every Christian temperance woman to increased effort to secure the weapon which friend and foe alike believe will be most succesful."

Surely the fruits of the labors of the Woman's Christian Temperance Union were manifest when, early in 1916, the Manitoba Legislature, by a unanimous vote, enfranchised its

PROHIBITION IN CANADA.

women, and before the year was gone British Columbia, Alberta, and Saskatchewan had adopted adult suffrage. Ontario followed up in 1919.

Because of the steady witness of modern science to the harmful effects on the growing boy of nicotine, especially in the form of the cigarette, and because of the same verdict given by educationalists, juvenile delinquent specialists, men of commerce, and judges on the bench, from the very foundation of the Woman's Christian Temperance Union, antinarcotics has been a shibboleth.

Through the efforts of the Woman's Christian Temperance Union, the wet canteen was removed from Canadian military training camps some years before the war. There had been much liquor selling and drunkenness at the annual training camps at Carling Heights, London, Ontario. Complaints had been made from to time to the officers in charge, without results, until, on the occasion of a visit to the camp by the then Minister of Militia, Sir Frederick Borden, a regrettable incident occurred in which a soldier was shot by another while under the influence of liquor. Following this, a strict regulation was passed forbidding the sale or use of intoxicants within the bounds of any military training camp. This regulation was known only to the military authorities, and was not observed. It was finally unearthed in the course of correspondence between Mrs. May R. Thornley, London, Ontario, and the Department, and a protracted struggle for its enforcement ensued, which, under the régime of Sir Sam Hughes as Minister of Militia, became successful. So it came to pass that Canada had " dry " camps in which to train her soldiers for the war.

During the war the Woman's Christian Temperance Union devotedly served Canadian soldiers overseas. The work done by the Ontario Provincial Union is perhaps the most striking. From 1915 to 1917 they paid $9,526 to the working allowance of individual Y.M.C.A. men whom they supported. From 1918 on, they concentrated on the supplying of free drinks, for which they raised in 1918, $26,600 (to which Nova Scotia

ORGANIZATIONS.

and Manitoba unions contributed); in 1919, $15,000. Also in 1918 they contributed $6,000 to the Soldiers' Christian Association in France. In the early part of the war the Woman's Christian Temperance Union (Dominion and Provincial unions co-operating) endeavored to prevent the establishment of wet canteens for the Canadian camps in England. In Ontario, inside of six weeks, a petition to this end, containing 66,186 names and signed only by mothers, was gathered and presented by Sir Robert Borden to the British War Office.

A heartfelt tribute to the Woman's Christian Temperance Union was paid by F. S. Spence in the *Canada Citizen* in 1887

"Bluff Germans are very fond of claiming the victory at Waterloo for their stern old Blücher, who marched on to the field with fresh troops late Sunday afternoon. Members of the Guards, who had rested in safety all day at the rear of the army, would insist that their fresh blood put impetus into the final sweeping charge, and that to them must be accorded the honor. But history tells us of certain battalions that marched to the front through the thick morning rain and stayed there all day under fire and charge; round shot traversed their 'hollow squares,' musketry thinned their numbers, and the finest cavalry in Europe were hurled again and again with crushing force against their ranks—but they stayed there; and when at last the bugles rang out the welcome 'Charge!' these battle-stained, patient squares dissolved into 'thin red lines,' and with the vigor of victory well-won, swept from blood-soaked Waterloo the magnificent army of the Empire. And when the Waterloo of prohibition is won, the credit will not be given the Blüchers who have been off attending to other matters and arrive just in time to join the pursuit; neither will it be accorded the Guards, who have watched the fight from a safe distance, ready to lead the retreat or join in a sure victory with a shout and a rush and a boast; but it will belong to those who have fought all day amidst shot and shell and charge. And when the roll of these battalions is called, there will answer a large body of light infantry who have done skirmishing, guarded the ambulance, and in times of great need headed fierce assaults and seen hard fighting; where heavier troops dared not venture they entered with safety; and oft, when dragoons and artillery were cumbered with burdens and harassed by uneven ground, they

PROHIBITION IN CANADA.

marched lightly on in advance and held the position till the clumsier soldiery could come up; whenever seen through the smoke of battle or mounting the heights, they are marked by a white badge, and upon their dazzling banner, always pure white amid the grime of war, is emblazoned the motto: 'For God and Home and Native Land.'"

V. DOMINION ALLIANCE.

The Council of the Dominion Alliance has been in existence and active for a good many years. Its efforts secured the passing of the Canada Temperance Act in 1878, the appointment of various commissions to investigate the liquor traffic, the enactment of other national legislation, and the settlement of the question of jurisdiction. Its constitution makes it representative of the prohibition and temperance organizations in the different provinces.* It also includes representatives from synods, conferences, unions, and such bodies. The following is its declaration of principles:

1. That it is neither right nor politic for the state to afford legal protection and sanction to any traffic or system that tends to increase crime, to waste the national resources, to corrupt the social habits and to destroy the health and lives of the people.

2. That the traffic in intoxicating beverages is hostile to the true interests of individuals, and destructive of the order and welfare of society, and ought therefore to be prohibited.

3. That the history and results of all past legislation in regard to the liquor traffic abundantly prove that it is impossible satisfactorily to limit or regulate a system so essentially mischievous in its tendencies.

4. That no consideration of private gain or public revenue can justify the upholding of a system so utterly wrong in principle, suicidal in policy, and disastrous in results, as the traffic in intoxicating liquors.

5. That the total prohibition of the liquor traffic is in perfect harmony with the principles of justice and liberty, is not restrictive of legitimate commerce, and is essential to the integrity and stability of government, and the welfare of the community.

* See Appendix I.

ORGANIZATIONS.

6. That, rising above sectarian and party considerations, all citizens should combine to procure an enactment prohibiting the manufacture, importation and sale of intoxicating beverages as affording most efficient aid in removing the appalling evils of intemperance.

THE ONTARIO BRANCH OF THE DOMINION ALLIANCE.

The Ontario Branch of the Dominion Alliance, which has grown with the movement till it has become a powerful organization, is not a society, but simply what its name signifies, an alliance of the churches and organizations of the Province of Ontario that favor the suppression of the liquor traffic.*

The Alliance work is divided into departments. There is a general executive committee, which meets three or four times a year. During the interim the work is carried on by sub-committees, the chief of which is the Managing Committee, to which all other committees report, and which generally supervises and co-ordinates the work in each department. Other sub-committees are the Finance, Campaign, Legal and Law Enforcement, and Publication. *The Pioneer*, of which Mr. F. S. Spence was the founder and the editor until his death, and which is still published by the Alliance, has been a tremendous factor in the prohibition movement of Ontario. Its circulation has grown until to-day it goes into over twenty-five thousand homes weekly.

Another department of Alliance work is Field Day, which is carried on from week to week. By previous arrangement of the Field Secretary in charge, speakers are massed in a county, city or district, and the pulpits of various churches occupied by representatives of the Alliance. This unites the churches, regardless of denomination or creed, and is of value in creating and maintaining a vitalized public opinion. During the past ten years 22,817 Field Day meetings were held.

The Alliance plan of work contemplates organization in every municipality in the province. These are linked together by counties in a County Alliance; County Alliances

---

* See Appendix II.

PROHIBITION IN CANADA.

are again federated in a provincial body. To secure the effective carrying out of this plan, the province is divided into districts with a Field Secretary in each district, having a general oversight of organization and Field Day work.

The present officials of the Alliance are:

Hon. Presidents, Jos. Gibson, Canon R. W. E. Greene, Theron Gibson; President, Chas. E. Steele; Treasurer, Henry Sutherland; Secretary, Ben. H. Spence; Chairman of Managing Committee, Jos. Oliver; Chairman of the Finance Committee, Miles Vokes; Chairman of the Publication Committee, R. D. Warren; Chairman of the Legal Committee, W. E. Raney; Chairman of the Campaign Committee, Dr. T. H. Cotton.

For over twenty years Mr. F. S. Spence was Secretary of the Alliance. He resigned that position in 1907, but to the very end he was the foremost figure in all the activities of the organization. The executive work was taken over by his brother, Rev. Ben. H. Spence, who was appointed Ontario Secretary in 1907. During his term of office the organization has grown to its present proportions.

SOCIAL SERVICE COUNCIL OF CANADA.

An interesting development of reform work in Canada has been the formation of the Social Service Council of Canada, which is a federation of churches and other Dominion-wide bodies for such united and co-operative efforts for social betterment as may be mutually agreed upon. Seventeen Dominion-wide bodies are now federated in the Dominion Council, and each of the nine provinces has a Provincial Social Service Council or analogous body. In a number of the provinces the provincial prohibition organizations have become merged in the Social Service Council, which has declared for the suppression of drink.

The Council publishes a monthly journal entitled *Social Welfare*.

The Dominion officers are:

President, Rev. L. Norman Tucker, D.C.L.; General Secretary, Rev. Dr. J. G. Shearer; Recording Secretary, Rev. Dr. T. Albert Moore; Treasurer, Mr. Frank Sanderson, LL.D.

SECTION IV

MAINE LAW PERIOD.

Great reform movements, mighty social upliftings, are often begun under very humble auspices. If, however, they are expressions of eternal truth, they win recognition, homage, allegiance, high repute and glorious success that blesses humanity.

I. NEW BRUNSWICK.

ABOUT the middle of the century the pledge-signing movement and the work of the temperance societies began to bear fruit in parliamentary action, both in the United States and Canada. In 1846, after a hard-fought campaign under the leadership of General Neal Dow, the first prohibitory law of the United States was passed in the State of Maine, which forbade the retail sale of spirituous liquors. A series of amendments, repeals, and re-enactments followed until 1858, when the Maine Law took practically the form which has prevailed to the present time.

New Brunswick followed the example of Maine and became the first part of British North America to enact a prohibitory measure. The New Brunswick law of 1855, which had but a short history, is ordinarily cited by opponents of prohibition as an example of the total failure of prohibitory legislation. Considerable information concerning its enactment, operation, and repeal was gathered by the Royal Commission of 1892, through information given by Sir Leonard Tilley, Lieutenant-Governor of New Brunswick, and several other witnesses who took part in parliamentary and popular action at the time. From that evidence the following facts were compiled in 1899:—

The agitation in the New England States which preceded the enactment of the Maine Law was paralleled about 1850 on the eastern side of the international boundary line in New Brunswick. Platform and press were vigorously utilized. Among the advocates of the new method was Mr. Samuel Leonard Tilley, then an active Liberal politician, later on becoming successively a member of the Provincial Government, a member of the Canadian Parliament, a Finance Minister of the Dominion, and Lieutenant-Governor of his native province.

PROHIBITION IN CANADA.

In 1854 a prohibitory bill was introduced into the New Brunswick House of Assembly by Mr. Scullar, but was not adopted. The petitions presented were very largely signed, great rolls of them being stacked up on the floor of the House, and the opinion was generally held that a great majority of the electors were in favor of the proposal.

In the year 1855 Mr. Tilley was a member of the Legislature and a member of the Government. A prohibitory bill, prepared by outside friends of the temperance cause, was placed in his hands. He did not introduce it, however, as a Government measure, but in his capacity as a private member of the Legislature. This course could not be followed to-day. Decisions and precedents have established the doctrine that responsibility for all measures affecting revenue must be taken by the administration, and any bill in Parliament or Legislature that affects the country's finances must be fathered by the Government and introduced into the House by a Cabinet Minister.

The debate on the bill was interesting. Advocates of the measure submitted a great array of evidence accumulated during three years' agitation, demonstrating that intemperance was the prolific cause of lunacy, poverty, mortality, and crime. The statistics adduced were comprehensive and effective. Men who at first opposed the proposal became advocates of it, and when the time for voting came it was supported by about three-fifths of the members of both branches of the Legislature.

This was in the year 1855. The bill provided that there should be no intoxicating beverages imported into, manufactured in, or sold in the Province of New Brunswick after the first day of January, 1856, except for medicinal, mechanical, or sacramental purposes. It is somewhat strange that there does not seem to have been any very strong or well-organized opposition to the movement which thus culminated. It was a popular agitation and swept the country. What little hostility it did evoke, outside those engaged in the liquor business, seems to have been among the lately arrived

MAINE LAW PERIOD.

English people and those who looked upon themselves as the "aristocracy" of the larger centres of population.

The new law of total prohibition went into operation in New Brunswick on January 1, 1856. The classes of the community that had not favored the measure were roused to a stronger opposition than had been manifested when it was under consideration. The unprecedented change in public policy raised a number of legal questions that had not before been dealt with by courts, and concerning which there were no definite decisions to guide judicial officers. The storm centre of the ensuing conflict was the city of St. John.

It is easy to understand how this interfered to prevent effective law-enforcement. At the same time the liquor party created disturbances amounting almost to riots in the City of St. John during the trial of some liquor cases. Enforcement was vigorous for about six weeks; then the heavy cost to the magistrates and the disturbances of the liquor party caused some revulsion of feeling. Even strong friends of the new law feared that it could not be made effective and that its enforcement was going to be a matter of much difficulty. Taking advantage of the situation, the liquor men threw open their doors and began to sell freely. A number of violations of the law were proved and the offenders convicted. Appeals from the decision of the convicting magistrates were taken to the Supreme Court, partly on the ground of irregularity of procedure.

Many of the justices were men lacking legal knowledge and experience, and it is not strange that some of them had made mistakes. Convictions were quashed and the justices making them had to pay costs running in some cases as high as $300 or $400. It is easy to understand the result. Some courageous magistrates made convictions; others were afraid to do so. Cases were undecided; appeals were held in abeyance. Charges were made of favoritism towards certain lawbreakers. Taking advantage of the confusion, some reckless liquor men risked punishment and sold openly. Many supporters of prohibition became discouraged or alarmed.

PROHIBITION IN CANADA.

There was another serious impediment to the success of the law in the strong and open hostility of the Governor, Mr. Manners-Sutton. This gentleman's personal view was that the bill was a very tyrannical one. He asserted that it had not been an issue in the preceding election, and that there ought to be an appeal made to the country upon it at once.

The members of the Government did not agree with the Governor. They claimed that the question had been discussed at the preceding general election in 1854; that it was made a prominent subject of debate at election meetings; that Mr. Tilley himself, besides a number of the other candidates, had openly advocated prohibition; and that, though other questions were prominent in the contest, many men had been elected mainly because of their favor for prohibitory legislation. The Governor sent a communication to the Council, expressing his views and urging a dissolution. Referring to the facts already stated concerning the conviction of some offenders and the escape of others, he said, "When justice ceases to be even-handed, it ceases to be justice." He urged the Government to dissolve the Legislature and appeal to the country without delay.

Naturally, the members of the Government resented this dictation. Some of them had not supported prohibition in the House, but when the Governor's message was received, they united in objecting to his high-handed proceeding. They argued that the new law had been in force but a very short time, that many cases were before the courts for settlement, and that the time was not opportune for deliberate public discussion and decision on so important a problem. They believed that the law ought to have at least a year's trial, and that no action ought to be taken before the next meeting of the Legislature.

Mr. Tilley was Provincial Secretary and Clerk of the Crown. To him the Governor addressed an order, officially instructing him to draft a proclamation declaring the Legislature dissolved, and calling for a general election. Mr. Tilley refused. The other members of the Government supported

MAINE LAW PERIOD.

his action. They informed the Governor that they did not approve of the course he was taking, that they declined to continue nominally as his advisers while their advice was not followed; and they tendered their resignation.

The Governor accepted the resignation of his Cabinet and called in other counsellors who were ready to meet his wishes. The new Government advised him to order the dissolution which he desired, and a general election came on, while there prevailed the chaotic and uncertain conditions which have been described.

New Brunswick had only just passed through the constitutional struggle that in most of the North American British communities preceded the full establishment of responsible representative government. The United Empire Loyalists formed a large element of the population, retaining their strong affection for British institutions. The electorate to which the dismissed Government had to appeal was specially susceptible to the cry that disrespect had been shown to the representatives of the Crown. The shouting of professed loyalty, that has drowned the voice of reason in many political contests, was a great help to the opponents of the new order. It will be noticed that prohibition had not been a Government measure, and that the election precipitated was not directly upon the issue of prohibition, but rather upon the question of the Governor's right to demand a dissolution of the Assembly when his constitutional advisors refused to sanction such a course.

The contest was close and bitter. It resulted in the election of twenty members who supported the late Government and twenty-one who opposed it. A special session of the Legislature immediately repealed the prohibitory law.

It is interesting to note that the new Government, with its bare majority, had a very short lease of power. After a Speaker was elected, the House tied upon different questions. It was found that the allegiance of at least one Government supporter was wavering and, barely in time to save itself from a vote of want of confidence, the new Government again dissolved the House after it had been in session for a little over a month. In the subsequent election, the party previously defeated on the constitutional question was reinstated in power by a large majority, having the support of fully two-thirds of the newly-elected House. A year after being dismissed, the old Government was back in office; but the prohibitory law had been repealed and was not re-enacted.

Many strong prohibitionists claimed, and still claim, that time and experience would have vindicated the constitutionality of the law and would have settled modes of procedure. They believe that a fair period of trial and the removal of the temporary defects would have resulted in such a measure of effective enforcement as would have made prohibition as permanent in New Brunswick as it has been in the adjoining State of Maine.

II. NOVA SCOTIA.

In Nova Scotia a sort of local option had existed since early times. In 1773 the power of granting licenses was conferred upon Justices of the Peace sitting in special sessions in all counties and cities, outside the Township of Halifax. In 1799 the law was amended to provide that the Grand Jury should nominate and recommend to the Justices of the Peace at the spring sessions "as many fit and proper persons of good fame and sober life and conversation as they judged necessary to be licensed." The justices were not, of course, bound to license all whom the Grand Jury elected. In 1851, ten of the seventeen counties refused to grant any licenses.

It was not, however, until the Grand Division of the Sons of Temperance committed itself to the principle of legislative prohibition, about 1851 or 1852, that an active propaganda was begun to secure the passing of a prohibitory law for Nova Scotia.

A singular circumstance occurred in 1852 in connection with this agitation. The opponents of prohibition, making

MAINE LAW PERIOD.

use of a time-honored cry to deflect the progress of the temperance cause, argued that education was more effectual than legislation for suppressing intemperance, and persuaded the House of Assembly to include in the supply bill a grant of £300 in aid of a series of temperance lectures to be delivered throughout the province. However, the Legislative Council, quite contrary to its custom of not interfering with supply bills, struck out the grant.

On February 23, 1854, the Hon. Mr. Johnston presented a bill concerning the manufacture, importation, and sale of spirituous and intoxicating liquors. It received its second reading on February 28th, and was ordered to be referred to Hon. Mr. Johnston, Mr. Archibald, Mr. McQueen, Mr. McLelan, Mr. S. Campbell, Mr. Fulton, and Mr. John Campbell, who should examine and report upon it with amendments or otherwise.

On March 1, 1854, 141 petitions from fourteen counties were presented to the Assembly, praying the House to adopt measures to effect the total abolition of the traffic in intoxicating drinks by enacting a law for the purpose. On the same day twenty-nine petitions from eleven counties were presented, asking for a grant in aid of temperance lectures. It was ordered that all these petitions should be laid upon the table. The bill was reported with amendments on March 11th by Mr. Johnston, and it was referred to a Committee of the Whole House and made the order of the day for March 15th. On that day it was killed in committee, largely through the influence of the Hon. Joseph Howe, who made a memorable speech against it.

He said that he would have been glad to be able to vote for the bill, because a very large, respectable body of his constituents were in favor of it. He admitted the extent of the evils of intemperance. He admired the self-devotion and earnestness with which large bodies of men had endeavored to eradicate these evils, so long as they sought reform by means of moral suasion. But he feared that they would sacrifice all the good they had done by carrying restraints

PROHIBITION IN CANADA.

too far. A prohibition law might be partially enforced for two or three years, but it would coerce people into resistance and occasion a revulsion of feeling to be followed by universal license. He resisted the bill, because by it the right of private judgment was denied.

On February 8, 1855, the Hon. Mr. Johnston again introduced a bill for restricting the use of intoxicating liquors. It was read a second time on February 21st, and a motion was made by Mr. Johnston that it be referred to a Committee of the Whole House. A warm and protracted debate ensued, which lasted through the whole sitting of the next day and three days of the following week. During this debate, the Hon. Joseph Howe moved an amendment to Mr. Johnston's motion to the effect that, instead of committing the bill, the House resolve that a Commission of three gentlemen be appointed to visit the United States, and investigate and report upon the operation and effects of prohibition legislation there. This motion was lost by a vote of 19 to 29, and Mr. Johnston's motion was carried by the same vote reversed. In Committee of the Whole, an amendment was made to the bill, to include cider among the prohibited beverages. Mr. Johnston, who represented the apple-growing county of Annapolis, objected to this amendment, and moved, when the bill was brought up, that it be recommitted for the purpose of striking out the cider clause. On March 12th the House divided on his motion, which was lost and the bill was read a third time and sent to the Legislative Council, where it was killed.

At a temperance convention held in Halifax on February 20 and 21, 1856, a resolution was adopted to petition the Legislature for a law prohibiting the sale of intoxicating liquors, except strictly for purposes of medicine and useful manufactures. If the Legislature should not enact such a measure during that term, the convention recommended the electors not to "assume the responsibility of lending aid to secure the election of any man to represent us in General Assembly or to any office having relation to carrying into operation and effect any such prohibition law, who is not distinctly and satisfactorily pledged to carry out the principles of prohibition."

The Legislature rejected the Prohibition Bill in 1856, on the ground that Nova Scotia should see how the New Brunswick law of 1855 would work, before committing itself. But the experience of that province was evidently such as to discourage the Nova Scotia legislators from undertaking prohibitory legislation; for in 1858, while the agitation for provincial prohibition was still being kept up, the Legislature enacted a new liquor license law. This measure effected very slight changes in the existing law but, unlike previous legislation, contained no provision limiting its operation to one year. Thus the act of 1856 was regarded as permanent in character and none but minor changes were made in it until 1886. In that year a new and very stringent act was passed, which formed the foundation of the license legislation in existence until the enactment of the Nova Scotia Temperance Act of 1910.

III. CANADA.

The influence of the Maine Law movement was felt also in Canada, which was then a single province divided into two sections, Canada East (now Quebec) and Canada West (now Ontario), even after the union familiarly known by their former names of Lower and Upper Canada.

In 1849 the Legislative Assembly of United Canada appointed a select committee, consisting of Col. A. Gugy, Chairman, and Messrs. DeWitt, Brooks, Flint, Taché, Bell, and Jobin, " to enquire whether any and what measures can be adopted to repress the evils of intemperance." Because of the expense that an extended tour would have incurred, the committee confined its investigations to the City of Montreal, of which they said they gave " a picture, not over-charged," and from which those interested might make their own deductions of the state of affairs elsewhere. They interviewed the Chief of Police of that city, the Gaoler, the High Constable, the Revenue Inspectors, the Collector of Customs, and the Coroners. Their report, delivered on March 28th, included a statement by those men, a letter signed by forty-three prominent physicians testifying to the evils of alcoholism and the benefits of total abstinence, and a table of crime in Montreal from January to December 31, 1842. As a result of their investigations the committee found that:

"Intemperance leads to crime, to insanity, and to pauperism. One-half of the crime annually committed, two-thirds of the insanity, three-fourths of the pauperism, are ascribable to intemperance. No other form of words would have been sufficiently comprehensive to express the deliberate convictions of your committee."

Amongst other radical measures they suggested greatly increased penalties for law-breaking, and the treatment of habitual drunkards as insane persons, incapable of managing their personal affairs. Also they recommended that municipalities be given the power to prohibit the traffic in intoxicating liquors.

The latter recommendation was before long acted upon by the Legislature. In 1853 a measure was passed entitled "An Act respecting the Municipal Institutions of Upper Canada," which enacted that "the sale by retail of liquors in inns and taverns in municipalities may be by a by-law prohibited, provided that before the final passing of such by-law, the same has been duly approved by the municipality." In 1855 the local option power was extended to the municipalities of Canada East.

On September 1, 1852, the first temperance measure introduced into the Canadian House of Assembly was brought in by the Hon. Mr. Malcolm Cameron, the Postmaster-General, "to restrain the manufacture, sale and

MAINE LAW PERIOD.

importation of intoxicating liquors in certain cases." This bill was supported by eighty thousand petitions from the people of both Upper and Lower Canada. The debate on the issue was deferred from time to time during the session, and finally, on April 13, 1853, the motion of the Hon. Mr. Cameron, seconded by Mr. Prince, that the bill be then read, was amended, postponing the reading for six months. Eloquent speeches in favor of the Prohibition Bill were made by the mover of it and by Mr. George Brown (Kent), and Mr. Sanborn (Sherbrooke County). The House divided upon the amendment, which was supported by thirty-two members and opposed by twenty-eight. Thus Mr. Cameron's motion was defeated by a majority of four.

The same year saw a new departure in the temperance movement. The work of the temperance societies up to this time had been mainly along moral suasion lines. In 1853 an organization was formed with the special purpose of bringing pressure to bear upon the Legislature for the enactment of a prohibition law.

Several gentlemen, resident in the town of London and its immediate neighborhood, resolved to form a Canadian Temperance League, which should combine not only the efforts of all members of temperance organizations, but of all favorable to the attainment of a prohibition law. For this purpose, a meeting was held in the Odd Fellow's Hall, London, on March 21, 1853, at three o'clock p.m., at which Simeon Morrell, Esq., presided and W. G. Telfer, Esq., acted as secretary. Besides the original movers in the work, there were present the following gentlemen: H. W. Jackson, G.S. of G.D.S. of T., Hamilton; C. H. VanNorman, Hamilton; T. J. Owens; Benj. F. Lazier, Wentworth County Branch; J. B. Jackson, Ingersoll; J. D. Waterman, Carlisle; John King and W. Glasgow, Fingal. After a full discussion, the meeting resolved upon a constitution and appointed the following executive committee to hold office until a general convention could be held:

PROHIBITION IN CANADA.

President.
John Wilson, Esq................London.

Vice-Presidents.

Charles Askew.........London.	Rev. R. V. Rogers.Kingston.	
B. F. Lazier............Dundas.	Hon. N. Cameron...Quebec.	
J. A. Jackson..........Ingersoll.	C. H. VanNorman.Hamilton.	
T. J. Owen..............Guelph.	J. C. Beckett......Montreal.	
Rev. Jonathan Shortt..Port Hope.	John McNab .....Toronto.	
John Dougall..........Montreal.	Rev. W. Ormiston...Clarke.	

R. J. Evans...............*Corresponding Secretary.*
Wm. Rowland, Jun........*Recording Secretary.*
D. J. Hughes.............*Treasurer*

On May 24th of the same year, a large convention was held in the Town Hall, St. Catharines. The object of the League, as set forth in the report of the executive committee, was " to advocate the necessity for and the advantages arising from a prohibition liquor law; to petition the Legislature for such, and enlist into the service all those who are willing to subscribe thereto. Although working in union with the present temperance associations, this declares as its definite object the interference of the law." In order to embody the purpose of the organization in its name, it was decided, after considerable discussion, that the union should be known as the Canadian Prohibitory Liquor Law League. The membership was not to be confined to total abstainers. It was argued that the eighty thousand petitioners of 1852 had not been all pledged abstainers, though they were anxious for the enactment of a prohibition law; and the League would not repudiate the aid of those who for various reasons were not identified with total abstinence societies.

The report of the executive committee, after summing up the work done since the inauguration of the Union, said:

"As to the propriety of soliciting the Legislature to put a stop to the liquor traffic, the Committee and the League generally have but one opinion. They believe it to be the duty of civil governments to suppress the existence of all evils which endanger and

MAINE LAW PERIOD.

injure the well-being of society. That the Government, by its present license system, admits the evil tendency of the sale of spirituous liquors by enacting laws for its regulation, but that the system of licenses as a means of restraint on intemperance has always been a failure; that the countenance of the Government should not in any degree be given to it, and that while the business is legalized and sanctioned by the Government all the efforts of moral influence will be futile. That an evil of such vast magnitude as this requires not regulation, but total suspension; and although such an enactment might appear to curtail the rights and privileges of some private individuals, yet that it is an acknowledged principle in all enlightened governments that private interests must be made subservient to the general interests of the community."

The convention, in adopting its constitution, inserted therein the following clause:

" And its object shall be to procure by the use of all constitutional means the enactment and permanency of a law in Canada to prohibit the manufacture and sale of intoxicating drinks as a beverage."

A manifesto issued by the Executive of the League embodied an early call to political action:

"As the enactment of a prohibition liquor law can only be effected by our representatives in Parliament, we call upon you to select men to represent you in Parliament who will not simply consult the wishes of a portion of the community, but will represent the interests and afford protection to the people at large by enacting a prohibition liquor law."

In 1854, through the activities of the Canadian Prohibition Liquor Law League, a bill providing for the prohibition of the sale of intoxicating liquors was introduced into Parliament by the Hon. Mr. Cameron. It passed its second reading by a vote of ninety-seven to five. But before the vote on its third reading, a point of order was raised that the bill had not been first introduced in Committee of the Whole, where measures affecting trade must originate, and it was thrown out.

PROHIBITION IN CANADA.

In 1856 committees of both branches of the Legislature were again appointed to inquire into the best means of suppressing intemperance. The committee of the Legislative Council approved of the Maine License Law. The committee of the Assembly, of which J. S. Sanborne was chairman, suggested placing before the people at the next municipal election the question of Prohibition *vs.* License Law. "The reason for regulating," said the committee, "is equally forcible for prohibiting if the object sought cannot otherwise be attained. The experience of other countries as well as our own proves that the license system at best is but a partial remedy for the evils of intemperance. From its nature, it can never be radical. It can only check, not remove, the evils."

On May 28, 1856, delegates from a number of temperance societies in convention at Prescott, appointed a standing committee to prepare a prohibition bill, confide it to a reliable member of Parliament, and watch over its progress in the Legislature. They also formulated a rigorous political action policy. Local committees were appointed for each electoral district to propose suitable candidates for the Legislature, and electors were to be earnestly requested to vote only for candidates to Parliament who were at the same time men of principle, who could be depended upon to vote for prohibitory legislation.

In 1859 a prohibition bill for Canada West was introduced by Mr. J. J. E. Linton, Clerk of the Peace, County of Perth. A great many petitions were presented to Parliament and referred by the Legislature to a select committee composed of: Mr. Simpson, Chairman, and Messrs. Cameron, Playfair, McDougall, Walker, Powell, McKellar, Hartman, and A. P. McDonald. The committee confined its investigations to Canada West. They interviewed several gentlemen actively interested in temperance (Messrs. Beatty of Cobourg, Farewell of Oshawa, and Burr of Toronto), and the Police Magistrate and Recorder of Toronto, the Governor of the Toronto Gaol, and the Episcopal Chaplain of the Provincial Penitentiary, as well as two gentlemen engaged in brewing and distilling. They obtained a communication from the Hon. Neal Dow on the history and working of the prohibitory system in the State of Maine. The statements of these gentlemen accompanied the report of the committee. They also forwarded a series of questions upon the subjects referred to them to the sheriffs and wardens of the counties; the mayors, recorders and police magistrates of cities; and the chief magistrates of towns and villages in Upper Canada. From the evidence obtained, the committee was fully convinced of the necessity of mitigating and, if possible, extirpating the evils caused by the use of intoxicating liquors in Upper Canada, and they recommended on March 30, 1859:

"That an Act be passed authorizing and establishing the prohibitory system in all the municipalities in Upper Canada, wherein in the month of July next, at a meeting of persons authorized to vote for school trustees, held for the express purpose of considering the matter, the majority of persons present at such meeting shall not vote against its taking effect within the limits of said municipality."

On March 26, 1859, an act, introduced by Mr. Linton, to restrain the sale of liquors from Saturday night to Monday morning, was passed by the Legislature.

The Dunkin Act.

On April 13, 1863, there was formed at Montreal the United Canadian Alliance for the Suppression of the Liquor Traffic, an organization that was largely instrumental in securing the passage of the Dunkin Act the following year. The first officers of the Alliance were: the Hon. Malcolm Cameron, President; Mr. Willett, Secretary; G. A. Sargeson, Montreal, Treasurer; and a long list of Ministers of the Gospel and Members of Parliament as Vice-Presidents. The declaration of principles of the society contained, among others, the following statements:

PROHIBITION IN CANADA.

"That the history and results of all past legislation in regard to the liquor traffic abundantly prove that it is impossible satisfactorily to limit or regulate a system so essentially mischievous in its tendencies.

"That, rising above class, sectarian, or party consideration, all good citizens should combine to procure an enactment prohibiting the sale of intoxicating beverages as affording most efficient aid in removing the appalling evil of intemperance."

A number of branch organizations were soon formed. Two travelling lecturers and agents were engaged—Mr. Thos. McMurray, Toronto, and Mr. John Moffat, Komoka—who sowed forms of petition for a prohibition law broadcast throughout the land. The Legislature was inundated with a flood of petitions from congregations, Sunday schools, temperance organizations, municipal corporations, and individual citizens. In 1864 Mr. Christopher Dunkin introduced a bill, "To amend the laws in force respecting the sale of intoxicating liquors and issue of licenses therefor, and otherwise for the repression of abuses resulting from such sale." The Alliance Council took in hand the business of carefully supervising the bill in committees and conferring with members of the House in reference to amendments and changes.

In the Upper House, the bill was in charge of the Hon. Jas. Ferrier. Some attempts at resistance were made by the opponents of prohibition, but Mr. Ferrier was strongly sustained by the Hon. Alexander Vidal and a large majority of the House, including the Premier and other Ministers of the Crown. The passage of the bill through the Lower House was a regular ovation; and its third reading was proclaimed with a unanimous shout of triumph by the Legislative Assembly.

The Dunkin Act gave to counties, cities, towns, townships, and villages of Ontario and Quebec, authority to prohibit by popular vote the retail sale of liquor within their respective limits.

Power was given to every municipal council to pass a by-law without submitting the matter to the electors, or

MAINE LAW PERIOD.

if they preferred they might order the by-law to be submitted to the electors for their approval. Thirty electors might propose by requisition the passage of such by-law in any given municipality and demand a poll where it should be adopted. The voting was to be done openly, not by ballot, each elector voting yea or nay. The poll might be kept open one day for every four hundred voters in the polling division. The warden was to count the votes on the close of the poll when the election was for a county. The by-law was to come into force on the 1st of March after its passage.

Licensed distillers or brewers were permitted to sell only liquors they manufactured, in quantities of five gallons, to be taken away at one time. Any merchant or trader having a store or place for the sale of goods might sell five gallons (or one dozen bottles) at a time. Collectors or agents violating the law were to be punished and incur the same penalty as their principal or employer.

Druggists might sell liquors for medicinal purposes; neither they nor the storekeepers were to sell any but between nine Saturday night and six Monday morning.

Prosecution might be brought in the name of the Inland Revenue officer of the district where the by-law was in force, or by the municipality, or in the name of any private person. Prosecution was to be commenced within three months after the alleged offence. Two or more offences by the same party might be entered in any given complaint. The maximum penalty imposable was $100. When the prosecution was brought in the name of an Inland Revenue collector, one-third of the fine was to go to the Government, one-third to the person on whose information the action was brought, and one-third was to be retained by the collector. When brought in the name of the municipality, the whole fine was to belong to the municipality, but it might pay one-half to the party on whose information the action was brought. There was no appeal from the decisions of the magistrate or other qualified officers. Any person obtaining liquor at an inn or other such public house contrary to the act, drinking to excess and being killed,

PROHIBITION IN CANADA.

committing suicide when intoxicated, or otherwise coming to his death while drinking to excess, the legal representatives of such persons might enter action against the innkeeper and recover damages. Any police officer might be authorised by two or more magistrates to enter a house of public entertainment to see that no infraction of the law was being committed.

The act was much more stringent than any previous local option law, yet it had many weaknesses which impaired its usefulness. It did not prohibit the sale of liquors by wholesale or by clubs. There was some uncertainty as to its constitutionality, which was finally established after various decisions of the courts on appeals against convictions. Such cases meant delay in enforcement in those places where the law had been carried. Another of the difficulties met by temperance workers was the ease with which an affirmative vote could be annulled on a legal technicality. For example, the act was carried in Lambton County, and was set aside by the courts because a polling place in one township had been closed for three hours before the specified time, although ample time had been given for all the electors to cast their ballots and although the act specifically provided that if at any time after the opening of the poll, one half-hour should elapse without a vote being offered, the poll might be closed.

Again, under the Dunkin Act, the penalty imposed for illegal selling was from $20 to $50, with no alternative of imprisonment. To render the law-breaker's position still more comfortable, a special clause prohibited the imposition of more than $100 aggregate fine upon one person, no matter how many offences he might be charged with. Want of provision for the enforcement of the law was one of the chief causes in many instances of its failure.

Notwithstanding the many imperfections of the measure, temperance workers made haste to avail themselves of its benefits. Mrs. Youmans, in her *Campaign Echoes*, tells several interesting incidents of Dunkin Act fights in which she participated.

MAINE LAW PERIOD.

In Prince Edward, her own county, the act had early been carried and was working admirably, when it was suddenly discovered that the seal of the municipality had never been attached to the by-law. Upon an appeal to the courts by the liquor party, the act was set aside. When the newly-organized Woman's Christian Temperance Union of Picton failed, after a valiant fight, to persuade the municipal council to cut off the licenses in the town, they determined to make an effort to have the Dunkin Act again adopted by the county. There were nine municipalities, from each of which a petition containing the names of at least thirty electors had to be presented to the County Council. This was accomplished, and matters seemed to be progressing when it was found that the clerk, through whose blunders the bill had been overthrown before, this time had omitted in one municipality to post the notice of votes at the specified time before polling day, thus making all the petitions void. The women had therefore to begin again. A new polling day was appointed; old bills were taken down, new ones substituted. During the strenuous campaign that followed, Mrs. Youmans was charged with having made libellous remarks at a public meeting, and steps were taken to bring her into court, " to scare her and stop her mouth for a while." But the suit was quietly dropped, and its effect, said Mrs. Youmans, " was to supply admirable kindling for the temperance fire." The result of the vote in 1875 was the adoption of the act by six hundred majority.

The following is an extract from a letter from G. D. Platt, of Picton, Secretary of the Temperance Committee, on the occasion of a repeal vote being taken in Prince Edward County at the end of the first year of the law. He said:

"It has done much good in our county, although it has frequently been violated, and for a long time, while litigation was going on, our magistrates were not as bold as they would have been under other circumstances. However, for the last three or four weeks there has been a decided change. Many convictions have been had and fines paid by the liquor sellers, who are begin-

PROHIBITION IN CANADA.

ning to confess that they have no hope but the repeal of the by-law. . . . The figures you refer to mean very little. The tavern-keepers here made all the drunkards they could and placed them on the streets to bring the law into contempt, while under license they try to conceal their work as much as possible."

The champion of the liquor interests during these campaigns was E. King Dodds, a powerful orator, who challenged the best efforts of the temperance forces to defeat him. Mr. Joseph Gibson, a young Englishman of Ingersoll, Ontario, was one of the temperance speakers selected to meet the liquor advocate, and ever since those strenuous days Mr. Gibson has been one of the most vigorous and valiant fighters in the cause of temperance reform that Ontario has had. In the early encounters with E. King Dodds, his keen logic, ready wit, inimitable power of illustration, made him a controversialist of great ability, while the intense earnestness of the man and his faculty for marshalling facts and arguments made him a power on the platform.

Mr. F. S. Spence's first participation in the public temperance work was in the Dunkin Act campaigns of the early seventies. He was teaching school in Toronto at the time, but he offered his services for such meetings as he could reach and return from every evening. We are indebted to Rev. A. Brown of Picton, for a personal reminiscence of one of those meetings held on February 19, 1877. Mr. Brown, who was responsible for supplying some one to oppose the liquor orator, wrote to Toronto to secure the services of a " Mr. Spence, a young man who did good service at Woodbridge." He writes:

" I have a vivid impression of this meeting, though the details are largely forgotten. It was at the village of Maple and during a Dunkin Act campaign. Posters announcing King Dodds, the champion of the liquor traffic, were distributed only two days in advance of the meeting. We were taken by surprise, and much disturbed—hence the haste and earnestness of our appeal to Toronto. The community was stirred. Villagers and people from the surrounding country crowded the hall. King Dodds, with his

MAINE LAW PERIOD.

big physique, strong oratorical powers, and boldness of countenance, seemed a very Goliath of Gath from the camp of the Philistines. Frank S. Spence, a mere stripling and unknown to the audience, was like David, the shepherd youth, in comparison. It certainly looked like an unequal combat. The giant was in armor of *brass* with sword and spear sharpened for the fight. As he roared his challenges, slashed with the sword and thrust with the spear, our hearts quailed. But F. S. Spence met him with unquestionable facts, undeniable testimony, invincible arguments, forceful illustration, and above all with a sincerity and beneficence of purpose that shattered the attack and left the temperance forces victorious. When the fight was over, King Dodds resembled Goliath smitten in the forehead and slain with his own sword. And when the liquor men saw that their champion was slain, they fled. It was one of the earliest efforts of the man who, by voice and pen, became such a powerful advocate of prohibition, and who, in the providence of God, was privileged to see the triumph of the cause for which he gave his life."

The Dunkin Act was voted upon in York County from March 29 to April 3, 1877. For this campaign the Toronto Woman's Christian Temperance Union issued the *York County Dunkin Act Advocate*. Only four of the seventeen municipalities of the county recorded majorities against the law, which was carried by a total majority of 455 in an aggregate vote of 7,769.

A vote was taken in Toronto in the summer of 1877. The regulations for voting provided only one polling place for each municipality and that one to be kept open one day for every four hundred names on the voting list. In Toronto the poll was held in the old drill-shed, where the St. Lawrence market now stands. It was evidently a time of considerable excitement.

The following account of the first day's proceedings is condensed from the report of the Toronto *Mail:*

"Before the doors of the drill-shed were opened, a crowd of anti-Dunkinites had surrounded the entrance and were kept in possession by a cordon of their companions, who, facing outwards, prevented all not of their party from getting near. Tickets with

PROHIBITION IN CANADA.

'Nay' on them were distributed among those known to be in sympathy with the Licensed Victuallers, and as soon as the possessors of the proud distinction were espied by the faithful guard, the word was passed to admit 'the solid man,' who was then accommodated within the charmed circle. Did any zealous Dunkinite try to worm himself in, he was quietly put back, or if he inclined to be in the slightest aggressive in indicating his right to get a little further, was unceremoniously bundled out. These tactics were pursued until the doors were opened, when the anti-Dunkinites obtained possession of the entrance leading to the polling place. There again were the obstructionists working with an ardor that would have done justice to a better cause. As was to be expected, the more prominent advocates of the measure came in for an extra share of the attention. The first who experienced the courtesy of the anti-Dunkin party was Alderman Hallam. He came to exercise his rights as a citizen, when he was surrounded by a crowd who jostled and hustled him around the building, at last bringing him to against the barricade. He finally got out of the hands of the 'free and enlightened,' apparently nothing worse of his warm reception. Mr. Spence was another prominent Dunkinite whose presence seemed obnoxious to the obstructionists. Mat Evans, a prominent Licensed Victualler, is reported to have prevailed upon 'the Mayor of Stanley Street' to attend to Mr. Spence's comfort; but Mr. Spence, not wishing to have such attentions obtruded upon him, firmly rejected them when the anxious Evans detailed six men to see that the bull-dozing was efficiently carried out. The civilities extended to Mr. Spence, if too demonstrative, could not but have been accepted by his friends as a high compliment to that gentleman's efforts in agitating the bill. Mr. Spence, after four or five attempts, with the loss of coat-tail and the assistance of the police, was enabled to poll his vote, thus getting somewhat the better of those who said that he, at any rate, would not be allowed to poll his vote on the first day. Evans, who seemed to be a leading spirit in the crowd, met his match when the Rev. John Potts came up and said, 'Come along, Evans, and I'll take care of you.' He went meekly amid some laughter and polled. One of two worthies in passing said to the other, 'Come on and let us give them another ruff-up.' This plan was followed throughout the day, and the marvel is how one hundred and ninety-nine men in favor of the act managed to force their way through."

MAINE LAW PERIOD.

The voting in Toronto lasted fifteen days. The total vote polled was 7,010: against the law, 4,063; for the law, 2,947.

In the *Canada Casket* in 1878 there was printed a summary of the Dunkin Act votings up to that date. They were as follows:

PROVINCE OF ONTARIO.

In force in·
> Counties of York, Durham, Northumberland, Ontario, Prince Edward, Lanark, Grey, Bruce, Haliburton.
> Townships of Pelham (Lincoln County), Richmond and Ernesttown (Lennox County), South Gower (Grenville County), Front of Lansdowne and Yonge (Leeds County), McDougall (Muskoka County), Melancthon (Dufferin County), Malden (Essex County), Kennebec, Olden, Garden Island, Clarendon (Frontenac County), Romney, Tilbury, Raleigh (Kent County), Euphemia (Lambton County), Pelham (Monck County), Roxborough (Stormont County).
> Town of Peterborough.

Quashed by technicalities in:
> Counties of Frontenac and Kent Oxford, Peterborough, Lambton.

Defeated in:
> Counties of Peel, Wellington, Haldimand.
> Cities of Ottawa, Kingston, Toronto.
> Towns of Port Hope and Cobourg.
> Township of Logan.

Adopted and repealed in preceding ten years in:
> Counties of Lennox and Addington, Brant, Halton.
> Townships of Iroquois, Ancaster, Darlington, Merrickville, N.-E. Hope, Charlotteville, Morrisburg, W. Flamboro, Elizabeth, Otonabee, Asphodel, Smith.

QUEBEC PROVINCE.

In force in:
> Counties of Missisquoi, Argenteuil, Brome.

Defeated in:
> County of Ottawa and City of Hull.

PROHIBITION IN CANADA.

Because of its weaknesses, the Act did not give great satisfaction, and in very many cases it was repealed after a term of imperfect enforcement. Notwithstanding these facts, the law did good in reducing crime and drunkenness in places where it was employed and enforced, as testified by the official returns of the criminal statistics. Five municipalities in Ontario are still under the Dunkin Act; viz., Bloomfield, Colchester, Hallowell, Pelham, and Sarawak.

THE ONTARIO LICENSE LAW.

Since 1849 the regulation of liquor licenses had been left chiefly with the municipal councils, but the arrangement had not worked well. In 1860 a provincial enactment limited the number of licenses to one for every two hundred and fifty people; this clause was omitted from the Act of 1868 and the number was again left to be fixed by the local authorities, few of whom were bold enough to place any limit. In 1873 the Ontario Provincial Legislature provided for the inspection of liquor selling premises and the accommodation offered by licensees, but an investigation made in 1874 showed that "the municipal inspectors had been inefficient, and that the municipal councils had allowed too many taverns to be licensed, more in many cases than were required for the wants of the community. There had been a great amount of apathy and indifference on the part of those bodies, whose duties it should have been to see that the requirements of the law were carried out."

In 1876 the Hon. Adam Crooks introduced into the Ontario Assembly and carried through a licensing act which bore his name. It provided for entrusting the granting of licenses to a board of responsible men appointed by the Government for each riding.

"There can be no reason why," said Mr. Crooks in introducing the bill, "in such an important matter as this the Government should not assume the same responsibility to the House and the country as it did in many other important

MAINE LAW PERIOD.

matters affecting the welfare of the people, such as the administration of justice, the public health, and kindred matters." The failure to limit the number of licenses led him to add: "It appears to me that upon the number of licenses largely depends the question of intemperance." In addition to withdrawing municipal control, the Crooks' Act limited the number of licenses to be granted in every municipality and authorized each council and board of commissioners to still further limit the number, required all taverns to be well-appointed eating-houses, imposed a minimum fee for each of the three kinds of licenses, wholesale, tavern, and shop, and provided for other restrictions. In the first five years under this act the reduction in the number of licenses was 2,165, or 433 per year. The foundation of the Ontario licensing system was thus laid in the Crooks' Act, which was gradually amended during succeeding years in response to the rising tide of public opinion in favor of increasingly stringent liquor regulation.*

---

* See Appendix III.

SECTION V

SCOTT ACT PERIOD.

No one expects that the tastes and habits of a nation can be revolutionized in a day. No one imagines that the coming into force of the Scott Act means the immediate extermination of drinking and drunkenness. All that is claimed is that the Scott Act will at once materially diminish the terrible evils of intemperance, that it will abolish the danger and curse of the open bar, that it will prevent the acquirement of drinking habits, that it will educate the public conscience, and that it will lead to still better legislation in the not-far-off future.

I. THE ONTARIO TEMPERANCE AND PROHIBITORY LEAGUE.

SOON after Confederation the need was felt for some union of the various forces in order that the strength of the temperance sentiment throughout the Dominion might be concentrated and directed towards political action. Consequently, on February 16, 1868, at a joint committee meeting of the Grand Lodge of Canada of the Independent Order of Good Templars and the Grand Division of the Sons of Temperance it was agreed that those two societies should call a convention in Toronto to organize a Temperance Union. Circulars were issued inviting the co-operation of the leading temperance men of kindred organizations and societies, churches and Sabbath schools. The subjects announced for consideration were:

1. The perpetuity of the Temperance Union.
2. Political action regarding temperance legislation.
3. More thorough deliverance of the country from the liquor traffic on the Sabbath day.
4. More extended circulation of wholesome temperance literature.
5. Relation of the Church to the temperance enterprise.

The circulars were signed by Rev. John Finch, G.W.P., S. of T.; E. Stacey, G.S., S. of T.; Rev. Jay S. Youman, P.G.W.P., S. of T.; A. M. Phillips, W.G.C.T., O.B.T.; Oronhyatekha, M.D., G.W.C.T., I.O.G.T.; W. S. William, P.S., W.C.T., I.O.G.T.; J. W. Ferguson, M.D., G.W.S., I.O.G.T.

In response to this call, a large number of representatives from Ontario, with a few from Quebec, met on February 23, 1869, in Temperance Hall, Toronto, which had been offered by the Toronto Temperance Reformation Society for the services of the convention. The distinguished guest of the occasion was

PROHIBITION IN CANADA.

Mr. John N. Stearns, of New York, P.M.W.P., S. of T. of North America, and publishing agent of the National Temperance Society and Publishing House. The convention lasted for three days. The organization of the Canada Temperance Union was completed and a constitution drawn up. The object of the Union was defined as follows:

To unite and concentrate the efforts of all temperance men and organizations favorable to the cause of total abstinence; to instruct and enlighten the public mind in regard to the great principles and truths of the temperance question; to promote temperance legislation and by immediate political action to secure, within the least possible time, the entire prohibition of the liquor traffic. One of the planks of the platform was: "That the temperance war must be fought out by the people at the polls, and it is therefore advisable as soon as possible to organize a Temperance Political Party."

The membership of the organization was to be composed of officers and members of all regularly organized temperance societies in the province, and all others who were pledged abstainers. The officers elected for the ensuing year were: Hon. M. Cameron, Ottawa, President; W. S. Williams Napanee, Secretary; E. W. Holton, Belleville, Treasurer.

The work of the Union was outlined as follows:

1. To continue the work of forming total abstinence societies.
2. To influence public opinion through the regular press and by employing an agent or lecturer.
3. To enlist the aid of the Evangelical Churches in the temperance movement.
4. To petition the Legislature for improvements in the law.

In this new organization was merged the work of the earlier United Canadian Alliance.

In 1870 the Canada Temperance Union resolved to confine its operations to Ontario and took the name of Ontario Temperance and Prohibitory League. Friends of temperance in each of the other provinces were asked to organize a pro-

SCOTT ACT PERIOD.

vincial society with a view to creating at an early date, by delegates appointed from each province, a national society as the executive head of the moral, religious and political temperance work of Canada. On November 10, 1870, the Quebec Temperance and Prohibitory League was organized. In 1871 the Montreal Temperance Society held its thirty-eighth annual meeting, after which the Quebec Temperance and Prohibitory League practically took its place and carried on its work. A conference of the Ontario and Quebec Leagues was held at Ottawa on April 22, 1873. The New Brunswick League was formed on September 4th of that year. The secretary of the Ontario League at this time and for many years was Jacob Spence, and the League had offices at 32 King Street East, Toronto.*

II. ROYAL COMMISSION OF 1874.

About 1873 an agitation was begun which ultimately led to the passing of the Canada Temperance Act. The Dunkin Act had proved defective in many particulars. It applied only to Ontario and Quebec, although petitions had come at different times from Prince Edward Island, New Brunswick, Nova Scotia, Manitoba and British Columbia to have its scope extended to these provinces. Furthermore, the machinery for enforcement was inadequate. In 1873 the Temperance Prohibitory Leagues led in an active petitioning campaign to secure the enactment of a law of total prohibition

The petitions presented to the Assembly were very numerous, and on Sir John A. Macdonald's motion they were referred to a select committee of the House of Commons. The committee in its first report, April 24th, asked for a grant of money to be used in having samples of liquor analyzed by a competent person in order to disclose a system of adulteration, destructive to health and injurious to the revenues of the Dominion. The money was granted. On

---
* See Appendix III.

PROHIBITION IN CANADA.

May 9, 1873, the committee presented its second report which declared in strong terms that the traffic in intoxicating liquors was an unmitigated evil.

They reported the receipt of 384 petitions signed by 39,223 individuals, as well as petitions from 82 municipalities and from the Legislature of the Province of Ontario, praying for a prohibitory law. In the opinion of the committee these petitions formed an unequivocal demand upon the House to remove if possible the evils complained of.

From the statements of 114 sheriffs, prison inspectors, coroners and police magistrates, the committee found that four-fifths of the crimes in Ontario were directly or indirectly connected with the liquor traffic; that out of 28,289 committments to jail for the three previous years, 21,236 were either for drunkenness or for crimes perpetrated under the influence of drink. Upon inquiry into the operation and effect of the Maine law, the committee was convinced that a prohibitory liquor law would mitigate, if not entirely remove, the evils complained of.

With regard to the revenue question, they believed that the diminution in the expense of the administration of justice and the maintenance of asylums, hospitals and penitentiaries would very considerably offset the amount lost to the revenue; that, "apart from all considerations of gain or profit, the interests of the subject should not be sacrificed even to the existence or maintenance of the revenue."

The committee respectfully submitted the importance of speedily enacting a law prohibiting the importation, manufacture and sale of all intoxicating liquor, except for medicinal and mechanical purposes, regulated by proper safeguards and checks.

The committee of the Senate, which had been appointed to consider the petitions presented to the Upper House, reported on May 14th, and fully sustained the findings of the House of Commons committee. They said in part:

"Your committee are fully convinced that the traffic in intoxicating liquors, in addition to the evils mentioned, is detrimental

SCOTT ACT PERIOD.

to all the true interests of the Dominion, mercilessly slaying every year hundreds of her most promising citizens; plunging thousands into misery and want; converting her intelligent and industrious sons, who should be her glory and her strength, into feeble inebriates, her burden and her shame; wasting millions of her wealth in the consumption of an article whose use not only imparts no strength but induces disease and insanity, suicide and murder, thus diverting into hurtful channels the capital that should be employed in developing resources, establishing her manufactures, and expanding her commerce; in short, it is a cancer in the body politic, which, if not speedily eradicated, will mar the bright prospects and blight the patriotic hope of this noble Dominion.

"Your committee regard it as the first and highest duty of Parliament to legislate for the peace, happiness and material prosperity of the people, and consequently for the removal and prevention of evils such as are proved to be now injuring and threatening the country through the common use of intoxicating liquors; and concurring in the opinion of the Legislative Assembly of Ontario, as expressed in their petition, 'that a prohibitory liquor law, such as prayed for by the petitions, would be most beneficial in its results' to the Dominion, would respectfully recommend that the prayer of the petitioners be favorably entertained."

The matter was discussed in the House and referred to the committee to report again.

In 1874, in view of the introduction of the prohibition question into Parliament, the Temperance and Prohibitory Leagues of Ontario, Quebec and New Brunswick called a conference of the several Grand Divisions of the Sons of Temperance and the Grand Lodges of the British American and the British Templars of the Dominion, to meet at Ottawa on April 22nd, during the session of the Dominion Legislature, in order to offer an opportunity for consultation with the friends of temperance in Parliament. Representatives from the three provinces mentioned were present, and there were also in attendance four senators and twelve members of the House of Commons.

PROHIBITION IN CANADA.

A resolution was adopted to the effect that in the opinion of the conference the time had arrived when a prohibitory law (if enacted by the Legislature) would be sustained by public sentiment. The conference approved of the appointment of a Royal Commission to investigate the success of prohibitory legislation in other countries, being fully satisfied that the result of the authoritative information thereby secured would fully justify the conclusion at which they had arrived in favor of a prohibitory law.

The action of the Ontario Prohibitory League in confining its activities to the Province of Ontario had again created a need for a national federation to correlate the temperance activities of the Dominion. The Ottawa conference took steps to meet the situation by adopting the following resolution:

"Whereas there are now in active operation Provincial Temperance and Prohibitory Leagues for the Provinces of Ontario, Quebec, and New Brunswick, and whereas the interest manifested in the various provinces of the Dominion in favor of the prohibition of the liquor traffic, and introduction of the question into the Senate and the House of Commons with the reports of the respective committees of both Houses, have gained for the temperance question, more especially in its relation to the liquor traffic, the position of a great national question, demanding the heartiest co-operation of all its supporters, the fullest and most intelligent discussion of its claims, and the adoption of such modes of action as may be required to remove the difficulties that exist, and secure for Canada a prohibitory law; therefore it is resolved:

"1. That this conference strongly desires the speedy formation of leagues in those provinces where such are not yet organized.

"2. That we recommend the formation of a General Council of consultation, composed of delegates from the various provincial leagues and grand bodies of the temperance organizations, the chief object of such council being to keep the temperance bodies in constant communication with each other and with our friends in Parliament, and to secure united action in all efforts for the overthrow of the drink traffic."

SCOTT ACT PERIOD.

A committee was appointed to communicate the resolution to the various temperance bodies, and if it proved acceptable to them, to call delegates together for organization.

A week later, on April 29th, the House of Commons discussed the adoption of the second report of the Select Committee on Prohibition. Speaking to the motion, Mr. George W. Ross called the attention of the members to the significant fact that already that session there had been received by the Assembly petitions for a prohibitory law showing an aggregate of 100,687 signatures—petitions signed by individuals of all ranks and classes, by municipal officers in their official capacity, by a majority of the representatives in the New Brunswick Legislature, and by the entire Legislative Assembly of Ontario. Mr. Ross scouted the idea that even if these petitions were in some cases signed by women and children they therefore carried less weight as an exponent of public opinion. "I mistake very much the temper of this House," he said, "if the simple fact of many of the class named having petitioned for a prohibition of the liquor traffic, does not give additional force to the petition, their very helplessness in distress deepening the anxiety which will be evinced in protecting them, where they are unable to protect themselves."

He quoted extensively from the report of the committee to show the alarming increase of crime out of all proportion to the increase in population. He challenged the term liquor trade, questioning whether an institution which caused such destruction of life and property and which needed to be increasingly restricted by law, could consistently be classified as one of the trades, which it was the duty of Parliament properly to protect and encourage. He concluded with an eloquent peroration:

"For my own part I have decided my course. On a question like this, when the choice is between the paltry revenue of a few millions—paltry because life is invaluable as compared with money—and the sacrifice of many of the noblest and best of our young men, I decide in favor of humanity. I stand on the side

PROHIBITION IN CANADA.

of the young men. When the choice lies between national morality and happiness and the Minister's financial balance sheet, I stand on the side of morality. When the choice is between the best interests of the many and the selfish interests of the few, I stand with the majority. And I do hope that the House, animated by those considerations of patriotism which should always guide its deliberations, will rise to the realization of the full magnitude of this important question, and in its wisdom devise such legislation as will protect society from the destructive influences of intemperance."

The House of Commons adopted the committee's report, and once again referred to them the petitions, which continued to pour in from every province of the Dominion. The Senate reported that year an aggregate of ten times the number presented to that body the preceding session.

Finally, since all the investigations by committees seemed to be fruitless of any practical results, the committee of the House of Commons, in their third report, delivered May 27, 1874, recommended that Parliament make more extended inquiries upon the subject of prohibitory law and take " such steps as would put the House in possession of full and reliable information as to the operation and result of such laws in those states of the American Union where they are now, or have been, in force, with the view of showing the probable working of such laws in Canada." The committee of the Senate made a similar recommendation, which was also the course approved of by the Prohibition Conference in April. Consequently, at the close of the session, on August 1, 1874, a commission was issued by the Government to Rev. J. W. Manning, former President of the Sons of Temperance, and Col. F. Davis, an anti-prohibitionist, to visit the states of the neighboring Union and to report on the success attending the working of prohibitory legislation there.

The Commission began work on August 25th. They visited the States of Maine, Massachusetts, Rhode Island, Vermont, Michigan and Ohio, and in Maine and Massachusetts they

SCOTT ACT PERIOD.

made special investigations in the rural districts. To use their own words·

"Your Commissioners sought and obtained interviews with governors, ex-governors, secretaries of state, members of Congress, judges of the Supreme, Superior and Police Courts, district attorneys, mayors, ex-mayors, aldermen, overseers of the poor, selectmen, jailers, trial justices, city marshals, editors, chiefs of police, employers of labor, and influential citizens. They also endeavored to obtain extracts from public documents and records, and brought with them for further reference about one hundred and forty state and municipal documents, varying in size from twenty to over one thousand pages. Under the guidance and protection of policemen they visited the lowest quarters of various cities in the states mentioned. They embraced every chance of going where large crowds were likely to be gathered, and, in short, lost no opportunity that they thought would enable them to advance the accomplishment of their object."

They reported that the loss of many public records by fires deprived them of valuable information, while the frequent changes of officials in the United States was not favorable to the preservation of statistical information. Nevertheless, they amassed a great collection of valuable facts and figures. The subject of the inquiry was divided into the following questions:

1. What are the provisions of the law in force in each State?
2. Is the law enforced, and if not, why not?
3. What has been the result in any State of a change from prohibition to license, or *vice versa?*
4. What have been the effects of prohibition upon the social and moral condition of the people?

Their report contains a synopsis of the state acts then in force. It records what was said by each individual interviewed in answer to the above questions. In conclusion, the Commission found "the testimony as to the partial operation of the law in many of these cities and its general enforcement in towns and rural districts to be uniform." The Commission

PROHIBITION IN CANADA.

refrained from making any specific recommendations, leaving the results of their investigations to speak for them. It is worthy of remark, however, that the anti-prohibitionist member returned from his tour of investigation completely converted to prohibition.

The report, presented in 1875, was thoroughly considered by the Houses of Parliament, and on the strength of it a resolution affirming the principle of prohibition was carried in the Senate in March, 1875, by a vote of twenty-five to seventeen.

The agitation was kept up. The number of petitions presented was very great. Mr. G. W. Ross moved to have the House of Commons resolve itself into a Committee of the Whole to consider a resolution in favor of the enactment of prohibition, as far as was within the competence of Parliament, as soon as public opinion would efficiently sustain such legislation. Dr. Schultz moved an amendment declaring that it was the duty of the Government to introduce a prohibitory measure at the earliest moment practicable. Mr. Oliver moved in amendment to the amendment that the House go into Committee of the Whole to consider means to diminish the evil of intemperance. This amendment was adopted. In Committee of the Whole, Mr. Ross moved the following resolution:

"That it is the opinion of the House that a prohibitory law fully carried out is the only effectual remedy for the evils inflicted upon society by temperance, and that Parliament is prepared, so soon as public opinion will efficiently sustain stringent measures, to promote such legislation as will prohibit the manufacture, importation and sale of intoxicating liquor so far as the same is within the competency of the House."

An amendment was offered by Mr. Bowell declaring it to be the duty of the Government to propose such a measure. The committee decided in favor of the motion offered by Mr. Ross and reported the same to the House. No action seems to have been taken upon this report.

SCOTT ACT PERIOD.

III. FORMATION OF THE DOMINION ALLIANCE.

In 1875 sixteen members of the House of Commons united to call a general convention of prohibition workers. About 285 delegates, representing Ontario, Quebec and the Maritime Provinces, met in the Y.M.C.A. Auditorium, Montreal, on September 15th, 16th and 17th. General Neal Dow was the honored guest on that occasion.

Senator Vidal took the chair. The purpose of the convention, as outlined by Mr. G. W. Ross, was to consider whether the temper of the public was sufficient to maintain a prohibitory law if once it were placed on the statute book; also whether prohibitionists should press Parliament for the immediate enactment of such a law. He cited the case of New Brunswick, in 1855, as illustrating a too hasty piece of legislation. The convention had also to decide, he said, in view of the difficulty in getting a prohibitory law, whether it would not be wise to accept some partial and more restrictive measures which would forbid the sale in public bars of liquors to be drunk on the premises. Before any motions were submitted for consideration, the meeting was thrown open for five-minute speeches on the questions:

(1) Would the abolition of tavern, shop and saloon licenses, without interfering with the domestic uses of intoxicating liquors, meet the wishes of temperance men at the present stage of the movement?

(2) Would a prohibitory liquor law, if now passed, be effective?

(3) Would the passage of a prohibitory law, dependent for ratification upon the decision of a majority of the electors of the Dominion by a plebiscite, accomplish the object in view?

A day and a half was given over to the discussion of these questions, during which time views were freely exchanged and the general temper of the convention was clearly evidenced. The consensus of opinion of the delegates seemed to be that they had had enough of half-way measures in the Dunkin Act, and that nothing short of total prohibition would be satisfactory.

In the remaining day and a half the following resolutions were formulated and adopted:

1. That the manufacture, importation and sale of intoxicating liquor as common beverages is found by the evidence of parliamentary committees, as well as the experience of society, to be a fruitful source of crime and pauperism, alike subversive of public morality and social order.

2. That all attempted restrictions of the traffic by license regulations are unsatisfactory, in as much as intemperance and all the evils connected therewith are constantly increasing.

3. That nothing short of the entire prohibition of the manufacture, importation and sale of intoxicating liquor as a beverage would be satisfactory to this convention.

4. That in order that a prohibitory law, when passed, may have that sympathy and support so indispensably necessary to its success, it is the opinion of this convention that the Dominion Parliament should be urged to enact such a law, subject to ratification by popular vote.

The first three resolutions passed with little debate. The fourth evoked considerable discussion. An amendment was proposed asking Parliament to proceed with the ratification of the law with all speed; but it was thought better not to tie the hands of Parliament in any way, and the amendment was lost.

A committee was appointed to draft a plan for a Dominion organization such as would serve to co-ordinate the scattered forces for united action. They presented the following report, which was adopted by the convention:

"That we recommend a union organization to be known as the Dominion Prohibitory Council, to be composed of twenty-five members and distributed among the respective provinces as follows: Ontario, eight; Quebec, six; Nova Scotia, four; New Brunswick, four; Prince Edward Island, two; Manitoba and British Columbia, one.

SCOTT ACT PERIOD.

"The objects of this organization shall be to continue the temperance efforts of the different provinces in such a way as will best promote the suppression of the sale and use of intoxicating liquors throughout the Dominion, and direct the action of the Provincial Leagues and organizations so as to secure uniformity; and we further recommend that the Council be filled by appointments from the Provincial Leagues at their annual meetings."

An interim council was appointed to act until such time as the provinces could select their own representatives.

Immediately after the Montreal convention, the council representing the provinces met and chose as its officers: Senator Vidal, President; Thos. Gales, Secretary; and Robt. McLean, Treasurer. In order that there might be a proper understanding of the work to be undertaken, suggestions were solicited from all members of the council, and a meeting was called at Ottawa on February 16 and 17, 1876, to which were invited members of the Legislature known to be favorable to prohibition. Here it was decided to form a national organization to be called the Dominion Alliance for the Total Suppression of the Liquor Traffic. The sympathy and co-operation of all existing temperance orders and associations were asked. Provision was made for the appointment of a representative council of members elected in each province by the several leagues and bodies. The council appointed at Montreal was retained for the first year.

In an interview with a deputation from this meeting, the Premier, the Hon. Alexander Mackenzie, said that he did not consider public sentiment in favor of prohibition sufficiently strong to warrant immediate legislative action. He expressed doubts as to the constitutionality of the plebiscite desired by the convention, but he thought provision might be made to take a direct vote upon the prohibition question at the next general election. He alluded to the apparently conflicting jurisdictions of the Dominion and Provincial Legislatures with regard to the prohibition of the liquor traffic, and suggested the necessity for a decision of the

PROHIBITION IN CANADA.

Supreme Court of the Dominion in reference thereto as a preliminary step.

The Premier's answer indicated clearly the obstacles to be encountered in the passing of a prohibition law. Nevertheless the Council determined to continue all the more earnestly in their efforts to influence public opinion in favor of such legislation, and to attempt either to secure parliamentary action, or through legal proceedings in the law courts to obtain the settlement of the constitutional difficulty.

Plans were made to hold Alliance meetings in the principal cities and towns of the Dominion, and to call upon the friends of the movement generally to petition Parliament at its next session in favor of prohibition.

It soon became clear that the Dominion Alliance and Provincial Leagues could not carry on work in the same districts without overlapping. On January 24, 1877, the Quebec Temperance and Prohibitory League, at its seventh annual meeting, dissolved in order to identify its work in the province with that of the Alliance. At the first annual meeting of the Alliance, on February 14th, it was decided to correspond with the other Leagues with a view to securing union. On September 18th and 19th the Alliance met in Toronto. A meeting of the Ontario League was held at the same time, and after some discussion a plan was agreed upon by which the provincial organization amalgamated with the Dominion Alliance.* Provincial branches of the Alliance were subsequently formed as follows: At Sherbrooke, Que., Sept. 25, 1878; at Halifax, Nova Scotia, Nov. 28, 1878; at Toronto, Ont., Jan. 14, 1879; at Winnipeg, Man., March 11, 1879; at St. John, New Brunswick, July 15, 1881; at Charlottetown, P.E.I., July 19, 1881; at New Westminster, B.C., Oct. 5, 1881.

The Council of the Dominion Alliance has ever since been recognized as representative of the organized prohibition movement of Canada, and has co-ordinated the work of the various Provincial Branches or analogous organizations so far as their activities are brought to bear upon Dominion issues.

---

* See Appendix IV.

SCOTT ACT PERIOD.

IV. JURISDICTION DIFFICULTY.

The pressure on the Government was continued from all sides. Deputations, petitions, resolutions voiced the growing demand for definite parliamentary action. On November 29, 1876, the Alliance Council met at Ottawa and adopted a resolution in favor of the enactment of a local option law for the Dominion. In 1876 the Nova Scotia Legislature adopted the following resolution:

"Whereas, it is a recognized principle that private interest or personal advantage should be subservient to the public good, and the voluntary conduct of individuals injuriously and prejudiciously affecting the welfare or the interests of society generally is a violation of the unalterable laws of justice, and consequently should be regulated by the laws of the state;

"And whereas, the manufacture, sale and use of intoxicating liquors as a beverage is inseparably connected with the direct evils to the human race and is the most fruitful source of misery, degradation and crime known to the civilized world;

"Therefore, resolved, That it is the opinion of this House that the manufacture, importation and sale of all intoxicating liquors, except for medicinal and mechanical purposes, should be prohibited by law in the Dominion of Canada."

During the years 1876 and 1877, however, in spite of the earnest efforts of friends of temperance, both in the House and out of it, action was deferred by Parliament on the ground of the uncertainty that existed as to the extent of the Dominion's jurisdiction in the matter of prohibitory legislation.

J. J. Maclaren, Q.C., D.C.L., in the *Vanguard* of October, 1893, gave an exposition of the jurisdiction controversy, from which the following extract is quoted:

"The British North America Act does not mention the prohibition of the liquor traffic among the subjects assigned to either the Dominion Parliament or the Provincial Legislature. In consequence of this, very soon after Confederation, the controversy

PROHIBITION IN CANADA.

began as to where this power lay. On one side it was said to belong to the Dominion as coming under the head of trade and commerce or the criminal law; on the other, that it belonged to the provinces under property and civil rights, municipal institutions, licenses, or local matters.

"The decisions of the courts were very conflicting. In Ontario, in 1875, it was decided that municipal prohibitory by-laws under the old provincial act were valid, and in the same year the provincial courts held that the provincial statute requiring brewers to take out a license was constitutional. In 1877 the latter decision was reversed by the Supreme Court on the ground that it was an interference with trade and commerce, which were under the exclusive control of the Dominion Parliament.*

"In Quebec it was held by the courts that the province had not the power to pass a prohibitory law, or to repeal the Dunkin Act, which had been passed prior to Confederation.

"In Nova Scotia a provincial law prohibiting licenses except on the petition of two-thirds of the electors in the district was upheld, while in New Brunswick a similar act was declared to be unconstitutional."

In 1876 Senator Vidal introduced a motion in the Senate for an address to the Governor, praying that the opinion of the judges of the Supreme Court should be obtained as to the extent of the jurisdiction of the Dominion and Provincial Legislatures respectively. Senator Vidal, when urged to withdraw this motion because of its inconvenience at the time, did so only after being assured by the Leader of the Government that the matter would receive consideration and the required information would be obtained at the next session.

The New Brunswick Legislature the same year took the matter up. Correspondence between New Brunswick and the Dominion Government showed that the Minister of Justice thought it would be better not to have the question argued in abstract, but to have a concrete case involving the points at issue tried before the court. The Premier expressed the same

---

* See Severn *vs.* Queen, p. 121.

SCOTT ACT PERIOD.

opinion to a temperance delegation from Montreal on November 10, 1876. Mr. Ross moved in the House of Commons for an address asking for the submission of correspondence between the Dominion Government and the Province of New Brunswick. Hon. Mr. Vidal made a similar motion in the Senate the following year. The return asked for was finally presented in 1877.

The same year Dr. Schultz moved a resolution declaring it to be the duty of the Government to submit to Parliament a prohibitory law as soon as practicable. Mr. Ross, the recognized temperance advocate in the House, and the members of the Government refused to support the resolution on the ground of the jurisdiction uncertainty. Mr. Ross moved in amendment that "Whereas the House has grave doubts as to whether under the provisions of the British North America Act it has power to deal with the sale of intoxicating liquor as a beverage, and whereas the Court of Error and Appeal in the Province of Ontario has referred a case involving such question to the Supreme Court, therefore it would be inexpedient to express an opinion as to the duty of the Government in the matter."

The case referred to was that known as Severn vs. the Queen, which was argued before the Supreme Court of Canada in June, 1877. A brewer of Ontario appealed against the imposition of a license fee by the local Legislature on the ground that the control of such licenses lay within the power of the federal rather than the local Parliament. The local Legislature had acted under a decision of the courts given in 1875, holding that the provincial statute requiring brewers to take out a license was constitutional. The decision of the Supreme Court, rendered February 8, 1878, reversed that finding and declared the provincial act *ultra vires,* judgment being given against the defendant with costs. The argument of the judge was that the power of regulating trade and commerce rested exclusively with the Dominion Government, which had the right to raise money by means of individual taxation except so far as is expressly given to local legislatures. To make it necessary to take out a brewer's license was to raise money by indirect taxation. The only method of indirect taxation allowed to local legislatures was defined in section 92, B.N.A. Act.

So far as clearing up the jurisdiction difficulty, the decision of the Supreme Court was a distinct disappointment, since it confined itself to the specific question of the Provincial Parliament's right to raise a revenue by licensing and left the whole question of jurisdiction as to legislation still unsettled.

V. CANADA TEMPERANCE ACT.

In 1878 the petitioning was continued for total prohibition, for the amendment of the Dunkin Act, and for other legislative measures. On March 18th the Hon. R. W. Scott, Secretary of State, introduced into the Senate, on behalf of the Government, a bill, the basis of which was a measure drafted and submitted to the Government by the Alliance Council. The Canada Temperance Act Senator Scott defined as an enlargement of the Dunkin Act. Whereas the law of 1864 applied only to Ontario and Quebec, the new measure was a local option or permissive bill, applicable to all parts of the Dominion.

"My own impression," said Senator Scott, "is that you cannot entirely control the drinking usages of society by prohibitory laws. I think that is impossible. People must be educated to correct views on the subject before they can be kept sober. But you can remove temptation from a considerable number of people who will not yield to vice unless tempted. I should consider it a farce to pass a prohibitory law in America at present or to prohibit the importation of liquor, because it could not be enforced. The people would not be impressed with the moral sense that the law ought to be observed, and it would be violated; but there are considerable sections of the country where a large majority of the people are impressed with the belief that society

SCOTT ACT PERIOD.

would be very much better without the use of intoxicating liquors; that if it were banished from their precincts crime would decrease, and they and their neighbors would enjoy better health and morally and physically would be superior if deprived of the use of that stimulant. In such sections I believe the people are entitled to prohibition if the majority desire it, because the traffic in intoxicating liquors is not like the trade in any other article."

Senator Vidal heartily approved of the measure, but thought that, considering the still unsettled state of the jurisdiction question, its validity should be ascertained before the Governor-General's signature made it the law of the land.

The bill was introduced into the House of Commons by the Premier on May 3rd. Mr. Mackenzie said he had always felt that the whole people had absolutely the right to such legislation as would practically prohibit the sale and manufacture of intoxicating liquor, yet that it was one of those moral questions which must ultimately be determined by the general will of the people. In speaking to various temperance deputations within the last two or three years, he had pointed out that it was essential that they should use the means which they had in order to manifest in a practical way their own belief in their statements as to the popular support of such a measure. He had been met with the argument that the law as it stood did not elicit a true expression of public opinion. The present bill had been prepared with a view to have an effective permissive bill placed in the hands of the people in all the provinces, with its machinery adapted to a prompt response of public opinion upon the question of local prohibition.

The bill went through the various stages of enactment, several amendments being made by the Senate, and finally became law on May 8, 1878.

The Canada Temperance Act, or Scott Act, as it is usually called, was a measure of local option available for cities and counties. It was divided into three parts. The first provided the machinery by which the second part might be adopted or rejected. The second related to prohibition and did not come into force until adopted by a vote of the electors. The third provided for the enforcement of the law after its adoption. The following are the chief features of the act:

A petition by one-fourth of the electors in any city or county required the taking of a poll. A majority vote in favor of the law secured its enactment. It provided for total prohibition, which could not be revoked for three years, and then only upon a reversal of the poll. If the measure were defeated, no similar petition could be presented for three years.

From the day on which the act came into force, no intoxicating liquor could be sold within the prohibited region, except for medicinal, sacramental, or industrial purposes, by druggists and specially licensed vendors, under strict regulations as to quantity and conditions of sale. The law permitted the sale by any producer of cider, or licensed distiller or brewer, of liquor of his own manufacture in specially defined wholesale quantities to druggists or licensed vendors within the prohibition area, or in retail in districts where the law was not in force. This provision was for the purpose of supporting home industries. The manufacture of native wines has always received special consideration in measures of liquor legislation.

The penalties for violation of this law were fixed at a maximum fine of fifty dollars for the first offence and one hundred dollars for the second, and imprisonment for two months upon every subsequent conviction.

The Scott Act improved upon the Dunkin Act in many particulars. The machinery of the Dominion Government, instead of that of the municipal authorities, was to be employed for the taking of the vote, thus removing the question from local politics. Voting was to be by ballot and was to be completed in one day. There were strict provisions against the corrupt practices in voting that had hampered the effectiveness of the earlier measure. Law enforcement was facilitated by the provision that no smaller territory than a city or county could adopt the Scott Act, and so there could not be a small prohibition area in the centre of a licensed district. The quantity permitted to be sold at one time by wholesale dealers was raised from five gallons to ten, and liquor could not be consumed in Scott Act territory.

VI. THE ACT ESTABLISHED.

During the first few years of its history the enforcement of the act was badly hampered. There were various test cases in the courts, involving the constitutionality of the act and various other points, such as whether an appeal could be taken from the judgment of a police magistrate, and how the act applied in counties where no licenses were in force. The Canada Temperance Act provided that a certain time was required to elapse after the expiration of the licenses in a county or city adopting the act before it could come into force. In several counties in Nova Scotia which adopted it, no licenses were running when the proclamation was issued; hence the lawyers claimed that the date of the expiry of the licenses had never been reached and therefore that the act could not come into force.

The validity of the Canada Temperance Act was finally established in the following manner: It was adopted and went into force in Fredericton, N.B., on May 1, 1879. After its adoption a liquor dealer, Grieves, was convicted of selling illegally. He appealed to the Supreme Court of the province on the ground that the Canada Temperance Act was *ultra vires of the* Dominion Legislature, since it did not deal with trade and commerce, but with civil rights and property. The Supreme Court on August 12th gave judgment against the act, Judge Palmer alone dissenting. On appeal to the Supreme Court at Ottawa this decision was reversed on April 1, 1880, and the act declared to be constitutional, Judge Henry alone dissenting.

Subsequently another Fredericton liquor dealer received permission to appeal to the Privy Council against the decision of the Supreme Court. The case was Russell *vs.* Woodward. Mr. Benjamin, Q.C., was retained by the liquor dealers. The Dominion Alliance urged the Government to employ Mr. Scott, the originator of the law, as counsel in defence of it. The Government at first refused to take any action, and the Dominion Alliance appointed a Canada Temperance Act defence committee, who engaged Mr. Justice Maclaren, Q.C., as senior counsel. Finally the Government agreed to take the matter up and lawyers were employed to argue both sides, Mr. Lash, Deputy Minister of Justice, in favor of the act, and Mr. Christopher Robinson against it. The Alliance employed Mr. Maclaren and Mr. McKay.

The case came up before the Privy Council on the 2nd of May, and the argument lasted two days. Mr. Lash contended that in order to show that a certain power was not vested in the Parliament of Canada, it must be demonstrated that it was vested in the local Legislature. This was not the case with the Canada Temperance Act. Mr. McKay held that the Parliament of Canada could not take away the right of the local legislatures to get revenue from taverns and other authorized sources. Mr. Maclaren's argument was that the right to regulate commerce involved also the right to prohibit. To show that a prohibitory act was a regulation of trade, he cited a decision of the Speaker of the Assembly in 1855, throwing out a prohibitory law which had come to its third reading because it had not originated in a Committee of the Whole, where trade acts must originate.

The judgment of the Lords of the Council, delivered on June 3, 1882, fully sustained the act and finally established the fact that the Parliament of Canada had power to prohibit the liquor traffic.

SCOTT ACT PERIOD.

VII. THE ACT IN OPERATION.

The first place in the Dominion to vote on the Scott Act was the city of Fredericton, N.B., which adopted the law in 1878 by a majority of two hundred. Since then there have been four unsuccessful attempts in that city to repeal the law, which remained in force until the passing of provincial prohibition in 1916.

The act was adopted also in Portland, N.B., and in ten of the fourteen counties of the province. It was subsequently repealed in Portland and in one of the counties. The city of Moncton was erected from a Scott Act county after the coming into operation of the law. Thus, at the time of the passing of provincial prohibition in 1916, nine counties and two cities were under the operation of the Scott Act. Parts of other counties also had local prohibition by municipal option.

Prince Edward Island, which has always been noted for its strong temperance sentiment, within a few years of the passing of the Canada Temperance Act, had adopted it in the three counties of the province and the one city, Charlottetown. The counties maintained the law against one or two attempts at repeal until the passing of provincial prohibition. In Charlottetown, however, the liquor men concentrated their attack upon the city and brought on successive repeal contests. In 1884 the law was sustained by a vote of 775 in favor and 715 against. In 1887 the temperance forces were a little weaker, the vote being 689 for and 669 against. Finally, in 1891, the repeal movement succeeded.

In the *Vanguard,* January, 1894, B. D. Higgs, editor of the Charlottetown *Morning Guardian,* gives an account of that contest and the results that followed:

" The liquor dealers, of course, were fighting for their living and stopped at nothing. Circumstances favored the lawless, too, in peculiar ways. When the city was smaller than it is now it was divided into wards, each ward having the same number of

PROHIBITION IN CANADA.

representatives in the city council. No provision was made for additional wards when the city grew. In time the two northern wards extended far beyond their first boundaries, and here the great bulk of the best class of citizens resided. In the lower wards the rum party was pretty well hived, and the result was that it managed to secure control of the council and of the police. A special Scott Act prosecutor who had been appointed, was dismissed. Several of the councillors sold liquor themselves and made every effort to hamper and obstruct the law.

"Another obstacle, almost insurmountable for a time, was a stupid decision of a Supreme Court judge that a liquor known as 'hop beer' was not an intoxicating but an 'exhilarating' beverage, and therefore not prohibited from sale by the law. This decision was at once followed by a deluge of beer-drinking in Charlottetown, which had most demoralizing results. To overcome these the temperance people worked strenuously. The beer nuisance was largely stopped by decisions of other Supreme Court judges convicting the liquor dealers for the sale of hop beer. The trouble with the city council was only overcome some time after the Scott Act was repealed, when a redistribution bill for changing the divisions of the city was passed.

"With these disadvantages the prospect at times was most disheartening, but our temperance workers never lost courage. They felt it would be wrong to retract from what they had gained, and they saw light ahead. Besides they knew that, even at its worst, the Scott Act had proved better than the old license law. It had made drinking disreputable, and by hiding the saloons had done great good. While before its enactment our county roads were unsafe to travel on at night after a market-day, under the Scott Act all this was changed. Excepting during the hop beer nuisance, a woman might safely drive any night on any road leading to the city. The country, too, was gradually growing in sobriety.

"There was, however, enough in the difficulties enumerated to discourage some, and three years ago the liquor men brought on a vote on the question of repeal. For this they had been preparing for many a day. They had done all they could, spending time and money to discredit the law, and now they determined to make a strong effort for license.

SCOTT ACT PERIOD.

"In the year 1891, by some way or other, in a revision of the Dominion voters' lists, there were left off the list names of a large number of men who were known to be in favor of prohibition. The liquor party eagerly seized on this opportunity, and a petition for another repeal vote was hurried off to Ottawa. The contest came on. The campaign was an eventful one. Nearly every clergyman in the city was for the retention of the law. Mr. Spence stirred the hearts of the people as never before, and had he been able to join us sooner in the fight it is likely the act would have been retained. The repealers won with a narrow majority. Their victory may be ascribed partly to the defect in the voters' list just named and partly to the indifference or discouragement of men who foolishly thought that the Scott Act should be a machine that would supply its own fuel, make its own steam, and consume its own smoke.

"The sentiment of the people of Prince Edward Island is pretty well shown by the figures of the votes polled in the different contests to which reference has been made. . . . Adding together the results of the latest voting in the three counties and Charlottetown, we find that the last recorded verdict of the electors through the Scott Act on the question of prohibition stands thus:

    For prohibition 6,018
    Against prohibition 1,923

        Majority 4,095

"After the repeal there came a period of free rum. During the time the Scott Act was the law of the whole province, the provincial license law was inoperative, and the probability of its being required again was so small that it was dropped from the statute book. Charlottetown, therefore, when the Scott Act was repealed, had in operation no law whatever relating to the sale of liquor. The sentiment against the liquor traffic and any legal recognition of it was so strong throughout the province that the Legislature refused to enact a license law. Even under free rum for a time the wonderfully educative effects of the Scott Act were apparent. Men still hesitated to enter the saloons, branded as they were by public opinion.

"Gradually this feeling began to wear away. The evils were so manifest that the Legislature in 1892 was obliged to recognize

PROHIBITION IN CANADA.

them, and on an urgent petition of the temperance people proceeded to pass a law of an unique character. This measure did not license the sale of liquor, did not authorize anyone to carry it on; it simply provided rigid restrictions which all who sold liquor were required to observe. The sale was only permitted during certain hours, in premises having unscreened windows open to the street, having only one entrance and no seating accommodation. A number of other restrictions were also imposed."

In 1894, when the Regulation Act was in force in Charlottetown, the *Island Guardian* made a survey of the city and found ninety-two places open for the sale of liquor. The results of its investigations were summarized as follows·

" The population of the city was, by the last census, then recently taken, 11,485. There was, therefore, one open saloon for every 125 inhabitants.

" Probably not more than one-fourth part of our people were actively contributing to the support of these saloons, the other three-fourths being made up of women, children and adult men who did not drink. Assuming this rough estimate to be approximately correct, the average number of regular customers within the city for each rum-seller was about thirty-one.

" At the same time we had in the city nine church buildings, or one for each 1,276 people, great and small, and three public schools, or one each for the children out of each population of 3,828.

" It would seem that under the system of free rum there was a surprising number of rum-saloons in proportion to the number of places ministering to the religious, moral and intellectual development of the city. Think of it! Ten rum dens for every church. Thirty rum dens for every public school. Thus it was under the Liquor Regulation Act."

In 1894 the Canada Temperance Act was again voted on in Charlottetown and carried by a slight majority, with 734 for it and 712 against it. There followed four years of vigorous law enforcement, during which time arrests for drunkenness were materially decreased.

SCOTT ACT PERIOD.

	Year.	Arrests for Drunkenness.	Convictions for Violation of the Act.
Free Rum	1891	304	
	1892	222	
	1893	198	
C. T. A......	1894	140	41
	1895	150	70
	1896	160	78

In 1897 the act was again voted on and this time it was rejected by a vote of 786 to 673.*

In Ontario twenty-five counties and two cities adopted the act. It was repealed in all of them. The history of the law in Ontario has been summarized by Mr. Spence as follows:

"It has been alleged that in the Province of Ontario the Canada Temperance Act, commonly called the Scott Act, became unpopular because of not being effective from a temperance standpoint, and that dissatisfaction led to its being repealed in the counties which had adopted it. It is true that the repealing occurred, but the statement referred to as the cause of repeal is incorrect. It would be nearer the truth to say that the Scott Act was repealed because of its success, which roused against it the strong hostility of all the interests affected by the curtailment of the liquor traffic which was brought about by the operation of the law.

'Roughly speaking, the period of Scott Act operation in Ontario ran from May 1, 1885, to May 1, 1889. Some counties changed from license in 1885, and some in 1886. Some changed back in 1888, and some in 1889. The criminal year does not coincide with the license year, and there was only one full criminal year, namely, that of 1887, during the whole of which all the counties referred to were under the Scott Act. Some of these counties include within their limits large cities in which the Scott Act was not carried. There were only seventeen counties which came entirely under the act, and in those counties the commitments to jail for drunkenness in 1887 were less than one-half of what they were during the last preceding full criminal year in which they were all under license, and also less than one-half of the number for the first full criminal year in which they were all under license after the Scott Act was repealed.

---
* See Appendix V.

PROHIBITION IN CANADA.

"The lessening of drunkenness under the Scott Act was too manifest and too well attested to be successfully disputed in any place in which the facts are familiar to the residents. Nevertheless, the law was repealed although it did good, and the actual reasons deserve consideration. They were in part as follows:

"As already stated, there were within the limits of Scott Act counties large cities under license. There were also in some Scott Act counties large towns which voted against the adoption of the act, their majority being swamped by the larger Scott Act majority in the surrounding rural districts. In these large towns which did not endorse the Scott Act there was much difficulty in enforcing the law, as the administration of justice is a county matter in Ontario. The expense of maintaining the results of drinking in licensed cities and in law-breaking towns had to be paid for in part by the other municipalities in the county, which were thus put to expense by a liquor traffic from which they derived no revenue. Much of the drunkenness remaining in the counties fully under the Scott Act had its sources in the large towns which voted against the law and in which was the discouraging law-breaking and drinking that remained.

"This explains to some extent the fact that after repealing the Scott Act the rural municipalities of Ontario have taken hold vigorously of a local option system which applies only to the local municipalities that adopt it and which is steadily becoming more and more popular.

"The Scott Act came into force in the Ontario counties at a time when there was a controversy between the Dominion and Provincial Governments as to which body had the right to control the liquor traffic. This control, of course, included the issuing of vendors' licenses under the Scott Act. The Dominion Government and the Provincial Government both appointed boards of commissioners and license inspectors, and both assumed authority to issue vendors' licenses. This conflict of authority interfered very much with Scott Act enforcement at the outset.

"After the jurisdiction question was settled, the Provincial Government vigorously took up the work of Scott Act enforcement and accomplished excellent results in the punishment and restraint of law-breakers and in the lessening of drinking and drunkenness. This policy was vigorously resented by the law-breakers, who were largely persons who had previously held

SCOTT ACT PERIOD.

licenses. They endeavored to make the proceedings taken against them as disagreeable as possible to the community, summoning as witnesses in some cases persons who had no connection with the matters inquired into—ladies who were members of the Woman's Christian Temperance Union, and the like. Convictions for liquor selling and unsuccessful evasions of conviction all tended to create local discord, which found its way into political affairs.

"All liquor laws were administered by local boards of commissioners appointed directly by the Provincial Government from year to year. This system necessarily made the issuing of licenses to sell liquor a piece of party patronage and brought the liquor traffic actively and interestedly into provincial politics. Liquor men endeavored to create feeling against the Government, and this led to impatience among Government supporters, who sometimes thoughtlessly blamed the Scott Act for a political opposition which the Scott Act was actually weakening.

"The enforcement of the law was defective and irregular. Where it was fairly and effectively carried out, the liquor traffic became arrayed against the party in power. Where it was not properly enforced, friends of law and order were disgusted and offended. Persistent, steady enforcement would have overcome these difficulties, but just about the time when the irritation had reached a climax the liquor traffic took advantage of the opportunity, and when the question of repeal was submitted to the electors, the active political workers, who cared more for party than principle, united in 1887 and 1888 to defeat a measure that was to them an annoyance, although a blessing to the community. The law was repealed in every place in Ontario in which it had been adopted."

VIII. THE ISSUE IN PARLIAMENT.

In 1879 two acts were passed for the amendment of the Canada Temperance Act, one of which authorized the application of the act to electoral districts in Manitoba, and the other made provision for the repeal of the Dunkin Act. In the closing days of the session of 1880 a bill was introduced into the House of Commons by Mr. Boultbee (York), providing that the adoption of the law should require an affirmative vote of a majority of the electors on the voters' lists of the county or city affected. The result of this amendment would have been to hamper seriously the working of the law, if not to render it absolutely useless, for the reason that, in the county voters' lists, a man's name might appear in every township in which he had property. One case is on record in Ontario where the same man was entered thirteen times on the list. Again, the lists rapidly became inaccurate through the death or removal of residents. Thus a proportion of the number of names in the list was no adequate representation of the actual voting strength of the district. Mr. Boultbee's bill passed the Commons by a narrow majority, the vote being ninety-six to seventy-three. The measure was rejected, however, by the Senate and did not become law.

The same motion was introduced again the next year, but this time the House of Commons voted it down by eighty-two to fifty-four.

In compliance with the wish of the Council of the Alliance, the President, the Hon. Senator Vidal, prepared and introduced into the Senate a bill making a certain necessary amendment to the Canada Temperance Act. The bill passed through its preliminary stages without serious alteration, but upon its third reading the Hon. Mr. Almon moved the insertion of a clause exempting ale, porter, lager, beer, cider, and light wines from the operations of the act. This attempt to mutilate the act was promptly resisted by our President and by other friends of temperance in the Senate. Senator Vidal endeavored to throw out his own bill rather than have it pass with the addition of the objectionable clause proposed by Senator Almon. The bill, however, with the clause added, passed the Senate by a vote of twenty-eight to twenty-six, and was sent in due course to the House of Commons. The proposition of Senator Almon called forth a general expression of disapproval. The Provincial Legislatures of Nova Scotia, New Brunswick and Prince Edward Island, several

SCOTT ACT PERIOD.

religious bodies and the large temperance organizations passed condemnatory resolutions.

In the same year the House of Commons voted to close the bars for the sale of liquors and to exclude from the House of Commons refreshment room all strangers not accompanied by members of the House.

When the judgment of the Lords of the Privy Council in the case of Russell was announced, it was agreed that the Dominion Parliament's exclusive control of legislation dealing with the liquor traffic had been thereby established. Consequently a bill providing for the issue of licenses and the regulation of the liquor traffic was passed in the Dominion Parliament. This measure was called the McCarthy Act, after the member of the Commons who introduced it.

In 1884, upon the passing of the measure to amend it, the McCarthy Act was referred to the Supreme Court at Ottawa and to the Judicial Committee of the Privy Council for an expression of opinion as to its validity. The judgment of the Supreme Court was that the license act was unconstitutional as far as it related to tavern or shop licenses, but valid as to vessel licenses and wholesale licenses. The Privy Council ruled that as to these latter also it was invalid, thus establishing the principle that the licensing power rested exclusively with the provinces.

In the year 1884 an historic debate upon the prohibition question took place in the Dominion House of Commons. On March 5th Mr. Geo. E. Foster moved:

"That the object of good government is to promote the general welfare of the people by a careful encouragement and protection of whatever makes for the public good, and by equally careful discouragement and suppression of whatever tends to the public disadvantage.

"That the traffic in alcoholic liquors as beverages is productive of serious injury to the moral, social and industrial welfare of the people of Canada.

"That despite all preceding legislation, the evils of intemperance remain so vast in magnitude, so wide in extent, and so

PROHIBITION IN CANADA.

destructive in effect, as to constitute a social peril and a national menace.

"That this House is of the opinion, for the reasons hereinbefore set forth, that the right and most effectual legislative remedy for these evils is to be found in the enactment and enforcement of a law prohibiting the importation, manufacture and sale of intoxicating liquors for beverage purposes."

The following is an extract from the memorable address made on this occasion by Mr. Foster:

"All preceding legislation has failed to diminish the scope of the evils which result from the traffic, and has failed to minimize those evils, as they should have been minimized. And we must take another thing into consideration when we come to discuss that part of the question; we must take into consideration this fact, that not only has law been doing its work for the last fifty or the last twenty-five years quite effectively, but alongside of law there has been also a very strong and increasing force of education and of the spread of information. Take that into consideration, and yet come to the test by results, and what do we find. We find that in 1831 the liquor bill per capita of the people of Great Britain was £2 15s.; in 1875 it had risen to £3 5s. In 1831 the absolute consumption of alcohol was sixteen pints per head; in 1879 it had risen to seventeen pints per head. What do these results show? They show that along with the restrictive license legislation, which has been growing in strictness for the last twenty-five years, aided by all the methods and teaching that philanthropy and religious fervor could bring about, there has been an absolute increase in the consumption, the cost and the evil results which flow from intoxicating liquors. So, I say, the necessity for a prohibitory law is shown by the failure of preceding attempts at legislation to minimize the evils which result from the traffic, or to diminish the scope of that traffic sufficiently to meet the wants and the wishes of the people."

Mr. Thomas White moved to amend Mr. Foster's resolution by the addition of the following words: "And this House is prepared, so soon as public opinion will sufficiently sustain stringent measures, to promote such legislation, so far as the same is within the competency of the Parliament of Canada."

SCOTT ACT PERIOD.

This amendment was accepted by the House. Mr. Thos. Robertson moved in amendment to the amendment that the following words be added: "And that this House is of the opinion that the public sentiment of the people of Canada calls for legislation to that end." The amendment to the amendment was defeated by a vote of 107 to 55. The amended resolution was adopted by a vote of 122 to 40.

In the year 1885 an act was passed suspending such portions of the McCarthy Act as had been declared unconstitutional by the Supreme Court, pending an appeal to the Privy Council. Many returns relating to the Canada Temperance Act were laid before the House. Many petitions relating to the temperance question were received. A number of bills proposing to amend the Canada Temperance Act were introduced, but not passed. One of the most important of these was the bill agreed to by the representatives of the Dominion Alliance and introduced by Mr. Jamieson. It passed the House of Commons, but was returned from the Senate with an amendment exempting beer and wine from the operation of the Scott Act. The House of Commons refused to assent to this amendment, and the bill did not become law. A motion was submitted by Mr. Kranz, declaring that when a prohibitory law would be enacted, provision should be made for the compensation of brewers, distillers and maltsters. An amendment was offered by Mr. Fisher declaring that the time when Parliament proceeded to discuss the details of a prohibitory law would be the occasion to discuss the question of compensation. The amendment was adopted by a vote of 105 to 74. Mr. Beatty introduced a bill providing for the severe punishment of excessive drunkards, and another bill aimed against the traffic in spirituous liquors but favoring the traffic in beer and wine. Neither of these measures passed the House.

A resolution in favor of total prohibition was introduced in the House of Commons by Mr. Jamieson in the session of 1887. Many amendments offered relating to the Canada Temperance Act were defeated. An amendment was sub-

PROHIBITION IN CANADA.

mitted by Mr. Sproule declaring in favor of compensation. An amendment to this amendment, moved by Mr. Fisher, similar to that submitted by him in 1885, was adopted. The amended resolution was defeated, the vote upon it being 70 for, 112 against.

In 1888 Mr. Jamieson again introduced a resolution in favor of total prohibition. It was not voted upon.

A bill was introduced by Mr. Jamieson making the Scott Act applicable to British Columbia and the unorganized districts in the provinces, and amplifying the provisions referring to prosecutions under the act. Mr. McCarthy introduced another amendment simplifying the form of voting in contests for Scott Act repeal, and exempting from the prohibition of the Scott Act medicinal preparations containing alcohol. Both of these measures became law.

Mr. Jamieson, in 1889, again introduced a resolution declaring it to be the duty of Parliament to enact a prohibitory law. An amendment was proposed by Mr. J. F. Wood, making an additional statement that such prohibition should be enacted when public sentiment was ripe for the reception and enforcement of such a measure. This was adopted by a vote of 99 to 59. An amendment offered by Mr. Taylor in favor of a plebiscite and compensation was defeated, as was also an amendment by Mr. Mills in favor of a plebiscite. An amendment offered by Mr. Moncrieff, favoring the exemption of beer and wine from the operation of the Canada Temperance Act, was ruled out of order. Mr. Jamieson's resolution was adopted without a division.

SECTION VI.

POLITICAL ACTION.

It is not too much politics that is the trouble with the temperance cause, but too little. Politics is a part of religion, and religion that has no politics in it is only half a religion at best.

I. CANADA'S NEW PARTY.

IN 1887 the dissatisfaction, long felt and repeatedly-expressed by temperance workers over the way in which both political parties shifted and evaded responsibility on the prohibition question, gave rise to a division in the temperance ranks. A section of prohibitionists advocated the formation of a new party along the line already being tried in the United States, with the idea of building up around a prohibition platform a party of candidates and electors who would abandon all former political connections and pledge themselves to the support of a prohibition policy.

The Dominion Alliance had repeatedly insisted upon the necessity for consistent prohibitionists to put the temperance issue before party considerations and vote for the temperance candidate, regardless of his political color. They thought that, so far as possible, temperance workers should make use of the strength and organization of the established parties, wherever temperance sentiment was found to exist within their ranks. A new organization, they said, would begin by ostracizing the prohibition parliamentarians who, in both political parties, had been using their influence to raise the temperance tone of Parliament, and would end by leaving the old parties, as a whole, less favorable to temperance, while the new party, at best one against two, would not have the strength or position to accomplish anything of practical value. These believed in securing the support of the man; the others pinned their faith to the party.

In accordance with this recognized policy, at the Dominion Alliance Convention in September, 1887, the Committee on Political Action recommended that friends of temperance should take immediate steps to prevent the election of such candidates to Parliament as were not in favor of or could not be trusted to support the immediate enactment of a national prohibitory law; that if no outspoken prohibition candidate should present himself in a constituency, the temperance people should put one forward or, if they could not do so, should withhold their votes.

This was not satisfactory, however, to some members of the convention. Rev. Dr. Sutherland had moved the following amendment to the committee's report:

Whereas, the experience of thirty years in Great Britain, the United States, and Canada shows that no advanced temperance legislation need be expected from the existing political parties, as such; and,

Whereas, the public utterances of party leaders in the Dominion afford no ground of hope that prohibition will be made a plank in either platform in the near future, if at all; and,

Whereas, there is no distinct issue of principle between the existing parties which renders their continued existence either necessary or important;

Therefore, be it resolved, that this convention is of opinion that the present juncture is peculiarly favorable for the organization of a new party, with prohibition as a chief plank in its platform.

After a spirited discussion that amendment was adopted by a vote of thirty-two to twenty-five, but no further action was taken upon the matter during the convention.

After the adjournment of the convention, however, a call was made for the supporters of Dr. Sutherland's resolution to remain for further consultation. About thirty or forty members met and appointed a provisional committee, consisting of Rev. Drs. Brethour and Burgess and Messrs. Munns and Wigle, to draft a platform on which such a party might be organized. One of the leading spirits of this movement was Dr. Alexander Sutherland. The following platform was drawn up and published in the press of Ontario and Quebec, with an invitation to all temperance electors of the Dominion who were prepared to organize on that basis to meet in Toronto on March 21, 1888, in the old Y.M.C.A. parlor, Shaftesbury Hall.

POLITICAL ACTION.

(1) Righteousness and Truth in public affairs as well as in private business, and no compromise with wrong.

(2) Equal Rights for all Creeds, Classes and Nationalities, but exclusive privileges to none.

(3) A National Sentiment, a National Literature, and in all matters of public policy—Our Country First.

(4) The Prompt and Absolute Prohibition of the Liquor Traffic, and the honest and vigorous enforcement of all laws for the repression of vice and intemperance.

(5) Retrenchment and Economy in Public Expenditure, with the view of reducing our enormous National Debt.

(6) Manhood Suffrage, with an educational qualification. That is, a vote to every freeman of legal age who can read and write.

(7) The Extension of the Franchise to Women.

(8) An Elective Senate.

(9) Civil Service Reform.

About half of those who came to attend the Shaftesbury Hall meeting found the plan of procedure such as they could not approve. They were expected, before entering, to sign their names, subscribing to all the planks of the platform. They were assured by Dr. Sutherland that it was the intention of the promoters of the movement to organize upon the prearranged platform, without allowing any discussion or amendments. Only those who signed the declaration were to be admitted to the meeting. Some of those who refused to comply with the terms of admittance declared themselves as heartily in favor of every plank of the platform, but they protested with vigor against what they considered a high-handed mode of procedure. They withdrew from the building, followed by a number who had already entered the meeting, but who, overhearing the heated debate outside the door, said that they had failed to notice that the book presented to them for signatures was anything more than a register of those in attendance.

Some of these gentlemen gathered in the office of the *Canada Citizen*, where they organized an impromptu meeting, presided over by Dr. Griffin, and adopted a resolution

PROHIBITION IN CANADA.

regretting that the conditions of admission to the Third Party Convention were such as to prevent their entering and taking part in the proceedings.

Those who remained in Shaftesbury Hall conducted the meeting, with Dr. A. Sutherland as Chairman and Mr. J. T. Moore as Secretary. A scheme of organization was adopted and the following officers were elected: President, Dr. Sutherland; Executive Council, Messrs. Gordon, Wigle, D. L. Brethour, C. H. Bishop, W. K. Ireland, A. C. Steele, W. R. Watson, G. E. Armstrong, J. T. Moore, and W. Munns. The newly-elected president delivered a rousing address, which was afterwards printed and circulated by order of the executive. At a later date the name of "Canada's New Party" was chosen for the organization.

Members of the New Party were to be organized in clubs of ten with a marshal as the controlling officer. When ten clubs should be organized within a convenient distance of each other, they were to form a company with a captain at its head. Ten companies should form a battalion, with an officer known as deputy marshal. The captains, deputy marshals, with the marshal as chairman, should constitute the Executive and Finance Committee of the party in a constituency. The movement gained adherents in all the provinces, though its main strength was in Ontario. It included in its ranks many clergymen. In February, 1889, the *New Party Bulletin* was started as a monthly publication. Later the *Canadian Nation* was established as the organ of the party.

The organization assumed a very hostile attitude to Roman Catholicism. Rome and Romanism were grouped together to represent organized selfishness. This policy was deplored by many people as unwise and unjust, considering the great help given to the temperance cause by many members of the Roman Church in Canada and elsewhere.

The *Templar* described Dr. Sutherland as a man of genius and power, a born polemic, strong in argument, intrepid, implacable, a doctrinaire, restive, determined, asser-

POLITICAL ACTION.

tive, and unyielding, and added the following criticism of his methods:

"He repels the greater number of independent thinkers who admire his motives, agree with him in part, but dare to differ with and question the wisdom of some of his plans. We are impressed with the notion that the New Party as a whole has been permeated with this spirit of the leader. There has been a disposition to flagellate every critic of the party. There has been a failure to recognize the great independent but unorganized body of independent electors, from whose ranks alone the new party can be built up."

The *Canada Citizen* published a series of letters discussing, both favorably and unfavorably, the Third Party movement. A variety of opinions were expressed on both sides. The *Citizen* gave its own attitude in an editorial. After reiterating his firm belief in the necessity for independent political action on the part of conscientious and consistent temperance men, the editor pointed out the mistakes in judgment of the organizers of the Third Party. Their error lay in a mistaken idea of the nature of political organization. A party is organized not upon a platform, but upon an issue. A great moral question may be the central idea, but there will be differences of opinion on minor points, which must sometimes be yielded for the sake of harmony and strength. The order of development is: (1) the issue, (2) the party, (3) the platform. It was absurd of the New Party to ask unconditional support of a platform, no matter how perfect it might be, without recognizing the rights of free thought and free speech on the part of those concerned. The platform was defective as a platform, for it made no mention of a fiscal policy. But above all its temperance plank was behind the times. Instead of " Prohibition Now," it advocated an " In the Meantime " policy. In this it went no further than the declarations of present political parties.

In a personal letter to his brother, Mr. Spence clearly explained the attitude which he consistently maintained regarding the political duty of prohibitionists.

PROHIBITION IN CANADA.

TORONTO, January 15th, 1896.

REV. J. M. A. SPENCE,
    Manitou, Manitoba.

My dear Joe,—I have your letter of the 11th inst., and very thankful for your kind congratulations about election. It was a stubbornly fought-out contest in which the lines were definitely drawn on the temperance question. One of my strong opponents was Davies the brewer, and the liquor men generally made a dead set on me. They also did their best to defeat Mr. Fleming.

In reference to your P. P. movement, I have been watching it closely, and while of course not fully understanding the situation, have felt some regret at the language used in some papers, notably the Manitoba correspondent of the *Templar*. It is right for us to stand unflinchingly by our cause and always by the best men, but we have to keep in mind that a great mass of the people are after all indifferent toward this important question, and language that seems violent creates prejudice, makes enemies and thus actually harms our cause. We are bound to be fearless in rebuking evil, but we are not bound to hit anyone, unless the hitting benefits either the hitter or the hit, or the cause for which we hit.

The general opinion here has been that the definite statement made by the leader of the Manitoba Liberal party is such as temperance men ought to highly appreciate. We want to encourage right action that does not go at all as far as we would desire.

After all, is not the trouble with the Liberal party as well as the Conservative party in Manitoba, just what has caused our dissatisfaction here? That is, our good people, church members, active Christians, will not soil their hands with politics, cannot be dragged to political conventions; they are eloquent in denunciation of political wrongdoing and calling upon electors to put their principles in their ballots, but will never lift a finger to put us in such position that we can have an opportunity to do this. They deliberately leave politics to bad men and then piously lament the badness of politics.

If we simply want to make a noise about badness and goodness without practical progress, then independent political action gives the best opportunity. If we are really anxious to accomplish the best results, then, as matters now stand, twenty men in their respective parties can help more towards better laws and purer

POLITICAL ACTION.

government than can two hundred independents. There is probably hardly a constituency in Ontario where twenty determined men could not practically control the management of either political party in that constituency.

This is very hard work. It is much easier to get out and fight as a foe than to stand up and fight as a friend. Moreover, in Ontario at any rate, the man who conscientiously endeavors to better politics inside party lines has to stand a fierce fire of abuse and misrepresentation that is hardly credible, from those who take the position that nothing is right except the particular independent policy which they advocate.

I do not know how Patronism stands in Manitoba. In Ontario it is sensibly weakened. I was hoping that it would take strong prohibition ground as an organization, but there is no immediate prospect of that now. Then in political methods it has unfortunately not got away from the wrong practices of the old parties, as our courts have shown. It also has imposed upon its members ironclad restrictions, which are difficult for a self-respecting, independent-minded man to observe.

After all, is not the fault with the people who make up the parties? Calling a man a Patron instead of a Conservative does not change his nature and therefore ultimately will not change his conduct. There are lots of things I would like to say on this important question, but, as you can imagine, I am pretty well driven for time. I sincerely hope that the outcome of your struggles will be really the advancement of what is right, though it seems to us here just now that prohibitionists would be stronger, more influential and more successful in compelling wise legislation from the party certain to be dominant in your Legislature, if you had approved that party's right-doing on the temperance question instead of merely denouncing its wrong-doing, when there was an opportunity for both. My ideas are, of course, only those of a spectator.

Sincerely and affectionately,

F. S. Spence,

PROHIBITION IN CANADA.

II. *NOVA SCOTIA PROHIBITION PARTY.*

In Nova Scotia in 1889, a movement was started which was similar to the New Party in many respects but different in some details. Disappointed at the failure of leading prohibitionists in Parliament—notably Edward Blake amongst the Liberals and Mr. Foster amongst the Conservatives—to persuade their respective parties to the adoption of a prohibition plank, some people in Cumberland County, N.S., led by J. T. Bulmer, started a prohibition party in the county which soon spread its influence throughout the province.

On November 13, 1889, a convention representing the churches, Sons of Temperance, Good Templars, Woman's Christian Temperance Union, Reform Clubs and Prohibition Clubs, met in Moncton. Mr. Bulmer, who was called to the chair, stated that the leading temperance organizations of the country, who were represented at the convention, were all in sympathy with the movement. A committee was appointed to draft a platform for the party to be presented to the convention.

There were some present who opposed the idea of forming a new party, and advised working along the old lines and influencing the old parties to prohibitory action, but they were voted down and, after considerable discussion, the following platform, presented by the committee, was adopted:

(1) We acknowledge our dependence upon the righteous Ruler of the universe.

(2) It is the recognized duty of the state to protect and conserve by law the national welfare, health and morals of the people. It is equally acknowledged that the liquor traffic works the greatest injury to all these interests of the individual, home and community. It is, therefore, a most evident right and duty of the state to prohibit this traffic, which is the greatest foe to those interests which the state is pledged to protect and conserve.

(3) With the greatest organized influence of the liquor interests in the old political parties, we have no ground to hope that either the Government or the Opposition will make prohibition a plank in their platform in the near future, if at all.

POLITICAL ACTION.

(4) We fail to distinguish any distinct issue in principle between the existing political parties at all comparable with that of prohibition.

(5) We therefore declare the total suppression of the liquor traffic to be the chief plank of the platform on which we stand, and believe it to form a political issue which claims the sympathy and practical support of all good citizens who have the highest welfare of the country at heart.

(6) We recognize the fact that when the prohibition party may have to assume the responsibilities of power, the minor issues affecting the welfare of the country will have to be considered. Until, however, this time has nearly come, we do not consider it best to risk the division of prohibitionists by introducing these issues before they require immediate practical consideration.

(7) In the meantime our representatives in Parliament are expected to give an independent support to all measures they consider for the best interests of the country.

The following officers were elected: President, J. T. Bulmer, Halifax; Secretary, Rev. A. S. Thompson, Petitcodiac; Treasurer, B. D. Rogers, Stellarton; Vice-Presidents and Executive Committee representing the various counties.

The *Canadian Voice,* published at Halifax by Mr. T. W. Casey, was made the official organ of the prohibition party in the Maritime Provinces. It was also the organ of the Good Templars in Nova Scotia. On the editorial page the following statement of principle appeared weekly: "Until the Liquor Question is rightly settled, I will never vote for a man for municipal, provincial or national office, whom I do not believe to be a prohibitionist and the nominee of a party that believes in prohibition."

There was a suggestion that the Maritime Prohibition Party should unite with the Third Party organized in Ontario, but the two were not in absolute accord, and the union was not effected. The chief point of difference between the parties was the policy of Dr. Sutherland's organization of including in his platform several planks not wholly connected with the prohibition idea.

PROHIBITION IN CANADA.

III. MONTREAL CONVENTION, 1888.

Political action was the theme of the great Alliance Convention which was called in Montreal in 1888. The plan of representation was calculated to make this more representative than any previous gathering of Canadian prohibitionists, and a special request was made for the co-operation towards this end of all temperance societies and friends of moral reform.

The situation that confronted temperance workers was in brief this, as set out in a *Citizen* editorial. Prohibitionists had asked for total prohibition and had been offered the Scott Act as a temporary measure, on the distinct understanding that a large vote in its favor would be accepted as an evidence of the approval of prohibition. The act was fought for by prohibitionists on the understanding that by supporting it they were making stronger their demands for a more comprehensive measure. That demand the Dominion Parliament had persistently ignored, and prohibitionists could not but consider this deliberate disregard as a breach of faith on the part of the legislators.

There was the further fact that about seventy prohibitionists in the House were ready to act in accordance with the pledge of ten years before, but the others, irrespective of party, had united to support the liquor interests, some ignorantly, some deliberately. Both political parties were directly hostile to prohibition and in joint conspiracy against it. The enemies of prohibition were strong because they were united and could prevent either party from declaring for prohibition. The friends of prohibition were weak because they did not stand everywhere shoulder to shoulder, so as to compel either party to make prohibition a political issue.

" What our cause needs," said the editor of the *Citizen*, " is union. Our friends must stand together without jealousy, without sectionalism, ignoring partisanship, but combining in a solid phalanx, determined by God's help to win. Let us have full discussion as to the best line of action to secure

POLITICAL ACTION.

this union, and then let every man sink his predilections for any other policy and go in heart and soul with the majority. So only can we hope to win."

It was an impressive gathering of 175 delegates, representing Ontario, Quebec, New Brunswick, Nova Scotia, and Manitoba, which met at Montreal on July 2, 3 and 4, 1888. There was an earnest conviction that, with the epidemic of Scott Act repeals, a crisis in the prohibition movement had been reached which demanded a new and aggressive step, one which would force the issue of prohibition upon the country. The history of the Canada Temperance Act showed that prohibition did prohibit, and consequently the liquor interests were fiercely antagonistic and fighting for their lives. Temperance sentiment demanded not a retreat but a more advanced law, and parliamentary representatives who would enact and enforce it.

On the evening of the first day, there was a mass meeting at which the Hon. Geo. E. Foster presided. Addressing the meeting, he expressed his hearty sympathy with the temperance cause, in which he had been interested for twenty-five years. He would offer a friendly word of caution: the friends of prohibition were not on the eve of victory; rather, one of the fiercest battles was yet to be fought. Prohibition would come, not perhaps for generations, but in God's good time. In this country temperance reform had reached the highest possible point, considering the time and circumstances. Everything possible had been done. The progress made had been great. It was now a political question; however, they must not forget the educational aspect. Education made and sustained the law. Laws could not be passed without public consent and sympathy; therefore the railing of temperance people against politicians was not fair. If members of Parliament did not vote for a prohibition measure now, it was because their constituencies did not want it.

The *Witness* recounts a characteristic incident:

"Before Mr. Foster sat down Mr. Spence ran on to the platform and with flashing eye, but cheek as pale as death, arrested the attention of the assemblage by asserting that the evidence before the country and the personal knowledge of the delegates was that the work of education, while necessary to be continued, was not the only thing to be done, and indeed not the greatest, for the electors were sufficiently educated to strike. As the heroic boys from this and other provinces went to the North-West to put down the rebellion, so now the time had arrived for the people, by their vote, to show they were ready for prohibition.

"An almost indescribable scene of enthusiasm was then witnessed. The applause that broke out was prolonged for several moments, and suddenly changed from clapping to cheering, until the hurrahs almost lifted the roof. The honorable chairman sat watching the demonstration with profound gravity.

"Mr. Howland moved a vote of thanks to the Hon. Mr. Foster, who presided. 'Of course,' said Mr. Howland, 'I differ very much from the stand taken by Mr. Foster.'

"'I will step up with you every time,' said Mr. Foster.

"Mr. Foster, returning thanks, said that it was a cause of rejoicing that men, agreeing in spirit, could meet on a public platform and in Christian spirit discuss methods upon which they differed."

The convention spent three days in careful deliberation of the various problems of the situation. The question of the Scott Act was a live one. It was decided that the act should not be repudiated by temperance workers in spite of the repeal movement, which was being used by opponents of prohibition to bring the whole temperance cause into disrepute. The law had done good where it had been given a chance, and should be adopted as extensively as possible until something better could be obtained.

The convention took a firm stand on the subject of law enforcement, and demanded that properly constituted authorities should be held responsible for the enforcement of the law. To this end it recommended the formation of Law and Order Leagues to see that the duly authorized representatives of the law enforce the same. The work of the Montreal Law and Order League was eulogized.

POLITICAL ACTION.

A plebiscite on the temperance question was not to be accepted by the temperance people under any consideration. It was strongly condemned as a political pretext for needless delay. The demand upon the Government was to be for an act of total prohibition. Neither would the convention entertain the idea of compensation for liquor dealers, but utterly denied that they were in any way entitled to compensation.

A memorable debate occurred on the report of the Committee on Political Action, which read as follows:

(1) That it is of the highest importance to obtain united political action on the part of all those who are in favor of immediate total prohibition of the liquor traffic.

(2) That we endorse the action of our friends in the House of Commons in introducing and supporting the prohibition resolution of 1887, and we request them to take like action at every session of Parliament until the resolution be adopted and prohibitiou secured. The following is the resolution of 1887: "That in the opinion of this House it is expedient to prohibit the manufacture, sale and importation of intoxicating liquors except for sacramental, medicinal, scientific and mechanical purposes. That the enforcement of such prohibition and such manufacture, importation and sale as may be allowed, shall be by the Dominion Government, through specially appointed officers."

(3) That we call upon the friends of prohibition to organize each of the constituencies for the purpose of preventing the re-election of any member who does not favor such a resolution, and for securing the nomination and election of candidates who are known and publicly avowed prohibitionists.

(4) That where the nomination of such a prohibition candidate is not otherwise secured, an independent prohibition candidate be nominated and supported at the polls.

The report was opposed by representatives of the recently organized New Party. Dr. Sutherland moved an amendment to substitute for the committee's report the following resolutions:

(1) The convention records its deliberate conviction that the prohibition of the liquor traffic is a question of the hour, affecting

PROHIBITION IN CANADA.

more deeply the welfare of the people than any other question now before the country.

(2) That the experience of many years leads to the conviction that prohibition will not be adopted in the near future by either of the parties now in the Dominion Parliament; and that independent political action is necessary to the success of the prohibition movement.

(3) That in our judgment a platform framed in the interests of the whole people, with prohibition as its central plank, would rally a strong force of public sentiment and lead to the speedy adoption of a comprehensive law for the abolition of the liquor traffic.

The following account of a few of the speeches is condensed from the report of the *Montreal Witness:*

Dr. Sutherland considered the report of the committee was a "jellyfish" arrangement. He would like to know how many more times prohibitionists were to threaten the existing parties with something terrible. Some people believed in a third party, just as they believed in the Millennium. They had no desire to make it come now. He believed that the members of Parliament wanted educating, but a dozen votes in a ballot box would educate a member of Parliament quicker than ten years of moral suasion. The report talked about bringing out candidates. How could they be brought out without an independent party? If they would be independent candidates, why not say so and not sail under false colors?

Hon. Senator Vidal resented the "jellyfish" allegation. He had fought for prohibition for forty-eight years. He was first and foremost for prohibition, and he would not for any party be untrue to the cause. The third party movement, in his opinion, would force out of the temperance ranks such prohibition champions as Mr. Fisher and Mr. Jamieson and be disastrous. He thought the country was ripe for prohibition, and if the temperance workers acted wisely they would get a majority in the House at the next election. Then, if a prohibition resolution was carried, the Government would have to carry it into effect or resign and go to the people on the question; then they would have a true temperance party, and it would secure prohibition within a few years, while a third party would need years for growth.

POLITICAL ACTION.

Mr. F. S. Spence said that they must do something practical. It did not occur to him that in the question of a third party any principle was involved. It was a question of policy. In prohibition there was a principle involved upon which they all agreed. They wanted to unite, so that in future their votes would not be thrown away, as in the past. They wanted to use their votes so that they would tell. He liked the Third Party Convention, as he thought it a healthy sign and meant business. They had done something like this before, but in the proposition of the Committee on Political Action they had machinery for the supply of funds and men. If they struck political action out of the cause, they might strike out prohibition altogether, as they could obtain it no other way. It was only three years since the electoral union scheme was first devised and it had been a success. If they could give him a scheme likely to give better results than the Electoral Union, it would be a grand thing. He didn't care a slap in the face for either political party. What they wanted was to take action as united Grits and Conservatives. They had the Presbyterians and Methodists at their back, and in the name of union, in the name of prohibition, let them go on increasing the temperance men in the Dominion Parliament until they had a majority.

Rev. Dr. Shaw, Toronto, said that in the present scheme of the Alliance there was no advance on what had been formulated ten years ago.

Mr. J. R. Dougall said that, if the Third Party was formed, it would mean two old parties against one prohibition party. They would undoubtedly have candidates, but would they send them to the House? He feared that the result would estrange the seventy men they had fighting for them now.

Mr. Jamieson, M.P., said he had always been a prohibitionist and had been elected by Conservative votes. He thought it not fair to characterize the Conservatives as a party of saloon-keepers.

Mr. S. A. Fisher, M.P., understood that the proposal was for a party to adopt the seventy temperance members in the House. But what if they refused to be adopted? It would put them in an unfortunate position. He was a member of the Liberal party and worked with that party because he believed that in so doing he was serving the best interests of his country. At the same time he was a prohibitionist, and the moment the Liberal party went against prohibition, he left the party. The New Party for some time would have very few men in the House. Was he to leave the body who had influence, and could do some good, and join one that would have little or no influence in the House for years to come?

The report of the committee was adopted with the addition to the third clause of the words, " and who will agree to act in concert with the other members of the House who favor prohibition."

A thoroughly revised form of constitution for the Alliance was prepared and adopted. It provided for a Committee on Political Action of twenty-one members, elected annually, to plan and direct the local organization in accordance with the political platform adopted by the convention. Also provision was made for a special Standing Committee on Legislation, composed of members of Parliament and other members of the Council who were in harmony with the declaration of principles of the Alliance. This committee was to hold a special meeting at Ottawa during each session of Parliament to watch and advise concerning legislation. The Alliance was made more representative, the membership being extended to include henceforth, as at this convention, in addition to delegates from the provincial branches, delegates also from provincial temperance organizations and religious bodies.

The General Conference of the Methodist Church, meeting at Montreal in September, 1890, endorsed the political platform of the Alliance as adopted at the Montreal convention, and strongly recommended that such political candidates as were approved by the Alliance should be given the earnest and undivided support of the members and adherents of the Methodist Church.

" It is only by thus showing ourselves independent of party influence on this supreme moral question that we can secure for our convictions the consideration they deserve, and force the early solution of this prohibition problem," was the declaration of the Conference.

POLITICAL ACTION.

Dominion elections on March 5, 1891, gave to temperance workers an opportunity for carrying out their plan for political action. It was early evident that they intended to make prohibition a live issue in the coming session. Letters were sent by the Alliance Executive to Dominion candidates, questioning them as to whether or not, in the event of their election, they would support the prohibition resolution in Parliament, and from their replies a temperance ticket was drawn up. Before voting day an electoral address was sent to Canadian prohibitionists, urging their support of temperance candidates and setting forth in full the political platform adopted in 1888 and confirmed by subsequent conventions. Voters were urged to support absolutely reliable candidates, and if need be "to sacrifice party predilections for the sake of patriotism and principle." There was submitted the voting record in Parliament of the previous House of Commons on the question of immediate total prohibition in the divisions taken in 1887 and 1889. Those who had voted for prohibition resolutions but had backed down upon the need for immediate action were, much to the indignation of some such, not classed with the radical prohibitionists.

The results of this vigorous campaign were gratifying to the workers. The temperance question had been made an issue in the elections to a greater extent than ever before. It was believed that amongst the seventy-five new members sent up to the House there were a considerable number who would favor the enactment of prohibitory legislation, and many members were pledged to support the prohibition resolution.

A movement for petitioning the Dominion Parliament in favor of prohibition had been inaugurated in 1888 by the General Assembly of the Presbyterian Church, in which other denominations and temperance societies quickly co-operated. By 1891 there were fifteen Christian bodies actively engaged in the work.

From the opening of the new Parliament in 1891, these petitions came pouring in, occupying about an hour each day

PROHIBITION IN CANADA.

in their formal presentation to the House of Commons. official returns of the Clerk of the House showed a tota 2,626 petitions received during the year, with 304,808 sig tures, twenty-two of which were those of presidents secretaries in behalf of societies.

SECTION VII.

ROYAL COMMISSION OF 1892.

There is a deal of cowardice that masquerades as caution and laziness that poses as wisdom.
The dilatory and cowardly course is never the prudent and wise one.

I. PARLIAMENTARY ACTION.

IN drawing up its resolution in 1891, the Legislative Committee of the Council of the Dominion Alliance set itself to forestall the habitual parliamentary shuffle on the prohibition question. Since the passing of the Canada Temperance Act, the tale of evasions had been a long one. Practically every year since 1884, there had been a resolution before the House to the effect that it was the duty of Parliament to enact prohibitory legislation, to which resolution an amendment had been regularly proposed that such legislation should be enacted when the country was ripe for it.

One result of this routine procedure was that, alongside those who voted against the prohibition amendment because they were in favor of immediate prohibition, were lined up those who voted against both resolution and amendment, and who were opposed to prohibition at all times and seasons. On the other hand, those who voted for the amendment claimed that those who had voted against it were really the opponents of prohibition. It was a bad muddle.

The resolution adopted after considerable discussion by the Alliance Committee at Ottawa on May 5, 1891, read as follows·

"That in the opinion of this House the time has arrived when it is expedient to prohibit the manufacture and sale of intoxicating liquor for beverage purposes."

They hoped that they had here an issue upon which a clearcut division could be made and for which it would be difficult to devise a subterfuge.

Hon. Mr. Jamieson was entrusted with the responsibility of introducing the resolution in the House and arranging for its discussion. The caucus of prohibition members who, at Mr. Flint's suggestion met in the Tower Room on May 13th,

PROHIBITION IN CANADA.

evinced a disappointing lack of harmony in the ranks of parliamentary prohibitionists. Mr. Jamieson, in taking the chair, presented to the meeting the resolution adopted by the Legislative Committee of the Dominion Alliance, which he intended to move in the House of Commons. This announcement called forth a protest that the caucus was not to be allowed to draft its own measure or to alter the one given to it. Objection was raised to the declaration for immediate prohibition by Mr. Taylor, of Leeds, Conservative Whip. Mr. Taylor had a grievance against the Alliance for having listed in their election circular, amongst the opponents of prohibition, those who had not supported the prohibition resolution or who had favored compensation and so many other qualifications and restrictions as, in the opinion of the Alliance, to nullify their support. After half an hour of disputation, a number of the objectors left the room and the resolution was adopted.

A circular letter was sent by the Alliance Executive to the members of the House of Commons, announcing the proposed resolution to be introduced as an independent measure and asking for non-partisan support of it. A similar letter was sent by the Ontario Branch of the Alliance to the Ontario members.

The resolution came up in the House on May 20th. Mr. Jamieson, on rising to make the motion, reviewed the action taken by former Parliaments in assenting to the prohibition principle from 1873, when a Senate committee had reported to the effect that "the traffic in intoxicating liquors was detrimental to the interests of the Dominion, destructive to her wealth and subversive of her prospects," and had recommended the enactment of a prohibitory law. He reviewed the Dominion-wide situation, adducing the Scott Act repeals, not as a retrogression of the temperance movement, but as an evidence of dissatisfaction with that peculiar kind of local option. Its success in lessening crime and drunkenness from Prince Edward Island to Manitoba was established by a comparative study of conviction statistics.

ROYAL COMMISSION OF 1892.

Mr. Fraser, of Guysboro', seconded the resolution from the Opposition benches, urging the benefits to the country of a prohibitory measure and the educational value of a strong statement on the subject by the House.

In discussion there came up the questions of loss of revenue, compensation for liquor dealers, difficulty of enforcement, and the uncertainty of popular support of the measure. It was suggested that the Finance Minister make a statement, a challenge which he did not at the time accept. Two amendments were introduced, one by Mr. McIntosh proposing a select committee to inquire into the whole question of prohibitiou, and one by Mr. Taylor advocating a plebiscite. It was clear from the tenor of the discussion that the prohibition petitions had created considerable impression upon the House. It was clear also that the Government was anxious to avoid a vote, while the Opposition desired to press the issue. At the close of the second day, after one unsuccessful attempt, the Government succeeded in carrying a motion for adjournment of the debate, opposed solidly by the Liberals, and by Mr. Jamieson alone from the Government benches.

A week later an influential deputation waited upon the Government in support of Mr. Jamieson's resolution and the numerous prohibition petitions before the House. It was composed of accredited representatives of the Methodist General Conference, the Presbyterian General Assembly, the Disciples of Christ, the Congregationist Union, Salvation Army, W.C.T.U., Sons of Temperance, Royal Templars of Temperance, and Independent Order of Good Templars. There were present also of parliamentary members, Senator Vidal, President of the Dominion Alliance and Chairman of the Legislative Committee, and Messrs. T. B. Flint, J. Jamieson, J. Scriver, J. P. Brown, C. C. Bowers, and J. Charlton. Owing to the illness of Sir John A. Macdonald, the deputation was received by the Hon. Mackenzie Bowell and the Hon. Geo. E. Foster. The speakers were introduced by the Hon. Mr. Jamieson. Mr. Bowell's reply was non-committal. Mr. Foster's speech—his first on the question for a long time—

PROHIBITION IN CANADA.

was very unsatisfying to the prohibitionists. He was reported in part by the *Toronto Mail* as follows:

"The position he took was briefly this, that if it was the desire of the majority of the people to have prohibition they should have it by all means, but care must be taken not to put upon the statute book a prohibitory enactment before the sentiment of the country was sufficiently strong to sustain and enforce it. He also pointed out many practical difficulties in the way of immediate prohibition of the liquor traffic, the principal among which would be the diminution in the annual revenue of the country of $7,500,000, to make up for which it would be necessary to resort to direct taxation."

The *Globe* commented on the Minister's position as follows:

"We advise the Mr. Foster of 1891, who is troubled about revenue, to commune with the Mr. Foster of 1884, who will speedily settle his doubts. What (so the earlier Mr. Foster will argue) is a mere change in the mode of collecting a revenue of $7,500,000—not a loss of that amount—what is that compared to the loss of $40,000,000 a year of the people's earnings now spent in poison, or to the loss of the labor of twelve thousand men, the waste of human powers and talents, and the misery, crime and degradation that drunkenness brings in its train?"

Debate on the Jamieson resolution was, by arrangement, resumed on June 24th, when Mr. Foster, speaking for the Government, made a somewhat memorable utterance, declaring his fidelity to his prohibition principles and his desire to carry out the will of the people. He went on to say:

"The only inconsistency which has been urged against me is that on one occasion I voted for immediate prohibition, when Mr. Robertson of Shelburne brought that up as an amendment. I did it and I did it in a moment of weakness. I did it not because I was convinced that the country was then ready for immediate prohibition, but because I felt that the lash was raised outside of that criticism, and that anathema which would be hurled against me if I did not vote for immediate prohibition, and I voted for it.

ROYAL COMMISSION OF 1892.

There is my candid confession. Take it and make what you please of it. But from this time forth I propose to do what I consider to be right and honest, and I will do nothing further and nothing less."

He then moved the following amendment to Mr. McIntosh's amendment to the Jamieson resolution:

"That in the opinion of this House it is desirable without delay to obtain for the information and consideration of Parliament, by means of a Royal Commission, the fullest and most reliable data possible respecting

"'1. The effects of the liquor traffic upon all interests affected by it in Canada.

"'2. The measures which have been adopted in this and other countries with a view to lessen, regulate, or prohibit the traffic.

"'3. The results of these measures in each case.

"'4. The effect the enactment of a prohibitory liquor law in Canada would have in respect of social conditions, agricultural, business, industrial, and commercial interests, of the revenue requirements of municipalities, provinces, and the Dominion, and also as to its capability of efficient enforcement.

"'5. All other information bearing on the question of prohibition.'"

It was pointed out by the Opposition that, while Mr. Foster presented the revenue difficulty as the principal obstacle to the passing of a prohibitory law, and insisted upon the importance of knowing the people's will in the matter as an earnest of the success of its enforcement, his commission proposal touched upon neither of these vital questions but sought other information, with which it was deemed the country was already quite familiar.

The division on the Foster amendment was: 107 yeas (all Conservatives) and 88 nays (85 Liberals and 3 Conservatives).

Few were deceived by the subterfuge of the Royal Commission. The disappointment of many prohibitionists over this move is expressed in a letter to Mr. Spence from Mr. T. B. Flint, M.P.:

PROHIBITION IN CANADA.

" Under Foster's lead the House has agreed to the appointment of a Royal Commission of 'Inquiry,' with a view to ascertaining facts with which the country is perfectly familiar, but with the real purpose and aim of postponing till a more convenient season any decided action by Parliament on the subject of the liquor traffic. . . . As regards the solid Liberal vote against this absurd resolution, it would not be correct to assume that they were all for Jamieson's resolution, pure and simple, as quite a number would have voted for a plebiscite, but they all realized that the Government's scheme was one of mere humbug and delay."

Not once nor twice in the story of Canada's temperance reform have her people needed to discriminate between genuine and spurious wisdom in remedial measures. The cloak of caution has been worn threadbare.

II. THE COMMISSION AT WORK.

The Commission was issued on March 14, 1892, in the following terms:

Seal.
STANLEY OF PRESTON.
CANADA.

VICTORIA, by the Grace of God, of the United Kingdom of Great Britain, and Ireland, Queen, Defender of the Faith, etc., etc., etc.

TO SIR JOSEPH HICKSON, of the City of Montreal in the Province of Quebec, Knight; Herbert S. McDonald, Esquire, Judge of the County Court of the United Counties of Leeds and Grenville, in the Province of Ontario; Edward F. Clarke, Esquire, of the City of Toronto, in said Province of Ontario, and a member of the Legislative Assembly of the said Province; George Auguste Gigault, of St. Cesaire, in the Province of Quebec, and the Reverend Joseph McLeod, of the City of Fredericton, in the Province of New Brunswick, Doctor of Divinity, and to all to whom the same may in any wise concern,

ROYAL COMMISSION OF 1892.

GREETING.

Robt. Sedgewick,
Deputy Minister
of Justice, Canada.

WHEREAS it is deemed expedient to obtain for the information and consideration of Parliament the fullest and most reliable data possible respecting:—

1. The effect of the Liquor Traffic upon all interests affected by it in Canada;
2. The measures which have been adopted in this and other countries with a view to lessen, regulate or prohibit the traffic;
3. The results of these measures in each case;
4. The effect that the enactment of a Prohibitory Liquor Law in Canada would have in respect of social conditions, agricultural business, industrial and commercial interests, of the revenue requirements of municipalities, provinces, and of the Dominion, and also as to its capability of efficient enforcement;
5. All other information bearing upon the question of Prohibitiou.

AND WHEREAS it is expedient that a Commission be issued to competent persons for the purpose of obtaining such data and information.

AND WHEREAS it is in and by "The Revised Statutes of Canada," Chapter 114, entitled "An Act respecting inquiries concerning Public Matters," amongst other things in effect enacted that whenever the Governor in Council deems it expedient to cause inquiry to be made into and concerning any matter connected with the good government of Canada or the conduct of any part of the public business thereof, and such inquiry is not regulated by any special law, the Governor in Council may by the Commission in the case confer upon the Commissioners or persons by whom such inquiry is to be conducted the power of summoning before them any witnesses and of requiring them to give evidence on oath, orally or in writing, or in solemn affirmation, if they are persons entitled to affirm in civil matters and to produce such documents and things as such Commissioners deem requisite to the full investigations of the matters into which they are appointed to examine.

AND WHEREAS it is expedient that inquiry under oath should be made into and concerning the matters and things hereinbefore mentioned and set out.

NOW KNOW YE that under and by virtue of all and every powers and power vested in US in that behalf, and by and with the advice of OUR PRIVY COUNCIL for CANADA, WE, reposing trust and confidence in your loyalty, integrity and ability have nominated, constituted and appointed and do hereby nominate, constitute and appoint you the said SIR JOSEPH HICKSON, Knight, you the said Herbert S. McDonald, you the said Edward F. Clarke, you the said George Auguste Gigault, you the said Joseph McLeod to be OUR Commissioners for the purpose of obtaining the desired data respecting:—

1. The effects of the Liquor Traffic upon all interests affected by it in Canada;
2. The measures which have been adopted in this and other countries with a view to lessen, regulate or prohibit the traffic;
3. The results of these measures in each case;
4. The effect that the enactment of a Prohibitory Liquor Law in Canada would have in respect of social conditions, agricultural business, industrial and commercial interests, of the revenue requirements of municipalities, provinces, and of the Dominion, and also as to its capability of efficient enforcement;
5. All other information bearing on the question of Prohibition.

AND under and by virtue of the powers vested in Us by the Statute lastly hereinbefore recited, We do hereby authorize and empower you or any or either of you, as such Commissioners or Commissioner, to summon before you any witnesses and to require them to give evidence on oath orally or in writing or on solemn affirmation, in case they are persons entitled to affirm in civil matters, and to produce such documents and things as you OUR said Commissioners shall deem requisite to the full investigation

ROYAL COMMISSION OF 1892.

and report of the matters into which you are hereby appointed to inquire and report.

TO have, hold, exercise and enjoy the said office, place and trust unto you the said Sir Joseph Hickson, Knight, you the said Herbert S. McDonald, you the said Edward F. Clarke, you the said George Auguste Gigault, and you the said Reverend Joseph McLeod, together with the rights, powers, privileges and emoluments unto the said office, place and trust of right and by law appertaining during the pleasure.

AND WE do appoint you the said Sir Joseph Hickson to be the Chairman of Our said Commissioners.

AND we do hereby require and direct you to report to Our President of our Privy Council for Canada the result of your investigation together with the evidence taken before you and any opinion or remarks you may see fit to make thereon and any recommendation in respect thereof.

IN TESTIMONY WHEREOF We have caused these OUR LETTERS to be made Patent, and the Great Seal of Canada to be hereunto affixed.

WITNESSES: Our Right Trusty and Well beloved THE RIGHT HONORABLE SIR FREDERICK ARTHUR STANLEY, Baron Stanley of Preston, in the County of Lancaster in the Peerage of the United Kingdom, Knight Grand Cross of OUR MOST HONORABLE Order of the Bath, Governor-General of Canada.

At Our Government House in our City of Ottawa this fourteenth day of March in the year of Our Lord, one thousand eight hundred and ninety-two and in the fifty-fifth year of Our Reign.

BY COMMAND·

(Sgd.) L. A. CATELLIER,
Under Secretary of State.

Until the publishing of the names of the Commissioners, some temperance people had trusted the Government's good faith in appointing the Commission and had hoped for results from the official investigation. But they lost heart at the outset of the work.

PROHIBITION IN CANADA.

The *personnel* of the Commission was a deep disappointment to the friends of the temperance cause. It had been hoped that there would have been on the Commission at least a fair proportion of persons who were not specially hostile to prohibition. Some of those appointed were men who were looked upon as warm friends of the traffic. In the subsequent work of the Commission it became manifest that all the Commissioners, excepting the Rev. Dr. McLeod, were bitter in their opposition to a prohibitory law. In every part of Canada in which the Commission took evidence, this opposition was strongly manifested in the methods of questioning used and in the persistent efforts made to shake the evidence of witnesses opposed to the liquor traffic. In some cases this action on the part of the Commissioners passed far beyond the bounds of civility.

The Woman's Christian Temperance Union and several other temperance organizations had asked that certain men be put upon the Commission, but their requests were not granted. The Dominion Alliance had decided to stand aloof on the grounds that the Royal Commission was purely a government affair, and a project, moreover, of which the Alliance could not approve; and further they held that it would be unwise for them to commit themselves in advance to the Commission by recommending or endorsing any person for appointment.

The brewers and distillers had engaged to look after their interests Mr. Louis P. Kribs, editor of *The Advocate,* a liquor journal published in Montreal and Toronto. It was urged at a meeting of temperance people in Montreal that an able temperance representative should be in attendance on the Commission to insure a fair statement before them of the case for prohibition. Accordingly the Dominion Alliance, when asked to take action in the matter, appointed their Secretary, Mr. F. S. Spence, for this purpose.

Fully realizing the unpromising nature of the undertaking, and without expectation of any positive results, Mr. Spence gave himself to the task, determined that the liquor

ROYAL COMMISSION OF 1892.

interests should not win by default. It was largely due to his indefatigable efforts, combined with his wide knowledge of every phase of the question, that the evidence presented was so overwhelmingly and conclusively in favor of prohibition. During a part of the inquiry at which Mr. Spence was not able to be present, Mr. J. H. Carson, of Montreal, Corresponding Secretary of the Alliance, took his place.

A great deal of work was done by the Commissioners. They prepared questions which were submitted to clergymen, medical men, magistrates and others, and the answers to which were classified and summarized. Extensive correspondence was carried on with public officials, both in Canada and other countries, for the purpose of obtaining information relating to the questions to be considered. A great mass of statistics was collected and arranged. Evidence was taken in leading cities and towns in all the provinces and in nine American states.

At the opening session of the Commission's proceedings, Mr. Spence asked for the privilege of addressing the Commission from time to time, questioning witnesses, and calling such witnesses to be examined as he thought necessary to secure the presentation of information that would be useful in promoting the inquiry. Mr. Kribs made a similar request, as did also Mr. J. F. L. Parsons, of Halifax, who had been appointed by the Nova Scotia Grand Division of the Sons of Temperance to act for that body.

The Commissioners considered these requests, and replied that they did not think it necessary to hear advocates on any phase of the matter they were appointed to investigate. They stated, however, that they were prepared to hear any witnesses who would present themselves and to consider whether or not they would ask such witnesses any questions that might be suggested. They said also that they would consider whether or not they would call any witnesses mentioned by the gentlemen named. Then the inquiry began.

The course usually carried on at the public sittings of the Commission was the following: A number of witnesses were

PROHIBITION IN CANADA.

selected and called by the Commissioners. Many of these were public officials, the mayor of the city or town in which the inquiry was held being usually the first. Then followed such local officials as the Sheriff, president of the Board of Trade, City Clerk, Inspector of Licenses, Collector of Customs, Collector of Revenue, superintendents and other officials of asylums, prisons and charitable institutions, and any other persons selected by the Commissioners. After this list was gone through, the Commissioners took the names of witnesses submitted by Mr. Spence and Mr. Kribs, generally calling one from each list alternately. Mr. Kribs and Mr. Spence submitted to the Commissioners in writing such questions as they desired to have addressed to the different witnesses examined.

Some of the difficulties under which Mr. Spence worked may be made clear by the following extract from a letter from him to Sir Joseph Hickson, Chairman of the Royal Commission, written on September 1, 1892:

"The Commission has called at my suggestion a great many witnesses supposed to be in possession of valuable information bearing upon the questions to be inquired into. In selecting these witnesses, I have taken great pains to secure persons whose special experience and knowledge in relation to specific matters would be likely to be valuable. By a decision of the Commissioners, however, I have not been permitted to question these or any other witnesses appearing before you. You will readily see that this decision makes it absolutely impossible for the parties whom I represent to have placed fairly before your honorable body the facts which they desire you to consider. The Commissioners cannot know what facts the witnesses are possessed of. The inquiry being by question and answer, these facts are not likely to be brought out unless questions directly relating to them are asked. It is true that I have been permitted to write questions and hand them to the Commissioners to be asked or not, at their discretion. This plan absolutely precludes any effective cross-examination and prevents the immediate following up of questions which are only partially answered. The friends of prohibition are therefore placed at a serious disadvantage in the inquiry being conducted.

ROYAL COMMISSION OF 1892.

A large portion of the evidence they desire to lay before the Commission is practically excluded, and your honorable body, and therefore the Government to which they will report, is prevented from having a full knowledge of many subjects and details that are, in the opinion of the temperance people, of very great importance. In view of these facts, and on behalf of the very extensive interests that I represent, I again respectfully ask your honorable body to reconsider their decision in this matter, and to permit me, within proper limits, to question the witnesses that I am allowed to present to the Commission, and also to cross-examine any other witnesses that may be called. You will readily see that this course is absolutely necessary if the Commission is to fully perform the work for which it was appointed.

"Another matter to which I desire to respectfully call your attention is this: Under the present plan of taking evidence a great many important witnesses are crowded out. Your Commission calls in each place the gentlemen holding certain public offices. The examination of these gentlemen occupies a great deal of time, and other important witnesses are thus excluded. For example, at the last session of the Commission in Summerside, P.E.I., I had fifteen witnesses, who had been carefully selected by a committee of representative workers from different points in the western section of the province. The time devoted to the investigation in that place was so brief, and the examination of the official witnesses occupied so much time, that only two of the fifteen gentlemen mentioned were heard. The temperance people were therefore deprived of the opportunity of laying before the Commission a number of important facts, as well as the opinions of a number of thoroughly representative men. As matters now stand, there is shut out a great deal of valuable evidence that prohibitionists desire to present. On their behalf I would respectfully request that your Commission will make some arrangement by which they can hear the witnesses that are prepared to testify in reference to the matters into which the Commission is inquiring."

These requests were not granted, however, and the prohibition advocate continued to work under unfavoring conditions.

Beginning in the east, the Commission worked its way across the country, taking evidence at Halifax, North

PROHIBITION IN CANADA.

Sydney, Truro, and Yarmouth in Nova Scotia; at St. John, St. Stephen, Fredericton, and Moncton in New Brunswick; at Charlottetown and Summerside in Prince Edward Island; at Quebec City and Montreal in Quebec; at Winnipeg and Brandon in Manitoba; at Regina, Prince Albert, Calgary, Fort McLeod, and Banff in the North-West Territories; at Victoria, Nanaimo, New Westminster, and Vancouver in British Columbia. They reached the west coast on November 22, 1892.

From British Columbia was taken the most extended excursion with least object and results. At Winnipeg a witness had informed the Commissioners that the town of Pasadena in Southern California was under prohibitory law, and Judge McDonald earnestly desired to see the law in operation. Accordingly the Commissioners went to Southern California and visited the two towns of Riverside and Pasadena. They were in Riverside for a few hours on December 2nd and interviewed three liquor-sellers, one bank president, and one clergyman. The following day they spent a very short time in Pasadena, interviewing the city marshal and three business men. This was all the work done in California.

The Commissioners worked in groups, dividing up the itinerary amongst them. They met at Montreal in January, 1893, for another public inquiry, which closed the first term of their investigations.

In the spring of 1893, work was continued in the United States, interviews being conducted in the western States of Missouri, Kansas, Nebraska, Iowa, Minnesota, and Illinois. Maine, the pioneer prohibition state, was visited in the summer, and also Massachusetts.

The Province of Ontario was left almost until the last, when, in the fall, investigations were held in Brockville, Peterboro', Hamilton, Woodstock, Windsor, Walkerville, London, Berlin, Guelph, Owen Sound, and Toronto.

In March, 1894, Mr. Spence and Mr. Kribs were examined before the Commissioners at Montreal. A full session at

ROYAL COMMISSION OF 1892.

Ottawa on March 9th closed the general public inquiry. Mr. Carson was examined by Dr. McLeod on his visit to Maine and his evidence appears in Dr. McLeod's report.

III. REPORT OF COMMISSION.

During the period of the Royal Commission's investigations, there was considerable criticism of the Government's plan, both in Parliament and out of it. Sometimes long intervals elapsed between sessions, when people grew impatient over the apparently unnecessary delay. The *Templar,* in 1892, while disapproving of the Royal Commission as a parliamentary evasion of duty, had enthusiastically helped to raise a fund to pay the expenses of a temperance representative; in 1893 it was bitterly denouncing "the fool chase" and "the outrageous political farce," and regretting the assistance it had given.

In 1893 there was a spirited argument in the House upon the Royal Commission item in the estimates, a matter of $15,000, for the first year. Dr. Thos. Christie, member for Argenteuil, an old and ardent temperance advocate, said in debate:—

"It appears to me that this Royal Commission can be of no service whatever. Its appointment is a perfect waste of money. It appears to me that it was only intended to stave off a difficult question for an indefinite number of years, and that it would be wise to bring this expenditure to a close. It is an enigma to me which I cannot solve, how this Royal Commission, by wandering about the country from Dan to Beersheba, and getting the opinions of people for and against prohibition, will ever advance the temperance cause. I think that nothing has occurred during the past decade so injurious to the cause of temperance as the appointment of this Royal Commission. It has completely sidetracked the prohibition movement, paralyzed all efforts and acted like a *placebo* to keep the temperance men quiescent. I think it is a useless waste of money, and that we should not sanction it. We

PROHIBITION IN CANADA.

all know that there is a very strong public sentiment in this Dominion in favor of prohibition."

After the completion of the evidence, there was further delay in the preparation and presentation of the Commission's report to Parliament. A preliminary report accompanying copies of the evidence taken in Nova Scotia, New Brunswick, Prince Edward Island and Quebec, was presented to the Governor in Council on June 4, 1894. The final report of the Commission is dated March 29, 1895. It was a majority report, being signed by all the members of the Commission except Rev. Dr. McLeod. In a few lines added to it, Mr. Gigault dissented from the findings of the majority in regard to some minor matters relating to light beer and wines.

These reports, with a number of appendices and the evidence taken by the Commissioners, comprise seven large blue books, aggregating 5,870 pages. A summary of the most important statements and opinions which they embody was compiled by Mr. Spence and published by the Dominion Alliance. This book, "The Facts of the Case," was divided into five parts corresponding with the five heads or subdivisions of the subjects for investigation assigned to the Commissioners. It has ever since been the standard work of reference for students of the prohibition movement in Canada, and has been recognized as one of the most able, succinct presentations of the case for prohibition ever published.

The majority report, which was published in six large volumes, declared in favor of the registration of all persons engaged in the liquor traffic and the imposition upon them of a special tax, as in the United States; the establishment of reformatories for intemperate persons; the making of license certificates permanent; reduction in the number of licenses; higher license fees; and various other reforms in methods of controlling the liquor traffic. The majority conclusions further condemned prohibition, directly and indirectly, in the face of an enormous mass of evidence that

ROYAL COMMISSION OF 1892.

had been accumulated to show the value of prohibitory law wherever fairly enforced.

The minority Commissioner summed up, at the end of his report, his conclusions in the following terms:—

In view of the facts hereinbefore recited, and after a careful consideration of all the evidence taken by the Commission, and of all other information and knowledge obtained, the undersigned respectfully submits the following as his conclusions in reference to the whole subject which the Commission was instructed to investigate:—

1. That the House of Commons of the Dominion of Canada made a right and wise declaration in relation to the subject when it declared, in 1884, "That total prohibition is the right and only effective remedy for intemperance"; that the House of Commons was right in declaring, at the same time, "That this House is prepared to enact such legislation as soon as public opinion will sustain them in doing so"; and that the House of Commons was well advised in reiterating from time to time, as already set out, this declaration.

2. That all the information which your Commission has been able to obtain has made clear to the undersigned that the effect of the liquor traffic has been and is seriously detrimental to all the moral, social and material interests of the nation; that the measures employed to "lessen, regulate or prohibit" the traffic have been of value and effective only in proportion as they have approximated, in their operation, to the absolute prohibition of the traffic in intoxicating beverages; and that the revenue requirements of the country should not be considered a reason for the continuance of an admitted evil, and, moreover, could be met without the continuance of that evil.

3. That the endorsement which the electorate of different sections of the Dominion of Canada have given, at the ballot box, to the principle of prohibition, whenever submitted, as well as many petitions, memorials and declarations of church courts, temperance organizations, municipal councils, and other representative bodies, make it sufficiently clear that a majority of the people of Canada are in favor of the total prohibition of the liquor traffic.

PROHIBITION IN CANADA.

4. That it would, therefore, be right and wise for the Dominion Parliament, without further delay, to carry out the promise given, and give effect to the principle stated in its several resolutions, by the enactment and thorough enforcement of a law prohibiting the manufacture, importation and sale of intoxicating liquors—except for medical, sacramental and scientific purposes—in and into the Dominion of Canada.

Mr. Kribs, the liquor representative, also published a report of the evidence from his point of view, and summarized it as follows:—

I am therefore opposed to prohibition because:—

(1) It is wrong in theory and impossible of effect.

(2) It contemplates a tyranny that cannot be justified by even the good its promoters ostensibly seek.

(3) It increases the evil sought to be removed, and develops other and far greater evils.

(4) It is based upon an atrocious injustice to a large section of the community, and boundless brigandage towards a large, legitimate trade.

(5) It is fostered by gross exaggeration, moral and scientific error, and immoral and un-Christian doctrine.

(6) It breeds perjury in the courts, knavery in politics, unrighteousness in the pulpits, and contempt for law among the people.

(7) Where attempted to be enforced, it destroys a reputable and open traffic only to drive it into the hands of the most disreputable classes, robs the community of those wise restrictions they are content to submit to, opens the way for wholesale adulteration, gives free play to all that is evil in the traffic, and offers opposition to only that which is good.

(8) Under it crime increases while prosperity decreases, drunkenness increases while immigration decreases, it destroys industry while furnishing ready avocation to the blackmailer, the bootlegger and the professional prohibition agitator.

(9) It asks, for its success (which it even then fails to attain), powers not granted under any other law, robs the citizen of a fundamental principle of British law, viz., that he

ROYAL COMMISSION OF 1892.

shall be held guilty until proven innocent; elevates to the magistrate's bench men utterly unfit for the position, and in whose hands justice becomes a mockery; depends for evidence to convict largely upon the scum of creation—the base professional informer, the character assassin, and the social thug who betrays his host through the very means by which hospitality was offered.

(10) It robs the young man of his manliness and his moral sense and develops in him sneaking, quibbling, lying or open defiance of law; where attempted to be enforced, shields him from the temptation of the open saloon but initiates him into the mysteries of the disreputable "joint," the unsavory "dive," the grossness of the kitchen bar, the dangers of the "jug" and "bottle" brigade and the drinking club; when not attempted to be enforced, familiarizes him with open, constant, flagrant violation of the law until he loses all respect for the majesty of the law.

(11) Professedly designed for the moral regeneration of man, it throws aside the Word of God to take in hand the policeman's club.

(12) It is based upon a false assumption, presupposing a condition of affairs that does not exist.

(13) It deprives the country of a large revenue under false pretences.

(14) It is un-Christian, unjust, unworkable and unnecessary.

The complete report of the Commission was duly laid before the House of Commons and the Senate, but no action was taken upon it.

SECTION VIII.

PROVINCIAL PLEBISCITE PERIOD.

No government, no party, no policy, no proposition, ever received so overwhelming an endorsation by the electorate as that which has been received by the proposal to totally prohibit the traffic in intoxicating beverages.

I. THE NORTH-WEST EXPERIMENT IN PROHIBITION LAW.

THE history of prohibition in the Canadian North-West is instructive. From the earliest time of that region's control by the Dominion Parliament, down to 1892, there was on our national statute books a clearly worded enactment for the protection of natives and settlers from the dangerous and aggressive liquor traffic. The law relating to the subject was in the following terms

"No intoxicating liquor or intoxicant shall be manufactured, compounded or made in the territories except by the special permission of the Governor in Council; nor shall any intoxicating liquor or intoxicant be imported or sold, exchanged, traded, or bartered, or had in possession therein except by special permission, in writing, of the Lieutenant-Governor."

The results of the operation of this legislation were incalculably good. As long as it was enforced there was among the North-West Indians comparatively little of the drunkenness that is so fatal to the aboriginal race. Statesmen have vied with each other in testifying to its benefits. Well-posted officials in high positions have spoken strongly of its advantages.

Additional evidence of the effectiveness of the law will be found in the Royal Commission Report, in the details given of methods by which law-breakers sought to evade it. Liquor was said to have been run into the country in nearly every imaginable disguise—in barrels of sugar and salt, in ginger-ale bottles, in neatly-constructed eggs, even in the interior of imitation Bibles, and in innumerable ingenious devices, all showing the straits to which persons who wished to evade the law were driven to carry out their plans.

It was not expected that under the regulation quoted there would be any free issue of permits for the bringing in of

PROHIBITION IN CANADA.

liquor. For a long time the issue of such permits was limited, and probably most of the liquor imported under them was for medicinal, sacramental and scientific purposes.

In 1882, Hon. E. Dewdney was appointed Lieutenant-Governor. Under his régime the issue of permits became more frequent, and a great deal of liquor was brought in for what was called domestic use. The police officials complained bitterly of the difficulty of enforcing the law when permits were so freely issued. In his report for 1886 Superintendent Perry said: "Permits are often used to cover unlawfully-obtained liquor. . . . They are frequently abused, thus preventing the carrying out of the law."

The officers met with another difficulty. A judge ruled that liquor once admitted under a permit could be held by anyone whether he was the party to whom the permit was originally issued or not. This decision practically allowed a permit to cover any liquor with which the holder could associate it. It was only necessary to get the stuff into the country and some old permit would protect it. The Commissioner declared that this decision almost completely killed the enforcement of the North-West Act. The effectiveness of the law was destroyed by the action of the Governor who ought to have upheld it and the decision of the judge who ought to have facilitated its enforcement. Commissioner Herchmer said in 1887

"The permit system should be done away with in the first place if the law is to be enforced, and the law itself should be cleared of the technicalities that have enabled so many to escape punishment this last year."

The people of the North-West favored the law. Protests were continually made by leading settlers, not against the prohibition, but against the facilities provided for its violation. The North-West Council was petitioned to urge the Dominion Government to bring about a reform. In the session of 1887 a motion, favoring a change from prohibition, was carried in the North-West Council, but it was carried by the

PROVINCIAL PLEBISCITE PERIOD.

appointed members, a majority of those elected by the people voting against it. Then it was proposed that no change should be made in the law until a vote of the people should be taken on the question of the continuance of prohibition. In 1888 the new Legislature declared in favor of such a plebiscite by a vote of fourteen to six, the six dissidents supporting an amendment offered in favor of a change to a stringent license system.

Hon. Joseph Royal was appointed Lieutenant-Governor in 1888, and he at once proposed to inaugurate a new method of dealing with the liquor traffic. The Legislature had declared against license. Citizens had petitioned against it. The best men and women of all Canada were in sympathy with prohibition for the new country. Deliberately the Lieutenant-Governor set himself to break down the law. He declared his intention of interpreting it as authorizing him to issue permits for bringing in and selling liquor, and he made provision for the sale of beer containing four per cent. of alcohol. He practically stated his intention of administering the law so as to establish the dangerous bar-room all through the great North-West.

As might be expected, this action raised a storm of indignation. The proposal to flood the country with beer was received with alarm. Journals all over the North-West declared their dissatisfaction. Protests were wired to the Dominion Government at Ottawa. A large convention gathered at Regina from nearly every part of the Territories to protest against the outrage. The chairman stated that some time ago a widely-circulated petition, praying the Dominion Parliament to make no change before a vote of the people was taken, had secured 2,143 signatures in a very short time. A committee waited upon the Lieutenant-Governor and urged him to delay his action until a vote of the people could be taken. Strong resolutions declared in favor of prohibition, and again urged the Dominion Parliament to enact legislation allowing the people to vote on the Lieutenant-Governor's proposal before it should be carried out.

PROHIBITION IN CANADA.

The Lieutenant-Governor would not heed the appeals. The Governor at Ottawa turned a deaf ear to them. The North-West Legislature met and declared its opinion by throwing out a license-favoring motion by a vote of fourteen to six and declaring in favor of a plebiscite. All was in vain. The disgraceful maladministration went on. The amount of liquor imported under permits in 1888 was 56,388 gallons, as compared with 21,636 gallons in 1887. The following year the liquor imported increased to 151,628 gallons, while the C.P.R. dining cars sold thousands of gallons of wine and beer. Theoretically the liquor brought in contained four per cent. of alcohol. This was simply nonsense. As Superintendent Perry, of the North-West Police, reported, "None but a chemical expert could determine the amount of alcohol in any particular beer." Strong ale was freely imported under four per cent. permits. Spirits were freely sold.

The Police Commissioner had by this time established canteens at the different mounted police posts, at which liquor was sold to the men. Thus the officers who should have carried out the prohibition law engaged in buying and selling liquor under the authority of the chief officers of the state. The result may readily be imagined. Superintendent McIllree, in his report for 1888, said·

"At the present time the existing law is not obeyed or respected by the mass of the inhabitants of this part of the North-West. It is evaded and set at naught by very many. . . . Under these rulings (of the Court) it is almost impossible to get a conviction."

Commissioner Herchmer wrote in 1890:

" The liquor question is still in a very unsatisfactory condition, and while the importation of beer has, I think, lowered the demand for stronger liquor, the ruling of the court that liquor once admitted under permit can be held by any one, and the fact that counterfoils of permits belonging to other people can protect liquor, almost completely kills the enforcement of the North-West Act, in spite of the efforts of the Lieutenant-Governor of the

PROVINCIAL PLEBISCITE PERIOD.

North-West Territories to prevent the transfer of permits, and places the police in a most unfortunate position; in fact, as at present interpreted, it is impossible to enforce the act."

Evidence given before the Royal Commission showed that sometimes when the mounted police seized contraband liquor, permits were issued to protect it, and this was done even subsequent to the seizure. The transference of permits went on. Hotel-keepers got permits for four per cent., carried heavy stocks of all kinds of liquors, and borrowed permits from friends to cover their ardent spirits. A police superintendent reports: "Hotels and saloons were well provided, as usual, with other people's permits."

In 1891 a new constitution was granted to the Territories. The Dominion Government had rejected all petitions of the North-West people for a vote on the prohibition question, and had refused to interfere with the Lieutenant-Governor's course, although appealed to by petitions and deputations from different parts of the Dominion. An election for the North-West Assembly was about to be held under the new law. To the new Assembly was to be relegated the whole question of how to deal with the liquor traffic.

In September of the same year, Mr. Spence was sent by the Ontario Alliance to assist in pressing the prohibition question to the front in the election campaign. He reported that the situation was really worse than had been anticipated. It was the freely expressed opinion of well-informed people that the administration of the law was such that there was imported into the territories not less than twice as much liquor as the regularly issued permits represented. Again, the municipal councils of the different towns in the North-West, in view of the free sale of liquor, had undertaken to use that sale for revenue purposes and had passed by-laws providing for licensing places for the sale of liquid refreshments. In these towns the mounted police hardly ever interfered with the sale of liquor, and of course the municipal police interfered only with places not licensed. There was thus the freest kind of liquor-selling; no restrictions practically existed such as are usually embodied in license laws.

This condition of affairs was pointed to as the "working of prohibition," though it was really a breaking down of prohibition and the converting of it into a license system of the loosest kind. The Lieutenant-Governor had announced that permits for the importation and sale of liquor, as already mentioned, would be issued on the recommendation of members of the Legislative Assembly. Nearly all the members of the old Legislative Assembly had made such recommendations, and were thus committed to the licensing principle. The North-West Territories therefore approached a general election with a nominally prohibitory law discredited, and with a number of probable candidates committed to the principle of license.

Under the direction of the Alliance Executive a vigorous campaign was immediately commenced. Meetings were addressed by the Ontario Secretary at Moosomin, Whitwood, Broadview, Grenfell, Wolseley, Indian Head, Qu'Appelle, Regina, Prince Albert, Fort Qu'Appelle, Moose Jaw, Swift Current, Maple Creek, Lethbridge, Macleod, Medicine Hat, Calgary, Red Deer, Banff, and other places. An immense quantity of literature was printed and circulated, in addition to that generously supplied by Ontario friends. The co-operation of temperance societies and churches was enlisted as far as possible and permanent organizations were formed in many localities.

The political situation prevented the temperance question from monopolizing interest in the election. Nearly every candidate, however, made a definite declaration of the determination to support more effective measures for dealing with the liquor traffic. The number of prohibitionists elected on November 7th was small, but there was returned a large majority in favor of a license law; accordingly the new Legislature proposed at the very earliest opportunity to change the prohibitory law, the administration of which had become a farce and disgrace. At its first sitting there was enacted a

PROVINCIAL PLEBISCITE PERIOD.

rigid system of license with local option provisions. Prohibition was broken down and the liquor traffic had fully opened up to it our great, new, rich North-West Territories.

The license system went into operation May 1, 1892. The Royal Commission visited the Territories in November of the same year. Everywhere they were met with the same unhesitating statement, "Drinking and drunkenness have greatly increased." This was the testimony of reliable men who favored prohibition. It was the admission of those who had advocated license. Not only had the sale and consumption of liquor increased among the white population, but also among the half-breeds and Indians. Sad stories are told of homes broken up, families robbed of necessaries, Indians debauched, drunkenness become more common, and an alarming increase of all the usually attendant evils. Commissioner Herchmer says in his report for 1892:

"Even in the best regulated districts there has been, I think, more general drinking than under the permit system, and one result is established beyond contradiction, viz., that the half-breeds and Indians can get more liquor than under the old law. Under the permit system liquor was expensive and dealers were afraid to give to people they could not trust, and, consequently, the lower classes of whites and half-breeds could very seldom get any. Now half-breeds with money can get all they want, and as many of them are closely related to the Indians, and in some cases live with them, it is impossible, when liquor once gets into their possession, to prevent Indians camped with them from getting it also; again, it is impossible for anyone not personally acquainted with them to tell, on sight, half-breeds from the better class of Indians, the latter in many cases dressing like whites, cutting their hair and speaking good English and French. In some cases very little exertion is made to establish their identity, and undoubtedly Indians very often buy liquor as half-breeds."

This strong evidence of the head of the police force is fully borne out by the statement of his subordinates. Superintendent Cotton says:

PROHIBITION IN CANADA.

"Inspector Huot, who is stationed at Duck Lake, is of opinion that some half-breeds have, when without ready cash on hand, sold cattle at a sacrifice in order to procure liquor, the sale of which is constantly going on about them. Under the old system it would have been impossible for such persons to obtain permits at will."

The reports of other officers all evidence the same sad condition of deterioration. It was one of the most disgraceful blots upon our country's history.

II. MANITOBA PLEBISCITE.

Because of the clearly recognized determination of the Government to prevent a decision being made by the Commons on the prohibition question, temperance workers felt that it would be of no use to have a motion for prohibition brought before the House while the Royal Commission was at work. Consequently, during the sessions of 1892 and 1893, no prohibition resolution was presented in Parliament. The question had undoubtedly been laid upon the table.

But the growing demand throughout the country for prohibitory legislation, obstructed in one outlet, inevitably sought other channels. When the prohibition question was temporarily removed from the House of Commons, the advocates of reform turned to the local Legislatures in order to secure from them the maximum measure of restriction of the liquor traffic that lay within their power to enact. Here they were met by the jurisdiction difficulty, which had delayed the enactment of the Canada Temperance Act. Uncertainty still existed as to the respective extent of Provincial and Dominion authority in prohibitory legislation.

Since 1878 judgment had been passed by the Privy Council upon the Canada Temperance Act and the McCarthy Act. Since that time, too, courts in various provinces had upheld various restrictive provisions of the provincial license laws. The Supreme Court had recently decided in favor of the right of a province:

PROVINCIAL PLEBISCITE PERIOD.

(1) To compel brewers to take out a license.

(2) To require an applicant for a license to produce a petition signed by a certain proportion of the electors.

(3) To disqualify a licensee from holding certain provincial and municipal offices.

Thus by 1892, through a long series of decisions in various courts, it had been established beyond a doubt that the Dominion Parliament had power to prohibit the liquor traffic, and that the provinces also had the right to exercise important powers in that direction, the nature and extent of which powers were, however, still open to serious doubt.

In Manitoba the advocates of reform, feeling confident of success, desired an opportunity of demonstrating to their legislators the strength of the sentiment that existed in favor of a prohibitory law. At a convention of temperance workers held in Winnipeg in April, 1892, a resolution was adopted favoring the taking of a plebiscite on the prohibition question at the time of the ensuing general election for the Provincial Legislature, and the Manitoba Prohibitory League was formed to promote this movement.

An enthusiastic mass meeting of Winnipeg citizens called by the League endorsed the proposal and sent a large deputation of over one hundred members, consisting of the executive of the League, the presiding officers of all temperance bodies, and clergymen of various denominations, to proffer the request to Parliament. Mr. W. R. Mulock, Q.C., President of the League, presented the petition on this question, signed by thousands of electors. Hon. Mr. McLean observed that a plebiscite was against the spirit of the British constitution, since it involved simply getting an opinion from the people without action necessarily following. Mr. Mulock was of the opinion that, in as much as the people ruled, a plebiscite could not be construed into a violation of the constitution. Other speakers pointed out that the deputation approached the Legislature in no party spirit, but believed that it was necessary to ascertain the moral sentiment of the people to make a prohibitory law effective.

PROHIBITION IN CANADA.

The Legislature agreed to the request, and on July 23, 1892, the voters were asked to express by a direct ballot their favor for or objection to the enactment of a law of total prohibition for the Province of Manitoba. The vote polled was as follows·

In favor of prohibition.................... 19,637
Against prohibition 7,115

Majority in favor of prohibition........... 12,522

III. NEW BRUNSWICK.

The Legislative Assembly of the Province of New Brunswick on the 7th of April, 1893, adopted a resolution in the following terms:

"Whereas, in the opinion of this Legislative Assembly the enactment of a prohibitory liquor law would conduce to the general benefit of the people of this province and meet with the approval of a majority of the electorate; and

"Whereas, legislative power in respect of the enactment of such a law rests in the Parliament of Canada; therefore

"Resolved, that this Assembly hereby expresses its desire that the Parliament of Canada shall, with all convenient speed, enact a law prohibiting the importation, manufacture and sale of intoxicating liquors as a beverage into or in the Dominion of Canada."

Thus, while there was no direct expression of the will of the people by means of a plebiscite, as in some other provinces, New Brunswick opinion was clearly voiced on the prohibition issue.

IV. PRINCE EDWARD ISLAND PLEBISCITE.

The result of the plebiscite campaign in Manitoba stirred Prince Edward Island prohibition workers. They felt an earnest desire to have their province similarly placed on record. Accordingly an act was passed by the Provincial

PROVINCIAL PLEBISCITE PERIOD.

Legislature providing for the taking of a popular vote on the question of prohibition. This vote was taken along with the general provincial election on December 14, 1893. The total result is given in the following table. The figure for the City of Charlottetown are included in those of Queen's County. They showed in the city proper a majority of 558 in favor of prohibition.

THE VOTE BY COUNTIES.

	For.	Against.
Queens County	4,226	1,513
Prince County	3,579	1,109
Kings County	2,811	768
Totals	10,616	3,390

Majority for prohibition, 7,226

V. ONTARIO PLEBISCITE.

Many prohibitionists in Ontario believed that they could strengthen their cause and make more effective their demand for prohibitory legislation by following the example set by their co-workers in Manitoba, in having a plebiscite taken. Amongst them were some who had heretofore most vigorously opposed such a course whenever it was suggested in the Dominion Parliament, because they considered it to be an evasion of the direct issue of prohibitory legislation. Unwavering in their purpose, unremitting in their zeal, they were now facing a changed situation, checkmate in the Dominion House, jurisdiction complications in the Provincial Legislatures.

There were others who denounced the plebiscite plan and called for more aggressive action. They were for the most part proponents of a new movement known as "The Advanced Prohibitionists," that took its birth at the convention of Royal Templars of Temperance held at Hamilton on August 6, 1892. The delegates at the convention had expressed general dissatisfaction with the policy of the Dominion Alliance. Some

PROHIBITION IN CANADA.

criticized as not being sufficiently radical the political platform adopted by the Dominion Alliance Convention in 1888 and endorsed by the Ontario Branch—the support of only publicly-avowed prohibitionists for public positions and as members of Dominion and Provincial Parliaments; and when neither party representative measured up to the prohibitionists' demands, the nomination of an independent candidate. Some, while favoring this platform, condemned the alleged inactivity of the Alliance in carrying it out, especially the failure to organize the electorate into prohibition clubs, as recommended by the convention. All agreed that it was desirable to organize advanced prohibitionists into a close and compact body for independent political action and to commence the work at once by the institution of local societies or clubs, similar in character to the political party associations. They decided, however, that no new organization should be completed, but only provisional action taken with a view to unifying the forces at the coming Alliance convention. A provisional committee was appointed in order to push the work of organization if the Alliance should not do so. The committee meeting in Toronto, on August 26th, outlined a plan for the organization of the local clubs and drafted the following pledge of membership:

"I, ..., solemnly promise that I will not give my vote or influence to any candidate for parliamentary honors whose party is not distinctly pledged to the complete suppression of the liquor traffic, and I further promise to support the party making prohibition the supreme issue."

At the annual convention of the Ontario Branch of the Dominion Alliance in Toronto on September 14, 1892, the question of legislative policy came up for discussion. While temperance workers were unanimous in their demand for total prohibition of the liquor traffic, they had differences of opinion as to the best methods to be pursued in attaining it. Delegates from the provisional committee of the Advanced Prohibitionists were present to give the views of that new

PROVINCIAL PLEBISCITE PERIOD.

organization. Mr. W. W. Buchanan, chairman of the committee, Mr. Jas. Thompson and Mr. W. G. Fee addressed the convention on behalf of the movement, giving a brief account of its purpose and history.

A difference of opinion was first expressed upon the report of the Committee on Legislative Action. The committee advised a strong demand from the Legislature for a provincial prohibitory law, on condition that the recent decisions of the Court of Appeals as to the jurisdiction of the Provincial Legislatures were not over-ruled. Mr. Spence moved in amendment that the Ontario Legislature be requested to take action to secure a vote of the provincial electorate on the direct issue of provincial prohibition.

The Advanced Prohibitionists argued that since the Legislature had, on a previous occasion, asked the Dominion Government to pass a prohibitory liquor law, they could not consistently refuse a provincial act; that it was the Government's duty to take the responsibility of making the question a party issue; that the plebiscite plan left the political parties as they were, divided between the friends and foes of prohibitory legislation; that the passing of a law, and the subsequent appeal to the people by the Government, would drive out from the ranks of the Government's supporters all enemies of prohibition and win to their side all true friends of the movement, leaving them with a solid and united party to support them in an honest and impartial administration of the law.

The arguments of Mr. Spence and his supporters in favor of the plebiscite were that the result of the vote in Manitoba had given workers there encouragement and a greater determination than ever to win out; that a contest here would likewise arouse temperance sentiment and be educative and inspiring; that a victory would be a strong argument in favor of the demand for Dominion prohibition or a mandate to the Provincial Legislature if the courts should decide in their favor; and that even a defeat could be turned to advantage as an index of the temperance sentiment in different localities by showing the municipalities in which local option measures could be carried.

The amendment in favor of the plebiscite was carried by a vote of twenty-two to eleven.

In the discussion on political action, Mr. Spence strongly opposed the Advanced Prohibitionists' movement, as he had done the New Party a few years previous. He objected to the ironclad pledge which would bind a man to vote non-confidence in a government on every question, no matter what it might be, because that government had failed to bring in a prohibition measure. After a heated debate, the convention decided to continue the political policy heretofore followed by the Alliance, and to push on with the organization of the prohibition electorate in every municipality, an organizer to be placed in the field as soon as money could be provided therefor, to form prohibition clubs, in affiliation with the Ontario Branch of the Dominion Alliance.

At the annual meeting of the Dominion Council of the Alliance, later in the same month, similar discussions resulted in like decisions. The report on legislation, amended and adopted, was that other provinces should be urged to follow Manitoba's example in applying to their respective legislatures for the taking of the vote; that the several Provincial Legislatures be urged to enact such measures of prohibition as the British North America Act permits; and that a demand be made of the Federal Parliament for the immediate abolition of the liquor traffic. Also it was decided that an agent should be appointed to organize clubs, pledged to act in accordance with the accepted Alliance policy, it being understood that this work should be carried on through provincial branches wherever such existed.

In the plebiscite controversy feeling ran very high. Mr. W. H. Howland, President of the Ontario Alliance, resigned from his office because of the decision in favor of the vote. The Advanced Prohibitionists, quite dissatisfied with the results of the convention, went ahead with their own plans for political organization and formed clubs in all the provinces.

PROVINCIAL PLEBISCITE PERIOD.

They agitated for a provincial prohibitory law. Petitions asking for it were circulated from the Templar Office in Hamilton.

After the convention the Alliance Executive Committee met to take steps for the carrying out of the instructions given by the convention. It was agreed that forms of petitions asking for a plebiscite should be at once sent out to churches and societies. Before this could be done, however, further objections were raised to the plebiscite proposal, and another meeting of the Executive Committee decided to delay the petitions until friends of the prohibition movement could be more generally consulted. Accordingly a circular was prepared setting out the action already taken and reasons therefor, and submitting the following questions

(1) Do you think it would be well to have a vote of the electors taken on the question of the desirability of the enactment of a prohibitory law?

(2) Is it your opinion that your society would work to secure a vote in favor of prohibition if the question were to be submitted?

(3) In your opinion, would such a vote in your locality result in a majority for prohibition?

This letter was sent to the pastor of every church and to the listed representative officer of each branch of a temperance order in the province. When the Executive Committee again met to consider the subject, there had been received 1,191 replies to the different questions, as follows:

	Yeas.	Nays.	Indefinite.
Question 1	1,042	117	24
Question 2	896	82	78
Question 3	766	143	254

This was considered such a strong expression of approval of the plebiscite proposition that the committee decided to carry out immediately the instructions of the convention. Accordingly a form of petition was prepared and sent out, to be signed on behalf of the churches and temperance and municipal organizations and sent to the Legislative Assembly. The petition was in the following form:

To the Legislative Assembly of the Province of Ontario:

Your petitioners respectfully call the attention of your honorable body to the following facts:

1. That notwithstanding the restrictive legislation at present in operation, intemperance with its attendant evils still exists in our province to an alarming extent, is a constant source of misery, pauperism and crime, and a persistent hindrance to the moral and material well-being of our people.

2. That your petitioners believe that the only right and effective legislative method of dealing with this evil is by the speedy enactment and thorough enforcement of total prohibition.

3. That not only do your petitioners believe that such legislation would be right in principle and very beneficial in operation, but that it is also desired and would be approved by a large majority of the electors of this province.

4. Your petitioners further believe that it is very desirable that there should be an opportunity given for a clear expression of this strong public opinion, uninfluenced by partisan or other considerations, so that the Legislature dealing with the question may be fully aware of the attitude of the electors towards it.

5. Your petitioners therefore pray your honorable body to make provision for the immediate taking of a direct vote of the electors of Ontario, in such form as will show what number of such electors would approve of a law prohibiting the importation, manufacture and sale of intoxicating liquors into and in the said province, and what proportion of the electors would be opposed to such legislation.

And your petitioners will ever pray.

The petition, denouncing the liquor traffic in strong terms, and affirming the soundness of the prohibition principle, made earnest and definite prayer for the taking of a vote of the electorate on the question of total prohibition. When the

PROVINCIAL PLEBISCITE PERIOD.

Legislature convened in 1893, 822 of these petitions, uniform in text, were presented from representative bodies. There were laid before the House petitions from—

- 199 Methodist Churches.
- 77 Presbyterian Churches.
- 32 Baptist Churches.
- 9 Congregational Churches.
- 7 Episcopal Churches.
- 7 Evangelical Associations.
- 112 I.O.G.T. Lodges.
- 98 W.C.T. Unions.
- 46 S. of T. Divisions.
- 29 R. T. of T. Councils.
- 153 Township and Village Councils.
- 20 Town Councils.
- 6 County Councils.
- 6 City Councils.
- 21 Miscellaneous.

There were also presented three petitions praying for a provincial prohibitory law.

THE BILL.

The matter was brought to an issue by Mr. Geo. F. Marter, who introduced as the first bill of the session in the Ontario Legislature, an Act "to amend the Liquor License Act by prohibiting the sale of intoxicating liquors by retail."*

---

*THE MARTER BILL OF 1893.

An Act to amend the Liquor License Act by prohibiting the sale by retail of intoxicating liquors.

HER MAJESTY, by and with the advice and consent of the Legislative Assembly of the Province of Ontario, enacts as follows:

(1) This Act shall be read with and as part of the Liquor License Act.

(2) On and after the 1st day of May, 1894, no tavern licenses or shop licenses shall be issued, renewed or extended within the Province of Ontario.

(3) All the provisions of the Liquor License Act and Acts amending the same, providing for the issue, renewal or extension of "tavern licenses" or "shop licenses" inconsistent with this Act shall be on, from and after the 1st day of May, 1894, repealed.

(4) From and after the 1st day of May, 1894, it shall not be lawful for any person or persons to sell or expose for sale, by retail, liquor or liquors, as defined by the said Acts, within the Province of Ontario, and any person offending against the provisions of this section of this Act shall be liable to the same penalties as are by the said Acts provided for in the case of sales of liquor without a license as by law required.

PROHIBITION IN CANADA.

A meeting of prohibitionists with members of the Legislature was called by the Alliance Executive in the reception room of the new Legislative Buildings in Toronto on April 10, 1893, to consider the Marter Bill and the plebiscite plan. The discussion showed that unanimity had not yet been reached.

Mr. Spence declared his endorsation of the Marter Bill, which was good so far as it went, he said, but only a part of what was wanted. His argument for the bill was set forth in a letter to the press written about this time. He compared the bill to the Dunkin and Scott Acts, partial measures, which were given in response to the demand for total prohibition. These measures were right in so far as they prohibited the liquor traffic, but defective in so far as they permitted it. From the defect evil resulted and the law was discredited. As the Parliament of Canada had repeatedly declared, total prohibition was "the right and most effective legislative remedy for the evils of intemperance." Nevertheless, the laws, imperfect as they were, had done good. Prohibitionists did right to accept what they could get, when they could not get what they had asked.

The Marter Bill created a similar situation. It was not what prohibitionists wanted, for it could not accomplish the good that total prohibition would accomplish. It dealt with the retail trade, which, according to the idea of many people, was the extent of the Ontario Legislature's power to control. Others, however, believed that power was greater, and the question was before the Supreme Court of Canada for adjudication.

The Marter Bill would delegalize bars and prevent treating. It would probably have little effect upon the consumption of liquor in the homes, but in as much as it would hamper and curtail the sale of liquor it would be productive of incalculable good. It ought to be supported by temperance people, who would not accept it as what they had asked for, or as what they wanted, but who would be willing to use any means of limiting or weakening the ruin-working liquor traffic.

PROVINCIAL PLEBISCITE PERIOD.

But while endorsing the bill, Mr. Spence made a strong appeal for a plebiscite. He argued that it was not intended to stave off the discussion of provincial prohibition in the Legislature. It would indicate exactly what might be the real strength of the prohibition sentiment. Therefore he moved, "That Mr. E. J. Davis and Mr. G. F. Marter be requested to act as our representatives in the Provincial Legislature in introducing a measure providing for the taking of a plebiscite of the electors of Ontario on the question of total prohibition, and pressing the same to an issue."

Mr. W. W. Buchanan, speaking for the Advanced Prohibitionists, opposed the plebiscite and declared that the Alliance in asking for it did not represent the organized temperance bodies of the province. The plebiscite was something entirely inconsistent with the country's system of representative and responsible government; it was no part of any process of legislation. Even if the Government did pass a prohibitory law in response to the plebiscite vote, such action would be disastrous to reform because the political conditions would be unfavorable to its proper administration. Mr. Marter's bill was the embodiment of resolutions deliberately adopted by the various temperance organizations and church courts with respect to provincial prohibition, and it was the immediate duty of all committed to these resolutions to come up solidly to its support.

Mr. Malcolm Gibbs, who seconded Mr. Spence's motion, spoke for the Woman's Christian Temperance Union. That influential organization, he said, wanted a plebiscite, but they wanted also provincial prohibition. Sir Oliver Mowat had told them that they must voice the sentiment of the province before any legislation on this question could be adopted. They desired to have the votes of the people at their back in order to carry prohibition to a successful issue.

Senator Vidal, President of the Dominion Alliance, saw no inconsistency in supporting both measures, but urged the plebiscite for the sake of its influence on the Dominion Parliament, and for the reason that prohibitionists wanted more prohibition than the Provincial Legislatures could give. Only the Dominion Parliament had the power to enact the prohibition of the manufacture and importation of liquor.

Mr. Marter declined to act in the Legislature to secure a measure for the taking of a plebiscite, fearing that such a measure would be used to kill his bill. He suggested that friends of the plebiscite hold over their question until next session. This would give his bill a clear field, and once it was passed he would not object to the plebiscite. If his measure was passed it would go into effect in May of the coming year, while a plebiscite would not be taken until the next general election, and thus no benefit could be expected from it, even if acted upon, in less than three years.

Dr. Dewart expressed the opinion that, as the plebiscite and the Marter Bill related to totally different phases, the one could not be moved as an amendment to the other, and that Mr. Marter's fears on that point were not well-founded.

Mr. Marter's name was taken out of Mr. Spence's motion, which was carried. Then a second motion was put and carried, "That this meeting heartily endorses Mr. Marter's bill and expresses the earnest hope that the said bill may be endorsed by the Legislature and may become the law of this province before the rising of the House."

Consistently maintaining their stand with regard to the Marter Bill, the Advanced Prohibitionists, in the name of the Royal Templars, issued an urgent call to prohibitionists, dated April 13th, to press on with petitions favoring the bill and to rally in support of it on the day when its second reading was expected. Their gathering in Richmond Hall on the afternoon of April 20th was, in spite of very inclement weather, a large one. The Marter Bill was strongly endorsed, but the meeting refused to consider the plebiscite question at all. The action taken by the Alliance was termed by one speaker "an emphatic pause." The opinion was expressed that it was the duty of the Government to pass the bill and to test its validity afterward.

PROVINCIAL PLEBISCITE PERIOD.

Mr. Spence was almost alone in the meeting in opposing this line of action. He reaffirmed his position with regard to the Marter Bill and declared that if the Legislature had the power to enact it, it was the duty of friends of temperance to take the Legislature by the throat and wring the concession from them. But, on the other hand, if that body had not the power, the passing of the law would only damage the cause. In either case, if Mr. Marter's bill became law in 1894 it would repeal all the clauses and provisions of the law then in force. The jurisdiction of the province would then have to be tested in the courts, and while the test cases were being dragged through the courts, Ontario would have an *interregnum* when there would be no liquor law, but the free sale of whiskey. There had been a disastrous case of that kind in Charlottetown, Prince Edward Island, from 1891 to 1893. The Scott Act had been carried in that province, and the local Legislature consequently repealed the license law. Then the Scott Act was repealed by counties and, there being no law to take its place, liquor was sold everywhere.

Mr. Mowat had said only the previous day that he would not assume the responsibility of the bill until its constitutionality was proven. The Ontario Government proposed to find just what their jurisdiction was, and at the same time to let the people of the Province say distinctly by a plebiscite whether or not they wanted prohibition. Then, if the Government found that they could enact such a law, constitutionally, and if the people had spoken in favor of prohibition the Government would give the legislation demanded. Mr. Spence concluded by appealing to the convention to support a prohibition measure which they knew was all right.

In the evening these resolutions were presented to the Premier. Rev. Dr. McKay, Rev. Wm. Kettlewell, and Mr. W. W. Buchanan spoke for the deputation. In reply, Sir Oliver said that he was going to speak frankly and not pretend to do that which he could not do, or say that which he did not believe. He had no doubt that if Ontario had a prohibition law that could be enforced it would be beneficial. But such

PROHIBITION IN CANADA.

a law unenforced was a thousand times worse than no law. If there was any reasonable doubt regarding the validity of the law, then its enforcement was practically hopeless. He continued:

"You see, therefore, I am not going to support Mr. Marter's bill, but the time may come when I will be able to support that and something more. The bill of Mr. Marter, for instance, proposes to prohibit the sale by retail, stopping there. What are you going to stop at retailing for? The Privy Council has repeatedly held that there is no distinction between retailing and wholesaling. What, then, is the use of stopping at retailing? I say, therefore, if it comes to be decided—I don't speak for others in this matter, I don't speak for my colleagues but for my own personal sympathy in regard to it—so that there could be no further question about it in our courts, that we have the power to pass a prohibitory law, I am prepared to go in for it. But whatever the consequences may be, I believe it to be my duty not to adopt such a measure until its constitutionality can be assured."

On May 1st, on the motion for the second reading of the prohibition bill, affairs took the turn which Mr. Marter had feared and which the plebiscite advocates had neither anticipated nor desired. The proposal for a provincial plebiscite was offered by the Government as an amendment to the motion for the Marter Bill. The Hon. G. W. Ross introduced the amendment, stating that as the authority of the Legislature was doubtful, it should be defined before prohibitory legislation was enacted, and that the House had confidence that the Government would take the necessary steps to secure a definition of the Legislature's jurisdiction. He said:

"I think, as a temperance man, the greatest calamity that could overcome the temperance people of this country would be to legislate in such a way as to raise uncertainty and doubts as to what our powers are, and in that way give those who are not favorable to temperance legislation facility for litigation and going on with appeals, and in that way weaken the efforts of temperance men."

PROVINCIAL PLEBISCITE PERIOD.

The leader of the Opposition, Mr. W. R. Meredith, supported the Marter Bill on the ground that it was not in excess of the ascertained authority of the Legislature, for it was not a provincial prohibitory law. It dealt only with retail trade and did not propose to interfere with the importation and manufacture of intoxicating liquors. Hence it was a regulating law, restricting the mode in which liquor might be sold, and as such it lay clearly within the jurisdiction of the province under the Ontario Liquor License Act.

Mr. Mowat supported the amendment and opposed the bill. He did not agree with Mr. Meredith's reasoning that the Marter Bill was not a prohibitory measure because it did not involve total prohibition, and he referred to the Canada Temperance Act, a Dominion prohibitory law, which yet made allowance for certain kinds of sales. The legal question, he said, did not depend upon the amount of prohibition but upon the effect of it. He quoted the judgment of the Privy Council in the case of the McCarthy Act, stating that there was no distinction between wholesale and retail trade in the matter of jurisdiction. Speaking as Attorney-General, he declared the intention of the Government to submit the question of jurisdiction to the courts. He said:

"The speediest way of getting a decision is by a direct reference under the powers that the Dominion Government has to refer to the Supreme Court, or the power the Provincial Government has to refer to the Court of Appeal. I want to take the shortest and speediest course of ascertaining the jurisdiction of this House."

He went on to say that he had entered into correspondence with the Dominion Government with a view to obtaining the consent of the latter to have the question of jurisdiction submitted at once to the Supreme Court, obviating the delay that would arise if the question were submitted by the Provincial Government alone, which would necessitate it being first submitted to one of the courts of this province, from which would arise an appeal to the Supreme Court or the Privy Council.

The amendment submitted by Mr. Ross was carried on a straight party division. This precluded a direct vote on the second reading of the Marter Bill.

Later on, a bill was introduced by the Hon. Mr. Ross, providing for the taking, at the next municipal election, of a vote of the electors of the province, and the women who were municipal voters, on the question: "Are you in favor of the immediate prohibition by law of the importation, manufacture and sale of intoxicating liquors as a beverage?" The printed instructions furnished in the bill for the guidance of voters explained the meaning of this question in the following terms:

"Electors in voting 'yes' on this question will be considered as expressing an opinion in favor of prohibition to the extent to which the Legislature of this Province of the Parliament of Canada has jurisdiction, as may be determined by the court of final resort."

A majority affirmative vote, Mr. Ross declared, would be a command or a request to those authorized to grant prohibition to do so without delay. This Plebiscite Bill passed through the several stages of enactment and was assented to by the Lieutenant-Governor on May 27, 1893.

At the first opportunity after the closing of the session of the Legislature, the Government prepared and submitted to the Court of Appeal for Ontario the following questions:

1. Has a provincial legislature jurisdiction to prohibit the sale within the province of spirituous, fermented or other intoxicating liquors?

2. Or has the legislature such jurisdiction regarding such portions of the province as to which the Canada Temperance Act is not in operation?

3. Has a provincial legislature jurisdiction to prohibit the manufacture of such liquors within the province?

4. Has the provincial legislature jurisdiction to prohibit the importation of such liquors into the province?

PROVINCIAL PLEBISCITE PERIOD.

5. If a provincial legislature has not jurisdiction to prohibit sales of such liquors, irrespective of quantity, has such legislature jurisdiction to prohibit the sale by retail, according to the definition of a sale by retail, either in statutes in force in the province at the time of Confederation, or any other definition thereof?

6. If a provincial legislature has a limited jurisdiction only as regards the prohibition of sales, has the legislature jurisdiction to prohibit sales subject to the limits provided by the several subsections of the 99th section of "The Canada Temperance Act," or any of them? (R.S.C., p. 105, s. 99.)

7. Had the Ontario Legislature jurisdiction to enact the 18th section of the Act passed by the Legislature of Ontario in the 53rd year of Her Majesty's reign, and entitled, "An Act respecting Local Option in the matter of Liquor Selling"?

Before the case was reached in the Court of Appeal, it was announced that the Dominion Government had accepted these questions as fully covering the disputed points of provincial jurisdiction, and had on October 26, 1893, submitted them to the Supreme Court of Canada. The decision of the Supreme Court was ultimately appealed to the Privy Council. The judicial process occupied a number of years.

THE CAMPAIGN.

On October 3 and 4, 1893, the active plebiscite campaign was initiated at a general prohibition convention in Toronto, called by the Union Committee of provincial temperance bodies. That committee, which had been formed at Toronto on March 3rd, was the result of a feeling in certain quarters that the Alliance was not sufficiently representative of the province to summon a convention at this critical time. There were some who thought that the committee, having called the convention, should continue in charge of the campaign, and thus supersede the Alliance. Other opinions prevailed, however, and the convention resolved itself into the annual Alliance meeting, and was invited to make any changes in the Alliance constitution deemed necessary for the better furthering of united work in Ontario.

PROHIBITION IN CANADA.

It was an enthusiastic gathering. There were 1,114 delegates reported present. Great mass meetings on the two evenings crowded the Horticultural Building to its utmost capacity. On October 4th, the Hon. G. W. Ross, speaking of the duty and prospects of the temperance workers in the plebiscite campaign, said in part:

"But it is said we have no guarantee that if public opinion is favorable to prohibition, even if the Ontario Legislature has the power, that it will pass a prohibitory liquor law. You have no guarantee? What guarantee do you want? The contract between a representative and the electors is not a contract between two parties of equal status, but it is a contract between master and servant. You are the master, the Legislature is the servant. Did you ever hear of a Legislature that refused to bow to public opinion? Such Legislatures are known by their epitaphs, not by their legislation.

"The English House of Commons for some years refused to listen to the voice of Grenville, Sharpe, Clarkson, and Wilberforce when they pleaded for the emancipation of the slave, but by and by there arose a House of Commons so transformed and renovated by public opinion that they paid the slave-holder twenty millions sterling for the fetters with which he had bound the slaves, that they might be free.

"There was a House of Commons that taxed the bread of England's millions in the interest of the agricultural landlord. There came up from the battlefields of public opinion a House of Commons that said: 'It is not meet for us to tax the children's bread for the sake of the landlord,' and bread was made free.

"There was a House of Commons in England that said: 'The franchise is for the capitalist and the landed aristocracy.' By and by there came a House of Commons that said the franchise should represent manhood, not money, and it is possible the time may come when the House of Commons may say that the franchise will represent womanhood as well.

"You want guarantees from the Legislature? You want the Legislature to open the door while you have the key in your own possession? You want the Legislature to sign a bond not to trespass on your property, while you hold a title to it in fee simple. The Legislature can have no permanent opinion of its

PROVINCIAL PLEBISCITE PERIOD.

own. A few individuals may endeavor to control it, and sometimes do control it for a time, but just so sure as the superior force of the allied armies of Wellington and Blucher crushed Napoleon at Waterloo, so sure will every Legislature that resists public opinion be itself obliged by and by to obey the mandate of the people, or be relegated to a position of retirement where its opinions will be as harmless as the rhapsodies of Napoleon at St. Helena.

"The people of this country are supreme, and when their will is decisively expressed, Legislatures dare not offer opposition, even if they would. Will we have prohibition then? Certainly, if we want it, and there is nobody who can say 'nay' to our demand. Will it come soon? It is for you to say, and after it has come it will be for you to say whether the opinion you expressed was based upon an honest conception of the issues involved, or an opinion open to reversal the moment it encountered the first onslaught of its enemies."

The Campaign Executive Committee of thirty-five prominent men and women, appointed to have general charge of the campaign, lost no time in setting to work. Dr. J. J. Maclaren, Q.C., was elected chairman, Mr. F. S. Spence, secretary, and Mr. E. Coatsworth, M.P., treasurer. Under the guidance of the Executive a most thorough organization of the prohibition forces was effected, with seventy central committees for counties, ridings, and cities, and sub-committees in municipalities and wards. Those who had previously opposed the vote and advocated the prohibition bill, now that the bill was defeated, threw in their forces with the plebiscite workers, determined, even while lacking faith in the issue, to roll up a big vote for the prohibition principle.

Never before in the history of the country were there held in the same time so many prohibition gatherings. There were found to be available a great number of volunteer speakers, including leading citizens and clergymen of nearly every denomination. The platform staffs of the different temperance societies offered their services. An idea of the work done by the Salvation Army may be obtained by the following

PROHIBITION IN CANADA.

extract from a letter sent out by Commandant Herbert Booth to local corps:

"December 7, 1893.

"My dear Comrade:

"*Re* The Prohibition Movement.

"I think it most desirable that the Army should take some active part in this campaign. None are more able to speak out clearly upon this question than we. In order that there may be uniformity of action throughout the province, will you please observe and carry out the following instructions:

" (1) The local corps should arrange to hold one meeting in each town of the province of any size and where there are prospects of a successful gathering.

" (2) The meeting should be arranged in conjunction with the local temperance people, to whom the dates should be submitted, and who should be asked to join us in the undertaking.

" (3) The meeting will, of course, be conducted either by yourself, as the district officer, or by the local captain.

"(4) Outside friends interested in this matter, always providing they are Christian people, should be invited to address the meeting, but the addresses should be as short as possible in order to secure interest and diversity.

" (5) When at all possible there should be two or three testimonies from converted drunkards, who, as working men, and as those having had experience in the curse of drink and the ease by which it can be obtained, should be permitted to give their opinion on this question."

A distinctive feature of the campaign was the literature circulation. Following the famous example of General Neal Dow in Maine, prohibitionists "sowed the State knee-deep with literature," but the committee restricted itself chiefly to circulars of official information necessary for the guidance of the workers. In addition to these, however, a vast number of educational documents were distributed by other institutions, such as Sons of Temperance, Grand Templars, the *Citizen* and the *Templar* Publishing Houses, the Methodist

PROVINCIAL PLEBISCITE PERIOD.

Book Room, and the Woman's Christian Temperance Union. Very many of the religious and secular journals of the province took up the matter, while campaign matter largely filled the columns of *The Templar, The Home Guard, The Canada Citizen, The Sons of Temperance, The Good Templar, The Woman's Journal, The Vanguard. Onward,* the organ of the Methodist young people's societies, was of special value in the contest.

The expression of opinion recorded at the polls on January 1, 1894, was an amazing victory for the prohibition cause. The aggregate results of the voting were as follows:*

	Men.	Women.	Total.
Votes polled Yes	180,087	12,402	192,489
Votes polled No	108,494	2,226	110,720
Total votes polled	288,581	14,628	303,209
A net majority Yes	71,593	10,176	81,769

SIR OLIVER MOWAT'S PLEDGE.

The electorate of Ontario had spoken in decisive tones upon the prohibition question, but the Privy Council had not yet answered the inquiries submitted to it concerning the jurisdiction of the province.

There were divided opinions as to what action the Legislature would take in face of the plebiscite returns, and the relative wisdom of the courses that lay open to it. Some people demanded the immediate total prohibition of the retail sale of liquor. Others favored the enactment of a law to be, for the time being, inoperative, but upon the announcement of the Privy Council's judgment to be brought into force by a proclamation covering as much of the enacted measure as the courts should have declared constitutional. Others, again, urged that no provincial prohibitory legislation be passed until the jurisdiction of the Legislature should have been positively defined, fearing that legislation respecting which any uncertainty existed would be ineffective, that its enforcement would be hampered by litigation and that the difficulties

---
* For detailed results see Appendix VI.

PROHIBITION IN CANADA.

connected with such conditions would be harmful to the cause of prohibition. No one questioned that the final delivery of the courts would lay upon either the Dominion or the Provincial legislative body the responsibility for prompt, progressive and thorough legislation.

While anxious that no precipitate step, useless or harmful, be taken, Mr. F. S. Spence strongly advocated continuance of local option work throughout the municipalities of the province. Indeed, one of the arguments used in favor of the plebiscite had been that such a vote would be a useful index of public opinion for local campaigns.

The local option situation was peculiar. It was discovered that, because of the Canada Temperance Act, the old municipal local option legislation of Ontario had been dropped from the provincial statute books. The Government was asked to replace it. This was done in 1890, and the old legislation was re-enacted. The law provided that any municipality might enact a by-law absolutely prohibiting the retail sale of liquor within its limits, such a by-law to be first passed by the municipal council and then ratified by a vote of the electors.

From September, 1890, to April, 1891, local option by-laws had been voted upon in twenty municipalities and carried in sixteen of them. Then its constitutionality had been challenged. In April, 1891, Chief Justice Galt gave decisions setting aside all but two of these by-laws, on the ground that the act authorizing municipalities to enact them was *ultra vires* of the Provincial Legislature. Immediately the opponents of prohibition in other municipalities in which the by-laws had been carried made application to have them set aside, and it became evident that until the question of jurisdiction was settled local option work would be at a standstill.

At the earnest urging of the Dominion Alliance Executive, the Ontario Government took prompt steps to have the validity of the law passed upon by a higher court. On April 28th the Attorney-General introduced into the Legislature a bill providing for an early reference of the question to the Court of

PROVINCIAL PLEBISCITE PERIOD.

Appeal of Ontario. The bill also provided that no further by-laws should be quashed until the decision of the Court of Appeal was given. The measure was hurried through the Legislature, and a case was prepared by the Government and ably argued before the Court of Appeal on May 28, 1891, by Æ. Irving, Q.C., and J. J. Maclaren, Q.C. The court sustained the law. This decision was subsequently carried to the Supreme Court of Canada, and in 1894 was still under consideration by that body.

In spite of this situation, Mr. Spence claimed that it was not necessary to wait for the settlement of the jurisdiction question to obtain some advantage from the victory won in the plebiscite. He argued that if a mischief-working barroom could be immediately closed it would be criminal to refrain from closing it, and that the carrying of a number of local measures would do much immediate good. Such a course would be by no means a substitute for advanced legislation. It would simply be using to the full the powers already possessed, while working to obtain something better.

"We must press the Legislature and Parliament for everything we can possibly get from them; but urging others to do their duty does not absolve us from our own responsibility," he said. "An advance on this line will not weaken, but rather strengthen our determination to insist upon further legislation. Total national prohibition is the end in view, short of which we will not stop. Meantime we fling our banner to the breeze, and push on the battle in which many outposts of the enemy will be taken and the full victory made easier and more complete.'

This has been the policy of the Dominion Alliance all through the fight for national prohibition, to strive unremittingly for the largest good but never to despise the small gains. It has been uncompromising in the principle embodied in its name: "For the Total Suppression of the Liquor Traffic," but in many a battle it has fought its way inch by inch. Over and over again it has had to take what it could get and be thankful.

PROHIBITION IN CANADA.

Mr. Spence was vehemently criticised, however, for his local option policy, which he outlined in the daily press. Some people objected to making use of local option by-laws on the ground that the law had not yet been finally settled by the Supreme Court. The plan was termed by those who judged it unwise "a retreat upon the eve of victory," and more unkindly still, "a political scheme to relieve the Liberal Government of responsibility and pressure." Some earnest workers, impetuous in their zeal, attributing a difference of opinion to unworthy motives, created division instead of striving for that unity which would have meant redoubled strength.

The situation was felt to be a critical one. In calling the prohibition convention in 1894, temperance leaders expressed the desire that all discordancy and diversity of opinion might be harmonized, and that in adopting a method of procedure and in carrying it out the unity and co-operation which had brought one victory to the temperance cause might be sustained for the accomplishing of another.

Fifteen hundred delegates met in the Pavilion on February 6th. The secretary read an historical report of the work done by the Plebiscite Campaign Committee, and said, in conclusion, "Your committee earnestly desires to express its deep gratitude for the signal success that has attended the recent movement, which it has been their high privilege to assist, and hearty thanks to the loyal workers who have so faithfully, earnestly and generously striven to secure the attainment of the strong and advanced position in which our cause to-day stands."

Mr. Spence then read the report of the Union Committee, the critical point of which was the recommendation, "That a deputation be appointed to wait forthwith upon the Ontario Government, and respectfully request them to declare in favor of total prohibition of the traffic in intoxicating liquors to the full extent of the power invested in the Legislature." The question at issue was, "What should the deputation ask of the Government?" The whole question of the relative

PROVINCIAL PLEBISCITE PERIOD.

wisdom of immediate legislation or of awaiting the settlement of the jurisdiction controversy was discussed from many points of view. The convention finally decided that it would be unwise to ask the Government to repent of its resolution made the previous year and, after submitting the question of jurisdiction to the courts, to legislate without waiting for their decision. The clause of the Union Committee's report was adopted without change.

At five o'clock a deputation of eighty-nine men and women gathered in the Members' Reception Room, in the west wing of the Parliament Buildings. Sir Oliver Mowat entered the room, followed by Messrs. Hardy, Ross, Dryden, and Harcourt. Mr. E. J. Davis, M.P.P., presented the deputation, which was headed by Rev. Wm. Kettlewell. Mr. F. S. Spence read the resolutions of the convention. Doctor Potts, Mrs. Thornley, President of the Woman's Christian Temperance Union, and Mr. John Cameron, laid the views of the convention before the Premier and the members of his Cabinet.

In response, Sir Oliver expressed his deep sense of the importance of the prohibition movement and the strength of public sentiment behind it, as evidenced by the plebiscite, the result of which was so eminently satisfactory. He then read to the deputation the following statement

"If the decision of the Privy Council should be that the province has the jurisdiction to pass a prohibitory liquor law, as respects the sale of intoxicating liquor, I will introduce such a bill in the following session, if I am then at the head of the Government.

"If the decision of the Privy Council is that the province has jurisdiction to pass only a partial prohibitory law, I will introduce such a prohibitory bill as the decision will warrant, unless the partial prohibitory power is so limited as to be ineffective from a temperance standpoint."

The Premier's reply was greeted with enthusiastic applause upon the part of the deputation. It was declared eminently satisfactory, and the proceedings were closed with three cheers for Sir Oliver.

In the evening an immense crowd gathered in the Pavilion to hear the report of the deputation and to bring the great convention to a close. "Onward, Christian Soldiers" they sang with all their hearts, and in the song was the ring of victory. There were a number of stirring addresses from leaders in the fight. The Hon. G. W. Ross recalled his expressions concerning the value of the plebiscite and the obligation of the Government to obey the will of the people. "It is what you had a right to expect," he said. "It is what it ought to do, and it is the only kind of a government I would be a member of."

The convention, in closing paid a graceful tribute to one on whom had fallen a great part of the burden of detail work in the fight, in the following resolution, adopted unanimously by a standing vote:

"That this convention desires to express its appreciation of the service rendered during the campaign by the Secretary of the Plebiscite and Campaign Executive, Mr. F. S. Spence, who, by his wide experience, untiring energy, and unflagging zeal, has contributed so largely to the magnificent result achieved on the first of January."

VI. NOVA SCOTIA PLEBISCITE.

D. Stiles Fraser, writing from Upper Stewiacke, N.S., in *The Vanguard* of October, 1894, gives the following account of the plebiscite in that province:

"The Sons of Temperance in Nova Scotia claim that they originated the movement for a plebiscite on prohibition in Canada. They base this claim on the action of their Grand Division at the annual session held in Halifax in November, 1887. On recommendation of the Committee on the State of the Order it was resolved: 'That the executive of this Grand Division be empowered to communicate with the executives of other Grand Divisions

PROVINCIAL PLEBISCITE PERIOD.

of the Dominion, and ask for concerted action in an appeal to the Government and Parliament of the Dominion for the passage of an Act, at an early date, providing for submitting, within the borders of Canada, the question of prohibition of the liquor traffic to a "Yes" or "No" vote of the electorate of the whole Dominion.'

"This is claimed to be the beginning of what is now so well known as the prohibition plebiscite movement. Though it may not be easy to trace the connection between the action and the plebiscite as so far realized, there can be no doubt that the seed then sown amidst opposition and fears has already borne abundant fruit, which is, we trust, only the firstfruits of the grand harvest to be gathered in when prohibition shall have become a living reality.

"The intention, as the resolution shows, was to have the vote taken under the direction of the Dominion Government. Efforts were made to carry out this intention, but without success, until in 1892 the action of temperance workers in Manitoba gave a new turn to the movement in having the vote taken by provinces. It was not, however, until after Prince Edward Island and Ontario had both followed the example of Manitoba that Nova Scotia came into line on this new plan.

"At the quarterly session of Grand Division, held in Lunenburg in August, 1893, it was agreed to petition the Provincial Government and Legislature to pass an act for the taking of a plebiscite on the question of prohibition in connection with the general election to be held in 1894. As a result very largely signed petitions were presented, an act was passed in accordance with the prayer, and the vote on prohibition was taken on the 15th of March, 1894. The time for the work was short, for very soon after the Legislature was prorogued, the House was dissolved, and the election brought on in about a month. But the time was well utilized. A provincial convention was held in Halifax as soon as possible, followed by various county and district conventions, and the whole province was well organized. The Woman's Christian Temperance Union did excellent work in circulating literature and in otherwise helping to make the campaign a success. Many meetings were held, and it is safe to say that never before did the great question of prohibition get such an airing in Nova Scotia. In many places the candidates at their meetings explained how

PROHIBITION IN CANADA.

the vote was to be taken. The presiding officer at each polling booth was required to tender to every voter a prohibition ballot, so that if he did not want to vote he had to decline the ballot."

The official return of the voting on the question of prohibition on March 15th was as follows:

	Vote.		Majority.	
County.	Yes.	No.	Yes.	No.
Annapolis	2,628	350	2,278	
Antigonish	883	948		65
Cape Breton	2,644	1,916	728	
Colchester	3,053	382	2,671	
Cumberland	4,595	511	4,084	
Digby	1,695	297	1,398	
Guysboro	1,362	392	970	
Halifax	5,387	2,351	3,036	
Hants	2,698	439	2,259	
Inverness	1,973	800	1,173	
Kings	3,170	249	2,921	
Lunenburg	2,567	916	1,651	
Pictou	4,100	1,192	2,908	
Queens	1,137	225	912	
Richmond	978	436	542	
Shelburne	1,838	166	1,672	
Victoria	1,165	284	881	
Yarmouth	1,883	501	1,382	...
Total	43,756	12,355	31,466	65

Net majority, 31,401

The number of voters who voted for candidates and the number who voted for prohibition, are given in the following table. It must be borne in mind, however, that the number of names on the list was much in excess of the possible pollable vote. Persons had died since the lists had been made up, or had moved away, or had become disqualified. The same names were frequently found on different lists. It was not possible to ascertain exactly the number entitled to vote.

PROVINCIAL PLEBISCITE PERIOD.

County.	No. on Voters' Lists.	No. who voted for Candidates.	No. who voted on Prohibition.
Annapolis	4,154	3,357	2,978
Antigonish	3,186	2,345	1,831
Cape Breton	7,331	5,323	4,560
Colchester	5,287	3,759	3,435
Cumberland	7,734	5,791	5,106
Digby	3,893	2,419	1,992
Guysboro	2,852	2,170	1,754
Halifax	14,558	8,839	7,738
Hants	3,386	3,386	3,137
Inverness	5,083	3,859	2,773
Kings	4,572	3,738	3,419
Lunenburg	6,240	4,969	3,483
Pictou	8,492	6,049	5,292
Queens	2,164	1,586	1,362
Richmond	2,571	1,974	1,414
Shelburne	3,284	2,728	2,004
Victoria	2,199	1,683	1,449
Yarmouth	4,372	2,847	2,384
	81,358	66,822	56,111

Majority voting "Yes" on prohibition.......... 31,401
Percentage of those who voted on the question of prohibition who voted for it, about......... 78
Percentage of those who voted for candidates who voted in favor of prohibition............. 65½

It will also be noticed that the number of votes polled for prohibition was even in excess of half the number of names on the voters' lists.

VII. THE PRIVY COUNCIL DECISION.

On May 9, 1896, the Lords of the Judicial Committee of the Privy Council delivered their decision of the jurisdiction question. It was a lengthy judgment, but it dealt almost exclusively with the seventh question, concerning the constitutionality of the Ontario Local Option Law, sustaining the legislation referred to therein. It was stated that the argument upholding the Ontario Local Option Act contained a sufficient answer to Questions Nos. 1, 2, 5, and 6. The judgment said further, that a provincial legislature had no power to prohibit importation, but had absolute power to prohibit any liquor selling or manufacturing transaction so carried on as to make its prohibition a merely local matter in the province. The *Montreal Witness* gave the following condensed report of the decision:

"The Privy Council discussed fully the seventh question, as that was the only one which related to an actual case, remarking as follows:

"'Their Lordships think it expedient to deal in the first instance with the seventh question, because it raises a practical issue to which special arguments of counsel on both sides of the Bar were chiefly directed.' After deciding the seventh question in the affirmative, referring to the other six, they say further: 'These differ from the question which has already been answered, in this respect, that they relate to matters which may possibly become litigious in the future, but have not yet given rise to any real and present controversy. Their Lordships must further observe that these questions, being in their nature academic rather than judicial, are better fitted for the consideration of the officers of the Crown than of a court of law. The replies to be given to them will necessarily depend upon the circumstances in which they may arise for decision, and these circumstances are in this case left to speculation. It must, therefore, be understood that the answers which follow are not meant to have, and cannot have, the weight of judicial determination.'

"In discussing the seventh question, however, they go over the whole ground pretty fully, and we may fairly infer what would be their probable decision if the other questions were submitted, as the seventh question was. To the first and second questions they simply refer to the opinions expressed by them in disposing of the seventh question. To the third question they say that in the absence of conflicting legislation by the Dominion of Canada, they are of the opinion that the provincial legislatures would have jurisdiction if it were shown that the manufacture was carried on under such circumstances and conditions as to make its prohi-

PROVINCIAL PLEBISCITE PERIOD.

bition a merely local matter in the province. The fourth question was decided in the negative. The fifth and sixth questions they answered as in the case of the first and second, by referring to the opinions expressed in giving the judgment on the seventh. A careful reading of the whole report leads to the following conclusion:

"(1) That the Ontario law referred to relates to the retail sale only, and, therefore, the simple fact that it is declared to be constitutional gives no warrant for saying that it would have been constitutional had it also included the wholesale sale.

"(2) That Dominion enactments, when competent, override but cannot directly repeal provincial legislation in force at the time of Confederation, and that the Scott Act, in so far as it purported to repeal the Dunkin Act, was *ultra vires*, but being a competent Dominion enactment would over-ride the Dunkin Act wherever it was brought into force.

"(3) That the provincial legislatures have the right to pass prohibitory legislation so long as no Dominion enactments covering the same ground are in force in the province.

"(4) Such prohibition, however, would probably not extend to the importation or to manufacture or sale by wholesale, that is to say, the importation could not be prohibited through a port situated in the province, and the manufacture and sale by wholesale could not be prohibited if the delivery and consumption was at a point outside the province. These conclusions must, however, be subject to the limitation made by the Privy Council as above quoted, namely, that they will necessarily depend upon the circumstances in which they may arise for decision, and these circumstances are in this case left to speculation.

"It would appear, therefore, that the Dominion Parliament has power to prohibit the importation, manufacture and sale, and until such legislation is enacted the provinces have power to give a very large measure of prohibition. Until an actual case shall arise for the decision of the courts, it is impossible to define the exact limits of the provincial authority in reference thereto."

PROHIBITION IN CANADA.

VIII. PREMIER HARDY AND THE HARCOURT BILL.

The decision of the Privy Council was announced on May 9, 1896. On July 18th a temperance deputation waited on Premier Hardy, Hon. Mr. Ross and Hon. Mr. Gibson, of his Cabinet, to ascertain what were the prospects for prohibitory legislation, in view of the change of the Government and final settlement of the long jurisdiction controversy.

Mayor Fleming introduced the speakers—Senator Vidal, Rev. Dr. McKay and Justice Maclaren. They reminded the Premier of the promise given to the temperance people by his predecessors that prohibitory legislation would be granted so far as lay within the power of the Provincial Legislature. According to the decision of the final Court of Appeal, said Justice Maclaren, that power had been declared even larger than was expected, and therefore the deputation came with confidence to ask from Premier Hardy the fulfilment of Sir Oliver Mowat's pledge.

Mr. Hardy replied that he recognized that the temperance sentiment in the province had not abated within the last two years, and that he saw no reason to withdraw from the opinions expressed by Sir Oliver Mowat and his colleagues in 1894. He was bound to say, however, that the decision of the Privy Council did not remove all doubt and difficulty respecting the jurisdiction of the province. For instance, it had not answered the question of whether or not the Provincial Legislature had power to prohibit the manufacture and sale of spirituous, fermented and other intoxicating liquors. Since the delivery of the Lords there had been some talk of license legislation. But he declared that the Government was a temperance Government; they believed in temperance reform and would take no backward step, but would go forward as rapidly as their jurisdiction and public sentiment would allow.

In November of the same year, another temperance deputation interviewed the Premier, with the request for definite

PROVINCIAL PLEBISCITE PERIOD.

and immediate amendment to the license law in the reduction of licenses and the shortening of the hours of sale. They received the Premier's assurance that the matter would be dealt with at the next session of the Legislature.

On February 25, 1897, a liquor bill was introduced on behalf of the Government by Hon. R. Harcourt, Provincial Secretary, and the temperance people called an emergency meeting on February 27th to consider it. The bill was a distinct disappointment. Apart from the fact that it was a liquor regulating bill instead of the prohibitory measure so long looked for, it could not but be regarded as favorable to the liquor trade. The proposed amendments to the license law were meagre. As many prominent temperance workers vehemently declared, the bill was "an insult." It was agreed to hold indignation meetings throughout the province and to call a convention immediately to protest against this breach of faith on the part of the Government. A committee consisting of Mrs. Thornley, Rev. Dr. A. C. Courtice, and F. S. Spence was appointed to prepare a resolution of censure.

Under the auspices of the Alliance, a mass meeting of Toronto citizens was held in the Association Hall on March 4th. The characteristic feature of the gathering was the unanimity with which the speakers, irrespective of political inclination, expressed disappointment in the bill before the House, denouncing it as retrograde in tendency and utterly out of sympathy with the sentiment of the province.

The regular Alliance convention, attended by five hundred temperance workers from all over the province, was held on March 11th. A report on the bill was drawn up and adopted at the afternoon session. The proposed legislation as to the number of licenses to be issued in proportion to the population and as to method by which electors might prevent the renewal of licenses was condemned. The withdrawing from municipal councils of the powers they had possessed of annually reducing the number of licenses was characterized as retrograde legislation. The closing hours proposed did not meet with their approval. There was no provision for restricting the sale and drinking of liquor in clubs. While considering the bill unsatisfactory, the convention went on record, however, as favoring the following points: (*a*) the raising of the age limit, (*b*) the reduction of licenses, (*c*) the restrictions of the sale of liquor by druggists.

This report was presented to the Premier late in the afternoon by a large deputation which filled the reception room of the Parliament Buildings. In reply to the speakers, Mr. Hardy reaffirmed the interest of the Government in temperance, and with reference to the pledge of Sir Oliver Mowat and himself said: "There is no dispute as to what Sir Oliver said. The only dispute is as to how you apply it, as to whether he was discussing a license or a prohibitory law. And I submit that the discussions and the questions which were submitted to the Privy Council and their decision give a complete answer as to what was being discussed. As to my own promise—'As far as our jurisdiction will permit and public sentiment will approve'—now we are called upon to legislate. My observations were made in reference to what we can do in the Legislature. We are not expected to attempt to carry something through which we cannot carry through, and my observation must be accepted as to legislative public sentiment. Now we have a majority of eight, or nine at the most; if five will not follow us the bill drops and the Government drops. That is the position." He went on to defend the bill against the charge of retrogression, and declared that the Government had been unanimous in reference to it.

At the evening session of the convention strong dissatisfaction was expressed over the Government's reception of the delegation in the afternoon. A committee was appointed to watch the progress of the bill through the House, and to promote so far as possible amongst the members of the Legislature the policy adopted by the convention.

The Ontario liquor dealers presented their case to the Premier on March 18th. Mr. James Haverson, K.C., their solicitor and spokesman, declared that the Government

PROVINCIAL PLEBISCITE PERIOD.

pledges were wiped out by the Privy Council decision, and asked for certain changes in the Government License Bill favorable to the liquor interests.

Amendments to the bill were announced on March 26th. On March 30th the measure came up for discussion in the Legislature, in a form differing materially from that in which it had been first read in the House, but only two of the twenty-three changes asked for by the temperance people had been granted.

Mr. Harcourt, in moving the second reading of the bill, referred to the great amount of hostile criticism to which, since its first appearance, it had been subjected by the temperance people, who complained that it did not go far enough. He thought great benefit lay in its moderation. The careful, moderate restricting of the liquor trade by the Government during the last twenty years had been eminently satisfactory. It had effected nothing short of a revolution in the drinking habits of the people, and the policy owed its success to the fact that the Legislature had never gone a step too far to carry with it the well-ascertained and serious conviction of the people in support of it. He then reviewed in detail the Liquor License Laws passed by Parliament since 1876. He quoted from the statistical records of the Dominion to show the efficacy of those laws in decreasing crime, and by a comparison of the figures with those of the prohibition State of Maine, claimed that Ontario showed a decided advantage in this respect.

He then took up the amendments made in the new License Bill since its first reading. These were:

1. Licenses were to be reduced from four to three for the first one thousand of the population, and after that to one for every five hundred instead of six hundred. The effect of this change would be to cut off some one hundred and fifty licenses in the province. Mr. Harcourt believed that such a reduction was sufficiently radical, considering the additional power to reduce that lay with municipal councils and license commissioners, and considering the fact that the action so far taken by municipalities

did not evidence any very strong popular sentiment in favor of drastic measures.

2. Hours of closing were fixed at eleven o'clock in towns and cities and ten o'clock in other municipalities. But the power of shortening these hours, which had heretofore rested exclusively with license commissioners, was henceforth to be vested in municipal councils through the submission of a by-law, so that the electors might have more direct control of this regulation.

3. Liquor was not to be sold to any person under twenty-one years of age. The limit set by existing law was only over eighteen years. This regulation was also to apply to all kinds of clubs as well as taverns.

4. A tavern was not to be erected within three hundred feet of a church or school.

5. If a licensee knowingly allowed liquor to be sold during prohibited hours, and if he were three times convicted on three different days within two months, the license commissioners should revoke his license and he should be disqualified from holding a license for three years. This clause, it was believed, would be valuable in enforcing prohibition of Sunday selling.

6. The thirty-four existing saloons of the Province were to be wiped out, one-half in May, 1898, and the remainder a year later.

7. Druggists were to be limited in selling liquor to quantities of not more than six ounces, unless the liquor were mixed with other drugs; should it be so mixed with other drugs the limit was to be one pint. Further, a druggist was obliged to have a prescription from a *bona fide* physician for the authorization of every sale and to keep a record of all sales.

8. Licenses were not to be issued in residential districts provided that a majority of the voters in the subdivision petitioned against it. Before such petition was undertaken, the electors might obtain from the license commissioners a statement as to whether or not the district would be considered by them a residential one.

In conclusion, Mr. Harcourt referred to the Nova Scotia License Law, which was held up by prohibitionists as being a very stringent and a very enviable measure. He quoted from the license inspector of Halifax to the effect that the law was not by any means enforced. Thus, he said, it was

PROVINCIAL PLEBISCITE PERIOD.

idle to legislate beyond the point reached by general public sentiment. He believed that the enormous advance in sobriety in Ontario was not due solely to legislation, but had been assisted by the pulpits, the schoolhouse, the press, and the well-regulated homes of the land. He concluded by saying:

"I ask this House to agree with me, all things considered, in the light of all that has been accomplished—our licenses thirteen thousand less in number than they were twenty years ago, our people more temperate than those of any province or state on this continent, the number of those committed for drunkenness one-third of what it was twenty years ago. I ask you to remember with me that this has been accomplished under moderate legislation, step by step legislation, under the policy of 'hurry slowly,' and, judging from the past, I ask you to agree with me that if the legislation of this bill is to be effective, is to be useful, is to lead to grand results, it can only be effective in proportion to its moderation, and in proportion to the extent in which it shall carry with it the moral sentiment of the whole community."

Mr. Marter criticized the Government's action in shirking responsibility by handing over powers to the councils and retaining only the appointment of inspectors and commissioners who would be useful for election purposes. This move would result in a lack of uniformity in the different parts of the province. He scored the Government for failure to carry out Mr. Mowat's pledge.

Mr. Hardy replied, defending the Government at some length. "Mr. Mowat's pledge," he said, "had no reference to a license law."

"It dealt only with total or partial prohibition. Who can stand up therefore in the face of men of intelligence and pretend for a moment that we have been false to our pledge or that we have made any pledge which we are violating in any sense of shape because we do not turn a License Bill, and attempt to screw the License Act into what might be called a partial Prohibition Act? I repudiate in the strongest language which I am capable of, that there has been any breach of faith or of pledges."

PROHIBITION IN CANADA.

He read the following letter from Sir Oliver Mowat in support of this argument:

"I do not know whether your temperance bill this session goes as far in the direction which temperance people desire as it would be practicable for you to go at present, but I concur in what I notice you have said as to the nature of the pledges given to a deputation in February, 1894. I agree with you that the pledge had exclusive reference to a License Law.

"The amendments which your bill proposes to the License Law, and the further amendments which temperance organizations desire ought to depend upon their merits, and not on any alleged pledge on the part of your Government."

The judges of the Privy Council had not decided, continued Mr. Hardy, the question of the power of the province to prohibit. Therefore, because of the wording of Sir Oliver Mowat's statement, there was now no pledge in existence; the Privy Council decided that we have jurisdiction. Further, regarding the demands of the temperance people, he said that, with the greatest respect for these men and women, the Government and Legislature had to be the judges in the last resort of how far public opinion demanded that a license bill should go, and whether its demands would allow anything more stringent than the bill which they had the honor to lay before the House.

The position taken by Mr. Whitney, the leader of the Opposition, was that his side of the House had nothing to do with the matter at all and did not propose to be badgered into it. Being in the minority they had no chance to pass a bill. When the time came that in a constitutional way the responsibility should rest upon the Opposition to deal with the question, they would deal with it like men and not dodge it for twenty-five years nor shirk the responsibility. The bill was given its second reading without a division.

SECTION IX.

DOMINION PLEBISCITE.

In the plebiscite campaign the liquor traffic did its best. It spent money freely. It appealed to unworthy prejudices. It strove to rouse race feelings. It used every device that desperation and dishonesty could suggest. Yet the liquor traffic was beaten. The electors it prejudiced and the electors it bought were not enough to equal the earnest, honest men who marked their ballots in condemnation of the traffic. The traffic was beaten and the people won.

By its action the Dominion Government has forced into politics the question of whether the law is to be in favor of the minority and the wrong, or on the side of the majority and the right. It looks as if we must fight again at the ballot box the question of whether or not the people have a right to rule.

I. LIBERAL CONVENTION OF 1893.

THE centre of interest swings again into the arena of Dominion politics. Ever since 1884 the Parliament of Canada had ostensibly been waiting for such evidences of public opinion as would justify them in the enactment of a law of total prohibition, in accordance with their official acceptance of the prohibition principle. In 1898, following the example of several of the provinces, the Dominion Government tested that opinion by a direct vote of the electors on the prohibition question.

In order to understand the history of the Dominion plebiscite, it will be necessary to go back to the period when the Federal Parliament last took action on the temperance question by appointing the Royal Commission to investigate the effects of the liquor traffic and the working of prohibition in Canada and the United States.

While awaiting the results of that investigation, temperance workers did not relax their efforts to keep the prohibition question before the eyes of the country's legislators. At the Dominion Liberal Convention, held at Ottawa on June 20 and 21, 1893, prohibitionists raised their voices and forced the prohibition issue upon the consideration of the Liberal Party. The convention was an historic event, the first gathering in council of the Liberals of all Canada since Confederation.

In view of the coming general elections, and the widespread disturbance of public opinion over the reciprocity question and the fiscal policy of the Government, the deliberations of the convention were of special interest. That the Liberal Party should make an expression upon the prohibition question was considered by the friends of prohibition to be a matter of great importance.

PROHIBITION IN CANADA.

The Hon. Wilfrid Laurier broached the subject in his opening address by saying:—

"Within the last fifteen days I have received several applications from different parts of the country asking me, 'What are you going to do about temperance? What are you going to do about prohibition?' I ought to speak frankly about this. I don't pretend at this moment to give you any more than my views. On a former occasion I already announced that this was a free, democratic convention, in which no cut-and-dried resolutions are to be placed before you. You are free to move upon prohibition or anything else that you choose, but I ask you simply to allow me to give you my views. You are aware that two years ago, against our protest, however, the Government of the day appointed a commission to investigate the liquor question, not only in this country, but in other countries as well. This was done against our protest. We believed—I still believe, for my part—that we have all the information we require on which to form an opinion on this subject. . . . As long as the commission is deliberating, it would be impossible for us to frame a policy. If we did, the Government would go to their friends and say: This is not fair towards us; we are seeking information at your request, and therefore do not ask us to have an issue on this. We could not have an issue on this subject, and, gentlemen, I want to have an issue with the Government on every subject that comes up."

Notwithstanding this rather discouraging opening, Mr. F. S. Spence, who was a delegate to the convention, presented the following resolution, which was referred for consideration to the committee on resolutions:

Whereas it is universally admitted that the common traffic in intoxicating liquors is universally recognized as the most prolific cause of poverty, disease and crime, that it is inimical to the welfare of the nation, and that it is the most formidable obstacle to the moral, social and material progress of our people; and

Whereas the Dominion Parliament has admitted the facts above set out, and declared by an overwhelming majority that total prohibition is the only right and effective legislative method of dealing with the liquor question; and

DOMINION PLEBISCITE.

Whereas the numerous strong declarations of the great ecclesiastical and civil bodies, the many petitions laid before the Dominion Parliament and Provincial Legislature, the extent to which our citizens have taken hold of local option laws embodying the prohibition principle in a necessarily limited and therefore defective form, the immense votes cast for this principle whenever independently submitted, and the strong feeling in favor of it everywhere finding emphatic expression, all make it absolutely clear that the vast majority of electors desire immediate and definite legislative action in harmony with the principles already admitted.

Therefore, resolved, that this representative convention of the Liberal Party declares that the time has come when the Dominion Parliament should enact a law prohibiting the manufacture, importation and sale of intoxicating liquors except for sacramental, scientific and medicinal purposes, and calls upon the Liberal Party to adopt the principle as a part of its policy.

The committee refused to recommend the resolution in the form presented, advocating, as it did, the adoption of a straight prohibition plank in the Liberal platform, but the following resolution was presented to the convention by Mr. S. A. Fisher, ex-M.P. for Brome, Quebec:

"That whereas public attention is at present much directed to the consideration of the admittedly great evils of intemperance, it is desirable that the mind of the people should be clearly ascertained on the question of prohibition by means of a Dominion plebiscite."

In speaking to the motion, Mr. Fisher said:

"We know that in three of the provinces the Liberal Governments of those provinces have brought about local or provincial plebiscites, thus giving the temperance people the opportunity to show what they believe to be the truth, that the temperance sentiment of this country is strong enough to enforce a prohibition law if it is given to it. I propose to read the resolution which will bring about this result, and which pledges the Liberal Party, if returned to power, to give the people of Canada an opportunity to express their views upon this question, and the Government in power must necessarily carry out the expressed will of the people. There is no doubt that this is what the Liberal Party would do, for we know their pledges can be trusted. This will bring the question clearly before the people of Canada, and will enable the Government to know just what the sentiment of the country is, and I have enough confidence in the people to believe that the result will be so pronounced that the Legislature and the Government will be only too glad to meet the wishes of the people, and that we shall be able to get a law of total prohibition."

Hon. A. T. Anglin, Toronto, opposed the resolution. He said:

"It is, in my opinion, of very great importance that the Liberal Party of the Dominion of Canada should not present itself to the people of Canada as a prohibitory-law party. The adoption of this resolution will have no other effect than to present it in that light, should it be adopted without objection.

"It may be said, indeed, that this resolution only asks for a plebiscite. But what do we mean when we ask for a plebiscite, if we are in earnest? Is it not that we desire to know what the opinion of the people is on this question; that we desire to ascertain their opinion in a particular way, and that we will do all in our power to give effect to their decision as thus ascertained? It may be that not one-half of the adult male population will vote. Nevertheless, should a majority be obtained at the polls, when this question is submitted, the friends of prohibition will be in a position to call upon the Liberal Party to follow up their resolution logically by assisting in the passage and enforcement of a prohibitory liquor law. There are many of us who do not believe prohibition to be the best means of promoting temperance. I am one of these."

Mr. F. S. Spence objected to the amended resolution because it did not go far enough. However, if he couldn't get an ell he would take an inch. He would rather have that resolution than nothing at all. "What need we of a plebiscite," he asked, "in order to ascertain public opinion? Ontario is taking her plebiscite; so is Prince Edward Island; Manitoba has taken hers. There is not a liquor license in Nova Scotia outside the City and County of Halifax. The

DOMINION PLEBISCITE.

Province of New Brunswick has memorialized the Dominion Parliament for total prohibition. All these signs indicate that public opinion is ripe for prohibition, and everywhere prohibitionists will be disappointed that you have not gone far enough in the right direction. We can see no reason why you should stop short at this resolution. Nevertheless, I think a plebiscite will do good. It will give us the opportunity of an educating campaign of great value to this country."

Mr. H. A. McKeown, St. John, N.B., made the closing speech of the debate. He said:

"We must be prepared to face the issue. Some provinces might be overwhelmingly for prohibition; others might be the other way. Then, sir, I consider it would not be a problem impossible of solution, or impossible to the statesmanship and genius of the Liberal Party in this country, to make such an amendment to the constitution as would enable us to have prohibitiou provinces in this Dominion, in the same way as they have prohibition states in the American Union. All the objections that can be urged against prohibition can be fought out when the question comes to be taken on a plebiscite. All the committee asks of the convention here assembled is to declare in favor of the will of the people being expressed upon this subject, and the Liberal Party will have lost its Liberalism if it is not willing to give the people what they want."

The resolution as amended was put and carried by an overwhelming majority.

In a personal letter written on October 25, 1901, Mr. Spence said, referring to the convention:

"I know positively that whatever may have been the secret thought of some person or persons who did not express it, there was no intention or expectation in the mind of the convention, excepting that an affirmative vote for prohibition would be followed by a prohibitory law. Further, if any leading member of the Liberal Party at that time, or subsequently, prior to the vote, had in his own mind any other idea, he kept it concealed.
There was never any suggestion or expectation that the Government would fail to give us a prohibitory law if we polled a

majority vote, and I am still as strong as ever in the conviction that the Government's treatment of the temperance party and the temperance cause cannot be excused or satisfactorily explained."

II. DOMINION ELECTION, 1896.

The Ontario Alliance convention, which met in 1894 after the provincial plebiscite vote, appointed a deputation to wait upon the Dominion Government. Representatives from every province united with this deputation, and shortly after the opening of the present session of the Dominion Parliament a great delegation was received at Ottawa by Sir John Thompson, leader of the Dominion House, and most of the members of his cabinet. The deputation urged the Dominion Government to immediately promote prohibitory legislation, the power of the Dominion Government to do so being unquestioned. Sir John Thompson, on behalf of the Government, expressed his sympathy with the deputation, but stated that until the report of the Royal Commission had been received and considered he would not make any promise in reference to the matter which the deputation had pressed upon his attention, beyond the assurance that it would receive careful consideration.

In 1895 the House of Commons was once again called upon to face the prohibition question, which for three years it had successfully avoided. At that session Mr. T. B. Flint, with the endorsation of the Legislative Committee of the Alliance Council, and according to the suggestion of the Dominion Alliance convention held in Montreal in July, introduced this prohibition resolution:

" That, in the opinion of the House, the manufacture, importation and sale of intoxicating liquors in Canada, except for sacramental, scientific, manufacturing, and medicinal purposes, should be prohibited by law."

The resolution was sidetracked by an amendment deferring consideration of the question until the decision of the

DOMINION PLEBISCITE.

Imperial Privy Council upon the jurisdiction question should have been received. In 1896 Mr. Flint again introduced his resolution, but it was not brought to a vote.

The Royal Commission, which had been so long holding the prohibition question in abeyance, presented its final report in April, 1895, and in May, 1896, the long-expected decision of the Imperial Privy Council upon the question of provincial jurisdiction of the liquor traffic was announced. In view of the decision and the general election which was soon to take place, the Alliance issued the following address:

TORONTO, May, 1896.

Electors of Canada,—

You are earnestly urged to take advantage of the opportunity now offering itself, in a general Dominion election, to secure a Parliament pledged to prohibit the traffic in intoxicating liquors. The judgment of the Privy Council, just rendered, having in effect reaffirmed the position that the Dominion Parliament alone can pass a law for the total prohibition of the liquor traffic, emphasizes the necessity for electing sound prohibitionists to the House of Commons.

The majority report of the Royal Commission, presented to the late Parliament, estimates that the cost of the intoxicating liquor annually consumed in Canada, at average retail prices, would amount to $39,879,854, and the amount paid therefore by the consumers is "considerably in excess of that amount."

This appalling outlay, however, is only a fraction of the evil with which the liquor trade is burdening our country. It lays upon our citizens a fearful load of suffering, poverty, disease, mortality and crime. It is an aggressive, debauching and dangerous influence in political affairs.

The overwhelming majorities in favor of prohibition in the plebiscites taken in Ontario, Nova Scotia and Prince Edward Island, and the prohibition memorial unanimously adopted in the New Brunswick Legislature, clearly demonstrate that the electorate of Canada desire immediate legislation against this giant evil.

This is the most important political question before the country to-day. Earnestly we appeal to you not to allow it to be side-tracked by others, or ignored by the candidates for your suffrage.

The platform adopted at the Montreal convention in 1894 details a plan which, if fairly carried out, will compel recognition of the prohibition reform and secure the return of a Parliament pledged to put that reform into practical operation.

Our friends are therefore recommended everywhere to take an active part in political organization and work, doing all that is possible to secure the nomination and election of representatives who are known and avowed prohibitionists, and who will loyally support prohibitory legislation regardless of party exigencies.

There is not a moment to lose. We cannot spare the aid and influence of any friend of our cause. Earnestly we appeal to you to act unitedly, fearlessly, determinedly, and at once. Do not wait for some one else to begin. Consult known friends of our cause in your locality. Question every candidate who is nominated. Work loyally and earnestly for those who will stand by our cause and thus aid in securing the speedy triumph of our principles in practical legislation.

By order of the Executive Committee.

The following questions were also prepared by the Alliance Executive and pressed upon parliamentary candidates who had not publicly declared themselves upon the prohibition question:

(1) Are you in favor of the prohibition of the liquor traffic?

(2) If elected to the House of Commons, will you do all in your power, in co-operation with the other members of Parliament who favor prohibition, to secure the introduction and enactment of prohibitory legislation at the earliest possible opportunity?

Parliament was dissolved on April 23, 1896. The Liberals appealed to the temperance people for support in the elections on the strength of the plebiscite resolution adopted at the convention of 1893. Then the question was raised as to just how definitely that resolution had committed the party to prohibitory legislation.

Mr. Fisher, in moving the resolution, had explicitly declared that the party pledged itself, if in power, to take a

DOMINION PLEBISCITE.

vote, and that the Government was obliged to carry out the expressed will of the people. No one had seemed inclined to contradict him. His interpretation of the move had been accepted as the correct one.

To a deputation of Winnipeg prohibitionists, the Hon. Mr. Laurier had made a statement in 1894, which was reported as follows:

"He would pledge his honor that as soon as the Liberals came into power in Ottawa they would take a plebiscite of the Dominion, by which the party would stand, and the will of the people would be carried out, even were it to cost power for ever to the Liberal Party."

In October, 1895, when questioned by Rev. Mr. Huxtable of Montreal, as to what would be done about prohibition if the Liberals came into power, Mr. Laurier had replied:

"The Liberal Party has pledged itself in convention at Ottawa that, whenever in power, they would take a plebiscite on the liquor question as to whether the people want a prohibitory liquor law or not. The answer is not in my hands. It is in the hands of the people, and according to their answer such legislation they will have at the hands of the Government."

Mr. Wilfrid Laurier, during the election campaign, when questioned directly upon the subject, said:

"The answer is plain. I am by nature a democrat. I believe in democratic government and, above all, in a constitutional government, and the only way to act under a democratic and constitutional government is that the people must govern and their command must be obeyed. As the people shall speak, so shall be the duty of the Government, if that Government be in the hands of the Liberal Party."

On the strength of these statements, friends of temperance polled a large vote for Liberal candidates and thus assisted materially in the sweeping Liberal victory of June, 1896.

PROHIBITION IN CANADA.

III. DOMINION PLEBISCITE CAMPAIGN.

The Cabinet which was formed under the leadership of the Hon. Mr. Laurier was an exceptionally able one, with outstanding representatives from every province, amongst them the former Premier of Ontario, Sir Oliver Mowat, as Minister of Justice.

On September 3, 1896, a deputation from the Dominion Alliance waited on the new Government and requested the introduction of prohibitory legislation at as early a date as possible. In reply to the deputation, Mr. Laurier stated his interest in the work promoted by the delegation, his gratification at the progress that had been made in temperance during the years of his political life, and the intention of the Government to carry out fully the policy which had been laid down. He said:

"It is the intention of the Liberal Party to carry out to the letter every article in its programme within the very shortest possible limit. There is no intention to delay. On the contrary, speaking even politically, it is perhaps the best policy of all to deal with the question within the shortest time. It is not our intention this session, but I have every hope that next session, and not later, we shall introduce the legislation promised."

The Speech from the Throne in 1897 promised a plebiscite bill that session. The introduction of the measure was delayed, however, owing to the Premier's absence from Canada to attend the Queen's Diamond Jubilee, and his special desire to be present when the matter should come up in the House.

Meantime, the subject of prohibition was being widely discussed by both friends and foes of the movement. The revenue problem was the centre of interest. Anti-prohibitionists argued that if prohibition were enacted it would involve, through loss of revenue and expense of enforcement, an increased taxation of about two dollars per head for the

DOMINION PLEBISCITE.

population of the Dominion, and that this additional amount would have to be raised by direct taxation.

Leading prohibitionists pointed out the fallacy of this stock argument. They showed that under prohibition the producing capacity of the people would be increased, while the cost of government would be greatly reduced, since three-quarters of the crime would be done away with. The capital, enterprise, and mental and physical energy employed in the liquor traffic to unproductive or destructive ends, would be, under prohibition, diverted into channels of revenue-producing industry within the Dominion.

Mr. F. S. Spence discussed the question at length in the daily press, and summed up the arguments as follows:

"The prohibition of the liquor traffic would prevent a vast waste of wealth and would promote the material prosperity of the country, so that in a very short time the increase thus brought about in taxable wealth would make it easy to provide even more additional revenue than the liquor traffic at present pays. Furthermore, a stoppage of this waste would immediately largely increase the revenue received through existing channels. Prohibition, from the standpoint of revenue-raising alone, would speedily prove a boon to the Parliament and Government wise enough to enact and enforce it."

The liquor interests pressed their point by a large deputation headed by Mr. Jas. Haverson and Mr. R. Dickie, Solicitor and Secretary, respectively, of the Ontario License Holders' Protective Association. They waited on the Government on May 13, 1897, and expressed their desire that the question to be submitted to the people should be so framed that those voting in favor of prohibition would also be voting for increased taxation. It was urged that provision should be made for compensating those engaged in the liquor traffic if prohibition should be enacted. The deputation wished to have it understood that prohibition would not be enacted unless the votes in favor of it amounted to at least fifty per cent. of the names on the voters' lists.

PROHIBITION IN CANADA.

In replying to the deputation, the Premier declined to commit the Government to the proposition that before legislation it was necessary to have any particular portion of the whole vote polled in favor of such legislation. He stated "that a law to be effective must be based upon the popular will, absolutely and unmistakably expressed," and that, if the people thus declared in favor of prohibition "it must be the duty of the Government to stand by the will of the people." He expressed the view that it was not necessary to submit the question of compensation to the electors, and promised that the matter of submitting the question of taxation would be considered by the Government in framing the bill.

A statement was subsequently published in some newspapers to the effect that the Government had resolved upon submitting to the electors, along with the question of prohibition, the question of whether or not the electors desired to have the loss of revenue replaced by direct taxation.

Immediately the friends of temperance and other fair-minded citizens protested. They considered that it would be exceedingly unjust to refer in the ballot to any possible undesirable results of prohibition, while mentioning none of the advantages that prohibition would bring. Such a plan would tend to array against the measure that large section of the community that did not believe in the direct taxation plan, and would complicate the question of prohibition with the question of what fiscal policy was most desirable. It would also tend to invite the opposition to prohibition of those people who objected to an increase of taxation. Moreover, the political party in power, before being endorsed by the electorate, had promised a plebiscite on prohibition. The people expected, from the statement made, that the proposed plebiscite would be such as had already been taken in the Provinces of Manitoba, Ontario, Prince Edward Island, and Nova Scotia. The taking of a vote on another plan, or in regard to other questions, could then not be looked upon by friends of temperance as a faithful fulfilment of the promise given.

DOMINION PLEBISCITE.

Many deliverances regarding this matter were made by different church bodies and provincial temperance organizations. The Dominion Alliance prepared a pamphlet containing thirty of the strongest of these declarations, all from bodies representing large constituencies, and sent a copy to every member of the Dominion Parliament. A circular was sent also to friends all over the Dominion, asking them to communicate directly with their respective representatives in Parliament, protesting against the Government's yielding to the liquor party's desire to handicap the temperance party in the contest. This request met with a prompt response. The matter was taken up and vigorously discussed by ecclesiastical bodies, temperance organizations, and leading journals. Deputations waited upon the Government regarding it, and finally the plan was dropped. A clear-cut and direct bill on the straight issue was presented by the Government.

Immediately after the adjournment of the convention, campaign organization was pushed with vigor in the different provinces and in the North-West Territories. All available suggestions were forwarded, and as much information as possible was supplied by the Alliance headquarters in Toronto. Special emphasis was laid upon literature circulation. A committee was appointed for this department of the work and a literature fund was created in order to make possible distribution at very low prices. It was considered that the literature would be used to better advantage if paid for than if sent out gratuitously.

Under the direction of the committee, the Secretary prepared twelve four-page leaflets and twelve two-page leaflets, each dealing with some particular feature of the prohibition controversy. Eleven of these were printed in German as well as in English. There were also a series of sixteen small slips called "Campaign Pointers," containing short, pithy statements, with portraits of eminent men whose words were quoted. Later on a series of cartoons prepared by Mr. J. W. Bengough, and a set of posters dealing with the financial aspect of the drink question, were published. The General

PROHIBITION IN CANADA.

Conference of the Methodist Church had an address prepared by Rev. Dr. Carman, which was also sent out from the Alliance office. The demand for these goods was enormous, necessitating the running of a number of presses day and night and the employment of a large staff of office assistants to attend to shipping. The total amount of literature thus supplied was as follows: Leaflets, 8,757,000 (pages, 24,964,-000); cartoons, 40,000; posters, 10,000.

Besides the literature prepared by the Dominion Alliance Executive, large quantities were furnished by other organizations. The Dominion Woman's Christian Temperance Union sent out a great quantity, and the *Witness* Publishing House of Montreal produced and distributed supplements to their regular journals and special issues of illustrated campaign sheets.

Details of work connected with public meetings, local organizations, canvassing of votes, and polling arrangements, were superintended in the different parts of the Dominion by the various central provincial campaign executives. In Ontario the work was carried on in connection with the Dominion Alliance Council work, the Secretary of the provincial Alliance, Mr. F. S. Spence, being also Secretary of the Council, so that much of the work done at the Ontario office had relation to the contest throughout the Dominion. For instance, at the beginning of the campaign, it was agreed that the Ontario Branch should provide funds to meet the deficit incurred in the literature production.

Special efforts were made in Ontario to secure thorough organization of the electorate, and on the whole the work was better done than in any former prohibition campaign. Special men were engaged by the Executive to secure the inauguration of the work in each locality, and subsequent campaigning was carried on almost entirely by local agencies. A great many meetings of the Executive and sub-committees were held during the contest, and as voting day drew near arrangements were made for a daily session of the local members of the Executive, to consult and advise regarding

DOMINION PLEBISCITE.

emergencies and matters needing consideration from time to time.

In Quebec, in order to secure the most united action possible among the prohibition workers of the province, the Provincial Plebiscite Executive and the Alliance Executive amalgamated, with Major E. L. Bond as chairman. A serious difficulty to be met with in Quebec was the preponderance of the French, who formed about six-sevenths of the population. The Roman Catholics numbered about 1,488,800 to 196,800 Protestants.

It was found that voluntary help could be expected only where Protestant churches were established, as apparently all prohibition work had crystallized around these churches. The Church of Rome taught temperance with splendid results, but she was not ready to commit herself to a policy of prohibition. The committee approached the Roman Catholic bishops of the province, with the request that they would endorse the movement and use their great influence towards having their people vote in favor of prohibition. After full consideration of the matter, the bishops decided not to interfere in the matter, but to allow their people to vote as they chose.

The committee then secured the services of two competent French-Canadian Roman Catholic gentlemen, one taking the north side of the St. Lawrence and the other the south shore. They visited the central points in each county. For the first week they sent in encouraging reports. They found many parish priests favorable to the prohibition movement and quite a number of people willing to watch the polls, so as to prevent fraud. However, about ten days before the vote was taken, the whole situation was changed. Persons who had promised to act as scrutineers withdrew, and the tide set overwhelmingly against prohibition. The reasons given for this change were the active entry of four Dominion Cabinet Ministers into the field against the movement and the report, industriously spread, that Sir Wilfrid Laurier wished all his supporters to vote against prohibition, for if this were not done the Liberal Party would be seriously endangered. An

PROHIBITION IN CANADA.

appeal was promptly made to Sir Wilfrid, who repudiated the use of his name in this connection; but the damage was done. But even a greater factor militating against the success of the prohibition cause in the province was the existence of organized fraud.

In the North-West Territories there was serious difficulty to be met with in the great distance between railway stations and centres of population, the long drives, and the labor involved because of imperfect means of communication. Moreover, owing to the mixed population of the country, it was found necessary to send out some of the campaign literature in three languages. Over a ton of literature was circulated. At a convention held at Regina to organize, Rev. W. A. Vrooman and W. J. Brotherton were put in charge of the work. A central committee was formed, composed of one minister and one layman for each religious denomination, two members of the Royal Templars of Temperance, the Woman's Christian Temperance Union, and the Salvation Army.

In British Columbia, also, the immense distances between various points of settlement, the geographical separation of the province into sections, and the varied character of the population, were serious impediments to organization and to work. At a well-attended convention held in Vancouver, however, a branch of the Dominion Alliance was formed and plans laid out. Various churches and temperance societies joined in heartily with the new organization. A weekly paper entitled *The Campaign Bulletin,* under the editorial management of Rev. Dr. Eby, was published and distributed gratuitously. Beginning at four pages, it increased to eight, with a circulation of 12,500. The press of the province as a whole was not in sympathy with prohibition, which made this independent publication necessary. Campaign meetings were held in every part of the country, at street corners and outdoor places as well as in churches and schoolhouses.

DOMINION PLEBISCITE.

In August it was announced that voting would take place on September 29th. Early in September "A Final Appeal" to workers was prepared by the Central Committee in Toronto, earnestly urging special effort to secure a full vote, giving additional information regarding literature and methods of work, and setting out a number of facts relating to questions and issues that had been brought into the campaign by the advocates of the liquor traffic. A very large edition of this document was scattered all over the Dominion.

The Provincial Woman's Christian Temperance Union actively co-operated in the campaign. Their delegate to the Dominion Woman's Christian Temperance Union Convention in Toronto, Mrs. Gordon Grant of Victoria, was appointed organizer by the National Prohibition Federation, a co-operative union of temperance societies arranged by the Royal Templars of Temperance in Toronto in October, 1897. Mrs. Grant organized a branch of the Federation in British Columbia, and at a well-attended convention, which was called by that association in Vancouver on August 9th, the report of the Dominion Alliance Plebiscite Convention was read, setting forth in full their plans of campaign. The result was that, for greater co-operation and unity of effort, the Federation Association merged itself into a Provincial Branch of the Dominion Alliance.

The Plebiscite Bill was introduced by the Hon. Sydney Fisher, Minister of Agriculture, on April 15, 1918. It provided for a vote on the question, "Are you in favor of passing an Act prohibiting the importation, manufacture, or sale of spirits, wine, ale, cider, and all other alcoholic liquors for use as a beverage?"

The bill passed through the various stages of enactment with little discussion and without being amended. A proposal to give women an opportunity of speaking on the question by allowing all municipal electors to vote, was lost.

The vote was taken on September 29, 1898, and the result in the different provinces was as follows:

PROHIBITION IN CANADA.

Province.	For.	Against.	Majority For.	Majority Against.
Ontario	154,498	115,284	39,214	....
Quebec	28,436	122,760		94,324
Nova Scotia	34,678	5,370	29,308	....
New Brunswick	26,919	9,575	17,344	
Prince Edward Island.	9,461	1,146	8,315	
Manitoba	12,419	2,978	9,441	
British Columbia	5,731	4,756	975	
N.-W. Territory	6,238	2,824	3,414	....
Total	278,380	264,693	108,011	94,324

Net majority for, 13,687.

By another method of stating the results, taking the territories for convenience as a province, the vote stood as follows:

	For.	Against.	Majority.
Provinces	7	1	6
Constituencies	125	81	44
Representatives	128	85	43

Another analysis of the vote:

Total names on voters' list.............................1,233,627
Total number of votes polled......................... 543,029
Votes polled for prohibition........................... 278,477
Votes polled against prohibition...................... 264,552
Majority for prohibition............................. 13,925

Percentage polled of names on list.................... 44.
Percentage of list voting for prohibition............... 22.5
Percentage of list voting against prohibition........... 21.5
Percentage for prohibition of vote polled............... 51.3
Percentage against prohibition of votes polled......... 48.7

The vote that went against prohibition was mainly a French vote. Leaving Quebec out, the results in the other six provinces and in the North-West Territory were as follows:

DOMINION PLEBISCITE.

Total names on voters' lists........................	898,992
Total number of votes polled......................	391,833
Votes polled for prohibition.......................	249,895
Votes polled against prohibition....................	141,938
Majority for prohibition...........................	107,957
Percentage polled of names on list.................	43.6
Percentage of list voting for prohibition............	27.8
Percentage of list voting against prohibition........	15.8
Percentage for prohibition of votes polled..........	64.
Percentage against prohibition of votes polled......	36.
Number of members of Parliament..................	148
Number whose constituencies voted for prohibition...	120
Number whose constituencies voted against prohibition.	28
Average majority for prohibition...................	1,042
Average majority against prohibition...............	611

The vote was, under the circumstances, a large one, as the Dominion Alliance Executive Committee pointed out in a message to the prohibitionists of Canada, issued on December 18, 1898. Forty-four per cent. of the people on the lists went to the polls, which was a large proportion, considering that there were no inducements, such as the spoils of office or political patronage, to offer the successful workers, and that there was not the force of partisan feeling or party organization to bring out the vote. Leading political workers of different parties gave practically no assistance to the temperance workers. The vote for prohibition was a purely voluntary and unselfish vote; and while, no doubt, many electors marked their ballots against prohibition out of honest conviction, there were also arrayed on that side selfish interests and desire for opportunities of personal indulgence and personal gain.

Moreover, in many places *prima facie* evidence showed that the vote against prohibition was swelled by impersonation and other improper practices. The vote in the Province of Quebec was remarkable. It was ridiculously small, there being no organization among the majority except that of the liquor interests, to urge the people to the polls. Outside the

PROHIBITION IN CANADA.

few English-speaking counties, the vote was practically all against prohibition. It is necessary to consider this fact, along with the other fact forcibly presented by Sir Wilfrid Laurier, that a large part of the Province of Quebec was practically under prohibition. Out of 933 rural municipalities, there were licenses issued in 1897 in only 330. It was manifest that the French electorate was actuated by some other motive than favor for the liquor traffic.

In many places in Quebec the friends of Laurier were strongly urged to vote against prohibition on the ground that a favorable vote would embarrass the Liberal Government and Party. Their pleading cost the prohibition cause thousands of votes. In the Province of Quebec a number of Cabinet Ministers and many other leading Liberal politicians came out in opposition to the proposed reform. The French people, whose admiration and affection for Sir Wilfrid were great, were told that a majority for prohibition would injure his position and influence. It was certain that the Quebec vote was largely influenced by this political consideration. Moreover, in many parts of the province, the most dense ignorance prevailed as to the meaning of the issue. There is an historic instance of one worker being asked, " Who is this man ' Plebiscite ' that's coming out against Laurier?"

These facts were laid before the Government on November 3rd by a strong deputation, which was kindly and courteously received. The Premier agreed with the deputation that the vote was large. He said that the question was too important to be trifled with, and that the Government would carefully consider what was to be done under the circumstances. The result of the Government's deliberation is expressed in the following letter to the Secretary of the Alliance:

OTTAWA, 4th March, 1899.

Dear Mr. Spence,—

When the delegation of the Dominion Alliance waited upon the Government last fall to ask, as a consequence of the plebiscite, the introduction of prohibitory legislation, they based their demand

DOMINION PLEBISCITE.

upon the fact that on the total of the vote cast there was a majority in favor of the principle of prohibition. The exact figures of the votes recorded were not at that time accurately known, but the official figures, which we have now, show that on the question put to the electors, 278,487 voted yea and 264,571 voted nay. After the official figures had been made public, it was contended by some of the opponents of prohibition that the margin of difference between the majority and the minority was so slight that it practically constituted a tie, and there was, therefore, no occasion for the Government to pronounce one way or the other. The Government does not share that view. We are of the opinion that the fairest way of approaching the question is by the consideration of the total vote cast in favor of prohibition, leaving aside altogether the vote recorded against it.

In that view of the question the record shows that the electorate of Canada, to which the question was submitted, comprised 1,233,849 voters, and of that number less than twenty-three per cent., or a trifle over one-fifth, affirmed their conviction of the principles of prohibition.

If we remember that the object of the plebiscite was to give an opportunity to those who have at heart the cause of prohibition, who believed that the people were with them, and that if the question were voted upon by itself, without any other issue which might detract from its consideration, a majority of the electorate would respond, and thus show the Canadian people prepared and ready for its adoption; it must be admitted that the expectation was not justified by the event. On the other hand, it was argued before us by yourself and others, that as the plebiscite campaign was carried out by the friends of prohibition without any expenditure of money, and without the usual excitement of political agitation, the vote recorded in favor of it was comparatively a large one. This statement I did not then controvert, nor do I controvert it here and now. I would simply remark that the honesty of the vote did not suffer from the absence of those causes of excitement, and that even if the totality of the vote might have been somewhat increased by such a cause, its moral force would not have been made any stronger. I venture to submit for your consideration, and the consideration of the members of the Dominion Alliance, who believe in prohibition as the most efficient means of suppressing the evils of intemperance, that no good purpose would be served by forcing upon the people a measure which is shown by the vote to have the support of less than twenty-three per cent. of the electorate. Neither would it serve any good purpose to enter into further controversy on the many incidental points discussed before us. My object is to simply convey to you the conclusion that, in our judgment, the expression of public opinion recorded at the polls in favor of prohibition did not justify the introduction by the Government of a prohibitory measure.

I have the honor to be, dear Mr. Spence,

Yours very sincerely,
WILFRID LAURIER.

IV. PARLIAMENTARY INACTION.

Sir Wilfrid Laurier's reply was received by prohibitionists with intense disappointment. The Government based its refusal to grant prohibition on the ground of the smallness of the prohibition vote. They had promised to obey the mandate of the people; now they declared they must obey the mandate of those who had given no mandate. The opinion of the people was to be respected; that is to say, the opinion of those who had not expressed their opinion.

Speaking on this point in the House of Commons on April 13th, Mr. Foster referred to Mr. Sydney Fisher's speech at the Liberal convention of 1893 when, in introducing the plebiscite resolution, he declared the Government's obligation to carry out the will of the people. Then he asked leave to inquire:

"Whether my honorable friend meant there, as his words say, that it should be the expressed will; and, as the expressed will was the only will, as was shown in the votes for and against, and as a majority of that vote was in favor of the principle of prohibition, whether he does not think his own words hold him to the expressed will being shown by the majority of those who came out to express their will by their vote."

DOMINION PLEBISCITE.

Mr. Fisher replied:

"I will answer the honorable gentleman very frankly that I do not think it does. As I have said, the plebiscite was for the purpose of obtaining the opinion of the people upon this question. If the people did not have an opinion, or did not express their opinion, the plebiscite does not show the true opinion of the people of this country as expressed in the vote; and until the responsible advisers of the Crown in this country can be assured of what they believe to be the opinion of the people, they can only carry that out by their judgment."

The Executive Committee of the Dominion Alliance, which was called immediately on receipt of the Premier's letter, protested against the Government's decision and called upon Parliament to carry out the mandate of the people at the polls. Their protest was endorsed throughout the country. Resolutions by churches, presbyteries, committees, divisions, lodges, councils, unions, and all kinds of organizations, as well as personal letters, poured in upon the members of Parliament. The press took up the cry. Many people who did not believe that the prohibition vote was sufficient to warrant national prohibition, declared their belief that Parliament ought to enact such legislation as would suppress the liquor traffic in those provinces which had voted so overwhelmingly for prohibition.

There was diversity of opinion as to how the question of prohibitory legislation should be brought before Parliament. The different viewpoints were represented in a sub-committee of seven members of Parliament appointed on March 22nd by the Legislative Committee of the Dominion Alliance at Ottawa, to consider methods of broaching the subject in the House. A majority of the sub-committee favored the introduction of legislation extending the scope of the Canada Temperance Act so as to make it applicable to provinces. The minority recommended calling upon the Government to introduce a law of prohibition for the whole Dominion.

The discussion of these reports, which were presented to the Legislative Committee on April 20th, was carried on

PROHIBITION IN CANADA.

largely on party lines. Liberal members of Parliament favored the majority report, claiming that the overwhelming vote against prohibition in the Province of Quebec made it undesirable to ask for a prohibitory law that would include that province. They argued further that since the Government had definitely refused to enact a prohibitory law, a resolution requesting such action would be considered a motion of want of confidence in the Government and would result only in a straight party division defeating the resolution. Conservative members claimed that, as the opinion of prohibitionists was that the Government was in the wrong, the committee should take that ground and should secure a division in the House of Commons to show prohibitionists who were their true friends. The meeting, unable to come to any agreement on the question, voted down both propositions, and then adjourned to allow the sub-committee to try again.

When the Legislative Committee reassembled the same evening, the sub-committee's report was adopted without any dissenting vote. It reaffirmed the principle of total prohibition as the goal of prohibitionists. In view of the Government's refusal to enact prohibitory legislation, it recommended the enactment of a prohibitory law to come into force in such provinces as should ratify the same at the time of the general federal election. The resolution embodying such legislation was introduced into the House by Mr. T. B. Flint, seconded by Dr. T. Christie. It was debated from three o'clock in the afternoon of July 28th to three o'clock a.m. the following day. There was very little approval of it in the House. An amendment was moved declaring in favor of total national prohibition; another declaring that a prohibitory law should not be passed. The debate was at length adjourned without the taking of a vote.

In October, 1899, the Dominion Alliance Executive appealed to the prohibition electors of Canada for co-operation in a great political effort, a proposal to enroll one hundred thousand electors pledged not to support at the next

DOMINION PLEBISCITE.

general Dominion election any candidate who would not aid in securing effective legislation against the liquor traffic. Before adopting this policy, the Executive Committee submitted it in detail to leading friends of prohibition in every part of the Dominion, inviting criticism upon it and asking advice concerning it. About one hundred replies were received, of which ninety promised co-operation and some six expressed disapproval of the proposals. Of the disapprovers, some thought that the present duty of prohibitionists was to unite with the Conservative Party to defeat the Government, in retaliation for their breach of faith. Some thought that they ought to demand immediate enactment of prohibition for every part of the Dominion, and accept nothing less. The vast majority heartily endorsed the Alliance plan. Over and over again prohibitionists had been told that they could attain their object only by electing prohibitionists to Parliament. There were in Parliament many friends of reform, whose hands were weakened by the fact that prohibitionists had never made a demonstration in their favor. Now was the time for action. Political leaders were making preparation for a general election, and the speeches of party advocates only made more clear their determination to evade if possible the prohibition issue.

In the plebiscite of 1898 there had been polled 278,380 votes in favor of prohibition. The 100,000 Voters Movement asked that about one-third of these pledge themselves to carry into the next general election the principle for which they had already declared. One hundred thousand voters would be an average of nearly five hundred in each constituency. If distributed approximately as the prohibition vote was distributed in the plebiscite, and unitedly exercised, it would enable voters to elect a prohibitionist to Parliament from at least every one of the 129 constituencies that gave prohibition majorities, thus giving the temperance cause control of the House of Commons by a majority of about forty-five.

The object of the pledge was not to keep men from voting, but to have their votes count for prohibition. Where there was in the field no candidate favorable to prohibition, the pledged voters, in order to avoid being disfranchised, would be obliged to take action to nominate independent candidates of the right kind. The following was the pledge they were asked to sign:

"We, the undersigned, promise that at the next general election for the Dominion Parliament we will vote only for such candidates as will agree to do all in their power, if elected, to obtain the immediate enactment of such legislation as will secure the total prohibition of the liquor traffic in at least those provinces and territories that gave majorities for prohibition in the plebiscite.

"This pledge is to be null and void unless twenty-five thousand signatures to it are secured."

In 1900, in order to avoid delay and unfruitful discussion such as had occurred the previous year, the Executive Committee decided to have the form of parliamentary resolution prepared and placed in the hands of a member, rather than leave it to be prepared by a committee of members. Accordingly a draft resolution was given to Mr. T. B. Flint. He moved it in substantially the form given to him, and it was seconded by Dr. Christie.

The resolution was on the lines laid down by the convention of 1899, and was in harmony with the 100,000 Voters' League arrangement. Its object was to secure an expression of opinion of the House of Commons upon the prohibition question, and it simply declared that the will of a majority of the electors should prevail in a specific case. It set out the declaration already made by Parliament and the fact of substantial majorities being recorded in favor of prohibition in all the provinces but one, and made this further affirmation:

"That this House is now of the opinion, in view of the foregoing facts, that it is desirable and expedient that Parliament should without delay enact such measures as will secure the prohibition of the liquor traffic for beverage purposes in at least those provinces and territories which have voted in favor of such prohibition."

DOMINION PLEBISCITE.

It was debated on April 23rd. Seventeen members took part. Not one of them directly advocated a continuance of the liquor traffic and only three failed to declare themselves prohibitionists. An amendment was moved by Mr. McClure in favor of total prohibition. Mr. Parmelee moved an amendment declaring that a prohibitory law should not be enacted at present. The debate was adjourned at midnight and taken up again on July 3rd. Sir Wilfrid Laurier stated that the question was not a ministerial one. He claimed that the Government's plebiscite pledge had been fully carried out by the taking of the vote, the result of which, in his opinion, was not such as to make the enactment of a prohibitory law advisable. He said there was no unanimity amongst prohibitionists as to the course that ought to be taken. A number of propositions had already been advanced by different members of the House. He was strongly opposed to the enactment for any provinces of legislation that did not apply to the whole Dominion. Legislation ought to tend to promote unity rather than to separate the different communities. He believed that the country was not ready for prohibition and that the question of temperance was largely a question of education. The Premier declared that he was not a prohibitionist, but that he favored legislation that would be progressive. He believed that the Canada Temperance Act had rendered good service to the temperance cause, and if temperance people asked to have that act improved, the Government would be ready to respond to their request.

Mr. Parmelee's amendment was adopted by a vote of ninety-eight yeas to forty-one nays. It read as follows:

"That at the plebiscite of 1898 only about twenty-three per cent. of the registered electors of the Dominion voted for prohibition; in the provinces and territories, excluding Quebec, only twenty-seven per cent. of the registered electors voted for prohibition; that these results show that there is not an active prohibition sentiment sufficiently pronounced to justify the expectation that prohibition could be successfully enforced, and therefore, in the opinion of this House, such a prohibitory law should not be enacted at present.'

On motion of Rev. Dr. Douglas, M.P., the following words were added to Mr. Parmelee's amendment:

" But in as much as it is desirable that legislation be enacted having in view the further restriction of the liquor traffic, it is therefore expedient, in the opinion of this House, that the Canada Temperance Act be enlarged in its scope and the provisions for its administration perfected."

SECTION X.

PROVINCIAL ACTION.

One of the greatest struggles of the nineteenth century is the struggle between the home, for which all law exists, and the saloon, the enemy of the law.

The earnest efforts of Christian citizens, true to their responsibilities, cannot fail to secure wise laws and honest enforcement. When these are attained, not only will it be true that the welfare of the people is the supreme law, but equally so that the supremacy of law is the highest welfare of the people.

I. MANITOBA REFERENDUM.

THE refusal of the Dominion Government to enact a prohibitory law following the plebiscite of 1898 threw the burden of responsibility back upon the provinces to go as far as they could constitutionally in prohibitory legislation. Manitoba had been the first to undertake a provincial plebiscite. Once again the Prairie Province led the van in aggressive action.

Since the Manitoba plebiscite of 1892, the Liberal party in that province, under the leadership of Premier Greenway, had failed to make any substantial advance in prohibitory legislation. With a large majority recorded by that vote in favor of a prohibitory law, but with the existing uncertainty as to the extent of provincial power in the matter of liquor legislation, the Manitoba Government went to the Dominion authorities to request such action on their part as would ensure effective prohibition for the province. However, Ottawa was at the time delaying all action, pending the decision of the courts on the jurisdiction question. That decision, when it came at last in 1896, did not remove the uncertainty as to the authority of the local Legislature. Indeed, the conclusion reached by the learned judges was so vague and indefinite that the Manitoba Government retained Hon. Edward Blake and asked him to give a legal opinion interpreting the decision. Mr. Blake's interpretation also lacked clarity and definiteness, but was taken to mean that the province had authority to prevent the sale of liquor only by refusing to grant licenses.

The Dominion plebiscite in 1898 entailed another delay. After it, pleading the second big majority recorded for prohibition, Premier Greenway waited on the Federal Government and again asked that Manitoba be granted additional powers for provincial action. There had been no response to this request when the Premier, on June 12, 1899, addressing a

PROHIBITION IN CANADA.

large temperance delegation at Winnipeg, and in answer to a great prohibition petition movement, said that his determination was to pursue the course of trying to get their friends at Ottawa to give full power of action. He could not say whether or not these powers would be delegated. Anyway, the Manitoba Government would prohibit the sale of intoxicating liquors to the fullest extent of their powers. The temperance party looked upon this answer as being shifty and were dissatisfied with it.

During these years, while prohibitory legislation was thus being sidetracked, there had been a notable advance in prohibition made throughout Manitoba by the adoption of local option by-laws. Many towns and villages of the province prohibited the local sale of liquor and the license law was greatly increased in stringency, making it more difficult for applicants to secure licenses, and making it easier for householders to prevent their renewal. Despite the laxity of enforcement under the administration of the department by the Hon. Clifford Sifton, amounting in some instances to a scandal and disgrace, this movement, considered along with the two plebiscite votes, was clear indication of a strong prohibition sentiment in the country.

In 1899 the Conservative party, feeling the popular pulse correctly, took up the temperance banner. That party, which at the time had only six members in the Assembly, was re-organized under the leadership of the Hon. Hugh John Macdonald, son of Sir John A. Macdonald. A Provincial convention held in Winnipeg to form a platform on which to go before the people at the ensuing general provincial election, adopted a prohibition plank in the following resolution:

" That a measure be adopted to give effect to the will of the people regarding the prohibition of the liquor traffic, which measure shall go as far in the direction of prohibition as the power of the province will allow."

Mr. T. E. Greenwood, of Douglas, Man., proposed the resolution in the convention. *Forward* tells the story of " this

PROVINCIAL ACTION.

young western elector who went to the party convention and retained possession of his soul."

When Mr. Greenwood was asked by the nominating convention for North Brandon to become the Liberal-Conservative candidate for that constituency, he accepted on the distinct understanding that he would work for prohibitive legislation, regardless of party considerations. At a council of the nominees, he explained his position to his leader, who assured him that he regarded the position taken as good public policy. Mr. Macdonald stated that, though he had not been a prohibitionist himself, he would heartily advocate the adoption of the prohibition principle by the party. Mr. Greenwood carried his point in the convention against some opposition, and prohibition was thus made a direct issue of the election of December 7, 1899. The election resulted in a victory for the Conservative party.

On February 23, 1900, a union deputation from the Dominion Alliance and Royal Templars of Temperance waited upon Premier Macdonald and urged him to carry out his declared temperance policy. The Premier in reply promised to introduce in the first session of the new legislature a bill providing for the prohibition of the sale of intoxicating liquors so far as the law would allow.

The bill was brought in by the Premier on June 1, 1900. It was a rigid measure of prohibition of all liquor transactions originating and ending within the limits of Manitoba. The License Holders' Association declared that the bill interfered with certain rights of the Hudson Bay Company as set forth in the deed of surrender of 1869, which was an agreement between the Company and the Dominion and Imperial authorities, and maintained that the provincial measure would accordingly be nullified. The Hon. Mr. Macdonald replied to this objection that if the bill was passed by the House the Courts would be asked to give a ruling on the disputed points at once.

In speaking to the bill at its second reading, on June 11, 1900, Mr. Macdonald expressed the sense of responsibility he had in thus introducing legislation which was without Canadian precedent. It was true that the Legislature of Prince Edward Island had passed a prohibitory law just the week preceding, but in that, he claimed, they had followed rather than led, since their move was brought about by the action of the Manitoba Government in giving notice of the prohibition bill now under discussion. In fact, the Manitoba bill had served the sister province as a model. Mr. Macdonald explained that it was a political obligation which bound him to the course he was taking—the duty of a Government to give effect to the wishes of the people by legislation and to implement its specific election pledges.

Of the care with which the bill had been framed in order not to interfere in any respect with trade and commerce, matters of Dominion jurisdiction, he said:

" In preparing the measure to be submitted I found myself in this difficulty. It was known that I was not a prohibitionist on principle, and I knew that naturally enough the great majority of the temperance people would not place that confidence in my action which they would in that of a man who they knew was heart and soul with them. Hence I thought it better, instead of attempting to prepare a law myself, to confide it to a gentleman in every way qualified to draw it up, and one in whom the temperance people had confidence. Consequently I asked Mr. J. A. M. Aikins, one of Her Majesty's Counsel, learned in the law, to prepare the bill. His position at the bar removes all doubt as to his ability. For years past he, being a prohibitionist on principle and of a very advanced kind, had given more than usual attention to the law on the subject, and to decision, American, English, and Canadian, which bear upon it. The instructions he received from me were to prepare a bill in exact fulfilment of the pledge to the people, going as far as we could in the direction of prohibition. Any intelligent man will see that Mr. Aikins has carried out his instructions to the letter. His task was no easy one. If it had been to change the license system to either that of Sweden, or that of South Carolina, it would have been easy enough. Had he been asked to prepare an act of total prohibition the work would have been still easier. But we had to prepare an act which, while

PROVINCIAL ACTION.

going as far as we could, should yet keep within limits of the law, and not run the risk of being set aside by the courts of the realm as being beyond our powers. The task required unusual skill and unusual study. Both of these Mr. Aikins has given. I, as attorney-general, went very carefully into the matter with him. We considered the act clause by clause, and I came to the conclusion that it was a fulfilment of our promise and was a measure we felt justified in submitting to this House."

The bill gives evidence of this careful preparation. Collaborating with Mr. Aikins were Mr. E. L. Taylor, Mr. W. R. Mulock, and Mr. W. W. Buchanan. It has since become the basis of every provincial prohibition act in Canada.

Mr. Greenway, leader of the Opposition, concurred in the desirability of having an effective prohibitory law, but maintained that it could be obtained only with the assistance of the Dominion Parliament. He believed that the limited prohibition proposed in the Macdonald Bill could not be enforced. Nevertheless he would not vote against the measure, and he hoped that in committee many of its objectionable features might be removed.

The bill was amended in certain details by the Law Amendments Committee of the Legislature, but its principle remained inviolate. On July 5, 1900, the act received the assent of the Lieutenant-Governor and became the law of the province, to come into effect on June 1, 1901.

The general satisfaction of the temperance people with the legislation was expressed in an open letter from the Executive Committee of the Dominion Alliance, which said:

"For the moment the measure is somewhat obscured by the dust of the discussion of detail, the prejudice of political strife, and the misrepresentation of the daily press; but impartial examination will reveal its true character as an excellent enactment of provincial prohibition, well worthy of the endorsation already given by the Manitoba Convention of the W.C.T.U. and the Annual Conference of the Methodist Church.

"Candor compels an acknowledgment of the good faith of the Government in preparing and passing legislation which meets the

PROHIBITION IN CANADA.

promise of the party platform to the electors and the pledge of the Premier to the prohibitionists. At last we have a prohibitory law which is the voluntary policy of a political party and for which a government has assumed full responsibility."

TESTING THE ACT.

But the bright hopes of the prohibitionists that seemed so near realization were dimmed when Mr. Macdonald retired from the premiership to contest the constituency of Brandon in the federal election of November 7, 1900, and the Conservative leadership went to Rodmond P. Roblin. Amongst the members of the newly-formed cabinet was Robert Rogers.

On November 20th, Attorney-General Hon. Colin H. Campbell, Q.C., announced the questions that, in accordance with the plan of the Government at the time of the passing of the Macdonald Bill, were to be submitted to the King's Court of Manitoba, and subsequently to the Privy Council, concerning the validity of the Manitoba Liquor Act, as the Macdonald Bill was formally entitled. They were as follows:

(1) Has the Legislative Assembly of Manitoba jurisdiction to enact the Liquor Act, and if not, in what particular or respect has it exceeded its power?

(2) Had the Legislative Assembly of Manitoba jurisdiction to enact the provisions of the 47th, 48th, 49th, 50th, 51st, 52nd, 53rd, 54th, 55th, and 56th sections of the "Liquor Act," or any, and, if so, which of such provisions, without the explanatory provisions of section 119 of the Act.

(3) Had the Legislative Assembly of Manitoba jurisdiction to enact the provisions of the 47th, 48th, 49th, 50th, 51st, 52nd, 53rd, 54th, 55th and 56th sections of "the Liquor Act," or any of them, as interpreted by the explanatory provisions of section 119 of the Act, and, if so, which?

(4) Had the Legislative Assembly of Manitoba jurisdiction to make regulations, limitations or restrictions on the sale or keeping of liquor by brewers, distillers or other persons in Manitoba, duly licensed by the Government of Canada for the manufacture in Manitoba of spirituous, fermented or other liquors, as provided by sections 47, 51 and 54 of and elsewhere in said Act?

PROVINCIAL ACTION.

(5) Has the Legislative Assembly of Manitoba jurisdiction to prohibit or restrict the giving away in Manitoba, as a free gift by the owner thereof, of liquors which have been lawfully imported into Manitoba, or otherwise lawfully acquired by such owner?

(6) If the Legislative Assembly of Manitoba has no authority to prohibit the importation of liquor into the province, has it authority to declare it illegal for an importer to employ a *bona fide* agent residing in the province to make the importation on his behalf, or to prohibit importation through such agent?

(7) Has the Legislative Assembly of Manitoba jurisdiction to prohibit an agent in Manitoba retaining in such agent's possession in Manitoba on behalf of such resident liquor imported into this province through such agent on behalf of such resident, such liquor being the property of the importer, and not the agent, so that such agent may make delivery of portions thereof from time to time as such resident may desire?

(8) Has the Legislative Assembly of Manitoba jurisdiction to provide that no sale of liquor for export from the province shall be made within the province, unless such liquor shall be delivered by the vendor at some point outside the province?

(9) If not, has the Legislative Assembly of Manitoba jurisdiction to compel a person purchasing liquor in Manitoba to convey the liquor purchased to a place outside the province without breaking, or allowing to be opened or broken, the package or parcel containing the same as received from the exporter?

(10) Do the provisions of the Liquor Act interfere with or infringe on the rights of the Hudson Bay Company, as assured to that company by the conditions contained in the deed of surrender to Her Majesty, and the various orders-in-council and statutes passed in respect thereof, and if so, to what extent?

(11) Is the Hudson Bay Company subject to the provisions of the said Act, and bound to observe the same? If not altogether, then to what extent?

Mr. F. H. Phippen was counsel for the liquor men before the Queen's Bench; Mr. Howell represented the Hudson Bay Company; W. Redford Mulock, Q.C., and Mr. E. L. Taylor were retained by the Dominion Alliance; and J. A. M. Aikins, Q.C., the framer of the prohibition law, also spoke in defence of it. The decision of the Supreme Court, rendered on Feb.

PROHIBITION IN CANADA.

23, 1901, by Chief Justice Killam, Mr. Justice Baine, and Mr. Justice Richards, declared that the act was *ultra vires* in a number of important particulars; that it went beyond merely local matters, and was so framed as to affect to some extent the trade and commerce of the Dominion.

This judgment was duly appealed to the Imperial Privy Council, and the Legislature amended the act, providing for it to come into force upon proclamation by the Lieutenant-Governor in Council, the understanding being that the law, if upheld by decision of the Privy Council, would be forthwith proclaimed. Mr. Haldane, K.C., Hon. Colin H. Campbell, and Mr. R. O. B. Lane, Jr., appeared for the appellant, the Hon. Edward Blake, K.C., and Mr. F. H. Phippen for the respondents. Mr. E. L. Newcome, K.C., watched the case for the Dominion Government. On November 22, 1901, the Privy Council overruled the finding of the Court of the King's Bench and declared the Manitoba Liquor Law constitutional.*
To the subsidiary questions of whether the Hudson Bay Company and the Manitoba Liquor Manufacturers, licensed by the Dominion Government, were subject to the act, their lordships said no useful answer could be given.

REFERENDUM CAMPAIGN.

When interviewed concerning the Government's proposed action, in view of the decision of the courts, Premier Roblin refused to give any serious answer, saying merely that the Macdonald Act was not the work of the present cabinet. Later it was announced that the Government would test the will of the people in the matter of enforcing the act by taking a referendum on the question. On January 15th a delegation, eight hundred strong, representing the Ministerial Association and the Dominion Alliance, crowded the Legislative Chamber to protest against this means of evading responsibility for legislation which was enacted in fulfilment of the party pledge, and accepted by the present Government in its

---

* See Appendix VII.

PROVINCIAL ACTION.

act of taking office and in submitting the measure to the courts. The Premier made no announcement in immediate answer to the deputation, but in the evening a letter giving his reply was read at a mass meeting of Winnipeg citizens. It said:

WINNIPEG, Jan. 15th, 1902.

REV. E. J. CHEGWIN,
 Secretary, Dominion Alliance,
  City.

Reverend and Dear Sir,—

I have the honor to acknowledge receipt of yours of even date, asking an answer to the requests that were made to the Government and Legislature to-day jointly by the representatives of your body and those of the Ministerial Association of the city. In reply, beg to say that, after carefully considering the statements made to-day by members of the Ministerial Association and the Dominion Alliance, the Government, after consulting with their supporters in caucus, still believe it is desirable that a referendum should be held, such referendum deciding the fate of the act, if so brought in force by the referendum.

I have the honor to be,

Your obedient servant,

R. P. ROBLIN.

Great was the indignation of the meeting over the letter. The Hon. C. H. Campbell and Mr. Aikins had come to speak for the Government and to explain further their policy. All over the building people sprang to their feet in protest against hearing them. Rev. Dr. Sparling advised that an audience be granted, urged that it was well to hear both sides, and reminded the excited crowd of the need of calm judgment to guide enthusiasm. But some one announced that he had heard that Mr. Aikins had advised the Premier not to enforce the act. After that there was no mercy for Mr. Aikins with the meeting. By an overwhelming vote the audience refused to give a hearing to the gentlemen. Only after an hour of

PROHIBITION IN CANADA.

considerable confusion was the chairman able to proceed with the arranged programme. Later on in the evening, a statement from the Attorney-General was read, denying the allegation made against him, and affirming his approval of the adoption and enforcement of the act.

After the public meeting, the Dominion Alliance held an important business session. Two resolutions were prepared by the Resolutions Committee and adopted by the meeting, the first unanimously and the second with two dissenting votes. They were:

1. Whereas this convention has expressed itself already by unanimous resolution against the so-called referendum on the Liquor Act; and

Whereas such a referendum has been finally decided upon by the Government; therefore

Be it resolved, that the temperance people of this province ignore this referendum and abstain from polling their votes therein, and that the Executive Committee be instructed to prepare for distribution a fuller statement of the principles and considerations which have guided us in this conclusion.

2. Resolved that this Alliance, having lost confidence in the sincerity of the Government to enforce the Liquor Act, has therefore declared against the so-called referendum.

In compliance with instructions, the executive published and distributed a manifesto setting forth reasons for not voting at the referendum. The referendum was declared unconstitutional and unprecedented when applied to an act that had already become law, as was the case with the Manitoba Liquor Act; and the attempt to employ it was termed subversive of the principle of responsible government. It was unnecessary as an educative factor, after the two plebiscites already polled. The referendum, if accepted by the temperance people, would be treated by the Government as a fulfilment of its pledges, and the prohibition plank of its platform would then be discarded by the party. On the other hand, if the temperance people refrained from voting, the Government

PROVINCIAL ACTION.

could not declare the vote an expression of the people's opinion.

On February 19, 1902, Attorney-General Campbell announced in the Manitoba Legislature that the vote would be taken on March 27th, and that an order-in-council would be issued, putting the Prohibition Act in force on July 1st, (1) if the votes polled in favor of the act amounted to forty-five per cent. of the number of persons qualified to vote; or (2) if sixty per cent. of those qualified voted and at least sixty per cent. of those voting were in favor of the act; (3) if sixty-two and one-half per cent. of all the electors voting were in favor of it.

The Referendum Bill was given its second reading on the 26th, without a division. The liquor dealers of Winnipeg passed a resolution approving the Government's action, and the Ontario Licensed Victuallers gave aid to the Manitoba dealers in raising a fund to use in defeating the Manitoba Liquor Law at the polls.

Premier Roblin defended the action of the Government in thus side-stepping the prohibition issue, by means of an ingenious interpretation of the prohibition pledge of the Conservative party, "That a measure be adopted to give effect to the will of the people regarding the prohibition of the liquor traffic, which measure should go as far in the direction of prohibition as the powers of the province will allow." It did not mean the will of the people as already expressed, he explained, but the will of the people to be ascertained afterwards, as was usual in the case of such legislation; that will would be respected, whatever it might be. The proper way to ascertain it was by the referendum, and in passing the Referendum Act the Government was doing exactly what had been promised.

The tide of prohibition indignation kept rising. The Grand Council of the Royal Templars of Temperance in Manitoba, in session on February 18th and 19th, endorsed by a vote of sixty-one to two the non-voting policy formulated at the January convention of the Manitoba Branch of the

PROHIBITION IN CANADA.

Dominion Alliance. On February 25th the Alliance presented a petition to the Lieutenant-Governor, asking him to disallow the Referendum Bill. Their executive, on March 5th, unanimously carried the following resolution: "That we hereby reaffirm the referendum non-voting position taken by the Dominion Alliance at the late convention, and further declare that the events which have transpired since said convention have tended only to confirm us in the righteousness and propriety of that position."

There were some prohibitionists, however, who disapproved of the plan to ignore the referendum. Mr. J. K. McLennan, Vice-President of the Alliance, handed in his resignation on February 12th to indicate his objection to their policy, and on February 26th there was issued in his name a public announcement of the organization of the Prohibition Campaign League, to secure a large vote of the temperance people in favor of the Liquor Act. The action of the Alliance Convention, said the members of the League, was hasty and the result of fevered excitement in the crowd. The division of the temperance ranks created by that action was of immense aid to the liquor party. Moreover, for Manitoba to go back on her own law, which had been upheld by the highest judicial authority of the realm, would be a harmful example to Ontario in her impending struggle.

The Ontario Branch of the Dominion Alliance took the view of the League and sent a manifesto to Manitoba prohibitionists advising them to vote, in conflict with the plan of the Manitoba Branch.

The first vice-president and treasurer were pro-referendum, and so all through the organization the cleavage obtained. In the discussion the guns of the speakers were against one another instead of against the common enemy, the liquor traffic. The pro-referendum temperance organization carried on a vigorous campaign through the province urging the people to vote. The Manitoba Branch of the Dominion Alliance was equally active urging electors to stay at home.

PROVINCIAL ACTION.

In Selkirk Hall, Winnipeg, a monster mass meeting was held on March 1st by the Alliance. On March 4th an equally large meeting was held by the League. Prominent temperance workers addressed each meeting. In Brandon, Rev. Principal Patrick, head of the Presbyterian Theological College, opposed in public debate Rev. E. A. Henry, one of the most prominent Presbyterian pastors in the province, representing the League. In Winnipeg, Rev. Dr. Sparling, President of Wesley College, forcefully urged voting. Rev. R. P. Bowles, leading Methodist pastor of the province, was equally strong in persuading temperance people to abstain from voting.

The *Northwest Baptist,* the organ of that denomination, in its issue of March 1, 1902, said:

"If the temperance people keep hands off the unrighteous subterfuge of a misnamed referendum, the act will probably die by default. Our advice is to stay at home on the second day of April and touch not the unclean thing, and God will open a way by which we shall yet obtain the desire of our hearts. To lose is to gain and to gain is to lose for years to come."

In an attempt to harmonize the conflicting parties and secure co-operation in the temperance ranks, on March 25th a convention of temperance workers was called by the Prohibition Campaign League in the Y.M.C.A. Hall, Winnipeg. The meeting was a stormy one. It developed, during the course of the evening, that there had been misunderstanding as to who were invited. Temperance men of both opinions were present, while it was intended that only those who favored voting on the referendum should attend. Half-way through the proceedings, the meeting was dissolved and reorganized as a general convention.

There was a good deal of excited discussion over the resolutions laid before the meeting by the Resolutions Committee, and at times the speakers descended to personalities concerning their opponents. Neither party was willing to abandon its policy for the sake of unity. Finally a resolution was proposed deploring the division of opinion, acknowledging the sincerity of purpose of all temperance workers, and agreeing to the cessation of organized effort to influence the vote, each man to be left to the exercise of his individual judgment. The resolution was passed unanimously, and the meeting broke up at 1 a.m. with the singing of "Blest be the tie that binds."

Premier Roblin and the Attorney-General, the Hon. Colin H. Campbell, held meetings through the province to justify the Government's action. The Hon. Hugh John Macdonald, Mr. Roblin's predecessor, gave a public interview in which, speaking of the referendum, he said:

"It was his intention to have brought the act into force as soon as it had been declared valid by the courts, without any submission to the people. Had any other course been taken by the party it would not have been under his leadership, and he so gave his supporters to understand."

THE VOTE.

Never was there greater confusion in any voting. In the meantime the liquor interests were busy. The usual Business Men's Committee was formed and an active campaign conducted.

Voting conditions were of the wide-open kind. Indeed, the chairman of the liquor dealers' organization secured a legal opinion from F. H. Phippen and J. W. Ewart, L.S., which was as follows·

WINNIPEG, March 31st, 1902.

Mr. Andrew Strang, Esq.,
    City.

Dear Sir,—

I am of the opinion:
1. That all persons are entitled to vote at the coming referendum who would on such day be entitled to have their names registered anywhere as voters under "The Manitoba Election Act."

PROVINCIAL ACTION.

2. That there is nothing in any of the statutes limiting the exercise of that right to any particular polling place, municipality or electoral division.

3. In my opinion, therefore, a person entitled to be registered anywhere in the province can, on taking the oath, vote wherever he may happen to be on the day of the poll.

Yours very truly,
(Sgd.) JOHN S. EWART.

This opened the door to all kinds of looseness in the voting. Any man could go into any polling-place in any part of the province, declare that he was entitled to vote, and be given a ballot. In St. Boniface the poll stood 639 against prohibition, 29 for, there being more votes against prohibition than there were adult citizens in the municipality. In the City of Winnipeg the poll was 5,817 against prohibition, 2,450 for. In Winnipeg alone there were 3,954 persons voted by declaration, as their names were not upon the lists. When everything was counted, however, the vote was as follows:

> For prohibition 15,607
> Against prohibition 22,464
> Majority against 6,857

A comparison with the votes polled in the Dominion election of 1900 is interesting·

> Prohibition vote needed to win............. 32,515
> Prohibition shortage 16,908
> Total votes cast........................... 36,071
> Total votes available...................... 74,477
> Votes left unpolled........................ 46,406
>
> Votes available in 1900.................... 64,027
> Votes unpolled in 1900..................... 41,687
> Left unpolled 22,340
> Surplus unpolled in 1902 over unpolled in
>   1900 24,066

The *Winnipeg Tribune* recounted the story of the voting under the heading " A Howling Farce ":

PROHIBITION IN CANADA.

"Voting on the referendum in Winnipeg was a screaming comedy. Any one could go and vote at any poll and at as many polls as he chose, unchecked by anything save his own conscience. The voters were allowed to deposit the ballots. Any man, whether property owner or enrolled to vote, could go in at poll after poll and deposit worthless ballots at each poll. Carriage loads, presumably of voters, were driven hastily from poll to poll. In the polling booths men were standing around *ad libitum*. The whole performance was ludicrous, indecent, naked and unabashed. It was just such a caricature of the taking of the vote as might be on the stage in a farce of the broadest and most palpable variety. The Government and liquor men must surely have lost their heads completely to have gone so far as to turn the vote into such an outrageous absurdity.

"It was not at Winnipeg alone that the performance was put on the boards. Nearly 1,800 votes against the act were recorded in the small town of St. Boniface, a number far in excess of the male population of that small place. At many other French places the vote against the act was also remarkable."

When interviewed after the voting, the Hon. Robert Rogers, the Premier's right-hand man, said:

"I suppose we will carry out the will of the people now that we know it. The large vote polled was evidence that the Dominion Alliance non-voting policy did not carry many adherents."

"Did the result meet your anticipation?" he was asked.

"I cannot say. Things were so badly mixed up that it was very hard to decide whether Manitoba really wanted prohibition or not. Now we know, and know how to act."

On June 2, 1902, the Macdonald Act was repealed by order-in-council of the Lieutenant-Governor. The Manitoba referendum is known in history as the "Roblin-Rogers Riffyrandum."

In June, Rev. B. H. Spence was appointed Field Secretary of the Manitoba Alliance to superintend organization in the ensuing campaign. Mr. Spence was granted a year's leave of absence by the Methodist Conference for this work. On July 31, 1902, the Dominion Alliance met in convention in Winni-

PROVINCIAL ACTION.

peg. It was a council of war against the Government. The president, Mr. Mulock, said in his opening address that he hoped that there would not be a single member of the House returned at the next general election. A vigorous policy of election campaigning was adopted by the convention. The Executive Committee was instructed to appoint a standing Committee on Political Action, which committee should confer with the members of the local executive in every electoral division, and should be empowered to enter into negotiations with any organization that might be disposed to assist in the election of prohibition candidates. The meeting affirmed that:

"We are determined to see, through means of our local organizations, that in every constituency there shall be a candidate who can be definitely relied upon to give his independent support to prohibitory legislation. To this end we urge the immediate and thorough perfecting of our organization in each constituency in the province, with a view to unifying the temperance electorate."

In March, 1903, at the invitation of the Manitoba Branch of the Dominion Alliance, the Temperance Legislation League, the Ontario organization which published the *Liberator*, gave consent that the journal should be moved to Winnipeg to assist in the campaign. With it came Mr. W. W. Buchanan, the veteran prohibition campaigner, who stayed in the fight until within a short time of voting day.

Pursuant to the policy adopted, conventions were held in various ridings throughout the province. The movement for independent political action grew in strength, and such a vigorous campaign was made that when voting day came there were fifteen independent candidates in the field definitely pledged to the Alliance policy. In the voting on July 20th, however, none of these were elected.

The campaign had the effect of compelling both political parties to nominate a finer type of candidate, with the result that although the Government was returned to power, the new Legislature contained many strong temperance men. Indeed, the Legislature was one of the best ever elected.

Commenting upon the situation after the election, the secretary of the Alliance said:

"We are in a position to-day of having cast votes enough to secure this, were the Legislature thoroughly representative of the popular opinion, and yet of being unable to realize our desires. In round numbers there were polled at the election 50,000 votes; of these 26,000 were cast for Government candidates and 24,000 for Opposition candidates. Were the Legislature, then, truly representative, the relative strength of the Government and Opposition would be 21 to 19, which would leave the Government with a bare majority of one after electing the Speaker.

"That we occupy the position we do to-day is not due to our voting weakness, but rather to the accident or manipulation which enables a bare majority of the electors to secure such an overwhelming dominance of representation in the Legislature."

II. THE ONTARIO REFERENDUM.

Mr. Hardy retired from the premiership of Ontario in 1899 because of ill-health. He was succeeded by the Hon. G. W. Ross, Minister of Education.

Prohibitionists expected that under the new leader, who was known as a pronounced temperance man, Ontario would make a decided advance in temperance reform. Although the Ontario Government had come to the conclusion that the terms of the Privy Council's decision did not establish the power of local Legislatures to enact prohibitory legislation, nor warrant their taking any action along that line, until some guarantee of their authority should be received, nevertheless it was hoped that at the first opportunity there would be introduced into the Legislative Assembly some substantial measure of license law amendment, in view of the majorities polled by the temperance party in the two plebiscites and the strong declaration in favor of temperance legislation made

PROVINCIAL ACTION.

by the two preceding premiers. No measure of any value to the temperance cause, however, was passed.

A bill was introduced on March 23, 1899, by Mr. W. German proposing to permit the sale of intoxicating liquors on Sunday under certain circumstances, and otherwise to amend the license law in the interests of the liquor traffic. A bill was also introduced by Mr. Thos. Crawford proposing to prohibit the sale of liquor within three hundred yards of any premises used as a public park or recreation ground. Temperance people throughout the country hastened to write to members of the Legislature, urging them to support Mr. Crawford's bill and to oppose the extension of the liquor traffic advocated by Mr. German. Both bills were withdrawn before the Legislature adjourned.

A slight measure of assistance was given to license holders by making license fees payable in half-yearly instalments instead of annually in advance, as heretofore. The Government announced that at the next session of the Legislature the license law would be revised and consolidated. This promise was not fulfilled, although a memorandum suggesting certain badly-needed amendments to the law was forwarded to the Government by the Alliance executive.

Prohibitionists were determined, however, not to permit of any cessation of hostilities. At the annual meeting of the Ontario Branch of the Alliance, held in Toronto on July 17, 1900, the following deliverance was made:

"That while we can accept as final no legislation short of total prohibition, we believe that great good will result from the enactment and enforcement of laws similar to those recently passed in Manitoba and Prince Edward Island, and that a strong deputation be appointed to wait upon the Provincial Government to ask for the introduction into the Provincial Legislature, at its next session, of a measure prohibiting the sale of liquor in the Province of Ontario to the full measure of its power.

"That the said deputation wait also upon the leader of the Opposition, asking a pledge from his party that if they come into power they will grant legislation prohibiting the sale of intoxicating liquors to the full extent of their power in the Province of Ontario."

The Legislature convened on February 6, 1901. On February 13th a large deputation of men and women crowded the members' reception room in Queen's Park, and was received by the Premier and several members of his cabinet.

The speakers were introduced by Dr. J. J. Maclaren. Rev. Dr. W. A. McKay, President of the Ontario Branch of the Dominion Alliance, referred to current newspaper rumors that the attitude of the Government towards the temperance cause was a frigid one, and that the liquor interest was so strong that both sides of the House would bow to its behest. He appealed to the Premier for heroic action, and reminded him of one illustrious British statesman who was said to have "lost his office, but saved his country."

Mr. F. S. Spence spoke of Mr. Ross' temperance record and the hope that it held for the prohibition cause. He reminded the Premier of his declaration on the great night of the temperance workers, the night of Sir Oliver Mowat's pledge in 1894, when Mr. Ross said of the plebiscite results that a politician who would disobey such a mandate would be known "not by his acts, but by his epitaph." Mr. Spence reviewed the temperance legislation of the six years since the Ontario plebiscite, and declared it utterly insignificant when compared with what the temperance people had been led to expect. The old proposition of four licenses for the first thousand of the population has been changed to three, and one for the next four hundred to one for the next six hundred. The closing hour had been fixed at one o'clock instead of open-as-long-as-you-like, and that was practically the sum total. There were other alterations: a three-hundred-foot distance to churches and schools, but the method of measurement made that of little value. The law had been changed to forbid the sale to minors instead of to children under sixteen, but the certificate system had nullified the law and thrown the legislation back fifty years. No conviction was possible under that clause. Saloons had been abolished, but they had been

PROVINCIAL ACTION.

merely turned into handsome hotels, and thus made stronger than ever. The changes affecting the druggists had simply diverted more trade to the licensed liquor sellers.

Mrs. A. O. Rutherford, President of the Ontario Woman's Christian Temperance Union, said she spoke for the women and children, who were the greatest sufferers through the liquor law. She had no doubt that before long women would be accorded the franchise and they would be able to give full expression to their opinion.

Rev. Dr. Carman, "punctuating his sentence with blows on the floor with his walking-stick," says a contemporary account, said that the moral sentiment of the province would sustain any Government that had the moral fibre to take hold of this question courageously, and that it was the bounden duty, the solemn responsibility, of the members of the Government to deal vigorously with an evil so clear and so appalling as the liquor traffic.

The Premier replied that it would be right and wise to wait for the decision given on the Manitoba prohibitory law then before the courts before taking action. He had carefully studied the act and the questions concerning it, which had been submitted for the consideration of the judges, and he believed that all the vital points at issue were covered by the questions being considered.

"It is somewhat unsatisfactory," said Mr. Spence, "to be assured that when the courts have decided, the Government will consider what is best. We would like to know more definitely what would be the attitude of the Government when the courts had made the constitutional powers of the province clear through the Manitoba case."

The Hon. Mr. Ross replied: "The Government does not recede from the position previously taken, and is prepared to go to the limit of its power."

On February 20th, another deputation representing the Ontario section of the Temperance Committee of the General Conference of the Methodist Church waited on the Government. They had confidence, they said, that Mr. Ross would

PROHIBITION IN CANADA.

carry out his pledge of a week ago. The Premier assured the deputation of his sympathy with the object, pointed out the difficulties that the Government had in dealing with the question, and expressed a hope that there would be no difference of opinion between the religious bodies and the Government on the question of moral reform. "You know," he said, "what our past record has been, what our predecessors have agreed to, and what is the general policy of the Government upon that question. That need not be repeated over and over again, because you know exactly where we stand. We stand where we always stood."

At the Provincial Prohibition Convention in Toronto on July 9, 1901, much complaint was made concerning non-enforcement of the License Law. One of the most flagrant violations of the law was in the sale of liquor on Sundays. Dr. McKay, in his presidential address, made the statement that there was at that time more liquor-drinking in the province on the Sabbath day than at any other time in Ontario's history. It was strongly felt that, while the Government was delaying action pending the settlement of the Manitoba case, there should be immediate legislation to remedy some of the most glaring defects of the existing law. The convention recommended application to the Government and Legislature for a number of practical amendments to the license law.

The decision of the Privy Council on November 22, 1901, upholding the Manitoba Act, and thus finally establishing the power of the provinces to enact legislation prohibiting the sale of intoxicating liquor for beverage purposes, brought the question squarely to issue in Ontario, and in the opinion of prohibitionists cleared the way for an immediate advance. But they found that in the words of the Premier to the Methodist deputation in February, "the Government was standing where it had always stood," and it was still hesitant about making any move.

On January 3, 1902, a week before the opening of the Legislature, deputations representing the Methodist Church,

PROVINCIAL ACTION.

the Woman's Christian Temperance Union and the Dominion Alliance received the promise of the Hon. Mr. Ross that careful consideration would be given by the Cabinet at an early date to the question of prohibitory legislation.

There was much discussion throughout the country as to the Government's probable action. His political opponents described the dilemma in which the leader found himself with his prohibition pledges behind him, and no judicial decision available, to be drawn like a red herring across the track of his pursuers. There was talk of a prohibition bill to be followed by a referendum, similar to that taken in Manitoba, with the requirement of a two-thirds temperance majority for the ratification of the law. The temperance people objected vigorously to the taking of another vote, which they considered absolutely unnecessary. They were very hostile to the proposal of legislation limited by any condition that would permit the opinions of the minority of the voting electorate to prevail. The executive of the Dominion Alliance voiced this protest, and the Provincial Woman's Christian Temperance Union addressed an open letter to the Legislature and the electors of Ontario to the same effect.

At the call of the Alliance, mass conventions met in each of the electoral divisions throughout the province to consider the question. A prohibition deputation to the Government on January 23rd, protested against the taking of a referendum. The following day nearly one thousand men interested in the liquor traffic presented their case to the Premier and asked that no law be passed, but if one were submitted, that it should be approved of by a large percentage of the voting strength of the province. They put in a claim also for compensation. There were some who advocated government control of the liquor traffic, and who presented this view to the Government on February 4th. To all of these deputations the Premier replied that he would give their words careful consideration in drafting any legislation on the question.

PROHIBITION IN CANADA.

The Bill.

On February 12, 1902, the Hon. G. W. Ross introduced into the Legislature the long-looked-for bill respecting the sale of intoxicating liquors. The effect of it was to bring into force in Ontario on May 1, 1904, the Manitoba Liquor Act, provided that on October 14, 1902, it was approved of by a number of electors exceeding one-half of the total number of electors who voted at the coming provincial general election.

In introducing his bill, Mr. Ross spoke for over two hours. He reviewed the history of the Ontario License Law, Crooks Act and its various amendments, to show that under it drinking and drunkenness had been steadily and rapidly decreased in the province. Since 1897, license law amendments had been left in abeyance while the question of prohibitory legislation was being considered.

He then discussed the propriety of taking a referendum on this question, a question which had never really been made a party issue at the polls, and on which the opinion of the electors was now to be asked, irrespective of their party affiliations. As to the constitutionality of the referendum method by which the legislative body, while not delegating the final act of enacting legislation, yet relinquished its right of decision in favor of the people, he had consulted Sir John Bourinot, whom he quoted at length. Mr. Bourinot compared the referendum method to that in use in Canadian municipalities in the matter of by-laws. He referred to the referendum clause recently incorporated in the Australian constitution, and approved by the Imperial Parliament. He gave his own opinion that it was a legitimate method for use in a vexed question affecting the social and moral conditions of the people.

Mr. Ross then defended the referendum as a philosophic expedient which would be useful in a single chamber House to assist it in maintaining judicial poise to guard it against hasty legislation, possibly against being stampeded by the fervent zeal of the militant temperance party.

PROVINCIAL ACTION.

" We ought not to try to get away too far from that principle on which, I think, the security of British institutions depends, of occasional and frequent appeals to the electors. One of the great planks of the Chartists was triennial parliaments, bringing the House of Commons to account every three years if possible. We have to give an account every four years, but I want to point out, while this is our constitutional method, it may be well in a question of this kind, and this question seems unique, to have some resting-place where that second thought will be given and where those who, in the last analysis, will have to take the consequences for good or evil, shall have an opportunity of expressing their opinions upon it."

He referred to various precedents, to the constant resort to the referendum in Switzerland, to the recent referendum in Australia on a question of religious education, to its adoption in the United States in every constitutional amendment, to its extensive use in the same country on other questions, to an analogous method of procedure in Canada in connection with the Dunkin Act, Scott Act, and the various provincial local option laws, all measures demanding popular ratification of legislation. As to its employment on the matter of temperance legislation, he referred to the Prince Edward Island referendum of 1902, to the one in Manitoba of the same year, and to the Provincial and Dominion plebiscites on the prohibition question.

In discussing the terms of the voting, Mr. Ross took some time to quote various authorities on the necessity for an undoubtedly strong popular sentiment in favor of the law, to authorize its enactment and to ensure its proper enforcement. The first proposal to consult the people upon the passing of the prohibitory law had come, he said, from the great Montreal prohibition convention in 1875. The Legislature in 1902 was, in effect, carrying out the request of the Dominion Alliance committee, appointed in 1875, that a prohibitory law be enacted and put into force in the province or territory, when ratified by a majority of the qualified electors therein voting on the election.

PROHIBITION IN CANADA.

Mr. Ross interpreted this to mean not a majority of those voting, but a majority of the electors. A three-fifths majority of the votes recorded had been suggested as a fair proportion to ratify the law, but that might possibly mean only a small expression of public opinion. It had been decided to let the majority of the electors, of those who make or unmake political parties, rule in this question. Moreover, it should be a majority of those who were interested enough to come out to the polls specifically for the purpose of voting on the prohibition question. If the required majority should prevail, the question on compensation to liquor men was to be referred to a commission.

From all quarters was heard adverse criticism of the Government's bill. The annual provincial convention of the Royal Templars of Temperance, meeting in Guelph on February 18th, emphatically protested against it as an evasion of responsibility, and called upon the Legislature to amend the bill by striking out all reference to a referendum.

On February 25th, a rally was called in the Horticultural Pavilion in Toronto, which proved to be the largest convention of prohibitionists ever held in Canada. The floor was crowded with delegates from every section of the province, and the gallery filled with interested spectators. Excitement ran high. The delegates were loud in their scorn of the Government bill. The President of the Alliance declared that the action of the Government was like throwing a bone to a dog and saying, "Here, take that." Rev. Mr. Herridge, of Brantford, reading a resolution of unqualified approval of the Ross referendum, was greeted with gales of laughter.

The delegates were practically unanimous in their condemnation of the unfair conditions attached to the proposed referendum. The main difference of opinion was as to whether or not repudiation should be made of the referendum altogether. Discussion took place upon the third clause of the executive committee's report, which read as follows:

(1) That this convention hails with pleasure the decision of the Privy Council sustaining the Manitoba Liquor Act, thus

PROVINCIAL ACTION.

affirming the right of a Provincial Legislature to prohibit transactions in intoxicating liquors which take place wholly within the territorial limits of its jurisdiction by the residents of the province.

(2) That the bill introduced into the Ontario Legislature making prohibition conditional upon difficult, unreasonable, and unjust requirements, cannot be accepted as a fulfilment of the Government's pledges, and this convention expresses its deep regret that the Government has not carried out the simple, definite promise of Sir Oliver Mowat, reiterated by Hon. A. S. Hardy and Hon. G. W. Ross, to introduce a bill to prohibit the liquor traffic to the limit of the declared power of the province.

(3) That a specially objectionable and unfair feature of the bill is the provision that even if the bill is approved by a majority of the electorate voting thereon, it will not become law unless that majority attains very large dimensions, and this convention begs to respectfully inform the Government that legislation, limited by any condition that would permit the opinions of a minority of the voting electorate to prevail, would not be considered by the prohibitionists of Ontario as a fulfilment of the Government's promises, nor as entitling members of the Legislature who voted for it to their confidence and support.

(4) That this convention also objects to the unfairness of a method which makes it necessary for the prohibitionists to poll a large vote in order to secure legislation they desire, while anti-prohibitionists are not required to do so, but may succeed without taking the trouble of voting.

(5) That this convention further protests against the fixing of the date for the proposed voting at an inconvenient time, although such voting might be provided for at a time of a municipal election with an important economy of public funds and the time and effort of the voters, and we call for a vote, if at all, on that date.

(6) That a deputation be appointed to lay before the Government the foregoing resolutions, and to ask for the removal from the bill of the unfair conditions complained of, and that every member of the Legislature be urged to do all he can to secure the elimination from the bill of those conditions.

In amendment to the third clause of this report, Dr. Chown moved the following:

PROHIBITION IN CANADA.

"Whereas two plebiscite votes have been taken upon the question of prohibition, in which the principle has been adopted by overwhelming majorities, and whereas Sir Oliver Mowat and the Hon. G. W. Ross each expressed the conviction that the vote of 1894 indicated that the people were sufficiently educated upon this question, and whereas the Government had promised to introduce legislation to the extent of its powers, this pledge being reiterated by the Hon. G. W. Ross last February, and

"Whereas the prohibition bill recently introduced by the Government provides for a referendum vote to give effect to said bill.

"Looking upon the proposal for the so-called referendum as an evasion of the responsibility that belongs to the Government and Legislature, and which cannot be regarded as otherwise than a violation of a solemn promise of the Government, therefore the convention enters its emphatic protest against such an evasion of responsibility and breach of faith, and calls upon the Legislature to amend the bill by striking out the provision for a referendum."

This resolution was seconded by Rev. W. Kettlewell, and was taken as expressing the views of that section of the convention which believed that the cause would be best served by denouncing not only the manifestly unfair features of the referendum bill, but the taking of any further vote of the electors on the question of prohibition. The strong opinion of the convention was that any more voting by the people was unnecessary, and that the Government ought to have dealt with the situation by the introduction of a bill to be made law by the simple, ordinary act of the Legislature. It was felt, however, by a majority in the convention that while the referendum was not necessary, the temperance party had not a strong case for objecting to the ratification of proposed legislation by a fair vote, and that the wisest position to take was simply that of opposition to the unjust features of the bill as it had been introduced into the Legislature.

The following picturesque account is taken from a newspaper report of the meeting:

PROVINCIAL ACTION.

"Dr. Chown's amendment, which aimed at shaking the skirts of prohibition free of the referendum altogether, had strong support among the delegates. It might have passed had not Ald. F. S. Spence stepped into the breach at a dramatic moment. After sitting at the secretary's table in silence all day, as the strife and clamor of tongues tore the Ross referendum into shreds, Alderman Spence at last declared himself openly as being against the machinations of his friend and political leader, Premier Ross. Mr. Spence threw restraint to the winds and, having waited until Dr. Chown had said the last word, he seized his advantage, and in a tide of hot, impassioned speech, aroused the martial ardor of the convention to fight out the battle.

"Mr. Spence dug his dagger into the unfair conditions of the referendum, but if it could be mended he wanted prohibitionists to go to the polls and fight to the last ditch. His censure of the Government was as vigorous and direct as that of any Tory delegate on the floor of the convention. His counsel prevailed, and the convention passed the report of the executive and declared that they would accept a modified referendum and enter the field against the liquor trade."

The report of the executive committee was adopted without amendment.

There was a suggestion that the whole convention, in a solid phalanx, should make an immediate onslaught upon the Government and express their views, but this was judged impracticable. On the following day the Government received the deputation appointed by the convention. Although only a few representatives were chosen to convey the message, a large crowd of interested delegates were in attendance. There were also some representatives of the liquor trade to witness the proceedings. The deputation was introduced by Rev. Dr. McKay, and the speakers were Mr. A. B. Spencer, Mr. C. J. Miller, Mrs. May Thornley, and Rev. Dr. Carman.

In reply, the Premier argued that such a bill as the proposed prohibition bill ought to have the sanction of a conclusive majority of the electorate. He did not think it unjust to require the prohibitionists to poll a majority of the votes cast in the election of 1898, and he stated that he could hold out no hope that prohibition would be secured by a simple majority of the votes cast. He was favorable to a change of the voting time to a later date, but was not prepared to say what date would be chosen, and he promised on behalf of the Government a thorough enforcement of the prohibition law if it should come into operation.

"It is now 'to your tents, O Israel,'" quoted Dr. Carman, as the deputation withdrew to consider the Premier's answer.

It was agreed that the Alliance executive be instructed to put forth every effort to induce members of the Legislature to secure the changes desired by the convention. After the adoption of the bill a systematic campaign was to be organized against the return in the coming election of those who had supported any other basis than that of a bare majority of the votes cast.

The Provincial Woman's Christian Temperance Union at first refused to co-operate in the campaign if the vote were taken on any but a bare majority basis, and an official letter to that effect was read at the meeting, declaring the unanimous decision of the executive to repudiate entirely an unfair referendum, and devote themselves exclusively to the election campaign, but afterwards they did magnificent work in the campaign.

On March 5th, the Hon. G. W. Ross moved the second reading of the prohibition bill, entitled "The Liquor Act, 1902." The changes proposed from the form in which the bill was first submitted merely altered the voting day from October 14th to some day early in December not then announced, and changed the majority required to secure prohibition to a majority of the votes cast, providing such majority were also a majority of the number of electors who voted at the general provincial election in 1898:

Mr. J. P. Whitney, leader of the Opposition, opposed the bill. He denounced the referendum proposal and the unfair conditions attached to it, and went on to say

"Also I am opposed to the bill on the merits of it, without reference to the referendum. We cannot have prohibition in the

PROVINCIAL ACTION.

province, therefore it is idle to discuss that question. I believe the remedy is rather in using the powers that we possess, namely, wholesome restriction, decreasing the number of licenses, removing those charged with the administration of the law from political influence, and honestly enforcing the law.

"Therefore I am prepared to support and introduce and pass legislation to, first decrease the number of licenses; maintain intact and allow no relaxation of the restriction; remove the commissioners and inspectors from political and party influence; and fourth, enforce the law honestly and with the whole power of the Government."

Hon. J. M. Gibson, Attorney-General, advocated the referendum as a constitutional method, quoting many authorities in favor of his contention and commending the conditions attached to the bill.

Mr. G. F. Marter favored the bill as a useful measure of legislation, but did not think there was any necessity for a referendum to bring it into operation. He forcibly attacked the unfair conditions of the measure, which he proposed to endeavor to remove, but said he would support the Government in endeavoring to bring the bill into operation.

The second reading was carried by a majority of thirteen, all the Liberals present and Mr. Marter voting for the measure and all the Conservatives excepting Mr. Marter voting against it.

On the last day of the session, March 14th, after more than three hours' discussion, the bill was given its third reading and the Lieutenant-Governor's assent. Several amendments were proposed by members of the Opposition. Mr. Crawford declared that the bill was a violation, or at least an evasion, of a pledge given to the temperance people, and was in that sense an immoral measure and not in the interests of temperance. He attempted to kill it by moving to strike out the second and one hundred and fourth clauses of the bill, which were those that provided for a referendum and a special basis for the vote. The contention was that without those clauses the Government would not support the bill, which would then

PROHIBITION IN CANADA.

be a prohibitive measure. The amendment was defeated on a straight party division.

Mr. Marter then introduced an amendment, seconded by Mr. Tucker, providing that the vote should be on the date fixed for the holding of the municipal elections in the province in 1903. The bill, he declared, was defective but not immoral. The bad feature was the impossible majority asked for, a subterfuge on the part of the Government to prevent the bill's becoming law, which he deplored. He hoped the members would deal with this great moral question without regard to party affiliations. The amendment was defeated by seventy-five to four. Mr. Marter was supported by John Barr, M.D., Dufferin; Thos. Crawford, West Toronto, and Jas. Tucker, West Wellington.

Mr. Marter then moved two other amendments, the first to change the Act so as to provide that it would come into operation by a bare majority of the electors voting on the question. When this was defeated by seventy-six to four, he moved that the majority demanded be sixty per cent. of the votes polled. Messrs. Marter and Crawford alone supported this proposal.

The division on the main question followed, and the bill was carried by a majority of thirteen, Mr. Marter voting with the supporters of the Government.

The Campaign.

The Ontario Legislature was dissolved on March 17, 1902. In the provincial election campaign that followed, temperance workers took an active part.

A special organization for the support of independent political candidates had been formed in Toronto in February, with Rev. Dr. Chown as president. In March this Ontario Prohibition Campaign Committee joined forces with the Woman's Christian Temperance Union and the Royal Templars of Temperance to form the Union Campaign Committee. The organ of this body was *The Liberator*, a weekly,

PROVINCIAL ACTION.

first issued on May 2, 1902, to advocate the election of independent prohibitionists to the Legislature. After the election it was decided to make the Union Prohibition Committee a permanent organization and *The Liberator* was sustained as a regular periodical. At a provincial convention held in London on June 30th and July 1st, the name of the committee was changed to the Temperance Legislation League.

The Dominion Alliance pursued its accustomed policy. The executive committee met with the Temperance Committee of the Methodist Church in Toronto on March 25th to launch its electoral campaign. They issued the following manifesto:

To the Prohibitionists of Ontario:

Dear Friends,—In view of the approaching provincial election, we appeal to you to rally for another battle against the terrible drink evil that is to-day the prolific cause of physical, social and moral degradation and ruin, and that is seeking more and more to entrench itself in the vantage ground of political methods and institutions and to control the Government, the Legislature and legislation so as to thwart the efforts of earnest and philanthropic citizens for the restraint of its debauching influence and power.

A CRITICAL SITUATION.

The united and energetic liquor traffic has won a temporary victory. The reasonable requests of the convention of February 25th last have been refused by the Government and Legislature, only four members voting for them. Our only hope for success is in such electoral action, untrammelled by partyism, as will give us representatives who will fearlessly stand for our principles, uninfluenced by any subservience to the liquor interests or the dictation of any party machine.

Your special attention is asked to the following features of the critical situation which confronts us. The Liquor Act which has been passed by the Legislature, and which is to be voted upon in December next, is such a combination of useful prohibition and unjust voting requirements that careful discrimination is necessary in discussing it, and careful consideration in planning any action to secure its alteration or enforcement.

PROHIBITION IN CANADA.

A GOOD LAW.

The second part of this act is a prohibitory law of the most complete and comprehensive character that the limits of provincial jurisdiction will permit. It is not fair to compare it with the Scott Act or any other measure more local in its nature or less stringent in its provisions. It is an honest attempt to devise the most effective kind of a prohibitory law. It was the work of skilled and experienced professional men who were also earnest advocates of total prohibition, and it is probably the most thorough-going legislation of the kind in existence.

UNFAIR CONDITIONS.

The first part of the act makes the coming into operation of the second part conditional upon its being ratified by a majority of the votes cast at a special polling to be held on December 4th next, and upon the total number of votes cast for the act being equal to a majority of the total votes cast at the general provincial election held in 1898. The latter condition we consider exceedingly unjust.

The liquor party may be in a minority, as they were in 1894 and in 1898; they may even stay away from the polls, not troubling themselves to vote, and yet be considered as successful in the contest. Prohibition may be counted as defeated, although approved by a large majority of the voting electorate. Without questioning the ability of prohibitionists to secure the required vote, we must claim that the conditions are so framed as to make it difficult for them to succeed and easy for the liquor party to win. We must protest emphatically against these conditions as discriminating against temperance voters and being unfair class legislation in the interests of the liquor traffic.

PROHIBITION IS RIGHT.

We stand by the principle embodied in the unanimous declaration of the convention of February 25th. We cannot consent to the injustice of legislation in accordance with the wishes of a liquor-favoring minority and against the demand of the voting majority, that majority being on the patriotic and unselfish side. Prohibition is the right legislative method of dealing with the liquor traffic. It has been emphatically endorsed at the polls, and

PROVINCIAL ACTION.

only men who favor it have any claim upon your support as temperance electors.

ELECTORAL ACTION.

It is therefore our plain and imperative duty to strive to elect in the approaching campaign such men as can be depended upon to carry out this principle. We must secure the nomination and election of reliable candidates, who will undertake, regardless of party, to support the bringing into operation of prohibitory legislation to the limit of the ascertained jurisdiction of the Provincial Legislature.

The question of which nominated candidate is best entitled to the support of prohibitionists, and of whether or not it is desirable to bring out an independent candidate, must be settled by the workers of each constituency by themselves. The first duty is the holding in every constituency of a representative conference of workers to consider these matters and to take vigorous action to give effect to the decision arrived at.

THE REFERENDUM.

While we protest against the unjust requirements of the referendum plan, we deem it our duty to stand by the cause we have always supported, and we earnestly urge our people to organize everywhere and to do their utmost to secure another prohibition victory in the referendum on December 4th next.

In union is strength. * We earnestly appeal for concentration of effort on the lines of action above stated and on the plan agreed upon in each locality to carry them out. Let your ballot in the coming contests be consecrated to the temperance cause and your energies devoted to devising how that ballot may be made to count against the liquor traffic.

OUR DUTY TO VOTE.

Every vote is needed and every vote will tell. To the extent that our influence is felt in the approaching election we will be strong to compel respect and fair play from the next Legislature. We shall need that strength to compel law enforcement if the referendum brings us prohibition. We shall need it even if our vote should fall short of the unreasonable referendum require-

PROHIBITION IN CANADA.

ment, to secure the legislation which our certain majority will fairly demand.

IMMEDIATE ACTION.

Steps are being taken to secure the holding of a convention for each constituency at the earliest possible date. Do not fail to attend the one called for your electoral district. It will be the starting point for both the impending campaigns, and upon its character and action will largely depend the value and effect of your own work for our cause in the near future. Urge others to attend. Go prepared to sacrifice, if need be, all party prejudice and your personal convenience in a determined, earnest effort to win the great boon of prohibition for our fair province.

Two questions were prepared for presentation to candiates:

(1) Are you in favor of legislation to prohibit the traffic in intoxicating liquors for beverage purposes to the extent of the power of the Legislature?

(2) Do you believe that a prohibitory law ought to be put into operation if it is found that a majority of the votes polled on December 4th next are in favor of prohibition?

Mr. G. F. Marter was publicly thanked by a special resolution for the independent stand he had taken in the referendum debate in the Legislature.

The Alliance organizer, Mr. Nicholls, assisted in the eastern part of the province by Mr. J. H. Carson from the Quebec Alliance, pushed with vigor the work of organization, reaching every constituency either by personal visit or by letter, holding conferences with the workers and addressing a large number of meetings. In many cases committees waited upon candidates, ascertained their views, and reported them to meetings. The result of all his work was the nominating of eight independent prohibition candidates and the pledging in favor of prohibition of a number who were nominated by one of the political parties. Mr. Marter entered the field as an independent candidate in North Toronto.

PROVINCIAL ACTION.

Voting took place on May 29th, and the Ross Government was sustained by a majority of only six, which, through the decisions of the courts and cases of illness and death, was later reduced to three. Not one of the independent prohibition candidates was elected, but Mr. Marter, opposing a very strong Conservative, was only two hundred votes behind in a total vote of nearly eight thousand. The three Conservative members who broke with their party and supported the Marter amendments to the referendum bill were all re-elected. It was agreed that the Government had lost some support from the temperance people, who either voted against it or apathetically stayed at home.

An important event in the history of Canada's temperance reform was the starting of *The Pioneer* on July 4, 1902, a weekly paper to succeed the small monthly *Camp Fire*. Mr. F. S. Spence was managing editor. It was sustained for a time by the liberality of friends of the cause. It was found that the enterprise was not self-sustaining, but it proved so valuable to workers as an educational factor and as a means of producing a continuous record of the progress of the movement that it was officially adopted by the Alliance.

Another provincial convention was called for July 29th in Association Hall, to complete plans for the referendum campaign. A deputation from the Temperance Legislation League asked for the appointment by the Alliance of a number of representatives to act with a similar number from the League in management of the referendum campaign. Replying to the request, the campaign committee recommended:

" That we appreciate the desire and purpose of the Legislation League to co-operate with the Alliance in the coming campaign; that we deem it highly desirable that there be unity of action on the part of all prohibition forces of the province; and that we favor the co-operation of the committees and organizations of the Alliance with the committees of the League and of all bodies favoring prohibition."

It was decided to request all churches and temperance societies to inaugurate an active movement to secure signatures to a total abstinence pledge as an aid in the referendum campaign. Also, on the second Sunday of September, ministers were asked to preach sermons along the line of total abstinence and the suppression of the liquor traffic by the state.

Immediately after the July convention, the executive committee took hold energetically of referendum campaign work. Sub-committees to deal with different departments were appointed and many meetings of these committees were held. Correspondence was entered into with constituencies not yet organized and some places were visited by organizers. Many circulars and letters were sent out, giving information about campaign methods—over 200,000 documents in all. One of the most useful and effective methods adopted by the executive committee was a literature circulation plan by which a valuable series of twelve four-page leaflets and eleven two-page leaflets specially adapted for campaign work were issued in very large quantities and at low prices. Of these there were issued more than four and a half million copies, being upwards of thirteen and a half million pages.

On November 25th, a week before the vote, a final rally of the temperance forces was held in Association Hall, at which the Premier presided.

On December 2nd, two days before the vote, there appeared in Toronto a manifesto against the Liquor Act, signed by some 244 of the bankers, brokers, manufacturers and professional and business men of Toronto and Hamilton. It read as follows ·

"*Re* The Liquor Act, 1902.

"We, the undersigned, actively engaged in business in the Province of Ontario, are of the opinion that the Liquor Act, which is to be submitted to the people on December 4th next, is an unwise and impracticable measure, since it permits importation in any quantity from other provinces and countries, and would therefore merely transfer the drinking of intoxicants from licensed and well-regulated places to unlicensed and disreputable resorts and to the homes of the people.

PROVINCIAL ACTION.

"We believe that this measure would be detrimental to the best interests, both moral and commercial, of this province, and we therefore urge all voters to mark their ballots 'No.'"

Mr. Spence, in commenting on this document, said that it was more remarkable for the names that were not attached to it than for those that were.

Notwithstanding the great difficulties in the way, the discouraging circumstances under which the contest was carried on, and the very bad condition of roads in many rural districts, the vote polled exceeded the expectations of the most sanguine workers. The conditions imposed required a vote of 213,723 in favor of the act. The vote actually polled was 199,749. This was a larger vote than was polled in either the plebiscite of 1894 or that of 1898. The total result was as follows:

For the Liquor Act	199,749
Against the Liquor Act	103,548
Majority for the Act	96,201

Mr. Spence said: " I think it the most complete demonstration ever made of the strength of temperance sentiment. What would you think of a party that could carry almost every constituency in the province by a majority of five hundred? I think when the returns are all in we will have carried three-fourths of the constituencies by majorities over one thousand. Never in the history of responsible government was there a stronger representation of public opinion in favor of any party and policy or any question."

It was well known that, on voting day, in different parts of the country attempts were made to personate voters to such an extent as to lead to the conclusion that there was an organized effort being made to prevent the polling of the full strength of the temperance vote. The local workers in different places took the matter up and instituted prosecutions against persons who had committed the offence of personating or had permitted others to do so.

PROHIBITION IN CANADA.

On January 23rd a petition was presented to the Lieutenant-Governor in Council asking for the issue of a commission to examine into the conspiracy of personation and ballot stuffing. The names and addresses of upwards of 160 persons whose votes were affected by the impersonation committed accompanied the petition, and also a great number of facts showing that there was a well-organized conspiracy. It was shown that in South Toronto over eighty ballots were found in the boxes with the numbers differing from those delivered to the deputy returning officer for South Toronto. At one poll there were twelve personations and fourteen fraudulent ballots; at another nine personations and twelve fraudulent ballots; and at still another eight personations and nine counterfeit ballots; and in nearly every case the counterfeit ballot was folded inside the genuine ballot.

The Government delayed issuing the commission while the prosecution of those charged with improper practices was being carried on. Mr. Alexander Mills rendered valuable service in this work in the face of considerable difficulties. He objected to the law that imposed a penalty of only fifty dollars for impersonation, and he succeeded in having this changed to a fine of four hundred dollars and a year's imprisonment.

AFTER THE VOTE.

On December 16th, as soon as returns of the referendum voting could be secured sufficiently complete to give a fair idea of the results, a meeting was called in Knox Church of the Alliance executive committee with members of the special standing committees of the various representative church bodies. The following resolution was presented at the meeting of the Resolutions Committee:

"That in view of the recent expressions by the electors of the Province of Ontario in favor of the Liquor Act of 1902, we deem it advisable to appoint a deputation to wait upon the Government and request that effect be given to the said vote by the abolition of the open bar, the treating system and drinking in clubs, and

PROVINCIAL ACTION.

the imposition of such other restrictions on the liquor traffic as should most effectively curtail its operation and remedy its evils."

A minority resolution was also presented as follows:

"That we appoint a deputation to wait upon the Government to call their attention to the magnificent vote of December 4th and to make inquiry as to the intention of the Government with regard to that vote."

The adoption of the minority resolution was not moved, but an amendment to the original motion was made, namely:

"That we appoint a deputation to ask the Government to pass a law enacting the second part of the Liquor Act of 1902."

A stirring discussion took place over the resolution and the amendment. Earnest appeals were made for united action to secure the best results from the great victory that had been won. The amendment was defeated and the resolution of the committee adopted unanimously. It was resolved that the persons invited to the conference should be a deputation to lay the views of the conference before the Government. The Temperance Legislation League was not in harmony with the Alliance in their action and took objection to the last sentence of the resolution, fearing that it would be construed to mean Government control. Moreover, *The Liberator* eriticized the executive for holding "a stealthy meeting, called without consultation with officers and executive of the Alliance, a secret meeting of a picked few the day before to make the policy, . . . a short night session in which there was no time for deliberation and every opportunity of a snap verdict." Consequently the members of the Legislation League declined to accompany the deputation.

The deputation were received by the Premier on January 15th, when the resolution adopted on December 16th was presented. The following account is from the *Globe's* report:

"Mr. Spence, who was first called upon, began by congratulating the Government upon now being in a position to do what the temperance people wanted. They came to the Government, he said, not merely on the strength of the majority. They came because they were engaged in a conflict against a tremendous evil. They came because the Premier himself had promised that all would be done that could be done to remedy the evil, and because they knew his personal sympathy with the great work they were striving to do, and believing that he was ready when it was practicable to do exactly what they asked, and they had been striving hard to make it very easy for him. They were now backed by the greatest majority that in the history of civilization was ever behind any party, any policy or any principle. They had more than sixty-five per cent. of all the votes that were polled in that election. Twelve months ago the Government were of opinion that sixty per cent. of the votes cast would be sufficient to bring the law into operation. Now they had exceeded the original requirement by a majority of seventeen thousand votes. In Manitoba, on the same bill, the Government had only asked the temperance people to poll sixty-two and a half per cent. of the votes cast, and promised to bring the act into operation. They had obtained more than the requirement of Manitoba and in the face of tremendous difficulties, such as the discouragement of many of the workers at what they had considered the very hard terms and in the face of an unfavorable time of the year for voting, when thousands of men in the north country could not vote, as the lakes were not frozen hard enough for traffic. In 1894 they also had a vote and also had majority, and on that occasion Sir Oliver Mowat had said that that vote was of such a character as to demand all the prohibition that it was in the power of the Legislature to enact. And Mr. Ross, he was glad to say, had agreed with that statement, and said that a Government that would take that position was the only kind of a Government that he would belong to. They now came with a vote greater than that vote by 19,462, and with a majority greater than that majority of 23,610. In 1898 there had been another plebiscite. Sir Wilfrid Laurier had said that under the circumstances it was a very large vote; yet they now came with a vote larger, so far as Ontario was concerned, by 45,051 and a majority greater by 55,989. Yet the case was far stronger than that, for four out of every five women wanted prohibition, as was shown by the limited number who voted in 1898.

PROVINCIAL ACTION.

"There were ninety-seven constituencies in Ontario. The temperance people had carried eighty-four of them and thirteen had gone against them. The aggregate majority of those who went in favor was 103,941; therefore they had carried the eighty-four constituencies by an average majority of 1,237.

"'It is only fair to say,' Mr. Spence concluded, 'that there was a little difference of opinion as to the request we should make. There is no difference of opinion among the temperance people as to what we ought to receive. Some thought it was wise to ask simply for the act. Some thought perhaps a better act could be framed. But the great majority asked for legislation that would give us all the legislation and all the benefits for the people that would come from that law. In our deputation to-day there is no one who utters a word of objection to that act. We are not so anxious as to how to attain the end, but we want you to attain that end. We come to you now with the endorsation of an influence overwhelming, asking for the strongest measures you believe necessary to carry out that result. We ask you to do your whole duty in the matter as we have striven to do ours.'"

Others who spoke for the deputation were: Rev. Drs. Carman, Dickson (Galt), Sheraton (Wycliffe College), Goodspeed, and Chown, Rev. J. H. Hazelwood (Hamilton), Rev. D. S. Hamilton (London), Messrs. Jonathan Ellis (Port Dover), Thomas Baty (London), A. Parrott (Chatham), Joseph Gibson (Ingersoll), and Mrs. A. O. Rutherford, President of the Dominion Woman's Christian Temperance Union.

Premier Ross, in reply, repeated his conviction that the Government had acted judiciously in submitting the referendum, and said in part:

"The measure of a Government's responsibility under our constitutional system as it is worked out is its majority. Although the leader of the Government at the present time and the leader of the Liberal party, I am not the Liberal party. I can only go as far as my supporters in the Legislature will enable me to go. You say if we had as large a vote as you have we would have something like seventy-seven of a majority. I am sorry I have not that majority. It would add very greatly to my comfort to-night, and

PROHIBITION IN CANADA.

perhaps add to the efficiency of the Legislature. But whether my majority be large or small, if I am to exist it must be maintained intact.

"My duty, however, in connection with this question is to consult my supporters, and that I shall do at the earliest opportunity. The earliest opportunity will be when the House meets, when we will see how far the members will support the Government in implementing that vote. That is the only position I can take to-day. There are some phases of the question on which you do not agree yourselves. I hope we will agree, and when we have agreed I hope we will secure such legislation as will meet with the approval of the country. I would feel humiliated if you thought we would play fast and loose with this question or any question. I think the time has gone by when reflection should be cast on the position of those entrusted with the government of the country on this question. We have not played fast and loose. We have acted in all sincerity, within our constitutional rights and limitations; and though you may not approve of all we may do in the future, I hope you will at least give us credit that we are acting with as much forethought and advancing just as rapidly as we feel we have the confidence of the people.

"Your vote is very large. Our vote is comparatively small. If the whole vote that asked for prohibition had voted for the Government that was to give you prohibition the situation would be different. We express no repining. At all events we accept the situation. We hope for legislation when the House meets, and we trust that that legislation will meet with the approval and confidence of the country."

After the interview with the Government, letters were written to members of the Legislature by the Alliance executive and workers throughout the country, impressing upon them the strength and importance of the vote that had been polled, and urging them to support legislation carrying into effect the views of the people as expressed at the polls.

PARLIAMENTARY INACTION.

The Legislature met on March 10th. The Speech from the Throne outlined the proposed legislation, and contained the following relative to the temperance question: "The vote

PROVINCIAL ACTION.

polled on the 4th of December last in favor of the Liquor Act of 1902, though not large enough to bring the act into force, may nevertheless be taken as an expression of the electors favoring further legislation with respect to the liquor traffic. A measure with this object in view will be submitted for your consideration." However, for some weeks the time of the Legislature was taken up with the judicial investigation and discussion of a series of charges made upon the floor of the House against a member of the Government. When this measure concerning the temperance question had not been introduced by May 13th, another deputation waited upon the Premier to inquire what the Government's intentions were. The Premier said that the Government had intended to introduce early in the season a measure of advanced and useful legislation. A temperance bill had been prepared, but the Government's plans had been interfered with. He did not consider it practicable now to bring down the bill, since it was desirable and necessary to have such a measure before the House long enough to allow for its receiving the fullest consideration by the members and the Council before being passed. It had therefore been decided to hold over the proposed measure and introduce it early in the next session.

The Premier's statement as to his reason for delay was not satisfactory to the delegates at the Ontario Alliance convention in the Guild Hall, Toronto, on May 28th. They felt that if conditions were such as to prevent the immediate enactment of the measure, yet the bill should at least be introduced in order that the Legislature and country might know what the Government proposed to do. Moreover, they claimed that a question that was of sufficient importance to demand the time and the expense of a special vote of the electorate should have been of sufficient importance to receive the attention of the members of the Legislature for the time necessary to consider a measure giving effect to the vote taken.

Mr. Marter, who occupied the chair owing to the illness of the President, Dr. McKay, counselled moderation in spite of the indignation with the Government that many in the meeting felt. The need was the solidifying of the temperance forces of the country, and the danger was that by making a bone of contention of the Government's failure to fulfil its promises, they might drive out from their ranks many people who would say that this was a movement calculated to damage the Government rather than to advance the temperance cause.

The responsibility for the Government's daring to trifle with the temperance people of the province lay at the doors of those who had put their party ahead of their temperance principles. It was time that they learned something in the way of combining and solidifying from their opponents, the liquor interests, who declared that they had no politics. All they cared for politics was how they could use them. He continued:

"It is the duty of temperance men to support those who give us temperance measures. I do not mean the Government or the Opposition. Any party in our Legislature who will measure up to our views, who will vote and act accordingly, ought to feel confidence that in doing so he will have the support of every temperance man in the community. As soon as we let them feel that they can depend upon us there will be a very different state of affairs in the building yonder."

The most important action of the conference was the adoption of the resolution of the Committee on Electoral Action, which called for the organization throughout the province of a league of voters pledged to make right principle a political force. The first two clauses of the resolution describing the character of the temperance movement and the strength of public opinion were adopted without comment. Over the third clause a discussion arose. The committee's resolution read:

"This conference directs the executive committee to organize an electoral league in every constituency to be composed of *bona fide* electors who will pledge themselves to support only candi-

PROVINCIAL ACTION.

dates of whatever or whichever political party who fully engage on such moral questions to set themselves free from party caucus control and party affiliations to the extent that they may, according to their best judgment, compel whichever party is in power to grant the most advanced prohibitory legislation practicable within the power of the province, and to insist upon such measures and action, either by the Government or Legislature, as shall make such legislation effective."

An amendment to this clause was offered by Mr. R. W. Dillon:

"That this convention recommend the temperance people in both political parties to take a more active interest in the appointment of delegates to the party conventions, with a view to securing strong representation in such conventions, and thus assist materially in the nomination of candidates in both parties in full sympathy with the cause of moral reform as advocated by this Alliance and also help materially at the same time in moulding the policy of their respective parties in all questions affecting the moral well being of the state."

Mr. W. Munns proposed another amendment declaring for vigorous and independent political action. The two amendments were put and lost and the clause of the original resolution was carried by a very large majority.

During the course of the convention a presentation was made to Mr. F. S. Spence in recognition of his long years of service in the Alliance and of the special responsibility he had borne in the referendum campaign. "He has sacrificed in this cause more than many of his friends know," said Mr. Emerson Coatsworth. "He has brought to it not only zeal but ability. His experience and wise judgment have often guided our actions, and I readily say that it is right that we should have been guided by him in this way. He has been fearless and independent, a hard hitter. I have sometimes felt his blows, but honest, fair, and free from partisanship. I can say this, being on a different political line from him, and knowing how faithful he has been to principle. Last of all, and not least of all, we have had from Mr. Spence a most cheerful service, that could only be given by a man whose heart was in the work, that could only be given by a man who was prepared to sacrifice money and influence to what he believed to be the work that he was to lay down his life for."

The Alliance executive went energetically to work after the convention with the organization of Voters' Leagues. Literature was circulated amongst the electors giving full information concerning the movement and meetings were held in many constituencies. An address was drafted, approved, and widely circulated, giving full information concerning the movement, including a form of agreement to be signed by electors and a suggested constitution to be adopted in each locality for the making of the movement effective.

Mr. S. Holland was engaged by the executive to visit different electoral districts and plan conventions, with a view to organization. Later on the committee secured the services of Rev. Dr. R. H. Abraham as field secretary, to attend conventions, address meetings, and assist in presenting and advocating the new movement and in the organization of Voters' Leagues. Meetings were held in the following constituencies: East Lambton, West Lambton, East Middlesex, West Middlesex, Haldimand, Halton, Peel, East York, West York, North York, South York, North Ontario, South Ontario, West Durham, East Simcoe, Centre Simcoe, West Simcoe, Cardwell, East Northumberland, West Northumberland, East Durham, West Durham, East Toronto, West Toronto, North Toronto, and South Toronto.

The agreement to be signed by the voters, and the agreement recommended for submission to candidates, were in the following forms:

Voters' Agreement.

In view of the widespread evils resulting from the legalized liquor traffic, and recognizing our personal responsibility as citizens and our duty to strive earnestly for better conditions and laws—

PROVINCIAL ACTION.

We, the undersigned, do hereby agree with each other that in preparation for the next election to the Provincial Legislature of a representative for this constituency, we will earnestly endeavor to secure the nomination of a candidate who can be relied upon to do all that he can to secure effective temperance legislation at the earliest possible opportunity, and who will hold himself absolutely free from party dictation in relation to such legislation.

And we further agree that in the said election we will work and vote only for a candidate who will comply with these requirements, if such a candidate is nominated and is endorsed by the Voters' League of this constituency.

By effective temperance legislation we mean legislation abolishing the bar and the treating system and drinking in clubs, and imposing upon the liquor traffic such other restrictions as shall most effectually curtail its operation and remedy its evils.

This agreement is to be binding upon us as soon as one hundred signatures to it are secured in this constituency.

Candidates' Agreement.

I, ..., a candidate for the Electoral District of ...., do hereby agree that if elected to the Provincial Legislature as a representative of this constituency, I will do all I can to secure, at the earliest possible opportunity, such effective temperance legislation as the province has power to enact, and in so doing will hold myself free from party dictation in relation to my action.

By effective temperance legislation is meant legislation abolishing the bar and the treating system and drinking in clubs, and imposing upon the liquor traffic such other restrictions as shall most effectually curtail its operation and remedy its evils.

The following footnote was submitted along with the candidate's pledge:

"Any candidate who refuses to accept this agreement cannot be considered as satisfactory or as having any claim upon the Voters' League for support."

At the opening of the Ontario Legislature on January 14, 1904, the Speech from the Throne indicated that legislation concerning the liquor traffic would be brought before the

PROHIBITION IN CANADA.

House, but gave no details concerning what the Government proposed. In the debate on the address the question was briefly referred to by the Premier and the leader of the Opposition. The Premier is reported to have said that the important question of the licensing laws was one which the House would consider. The vote on the referendum indicated a strong feeling that this question should be dealt with along progressive lines. Mr. Whitney's statement was: He would like to see them deal with the sewage question and several questions of a moral nature which the Premier and the Government refused to deal frankly with. There was the local option law, for instance. It had been placed on the statute books, so the people might have the privilege of expressing their views with regard to the liquor trade, but unfortunately there were obstacles in the way of a fair expression of opinion, and they should be removed.

On the 8th of March, a caucus of Liberal members of the Legislature was held. Although the deliberations of the political council were not intended for publication, accounts of the proceedings found their way into the daily press. Opinions differed as to the Premier's position. Some people pictured him " with his back against the wall, fighting valiantly for a prohibition measure." Others condemned him for trading on his temperance record and doing nothing to redeem his promises. The statement published in the *Daily Star* was as follows:

" It was learned that the Premier presented a most drastic measure of reform. It included not only the abolition of the bars, but the complete abolition of hotel licenses throughout the province.

" This was supplemented by a regulation providing for the Government control of shops, the argument being that it would be most unfair to allow privately-owned shops to continue in business after the hotel licenses had been cancelled.

" The proposition, the skeleton of which is here outlined, was fully discussed in caucus, with the result that although the Premier urged its adoption very strongly, it was not entertained, the majority against it being considerable.

PROVINCIAL ACTION.

"An alternative proposition was next presented. It looks to the submitting of the question to the municipalities on the day of the next municipal election. Each voter will be asked whether he is in favor of the abolition of the hotel licenses, and also if he is in favor of the abolition of the shops. Each municipality that votes aye to these questions will automatically receive local prohibition. Along with this proposition are additional regulations looking to the more stringent control of the trade in the municipalities which do not vote for prohibition, and probably to Government control of shops in the municipalities which abolish the hotel but vote to retain the shops.

This plan was outlined to caucus and the whole subject deferred to future day without definite action being taken."

The pressure on the Government was continued. The Alliance executive on March 16th reiterated its insistence upon no compromise in the matter of prohibition legislation. It condemned the expedients outlined in the Liberal press as to the purposes of the Premier; and while some members insisted that nothing but immediate total prohibition should be accepted, the arguments of others prevailed, that it was wise to press first for the abolition of the bar—the course that the Premier had himself advocated—and when this was attained they could push on to the ultimate goal of total prohibition, which was their unalterable aim.

Members of the Government and Legislature were interviewed and strong letters were sent to them by their constituents. In a number of cases replies were received, stating that the representatives would cordially support any restrictive legislation introduced by the Government.

The Methodist and Baptist Ministerial Associations of Toronto, on April 4th, and the Presbyterian Ministerial Association on April 6th, sent deputations to interview the Premier and urge him to bring before the Legislature such a measure as the situation demanded and public opinion warranted.

The Premier's written reply was received by Rev. J. A. Rankin, President of the Methodist Association. It was as follows:

PROHIBITION IN CANADA.

"Toronto, April 6th, 1904.

"*Dear Sir:*

"In reply to the deputation which I had the honor of receiving yesterday, I desire to express my concurrence in the views presented by the different speakers, that nothing short of the prohibition of the sale of liquors in hotels and the strictest control over sales for purposes generally recognized as proper and legitimate, would fully protect society from the evil effects of excessive drinking, so far as legislation can be invoked for the purpose. Your decided preference for such a measure, as against amendments to the license laws, I understand to mean that you do not favor at present any other form of temperance legislation. If the Government are unable to give the measure desired this session it will be our duty to consider what means are available for further action.

"Yours truly,

"(Signed)   George W. Ross."

Mr. F. S. Spence was asked by a newspaper reporter what he thought of the Premier's reply.

"Reply? I have not seen any yet."

"What about Ross' letter?"

"Oh, I do not consider that an answer to the deputation. The letter is absolutely indefinite. It leaves us just where we were before it was written, as far as any declaration of the Government's intention is concerned. There will no doubt be a great deal of disappointment at the Premier's failure to state definitely that legislation would be introduced during the present session, as there has been general and well-warranted expectation that this would have been done.

"Still, I think that Mr. Ross rightly interprets the general opinion of the temperance people in the view that they would not accept anything short of the abolition of the bar-room as being a satisfactory fulfilment of the promises that have been made. There is some satisfaction in the fact that the Premier concurred with our views as to the necessity for legislation, and the kind of legislation that the situation demands, and recognizes the situation and the public's demand so far as to say that even if the

PROVINCIAL ACTION.

Government cannot give us such legislation this session they will consider what means are available for further action, though it is puzzling to know what that statement implies.

"My own personal opinion—different, I admit, from that of many other temperance workers—is that anything is better than nothing, and that the right thing to do is to go as far in legislation as it is possible to go. If the Government do nothing, then the Opposition could bring some effective and useful temperance legislation that would meet the gratitude and win the support of many temperance electors. This is a question that ought not to be dealt with merely from a political standpoint, and I believe that if the Government introduced such legislation as has been suggested they would receive considerable support from the other side of the House and would carry their legislation through, even if some Liberals failed to support it."

Election Campaign.

It was evident that the failure of the Liberal party and the Government to follow up the demonstration of public opinion made in the referendum had been a source of weakness for the party. Many ardent Liberals, who were also earnest temperance men, were not willing to accept the expressions given as reasons for inaction and were growing impatient of delay. Moreover, the smallness of the Government's majority in the Legislature and the number of vacant seats made desirable another appeal to the country so as to make the position of both parties in the House more definite.

It was generally understood that an appeal to the country, with no action taken nor any policy declared upon the temperance question, would be a sure courting of defeat. Thus, early in November, 1904, announcement was made of the Liberal Convention to be held in Toronto on the 23rd instant. It was also announced that the Conservative party would hold its conference on the following day.

Deputations were immediately appointed by the Alliance Executive to urge the leaders of both parties to ask their followers to declare in favor of advanced temperance legislation.

PROHIBITION IN CANADA.

In response to the call for the Liberal Convention, there gathered in Massey Hall, on November 23rd and 24th, over 3,000 delegates. Shortly after the opening of the Convention, a Committee on Resolutions, composed of a representative from every riding, with the addition of Cabinet Ministers and a few other delegates, was appointed to prepare a series of resolutions which would constitute a platform for the party.

The Resolutions Committee spent many hours discussing a score of resolutions regarding the temperance question. The committee voted down a resolution embodying the abolish the bar" platform, also resolutions looking toward Government control of the traffic and other allied propositions. Eventually the discussion simmered down to two propositions—one advanced by the Hon. J. M. Gibson for further restricting of the traffic by radical amendments to the license laws, and the other brought forward by Mr. John Ewan and Mr. Spence, asking that every municipality which carried the referendum in 1902 be given prohibition, to go into effect on Jan. 1, 1906, unless such municipality declared against it in the meantime.

Although the majority of the committee were opposed to Mr. Spence's motion, he declined to support Mr. Gibson in his high license restrictions. It was moved by the Hon. A. G. McKay that Mr. Spence and Mr. Gibson retire to another room and try to come to an agreement. This they did, and brought in the following resolutions:

" 1. That a vote shall be held at the municipal elections of Jan. 1, 1906, on the following questions, in each municipality:

" (a) Shall the bars be abolished?

" (b) Shall the shop licenses be abolished?

" 2. That a majority vote shall be decisive in each municipality.

" 3. That in the municipalities that vote to abolish the bars and the shop licenses, or either, the vote shall be final; that is, there shall be no provision for any future appeal to the electorate.

" 4. That in municipalities which declare against prohibition, the question may not be again submitted for at least three years after Jan. 1, 1906, but in three years the question must be again

PROVINCIAL ACTION.

submitted if 25 per cent. of the voters sign a petition to that effect.

"5. That in any municipality where the license system remains no license shall be granted unless it is petitioned for by at least 50 per cent., not of the ratepayers in the polling divisions, as at present, but 50 per cent. of the municipal voters in the district which includes a number of women.

"6. That no new licenses shall hereafter, forever, be granted in the unorganized districts of New Ontario.

"7. That no hotel sites shall be sold by the Government except on the understanding that no liquor shall be sold in them."

The resolution was submitted to the committee by the Hon. J. M. Gibson, who gave it his support. Mr. Spence spoke briefly, expressing his entire approval. The resolution was adopted by the committee, but not unanimously, some dozen votes being cast against it.

The temperance resolutions were presented to the convention in the afternoon of November 24th. The following summary of what was done at this session is condensed from the report of the *Toronto Daily Star:*

"The closing session of the convention, lasting from 2.30 until almost 6 o'clock, Thursday afternoon, was marked by the most intense excitement, and at the same time, generally speaking, with the most perfect good feeling. The pivot about which the battle raged was the temperance resolutions recommended by the Committee on Resolutions, and presented to the convention by Mr. Robert Holmes, ex-M.P. As soon as they were read, some of the pronounced opponents of prohibition made attempts to throw them out altogether.

"But the convention, as a body, was in no humor for any such negative action. Lashed to enthusiasm by orations from Messrs. F. S. Spence, Rev. F. Chisholm, Leeds; J. S. Grant, North Brant; Rev. G. B. Brown of Blenheim, and several other temperance advocates, it looked for a time as though the most radical platform of reform could have been put before the convention and carried unanimously.

"Among the first speakers was Mr. F. S. Spence, who was given an excellent hearing. 'There are a couple of reasons,' said

PROHIBITION IN CANADA.

he, ' but I will only mention one, for advanced legislation. One of them is the promises that have been given by our leaders. Some, I believe, will challenge that. I want to say right here, in view of the public sentiment of the province, as revealed in the votes that were taken, the leaders were right in giving the promise. Not only does the country need advanced legislation, but it was entitled to it because of the promise given, backed up by public sentiment. When Sir Oliver Mowat asked our opinion, we gave in favor of the suppression of the liquor traffic a majority of 82,000 —a magnificent majority. When Premier Ross submitted the question two years ago, we gave a majority of 96,000—such a majority as never was before recorded in this country on behalf of any Government, any party, or policy laid down by the people.

"Mr. Spence said he thought, personally, that those votes would have justified the convention in going a great deal further than the resolutions, but the committee had thrown out a plank to abolish the bar, and although some of his friends might not agree with him, he was willing to accept the compromise.

"Mr. A. B. Spencer, of Collingwood, and Mr. Stapleton Caldecott, of Toronto, favored the resolution, but Dr. Adams, of Kingston, told the people that they were asking a political party to commit political suicide.

"Mr. James McLaughlin moved an amendment to compensate those who had been affected by the passing of local option laws, but the amendment was voted down by an overwhelming majority.

"W. S. Buwell, of Brockville, seconded by J. McD. Mowat, of Kingston, moved that the third clause of the resolution, providing for a compulsory vote in 1906, be stricken out. They told the convention that if such a clause were adopted the Liberals would lose both Brockville and Kingston. Mr. Edward Devlin, of Ottawa, told them they would have no chance to win in Ottawa. Hon. A. G. McKay intimated that on such a platform his head might drop in North Grey. Mr. W. F. Summerhayes said that the passing of such a clause would lose them East York. Other members, who opposed the clause, were Alfred Wood, Ottawa; D'Arcy Scott, son of the author of the Scott Act; A. E. Dyment, Nipissing; J. B. Pense, Kingston; and J. R. Lumley, Fort William.

"Mr. J. S. Clark, of North Brant, Wm. Rickard, West Durham; Dr. Hunter, West Toronto; Henry Moyle, North Toronto; and Rev. George T. Webb, West Toronto, favored the clause.

PROVINCIAL ACTION.

"Hon. George P. Graham asked the delegates to pause and consider that there were at present scores of municipalities in Ontario that were not under local option, but which had not had a hotel license for years. The proposition was to make these municipalities take a vote. That was the purport of the resolution. He appealed to the temperance people whether they could not agree on the common ground that a petition by 25 per cent. of the electors should insure an appeal to the people on this important question.

"An amendment offered by Mr. N. W. Rowell to effect a compromise was voted down almost as soon as made. The next act of the convention was to vote clause 3 out of the resolution. The remainder of the clauses were carried amidst great enthusiasm. Premier Ross expressed his confidence in the platform the convention had given him, and referring to the temperance question, declared himself delighted with their decision."

The temperance question did not take the prominent place in the Conservative Conference that it did in the Liberal Convention, but the Hon. J. P. Whitney, in his address on the question of policy affecting the party's interest, made a deliverance indicative of his position on the question, which was endorsed by the convention. He referred to the attitude he had taken during the discussion of the Referendum Bill, and quoted his statement of policy made at that time, as a correct exposition of his views at the present time. He said:

"We cannot have prohibition in a province; therefore it is idle to discuss that remedy. I believe the remedy lies rather in using the powers that we possess, namely, wholesome restriction —a decrease in the number of licenses, removing those charged with the administration of the law from political and party influences, and honestly enforcing the law."

Mr. John George, ex-M.P.P., moved: "That this conference, recognizing that abuses exist in connection with the liquor traffic places itself on record as being in full sympathy with all well-directed efforts to promote temperance and moral reform."

The resolution, as moved by Mr. George, was adopted.

PROHIBITION IN CANADA.

The Alliance Manifesto.

The action of neither the Liberal Convention nor the Conservative Convention was considered satisfactory by the Dominion Alliance. They were especially disappointed in the Liberal results after all the promises given by successive Liberal Governments. Consequently, on December 2nd, the Executive Committee issued an important manifesto.* It was a lengthy document. It set out the history of the movement that resulted in the promise made by Sir Oliver Mowat and endorsed by his successors. It deeply regretted the course taken by the Liberal Convention in refusing to consider prohibitory legislation and in their makeshift of offering instead a referendum under "arbitrary and unfair requirements." It expressed special disappointment with the Premier's attitude. It strongly repudiated the Ross Government in these words:

"In view of the promises made, the overwhelming mandate of the electors, and the need for effective measures to check the evils of intemperance, the Alliance views the situation as it now exists with the deepest regret and disappointment. The Government has trifled with the great temperance question, has been unfaithful to the pledges and promises of its successive Premiers, and has by its record and recent course on this, the most important issue in provincial politics, forfeited all claim to the support of electors who put temperance principle above partisanship in political affairs."

Finally it emphasized again the principle of the Voters' Leagues and called upon ministers and temperance electors to take active steps for the election of reliable temperance candidates and the defeat of those who do not comply with the requirements set out.

Hon. G. W. Ross replied to the manifesto in the *Toronto Globe*. He considered that he had not in any particular broken Sir Oliver's pledge to introduce "such a prohibition bill as the decision of the Privy Council will warrant." He

---
* See Appendix VIII.

PROVINCIAL ACTION.

had submitted a prohibition bill to a referendum, but since Sir Oliver had made no expressed declaration on the subject of a referendum, the action of employing one would scarcely be called the breaking of a pledge. The conditions under which the vote was held, characterized by the Alliance as arbitrary and unfair, had been endorsed by the whole Legislative Assembly, with the exception of four members. As for the Liberal Convention, it was not a temperance convention, and for it to have placed itself in the hands of the advocates of any form of special legislation, would have been to weaken, if not to destroy, its influence. The views of the Alliance as to the closing of bars and shops had been considered by the Committee on Resolutions, composed of one hundred persons appointed by the convention, and had been rejected by that committee. How, then, could the Alliance expect its views to prevail in a convention of four hundred or in an electorate of over 600,000. Moreover, in blaming the Liberal party, the Alliance entirely ignored the significant declaration on advanced legislation heartily and unanimously conceded by the convention, a recommendation which would, if carried out by legislation and enforced, introduce a new era in temperance and moral reform. These recommendations were passed over by the Alliance in silence.

The Premier said he was heartily delighted with the convention's decision on the temperance question, though his delight was deplored by the Alliance. He was the first Premier of the province who ever saw the great party of which he was leader, in convention assembled, declare itself in favor of advanced temperance legislation. He suggested that the Alliance manifesto would be regarded as so unfair that it would alienate at a serious crisis in its history the great majority of Liberal friends of the temperance movement.

The Alliance, in replying to the Premier, maintained without retrenchment the charges against the Government, and urged temperance electors to rise above partizanship and act according to their judgment and conscience on this moral issue.

PROHIBITION IN CANADA.

The result of the provincial elections held on January 25, 1905, was the overwhelming defeat of the Government and the return of the Conservatives to power with a majority of forty-two in the Legislature. The consensus of opinion was that the overthrow of the Liberal party was in no small degree due to the course followed by the Government in regard to liquor legislation. Temperance men were indignant that their earnest desire for the promotion of moral reform had been traded upon for the benefit of a party. Men who took no interest in the temperance cause condemned the Government and the Liberal party because of their failure to stand honorably by the promises they had made.

SECTION XI.

PROVINCIAL PROHIBITION.

The old doctrine of so-called "Personal Liberty," as still reiterated by some of the retained retinue of the drink-power, was, in days gone by, a convenient theory for the protection of petty tyranny, domestic cruelty, and systematic plunder of the weak for the benefit of the strong or the privileged. It was invoked by wealthy men who sought to extort further gain from their less fortunate fellows. It was pleaded in behalf of the drunken husband or father who claimed the right to torture in his own home those that he ought to succor and protect. It was the cloak of assumed respectability under which brewers and distillers made themselves rich at the cost of starvation of women and children. It was the shield of the coward, the usurer and the brute.

Now it is swept away. The gospel doctrine that man owes a duty to his fellow men has been adopted by every organized Government; and in the present has been given an effectiveness before which the old, heartless, barbaric seeking only of personal welfare has been consigned to disreputable desuetude. For the good of their fellows, men are being called upon, or compelled, to sacrifice money and effort and life itself. The individual's duty towards others and his responsibility for the welfare of all, are real things of life to-day.

Let us hope that this uplift, this practical working out of the great Christ idea, will remain after the war clouds pass, and victory for the principles of honor and justice and liberty emerges from the conflict in which their preservation has been bought by self-sacrifice of the sublimest kind.

I. PRINCE EDWARD ISLAND.

PRINCE EDWARD ISLAND, with the exception of the City of Charlottetown, obtained prohibition under the Canada Temperance Act in 1881. The story of the temperance movement in the Provinces from that time on was a story of successive repeals and enactments of the law in Charlottetown. (See Canada Temperance Act, P.E.I.)

A second period of "Free Rum" followed the repeal of the Canada Temperance Act in 1897. Public opinion in the province was so strongly opposed to the liquor traffic that it was deemed unwise to enact a license law. But in 1898, at the request of the temperance people of Charlottetown, the Assembly passed a Liquor Regulation Act, practically a re-enactment of the Act of 1892, with some additional restrictions. The chief provisions of this act were·

"That liquor was not to be sold to anyone under 18 years of age; an hour for early closing was fixed; no liquor was to be sold on election days, Dominion, Provincial, or Civic, or on public holidays; anyone treating another to liquor was to be fined from $2 to $5, or to be imprisoned from 10 to 25 days; druggists were to keep open to inspection a record of sales made; doctors were liable to a penalty for false prescription; on the petition of a majority of residents of any street or block, for the closing of any place where liquor was being sold on their street or block, such place was to be closed; any person desiring to sell liquor was to register with the Colonial Secretary and to pay $100 registration fee, to be renewed every six months."

In 1898 the Premier introduced a bill to amend this act, by providing for taxation of liquor sellers. The measure was opposed in the Legislature by those who objected on principle to the raising of public revenue from the traffic or participating in any degree in the proceeds from it. Moreover, the Dominion plebiscite vote had just been announced, and it was hoped that the result would be a Dominion law which would supersede all provincial legislation.

Temperance workers suggested to the Assembly a measure that would, to some extent, meet the need of restriction and would cover the ground dealt with in the Premier's proposed bill, while it would leave out the objectionable feature of license revenue. Their plan was to have a registration deposit of $200 cash as a guarantee, on the one hand, of good faith on the part of the seller, and on the other hand, as security for fine in case of violation of the law, the deposit to be returned in full by order of a properly authorized official, if the person registered retired from business. There was to be no place of sale in any block where there might be a church, a school, or a hospital, or in any other block in the city unless by consent of three-fourths of the ratepayers. Places of sale were to be closed from 9 p.m. to 3 a.m., with the exception of Saturdays, when they were to be closed from 4 p.m. until Monday morning at 8 o'clock, and on market days from 12 noon until 8 a.m. the next morning. No sale was to be made by minors or to minors. Nothing but liquor was to be sold in places registered. Fitting penalties for law violation were to be exacted. These suggestions were not incorporated in the Government bill, which was defeated.

In 1899, the Tax Act, amending the Regulation Act, was introduced by Premier Farquharson and passed by the Legislature. It taxed not only the liquor stores and saloons $200 per annum, but also commercial travellers who dealt in liquor. There was a $400 tax on breweries. The hours for sale on market days were shortened from 10 p.m. to 7 p.m. No liquor was to be sold to anyone under 18. There was to be no treating.

When the Federal Government had refused to enact a prohibitory law following the Dominion plebiscite, prohibition workers strongly expressed their condemnation of that refusal and called upon the Provincial Government to give a provincial law.

PROVINCIAL PROHIBITION.

At the annual meeting of the Prince Edward Island Alliance on April 12, 1900, it was resolved that the Legislature be urged to enact such a law as would prohibit the sale of liquors in the City of Charlottetown. The Executive waited on the Government with its request. The Government, in reply, asked the Alliance to have a bill drafted at the Government's expense. While the committee was proceeding with this work, they were informed that an Act applying only to the city would not be considered by the Government. They were thus obliged, in the hope of getting any legislation whatever, to prepare a general Act.

On May 24, 1900, a bill was presented to the Premier and members of the Legislature by a deputation representing the leading temperance organizations of the province. The deputation asked that the License Law passed the previous year be abrogated, and that the Legislature enact the bill prohibiting the sale of liquor, which had been prepared with careful regard to keeping within the legislative powers of the Province. It provided for no interference with the Scott Act in the counties, but was to take effect in any county if the Scott Act should be repealed by a vote of the electors. It was to go into force in September, 1900.

The Premier told the delegation that he was awaiting an answer from the Hon. David Mills, Minister of Justice, regarding questions submitted to him concerning provincial jurisdiction in prohibitory legislation.

In June, there was introduced in the Legislature, not the measure asked for by the temperance delegation, but a bill "For the purpose of prohibiting the sale of intoxicating liquors within this Province where the Canada Temperance Act does not apply except for sacramental, medicinal and mechanical purposes by vendors thereto specially appointed, and by physicians, chemists and druggists under certain conditions, also by wholesale dealers to vendors, physicians, chemists and druggists as aforesaid, and to others if the liquor sold is not intended for consumption within this province." The act also imposed fines and penalties for violation of its provisions and authorized the Government to appoint inspectors to supervise its enforcement. It was to come into force on the 5th day of June, 1901. In the opinion of the temperance workers, this measure was much weaker than the one asked for.

In moving the House into committee for consideration of the prohibition Act of 1900, Mr. Farquharson said that he was going to fulfill his promise made at meetings throughout the country to give a measure prohibiting liquor-selling to the extent of provincial power. He did not know how the Opposition would vote. He hoped they would support the bill, but the Government could carry it without them. In anticipation of this measure, he had telegraphed to the Minister of Justice regarding the question of provincial jurisdiction, but had not yet received a reply. He had also telegraphed to the Hon. Hugh John Macdonald, Premier of Manitoba, asking for a copy of the prohibition bill that had been announced in the Manitoba Legislature. A copy would be sent to him as soon as it was out of the printer's hands.

The Prince Edward Island Prohibition Act was not to go into effect for a year. That was in order to give the Minister of Justice time to pronounce upon its constitutionality. The bill was absolute in so far as it could go. It could not prohibit importation and manufacture. That, a Dominion law alone could do; but, if they could not get Dominion prohibition, they could at least stop the sale of liquor.

Several amendments to render the act more stringent were moved in committee by the Opposition and rejected. The bill, in its original form, was passed by a unanimous vote of the Legislature.

After the passing of the Prince Edward Island Prohibition Law, the Manitoba law was declared invalid by the Court of the King's Bench of Manitoba. In view of this decision, it was suggested that the operation of the Island Act be suspended until the powers of the province should be defined by the decision of the Supreme Court of Canada or the Imperial Privy Council. There was a fear expressed that chaos

PROVINCIAL PROHIBITION.

would result from an attempt to enforce the law without a settlement of the case. Instead of suspending the act, however, the Government proposed, in April, 1901, the following amendment, with the idea of making the act doubly sure of enforcement:

"While this act is intended to prohibit and shall prohibit transactions in liquor which take place wholly within the Province of Prince Edward Island, except as otherwise specially specified by this act, and shall restrict the consumption of liquor within the limits of the Province of Prince Edward Island, it shall not affect, and is not intended to affect *bona fide* transactions in liquor between a person in the Province of Prince Edward Island and a person in another province or in a foreign country, and the provisions of this act shall be construed accordingly."

The amendment was agreed to without discussion and without change.

When the law was first put into force some little friction occurred on the question of where the responsibility for its enforcement should lie. The city council of Charlottetown decided by resolution that the municipal police officers should take no part in the prosecutions under the act, and that the enforcement should be left with the Provincial Government. The liquor interests hoped by this means to block the operation of the act. Their plans were frustrated, however, by the action of the Marshal of Police in serving the papers issued by the stipendiary magistrate in compliance with his oath of service.

The validity of the prohibition law was definitely established by judgment of the Supreme Court of Prince Edward Island, delivered on January 14, 1902. That decision was the result of the action of Angus McDonald, who, being convicted by the stipendiary magistrate for Charlottetown on July 22, 1901, of having unlawfully sold in Charlottetown intoxicating liquor, contrary to the provisions of the Prohibition Act, sought to have the conviction quashed by appealing to the Supreme Court of Judicature. He took the ground that the prohibitory Act was *ultra vires* of the Legislature that enacted it, in as much as it encroached upon a regulation of trade and commerce, a subject which, by section 91 B.N.A., was under the authority of the Canadian Parliament.

The act was defended on the ground that it dealt with property and civil rights in the province, or—" generally all matters of a merely local or private nature in the province." (Section 92 B.N.A.)

The decision of the Imperial Privy Council sustaining the Manitoba Liquor Act of 1900 was deemed to cover the case of the Prince Edward Island law, and to apply with equal or added force to Prince Edward Island, since the Island Act was less stringent than the Manitoba measure. The application of Angus McDonald for a writ of *certiorari* was refused with costs.

While rejoicing in the triumph of the prohibition law, temperance workers fully realized that the cause of reform depended not on legislation but on results. The machinery of the Act was still defective. A special meeting of the Charlottetown Branch of the Dominion Alliance was called on February 20, 1902, to consider the desirability of several amendments to the law in order to secure more rigid enforcement. The amendments considered necessary were, right of search, the possession of liquor and other equipments of the liquor trade to be deemed *prima facie* evidence of an infraction of the law; confiscation of the liquors to the Government; proprietors of saloon buildings to be held liable for the penalties incurred by tenants by violating the law; the delegalizing of the wholesale trade of liquor within the province; and placing of further restrictions upon the vendors appointed under the act.

The meeting appointed a committee to obtain legal advice and prepare a draft of such amendments to be submitted at the coming session of the Legislature. The committee was also instructed to urge upon the Premier the necessity of appointing an official assistant prosecutor, with power of

PROVINCIAL PROHIBITION.

bailiff, for the more thorough enforcement of the prohibition law, and the prompt collection of fines.

The amendments introduced by the Legislature in the session of 1902 were as follows

(1) All druggists and vendors were required to make returns of all liquors sold.

(2) Physicians giving fraudulent prescriptions were liable to a fine of from $20 to $40.

(3) Right of search was granted and force might be used to effect entrance to a suspected place.

(4) Liquor seized was to be destroyed.

(5) For interference with officers in the discharge of their duty, a fine of $100 was imposed.

(6) Beverages containing 3 per cent. alcohol were to be considered intoxicating within the meaning of the Act.

It was now strongly urged by the temperance people that the provincial law offered better machinery for enforcement and was altogether more satisfactory than the Dominion measure. Consequently, the Canada Temperance Act was repealed in the counties which had adopted it, and the entire island was thus brought under provincial prohibition.

II. NOVA SCOTIA.

Nova Scotia has always been a stronghold of temperance sentiment. It claims the first temperance organization in Canada. It has counties from which the legalized liquor traffic has been excluded for three-quarters of a century. Its Scott Act record is a demonstration of the hostility of the people towards the liquor trade, and in the provincial and the Dominion plebiscites the province rolled up large prohibition majorities.

Moreover, the Nova Scotia license law was an exceedingly stringent one, and made it very difficult for the traffic to retain a foothold. The law provided that, except in the City

PROHIBITION IN CANADA.

of Halifax, no license should be granted unless the applicant secured the consent in writing of two-thirds of the ratepayers in the polling subdivision in which the license was to take effect. In Halifax the proportion required was three-fifths. These petitions, verified by oath, had to be obtained every year; otherwise renewal of the licenses would not be permitted. As a result of this strong law, there were licenses in only three counties of the province, namely, Halifax, Cape Breton, and Richmond. Halifax City, with ninety liquor-selling places, acted as a centre of degrading influence, and made the enforcement of prohibition very difficult all over the province.

Various efforts were made to have amendments passed to remedy these abuses. One such attempt was the Labelling Bill of 1901, endorsed by the Presbytery of Truro. It was a measure requiring the labelling of all packages of liquor shipped within a county district, with the object of preventing mail coaches from carrying such liquors. The bill was deferred in 1901, was brought forward a second time the following year, and again failed to pass the Legislature.

The need was keenly felt for a comprehensive provincial prohibitory liquor law with adequate enforcing machinery. The only explanation that could be given by the Provincial Government for non-compliance with the will of the people, as expressed by the plebiscites of 1893 and 1898, was that the decision of the Supreme Court of Canada placed the subject beyond the provincial authorities. When this difficulty was removed by the decision of the Privy Council, a definite move was made by prohibitionists to press their demand upon the Government.

On January 15, 1902, a prohibition convention of one hundred and sixty-eight delegates at Truro adopted the following resolution:

"Whereas the Privy Council has, in a recent decision *re* the Manitoba Act, shown that the prohibition of the liquor traffic is within the power of the Provincial Legislature:

PROVINCIAL PROHIBITION.

"Resolved that this convention petition the Legislature of Nova Scotia, at its approaching session, to enact a law prohibiting the liquor traffic in this province, and that a committee of twenty-seven be appointed, each county to be represented, to wait upon the Legislature, and that this committee be empowered to assist in every way possible in maturing such legislation in order that it may be fully satisfactory to the temperance people of this province."

A deputation waited on the Government on February 19th with this request, to which, a month later, the following reply was given:

"HALIFAX, N.S., March 24th, 1902.

"*Dear Sir·*

"Sometime in the early part of the session a delegation of gentlemen, of which you were the head, waited upon the Government and asked for the enactment of a provincial prohibitory act. You were advised at the conclusion of the meeting that the Government would give the subject of your application their most careful consideration.

"I have to advise you that this matter has received the most careful and earnest consideration by the Government, and we have reached the conclusion that for various reasons it would not be expedient to introduce a provincial act at the present time.

"Yours very truly,

"(Signed) J. W. LONGLEY.

"A. M. Bell, Esq."

A convention held at Halifax on March 11, 1903, discussed the Government's reply to the Truro Convention. There were some delegates who saw no encouragement to press on with the demand for a provincial law. They argued that the Scott Act was in force in the parts of the province where prohibition sentiment was strong enough to sustain it, and that it was folly to think of a prohibition law for Halifax since the license law was there so indifferently enforced. They advised, therefore, concentration upon license law enforcement and amendments of the Canada Temperance Act. There were others who looked upon that attitude as endorsement of the Government's action and as an impossible surrender. It was the views of the latter which prevailed, and the convention adopted the following resolution:

"This convention affirms its conviction that while prohibition by the Government of the Dominion is the only satisfactory and final solution of the liquor problem, yet that it is the duty of the Legislature of Nova Scotia to promote prohibitory legislation by enacting, at as early a date as possible, the largest measure of prohibitory legislation within their jurisdiction, and that in the meantime the Legislature be requested to amend the Provincial License Law at the present session in the direction of making its prohibitory clauses more easily enforceable."

The Government's only response that year was to discuss the introduction of the Gothenburg system of licensing, and to defeat again the Labelling Bill of 1901 and 1902, introduced as Pearson's Bill with a somewhat wider scope.

In a personal letter from an Alliance worker, dated October 19, 1903, we read:

"The outlook at present is very discouraging in Nova Scotia. Partyism has taken all the life and hope out of the prohibition movement and advocates. Those who were leaders are so busy gathering in their harvest of good things that their former love is forgotten.'

Several amendments were made during the year in the license law, some of no practical value, some slightly favorable, one very good one, which made an inspector under the Canada Temperance Act liable to a fine of $100, and forfeiture of his office if he failed within ten days to prosecute, after having received information furnished by a ratepayer.

In 1904, Mr. Pearson (Colchester) re-introduced his bill to prevent the sale of intoxicating liquor in Scott Act or other prohibition territory, and again it was defeated.

But the same year a very peculiar legislative action was taken in amending the Assessment Act. This act contained

PROVINCIAL PROHIBITION.

only one section, to which was added section 2, containing three subsections, and section 3, dealing with the Stipendiaries Act and so amending that act as to cover up all reference to it excepting the mere mention of it in the title. Under provincial law, violators of the Canada Temperance Act might be summoned before the county stipendary instead of the local magistrate. The act of 1904 took away this power and gave exclusive authority to local magistrates. This made it almost impossible in some localities to secure convictions, especially for second and third offences. The strange part of the affair was that there was no record as to when the amendment was added. It was smuggled through during the closing hours of the session, and so irregular were the circumstances attending this enactment that Rev. H. R. Grant, speaking for the Presbyterian Synod and other churches, asked the Government to repeal the legislation and pursue an investigation as to its passing. Investigation was refused; the act was repealed, but a new one was adopted which made the principle of the former one applicable to the whole province.

In 1905, a measure of retrograde nature was passed by the Legislature, in a bill providing a special license law for the City of Halifax. It increased the city's interest in the traffic by raising the license fee. It removed the prohibition of the consumption of liquor on hotel premises on which it was sold, thus providing for bar-room drinking, which had been before this time prohibited in Nova Scotia. It repealed a provision of the existing license law which prohibited the granting of a license to any premises within 100 yards of a railway station, and lengthened the hours of sale on Saturday night from six to nine p.m., and on other nights from nine to ten.

The Provincial Prohibition Convention at Truro, on June 27, 1905, took a significant stand with regard to political action. The following resolution was adopted:—

"Resolved, that this convention hereby commits itself to the completion of the work begun at the convention of 1902, to take such steps as it deems necessary to replace in our Legislature those hostile to further legislation with those who will represent the churches and opinions of the majority on this question by the enactment and enforcement of provincial prohibition."

The political platform agreed upon was outlined as follows:

"This convention, believing that in the present circumstances provincial prohibition is the best possible method of dealing with the liquor trade, resolves to ascertain from the leaders of both political parties, within thirty days, their attitude on the question and pledges itself to support the representatives of the party that will undertake immediately to provide for the enactment of, and the efficient enforcement of the strongest prohibitory legislation possible under the constitution. In event of their leaders refusing to commit themselves to provincial prohibition, we pledge ourselves to work for the nomination and election of candidates, irrespective of party, who will pledge themselves to cast their votes for the enactment of prohibitory legislation when introduced by either of the parties or by private members."

As a result of this convention, the Nova Scotia Temperance Alliance was formed with the purpose of unifying the different temperance organizations and of carrying on a campaign for provincial prohibition. The following officers were elected for the ensuing year:

President............R. H. Eaton, Dartmouth.
Vice-President.........Rev. H. R. Grant, Trenton.
Secretary..............W. S. Sanders, Halifax.
Treasurer.............A. B. Fletcher, Truro.

An executive committee representing the counties was appointed.

Special mention should be made of the work of the Pictou County Temperance Association, of which Rev. H. R. Grant was secretary. The purpose of the organization was to secure the co-operation of churches, Woman's Christian Temperance Unions, and Young Men's Christian Associations, lodges, and temperance societies, to enlist the interest of earnest citizens in encouraging the officials to enforce the law, to strengthen the sentiment already exist-

PROVINCIAL PROHIBITION.

ing against the saloon, and to foster a more virile public spirit on the whole question. Various methods were employed, including a pledge-signing campaign, distribution of literature, and Gospel temperance meetings. When it was started there were in the county as many open drinking places as churches. In a little over two years there was not one open drinking place or bar-room in the county, and the arrests for drunkenness had been reduced over fifty per cent. The Association might well claim a share of the credit for the progress made, especially for its part in securing the co-operation of temperance forces.

On July 20, the Alliance Executive interviewed the members of the Government, presenting the following resolutions from this convention:

1. That provincial prohibition in the present circumstances is the best possible method of dealing with the liquor traffic.

2. That the time has come to ascertain from the leaders of both political parties their attitude on the question, and to ask a definite answer, "Yes" or "No," as to whether they will put a prohibition plank in their platform. Respectfully ask for such an answer.

The answer of the Government, given after deliberation, was to declare itself opposed to a prohibition law and in favor of the license system.

On the other hand, the Conservative convention in 1905 gave its pledge that, upon that party's accession to power, a plebiscite would at once be taken, and if the majority of votes polled were in favor of provincial prohibition, such a law would be immediately enacted. In the County of Pictou, two Conservative candidates, Messrs. C. E. Tanner and J. M. Baillie, showed themselves in earnest on the question, and were backed up by a declaration of the party convention that nominated them. Mr. C. E. Tanner, in a published address to the electors, declared for the Alliance policy in unequivocal terms. Consequently, the Alliance convention of 1906 endorsed these two men, and urged all temperance voters throughout the province to support them in the coming election. Both candidates were elected. The return of Mr. Tanner, who at the session of 1906 became leader of the Opposition, gave a great impetus to the prohibition movement, and from year to year the demand for prohibition became more insistent.

In 1906 was passed the McGregor Bill, a modification of the measure drafted by the temperance people the previous year. In its changed form, however, it was useless. While it forbade the shipment of liquor into Canada Temperance Act and no-license counties, to be paid for C.O.D., and enacted penalties on seller and carrier, its provisions were made unworkable. Proof was required that the sender had shipped liquor, "knowing or having good reason to believe that the person or persons to whom such liquor was sent were engaged in the sale of liquor contrary to law." Also it was provided that carriers were guilty only when knowingly took or carried liquor from or at the request of or on behalf of a licenser to be paid for C.O.D.

In the session of 1907, the temperance question occupied a prominent place in the Legislature. Since 1903 the temperance people had been pressing the Government, not for prohibition, but for amendments to the license law. In 1907 they revived their demand for a provincial prohibition law, which the Government again refused.

On February 28th, Mr. E. H. Armstrong, of Yarmouth, as a private member, introduced a bill based on the Provincial Act of Prince Edward Island. On motion for its second reading on March 26th, the Premier, the Hon. G. H. Murray, objected that it could not constitutionally be read since, as a measure affecting the revenue, it must be introduced by the Government. The Speaker sustained the point of order and ruled that the motion for the second reading could not be put. Mr. Armstrong at once gave notice that he would ask the Government to bring in a similar bill.

On February 15th, Mr. C. E. Tanner moved in amendment to the address on the Speech from the Throne:

PROVINCIAL PROHIBITION.

"That the House regrets that reference is not made to the traffic in intoxicating liquors, and is of opinion that the Government should immediately deal with that vital subject by means of a provincial prohibition measure."

After considerable debate, the motion was lost on a vote of 25 to 6.

On April 3rd, when Mr. Armstrong's resolution came up for discussion, an amendment was proposed by Rev. C. F. Cooper (Queens), favoring the Scott Act rather than provincial prohibition. The following day Mr. Tanner moved an amendment to the Cooper amendment:

"That in the opinion of this House the Government advise consent of his Honor the Lieutenant-Governor to the money clauses on the bill entitled 'An Act to prohibit the sale of intoxicating liquor,' introduced in this House on the 28th of February last, and proceed with the same this session as a Government measure.

"And further resolved, that this House requests the Dominion Government and Parliament to supplement the said measure by enacting a law prohibiting the importing of liquors into and manufacture of liquors in Nova Scotia."

After a lengthy debate, provincial prohibition was defeated overwhelmingly, the Conservatives and one Liberal (Mr. C. A. Campbell, of Kings) voting for it, and the Liberals voting against it.

Two government measures amending the license law were enacted during the session. One bill reduced the number of licenses in Halifax from 114 to 90 until the census of 1911, and after that one for every six hundred inhabitants. The liquor men made a strong, but unsuccessful, effort to have included in the measure a withdrawal of the provision by which petitions for licenses required certificates with the signature of three-fifths of the ratepayers. The other bill was an attempt to deal with the long-standing question of the shipment of liquor into prohibition territories. It was introduced by the Attorney-General, and passed the

PROHIBITION IN CANADA.

Lower House with slight alteration, and the Legislative Council without change.

It forbade licensees and other persons in Halifax to send liquor to any one other than a properly qualified vendor in Canada Temperance Act and no-license counties. It provided for proper labelling of packages and forbade carriers to receive packages improperly marked or sent to any one other than licensed vendors. It gave power to inspectors to open suspected packages. It empowered stipendiary magistrates to inquire of prisoners, drunk and incapable, where they procured liquor. It forbade commercial travellers and agents to solicit orders in prohibition territory. It imposed heavy penalties for any violation of the law.

On January 21, 1908, the annual prohibition convention at Truro decided to confine its representation to the Government to definite issues of (1) Provincial prohibition as far as possible; (2) Federal legislation to cover manufacture, importation and such other necessary points as might not lie within provincial authority; (3) Provision for all necessary enforcing machinery under thorough provincial control instead of municipal enforcement as heretofore.

On February 25, 1908, a representative body of men met in the Y.M.C.A. Hall, Halifax, at the call of the Alliance. In the evening they went to the Legislative Council Chamber, and were granted a two hours' conference with the Premier and his Cabinet. The speakers of the deputation submitted the draft of a prohibition bill drawn up by temperance workers. In reply, Premier Murray intimated that the policy of the Government was not to enact provincial prohibition, but to further amend the License Act, and in addition to seek federal legislation which would so amend the Canada Temperance Act as to prohibit importation into and manufacture in counties in which that act was or might thereafter be in force. The deputation declared that they could not assume responsibility for this policy.

In 1909, the Alliance decided to bring the question into the House of Assembly and ascertain the stand of individual

PROVINCIAL PROHIBITION.

members of the Legislature on the question, and a resolution favoring prohibition was introduced by an Independent member, Mr. C. A. Campbell (Kings), and seconded by R. H. McKay (Pictou). The resolution was defeated, but its introduction proved to be of immense value to the cause. The debates in the House were read throughout the province, and the arguments for and against aroused great interest and provoked discussion in every county.

In November of this year a by-election was held in Hants County. The Alliance made prohibition an issue, and the prohibitionist, Mr. Albert Parsons, won the day. Before the opening of the House in 1910, a by-election was held in Queens County, and the prohibition candidate, Mr. W. L. Hall, was elected.

On March 15, 1910, the Alliance again pressed upon the Government their petition for the enactment of a provincial law. Premier Murray expressed his sympathy with the deputation and indicated the Government's intention to make some improvements in the license law at an early date. Disapproval of this reply was voiced by a resolution moved in the House on March 30th, by C. A. Campbell, seconded by R. M. McKay, declaring in the words of the Alliance resolution of 1908 that it was the Government's duty to enact a provincial prohibitory law. The Premier immediately declined to discuss the resolution in view of the legislation soon to be introduced, and the debate on Mr. Campbell's motion was adjourned.

On April 13th, Attorney-General McLean introduced into the Legislature a bill which marked a distinct change of policy on the part of the Government. It made possible total prohibition of the sale in the province of intoxicating liquor for beverage purposes. It was so framed, however, as to require further action on the part of electors favorable thereto. The sale of liquor was to be prohibited except (*a*) in the Canada Temperance Act counties, which comprised eight of the eighteen counties of the province; (*b*) in Richmond County; (*c*) in Halifax.

PROHIBITION IN CANADA.

The prohibitory law was to come into force in Richmond County on the expiry of the licenses there; in Halifax, by proclamation issued any time after sixty days of the registering of a majority vote in favor of the law, such vote to be taken when petitioned for by one-fourth of the electors; in Canada Temperance Act counties, upon repeal of the Canada Temperance Act. Provision was made for the sale of liquor under specified conditions for medicinal, scientific and sacramental purposes. Municipalities were to enforce the law, but there was to be a Government inspection and Government officials were to take over the administration in case of failure by the municipalities. Especially valuable features of the law were the prohibition of shipment of liquor into prohibition territory, and the strict regulations to prevent abuse of the authorized sale.

The bill was taken up by the Law Amendments Committee on April 18th, when representatives of the temperance and anti-temperance interests were invited to discuss the measure. Rev. H. R. Grant objected to certain details, reiterating that the Alliance stood by its demand for absolute prohibition. The act was passed on April 22nd. In a statement issued in June, the Alliance expressed appreciation of the Government's move, which, while not a settlement of the prohibition question, was nevertheless a distinct step in advance. "The Alliance has great reason to be encouraged with the progress made, under the blessing of God, in temperance reform, and the Executive believes that by earnest and united efforts in every county the goal toward which the Alliance has been striving will soon be reached."

The Alliance convention in February, 1911, asked the counties not to take action to repeal the Canada Temperance Act until the Nova Scotia Temperance Act should be amended. A deputation presented to the Premier and the Attorney-General a list of desired amendments. They also reminded the ministers of the Alliance policy of pledging political candidates to support such measures and of uniting to oppose them if they did not comply. This policy the

PROVINCIAL PROHIBITION.

Attorney-General characterized as *unfair and undecent.* "Scallawags are more apt to consent to pledges than are respectable men," said he. Certain amendments increasing the power of enforcing officials were passed by the Government in March, but the change most desired by temperance workers, namely, the extension of the prohibitory law to Halifax, was not made, the Premier declaring it to be his opinion that special conditions existing in that city necessitated special legislation.

Under the amended law, the Scott Act counties set to work in 1914 to obtain repeals of the Scott Act in order that the Nova Scotia Temperance Act might come into force. In these contests, curiously enough, the liquor dealers, especially those in Halifax, worked to sustain Scott Act prohibition, which they regarded as the lesser of two evils. They feared a temperance victory that would establish legislation under which shipments from their warehouses might be seized. Further, they feared that victory in Scott Act counties would encourage temperance workers to direct their efforts anew to the suppression of the traffic in Halifax.

The *Wine and Spirit Journal* declared, after the repeal in Pictou, Hants, Kings and Cumberland, " The question of prohibition for Halifax is sure to come up at the next session."

Their fears were not ungrounded. In 1912, 1913 and 1914 the Government was repeatedly asked to place Halifax under prohibition; and while they persistently refused to do so, their resistance was gradually weakening. The argument for the extension of the act was strongly set forth in a statement by the Alliance Secretary, Rev. H. R. Grant, as follows:

" The province suffers as well as the city by reason of the existence of the licensed trade. It suffers in two ways: First, it suffers because hundreds of young men, for a time residents of the city, have been ruined by its clubs and bar-rooms; we could name not a few bright young men from country homes whom the licensed bars of the city have destroyed. Second, the province suffers because the Halifax liquor interests give encouragement to the illicit dealers in the counties; back of every dive-keeper in Nova Scotia is some wholesale Halifax dealer; these brethren of the traffic stand by each other and for each other. No illicit trader in the province is too disreputable to receive supplies fraudulently sent by the Halifax liquor trade. The Halifax trade is the stronghold of liquordom in Nova Scotia."

In 1915, the request of the temperance workers was repeated and the bill expressing it, moved by C. E. Tanner, was defeated only by the casting vote of the Speaker. On February 22, 1916, a bill to bring Halifax under the provincial prohibition law after June 30, 1916, was introduced as a private measure by H. W. Corning (Yarmouth), and solidly supported by the Conservative Opposition. Discussion on the measure was defeated by the Government several times, on the ground that amendments to it were being prepared, but it came up for a second reading on March 13th in its original form. It was debated for two days and three nights. Premier Murray finally announced that he would vote for the measure, though he professed little faith in prohibition because of the elaborate and expensive machinery necessary for its enforcement.

The bill met with some opposition also in the Legislative Council. There a small group of members did what they could to delay the coming into force of the measure until after September 15th, to allow liquor dealers to dispose of their stock, but after four divisions had been taken on as many amendments, the bill making Halifax a prohibition city and thus enacting total prohibition for the Province of Nova Scotia was passed on April 29th. It became effective on June 30, 1916.

PROVINCIAL PROHIBITION.

III. NEW BRUNSWICK.

The New Brunswick liquor license law of 1896 contained provisions for prohibiting the liquor traffic by local option. The conditions of voting were, however, inimical to the success of the temperance cause. Upon petition of one-fourth of the ratepayers of any ward of a city or town, or any parish of the township, the municipality was obliged to take a vote on the question of whether or not licenses should be issued in that locality. But the vote required to prohibit the licenses was a majority of the names on the voters' lists. That is to say, in a contest where there were 1,000 names on the list, if 500 votes were recorded in favor of prohibition, even if there were not a single vote polled against it, the temperance forces would be defeated, because 501 votes were needed for victory. All that the friends of the liquor traffic needed to do, was to refrain from voting. Every dead man whose name had not been erased from the list, every sick man, every man who failed to vote, was reckoned as an opponent of prohibition.

Because of the obvious unfairness of these conditions there was no attempt for many years on the part of temperance workers in the province to make use of the local option section of the license law, and the clause remained a dead letter. Instead, attention was concentrated upon securing local prohibition through the adoption of the Canada Temperance Act. By 1918 the Dominion law was in force in nine of the fifteen counties and two of the three cities, Moncton and Fredericton. The only instance of the repeal of the act after its adoption was in the old city of Portland, when it was amalgamated with the city of St. John.

Several appeals were made to the Government at different times to pass a provincial prohibitory law. Early in 1900, the Sons of Temperance in New Brunswick circulated for signature a petition to the Governor-General of Canada, calling attention to the failure of the Provincial Government to promote legislation in accordance with the majority of votes

PROHIBITION IN CANADA.

polled in the provincial plebiscite, and requesting the Governor-General to ask the Lieutenant-Governor to introduce a prohibitory law or else resign.

On March 22, 1902, a petition was presented to the Provincial Government, containing the names of 9,369 residents, and asking for legislation similar to that recently enacted in Manitoba. The speakers of the deputation urged, not only the force of the signatures, but also the sentiment of the province as evidenced by the plebiscite vote of 1898. Their request was refused.

Again in March, 1904, the Sons of Temperance, on behalf of the temperance people of St. John, asked that the Government should enact a provincial prohibitory law or, failing that, certain amendments to the existing license law. About thirty suggestions for improving the law were advanced by the temperance committee, which waited upon the Government. The answer given by Premier Tweedie on September 17th, was to the effect that the Legislature was sincerely desirous of advancing the cause of temperance by any rational means; that as far as provincial prohibition was concerned the Government had long been giving it consideration, but had come to the conclusion that such legislation would be premature and would thus have a tendency to set back the cause of temperance for many years. The Government, however, accepted a number of the committee's suggestions for license law amendments, among which were the following:

1. License commissioners were to be elected instead of appointed, and given power to refuse to grant licenses.

2. A liquor license applicant was to be required to obtain a certificate of qualification, signed by a majority of ratepayers in the ward where he proposed to do business.

3. The number of licenses in cities, towns and parishes was to be diminished.

4. No firm or corporation might hold more than one license.

5. Wholesalers were prohibited from selling, except to licensed retailers.

PROVINCIAL PROHIBITION.

6. Re-extension of licenses was made impossible.
7. Beer licenses were to be abolished.
8. Hours of sale were to be from 7 a.m. to 7 p.m.
9. The clause relative to minors working in the liquor business was to be widened.

In 1907, the Government, in response to the demand of a temperance delegation for a prohibitory law, appointed a Royal Commission of three to inquire into the working of prohibition in Prince Edward Island and of the Canada Temperance Act in New Brunswick. The Commission's report delivered on December 5, 1907, declared that a tremendous amount of liquor was being illegally sold on the Island, and that in New Brunswick the Canada Temperance Act, while fairly well enforced in the country districts, was being used in the cities and towns as a means of raising civic revenue, so numerous were the fines imposed for law-breaking.

In the same year attention was again directed to the local option law. Temperance advocates determined to demonstrate its unworkable nature by an attempt to apply it. Early in the winter of 1907, Rev. R. H. Stavart, of Harcourt, Kent County, began an agitation for a local option contest in his parish. He presented to the Kent County Council a petition with more than the required number of signatures, but the Council threw it out, on the grounds that it was not drawn up properly and that there should be some way of proving the names attached to be genuine. At the next Legislative Assembly an amendment was made to the license law, prescribing a form for such petition and requiring that an affidavit attesting to the genuineness of the names be attached by the party circulating the petitions.

In January, 1908, Mr. Stavert appeared before the Kent County Council with a second petition, which was found to be in accordance with the prescribed form; but it was held that only certificates and not affidavits had been given that names were genuine, and the petition was again thrown out.

PROHIBITION IN CANADA.

The case was appealed to the Supreme Court, who sustained the Council's decision.

In 1909, there was presented a third petition with the names of over 50 per cent. of the electors in the parish. On this occasion a new objection was offered. According to Section 20 of the Liquor License Act, the petition must be presented to the warden of the council on or before a certain day preceding the meeting of the council in any year. In the northern part of Kent County, one of the very large parishes had been divided into two smaller ones. The warden of the council to whom the petition was presented had been one of the councillors in the large parish, but had resigned the wardenship to be elected councillor of one of the smaller parishes just created. Mr. Stavert, on presenting to him the petition according to law, was told that he was not legally warden of the council on account of his having resigned to run in a new parish. The law made no provision for presenting the petition to any other than the warden. When the council met, it was decided that the petition had not been legally presented, and again it was thrown out. The case was a second time appealed to the Supreme Court, which once more upheld the decision of the council.

In 1908 the churches of St. John, Roman Catholic and Protestant, co-operated with other moral reform organizations in securing petitions for a local option vote in four wards of the city. The required number of signatures was secured and presented, with a request that the vote be held on the day of the civic election. The request as to the day was refused by the city council; the temperance workers refused to enter the contest under any other condition; and the petitions were withdrawn. Announcement was made that the Provincial Legislature would be asked for such legislation as should allow a fair expression of public opinion.

There was before the Government at the time a petition circulated by the Temperance Federation asking for a prohibitory law. Premier Hazen promised that the question

PROVINCIAL PROHIBITION.

of the liquor traffic would be dealt with at the coming session of the Legislature. The policy of the Government was not yet revealed, and St. John workers delayed further action while awaiting the Government's definite statement in answer to the petitions.

On January 21, 1909, a representative delegation from churches and temperance organizations pressed the Government for a provincial prohibitory law. The Premier gave a tentative verbal reply which was followed by a written statement in March, 1909. He expressed the opinion that the petition containing only 9,731 signatures from a population of 331,120 was not sufficiently strong to justify the enactment of a provincial prohibitory law. Counties might adopt the Canada Temperance Act in those localities where popular sentiment was able to enforce it. However, the Government would introduce amendments to the local option law, which would make the conditions fair.

Upon receipt of the Government's answer, the Moral and Social Reform Council of St. John met and adopted a draft of license law amendments which were presented to the committee of the Government by a deputation consisting of three Protestants and two Roman Catholics. His Lordship, Bishop Richardson, who came to town on the day of the deputation, joined the group. The Premier and two members of his Cabinet discussed fully with the temperance representatives the proposed amendments, which were:

1. Secrecy of the ballot.
2. The British principle of majority rule.
3. An opportunity to vote in the four wards in St. John on the day of civic election, April 20, 1909.

These amendments were subsequently embodied in a bill and enacted on April 6, 1909, as a Government measure. There were some additional changes made, amongst which were: hours of sale were shortened; liquor selling places were closed on holidays, and at 5 p.m. on Saturdays.

PROHIBITION IN CANADA.

The St. John workers immediately undertook the local option campaign in four wards of the city; they had only fourteen days in which to work. The following description of the campaign was given by Rev. Angus A. Graham, of St. John, in the *Canadian White Ribbon Tidings* on October 1, 1909:

"The contest was a spirited one. The forces of the united churches rented committee rooms as the headquarters in the different wards, and the usual machinery of an ordinary parliamentary election was in operation. There was no undisciplined mob, but a consecrated and well-organized band of workers earnestly engaged. Meetings were held, but the best work was done in the personal canvass. The situation was not complicated by the hotel question, as there were no clubs or hotels in these wards, but saloons only; and the watchword adopted was 'The Home Against the Saloon.'

"The campaign against us was a still one. They held no public meetings, nor did they appear at our meetings to present their side of the case. They went on the still hunt after the electors. They published in the daily press at advertising rates the names of the citizens who signed the petitions, which was a serious tactical blunder, as it reacted strongly against them in the contest. You can argue or plead with men and hope to win them, but when you attempt to drive them you have lost the day. It was an open challenge to the electors to go to the polls and sustain their action. Some of our men travelled over two hundred miles home to vote. Thus intimidation failed. . .

"But while intimidation and boycott were used, unfailing courtesy was shown towards those engaged in the reform movement. Both parties worked together round the polling places in a good-natured strife to get out the vote.

"The notable feature of these efforts after better temperance legislation and of the first local option conflict in this province, is the united action of the churches. The movement began in the church, and all the moral elements in the community were mobilized about the church to fight in defence of the home."

The result of the contest was gratifying. The question was submitted in Lorne, Lansdowne, Victoria and Duke's wards. In Lorne the temperance people won by a majority

PROVINCIAL PROHIBITION.

of 215; in Victoria by 55; and in Duke's ward by 78. This victory abolished eleven licenses.

In October of the same year, local option was carried in Harcourt by a vote of three to one. Taking advantage of the amendments of the Liquor License Act, a number of other places followed the lead of St. John and Harcourt. In several parishes, instead of bringing on local option contests, workers availed themselves of another clause in the license law to secure the abolition of license by petitions addressed to the Lieutenant-Governor in Council.

In February, 1912, a deputation presented to the Government a prohibition bill with a request that it be made law. No action was taken, and the request was reiterated a year later. Premier Flemming expressed his sympathy with the cause of temperance, but stated that since, under the license law, such rapid strides were being made in local prohibition, he doubted the wisdom of proceeding any faster.

THE PROHIBITION ACT.

For some little time organized effort for a prohibitory legislation almost ceased, but as a result of patient and persistent work the license law was gradually improved. In April, 1915, some special wartime amendments were made. Hours of sale were shortened for the period of the war; they were to be from 8 a.m. to 8 p.m., except on Saturday, when the closing hour was to be 4 p.m. It was made illegal to sell to soldiers or officers in uniform or partly in uniform. There were also a number of changes facilitating law enforcement in prohibition areas. Then at the end of that year, another prohibition campaign was begun.

At a very representative meeting held in the city of Fredericton on December 6 and 7, 1915, the New Brunswick Branch of the Dominion Alliance was thoroughly reorganized. The old debts were paid off and a new staff of officers appointed, consisting of: Donald Fraser, President; Rev. Thomas Marshall, Vice-President; W. G. Clark, Treasurer; and Rev. C. Flemington, Secretary. For the first time all the churches and temperance societies of the province were represented and able to present a united front. On December 10, 1915, a representative delegation waited upon the Government with five requests:

1. A prohibition bill.
2. The privilege of helping to frame the bill.
3. A referendum.
4. A majority vote.
5. An immediate answer to its request.

They were graciously received and their request was promised favorable consideration. On January 25, 1916, the Premier, the Hon. George J. Clarke, wrote the Alliance stating that, at the approaching session of the House of Assembly, legislation providing for prohibition would be enacted. At the interview with the Government, the Alliance had suggested that a committee of the Alliance should be associated with the Government in the preparation of the proposed new law. At the request of the Hon. J. B. M. Baxter, the following were appointed by the Alliance to act with S. B. Bustin, K.C., who had been instructed by the Attorney-General to prepare the bill for presentation to the House: Donald Fraser, President of the Alliance; Rev. Thomas Marshall, Rev. W. R. Robinson, Rev. Dr. W. H. Smith, J. Willard Smith, W. D. Ryan, and Rev. W. D. Wilson. Mr. Wilson had for some years been the secretary of the Prince Edward Island Alliance, and in February was appointed Field Secretary of the reorganized New Brunswick Alliance.

The committee, with Mr. S. B. Bustin, prepared carefully the necessary measure for presentation to the House. The Government assumed full responsibility for the bill as a Government measure and for bringing it into force without the necessity of a referendum. With only a few minor changes, under the leadership of the Hon. J. B. M. Baxter,

PROVINCIAL PROHIBITION.

in April, 1916, the bill was almost unanimously passed by the Assembly, only two members voting against it.

The principal features of the act are:

1. All licensed bar-rooms and clubs are abolished and thus the treating system is eliminated.

2. No liquor may be kept in hotels, clubs, offices, places of business or boarding-houses.

3. It is illegal to advertise liquor upon any vehicle of transportation, or at any public place or resort, or upon any sign or billboard in the province.

4. Treating and drinking in public places are prohibited. It is an offence to treat or offer liquor of any kind to any person in any street or car or upon any railway, passenger car, or coach or platform while the train is in the service of passenger transportation in the province.

5. The act prohibits anyone under the influence of liquor from driving, operating, or having charge of, the power or guidance of any automobile, motor-cycle, or any motor vehicle propelled by other than muscular power.

6. Provision is made for the sale of liquor for medicinal, mechanical, scientific and sacramental purposes through licensed drug stores.

7. Hospitals are permitted to keep liquor for the use of patients, and sick persons are allowed to have liquor in their rooms.

8. Properly qualified persons, such as druggists and doctors, can obtain alcohol for strictly medicinal, mechanical or scientific purposes.

9. A householder is allowed to keep liquor in his own home for his private use, provided it is not purchased within the province.

10. A fine of not less than $50 and not more than $200, and in default of immediate payment confinement in jail for not less than three months nor more than six months, is the punishment for first violation of this act. For a second offence no fine is made, but the offender will be committed to prison for not less than six months nor more than twelve months, and in the discretion of the magistrate he may be put at hard labor; and for a third offence be committed to jail for not less than nine months

PROHIBITION IN CANADA.

nor more than twelve months, and for every subsequent offence be imprisoned at hard labor for one year.

11. When any constable, policeman or local inspector sees any person in a state of intoxication or with liquor in his possession, that officer can cause said intoxicated person to go before a magistrate or a justice or any town clerk, and have him tell where he got his liquor. He shall make an affidavit or affirmation as to where he got such liquor, and on failure to do so to the satisfaction of the person taking the affirmation, he can be arrested and imprisoned until he makes such affidavit or declaration.

12. A civil remedy is provided by the act in the case of a person whose death has taken place while intoxicated. When any person who has drunk liquor which has been illegally furnished to him, comes to his death by suicide or drowning, or perishing from cold or other accident, the person who furnished the liquor becomes liable to an action for personal wrong at the suit of the legal representative of the deceased, who may recover damages of not less than $100 and not more than $1,000, as may be fixed by the court.

In every county of the province where the Canada Temperance Act was in force, the Provincial Prohibition Act was to come into operation immediately upon the repeal of the Dominion measure. In those counties where the New Brunswick License Law was in force, the prohibitory law became operative on May 1, 1917.

Between the passing of the act in April, 1916, and its coming into force on May 1, 1917, as the result of a general provincial election a change was brought about in the Government, but both the Opposition and the Government parties declared themselves in favor of the Prohibition Act, and have given it a fair and generous support.

The necessary steps were at once taken to bring about the repeal of the Scott Act, and elections were held in Sunbury and Charlotte Counties and in the city of Fredericton. In each case the repeal vote was carried. Petitions were circulated in the remaining counties. As the general sentiment of the province was so strongly in favor of prohibition, the Dominion Government, appealed to by the Alliance,

PROVINCIAL PROHIBITION.

passed a law whereby, on securing the necessary number of names to the petitions for repeal, the operation of the Scott Act was suspended so long as the prohibitory law remains in force. Since that time the whole of the province has been brought under the operation of the New Brunswick Temperance Act.

Between the passing of the act and its coming into force a very earnest and aggressive campaign of education was carried on by the Alliance, through public meetings, correspondence, advertising, and other methods to bring to the people generally a knowledge of the different sections of the act. A campaign of advertising was followed practically throughout the whole province. Advertisements were inserted in every newspaper, and much good resulted from the effort. A resolution was presented to the Government, recommending that a strong temperance worker and able, efficient administrator be appointed to the position of chief inspector under the prohibitory law. At the suggestion of the Alliance, Rev. W. D. Wilson was appointed to that office.

The act has been carried out in a very successful way and has met with general approval throughout the province. The results have been so satisfactory that a great many who were opposed to prohibition are now its firm friends. The great and marked improvement has been largely owing to the careful, prudent and effective way in which the act has been administered and the very satisfactory way in which the difficult and trying work of the inspectors has been done and the aid they have received from the officers and administrators of the law in the province.

IV. QUEBEC.

The prohibition movement in the Province of Quebec is unique, as Quebec herself is unique among the provinces of the Dominion. The Roman Catholic Church to which eighty-six per cent. of the population belongs, has always favored temperance. But, since the days of Father

PROHIBITION IN CANADA.

Chiniquy, it has looked with suspicion upon the organized temperance movement. Through the influence of the Church, indeed, the liquor traffic has been suppressed throughout the greater part of the province, with the result that Quebec has a moderate, temperate, law-abiding population with an exceptionally low criminal record, and a very high law-enforcing record. In the plebiscite of 1898, while Quebec recorded a majority of 94,324 against prohibition (the only province in the Dominion to give an adverse vote), there were at the time 603 municipalities out of a total of 933 in the province where the sale of liquor was prohibited. The policy of the Church, however, was to work by itself among the people, forming temperance societies, and giving temperance instruction in the schools, rather than to advocate temperance legislation; and for a long time they refused to co-operate with representative temperance organizations, and even opposed their fight for legislative reform. The Church worked on the principle of moral suasion and did not sympathize with legal methods of dealing with the traffic.

Hence, while every other province was advancing steadily and surely toward provincial prohibition, Quebec was content to see the liquor traffic remain a legalized, revenue-producing institution; and while in many rural districts local prohibition prevailed, conditions in the cities, notably in Montreal, were vicious in the extreme. For years that city had the reputation of maintaining ten times as many licensed places as any other city in Canada. Montreal, with less than half a million population, had more retail liquor licenses than Toronto, Winnipeg, Hamilton, Edmonton, Vancouver, Calgary, London, Ottawa, Quebec, Halifax, and St. John put together, although those cities had a combined population of more than a million people.

The Quebec Branch of the Dominion Alliance had been working since 1879 with the following fundamental principles:

" (1) That it is neither right nor politic for the State to afford legal protection and sanction to any traffic or system that tends

PROVINCIAL PROHIBITION.

to increase crime, to waste the national resources, to corrupt the social habits and to destroy the lives and health of the people.

" (2) That the history and results of all past legislation in regard to the liquor traffic abundantly proved that it is impossible satisfactorily to limit or regulate a system so essentially mischievous in its tendencies.

" (3) That rising above sectarian and party considerations, all good citizens should combine to procure an enactment prohibiting the manufacture and sale of intoxicating beverages as affording the most efficient aid in removing the appalling evil of intemperance."

But for many years the Alliance put up a doughty fight practically alone, working with a constituency that represented only a very small fraction of the population of the province. Because of the recognized strength of the opposition to a provincial prohibitory law, the Alliance for many years devoted their attention to securing where possible local prohibition under the Canada Temperance Act and the Quebec Temperance Act.

By the Quebec act the licensing authorities were the municipal councils in all municipalities, except Montreal and Quebec cities, where licenses were granted by a special Board of License Commissioners. No license, old or new, could be issued by the licensing authorities if there were placed in their hands an opposition signed by a majority of the municipal electors residing or doing business in the polling division where the premises were situated. In the act is embodied the principle of the old Dunkin Act, which provided that any municipality could, by the action of its municipal council, either enact a prohibitory law applicable to the locality or submit such a law to the vote of the electors for their approval.

There were some counties in which a number of contests occurred; for example, Richmond, a vanguard county in the temperance battle, where the Dunkin Act was retained for many years before the attempts to repeal it were successful.

Besides carrying on these local option contests, temperance workers gave much attention to the securing of improve-

PROHIBITION IN CANADA.

ments in the license law, restricting the traffic, shortening the hours, and increasing the penalties. The result was that Quebec Province had secured what might be fairly regarded as one of the best license laws in the Dominion.

Some attention was also given to political action in election contests. The line of action adopted was to secure, as far as possible, the nomination of men who were known and avowed temperance advocates. The Alliance did not nominate any independent candidate, but supported men in both political parties. The thing that the temperance people tried to avoid was any distinctive party affiliation, preferring to support known temperance men in either party, wherever such could be found. This policy resulted in the temperance forces being actively engaged on one side in one election and on the other in another election, sometimes supporting Liberals and sometimes Conservatives, until it was clearly established that the temperance people in Quebec were concerned in securing the election of good temperance men rather than of any party candidate. This influence was felt in municipal elections, as well as in parliamentary and provincial campaigns.

In the late eighties there was an active Law and Order League of Montreal, with Dr. J. A. Bazin as President, and J. H. Carson as Secretary. Major E. L. Bond was an efficient member and active worker. A number of prosecutions were instituted against violators of the license law and convictions secured against some of the most influential and notorious law-breakers. Sometimes these contests were very exciting, and members on both sides were battered and bruised. For example, the Richmond hotel-keepers, one or two in particular, were determined to break down Dunkin Act prohibition and by flagrant violation sought to bring the law into disrepute. On the other hand, a gentleman of that county, of considerable means, gave his time and money most generously to secure the enforcement of the law and the punishment of the law-breakers. There was keen interest aroused over the struggle. The temperance people found at

PROVINCIAL PROHIBITION.

last that there was not much use in having the law-breakers fined, and they planned another device. On a certain day Mr. Goodhue and Mr. Carson met on the Richmond Station platform, giving the idea that they were going to a temperance convention at Sherbrooke. They suddenly separated, raided the town and cleaned it up, particularly St. Lawrence Hall. The hotel-keeper refused them entrance, which was sufficient evidence to convict him. They went away, but soon returned, this time gained admittance, made a thorough search of the premises, and found a trapdoor, under which was concealed $400 worth of liquor. They shipped the liquor to Danville, where, on an order from the constable at Danville, the temperance people gathered, smashed the bottles, and poured their contents down the gutter. The chief value of such spectacular raids was that they kept up public interest in the subject of law enforcement.

Educational campaigns were also part of the Alliance work. Public meetings were held, temperance was taught in the schools, and temperance resolutions were passed at nearly every Church Conference and Synod.

FRANCISCAN CRUSADE.

But notwithstanding the efforts of the Alliance, the strength of the liquor traffic steadily increased in Quebec until the year 1906. That year was marked by the entrance of the Roman Catholic Church into the war for prohibition. Members of the Quebec Alliance Executive had several interviews with Mgr. Bruchesi, the Archbishop of Montreal, who expressed an earnest interest in the work of the Alliance. While he did not take such an advanced view as theirs upon the question of total prohibition, he was in entire sympathy with all the other declarations of their platform.

The Alliance had been urging municipalities where public opinion seemed favorable, to press the municipal councils to pass either local option by-laws or by-laws for early closing. At a meeting in Montreal for the discussion of this plan, the Archbishop made a noteworthy expression of

PROHIBITION IN CANADA.

opinion in favor of prohibiton. The enthusiasm of the great crowd was compelling. His Grace conceded afterwards that the audience had made his speech for him. He had caught the contagion of their zeal and had been borne along farther than he had foreseen. " We are asking," he said, " whether Montreal needs the open liquor shops for so many hours a day. I should like to ask whether we need them at all."

On December 20, 1905, Archbishop Bruchesi started a temperance crusade in the Diocese of Montreal which was formally inaugurated by a stirring pastoral letter. After dilating upon the physical and spiritual effects of alcoholism, not only of excessive drunkenness but of the habitual use of small quantities of liquor, he exhorted the people to assist the civil authorities in securing the enforcement of the license laws and outlined the plan of the special temperance campaign.

" 1. The clergy shall be the first to set an example of the temperance which they must preach. Consequently in the presbyteries and religious communities, on the occasion of pastoral visits, of gatherings for retreats and missions, of visits from priest or laymen, before or after meals, no alcoholic liquor shall be taken.

" 2. We request all families to do the same thing; to entirely give up the deplorable habit of offering and of taking spirituous liquors such as brandy, gin, rum, whisky, etc., on the occasion of gatherings, soirees, dinners, visits, and especially the visits and festivities of New Year's Day. Let all kinds of alcohol disappear from our homes; let us use it only in cases of necessity and upon the doctor's order. The pastors will not fail to often refer to this subject when giving advice to their parishioners.

" 3. We implore young men and fathers of families not to enter saloons and bar-rooms except for serious reasons; not to drink there intoxicating liquors, and especially to give up the, alas too common, practice of treating. We would feel happy to see all honest men league together against that social disorder which brings so many evils both to the family and to individuals. We particularly entreat the citizens who form the leading classes and the members of the liberal professions to preach by example in this respect.

PROVINCIAL PROHIBITION.

"4. We request the priests, the principals of colleges, and teachers in general to often refer to intemperance in the classrooms, and to adopt all possible means to inspire the pupils with horror for that vice.

"5. We order that in all parishes work be commenced at once to establish temperance leagues or societies: first among the children from the year of their first communion up to the age of eighteen years; second among young men; third among the heads of families. St. John the Baptist shall be the patron of those leagues, the members of which must pledge themselves not to use spirituous liquors except in cases of sickness and of real need. Those societies already exist in some parishes and do the greatest amount of good."

The sixth regulation appoints the reverend Franciscan Fathers special apostles of temperance to preach the crusade in all the parishes and makes the following appeal:

"We specially and earnestly request the greatest zeal in caring for the children and young men, upon whom we must rely to form the sober generation of the future."

The seventh and last regulation is in the following terms:

"7. It is also our will that temperance societies be founded in our colleges and in our university. The students of these important institutions are, as they know, the subject of our greatest solicitude and our deepest affection. It is our ardent desire that they may become one day men of character and of principle, men of science and of virtue, for the glory of their Church and of their country. They will become all this in as much only as they are really temperate. Let them call to mind the number of fine talents prematurely destroyed by the poison of alcohol. We do not wish them to have such a sad fate, and that is the reason why we are so anxious to see sobriety and temperance honored in our colleges and in our university."

The part played by the Franciscans as temperance missionaries is described in vivid, pictorial language in *Les Franciscains et la Croisade Antialcoolique,* from which the following paragraphs are extracted:

PROHIBITION IN CANADA.

"In the month of February, 1906, our fathers began their preachings in the diocese of Montreal; these teachings soon spread into the other dioceses, and for two or three years most of the missionaries of all the orders, Dominicans, Jesuits, Oblates, Redemptorists, etc., were busy preaching retreats, triduums, and temperance sermons throughout the Province of Quebec to its two million Catholics.

"It was laborious preaching. The matter involved an attack on desires and on old customs; it meant refuting a thousand objections and overthrowing the obstacles presented by those interested in the preservation and success of the saloons. The struggle was hard, but what a reward in the final triumph!

"The men who gave their names to the temperance society assembled in the sanctuary. In the nave the mothers, wives and children looked on with emotion at this interesting scene, so important to the happiness of their homes. After an address by the missionary and a hymn by the throng of people, the priest or preacher, wearing his stole, proceeded to bless the crosses piled up near the altar; then these were distributed to the candidates, who received them kneeling and kissed them. When the distribution was completed the following dialogue took place between the men and the missionary, being taken from the form in use by the Franciscan Fathers:

"Question. 'My dear brothers, for the love of Jesus Christ, and by the grace of God, you are about to undertake to practise temperance for life. Do you promise never to use strong drink except in case of sickness?'

"Answer. 'Yes, I promise.'

"Q. 'Do you promise not to treat any one?'

"A. 'Yes, I promise.'

"Q. 'Do you promise not to enter hotels, except for important reasons?'

"A. 'Yes, I promise.'

"Q. 'Do you promise to keep the rules of the society?'

"A. 'Yes, I promise.'

"Q. 'Do you promise to exhort your relatives and friends to temperance?'

"A. 'Yes, I promise.'

"'On your knees,' continued the missionary, 'you are now to declare your vow with me, and may the Lord help you.' And the voice of the missionary pronounced slowly the solemn declaration

PROVINCIAL PROHIBITION.

which, member after member, the hundreds of men bravely repeated in a loud voice and carrying the cross. .

"Such was the touching scene presented by several hundred parishes, following temperance preachings for some years. The women and children were also enrolled in the temperance society. Article 15 of the constitution of the temperance society promulgated by Mgr. Bruchesi on the 22nd of January, 1906, declared, moreover: 'Young women and mothers of families should be zealous apostles of temperance, which they will undertake to practise and to have practised around them.'

"What was the share of the Franciscans in this preaching crusade? *La Tempérance,* May, 1908, thus sums up the work of the first two years: 'Apart from a large number of individual sermons and 78 lectures with lantern slides, there were preached 160 triduums and retreats. During these preachings the number of people known to have adopted temperance is more than 80,000, divided as follows:

> Men and youths................. 39,765
> Women and girls................ 32,070
> Children 9,280

It is worthy of notice that among the number of men and youths enrolled, heads of families comprised more than half the number, that is to say, 20,863 people.

"'Large as this figure (81,115) appears, we must mention that it is furnished by only about a hundred parishes: the results of the crusade in the other districts having only appeared in the record under the vague information, two-thirds, three-quarters, etc., of the parish.'

"As to the number of our Fathers engaged in the crusade, all our preachers were in it more or less, and had their number been tripled it would scarcely have been sufficient for all the demands and needs. It is, however, simple justice to mention, in a memoir like this, the names of Father Ladislas Minette and Father Joachim—Joseph Monfette. The numerous preachings of Father Ladislas, his special work in the meetings with lantern slides, his position as first manager of *La Tempérance,* a position which he held till 1910, gave him a most important place in the crusade against alcohol from its beginning. . . . Father Joachim, also one of the missionaries of the early days, became and remained the chief and the most devoted as well as the most popular apostle of temperance. He traversed the country in all directions, with constant success. . . .

La Tempérance.

"From the beginning of the crusade the need of an anti-alcoholic paper was felt, and the Very Reverend Father Colomban-Marie Dreyer, then Provincial Minister, founded it in the spring of 1906, with the full approval and blessing of the Archbishop of Montreal. . Moreover, His Excellency Mgr. Donat Sbaretti, the Apostolic Delegate to Canada, and the Archbishop of Quebec gave the most friendly encouragement to the bulletin at its beginning, in letters which *Le Tempérance* published in June, 1906. *La Tempérance* received indeed at the beginning of its second year the highest mark of favor which can be desired, and its crowning reward. The Sovereign Pontiff himself, His Holiness Pius X, deigned to address to *La Tempérance,* under date June 20, 1907, an autograph letter of blessing.

"Thus encouraged, the missionaries of temperance have spared neither their time nor their devotion in developing and advancing, at the cost of much personal sacrifice, a work recognized as so useful to the Church and society. *La Tempérance* counts at least, from its beginning, twenty-five thousand subscribers. . . . We have published since 1906* tracts and pamphlets on temperance to the total number of five hundred thousand copies, representing fifteen million pages; two hundred thousand of these pamphlets and tracts, principally pamphlets, have been distributed gratuitously.

"By force of circumstances, the office of *La Tempérance* became gradually the centre of anti-alcoholic social action and a secretary's office for the information of and efficient assistance of the priests in the struggle against the saloons."

The pastoral letter of the Archbishop of Montreal was followed on January 22, 1906, by a similar letter from Mgr. Bégin, Archbishop of Quebec, and soon after the crusade was taken up in their several dioceses by the Bishops of Joliet, St. Hyacinthe, Chicoutimi, Rimouski, Valleyfield, and Three Rivers. While the crusade was inaugurated and fostered by

---

* The account from which this is taken is dated 1915.

PROVINCIAL PROHIBITION.

the Church, laymen were called to participate in the movement and to lead to a certain extent.

In 1906, as an outcome of the temperance sentiment working in the province, the La Ligue Anti-Alcoolique League of Quebec was formed, with Sir François Langelier as president, succeeded soon after by Sir François Lemieux. In 1907, the Anti-Alcoholic League of Montreal was created, with Judge H. Taschereau, Chief Justice of the Court of Appeal, as president, succeeded by Judge E. Lafontaine. Other officers of the Montreal society were: Honorary President, His Grace the Archbishop of Montreal; Secretary, Mr. Victor Morin; Treasurer, Mr. Arthur Gagnon. These leagues were not total abstinence associations, but advocated abstinence from distilled liquor and a moderate use of fermented and alcoholic beverages. Their object was to strengthen individual effort by organization and co-operation, to create temperance public opinion, to educate, to secure reforms in legislation and administration. With them were affiliated a number of temperance societies.

LICENSE LAW AMENDMENTS.

The influence of their work was shown in 1906, when a deputation of ten Roman Catholic priests and four Protestant ministers waited upon the Provincial Government to urge the reduction of licenses by one-third. They presented a largely signed petition. Premier Gouin promised to reduce the licenses by fifty.

In 1907, the following amendments were made to the license law:

1. The employment of any female to act as bar-maid, to serve or wait upon guests or the public in the bar-room of any tavern, hotel, wine-shop or restaurant licensed under the law was prohibited. This did not apply to the wife of any keeper of a tavern or restaurant.

2. The fee for distillers' licenses was increased from $250 to $1,000, and of brewers' licenses from $200 to $750.

3. A scale of license fees for towns and villages was adopted in proportion to the number of licenses.

PROHIBITION IN CANADA.

4. It was made illegal to supply intoxicants to persons in clubs under twenty-one years of age. This did not apply to restaurants, where the minimum age was eighteen years.

5. There was a readjustment of license fees for the duty payable to the collector of the provincial revenue for transfer of licenses.

In April, 1908, the Roman Catholic Total Abstinence Union, an organization of strong voting power, affiliated with the Provincial Alliance for the advantage of united effort.

During the 1908 session of the Legislature, petitions for reforms in the license law were presented, bearing no less than one hundred thousand signatures of members of both the Roman Catholic and the Protestant clergy, judges, college professors, senators, two ex-Premiers of the province and other representative citizens. Amendments were enacted by the Legislature as nearly as possible in compliance with the draft of the measure prepared by the temperance people and submitted to some of the members of the Government:

1. License holders were prohibited, under penalty of $20 or a month in jail, from cashing or exchanging cheques, employers' certificates or pay slips. This measure was especially important in such manufacturing cities as Hull.

2. Licenses were to be reduced in Montreal, Quebec, and other cities and towns by about 125.

3. The sale of liquor on Christmas Day, New Year's Day and Good Friday was prohibited.

On October 25, 1909, there was held in the town of Ville St. Pierre, near Montreal, an inter-parochial temperance congress for the west portion of the city of Montreal and Montreal Island. This congress, at which thirteen parishes and fifteen temperance societies were represented, was due particularly to the initiative of M. l'Abbé J. P. Desrosiers, curé of Saint Pierre aux Liens, who had devoted himself entirely to temperance work. The congress was the point of departure for a vigorous temperance campaign in Montreal.

There was an increased agitation on the part of Montreal citizens to secure the adoption of an early closing by-law,

PROVINCIAL PROHIBITION.

which Alderman S. J. Carter, President of the Provincial Branch of the Alliance, had for some time been trying to have passed in the municipal council. The proposal was to close liquor selling places at 7 p.m. on Saturdays and 10 p.m. on other days. It was in support of this Carter by-law that the anti-alcoholic leagues, representing the French Roman Catholics, and the Dominion Alliance, representing the English Protestants, began a signal movement of definite co-operation, which has been cordially and harmoniously continued ever since, and the wisdom of which has been manifested by sudden and rapid progress and a final magnificent triumph. Although the Leagues' platform did not at first include prohibition, the Alliance, while not offering the slightest compromise of their principles, went with the French as far as it was possible to go, and worked for measures of restrictive legislation that lay in the direction of total prohibition.

"The introduction of the by-law," said Mr. Carter, " was taken as a huge joke, and there was scarcely an alderman in sympathy with the measure. A great majority were antagonistic. Certainly it was a bold venture in a city like Montreal, the centre of the liquor interests of the Dominion.'

But the Montreal daily newspapers, as well as the press throughout the province, gave prominence to the measure. The Roman Catholic clergy gave it their almost unanimous support, some of them attending in person the meetings of the city council, and public opinion in favor of the by-law made rapid strides. This became very evident just before the municipal elections, and so many aldermen owed their seats in council to the support of electors favoring the by-law that there was finally only a small minority of the members who opposed it. But these, led by a member of the council who was also secretary of the Licensed Victuallers' Association, and backed up by the liquor dealers, put up a most strenuous fight and were finally successful in bringing the measure and also Mr. Carter (at the next civic election)

PROHIBITION IN CANADA.

to defeat. The temperance public opinion created by the campaign was, however, strong.

In 1910, the Alliance, as one of the law enforcement agencies recognized by the Quebec License Law, made war upon illicit liquor-selling in Montreal. They found the law being flagrantly violated and the police either in ignorance or indifference with regard to the conditions. Representations were made to the Provincial Government in regard to the action of the License Commissioners in granting nearly three hundred licenses for the current year to places not properly equipped as by law required. The Premier promised that an inquiry would be instituted. The License Commissioners, at one of their public sittings held soon afterwards, took occasion to criticize the action of the Alliance in the matter, upon which the secretary made a spirited rejoinder in the press. This led to a somewhat prolonged, and at times heated controversy, in which His Honor, Mr. Justice Lafontaine joined, endorsing the secretary's attack on the commissioners. Finally the License Commissioners, in a long document, appealed to the Attorney-General to vindicate them, and the secretary, replying to this, appealed to Sir Lomer Gouin to vindicate the law. The result of this appeal was that the Provincial Treasurer issued a memorandum to the License Commissioners, instructing them to grant no licenses to places not properly equipped, but to enforce the law as written, thus vindicating the law as requested and tacitly administering an admonition to the commissioners.

In March of that year, a union conference was held in the Monument National in Montreal. Mr. Justice Lafontaine, President of the United Anti-Alcoholic League, occupied the chair, and representatives of the League and the Dominion Alliance took a prominent part in the proceedings. The meeting decided upon a campaign to secure a better provincial liquor law. A number of amendments were recommended, and it was agreed that both organizations should circulate throughout the city petitions asking that these changes be enacted with other legislation. A

PROVINCIAL PROHIBITION.

splendid response was made to this appeal by churches, municipal councils and other bodies, seventy resolutions being passed by councils alone, approving of the proposed amendments.

The campaign culminated in a monster deputation to the Government. More than two hundred delegates from all parts of the province, representing temperance societies, municipal councils and labor unions, and made up of bishops, priests, Protestant clergymen, magistrates, merchants, working men and professional men, unanimously presented their request. Their prayers were not all granted, but a very important measure of restriction was introduced in an Early Closing Government Bill. All bars and restaurants in cities and towns were to close at 11 o'clock nightly, and at 7 p.m. on Saturdays, and they were not to open in the morning until 7 o'clock. In the country districts, the hours for closing were to be 10 o'clock on ordinary nights and 7 o'clock on Saturdays. The same hours were to apply to the sale of liquor in groceries. This amendment cut out from the liquor traffic approximately one day a week. It was the thin edge of the wedge of license reform. It came into force on May 1, 1911. Furthermore, the leader of the Government, Sir Lomer Gouin, frankly asserted that he and his Government were partizans of the temperance cause.

This action of the Government roused the hostility of the liquor forces, and they declared their intention of overthrowing the Ministry at the next election in May, 1912. The Executive Committee of the Dominion Alliance faced the issue with determination. A strong Political Action Committee was appointed, consisting of Messrs. S. J. Carter, President; J. H. Roberts, Secretary; J. H. Carson, W. Patterson, and C. Boon. Resolutions were adopted by the committee expressing hearty approval of the stand for temperance taken by the Gouin Government, and urging citizens of all parties to support in the forthcoming provincial election those Government candidates whose records showed that they

PROHIBITION IN CANADA.

were in harmony with the temperance policy of the Provincial Government.

Copies of the resolutions were sent to every Protestant clergyman and to every newspaper published in the province. In thus taking sides in the political campaign, the Alliance departed from previous method, but they felt their course was the only consistent one under the circumstances. The Government had been faithful to the temperance cause, while the Opposition leader had declared and voted against the Early Closing Law and the enemies of prohibition had lined up solidly with him. The result of the election was that the Gouin Government was triumphantly returned to power.

Among the first acts of the Government after its re-election was to appoint, on June 21, 1912, a Royal Commission, consisting of Justices Carroll (chairman), Cross, Lessier and a secretary, "To study the sale of intoxicating liquor and the changes which it is expedient to make in the license law." The Alliance and the Anti-Alcoholic League co-operated in drawing up a list of amendments and recommendations to be submitted to the commission. The Alliance secretary, Mr. Roberts, was requested by the league to represent the two organizations before the commission, and to explain and urge the amendments submitted.

The commission held public sittings in Montreal, Quebec and Sherbrooke. They made a study of the legislation of the several states of the American Union and the provinces of the Dominion, and that of foreign countries, questioned the revenue collectors of the province, the representatives of public bodies and, generally speaking, those whom they looked upon as being in a position to give useful information.

The commission reported in September, 1913. They reviewed the history of the license laws of Quebec from 1774. They discussed several broad aspects of the problem, such as sobriety and labor, and the physical effects of alcoholic liquors; they described and favorably commented on Gothenburg and Bergen systems. Opposing the principle of prohibition, they quoted the alleged failure of the State of

PROVINCIAL PROHIBITION.

Maine and utterances of Cardinal Gibbons and Archbishop Messiner of the Roman Catholic Church, and Bishop Foilly of the Montreal Anglican Church. They said in part:

"It was clearly proved a few years ago that the immense majority of the population of this province is opposed to prohibition. Such a measure would be contrary to public sentiment in the province. In so far as we are concerned, we are not prepared to say that such a measure would be in the interests of the province. Experience, the great teacher, has convinced us that prohibition in populous towns would not succeed here any more than it has done elsewhere. The liquor traffic is not like any other; it is dangerous and detrimental to the state, because it is hurtful to individuals who make up the state, while the other kinds of commerce are of assistance to the state and contribute to its progress. It is only by way of toleration that certain persons are allowed to sell intoxicating liquors, and these persons must be prepared to make sacrifices."

The following recommendations, among others, were made:

(1) Education of the people. "The law comes to the assistance of a well-prepared and matured public opinion."

(2) Teaching in schools, academies, Normal and Model schools by object lessons that leave out moral aspect and treat the physiological and economic phases of the alcohol question.

(3) Diminution in the number of hotel and restaurant licenses.

(4) Gradual suppression of all bars, which are worse than the retail shops.

(5) Retail shops not to exceed the number of hotels and restaurants.

(6) No general compensation except possibly in Quebec and Montreal.

(7) The division of the province into two districts with two license commissions, one in Montreal and the other in Quebec. That in Quebec was to consist of three members, one of these to be a physician.

(8) The commissioners had charge of the supervision and cancellation of licenses. The municipal councillors to have no control over the issue of licenses as regards beer and wine. These

PROHIBITION IN CANADA.

light liquors not to be exempted from the regulations governing ardent liquors.

(9) Inebriates to be given chance of rehabilitation.

This report, while in some respects a disappointing document to the temperance workers, especially in the recommendation of Gothenburg and Bergen systems, contained much for their encouragement.

The Legislative Committee of the Alliance, with the Committee of the Anti-Alcoholic League of Montreal and Quebec, waited on the Premier, Sir Lomer Gouin and laid before him their views regarding the necessity and character of legislation based on the findings of the commission. They especially emphasized the various recommendations submitted by the allied temperance forces, which had been approved by the committee. The deputation received the most sympathetic hearing and the assurance that their request would receive due consideration.

The Government bill, introduced shortly after, contained many amendments to the license law very satisfactory from a temperance standpoint. The Government ignored the commission's suggestion of the company system, but to the disappointment of temperance workers, and in spite of their protest, included a provision for compensating those dispossessed of licenses by the reduction of the number of licenses in Montreal. The bill, which was based on the Royal Commission's report, was to take effect on May 1, 1914, except in certain special cases on May 1, 1915. It contained the following provisions among others:

License Commissioners were appointed in Quebec and Montreal with power to suspend or cancel licenses and to compensate liquor dealers. The number of licenses was greatly reduced, and liquor sales were separated from groceries.

In 1913, the energies of the temperance forces were once again directed particularly to securing local prohibition through the Quebec Temperance Law and the Canada Temperance Act. The success of the movement was remarkable.

PROVINCIAL PROHIBITION.

Parishes, towns, counties and a number of cities voted dry. Great credit is due to the faithful work of the Roman Catholic priests in conducting educative campaigns with lectures, exhibitions and literature. In municipality after municipality prohibition was carried by a practically unanimous vote—a thing unheard of in any other province of Canada. This was true in Protestant as well as Roman Catholic centres.

In the session of 1915-1916, an Early Closing Law shortened the hours of sale.

PROHIBITION BILL.

In 1916, a campaign was launched for the securing of provincial prohibition. On October 4th, a very strong deputation waited on Sir Lomer Gouin and other members of his Cabinet to ask for early action. There were present about three hundred citizens representing many ecclesiastical and other organizations, and the Government listened for about three hours to their representations. In his reply, the Premier asked the deputation what would be its view of the prohibition of spirits, leaving the sale of beer and wine still licensed. Judge Lafontaine, President of the Montreal Anti-Alcoholic League, made a strong argument in favor of the same thorough-going form of legislation that had been adopted in other provinces. He argued that the wine sold in this country was largely adulterated, and that permission for wine-selling only would be looked upon as legislation in the interests of the wealthier classes. He denounced beer as an unsanitary and mischievous beverage, pointing to the brutality of the German nation as an evidence of its evil effects. The Premier expressed his appreciation of the representations made. He said that he had seldom attended an interview with a deputation of so interesting a character, and that he was impressed with the unanimity of the views stated. He added

"You say that the time has come to give prohibition; that the education of the people is complete. Other important persons believe that the time has not yet come. We must tell you that we are facing a very difficult problem, and opinions must be weighed. You have pleaded your case. Rest assured that you have not appealed to deaf ears. We shall give to your requests all consideration which they deserve, and rest assured that we shall remain worthy of the confidence of the people of this province."

The bill brought in by the Government fell short of prohibition, but was a much more stringent law than the one in force. While it did not give satisfaction to prohibitionists, it was looked upon with as much disfavor by the liquor interests. It was passed by both Houses and Legislature. The following were its principal features:—

Bar-rooms were practically abolished and the number of places in which liquor was sold, to be consumed on the premises, was very much reduced. All treating was prohibited. Shop or grocery licenses were to be lessened in number, and finally the sale of liquor was to be separated entirely from any other business. Hotel licenses were not to be granted to places that had less than twenty-five bedrooms. The hours of sale in hotels were from nine in the morning until five in the evening. By May, 1918, bar-rooms were to give place to cafés.

On May 3, 1917, the City of Hull voted on a local option by-law and achieved one of the most significant temperance victories ever won in Canada. The poll stood:

For prohibition	2,487
Against prohibition	1,306
Majority for	1,181
Spoiled ballots	17
Total vote	3,810

Hull was one of the strongest citadels of the liquor traffic; Ottawa, just across the river, was under prohibition, and from the Ontario city thousands of dollars poured into Hull, a fact which made the liquor interests all the more determined to maintain their hold. The victory was as valuable to Ottawa as to Hull.

PROVINCIAL PROHIBITION.

On October 4, 1917, Quebec City took her place in the line of progress by voting on the Canada Temperance Act. It was considered preferable to employ this act rather than Quebec Temperance Act, because as the latter called for open voting, the organized liquor interests in the city would have probably seen to it that the polls should never close. The vote was preceded by a hard-fought campaign of several weeks, which exceeded in bitterness the warmest political battle that Quebec Province ever witnessed. The clergy—Catholic and Protestant—united strongly against their churches' common foe. Many meetings were held, at which a number of the most influential men in Canada took the platform in favor of prohibition.

On the other side there was no lack of effort. The anti-prohibitionists were well organized, and among their spokesmen were some of the well-known public men of the province. The result seemed in doubt up to a few days before voting, when it was generally conceded that the temperance forces had good prospects of winning. When the ballots were counted, it was found that of the votes cast there was a majority of 3,251 in favor of prohibition.

The law went into effect May 1, 1918, and meant the closing of forty bars and seventy licensed groceries in the city.

A caucus of Quebec Province Liberals was called in January, 1918, to consider the situation created by the Dominion order-in-council, and the advisability of enacting provincial prohibition. Sir Lomer Gouin suggested a measure to take effect on May 1, 1919, giving the liquor dealers of the province a year's grace in which to liquidiate as well as possible. Mr. Peter Bercovitch, K.C., deputy from St. Louis, Montreal, suggested a referendum on the question. This was received by the caucus in silence.

Mr. J. N. Francoeur, deputy for Lotbinière, and author of the famous Francoeur motion on Confederation, suggested that it would be well to prohibit ardent spirits, and allow the sale of beer and wine in the province. This was also received in silence. The Prime Minister said that the Government would take the suggestions into consideration, and the tacit understanding was that it would be left to the Government to come to a decision.

In February, 1918, under what was practically a threat of the resignation of the Government, Sir Lomer Gouin succeeded in the Quebec Assembly in having carried unanimously "bone-dry" prohibition for the Province of Quebec, to come into force in May, 1919. Hon. Walter Mitchell brought in a bill for total prohibition, and the Prime Minister insisted that the members accept it or express want of confidence in the Government. "If we have not the confidence of the House we will submit to the consequences," declared the Prime Minister. The bill was then unanimously adopted on second reading, and it was sent to committee for study of clauses and was then given its third reading.

Explaining his bill to amend the Quebec License Act, Mr. Mitchell spoke of the prohibition wave that had swept over Canada while Quebec had remained the only province under license law. But, in spite of that, up to the time the war broke out, Quebec had made more progress towards temperance than any other part in Canada. He pointed to the strides made by the dry movement in the province, and then referred to the Federal order-in-council prohibiting the manufacture, importation, and transportation of intoxicating liquors. The Quebec Government was obliged to take this matter into serious consideration, for in about a year's time, with the new regulation, the stock of imported liquors would be exhausted. Besides, the prohibition of manufacture would mean that in about the same time the supply of distilled liquors would also run out. The Province of Quebec would then be in a position of issuing licenses for the sale of something which had no legal existence in the country. He said that, in view of the Ottawa enactments, and the sentiment of the people in the province and throughout the country, the Government had come to the conclusion that it was the will of the people that it should be passed.

PROVINCIAL PROHIBITION.

Between the adjournment of the Legislature in 1918 and its re-assembling in 1919, a determined campaign was carried on, particularly by the brewing interests, to induce the Gouin Government to recede from the position taken on the prohibition question.

After Parliament opened, this campaign was renewed with redoubled energy. Immense double-page advertisements were inserted in the papers of the province. Petitions were presented from labor organizations and others, asking that the act be amended to permit the sale of light beer and wine. Counter representations were made by the prohibition forces.

The temperance forces, however, were disorganized. The secretary of the Quebec Branch of the Dominion Alliance, Mr. John H. Roberts, had resigned a short time previously and had left for Australia. There was no rallying centre for the forces. In the emergency, the Dominion Council of the Alliance stepped in and arrangements were made for the holding of a great Union Prohibition Convention. The call for this gathering was signed by:

S. J. Carter, President, Quebec Branch of the Dominion Alliance; Chas. P. Rice, Treasurer, Quebec Branch of the Dominion Alliance; Robt. Neville, Jr., President, Anti-Liquor League of Quebec; R. L. Werry, Secretary, Anti-Liquor League of Quebec; W. H. Wiggs, Acting-President, Social Service Council of Quebec; W. Harold Young, Secretary, Social Service Council of Quebec; Mrs. F. H. Waycott, President, Quebec Provincial W.C.T.U.; Mrs. R. W. McLachlan, Secretary, Quebec Provincial W.C.T.U.; Mrs David Scott, President, Montreal Northern District W.C.T.U.; Mrs. Arthur Richardson, Secretary, Montreal Northern District W.C.T.U.; W. S. Wilkinson, G.C.T., International Order of Good Templars; W. Davis, Gr. Secretary, International Order of Good Templars; Isaac Collins, G.C., Royal Templars of Temperance; A. B. Parker, G. Secretary, Royal Templars of Temperance; John Montreal, Anglican Bishop of Montreal; Rev. Geo. Hanson, D.D., President, Montreal Protestant Ministerial Association; Rev. Chas. G. Smith, Secretary, Montreal Protestant Ministerial Association; J. R. Dougall, Hon. President,

PROHIBITION IN CANADA.

Council of the Dominion Alliance; Ben. H. Spence, Secretary, Council of the Dominion Alliance.

The convention was a huge success. A memorial was unanimously adopted to forward to Sir Lomer Gouin. This was as follows:

PROVINCIAL PROHIBITION CONVENTION,
MONTREAL, March 13, 1919.

SIR LOMER GOUIN,
Premier of the Province of Quebec.

At the Provincial Convention now in session at Montreal, the following resolutions were unanimously adopted:

"In compliance with the request of the temperance forces of Quebec, and in harmony with the wishes of the citizens of the province, the Provincial Government at its last session declared for provincial prohibition, and a bill was passed that such a law should become operative on May 1st of this year.

"This policy, embodying as it does the principles for which we stand, and meeting in our judgment the needs of the situation both then and now.

"We therefore protest that any departure from this right, wise policy and any modification of the prohibition law that would allow the sale of intoxicating liquors would be class legislation in the interests of the liquor traffic and inimical to the interests of the people of the province.

"By consensus of opinion of every Legislature in Canada, and the Liquor Law of the Province of Quebec, liquor containing more than two and one-half per cent. of proof spirits is conclusively deemed to be intoxicating. This is the maximum strength allowed by the Dominion war-time prohibitory Order-in-Council.

"The federal amendment to the constitution of the United States prohibits intoxicating liquors for beverage purposes. The Federal Government has fixed the standard for intoxicants to be one-half of one per cent. alcohol. For the Province of Quebec to stand out from amongst the commonwealths of the North American continent by passing legislation specially favoring the liquor traffic, and allowing the sale of intoxicating liquor will be to lower her in the eyes of the world and to give the liquor traffic a vantage

PROVINCIAL PROHIBITION.

ground from which it may continue to wage a campaign against prohibitory laws in other places.

"We earnestly call attention to the fact that nothing has occurred in the province during the past year to indicate any popular desire for any change in the commendable legislation of the last session, and that the only suggestion for such change has come from the organized interest of the liquor traffic.

"We believe that the reform for which we stand is too important and vital to the welfare of the people to be jeopardized by submission to a hasty verdict without the possibility of adequate preparations and at an inopportune time. For the honor of our province, we earnestly hope that the announced decision of the Government is not final, and that on further consideration the law will stand as originally passed and in accordance with the previously expressed purpose of the Government."

GEORGE HANSON,
Chairman.

G. J. TRUEMAN,
Secretary.

The convention closed with a great mass meeting in St. James' Methodist Church when the audience of 2,000 rose as one man, and with uplifted arms and clenched fists pledged themselves to the campaign. The *Montreal Star,* reporting this meeting, said:

"'We will see this thing through,' they thundered in unison, led by the Rev. Ben. H. Spence, who had suggested this dramatic manner of putting themselves on record as opposed to the passage of legislation permitting beer and wine licenses in the Province of Quebec.

"Earlier in the day several hundred delegates to the temperance convention had shown their determination to fight the refereudum by making a collective promise in the same dramatic way.

"The evening mass meeting of prohibition supporters was the culmination of the two days' convention, a convention which the Rev. Ben. Spence referred to as 'one of the greatest temperance conventions he had ever seen.' The speakers at the afternoon and evening sessions were largely representative. They included the Hon. Wayne Wheeler, of Washington, D.C., the national attorney

PROHIBITION IN CANADA.

of the Anti-Saloon League of America, and the man who framed the bone-dry act passed by the United States Congress; Bishop Farthing, who made his first public appearance on the temperance platform; Judge Lafontaine, president of the Anti-Alcoholic League of the Roman Catholic Church; Captain the Rev. A. C. Trivett, of the Y.M.C.A.; and the Rev. Ben. H. Spence, of the Dominion Alliance."

The Legislature, however, was stampeded and the bill, as introduced by the Government, was finally passed.

A few days later the Government announced that a vote would be taken on April 10th, leaving less than three weeks for preparation for the vote. The temperance forces lost no time in completing organization as planned by the convention.

A Campaign Committee was formed, with W. H. Wigg, Esq., of Quebec City, as president; Rev. Dr. E. I. Hart, of Montreal, as secretary; and Mr. George J. Trueman, Principal of Stanstead College, as campaign manager. Offices were opened at 204 Witness Building. A staff was engaged, and a vigorous campaign was launched.

The English-speaking Protestant clergy were practically a unit for prohibition and against permitting the sale of beer and wine. No official action was, however, taken by the Catholic clergy.

The Anti-Alcoholic League, the French temperance organization, was divided on the wine and beer issue. The Secretary, Mr. Victor Morin, declared for the beer amendment. The president, the Hon. Justice Eugene Lafontaine, came out with a strong deliverance for prohibition, in which he said that the League would not make any campaign, but urged electors to vote NO. Judge Lafontaine said in part:

"If we were dealing only, as it is erroneously said and too often thought, with the use in the family, or at meals, at the restaurant or at the hotel, of wine and beer, which would be bought at the grocery store or at the wine merchant's, the League would say: 'Let us give in and let us try it.' But the situation is entirely different, and what is proposed to us is the selling of these drinks by the glass in establishments exactly like those too

PROVINCIAL PROHIBITION.

well known to-day, only without the counters. In other words, it is the régime of the public drinking-house or of the open tap from the barrel running into ever-thirsty throats, as long as the pocket-book of the unfortunate customer shall not run dry. But of this régime the country has already had enough. All, except those who are interested, admit it, and it is high time that the death blow was given it.

"Except for the labels, it appears to us that nothing has changed—the 'license system' is the same and the license commissioners whom we must hold responsible for granting so many licenses against the law to unworthy persons are the same men. The licensed sellers, who in the past have been the distributors of alcoholic poisons and the cause of many a disorder and of the abuses which have made the old régime fall beneath our feet in universal disgust, these too will be the new licensed vendors for the selling by the glass of wine and beer. This means that the same old abuses will go on as before, if they are not even increased. For establishments where wine and beer will be sold can easily become places where illegally-manufactured alcohol will find an easy and continuous entrance. Finally, the authority whose task it is to execute the law remains the same; that is to say, as in the past the law will not be carried out, as this is left to the municipality, which has endeavored to get rid itself of the accomplishment of its duty, when it has not openly favored the violators of the law.

"We pass in silence the foolish spending of money at a time when living is so dear, which this wine and beer régime, as organized, will inevitably bring; and we will not speak either of the disorders which it will necessarily create, the same causes providing the same effects.

"But there is one thing which ought to make us call a halt: the determination of the capitalist to get rid of his products by means of a well-paid organization and high-priced advertising.

"How long are the people going to let themselves be fooled, defrauded and exploited for the profit of a few individuals? Who cannot see in this extraordinary activity to maintain the license régime, and in so much money spent in publicity without counting the cost on an advertising campaign, regardless of truth and sense, a deceitful movement of the capitalist to line up labor against prohibition in order to get hold of the worker's salary and live at his expense, throwing him afterward on the pavement with his health forever ruined?

PROHIBITION IN CANADA.

" Eight out of the nine provinces of our Dominion had adopted prohibition already. Quebec only remained, and last year she placed herself in line with the rest and decreed the closing of saloons for May 1, 1919.

" By a change of front, it is no more prohibition that is proposed to us, but a wine and beer régime unknown anywhere. Once more Quebec wants to stand alone; Quebec puts herself apart from the rest of the country and isolates herself in a matter in which uniformity of legislation is necessary.

" It is clear that if so much effort has been made to make prohibition in Quebec a failure, it is in order to make it a failure in Ottawa also, and to endanger it in the other provinces where a new offensive will then be started.

" Are the French-Canadians, whom they attempt in particular to gain to the cause of wine and beer, going to give themselves to this scheme, which will be most pernicious for them?

" Humanity has just passed through a terrible ordeal. The world is still as in a whirlwind. The sacrifices of human lives, the sum of sufferings and sorrows endured, is inexpressible; the material loss is beyond estimate; the greatness of the effort in work, in skill, in devotion and in courage displayed by the Allies for right, justice, civilization and freedom, surpasses all imagination. But all of these will have been in vain if the world does not triumph over alcoholism.

" Let Providence extend His protection over our beloved Province of Quebec and our country."

The liquor forces were well organized, had unlimited funds and spent prodigious sums in newspaper publicity.

In the closing days of the campaign the Hon. Napoleon Seguin, Minister without portfolio in the Provincial Government, raised the racial and religious cry, declaring prohibition to be a Methodist plot directed at the Roman Catholic Church to destroy the Sacrament by taking away wine, and stated that:

" An important bishop in the United States submitted to his confrères the original of a letter which was written by a high dignitary of the Methodist Church, and which letter declared, among other things, that if prohibition could be realized in all

PROVINCIAL PROHIBITION

America, the *coup de grace* would be given to the Catholic religion."

In the absence from the province of a great leader of the prohibition forces, Archbishop Bruchesi, and with the Church officially neutral, this last-minute lie had its effect.

A "Committee of Moderation" was formed with the stated object of putting before the electors the argument for a moderate use of beer and wine of a percentage of alcohol fixed by the Provincial Government. Honorary presidents of the committee were: Lord Shaughnessy; Sir Alexandre Lacoste, ex-Chief Justice of the Court of Appeal; Hon. L. O. David; Mr. J. T. Foster, President of the Trades and Labor Council. The president was Mr. Joseph Quintal, president of the Chamber of Commerce, and the secretary, Mr. J. E. Cote. A great number of other prominent citizens lent their names to this committee and, under this camouflage of respectability, the anti-prohibition campaign was conducted. The question submitted to the electors on April 10th was:

"Is it your opinion that the sale of light beer, cider, and wines, as defined by law, should be allowed?"

The result was an overwhelming majority for beer and wine, the figures being:

```
Yes ........................ 178,112
No ......................... 48,413
                             -------
Majority ................... 129,699
```

V. ONTARIO.

The decade following the Manitoba and Ontario referenda is the main period of the local option method, which had remained comparatively unutilized while vigorous efforts were being made to secure from Dominion and Province more comprehensive and thorough-going legislation.

PROHIBITION IN CANADA.

On February 24, 1905, shortly after the new Government's installation, a deputation waited upon Premier Whitney and members of his Cabinet. There had been some discussion at the Alliance Convention the preceding day as to what requests should be made of the Government by the temperance people; whether, considering the official declaration of the Conservative party at the conference the preceding year, the deputation should ask for specific amendments to the license law, or whether they should uncompromisingly stand by their demand for abolition of the bar, the treating system and drinking in clubs. The decision arrived at had been to continue the demand for prohibitory legislation. The Royal Templars of Temperance concurred in this decision and sent official representatives to the deputation.

The Premier, in reply to the speakers, said that the Government were anxious to hear any suggestions regarding the question, and the opinions of all classes of the people interested, and out of the results of the consultation held it would be their duty to evolve amendments to the present law which would be in the best interests of the province. Legislation of importance would, however, have to be postponed because of the shortness of the time since the Government had taken office.

In a vigorous debate in the Toronto and Hamilton Presbyterian Synod in May, 1905, strong ground was taken concerning the duty of Christian citizens and the Church at large on the temperance question. A deputation was sent to the Government to urge the protection of New Ontario from further inroads of the liquor traffic. Their answer, delivered by the Provincial Secretary, the Hon. W. J. Hanna, was to the effect that the policy of the Government was to refrain from increasing the number of licenses not only in New Ontario but in every part of the province.

During 1905 a bill was introduced into the Legislature by the Provincial Secretary, for the amendment of the Liquor License Act. It contained only one provision of value from a temperance standpoint—that of absolute prohibition of

PROVINCIAL PROHIBITION.

the sale of liquor to minors. As the law formerly stood, a minor might obtain liquor on an order from his parent or guardian. Another act extended the powers of brewers and distillers. It provided for a new kind of license to be called a Brewers' or Distillers' Warehouse License, authorizing the wholesaling of liquor in any localities in which licenses were taken out. It was claimed that under this act brewers might open warehouses in municipalities which had local option by-laws in operation.

A notable effort was made by the new Government, however, to improve the administration of the Liquor License Act. In the city of Toronto, three prominent citizens, Mr. J. W. Flavelle, Col. John I. Davidson and Mr. John A. Murray were appointed as commissioners. They adopted as their motto "The License Commissioners seek to enforce the law in a high-minded and just manner, and in doing so will know neither politics, creed nor corporation." The new commissioners took their duties seriously and personally visited the licensed houses for the purpose of ascertaining how fairly, in letter and in spirit, the requirements of the law were being observed. Some excerpts from the report are interesting:

" A common condition is that many houses are being kept merely as drinking places. . . . The sanitary appliances and conveniences are in many instances wholly bad, and unfit for either public or private use. . . . In many houses no attempt is made to serve meals regularly. . . . It has been the practice of the various brewers and wholesale dealers to acquire control of certain houses. The commissioners were struck with the number of women who were served through side-door entrances. . . . Many of the houses are nothing more nor less than saloons. . . . A common offence is the sale of liquor to men and women who are drunk."

The commissioners made an honest attempt to bring about better conditions, but encountered a difficulty in the attempted control of their actions by the License Department for political purposes, and in protest resigned at the end of the year. Another more amenable commission was appointed and things sank back into the old rut again.

In view of the fact that any legislation of importance would likely be postponed during the first year of the new administration, it was deemed advisable by the Ontario Branch of the Dominion Alliance to undertake a vigorous local option campaign to secure the closing of as many barrooms as possible. In response to an appeal from the executive, a great many municipalities worked to secure the submission and adoption of local option by-laws. The general plan followed was to have voting take place at the time of the municipal elections for 1906. In a number of cases, these efforts were thwarted by the unreasonable refusal of municipal councils to submit by-laws to the electors. In some cases friends of temperance thus treated promptly organized to secure councils more favorable to fair play, and in a number of cases were successful. Sixty-one municipalities voted on the first Monday, of January, 1906, and nine others shortly afterward. The prohibitory by-laws were carried in fifty-nine out of the seventy contests.

The success attained in these votings was so marked that it was deemed wise to call the attention of the Government to the matter. There was further reason for doing so in consideration of the probability that some liquor legislation would be introduced into the Ontario House in the ensuing session, according to the announcement of the Government. Consequently a deputation waited on the Cabinet on February 7, 1906, and asked for such prohibitory legislation as was demanded by the manifestation of public opinion in favor of bar-room abolition.

The Premier said that the Government felt it their duty to be ready to hear at any time representations on this question. Amendments to the License Act would be made from time to time, but the Government must keep in mind what was the policy announced by the Conservative party prior to the general elections of 1905. The Premier quoted the deliverances of the conference on the question, and went

PROVINCIAL PROHIBITION.

on to say that the success of the Conservative party in the election after that declaration, was evidence that the people approved of the policy thus set out. The deputation had asked the Government to banish the bars. For the Government to take any such step would be for them to do what they had no mandate from the people to do. The day had gone by when it was necessary for any one to take time to point out the evils of the drinking habit. The question was, how could they be ameliorated? Consistently with the course advocated when in Opposition, the Government were anxious to do anything in their power to minimize the evils resulting from the drink habit. He desired to state this position very emphatically and he was ready at all times to be held to it and reminded of it. He would carry it out to the best of his ability, according to his judgment.

THE THREE-FIFTHS CLAUSE.

Suddenly on March 20, 1906, without any previous intimation of intention to do anything else than to carry out their avowed policy of liquor traffic restriction, the Government introduced into the Legislature a license law amendment that was considered by prohibitionists decidedly reactionary and such as would hamper the temperance cause and give the liquor traffic a new lease of life. While municipal councils were to be compelled to submit prohibition by-laws to a vote of the electors when 25 per cent. of the electors petitioned for a vote, and were also to be under compulsion to pass such by-laws if the people adopted them, this advantage was partly counterbalanced by the proposal that a repeal contest might be brought on after two years' instead of three years' trial of the new plan. The bill permitted the Sunday sale of liquor, and also the sale on vessels and on dining and buffet cars.

The clause to which the temperance people chiefly objected was the one providing that in a municipality voting on a local option by-law, unless three-fifths of all the votes cast were in favor of it, the by-law would be considered defeated. A three-fifths vote was also required for the repeal of a by-law.

This proposal of requiring more than a majority vote was the one which the Liberal Government had made in reference to the referendum in 1902 and which had raised such a storm of opposition that the Government were compelled to withdraw it. The Hon. Mr. Hanna, in introducing the bill, said that the amendments proposed were intended to enable the Government better to carry out their policy with respect to the license laws. It was not intended to interfere in any way with local option.

The Alliance Convention in session in Toronto on March 27th and 28th expressed in strong terms condemnation of certain features of the proposed bill. "Positive abomination" Dr. Carman said of the clauses legalizing the sale of liquor on steamers and dining cars. A deputation was sent to the Parliament Buildings on the morning of the second day of the convention.

Hon. Mr. Hanna explained that the provision for Sunday liquor selling to hotel guests was in the draft of the bill by mistake and the Government did not propose to ask the House to adopt it. He defended the other features of the bill. The Premier said that the provision of the three-fifths majority was to make it necessary that the by-law should be backed up by a strong public sentiment. This was especially necessary when the act compelled the council to pass a by-law which had received a proper majority from the people. He argued that there must be a strong expression of opinion to warrant the passing of a measure which would depreciate the value of the property of a class of people. As for the statement of the deputation that the three-fifths vote was un-British, there were many other instances of the same kind. Bonus by-laws required a similar vote.

On April 4th a deputation from the liquor men also waited upon the Government and expressed their views upon the proposed legislation, advocating Sunday sale, deprecating increased license fee, objecting to municipal power to reduce

PROVINCIAL PROHIBITION.

licenses, complaining strongly of the severity of the penalties, but approving of the three-fifths clause. They asked that the local option by-law might be repealed by a majority vote where the original by-law was carried that way.

Other deputations waited upon the Government and strongly urged the elimination from the new bill of the three-fifths clause. Many electors in different parts of the province appealed earnestly to their representatives to oppose the measure. When the bill came up for its third reading on April 26th, the Hon. G. W. Ross moved an amendment striking out the three-fifths clause. The amendment was lost by a vote of 64 to 21 and the Liquor Act was passed without a division and with the objectionable three-fifths clause included in it.

It embodied some changes in the law that were advantageous from a temperance standpoint. In addition to the amendment requiring municipal councils to submit local option by-laws when such submission was petitioned for by one-quarter of the electors, another clause compelled councils to give a third reading to by-laws for which the electors had given the required vote. A third amendment prevented the quashing on mere technicalities of convictions for law violation. Changes which did not interest temperance workers very much were provisions for the increase of license fees and for the licensing of bar-tenders.

Regularly every year from that time on, the Alliance Conventions reiterated their denunciation of the three-fifths clause and sent a deputation to press home their demand for its appeal. Always they received the same answer.

Notwithstanding this serious obstacle, the progress made in local option contests was most encouraging. At the beginning of the campaign in 1904, there were only 187 "dry" municipalities to 607 under license. In 1916 the number had increased to 851. The swing from "wet" to "dry" in these years is illustrated by the following diagram and table:

PROHIBITION IN CANADA.

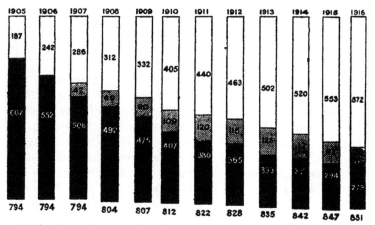

White shows the proportionate number of municipalities dry in each year. Black and shaded shows the proportionate number in which licenses are granted. The shading represents the number in which majorities were secured for Local Option, but in which we were defeated by the three-fifths.

LOCAL OPTION VOTING RECORD.

The following table gives the record of the Local Option voting in the Province of Ontario for thirteen years:

	Municipalities voting.	For.	Against.	Maj. for.	Carrying L.O.	Three-fifths.	Maj. Agst.
1904	6	2,204	1,717	487	6	0	.
1905	24	7,094	5,480	1,614	17	0	7
1906	70	23,432	16,194	7,238	59	0	11
1907	100	32,135	22,152	9,983	44	41	15
1908	84	24,127	18,795	5,332	31	29	24
1909	56	15,618	11,531	4,087	21	22	13
1910	158	55,658	38,595	17,063	77	55	26
1911	81	24,723	19,963	4,760	26	30	25
1912	69	16,597	15,763	834	18	21	30
1913	77	23,831	13,866	9,965	26	37	14
1914	41	14,888	10,727	4,161	17	20	4
1915	20	4,107	3,483	624	6	8	6
1916	47	20,922	16,953	3,969	20	19	8
Total...	833	265,336	195,219	70,117	368	282	183

The Dominion Government had asked for evidence of public prohibition sentiment; the Ontario Government had declared prohibition to be not practicable. The answer to both was given by the working out of the local option method.

PROVINCIAL PROHIBITION.

The voting showed the growth of public opinion in favor of the prohibition principle, while no stronger argument as to the soundness and effectiveness of prohibition could have been given than the fact of its spread. Had the local option law not been a success where tried, the movement would have had diminishing, not increasing force. It was because people saw the good results in other places that they adopted the measure for themselves. Moreover, during those years, opportunity was given for the repeal of prohibition, any time after it had been in force for three years. But such was its success that in the last six years of the local option period, out of 1,330 opportunities for repeal, in 1,260 cases the law was so firmly established that there was not even sufficient opposition to bring the matter to vote. Seventy repeal contests were brought on in six years. The law was sustained in sixty-nine of these cases.

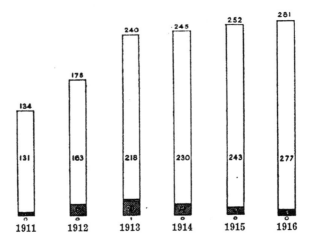

The accompanying diagram illustrates this outstanding fact. The whole column represents the total number of possible contests each year. The white represents the places where the liquor traffic was not strong enough to bring the matter to the polls. The shaded represents the contests brought on where the liquor forces were defeated. The one black line represents the one municipality (village of Acton) where Local Option was repealed.

PROHIBITION IN CANADA.

SUMMARY OF DIAGRAM FIGURES.

	1911	1912	1913	1914	1915	1916	Total
Possible Contests	134	178	240	245	252	281	1,330
No Vote	131	163	218	230	243	277	1,262
Local Option sustained	3	15	21	15	9	4	47
Local Option repealed.	0	0	1	0	0	0	1

The gaining of municipal prohibition by localities meant practical demonstrations or object lessons of the business, social and moral benefits of its operations. Thus, as the dry area spread, public opinion was built up and strengthened, and sure foundation was laid for a larger measure.

LICENSE REDUCTION.

In addition to the local option campaign, there was in 1909 a movement for license reduction in a number of places. In Toronto, the city council had passed a by-law early in 1908 reducing the number of bar-room licenses in the city from 150 to 110; but the by-law was quashed by the courts. At the municipal elections in 1909 the issue was put to the electors. Revelations made in the License Commissioners' report regarding conditions in Toronto hotels, were used with great force in the campaign. The fight was a close and bitter one. The temperance forces were well organized and won out by a vote of 19,338 to 18,492, a majority of 846 in favor of reducing the bars from 150 to 110.

In St. Catharines, a plebiscite was taken and a large majority secured for license reduction. A by-law was consequently passed by the city council reducing the number of bar-rooms. In Ottawa a reduction was made of nine bars and four shops.

Temperance workers in Peterborough, Brantford, Picton, Sault Ste. Marie, and other places, where a large majority was secured for local option, but where they were defeated by the three-fifths requirement, urged their municipal councils to pass license reduction by-laws, and as a result of their requests about 250 licenses were cut off.

A notable temperance victory was won in Hamilton in 1911. The city council, after defeating a license reduction

PROVINCIAL PROHIBITION.

by-law, took a plebiscite on the questions of cutting down the licenses from 66 to 60, and of paying compensation to liquor dealers. The Hamilton Temperance Federation took up the fight. The vote upon the question of license reduction was as follows:

    For reduction 6,555
    Against reduction 4,340

    Majority for 2,215

On the question of compensation it was as follows:

    For Compensation 3,894
    Against Compensation 6,767

    Majority against 2,873

License Law Amendments.

A notable feature of the amendments passed by the Legislature during these years was that they did not impose much further restriction upon the sale of liquor by license-holders, but were largely in the nature of making it difficult and dangerous to sell liquor without a license, and to secure a better enforcement of the law generally.

In 1907, several minor amendments to the license law were made. The only point where local option work was affected was a clause allowing for the filing of petitions requesting the taking of a local option vote, with the clerk of the municipality, instead of requiring their presentation before the municipal council. The provision regarding the sale of liquor to minors was greatly strengthened. Further restrictions were put upon clubs and club-selling. The section relating to the right of search was also improved.

The liquor legislation of 1908 was disappointing. It had been hoped that something would be done to remedy the intolerable situation which has been created by the imposition of the three-fifths requirement for the passing of the local option by-laws, but the amendments were few, and mostly dealt with unimportant details. There were, however, two commendable features. One was a clause to prevent the possible evasion of the law by bar-leasing; the other was the carrying out of the principle that the "people shall rule," and provided that even if by-laws approved of by the electors were quashed, no license should be issued within that municipality without the written consent of the Minister. This was made retroactive so as to include municipalities where by-laws had been passed in 1907, and resulted in the cancellation of licenses in several places.

When the amending bill came up for its third reading, Mr. T. H. Preston (Brantford) brought the question of the three-fifths requirement before the House in a motion to strike out the word "three-fifths" and substitute therefor a "majority." Mr. Preston clearly set forth that the clause was an infringement of a provision which had been in existence since Confederation, that the electors should decide such questions by a majority vote. Mr. Hanna, speaking in defence of the three-fifths, said that the Government intended giving the clause a fair trial. Mr. Preston's amendment was lost by a vote of 21 to 55.

Some of the principal features of license law amendment in 1909 were: the prohibiting of the sale of liquor in local option municipalities by the holders of Brewers', or Brewers' Warehouse Licenses; the repeal of the provision under which certain cities and towns had more licenses than should be permitted by the regular population limit; an increase in the penalties for a first offence in selling liquor without a license; giving fuller protection to witnesses who had unlawfully purchased liquor from persons charged with law violation; compelling intoxicated minors to give evidence as to where they procured liquor; provision that a penalty might be imposed for a proven offence, even though some other offence had been primarily charged; the simplification of procedure in appeals, and the sustaining of convictions; power for officials to seize liquors in transit when they

PROVINCIAL PROHIBITION.

believed such liquors were intended to be sold illicitly; improvement in the provision restricting canvassing for liquor in local option municipalities; providing that the finding in any lodging-house of more liquor than might be reasonably supposed to be for private use, should be evidence that such liquor was kept for sale; amending the clause which made it mandatory upon license commissioners to grant club licenses.

The matter of the three-fifths requirement was again brought up by Mr. W. Proudfoot, M.P.P. for Centre Huron, who introduced a bill providing for the repeal of that injustice.

Notwithstanding the continuously increasing temperance sentiment in the Province of Ontario and the growing demand for progressive restrictive legislation, the 1910 session of the Legislature came as near to doing nothing as was possible when any action at all was taken. The most important amendment to the license law was the closing of the licensed places on Christmas Day. An important amendment was passed to the Municipal Act, by which all the provisions of that act regarding corrupt practices at elections were made applicable to the voting upon local option by-laws.

The recommendations of the 1912 Alliance Convention in reference to proposed amendments to the Liquor License Act were incorporated in a bill prepared by Mr. W. E. Raney, K.C., at the request of the executive, and some of its proposals passed into law. The principal amendments of this year were: the keeping of liquor for sale was made punishable with the same penalties as the offence of selling; the storing of liquor for future delivery in a local option municipality was prohibited; persons found drunk in a local option municipality might be compelled to state where and from whom they obtained liquor; councils in cities were prohibited from passing by-laws reducing the number of shop licenses without a vote of the electors; local option districts were made subject to inspection, and reports concerning them to the Minister were authorized.

PROHIBITION IN CANADA.

When this bill was under discussion, the Leader of the Opposition moved an amendment providing for prohibition of the issue of club licenses in local option districts, which was defeated by an amendment declaring the satisfaction of the House with the Provincial Secretary's assurance that the Government's policy was not to issue such licenses.

PARTY PLATFORMS.

In November, 1911, it was announced that the Ontario Government would appeal to the country and that a general provincial election would be held on December 11th. The Alliance decided that in view of the failure of both Liberal and Conservative parties to accept the mandate of the people against the bar-room, as recorded in two special votings, and in many local option contests, they could not support directly either of the two parties. They reiterated in a manifesto to electors their time-honored principle of supporting avowed prohibitionists irrespective of party.

Shortly before the election, the leader of the Liberal party, Hon. A. G. Mackay, resigned, his place being filled by Mr. N. W. Rowell, K.C., a vice-president of the Alliance, and a gentleman who has always been recognized as a strong friend of the temperance cause. Neither of the parties in its appeal to the electors declared in favor of an adequate measure of provincial legislation. The platform of the Liberal party as published contained the following:

"The evils of intemperance constitute a grave social peril. During the ensuing parliamentary term, we will consider the best form of legislation to deal effectively with these evils, and the electors will have an opportunity of passing upon our proposals at the following general elections.

" We will immediately abolish the three-fifths vote in local option contests, and substitute a simple majority.

" During the continuance of the license system, we will secure the removal of its administration from political influence."

As the campaign developed, a number of Liberal candidates pronounced themselves clearly and definitely in

PROVINCIAL PROHIBITION.

favor of province-wide abolition of the bar. Many Conservative candidates also pronounced themselves as favoring progressive temperance legislation. The Conservative Government was sustained in the elections.

The growing public sentiment in favor of prohibition was reflected in the policies of the political parties. In 1912, Mr. N. W. Rowell moved the following resolutions in the Legislature:

That in the opinion of this House, the public interest demands:
(1) The immediate abolition of the bar;
(2) Such other restrictions upon the residue of the liquor traffic as experience may show to be necessary to limit its operations and effective to remedy its evils;
(3) The strict enforcement of the law by officials in sympathy with law enforcement, and the elimination of political influence from the administration of the law;
(4) Regulation and inspection of all houses of public entertainment, so as to insure reasonable accommodation for the travelling public.

The Conservative position was expressed by an amendment moved by Premier Whitney in the following words:

This House recognizes the duty cast upon it to minimize, as far as possible, the vile effect of the drink habit, by wise restrictions upon the traffic in intoxicating liquors. The House also recognizes that, having regard to the decision of the Judicial Committee of the Privy Council as to the respective jurisdiction of the Dominion and of the provinces, it is impossible for the people of the province, through its Legislature, to abolish or control the manufacture within, or the importation into, the province of intoxicating liquors; that the treating habit is now almost universally recognized as the most powerful factor in the evil results of the said traffic and habit, and no good object would be served by simply diverting the habit from the bar to some other place; that in the opinion of this House, legislation to prevent and put a stop to the said treating habit should be enacted and, if necessary, supplemented by regulations under which retail licenses are granted and held.

PROHIBITION IN CANADA.

The Legislature endorsed the amendment by a vote of 79 to 19. Each succeeding year Mr. Rowell raised its issue in the House on a similar resolution.

At the 1913 session of the Ontario Legislature, on February 18th, an amendment to the address, in reply to the Speech from the Throne, was moved by Mr. W. Proudfoot, of Centre Huron, in the following form:

That the following words be added to the motion
"And in view of the resolution submitted by the Government to this House at its last session, and approved by this House, which contains the following declaration: 'Resolved, That this House recognized the duty cast upon it to minimize as far as possible the evil effect of the drink habit by wise restrictions upon the traffic in intoxicating liquors;' that in the opinion of this House legislation, to prevent and put a stop to the said treating habit, should be enacted and, if necessary, supplemented by regulations under retail licenses are granted and held."

"And in view of the increasing demand throughout the province for advanced temperance legislation, this House regrets that the Government has failed to indicate its intention to introduce legislation pursuant to this resolution, or other and more effective legislation to curtail the evils of the liquor traffic."

This motion being offered as an amendment to the address, would, if carried, have been practically an expression of want of confidence in the Government, and to prevent a vote being taken directly upon it, the Hon. W. J. Hanna moved to amend it by substituting for it the following:

This House has confidence that the Government will, at the proper time, submit legislation for the consideration of the House that will place further restrictions on the liquor traffic and minimize the evils of the drink habit.

This amendment was declared adopted on a division

The temperance question was first brought to the attention of the Legislature in 1914 by a motion offered by Dr. McQueen, in which regret was expressed that the Government, notwithstanding the resolution declaring in favor of legis-

PROVINCIAL PROHIBITION.

lation against the treating practices, had failed to propose legislation to abolish the bar-room, to prohibit the treating system, or otherwise to curtail the liquor traffic. The motion was defeated by a vote of 52 to 15 on a straight party division.

A feature of that session was a proposal by Mr. Rowell that his party would give united support to any measure of temperance legislation more progressive than his own, if the Government would propose and support it. He also offered to join in an appeal to the people for ratification of such a measure if a ratifying vote upon it were deemed advisable. He further called attention to the fact that the policy embodied in his resolution did not originate with the Liberal party, but was first proposed by a representative convention called by the Dominion Alliance.

In his reply, Mr. Hanna reiterated the steps of progress that had been made in temperance legislation during the recent years, pointing out what had been accomplished in license reduction and law enforcement. He repudiated the charge of an alliance between the Government and the liquor interests and claimed that the license law was being administered from a non-partisan standpoint.

LICENSE COMMISSION.

There is no doubt that the outbreak of the European War helped to hasten the end of the legalized liquor traffic in Canada, an end, however, which was inevitable. The overwhelming evidence given by the events of the opening of that campaign to the mischievous effects of alcoholic indulgence, gave a force to the appeal for immediate action. But prohibition was not a moral whim brought about by war conditions. It was rather a culmination of progressive legislation.

Upon the death of Sir James Whitney in September, 1914, Mr. (afterwards Sir) William Hearst became leader of the Conservative Government. Mr. Hearst was known as a strong temperance man. He had taken an active part in local option campaigns and other temperance work in Sault

PROHIBITION IN CANADA.

Ste. Marie, and prohibitionists hoped for sympathy and help from the new Premier.

In a public address, Mr. Rowell, shortly after the outbreak of war, renewed to Mr. Hearst his offer to lift the temperance question entirely above the realm of party controversy. He said in part:

"If Mr. Hearst and his colleagues still believe that this question should be passed upon by the people, free from any political considerations, then, let us, at least, agree to close up these drinking places during the war, and submit to the direct vote of the people the question of whether the bars thus closed shall remain forever closed or be re-opened at the end of the war, the question to be settled by a majority vote. I have no doubt as to the result."

The bill to amend the Liquor License Act, introduced into the Legislature shortly after the 1915 Alliance Convention, was a great disappointment. It was felt that public opinion and the great Empire emergency demanded advanced progressive enactment, but only two restrictions of any moment were proposed: the closing of the liquor shops at 7 p.m. and the prohibiting of liquor selling on one holiday, Labor Day.

The main feature of the bill, however, was the providing for the appointment of a Board of License Commissioners for the province. The far-reaching effects of the new law were set forth in an official circular sent out by the Department in which it is stated the Board may

1. Subdivide the province into new license districts in such manner as experience and investigation may show to be advantageous to the better administration of the law.

2. Issue a restricted license such as a "beer license" in any locality.

3. Shorten the hours within which liquor may be sold in taverns or shops throughout the province or in any portion of the province, but cannot extend the hours of sale beyond what the law now provides.

4. In its discretion, suspend or cancel any license.

PROVINCIAL PROHIBITION.

5. Make regulations for improved hotel accommodation to meet the requirements in any locality, and enforce these regulations by either suspension or cancellation of the license if they are not carried out.

6. Conduct an inquiry into any matter deemed necessary in connection with the administration of the law, and require evidence to be given under oath.

7. Supersede the necessity for a vote on local option by prohibiting the sale or other disposal of liquor in any portion of the province, subject to ratification by the Lieutenant-Governor in Council:

    (a) For all time.
    (b) For any particular time.
    (c) For any specific period.
    (d) To any class of persons.
    (e) During prohibited hours.

The bill went through with very slight alterations.

When the personnel of the commission was announced general satisfaction was felt throughout the province. It consisted of Chairman J. D. Flavelle, Vice-Chairman W. S. Dingman, and Commissioners John A. Ayearst, George L. Smith, and Frederick Dane.

On May 12, 1915, a deputation from the Executive Committee of the Ontario Branch of the Dominion Alliance waited upon the Ontario Board of License Commissioners, requesting them, if it lay within their power, to prohibit entirely the sale of liquor in bar-rooms, licensed shops and clubs during the war. If the authority of the commission would not warrant such a step, they were asked to impose a number of specific regulations restricting the districts, hours and days in which liquor might be sold.

In the fall, strong representations were again made to the License Board and to the Government for early closing, with the result that an order was issued by the Board, and approved by the Government, fixing the closing hour for bars throughout the province at 8 p.m. every week-night except Saturday, at which time the closing hour remained 7 p.m. The order went into effect in November and was to continue in full force and effect during the period of the war.*

ONTARIO TEMPERANCE ACT.

During the year 1915 several conferences were held between a number of temperance workers connected with various organizations in the province, and a call was issued for a meeting which was held in the Royal Bank Building, Toronto, on October 15th, when about one hundred men were present. After some discussion the following resolution was adopted

"That a Committee of one hundred citizens of Ontario be forthwith formed, to be composed as nearly as may be of an equal number of Conservatives and Liberals, and that such committee proceed to organize constituencies and to secure the nomination of candidates for the next election who shall be pledged to the abolition of taverns, shop and club licenses and the prohibition of all sales of intoxicating liquors for beverage purposes."

A Citizens' Committee of One Hundred was then named, with Judge E. P. Clement, of Kitchener, as chairman; James Hales, Toronto, vice-chairman; Frank Kent, Meaford, treasurer; and Newton Wylie, Toronto, secretary. A campaign was planned to petition the Government of Ontario for provincial prohibition, and steps were taken to thoroughly organize the province for this purpose. At a meeting of the Managing Committee of the Ontario Alliance, on November 5th, a deputation representing the Citizens' Committee of One Hundred asked for the co-operation of the Alliance in this petitioning movement, and a resolution was passed promising full co-operation with and hearty support to the committee in the campaign. The services of Mr. G. A. Warburton were secured as chairman of the Campaign Executive Committee.

The following form of petition was circulated throughout the province:

---
* See Appendix IX.

PROVINCIAL PROHIBITION.

Voters' Petition.

Municipality of
County of

To the Premier and Government of the Province of Ontario:

Your petitioners, being (male) British subjects of the age of twenty-one years or over, and residents of the Province of Ontario, humbly pray:

That the Government at the forth-coming session of the Legislature bring down a bill for the prohibition in this Province of the traffic in intoxicating liquors for beverage purposes, up to the limits of the powers of the Legislature, such bill to become law—

(a) When enacted by the Legislature, or in the alternative,

(b) Upon submission to the electors, and upon receiving the approval of a majority of the electors voting thereon.

And your petitioners, as in duty bound, will ever pray.

Before this campaign was completed the Legislature met and the Government policy was announced in the Speech from the Throne in the following words:

"Legislation will be submitted relating to the prohibition of the sale of intoxicating liquors within the province and for the submission of the same to the electors."

The policy of the Government was further explained by the Premier himself, who said:

"This is not the time to speak of the details of the legislation. The authority of the province is not wide enough to prohibit the manufacture or importation of intoxicating liquors, and provision must be made for sale for mechanical and scientific and medicinal purposes; but I may say that it is the intention of the Government to have the legislation go as far as the powers of the province, as they have been interpreted by the Privy Council in connection with this matter, will allow us."

The Premier, in reply to various deputations, reaffirmed the position of the Government and stated that the policy

PROHIBITION IN CANADA.

had been only determined after careful consideration, and would be adhered to.

The Citizens' Committee, however, did not allow the action of the Government to hold up the work they had undertaken, and the petitioning campaign was pushed to a triumphant conclusion, as will be seen from the following table:

PETITION OF CITIZENS' COMMITTEE OF ONE HUNDRED.

Total number of names on voters' lists in Ontario at last election	728,624
Total number of votes cast in all constituencies at last voting	476,905
Total number of names of male British subjects twenty-one years and over signed to petitions	348,166
Other residents of Ontario (none being under eighteen years of age) signing petition	477,396
Total number of names on both petitions	825,562
Percentage of names signing potential voters' petition of total votes cast last election	73.4%
Percentage of names of potential voters signing petition of total number on the list last election	47.8%

Following up the petition, a monster demonstration was held in the city of Toronto, to which excursions were run from all parts of the province. On March 7th a banquet was held in Willard Hall, followed by a public mass meeting in Massey Hall, addressed by Sir Geo. E. Foster and others.

On March 8th a great parade took place, which, in spite of the unfavorable weather and hostile demonstrations by liquor sympathizers, was a success. The paraders carried through the streets the monster petition and presented it to the Government at the Parliament Buildings. The chairman of each county, bearing the petition from that county, together with a number of other persons, met the Premier and Cabinet, and Judge Clement, Chairman of the Citizens' Committee of One Hundred, presented an address, in which he said in part:

PROVINCIAL PROHIBITION.

"The committee are delighted to learn by the Speech from the Throne and by the remarks of the Premier in the House, that the Government, recognizing the growth of temperance sentiment and conviction in the province—a sentiment which the war has served to greatly increase and intensify—have decided to submit the question of prohibition to the people. As this action of the Government has anticipated the presentation of this petition, and as the measure proposed by the Government is in harmony with our alternative proposition, we are in the happy position of being able to congratulate the Government upon their decision and to pledge them our earnest support during the progress of the bill through the House. We will also exert ourselves to the utmost to secure a favorable vote when the bill is before the people."

Premier Hearst, in reply, said:

"The Government has come to the conclusion that a large proportion of our people desire, and desire earnestly, further legislative action on this question at the present time, and the decision the Government has come to is endorsed and emphasized by the petition you have presented to-day.

"This Government has announced its policy clearly in the Speech from the Throne, and I have defined it also in my address in the House. If that proposed law becomes effective, this Government will enforce that law to the utmost of its ability. We shall take care, so far as it is humanly possible, to see that no fault lies at our doors in connection with the enforcement of that law. And we have a right to expect that the gentlemen of your committee and the people throughout the province who ask for temperance legislation will do their full duty to back up the Government."

Prior to the presentation of the petition by the Citizens' Committee of One Hundred on March 22nd, the Hon. Mr. Hanna had introduced the "Ontario Temperance Act" in the Legislature. It is an admirable, comprehensive and strong measure, following with very slight variation the Manitoba Act, which had been approved by the Privy Council.

The announced intention of the Government was that the bill should be immediately submitted to a vote of the electors. Owing to war conditions and the absence of so many men overseas, however, this was found impossible, and it was decided to pass the measure, give it a fair trial, and then, at the close of the war and upon the return of the troops, submit the question to a vote. The bill was finally passed at 10 p.m. on April 12, 1916. It came into force at 7 p.m. on Saturday, September 16.

With the passing of the Ontario Temperance Act, upon which both political parties united, the temperance issue was removed from the controversial issues between the political parties in the Province of Ontario. This was set out by Premier Hearst in his great address before the Legislature in which he said:

"Our policy in 1914, and before and since, has been that this question should be removed, as far as possible, from the arena of party politics and from partisan controversy, and the policy we are submitting to this House for the final settlement of this question by means of a referendum provides the only way in which that policy can be effectually carried out."*

It was also emphasized by Mr. Rowell, when he referred to an appeal which he had previously made to the Government, in the words: "What a magnificent spectacle it would be if Ontario, the leader of the provinces of the Dominion, should have both political parties uniting and saying, 'For the public good, the bar must be wiped out.'" He added:

"To-day that vision is a reality, that dream has come true, and this province witnesses the spectacle of both political parties united to wipe out the bar and to suppress the retail sale of liquor in the Province of Ontario. I am sure it is an inspiring sight to the overwhelming mass of the people of the province, and it will have its effect on the question of the enforcement of the law in the future."

Each year the Ontario Temperance Act has been amended and improved, and is now an exceedingly effective piece of legal machinery for the remedying of the evils of intemperance.†

---

* See Appendix X.
† See Appendix XI.

PROVINCIAL PROHIBITION.

Upon the passing of the act, the Provincial Board of Commissioners already appointed was charged with the administration of the measure, and to their efficiency and integrity the success of the act is in a large measure due. The sale for permitted purposes was to be by licensed vendors. At first three were appointed—two in Toronto, and one in Hamilton. The number was afterward increased to seven, licenses being granted in Ottawa, Kingston, London and Windsor.

When the act had been in force for one year public men all over the province were asked to express their opinion as to the results of its operation. Sir William Hearst said:

"We have now had twelve months' experience of the Ontario Temperance Act, and I am thankful to be able to say that the operation of the law has come up to my greatest expectations. Reports from all parts of the province indicate the success of the measure as well as the great benefits that are resulting from it. One very gratifying result of the act is the increased efficiency of the workers of this province in every branch of production. Employers of labor are unanimously of opinion that our people are doing more and better work to-day than ever before. This is a good thing for the workers and for their families and for their employers as well, and is a great thing for the country at a time when all our energies are required to save the Empire from destruction. In this way a patriotic purpose of the highest order has been served. I am glad to know that in accomplishing this end we have not been compelled, as many people feared we would be, to put the travelling public to serious inconvenience. Our information is that the hotel accommodation in Ontario is, on the whole, better than before the act came into force, and constantly improving, though it may not be quite as extensive and in some cases not as cheap as it was when the sale of liquor was permitted.

"While there have been a number of violations of the act throughout the province, the law generally has been well observed, having regard to the somewhat drastic provisions of the act and the great change in former conditions and practices created thereby. Official figures indicate a large decrease in the number of convictions for drunkenness in the province. These figures, however, by no means indicate the full extent to which drunkenness

PROHIBITION IN CANADA.

has been reduced. Before September 16th last, men arrested for drunkenness, when no other charge was lodged against them, were usually discharged by the police when sober, without any conviction being registered. Now charges are lodged in all cases and record kept. The small number of criminal cases throughout the province and the absence of criminals in so many of our jails bear positive testimony of the good influence of this measure in reducing crime of all kinds, and there can be no doubt that the act has been instrumental in adding greatly to the comfort and happiness of thousands of our people.

"I feel confident that as years go by, and our people become accustomed to the changed conditions, still better results will ensue. A generation will grow up free from the associations and temptations of the open and public sale of intoxicating liquors; the taste and inclination for alcohol will gradually disappear, and we will escape the terrible evils with which the excessive use of intoxicants has so long been associated. Necessarily the first year's operation of the Ontario Temperance Act must be considered the most difficult and trying one of its experience. Many good people had doubts of the wisdom and the practicability of the step. To-day those who conscientiously opposed the measure are to be found among its strongest supporters, so that the public sentiment necessary to the proper enforcement of this law is constantly growing and guarantees alike its efficiency and stability."

Mr. N. W. Rowell, K.C., said:

"I am in receipt of the strongest testimony, from all parts of the province, of the great practical benefits which have resulted from the operation of the Ontario Temperance Act during the past year.

"The results have been so satisfactory that large numbers of those who were opposed to the adoption of the measure are now its warm supporters. Thousands of wives and children are better clothed, better fed, and know more of the real meaning of 'home' to-day than they ever knew before. Crime has been substantially reduced; the efficiency and earning power of the workers have been materially increased; business has been stimulated rather than depressed, and the whole country has been enjoying freedom from the constant menace of the open bar. It is evident that the bar now closed will never be reopened in this province.

PROVINCIAL PROHIBITION.

"Vigorous and impartial enforcement of the law must be maintained, and the act must be strengthened where necessary to make it more effective and to carry out its intent.

"Our grateful appreciation is due to the men and women all over this province whose untiring and unselfish labors through the years made possible this great measure of social reform."

Many other equally striking testimonies were received.

A questionnaire to the mayors of the principal towns and cities brought 69 telegraphic replies; 59 were decidedly favorable, 9 non-committal, and 1 unfavorable. A questionnaire to the principal newspapers of the province brought 58 telegraphic replies, not a single one being unfavorable. A letter to the members of the Toronto Board of Trade, comprising the principal business men in the city, brought 396 replies, of which 366 were favorable, 22 non-committal, 9 unfavorable. The response on the whole would indicate that prohibition had substantially grown in favor and good results were following its operation.

At the session of the Legislature in 1918, the Board of Provincial Commissioners was reduced to three, Commissioner Fred Dane retiring, Commissioner J. A. Ayearst being appointed enforcing officer for the province. The board was then constituted with J. D. Flavelle, chairman; W. S. Dingman, vice-chairman; and Commissioner George T. Smith.

At the session of the Legislature in 1919, Premier Hearst announced the Government's policy, which was to take over the sale of liquor for permitted purposes and place the same under direct control of the Provincial Board of License Commissioners, eliminating all private profit in connection therewith, and to provide for taking of the vote of the electors of the province upon the repeal or retention of the Ontario Temperance Act, the referendum to be held in the early fall. Bills were afterward passed in accordance with the Premier's statement. The bill respecting the referendum provided that the day should be fixed by the Lieutenant-Governor in

Council, and that the following four questions should be submitted to the electors:

	Yes.	No.
1. Are you in favor of the repeal of the Ontario Temperance Act?		
2. Are you in favor of the sale of light beer containing not more than 2 51-100 per cent. alcohol weight measure through Government agencies and amendments to the Ontario Temperance Act to permit such sale?		
3. Are you in favor of the sale of light beer containing not more than 2 51-100 per cent. alcohol weight measure in standard hotels in local municipalities that by a majority vote favor such sale, and amendments to the Ontario Temperance Act to permit such sale?		
4. Are you in favor of the sale of spirituous and malt liquors through Government agencies and amendments to the Ontario Temperance Act to permit such sale?		

VI. MANITOBA.

For some time after the Manitoba referendum, temperance work in that province languished. Party politicians seemed to be doing their utmost to discredit the movement and to hinder reform, and workers, holding the settled conviction that no good thing could be had from the Government then in office, were inclined to await developments. The legislation of 1905 was trivial: the raising of the license fee; the requiring of more extensive hotel accommodation in premises in which liquor was sold; and the prohibition of wholesale licenses in villages.

Then under the stimulus of the provincial general election, things began to stir. Since the Hon. Thos. Greenway's retire-

PROVINCIAL PROHIBITION.

ment in 1904, the Hon. C. Mickle had been acting Liberal leader. At the convention in Winnipeg in March, 1906, the party was reorganized under the leadership of Mr. Edward Brown, Mayor of Portage la Prairie, and chairman of the Provincial Liberal Executive. Speaking at Selkirk in the fall of 1906, Mr. Brown outlined the temperance policy adopted by each party at that convention. He said in part:

"We have promised to place it within the power of the temperance people in any community to have local option in any municipality where a majority, not of the property owners who reside elsewhere and therefore can have no particular interest in the matter, but of the actual residents, decide that the local option law shall go into force. This, I think, is as far as public opinion will justify any party in going under the existing conditions, and no party should be asked to go further than public opinion will warrant. We will also restore the franchise to married women, who have been deprived by this Government of the right to vote on these questions. We will see to it that the license commissioners are men in whom everyone has the utmost confidence. This is certainly not the case at the present time. The Government has sought to lay the blame for licenses wrongfully granted upon the license commissioners. They cannot shirk responsibility by any such excuse. The policy of the commissioners has been the policy of the Government.

"The Liberal party stands also pledged that it shall be within the power of any municipality to restrict the number of licenses within its borders, and that upon the presentation of a petition signed by twenty-five per cent. of the resident ratepayers the municipal council shall have no option, but must submit a local option by-law to the popular vote."

In the election campaign in the spring of 1907, considerable prominence was given to the temperance question. The Government saw fit to reply to denunciations of their license policy. Mr. J. A. M. Aikins, K.C., at Winnipeg on February 26th, at Virden on the 27th, and elsewhere defended the Government by reading from the Statutes of 1904 and of succeeding years a number of restrictive amendments to the license law added by the Conservative Government in the

PROHIBITION IN CANADA.

interests of temperance reform. The result of the election, which was held on March 7, 1907, was the return of the Conservative Government by a slightly reduced majority

In discussing the election vote, *The Pioneer,* of March 22, 1907, said:

"There is no question that the liquor vote went fairly solid for the present Administration. On the other hand it is equally certain that the temperance vote was divided. The reason good citizens supported the Government rather than the Opposition was not because they did not know the Government to be bad, but rather because they did not know the Opposition to be good.

"There was an open, brutal bravado about the attitude of the leaders of the Conservative party which could not be mistaken for anything like friendliness to the temperance cause. On the other hand, there was a shrinking, timid fearfulness on the part of the Opposition, which could not be construed into antagonism to the liquor traffic.

"The Liberal party, in their so-called 'temperance' platform, went too far to retain the support of the liquor element, but did not go far enough to obtain the support of temperance people.

"The situation demanded vigorous treatment and a strong pronouncement. This the Liberals were not prepared to give. They have only themselves to blame. The most advanced plank in the Liberal platform was 'local option by majority vote,' and in view of the strong sentiment in the Province of Manitoba in favor of bar-room abolition, this was a pitiably weak and inadequate policy. Had the Liberals shown strength the result would have been different."

In the spring of 1907 several deputations from churches and temperance societies waited upon the Government, asking for amendments to the license law, but each deputation made different requests, and in some cases the prayers were conflicting. It was an illustration of the need of some kind of federation of the religious and social reform bodies to garner up the strength of the temperance sentiment by co-operation.

Rev. S. D. Chown and Rev. J. G. Shearer, secretaries of the moral and social reform departments already established

PROVINCIAL PROHIBITION.

in the Methodist and Presbyterian Churches, by request called an Interdenominational Conference in the Y.M.C.A. at Winnipeg, on November 15, 1907. There were present representatives of the Presbyterian Synod, the Anglican Synod, the Roman Catholic Church, the Congregational Church, the Trades and Labor Congress, and the Royal Templars of Temperance. Mr. Czerwinski, chief officer of the R.T., presided, and W. W. Buchanan acted as secretary.

The delegation unanimously agreed that it was desirable to establish a permanent federation of the moral and social reform forces of the province for united action to secure progressive legislation. They approved of the employment of the local option method as the only available prohibitory legislation on the statute books, and planned for a campaign to secure the abolition of drinking places under the slogan of "Banish the Bar."

A second conference met on February 18, 1908, and included, in addition to the bodies represented at the first meeting, members of the Baptist Association and Salvation Army. A permanent organization was established under the name of the Moral and Social Reform Council of Manitoba. The following officers were elected: Wm. White, Hon. President; A. W. Puttee, Vice-President; W. W. Buchanan, Secretary; A. M. Fraser, Treasurer; and an Executive Committee representing the Roman Catholic Church, the Anglican Synod, Presbyterian Synod, Methodist Conference, Baptist Association, Congregational Union, Salvation Army, R.T. of T., and Trades and Labor Congress.

The temperance policy adopted at the conference of the preceding year was endorsed, and it was decided to inaugurate a petitioning campaign to secure the abolition of the bar-rooms. Since that time there have entered the federation, the Unitarian Church, the Good Templars, the W.C.T.U., the Scandinavian Anti-Saloon League, the Provincial Sunday School Association, the Provincial Union of Christian Endeavor, the Polish National Catholic Church, the Ruthenian Catholic Church, and the Russian Orthodox

Greek Church. Also the Provincial Grain Growers' Association endorsed the policy for the abolition of the bar-room.

On January 29, 1908, a strong petition of 9,000 signatures, headed by the Archbishop of St. Boniface, and supported by a deputation, asked the Government for legislation to close hotel bars at 6 o'clock. This request was refused on the ground that such a law would encourage illegal dives. But a number of important changes were made in the license law during the session. The three-fifths clause of the local option law was changed to a straight majority—an amendment which the Liberal party had urged strongly during their election campaign, and which had formed part of the Liberal platform. The petition of twenty-five per cent. of the resident electors was to be mandatory upon a municipal council to hold a local option contest at the annual municipal elections. Penalties for illegal liquor selling were increased, and the regulation of sales was made more stringent.

These amendments stimulated enthusiasm for a local option campaign, initiated by the Provincial Executive of the R.T. of T. and the recently organized Moral and Social Reform Council of Manitoba. Much hard and good work was done. One feature of the campaign was an auto-veto movement conducted by the Royal Templars.

There were at the time only twenty-seven of the one hundred and twenty-eight municipalities of the province under veto. Petition for a vote was signed and filed by sixty-seven municipalities. The requirement for such petitions was twenty-five per cent. of the resident electors, but none of the petitions had less than fifty per cent. of the electors' signatures, and one recorded ninety-two per cent.

Once again the temperance workers were tripped up. The section of the Liquor Act relating to petitions provided for the submission of a vote, "if the council received, not later than the first day of October in any year, a petition." The decision of the courts was that application, although filed with the clerk of the municipality before October 1st,

PROVINCIAL PROHIBITION.

was void unless the council were in session at the time of the filing of the petition. Thus forty-five municipalities were debarred from voting on December 15th. Of those that voted, fifteen carried local option by-laws. Repeal contests were brought on by the liquor men in ten municipalities, but they were successful in only one.

On February 19, 1909, a deputation of more than 1,000 persons waited on the Government, presenting an "Abolish the Bar" petition, with 13,500 signatures. They asked also that the local option law be made workable by the addition of a saving clause so that courts would not prevent a vote or quash a by-law upon a technicality; that non-residents should not be permitted to vote; and that a penalty be provided for personation. Premier Roblin promised consideration to the requests for local option amendments, but thought the country was not ripe for the abolition of the bar.

On February 23rd, the liquor men requested the Government to return to the three-fifths local option requirement, but their petition was refused.

In 1909, the local option law was amended, providing (1) a penalty for personation; (2) that petitions might be filed with the municipal clerk; (3) that liquor might not be imported into a local option town.

The next year a petition was filed for voting in sixty municipalities. The liquor party put up a hard fight. They appealed for an injunction to prevent the vote and secured from Judge Metcalfe one applying to the municipality of Pembina, because the petition had been pasted together. Some of the other trivial excuses that succeeded were: that names were spelled differently on the petition and on the voters' list; that a woman used her husband's initials instead of her own; that some of the signatures were attached a few months before the petitions were presented, although there had been no change of the voters' list. A petition was stolen from a clerk's office; in another case the clerk's office was burned and the petition with it. Although twenty-one petitions were thus headed off, thirty-nine municipalities voted and twenty returned local option majorities.

A deputation in 1910 repeated the request of the previous year, and the Government was requested to refuse to issue licenses in municipalities where the people had adopted local option by a popular vote, but where the by-law had been quashed. The Premier pledged his Government to carry out the temperance workers' request in this respect, but he repeated his conviction that the province was not ripe for prohibition legislation.

The amendments to the liquor law in 1910 were prejudicial to temperance interests: three-year periods between votes and local option petitions were to have affidavits attached, stating that one person had witnessed all the signatures.

In December, 1910, the R.T. of T. decided to abandon the local option method. They had used it because it was the only available weapon, said Mr. Czerwinski. Amendments to the liquor law, early in 1910, were unfavorable and calculated to make the adoption of the veto more difficult. They determined to ask the Provincial Legislature to submit the question of the abolition of the bar to a vote of the people. If this were not granted they would turn to the Canada Temperance Act and attempt to bring on a vote in the ten Dominion constituencies of the province. This plan was laid before the Government in February, 1911, by Rev. Principal Patrick, Rev. Dr. Crummy, W. H. Greenway, W. W. Buchanan. The request was supported by a petition signed by nearly 21,000 qualified electors, and a deputation of about 1,000 persons. The speakers pointed out also that since local option was on the statute books it ought to be made workable. Premier Roblin thought that the local option law gave little ground for complaint, and he made no promise concerning the proposal of the deputation for a referendum.

By June, 1911, no action on the referendum had been taken by the Government, and a special meeting of the Moral and Social Reform Council was called in Winnipeg to discuss

PROVINCIAL PROHIBITION.

the situation. It was decided to start a vigorous political action campaign, to request the electors to write to and to wait upon their members, asking explanation of their inaction. Since no amendments had been made in the local option law, it was decided not to encourage any general local option campaign, but to concentrate upon the demand for increasing restrictive legislation for the whole province, especially the demand for the abolition of the bar.

On March 1, 1912, a resolution was introduced by Messrs. S. J. H. Malcolm and J. B. Baird in favor of taking a referendum on the question of banishing the bars. The Government opposed the motion. Premier Roblin urged it should not be dealt with in a hurry and deprecated an immature conclusion lest it hurt the temperance cause. Two sittings of the Legislature were taken up with the discussion of the resolution, which was finally defeated by a vote of twenty to fourteen, two members of the Government (Messrs. Argue and Carroll) voting for it.

During the year 1913, the Federation circulated an electors' covenant, which was very largely signed in many constituencies. It pledged the electors at the forthcoming provincial elections to vote for only those candidates who would support a measure of bar-room abolition.

On January 8, 1914, a deputation from the Social Reform Council once again asked for amendments of the local option law and for a referendum on the question of bar-room abolition. Premier Roblin replied that to close the bars, opening up instead numerous wholesale places, would be a retrograde step. " Close the bars and the wholesale houses, too. That is the thing, and where that is the intention, I am with you."

There was considerable discussion of the prohibition question in the House during the early part of the session of 1914. On January 15th, a resolution was moved by J. H. Baird and seconded by S. J. H. Malcolm, that in view of a petition from twenty thousand electors of the province, a referendum should be granted on the question of abolishing the sale of intoxicating liquor in bar-rooms. The Premier and the Hon. H. Armstrong moved in amendment that "This House having declared for the prohibiting of the sale of intoxicating liquors, whether retail or wholesale, by the local option clause of the Liquor License Act, and excellent results having been secured therefrom, declines, until proof is given that some other method would be more effective, to endorse any action or policy regarding the liquor trade that may impair the securing of total prohibition as provided for in said local option clauses." The amendment carried by twenty-three to twelve, on a straight party division.

During the month of January, also, considerable excitement was roused over the club license question. Through the exposures made by a Royal Commission of Investigation on the murder of Arnold, a banker at Morden, by Krafchenko, the club business in Winnipeg was revealed as a hideous scandal. Many institutions were operating under the guise of licensed social clubs which were really drinking and gambling dens. On February 1st, the Social Service Council held a great mass meeting in Grace Church, at which public indignation on the club question was voiced. The speakers included Rev. Dr. Jas. L. Gordon, Rev. J. E. Hughson, W. W. Buchanan, R. C. Heners, Rev. G. B. Wilson, and W. R. Bartlett. A proposition to divert public attention to merely a few clubs "of that class" was overborne by a strong resolution condemning the whole bar and club system as a breeder of vice and crime.

On February 3rd and 5th, the Club License question was discussed in the Legislature. Wm. Ferguson and G. Stell urged the cancellation of all club licenses, and the immediate amendment of the law to restrict the hours of sale at meals, and to increase the restrictions under which licenses should be issued. The Premier promised that if any direct charge were laid by anyone against any of these clubs, the Government would appoint a Commission of Inquiry. A motion introduced by T. H. Johnson, and seconded by W. Armstrong, to repeal the act incorporating such clubs and to cancel their licenses forthwith was lost. An attempt on the part of the

PROVINCIAL PROHIBITION.

Liberal members to have nine specifically-named clubs investigated, was defeated.

On February 6th, a deputation presented to the Premier and his colleagues the resolutions adopted at the mass meeting on February 1st, one of them calling for a Royal Commission to investigate the whole subject of the clubs and bars. The Premier declined to promise a special investigation, but suggested that the time was ripe for giving the municipality much greater control over the licensing of liquor-selling places.

On February 10th, Messrs. Green and Baird moved for the appointment of the Royal Commission of Inquiry with wide powers. The Premier moved in amendment that no Royal Commission be appointed until definite charges had been made. The amendment carried. Mr. Green then made the charges: (1) That clubs sold day and night and that the law was not enforced in granting or administering licenses; (2) That clubs were not for social intercourse, but for financial profit.

Mr. Howden's amendment to the Liquor License Act, which passed, contained the following items:

1. Detailed rules for the formation and maintenance of clubs.
2. Sale between 12 midnight and 8 a.m. prohibited.
3. Gambling prohibited.

On February 19th, Mr. Norris moved in amendment that provisions be included in the liquor license law to limit voting in local option contests to resident electors, and to give electors power to prohibit by majority vote the retail sale of liquor. The amendment was defeated. At this time the Opposition, led by Mr. T. C. Norris, endeavored to aid the temperance cause by a bill to allow women to vote for the Legislative Assembly, but the attempt was defeated.

The House was prorogued on February 20th, and preparations were immediately made for the coming elections.

The provincial temperance convention in Winnipeg on the 19th and 20th of March was the greatest demonstration

PROHIBITION IN CANADA.

of enthusiasm, determination, and unanimity ever made by the temperance people of the province. The convention was called for the auditorium of the Oddfellows' Temple, but this big hall would not begin to hold the delegates, and a hurried adjournment was made to St. Stephen's Presbyterian Church, three blocks away. They declared for making temperance the chief issue in the provincial elections; that the abolition of the bar was the irreducible minimum as a province-wide measure which should come into operation on receiving the approval of the electorate by popular vote; that the enactment of the saving clause should warrant another campaign for local option at the next municipal elections; that the further amendments to the law should be urged upon the Government and Legislature; and that the local option provisions should be enlarged to enable the people of any municipality to reduce the number of licenses, to prohibit the use of any kind of license, to limit the hours of sale, and to prohibit sale on public holidays.

The provincial convention of the Liberal party was held in Winnipeg on the 26th of March, and in accordance with the instructions of the temperance convention, a delegation representing the Social Service Council visited the convention, and very strongly urged the adoption of an advanced policy upon temperance legislation. The deputation included Rev. Chas. W. Gordon, D.D., George Fisher, Prof. S. G. Bland, John Fleming, George R. Wilson and W. W. Buchanan. They were received with genuine enthusiasm and given ample opportunity to address the big convention. It was quite evident that their addresses met with sympathetic appreciation, as well as applause.

The convention included in its platform a clear-cut utterance upon the temperance question, declaring its sympathy with the temperance cause, and pledging the party if returned to power to enact a measure for the abolition of the bar and submit it to a popular vote, and to put the measure into thorough operation if it received the support of the majority of the electors voting. In addition to this specific

PROVINCIAL PROHIBITION.

reply to the petition of the Social Service Council, the platform further promised a reduction in the number of liquor licenses; the abolition of proprietary club licenses; prohibition on Christmas Day, Good Friday and Thanksgiving; giving municipalities power to limit, reduce or abolish any class of liquor licenses, and to shorten the hours of sale; the elimination of non-resident votes in local issues; the refusal of licenses in any municipality where local option is carried, even though it may be quashed by the court.

The lining up of all the Liberal candidates under the platform of the party in favor of granting the prayer of the petition for a referendum on the abolition of the bar, and the open opposition of the Government to that policy, put the temperance forces to the test, and the executive of the Social Service Council, after careful consideration, unanimously resolved:

"That the temperance resolution of the Liberal convention as interpreted by the leader of the party is acceptable and satisfactory to the Social Service Council."

The qualification, "as interpreted by the leader of the party," referred to an official statement of the leader that when the Liberal convention declared its sympathy with the temperance cause that included and should be interpreted to mean sympathy with the specific movement for the elimination of the bar-room and the abolition of the treating habit. This resolution practically committed the Social Service Council and its friends to the support of all candidates who were loyal to this declaration of policy, and the question became a keenly contested concrete issue in the election campaign.

The Liberal party went into the campaign with the support of the independent temperance electors, with whose views Mr. Norris had expressed his hearty personal sympathy. The Conservative party, on the other hand, had behind it the undivided strength of the liquor forces.

PROHIBITION IN CANADA.

At Neepawa, on April 16th, Premier Roblin made a bid for temperance support by reviewing the Conservative policy toward temperance, since the advanced Prohibition Act of 1900 had been rejected. It had included, he said, among other improvements, abolition of restaurant and saloon licenses, reduction of the number of licenses, raising of the standard of hotels, amendment of the local option law and the substitution of a majority for a three-fifths vote in local option. The *Winnipeg Tribune,* in commenting on the Premier's speech, pointed out that while restaurant licenses had been abolished in 1904, club licenses had been instituted in 1909. It published the following table of hotel, wholesale and club or retail licenses issued for the years 1900-1912:

Year	Licenses	Year	Licenses
1900	171	1907	269
1901	188	1908	267
1902	194	1909	282
1903	226	1910	274
1904	249	1911	284
1905	254	1912	296
1906	261		

The Social Service Council, in a manifesto issued by the President, Dr. Gordon, on June 6th, described the hopefulness of the situation, with the Christian churches, various organizations, social workers and all decent citizens lined up against the Roblin Government, the liquor traffic and every form of organized vice and crime.

"Our objective stands clearly visible—the elimination of Premier Roblin and his Government that back the bar. Let us be clear about this. It is not a question of party politics, but of ethics, of patriotism, of religion. For this election this is the paramount issue."

On June 20th, Mr. Norris issued a manifesto which set out at length the position of the Liberal party on the temperance issue.

PROVINCIAL PROHIBITION.

Mr. Norris' Manifesto.

The liquor problem has come prominently to the fore in recent years. In my judgment this is due very largely to the loose administration of our liquor laws and the manipulation of the liquor interests for political purposes. Our citizens have become completely disgusted with conditions as they exist. With the approval of the Government there has been allowed to grow up in our midst a system of saloons and clubs that are nothing less than breeding-places for vice. These must be swept out of existence. Besides, there has been growing sentiment in favor of abolition of the bar. As regards this question, the Liberal party stand by its pledge to enact such temperance legislation by way of reform as the majority of the people may desire, as indicated by a referendum. I hold that on an issue of this kind the will of the people should prevail, and that they should be given the fullest opportunity to decide the question on its merits apart from other issues.

Moreover, the Liberal party, in a provincial convention, had laid down a definite and practical policy of dealing with the drink question. The platform it had adopted contained the following statements:

"That this convention condemns the administration of the liquor license laws as grossly inefficient, corrupt and partisan, and declares that the Roblin Government is responsible therefor, and should on this account, and on account of its opposition to all proposals of reform, be condemned by all citizens who believe in moral progress and honest enforcement of the law.

"That the Liberal party, recognizing the grave evils, disorders and corrupt influences associated with the liquor traffic, especially the bar sale of liquor and the treating custom, reaffirms its declarations of unqualified sympathy with the temperance cause and pledges itself:

"(1) To pass an act for the abolition of the bar, to be prepared by the recognized temperance forces, and to submit such act to a referendum, which act, if endorsed by the electors, shall be put into operation and shall have the hearty support of the Liberal party in its thorough enforcement.

"(2) To amend the Liquor License Act so as to ensure a large reduction in the number of liquor licenses, the abolition of proprietary club licenses, and the prohibition of the sale of liquor on Christmas Day, Good Friday and Thanksgiving Day.

"(a) To limit, reduce or abolish any class of liquor licenses, as well as to shorten the hours of sale.

" (b) That resident voters only shall have the right to vote.

" (c) That no liquor license shall be issued where a local option by-law has been carried and subsequently quashed on technical grounds."

The election contest was exceedingly hot. A notable feature of it was the vigorous platform campaigning of Mrs. Nellie McClung, who mercilessly scored Sir Rodmond Roblin's Government for its rejection of the reasonable proposal to have a vote of the electors taken and to be governed by the result. The voting on July 10th resulted in the return of twenty-four Conservatives and twenty-two Liberals, the Government's majority, which formerly had been seventeen, being reduced to two.

Upon the outbreak of the war, Premier Roblin called a special session of the Provincial Legislature, and it was announced that the Assembly would hear delegations upon the proposed bills for raising money and for the establishment of a moratorium. The Social Service Council promptly appointed a delegation to ask for the closing of bar-rooms as a war measure to preserve the savings and food of the people. The deputation, accompanied by two hundred persons, was refused admittance, however, the Premier announcing that the House was in committee, and moreover, that the formal proceedings of presenting the petition had not been carried out. Mr. Norris championed the cause of the petitioners, and moved in the Assembly that the deputation be heard, but he was unsuccessful.

During the years 1911 to 1914 not a bar-room had been closed by local option. In Carman, a vote had carried for two successive years, but each time the by-law was quashed and licenses granted in violation of the Government pledge. In 1914 the local option law had been amended by the addition of a saving or curative clause, so as to remedy the

PROVINCIAL PROHIBITION.

hampering of work by technicalities. In the fall of that year, the new clause being operative, the Social Service Council issued a call for a vigorous local option campaign. Twenty-two places voted, including the two cities of Brandon and Portage la Prairie. The result was a sweeping victory. Sixteen places carried the by-law. One place tied the vote and five recorded adverse majorities. Portage la Prairie went for prohibition and Brandon against. The liquor men brought on one repeal contest, but the local option by-law was sustained by a majority of over three hundred.

At the end of the year the Government passed an order-in-council requesting bar-rooms and clubs to discontinue selling liquor at 7 o'clock every evening and requesting wholesalers to close at 6 p.m. No penalty could, of course, be imposed for failure to comply with the request. "The Government believes," said Premier Roblin, "that it will, in view of the strong opinion existing upon this matter in the province, and in view as well of the merits of the case, receive a not unwilling response to its request. The Government recognizes that in requesting this voluntary action upon the part of license-holding citizens, it is asking a measure of business sacrifice at their hands, but it also desires to point out that this is a time when citizens, no matter what their standing or calling in life, are necessarily required to make personal sacrifices for the common good. The same request will be made to all social clubs where liquor is dispensed." At the same time the Premier announced the intention of the Government to introduce into the Legislature at its next session a bill which would make the request effective.

On February 6, 1915, the Social Service Council sent another deputation to the Government. The Premier refused to grant total prohibition as a war measure at this time, saying he would rather wait a year or so and be sure of victory than suffer the humiliation of defeat. He declared his sympathy with prohibition as an ultimate objective, and his expectations of putting a prohibition law into the statutes

PROHIBITION IN CANADA.

before he left office. Meanwhile he stated it was the policy of the Government to bring about reform gradually and surely by local option. He proposed a great local option campaign for the coming fall, promising himself to take the platform in support of the measure. He hoped that even Winnipeg might be included in the contests, and he expected that the vote for local option would be so overwhelming as to warrant him in enacting provincial prohibition.

Meantime investigations were being carried on concerning certain scandals connected with the new Provincial Parliament Buildings, which showed that charges made against the Roblin Government were not without foundation. Political feeling waxed exceedingly strong, and in May, 1915, the Government resigned, and Mr. Norris was called upon to form a new administration. In July the Manitoba Legislature was dissolved and a new election was announced to be held on August 6, 1915.

The Conservative party was reorganized under the leadership of Sir Jas. Aikins, and a new platform was adopted, a leading plank of which was as follows:

"Total prohibition so far as is possible by the re-enactment of the Hugh John Macdonald's Act of 1900, with no provisions for referendum or repeal."

Thus, while the Liberal party stood by its promise of a referendum, the Conservative party abandoned its antiprohibition attitude and promised prohibition legislation. Moreover, the Conservative leader was known to be friendly to the temperance cause. But evidently the electors had little faith in a party promise made just before an election and after a policy of consistent hostility to the measure suddenly advocated.

In the election of August 6th, the Liberal party was returned, only four Conservatives being elected out of a total of forty-five. There is no doubt that a principal cause of this great overthrow was the revelation of political corruption made at the inquiry into the Parliament Buildings

PROVINCIAL PROHIBITION.

transaction. It is true also that the Roblin Government's practical opposition to temperance reform was a factor in rousing public opinion to rid the province of the misrule under which it had suffered so long.

The contest and its outcome were strikingly similar to the situation and result in Ontario in January, 1905. At that time there was, among temperance workers in this province, intense disgust with the Government's truckling to the liquor interests, which had been going on for some time; and although the Liberal party promised better temperance legislation than was promised by the Conservatives, the people refused to trust any longer the party that had been so long friendly with the liquor traffic. So in Manitoba the Conservative party, led by Sir James Aikins, a temperance man himself, promised more than the Liberals promised, but temperance men refused to support the party that had before worked hand in hand with the enemy of temperance reform.

In August, 1915, the new Government carried out its promise and asked the Social Service Council to draft a prohibition bill to be submitted to the people in the form of a prohibition referendum. The bill submitted by the Council was the H. J. Macdonald Bill of 1900. The Council asked that the vote be taken on December 1st, but the Premier announced in October that the referendum would be held in March, 1916, and that, if the measure were adopted, no new license would be issued, and there would be no renewals of licenses then in force, which expired on May 31, 1916. Thus the law would be brought into effect as soon as if the Council's request had been granted. The Council requested, further, that women be allowed to vote, but this was deemed impracticable by the Government on the ground of the delay and expense entailed in preparing new voters' lists. It was decided that the vote should be taken on the basis of the current provincial lists revised the previous spring.

PROHIBITION IN CANADA.

On March 13, 1916, the electors of Manitoba ratified the Macdonald Prohibition Act by a vote of nearly two to one. The vote stood as follows:

>   For prohibition................. 50,484
>   Against prohibition............. 26,502
>
>   Majority for prohibition........ 23,982

The complete returns of the referendum vote on March 13th, by constituencies, are as follows:—

	For.	Against.	Majority for.	Majority against.
Arthur	654	231	423	
Assiniboia	1,128	643	485	
Beautiful Plains	1,264	176	1,088	
Birtle	801	155	646	
Brandon City	1,547	1,210	337	
Carillon	509	360	149	
Churchill and Nelson	8	36		28
Cypress	837	198	639	
Deloraine	1,105	212	893	
Dauphin	1,036	378	658	
Dufferin	1,210	418	792	
Elmwood	1,614	1 381	233	
Emerson	698	530	168	
Gilbert Plains	1,196	516	680	
Ginli	879	421	458	
Gladstone	983	411	572	
Glenwood	892	246	646	
Grand Rapids	48	41	7	
Hamiota	1,158	195	963	
Iberville	361	228	133	
Kildonan and St. Andrews	1,167	646	521	
Killarney	770	181	589	
Lakeside	747	262	485	
Lansdowne	1,254	205	1,049	
La Verandrye	510	387	123	
Manitou	1,107	320	787	
Minnedosa	1,159	375	784	

426

PROVINCIAL PROHIBITION.

	For.	Against.	Majority for.	Majority against.
Morden and Rhineland	825	554	271	
Morris	675	443	232	
Mountain	1,251	217	1,034	
Norfolk	538	295	243	
Portage la Prairie	911	404	507	
Roblin	427	181	246	
Rockwood	970	523	447	
Russell	854	399	455	
St. Boniface	1,023	1,055		32
St. Clemens	654	606	48	
St. George	861	795	66	
St. Rose	561	274	287	
Swan River	567	282	285	
The Pass	232	75	157	
Turtle Mountain	648	198	450	..
Virden	1,096	353	743	..
Winnipeg North	2,820	2,885		65
Winnipeg South	5,360	2,507	2,853	..
Winnipeg Centre	5,569	4,094	1,475	

Total number 76,986
Total affirmative answers to the question............... 50,484
Total negative answers to the question.................. 26,502

Majority for the affirmative......................... 23,982

VII. SASKATCHEWAN.

Power of local option was granted to the municipalities of Saskatchewan by the license law of 1908. The Attorney-General, the Hon. A. Turgeon, on moving the second reading of the bill explained that the license system inaugurated in Saskatchewan in 1891 had always contained provision for local option under certain conditions, probably the best provision possible when the law was framed. But the municipal organization of the province was not well defined. The area in which local option was applicable was larger than it

PROHIBITION IN CANADA.

should have been and local option had remained a dead letter upon the statute books.

The Government bill of 1908 gave to cities, towns and rural municipalities the right to determine upon majority vote the question of license or no license. A by-law could be submitted only once in two years. The bill limited the number of licenses a community might have, forbade the issuing of club licenses, and provided for the closing of bars on religious public holidays. An attempt to introduce a three-fifths clause into the bill was supported by only two votes. Also a motion to lengthen the hours of sale from 10 to 10.30 p.m. was defeated. The actual operation of the new law was delayed until after the enactment in 1909 of the Rural Municipalities Bill, which completed the municipal organization of the province.

During the following year six local option contests were conducted by the Social and Moral Reform Council of Saskatchewan, in four of which the prohibition forces were successful.

A retrograde step was taken by the Government in 1909, in a measure to amend the License Act by making two notable concessions to the liquor party, namely

(1) Hours of sale were lengthened by half an hour for five days of the week in cities and provision was made for partial opening of liquor-selling places on polling days.

(2) The privilege of selling liquor was extended to clubs.

A temperance deputation representing the local Moral Reform Council and various churches, and temperance organizations of Regina voiced a strong protest to Premier Scott against these changes, but they received no satisfaction from the leader of the Government and the measure was put through on a straight party vote.

In 1910 amendments were made to the Liquor License Act, valuable from a temperance standpoint, as follows:

(1) It was made possible for local improvement districts to submit local option by-laws, and in doing so to include any village

PROVINCIAL PROHIBITION.

or villages within their areas. The villages and the surrounding country were to vote together. This was true also of rural municipalities and the villages within their boundaries.

(2) The right to vote was restricted to male British subjects who had resided in the province for a year and in the municipality for three consecutive months just prior to polling day.

Furthermore the Government pledged itself to the establishment of a secret service law-enforcing department.

In the same year a vigorous local option campaign was carried on throughout the whole province. Contests were held in December in seventy-three voting districts, among which were the cities of Regina, Moose Jaw, Saskatoon, and Prince Albert. Local option carried in thirty-seven places, of which Moose Jaw was the only large centre, although Regina came within 100 votes of victory. But a number of the by-laws were subsequently declared invalid by the courts.

The case of Moose Jaw is notable. Prohibitionists had a majority of 190 votes, but the liquor party brought in a charge of irregularities in the petition and in the procedure followed by the Council, and consequently the by-law was set aside. However, the Board of License Commissioners determined to respect public opinion and refused to grant licenses for the next year, although they stated in a rider that their action was not intended to establish a precedent in the matter. The liquor interests then presented a petition with 900 names, asking for reversal of the Commission's decision, and were told that their request would be disregarded unless supported by a majority of the 2,600 names on the voters' list. They came back with 1,557 names, and the Commission issued five licenses.

On January 26, 1911, the Social and Moral Reform Council petitioned the Government for the speedy enactment of a measure of provincial prohibition, immediate rigid enforcement of the license regulations and improvements in the local option law. Premier Scott replied that the Government had already lost votes by its policy of local option legislation inaugurated in 1908, and he calculated that similar results might easily follow the adoption of a prohibition policy. He favored an extension of the local option period from two to five years.

On November 23, 1913, a great convention was held in Regina, at which a new and aggressive step was taken, one that was to prove momentous in the history of prohibition in Saskatchewan. The meeting was called by the Social and Moral Reform League to consider a policy upon which temperance workers should unite for the coming year. Three hundred delegates met in the Y.M.C.A. auditorium under a flaring banner bearing the words: " Saskatchewan Must Go Dry." They undertook an immediate campaign to abolish the bar in the province.

Discussion arose as to the advisability of forming a separate organization for the work, but it was finally decided to entrust it to the Moral and Social Reform Council. A special committee of eighty members, including ten representatives of the W.C.T.U., was chosen, to be known as the " Banish the Bar " committee.

A special feature of the convention was a powerful address at the Sunday evening mass meeting by Bishop Mathieu, head of the Roman Catholic Church in the diocese, who promised to issue a circular letter to his clergy, instructing them to give their heartiest support to the temperance crusade. The warm sympathy and hearty support of the Anglican Church were expressed in a letter from the Bishop of Saskatchewan, who was unable to be present at the meeting.

Premier Scott, accompanied by the Attorney-General, attended the afternoon session, and received the recommendations of the convention presented by the chairman, Chancellor Lloyd, of Saskatchewan. They were as follows:

1. That a campaign be immediately launched for the abolition of the bar throughout the entire province of Saskatchewan.

PROVINCIAL PROHIBITION.

2. That this term, abolition of the bar, be interpreted to mean the doing away with the liquor licenses in clubs as well as bars in hotels and all sale of liquors to be consumed on the premises.

3. That local option be maintained as a means of dealing with the wholesale stores, and that the local option law to this end be made effective.

4. That a request be made, either by petition or deputation, to the Government, asking that it will at the present session of the Legislature introduce or receive and give three readings to a bill as above outlined.

5. That this bill, after being passed by the Legislature, be submitted to the people of the Province of Saskatchewan, and upon receiving a majority of the votes polled, that the law come automatically into force at the end of the then license year.

6. That the vote take place at the time of the municipal elections in December, following the passage of the bill by the Legislature.

7. That in order to cope with the hotel problem, municipal councils be given the power to erect or purchase buildings in order to lease or operate, or to take other desirable steps, for the purpose of providing accommodation to the travelling public.

8. That all houses of public entertainment be regulated, licensed and inspected, so as to ensure proper accommodation for the guests.

Premier Scott made no specific promises in reply to these requests, but said:

"Speaking on my own behalf, I believe that the line you are taking with regard to the temperance reform is the right line, the line that all legislators and statesmen are advocating; and further, I can assure you that your recommendations will receive the most careful and kindly consideration, both from myself and from the legislators."

In 1913 local option contests were fought in twenty-six districts, the first attempt for three years, because of the temperance people's objections to the conditions of the law. They were successful in six of the places voting.

PROHIBITION IN CANADA.

On December 15th Premier Scott presented in the Legislature a bill proposing to hold at the time of the municipal elections in December, 1914, a plebiscite on the question,

"Are you in favor of bringing into force an 'Abolition of the Bar' Act?"

The measure was to require an affirmative vote of not less than 50,000, and the Government took the ground that, since the proposed new system meant a radical change, and since the Government would be responsible for administering the law, it was necessary to safeguard against a measure lacking a sufficient body of public opinion to ensure satisfactory enforcement.

The Temperance Committee of the Social and Moral Reform Council discussed the bill with Premier Scott, and expressed strong dissatisfaction with the terms of the proposed requirements for the vote. They objected to the applying of any minimum on this question, and particularly to such a large one—larger than the Government itself had polled after an exciting campaign at the last provincial election. Moreover, the fact that the poll was to be taken in December when the weather might be bad, was a serious handicap. The deputation suggested a 30,000 minimum affirmative vote and a 10 per cent. majority; the Premier expressed himself as being in favor of a 40,000 minimum. After some discussion, the deputation accepted the compromise of a 40,000 minimum and a straight majority, and departed with the distinct understanding that the bill would be amended on those lines. Next day, without any further intimation to the committee, the Premier withdrew the bill, giving as his reason that the temperance leaders were dissatisfied with it and not united in their views.

In September, 1914, a delegation laid a petition before the Government on behalf of the United Brotherhood of Saskatchewan, supported by similar appeals from other organizations, to promote legislation closing up all the bars in the province during the ensuing winter. Several journals,

PROVINCIAL PROHIBITION.

notably the *Saskatoon Star,* gave the proposal cordial support, urging the great need of conserving resources to the fullest extent possible, in order to bear the strain of war conditions. The petition was a strong but moderately-worded appeal for action, which, it said, was fully justifiable for reasons stated in part as follows:

" That we have carefully considered the present condition of affairs, and we have given particular attention to the situation which is likely to arise during the forthcoming winter as a result of (*a*) the scarcity of employment during the past year; (*b*) the abnormal conditions created by the partial failure of the crops in the province; (*c*) the European situation. That the presence of the saloon will not aid to the solution of our present economic problem, and your petitioners are assured that if the economic waste caused by the saloon were eliminated for the next half year, our cities and towns would be materially assisted in their task of providing for those dependent on their charity.

"Your petitioners have been corresponding with every city and nearly every town in the province and have made careful enquiry from retail merchants, from travelling salesmen, and from those engaged in humanitarian work, and the verdict of those interviewed is that the saloons of the province should be closed for a period covering the forthcoming winter."

The movement however did not succeed. The emergency session of the Legislature, which opened September 15th, closed within a few days without taking any action on the prohibition question.

In November, 1914, the Committee of One Hundred of the "Banish the Bar" Crusade met in Regina and sent a deputation to ask the Government, as a war measure, to suspend all retail liquor license in the province until the end of the war. Some of the reasons in favor of the request of the committee were forcibly summed up by the *" Banish the Bar" Crusader* in the following form:

1. Owing to the fact that the emergency war session of the Legislature took the character of a regular annual session, there will be no session of the Legislature for a year, and consequently

PROHIBITION IN CANADA.

the referendum cannot be obtained until 1916 at the earliest, and if successful the bars could not be closed until July 1, 1917, which is a long way off—a long, long way, in fact.

2. On account of the economic conditions prevailing all over the world, no country can afford to waste its resources. Saskatchewan wastes $17,000,000 annually on the liquor traffic. This should stop as a war measure. Every available cent should be husbanded.

3. On account of the terrible conditions prevailing in certain parts of the province due to drought, the national and provincial governments are aiding men to obtain "grub stake," and much of this aid, so it is alleged, is finding its way to the bars.

4. On account of the mixed character of our population, brawls and riots are liable to break out in many places where these various nationalities frequent the bars.

5. It is more than hinted that some of the bars are meeting-places for our Empire's enemies and breeding-places for sedition. This is intolerable. Surely the province cannot continue to license convenient centres for spies and plotters against the country's peace.

6. Many of the British cities have taken steps in this direction, and the agitation is growing for its application all over the nation.

7. Russia closed all its grog-shops, and although this was begun as a war measure for a brief period, the economic and other results have been so good that the Czar has decreed that it shall be perpetual. We might reasonably plead to be put in as advanced a position as Russia has taken.

The Premier's reply was that, with the province facing the severe winter months with thousands of unemployed, it would be better not to take any action which might altogether close many hotels, and throw their employees out on the street.

In December, a "Banish the Bar" convention was held in Regina to decide upon an electoral policy. The President, Principal G. E. Lloyd, after reviewing the events of the preceding year, the proposed referendum on terms not satisfactory to temperance workers, and the subsequent withdrawal of the bill, went on to say:

PROVINCIAL PROHIBITION.

"We have not got one single thing from the Saskatchewan Government. Are we going to go on tramping back and forth between conventions and the Government building year after year without any satisfaction? On the other hand, the liquor interests have been given some eighty new licenses this year, and they are being encouraged while we are being ignored. Are you satisfied? If you are not, what are you going to do? That is what is to be decided at this convention. You will get absolutely nothing until you are absolutely unanimous and are prepared to stand behind the policy adopted in convention, whether it be to go after total prohibition or the banishing of the bars. You must put your Conservatism in one pocket and your Liberalism in the other, and be a temperance man first, last and all the time, before anything can be accomplished. I do not think it makes very much difference whether we have a Liberal, Conservative, or Coalition Government in the province; but it would make a great deal of difference if we had a Temperance Government for five years. Politics do not, after all, count for very much when the interests of the people at large are at stake, and you will have to learn to lay stress upon your political leanings where principle is at stake."

The alternatives suggested by the president were carefully discussed by the convention. A resolution was offered by Dr. Wylie Clark, proposing that the provincial organization change its platform from bar-room abolition to total prohibition. After some discussion, however, it was clearly seen that total prohibition in the fullest sense was beyond the power of the Provincial Legislature, and that other reasons militated against a change of programme at that time. The resolution was withdrawn, and instead of it the following was adopted, on motion of Dr. R. C. Manley, seconded by Bishop Newnham:

"Believing that considerable progress has been made in educating the people in favor of the 'Banish the Bar' movement during the past year, and believing it unwise to change the policy at this time, we recommend to the convention that the work be vigorously continued until we attain our object. Also we recommend that the Government be again urged to further limit the hours during which the bars may remain open."

PROHIBITION IN CANADA.

The policy on electoral action adopted by the convention was the familiar one of the Dominion Alliance—to support pledged temperance candidates irrespective of party affiliations, and if no candidate in a constituency would agree to stand upon the temperance platform, to bring out an independent man.

This significant declaration was added to the plan of campaign with reference to pledging parliamentary candidates:

"We further pledge that we will ask for an agreement to vote for a motion of want of confidence in the Government if it does not introduce at the first session of the House a bill to banish the bar, to be drawn or approved by our laws committee and submitted to the people on terms of an enabling bill, also drawn or approved by our laws committee."

On December 31, 1914, the temperance workers presented the following requests to the Premier:

1. That the Government refuse to grant any new licenses during the continuance of the present war.

2. That the hours of sale be shortened, making the opening hour 8 a.m. and the closing hour 6 p.m.

3. That the Government at the next session of the Legislature pass an enabling act, so that the question of "Banish the Bar" be submitted to the people at the municipal elections in December, 1915, and upon the municipal franchise, with a straight majority vote.

The reason urged for the submission of the vote the ensuing year was the desire that the question might be disposed of before the time of the next general election. The Premier sent a prompt reply to the Secretary on January 5th, in which he stated that the Government had decided to notify the Liquor License Board that no action would be taken for granting licenses for new premises before the end of the year. To the other requests, the answer was a repetition of the Government's answer in December, that economic conditions were such as to deter them from taking any action during the winter.

PROVINCIAL PROHIBITION.

On March 18th, Premier Scott at a meeting of his supporters at Oxbow, announced a definite course of action in temperance legislation to be taken by the Government, as follows:

1. To at once issue a proclamation curtailing the hours of retail liquor sale to seven o'clock in the evening from April 1st.

2. To convene the Legislative Assembly as early as possible in the month of May, and submit to the House a measure of which the outstanding features will be the abolition of all bar and club licenses from July 1, 1915, until the ending of the war, and the taking over by the Government of the wholesale liquor business throughout the province.

3. To provide in the measure that, following the ending of the war, the bar and club licenses shall not be revived except as the result of a referendum on the question to be taken at the time of municipal elections held after peace is declared, but not earlier than December, 1916, a majority vote to decide, and the provincial franchise to be adopted for the referendum; the Government to provide most carefully-framed safeguards against any irregularities, such as personations, false declarations, and the use of liquor or any other improper influences, and for the more secure discouragement of improper practices, to appoint a prosecutor and to follow and prosecute infractions.

4. To provide in the measure for maintenance by the Government, under a commissioner having status similar to that of the provincial auditor, of a liquor dispensary or dispensaries in each city or town where at present wholesale licenses exist, to be known as Saskatchewan Dispensaries for Sale of Liquor, which must not be consumed on the premises, and under strict regulations as to quantities, size of packages, etc.; the question of establishing such dispensaries in towns and villages where at present wholesale licenses do not exist to be determined by a referendum of the electorate, to be taken at the time of the municipal elections.

5. To provide that in the year 1919, or any subsequent year, on presentation of a petition signed by twenty-five per cent. of the number of electors who vote at the next preceding provincial elections, a provincial referendum shall be taken to decide the continuance or abolition of the proposed dispensaries. All dis-

pensaries taken over or opened to remain in operation until aforesaid referendum decides.

The Committee of One Hundred of the "Banish the Bar" Crusaders expressed its hearty appreciation of the proposals of the Government. While they restated their attitude of antagonism to the liquor traffic, whether under private or Government control, they considered the Government ownership plan acceptable as a temporary expedient looking towards total prohibition. They suggested several changes in the details of the Government plan, as follows·

1. That the Government confine the area for the submission of the referendum to electoral districts, and that there should be only one dispensary in each electoral district. This should require a petition from the liquor sympathizers before a vote could be taken on the same terms as required for the voting proposed in 1919.

2. That in places where wholesale licenses existed and where the people had not been consulted, they should be given opportunity to vote those dispensaries out of existence at the next municipal elections on the same terms as were provided for voting either in or out; that the vote should be taken not oftener than every three years; that these votings should be independent of the general referendum of 1919 on abolition of dispensaries throughout the province; that unless these proposals were agreed to, the twenty-five per cent. of the 1919 referendum should be reduced to fifteen per cent.

3. That a clause be inserted in the bill at once empowering town and village corporations and municipalities to buy, lease, administer, rent and bonus hotels and other places of such like public entertainment, and also provide for public inspection of the same.

The committee expressed the hope that the Government would see its way to aid in the solution of the hotel problem by helping the municipalities financially, or in some other tangible way would protect the travelling public. These suggestions were presented to the Premier and his Cabinet on April 1st, by Principal Lloyd, who explained that the

PROVINCIAL PROHIBITION.

decision of the committee in asking for the amendments was practically unanimous.

On behalf of the Government, Premier Scott thanked the delegation, and said that the proposals were all reasonable, and would receive the Government's earnest consideration. He referred at length to the Government dispensaries and said that the Government ownership of the liquor traffic was very distasteful to him, but was adopted in order to aid in the strict enforcement of the laws against the illicit sale of liquors. He stated that he was fully aware of the odium that would be attached to any failure to handle the matter wisely and the slurs that would be heaped upon the Government and himself especially, because of the Government's undertaking to handle the traffic. He was anxious for suggestions as to how the hotel problem could best be solved.

On April 5th a Royal Commission, consisting of Principal E. H. Oliver, Presbyterian Theological College, and J. F. Bole, M.L.A., of Regina, was sent to South Carolina to investigate the working of the dispensary system of that state, the only place in America where it had been put in operation. The commission reported on May 18th, and the report contained a good deal of valuable information concerning the liquor legislation situation in a community in which the people may choose between prohibition or public ownership of the liquor traffic. It was shown that the method had entirely extinguished the open saloon, but that there still went on a good deal of illicit liquor selling. This law breaking was facilitated by conditions that did not prevail in Canada.

The commissioners reported that in their investigation they discovered that the dispensary system in South Carolina was used as a political machine; that its operations were accompanied by graft; that it led to political corruption; that it was administered by too many poorly paid officials; that courts and public officials did not give it sufficient support; that the conditions under which it operated were complicated by the race question; and that

PROHIBITION IN CANADA.

advanced temperance men generally approved the restrictive features of the system, but did not approve the provision for liquor selling. It was found that, nevertheless, there had been under the system a marked decrease in drunkenness.

They recommended:

1. That the system be kept entirely ont of politics.
2. That the authority and responsibility for control and purchase be vested in one individual.
3. That the goods handled be restricted to the smallest possible number of brands.
4. That severe penalties be provided for graft of any kind.
5. That in the local dispensaries the sale of liquor be restricted at least to the period between 9 a.m. and 5 p.m., and be made for cash only.

They made a number of suggestions as to details of administration and concluded by saying:

"The commission is unanimous in its conviction that in view of all the circumstances the state dispensary can with certain very needful modifications, if taken out of politics and kept clear from graft, be applied to the Province of Saskatchewan."

No doubt the information supplied by the commission was carefully considered by the Government in forming the measure which was introduced into the Legislature in June by the Hon. J. A. Calder. The details of the bill were very comprehensive and manifested much careful study and provision. It prohibited after July 1, 1915, the sale of intoxicating liquors throughout the province except in stores operated by government officials, where certain kinds of liquor might be sold under specified restrictions. The number of such stores was to be strictly limited, and they might be entirely abolished in any locality at any time before 1919 by a majority vote of municipal electors, taken upon petition of the electors, and under the direction of the Government. In 1919, at the time of the municipal elections, the electors

PROVINCIAL PROHIBITION.

of the province were to vote upon the question of whether or not this government ownership plan was to be continued. Before that time a vote was to be taken on the question of whether or not the people desired to have the bar-room system re-established. The bill was given its second reading on June 3rd, and was carried by a vote of 44 to 5.

Referring to the threat of the liquor sellers to close their hotels, the Premier said that such an action would cause "such a revulsion of feeling amongst thinking people that nobody will even dare to suggest that the bar-room business be revived." Discussing the situation that would exist in 1919, he said:

"When the vote shall be put to the people in 1919 there shall neither be a strongly-entrenched liquor interest in the province to fight on their own behalf, nor will there be at that time any revenue coming to the Government from the sale of liquor, to prejudice people, for the profits of the system by that time will have been devoted to other objects. In the first year the Government will lose through this their revenue of $50,000. Our revenue from licenses hitherto has been $300,000. The first year, under the new system, profits to the Government will be restricted to $250,000. These profits will be annually reduced, until in 1919 they will be altogether abolished."

Mr. N. W. Rowell of Ontario paid the following tribute to the Premier of Saskatchewan on this occasion, saying:

"The courageous and patriotic achievement of Mr. Scott has won for him not only a commanding place in the heart of the province, but has also given him a unique position among the Premiers of Canada."

In the municipal elections of December 13, 1915, the dispensaries in six districts were voted out, three districts without dispensaries voted against the establishment of any, and three districts abolished those already in operation.

In 1916, a change was made in the Liquor Act, providing that the vote upon the continuance of the remaining twenty-three dispensaries, which was to have been taken in 1919, should be taken at the time of the municipal elections. The result of the voting on December 10, 1916, was:

$$\begin{array}{lr} \text{Against dispensaries} & 95,249 \\ \text{For dispensaries} & 23,666 \\ \hline \text{Majority against dispensaries} & 71,583 \end{array}$$

The success of the prohibition movement startled even the most optimistic of the workers for the total suppression of the liquor traffic. Women voted in large numbers and no doubt helped to swell the prohibition majority. The vote in cities and towns was especially noteworthy. The votes polled in the cities of Regina, Saskatoon, Moose Jaw, Prince Albert, Weyburn, and Swift Current, aggregated as follows:

$$\begin{array}{lr} \text{Against dispensaries} & 14,528 \\ \text{For dispensaries} & 2,286 \\ \hline \text{Majority against dispensaries} & 12,242 \end{array}$$

Fifty-seven places incorporated as towns registered a vote that might be stated in round figures as 10,000 against, and 1,000 for abolition. In a number of places there was not a single vote in favor of the government-operated liquor business.

Under the act providing for this vote, the Government was to have six months longer to continue the dispensary system if it so desired, but the manifest trend of public opinion and the Government's desire to act in harmony therewith were so strong, that the Attorney-General, the Hon. W. F. A. Turgeon, K.C., announced before the polls were closed: "I am authorized to state on behalf of the Government, that if the vote is against the liquor stores, they will be closed December 31, 1916." The law giving effect to the popular demand for total prohibition in Saskatchewan became operative on January 1, 1917.

PROVINCIAL PROHIBITION.

Regarding the effect of provincial prohibition in Saskatchewan, Mr. W. J. Stewart, of Regina, writing in *The Pioneer,* said:

"With prohibition came a well-recognized new epoch for the province. Our farmers, merchants, professional and laboring men are generally deeply gratified at the enormous saving to our economic, industrial and social life. The gains are so outstanding, and such strength of public opinion has been developed as to make it practically impossible for Saskatchewan to revert to the old order.

"That we have some who resent the restrictions of the Temperance Act is true, but happily they are few and usually are persons of little appreciation of their obligations to their fellows, and with feeble ministry to any phase of community welfare.

"The monetary saving has made possible large contributions to the Red Cross, Red Triangle, Red Shield, Patriotic and other funds. The praiseworthy investment of such a large amount of money in Victory Bonds was in no small measure due to the results of our temperance legislation and its effectual enforcement. Some hotels closed; others remained open, and generally are doing a wholesome business without the bar. We are confident that old King Alcohol is doomed to an early death. The surprise is that so many good people endured him so long. Let the doubter of prohibition take a trip into some territory where the law is enforced and where definite results are being obtained, and there will no longer remain any scepticism as to the worth of prohibition to society and to all commercial, industrial and moral relations. Give the people a chance and there will be no question as to how long alcohol will remain enthroned in power.

"The attitude and sentiment in Saskatchewan is briefly expressed in the following testimonies selected from many that might be quoted:

"Premier Martin says: 'Reports coming to us from various parts of the province indicate that there is very general satisfaction with the prohibitory law, economically and socially. I believe the measure has been a success.'

"C. A. Mahony, Chief of Provincial Police: 'Since the advent of prohibition a tremendous improvement has been noticeable in the economic conditions of the people of Saskatchewan generally.'"

PROVINCIAL PROHIBITION.

PICTURES OF PROHIBITION PROGRESS.

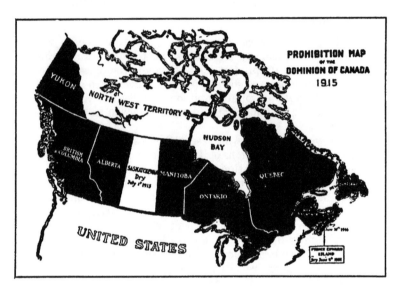

PROHIBITION IN CANADA.

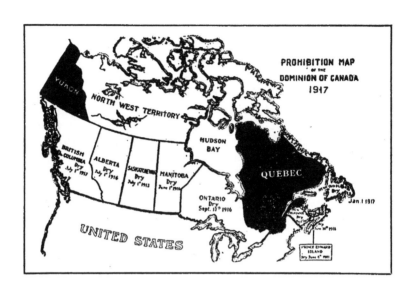

PROHIBITION IN CANADA.

VIII. ALBERTA.

The new Province of Alberta came into existence on September 1, 1905, but it was not until March, 1907, that the temperance forces of the new province were definitely organized for effective effort along aggressive lines looking toward propaganda and legislation.

This does not mean that no efforts whatever were put forth previous to the organization of the forces provincially. The district of Cardston, in Southern Alberta, which was settled very largely by Mormons, passed a local option by-law several years before there was any united effort. At the Calgary convention of the Territorial Woman's Christian Temperance Union, held early in the year 1905, before provincial autonomy became effective, it was resolved: "That we endeavor to secure a prohibitory clause in the Constitution when the Territories become a province." They memorialized the Territorial Grand Council of the Royal Templars of Temperance in February, 1905, asking that older organization to take the lead for these new provinces in the anticipated election campaign. Both organizations appointed representatives on a joint committee, called the Alberta Prohibitory Committee. Literature was distributed, and addresses made throughout the country in the interests of prohibition.

On November 2, 1905, some representatives of the Baptist, Methodist, and Presbyterian churches met in the Central Methodist Church, Calgary, to discuss the temperance situation in the new province, this meeting being called by the Rev. Dr. S. D. Chown, General Secretary of the Department of Temperance and Moral Reform of the Methodist Church in Canada. Plans were discussed and arrangements made for a deputation of those interested in the cause of temperance in the new province to wait on the newly-formed Government of Alberta to urge the best possible legislation to be enacted at the first session of the Alberta Legislature.

PROVINCIAL PROHIBITION.

On the evening of November 15, 1905, an important meeting was held in Alberta College, Edmonton, when several delegates gathered to discuss the proposals to be made to the Government at this first interview. It was decided to ask the Government to introduce a measure providing for the removal of the sale or distribution of intoxicating liquors from hotels and other places of public entertainment, the removal of the sale or distribution of liquor in clubs, the abolition of the saloon and the treating system, and the placing of such further restrictions around the liquor traffic as would most effectually curtail its operations and remedy its evils.

On the morning of November 16, 1905, the first temperance deputation to present their views and requests to the Alberta Government were received by the Hon. A. C. Rutherford, Premier, and members of his Cabinet, the members of the deputation being introduced by the Rev. Dr. John McDougall, the pioneer missionary to the Indians of Western Canada. The speakers in this deputation were: Rev. C. H. Huestis, M.A., Rev. H. A. Gray (now Bishop Gray of Edmonton Diocese of the Church of England), Mr. W. D. Mills, of Strathcona; Mr. John Benson, of Medicine Hat, and the Rev. Dr. S. D. Chown. The speakers emphasized the unique opportunity the newly-formed Government had in the matter of legislation effecting temperance reform, and the great importance of the initial action taken by them at the outset of the new province's career.

Growing out of the discussions and deliberations of this gathering, a Temperance and Moral Reform Committee of Edmonton and Strathcona was formed, to whom was committed the responsibility by that meeting of watching legislation, and taking such steps as might be deemed advisable in the way of negotiation and education. Growing out of the action of this committee a platform embodying several desirable amendments to the Liquor License Ordinance was formulated, including the following:

PROHIBITION IN CANADA.

1. Limiting the number of licenses in towns and cities as follows: Two licenses for the first one thousand of population and one for each additional thousand.
2. Closing all bars at seven o'clock each evening.
3. Closing all bars on the following religious holidays: Christmas, Good Friday, and Thanksgiving Day.
4. *Re* Local Option:
   (a) Permitting the vote for local option in a city, town, or village, instead of, as now provided, in a license district.
   (b) A straight majority to carry a by-law, instead of a three-fifths vote.
   (c) The expense of such campaigns to be borne by the municipality.
   (d) The law to remain in force and unrepealable for three years.
   (e) Permission to submit the question every year until carried.
5. A more satisfactory definition of the word "householder."
6. The granting of no licenses in any locality (village, town, or other place) where there are not at least forty occupied houses within an area of 960 acres, and within a radius of one mile from the house for which application was being made.

Copies of these proposals were submitted to individual congregations of the different denominations at work within the province, to temperance lodges, and branches of various temperance organizations in the cities and towns of the province, asking for careful consideration of each proposal, endorsation, and co-operation in bringing the necessary pressure to bear upon the members of the Provincial Government and Legislature. This may be regarded as the first effort to arouse public opinion in the new province on the matter of desired legislation, and to secure definite expressions of opinion from temperance workers in all parts of the province.

Growing out of these efforts of the committee in Edmonton and Strathcona, representatives from various parts of the province, appointed by congregations and temperance organizations, met in the McDougall Methodist Church, Edmonton, to discuss the proposals and make

PROVINCIAL PROHIBITION.

definite plans for the presentation of these requests to the Premier and members of the Government and Legislature. This meeting was held in the morning of January 25, 1907, and the interview with the members of the Government took place on the afternoon of the above date, in the Assembly Hall of the McKay Public School, Edmonton, the temporary meeting place of the Legislature of Alberta.

At this same meeting pressure was brought by several of the representatives present from different parts of the province, urging that steps should be taken immediately to call a convention of those in sympathy with temperance reform in the province, with a view to forming an effective provincial organization. A representative committee was appointed to issue the call for this convention, and to make the necessary preparation for it. In response to this call a large gathering of temperance workers, representing practically all parts of the Province of Alberta, met in the Oddfellows' Hall, Red Deer, on March 20 and 21, 1907. At this convention the Alberta Temperance and Moral Reform League was definitely formed, the constitution then adopted declaring the purpose of the League to be:

" To promote by educational and aggressive effort the growth of temperance sentiment and habit in the province, to promote temperance legislation in the direction of restricting, and ultimately abolishing, the liquor traffic, to put down gambling and other vices, to secure the stringent enforcement of the laws, and to endeavor to secure the election and appointment of men of good character and ability for all public positions."

The officers elected to guide the activities of the new organization in the initial year of its history were:

President..........J. D. Blayney, Esq., Edmonton.
Vice-President.....Thos. Underwood, Esq., Calgary.
Secretary..........Rev. Geo. G. Webber, Innisfail.
Treasurer.........Rev. Geo. R. Laing, Olds.

A provisional president for each of the provincial electoral ridings was appointed, with instructions to take steps for the formation of branches of the League in each of these districts, as well as in the cities, towns and villages of the province. Provision was also made for the employment of a field secretary, who would devote his whole time to this work, a special committee being named to secure the services of such a man. This committee ultimately named the Rev. W. G. W. Fortune, of Red Deer, who assumed the duties of this new office early in the following year.

In 1907 the Liquor License Ordinance was amended to make illegal the granting of licenses in rural places where there were not at least forty dwellings within an area of 960 acres, also forbidding the issuance of restaurant licenses, and raising the age limit of those to whom liquor might be sold from 18 to 21 years. The requests of the temperance people for a shortening of the hours of sale, and for the desired improvements to the local option law were disregarded, except that, at the petition of the Edmonton City Council, the hour of closing the bar-rooms was changed from 11.30 to 10 o'clock p.m.

On January 16, 1908, the Temperance and Moral Reform League interviewed the Government for the first time since its organization, and urged that the hour for closing the bar-rooms be changed to seven o'clock; that a local option by-law be procurable by a majority vote; that all bar-rooms be required to front on a public thoroughfare; that wholesale selling be restricted; that the fee charged for counter petitions against a license be abolished; and other minor amendments. In reply to this deputation, Premier Rutherford stated that, since the Government had made amendments to the Liquor License Ordinance the previous year, it was not their intention to deal with the matter during the coming session.

During the session of the Alberta Legislature in that year, Mr. Don Hiebert, Conservative member for Rosebud, introduced a prohibition resolution, but the resolution was defeated. Later in the same session Mr. Hiebert introduced a bill looking toward government control of the sale of

PROVINCIAL PROHIBITION.

liquors through government dispensaries, but on a motion for a second reading, the bill was ruled out of order and withdrawn.

In January, 1909, representatives of the League again interviewed members of the Government, this time supported by largely signed petitions from electors throughout the province, asking for the following amendments

(1) A local option law which gives the right to any municipality to outlaw the traffic in intoxicating liquors on a majority vote of the resident electors who vote on such questions, and the abrogation of the $100 deposit in connection therewith.

(2) The total elimination of intoxicants from all clubs, and forfeiture of charter upon first conviction for violation of the law in this regard.

(3) The closing of the bars and liquor shops on Christmas Day, Good Friday, and Thanksgiving Day.

(4) "Dwelling-house" to mean an actual separate inhabited dwelling with a separate door for ingress and egress, and occupied for at least three months previous to an application for a license under the ordinance.

(5) Amendment of the Liquor License Ordinance making it compulsory for minors, and any person who may be found intoxicated during prohibited hours, to give evidence as to where the liquor was obtained, as in the case of interdicts.

(6) That license inspectors be required to take affidavit in respect to every application for license under the ordinance, stating whether all legal requirements are met or not.

The annual convention of the League, held March 17 and 18, 1909, was noteworthy for another advance step in the work, by the decision to publish a monthly paper to give publicity to the propaganda of the League. The name chosen for the official organ then launched was *The Searchlight,* and A. W. Fullerton, Esq., of Edmonton, was appointed publisher and editor. The first issue of this new paper appeared in May, 1909. From the first it has proved to be a worthy organ of the League, and has done much to disseminate information, and stimulate public opinion on the important questions of public policy relating to temperance and moral reform.

During the years 1909 and 1910, no improvements were made in temperance legislation, but the work of organization and education was persistently pressed throughout the province. Efforts to secure satisfactory amendments to the local option provisions of the Liquor License Ordinance having been unsuccessful, it was decided to test the existing local option law by taking steps to bring on a vote in one or more license districts. Conventions were called for License Districts Numbers 2 and 3, and in both instances it was decided to proceed with the circulation of the necessary petitions, and such other steps as were likely to make these campaigns effective. These license districts comprised almost one-third of the settled area of the province, including a large number of towns and villages. Petitions were secured with more than the required 20 per cent. of the names of the electors within the areas indicated, but when the petitions came before the License Board for scrutiny, exception was taken by the License Commissioners to affidavits attached to the petitions. The demand for new affidavits necessitated another complete canvass for signatures, but in due time the petitions were again presented. The date ultimately set for the vote on local option in these license districts was November 30, and the efforts of the League were turned towards making these campaigns successful. Shortly before the time set for the holding of the poll in these districts, the secretary of the League was informed by the Deputy Attorney-General that the vote could not be held, giving as the reason for this action on the part of the Government that it was impossible to carry out the wishes of the Government in the short time at their disposal.

Naturally the friends of temperance, both within the areas directly affected and throughout the province, were greatly disappointed with this result, and the demand was made upon the Government that legislation should be

PROVINCIAL PROHIBITION.

enacted making the petitions secured at such effort valid for a vote in the following year. The legislation subsequently enacted provided for the use of these petitions in a vote to be taken during 1912, and giving these petitions the same status they held at the time they were taken. At the same session of the Legislature, amendments were also made to the local option provisions of the ordinance, removing some of the technical difficulties in the operation of those provisions, but these amendments were not made to apply to the petitions already presented for License Districts Numbers 2 and 3.

The work was taken up again during 1912, and campaigns entered upon looking towards the expected vote in that year. But, just when it was anticipated that the vote would be taken, application was made on behalf of the friends of the liquor traffic for an injunction against the holding of such a poll on the petitions of 1911. The legality of the petitions was attacked, and these were eventually set aside by the court, on the ground that, although the names secured represented more than 20 per cent. of the persons voting in the previous election (there being no voters' lists for these districts), this did not necessarily represent 20 per cent. of the persons entitled to vote in 1913. This second failure deepened the disappointment of the temperance people of the province, and really marks the time when attention was diverted from attempts to make use of what was regarded, at best, as an unsatisfactory local option law. Out of these repeated disappointments, as will soon be shown, there arose demands which led to larger plans, and greater efforts.

Another line of action was started in 1913 by a committee in Calgary. Instead of insisting upon immediate prohibitory legislation, they proposed a scheme of government control, pending the securing of a prohibitory law. The League, which had always stood for a prohibition policy, did not approve of the Calgary committee's plan. They condemned the principle of involving the government in

PROHIBITION IN CANADA.

partnership with the traffic, any further than it was already involved by the license system. Their aim was to free it from such trammels altogether, and they feared that the advocating of such a plan as government control would draw attention from the reforms for which temperance people were laboring, and which they believed were almost in sight. *The Searchlight* said, in comment on the situation:

" The Calgary policy is unacceptable, also, because it is unnecessary. It overlooks the steadily increasing prohibition sentiment throughout the province That sentiment, fostered and developed by such educational work as may be done within the next few years, will in that short time, we fully believe, be strong enough to put the liquor traffic out of existence, thus removing the occasion for any such doubtful expedient as government control. This is not sky-dreaming. Those who are in touch with the public sentiment know that there is reason and fact behind such a forecast."

At a convention of the Temperance and Moral Reform League in February, 1914, it was decided to submit to the Legislature a prohibition act, with a petition praying for its enactment the next session of the Legislature. The solicitors of the League took great pains in drafting the act. They consulted prohibitory laws in operation in the United States, also the Prince Edward Island Prohibition Act of 1900, the Nova Scotia Act of 1910, and the Manitoba Act, which, while it had never become operative, had been declared *intra vires* by the Imperial Privy Council. The bill, finally prepared by them, a most stringent piece of prohibitory legislation, was presented by a large deputation to the Government, with the request that it be submitted to the electors on the first Tuesday of June, 1915, under the initiative and referendum legislation of the province.

By the Direct Legislation Act, a bill, if approved by a majority of the electors, shall be put into effect by the Provincial Legislature without substantial alterations. Such a measure is thus pre-eminently a piece of popular legislation, in the enactment of which the Assembly takes only the

PROVINCIAL PROHIBITION.

formal part of implementing the popular vote. The committee of the Legislature which examined the names on the petition presented by the League, reported that it appeared to conform to the requirements of the Direct Legislation Act. On October 9th, Premier Sifton moved that it be referred to the electors of the province, the date to be decided by the Lieutenant-Governor in Council. The motion was passed without discussion.

Representatives of the Licensed Victuallers asked for delay that they might verify the signatures. They contended that the bill did not come under the Direct Legislation Act, since it was a charge on the revenue of the province. Their objections were overruled, however, the temperance forces merely being required to give affidavits that the greatest care had been exercised in compiling the lists. The date of voting was later set for July 21, 1915.

A lively campaign opened in January, 1915. The officers charged with the work of securing prohibition were: President, T. H. Miller; General Secretary, W. F. Gold; Campaign Organizer, A. W. Coone; Treasurer, J. H. McDonald; Finance Commissioner, A. T. Cushing. Mr. Clinton N. Howard, Rochester, N.Y., was engaged by the League for a month's meetings. Mr. N. W. Rowell, Leader of the Ontario Liberal Opposition; Archdean Lloyd, Principal of Emmanuel College, Saskatchewan, and many other men noted for their self-sacrificing advocacy of the temperance cause, spoke at conventions and mass meetings. Rev. Ben. H. Spence, Secretary of the Ontario Branch of the Dominion Alliance, and Rev. F. W. Patterson of Edmonton, were assigned the duty of meeting the opposition orator, C. A. Windle, of pro-German notoriety, and did their work well. The W.C.T.U., under the leadership of Mrs. L. C. McKinney, who addressed meetings in many places in the province, gave a most active and needed assistance in every phase of the campaign. Church organizations supplied efficient workers, and many newspapers gave unhesitating support to the prohibition measure. Literature and cartoons were published in English,

PROHIBITION IN CANADA.

French, Russian, German, Chinese, Greek, Italian, Spanish, Bohemian, Finnish, Swedish, Slovak, Yiddish, and Roumanian. Buttons, postcards, envelopes, posters, leaflets, lectures, and stereopticon views were requisitioned. About six and three-quarters tons of literature was distributed.

In connection with this campaign, an interesting memorial was received by the League at its convention in Edmonton in 1915. It read as follows:

"From the Blackfoot Anglican Mission, Gleichen, Alberta, January 16, 1915.

"To the Alberta Temperance and Moral Reform League, Ninth Annual Convention, Edmonton:

"We, who are Blackfoot Indians, have heard that a very big convention is taking place this week in Edmonton, in the hope of suppressing the manufacture and sale of alcoholic drinks.

"We are very glad to hear of such a convention. We are sorry we cannot be there, to let you know how glad we are.

"We are glad of this because for very many years intoxicating drinks have done us and our people very great harm. Because of it, many have died, very many have been imprisoned, and most of us have become very poor in horses, which we have had to sell in order to pay fines for drunkenness: therefore, we are very, very glad to hear of your meeting, and we shall think of you as our best friends, and will pray to our Father in Heaven that you may be successful in your efforts.

"We shake hands with you very heartily.

"Head Chief David Yellow Horse, William Water Chief, Joe Calf Child, Raw Eater, Frank Tried to Fly, James Appikoki, Bull Bear, The Calf, Doesn't Bake, Bill Bear Chief, Bernard Not Useful, Eagle Ribson Sleigh, Spotted Eagle, Little Backbone, David G. Forehead, Joe Fox, Black Face, Porter, Doesn't Bake, Jack Raw Eater, Tom Eagle Tail Feathers, Turning Robes, Black Rider, Fred McGuire, Albert Eagle Rider, Charlie Raw Eater, Martin Holy Rider, Rev. Backfat, Fred Stud Horse, A White Elk, Ghost Skin, Shief Child, Medicine Traveller, Ed. Costigan, Black Chief, Oldman Bull, Philip Backfat, P. Sarcee Medicine Wife,

PROVINCIAL PROHIBITION.

Blue Bird, Henry Fevershield, Paul, Tom Sarcee Medicine Pipe, Joe Turning Robe, Running Antelope, N. Calf Child Donald McMaster, Joe Weasel Child, Thos. Cutter."

The act was approved on July 21st. The vote was:

For prohibition 58,295
Against prohibition 37,209

Majority for prohibition......... 21,086

Calgary and Edmonton, to the surprise of many people, recorded large affirmative majorities.

The Legislature was now called upon to put the Act into effect. During the campaign it had been urged in various quarters that certain grave defects in the bill would make it unworkable, and that unless substantial amendments were introduced, attempts at enforcement would be disastrous. The prohibitionists, however, opposed any tampering with the measure which had received public sanction on the distinct understanding that no substantial change should be made in it. Any such action now, they contended, would be a breach of confidence with the people. This view was evidently the one taken by the Legislature, for when the bill came up for its third reading on March 8th, it was passed without debate and with only two slight amendments, one a grammatical correction, and the other removing the quantity restriction on the amount of liquor a clergyman might keep for sacramental purposes. The Alberta Prohibition Law came into force on July 1, 1916.

Elated by their triumph, temperance workers now directed their attention to the vital question of enforcement of the new law. In the Legislature, serious charges of neglect and inefficiency had been frequently laid by the Opposition against the Attorney-General's department, which had controlled the administration of the former license law. The Temperance and Moral Reform League urgently and repeatedly requested the Government for the appointment of a commission, independent of party control, to enforce the new law, as the only efficient method according to the experience of the different provinces of the Dominion. After a year of the old method, the Government having to replace the Mounted Police, created a new provincial police force, and gave it the enforcement of all law, including the Liquor Act. This force, under a commission of three, had full responsibility for the enforcement of the temperance laws; but after two years of trial the method proved ineffectual, the commission was disbanded, and the officials were placed under the Attorney-General's department. The special responsibility of enforcing the Liquor Act was placed under a separate force of plainclothes men, who were under an inspector appointed by the head of the force.

In 1917 the Alberta Prohibition Law was amended. It was forbidden to keep liquor in excess of one quart of spirits and two gallons of malt. This ruled out everything in the way of warehouses and commission firms. It was also provided that there should be no liquor advertising of any description by newspapers, electric signs, bill posters or circulars through the mail. In 1918 the sections relating to the quantity of liquor, having been found to be unworkable, were rescinded.

The history of prohibition in Alberta would not be complete without record of the fact that in the provincial elections of 1917, Mrs. L. C. McKinney of Claresholm, President of the Provincial Women's Christian Temperance Union, was elected to the Legislature, the first woman in Canada to be accorded this political recognition.

PROVINCIAL PROHIBITION.

IX. BRITISH COLUMBIA.

The liquor traffic has always had a powerful grip on British Columbia. The history of the opening up of the province, the nature of its industries, and the character of a large part of the population, help to explain the evil conditions. Trapping, mining, lumbering and fishing, almost exclusively masculine occupations, necessitate a peculiar isolation of the workmen for months at a time, followed by the possession of ready money and abundant opportunity for drinking and drunkenness. Further, the large foreign element of the population immeasurably complicates the liquor problem.

The provincial license law was long quite inadequate to control the situation. It contained a Sunday-closing clause which was almost a dead letter, in that it classified any person walking three miles to procure liquor as a *bona fide* traveller, who was therefore permitted to purchase it on Sunday. The granting of new licenses was in the hands of local boards of licensing magistrates, with the mayor of each town as chairman, *ex officio*.

Petitions of ratepayers against the issuing of licenses were openly disregarded. The whole traffic was in control of political party machinery, as Mr. A. I. Morley, Mayor of Victoria, in 1906 and 1907, testifies in an experience related in *The Pioneer*, September 25, 1918.

Early in 1906, Mr. Morley waited on the Premier and urged the wisdom and necessity of giving municipalities the right to elect license and police commissioners, but he received no satisfaction from the leader of the Government. In 1907 he renewed his plea, and described the unsatisfactory work of 1906. He was told that the commissioners for the ensuing year were already selected, according to the nominations of the Conservative Association. He expressed satisfaction with the personnel of the commission, but protested that the license nominees were not in the interests of the city, and received the reply that this matter was considered the prerogative of the party, and that the Premier was unable to do anything to remedy matters.

The Woman's Christian Temperance Union was the first agency to undertake definite action against the traffic. In 1907 they began a great campaign to secure the enactment of a local option law. Churches and temperance societies heartily co-operated. Miss Ada L. Murcutt, from London, England, was engaged to deliver a series of illustrated lectures, and she was successful in creating great interest and enthusiasm throughout the province. The movement speedily gathered momentum. The aim of the workers was to secure the name of every man in the province for the petition to be presented to the Legislature at the coming session.

On November 25, 1908, a most notable convention was held in Vancouver, at which almost every section of the province was represented; one hundred and twelve delegates coming from outside points. The British Columbia Local Option League was organized with the following officers:

President, Mr. E. B. Morgan; 1st Vice-President, Mr. T. T. Langlois; 2nd Vice-President, Mr. R. H. Cairns, Chilliwack; 3rd Vice-President, Mrs. Spofford, Victoria; 4th Vice-President, Dr. Ernest Hall, Victoria; 5th Vice-President, Mr. Joseph Patrick, Nelson; Hon. Sec., Miss A. L. Murcutt, Vancouver; Treas., Mr. F. R. Stewart, Vancouver.

An Advisory Council was formed, including all presidents of Local Option Leagues in the province, the presidents of the Independent Order of Good Templars, Royal Templars of Temperance, Christian Endeavor Unions and the Dominion Alliance, also the Bishop of Columbia, the Bishop of the Reformed Episcopal Church, the Archbishop of the Roman Catholic Church, and the presidents or chief officers of the Methodist, Presbyterian, Baptist and Congregational bodies, and the Salvation Army.

Among the resolutions adopted were the following:

(1) That a British Columbia Local Option League be now organized, to be composed of residents of the province, and on an

PROVINCIAL PROHIBITION.

absolutely civic basis, for the purpose of organizing a Local Option League in every part of the province, for securing a local option law and putting the same into operation in every municipality throughout British Columbia.

(2) That the membership of the League consist of residents of British Columbia who are in favor of local option, irrespective of race, creed or political affiliations, and that all monetary contributions be voluntary.

The plan of campaign was as follows:

(1) The obtaining of signatures to a petition to be presented to the Lieutenant-Governor in Council, asking for the passing of a local option bill at the next session of the Legislature.

(2) The education of the people in temperance reform.

(3) The organization of every municipality and district for local option purposes.

(4) The promotion of local option legislation.

The campaign work was superintended by Rev. Dr. D. Spencer of Victoria. Organizers found a strong sentiment in favor of the League throughout the country. From only one place did they report having obtained the signatures of less than sixty per cent. of those canvassed. The majority of places responded with from eighty per cent. to ninety per cent. By the beginning of the next year there were about fifty Local Option Leagues throughout the province. Dr. Spencer sent to every member of the Legislature a strong and vigorous letter, presenting the arguments in favor of a local option law and urging the right of the people to choose for themselves.

Meantime, the liquor party had been aroused, and a meeting of the Licensed Victuallers urged the Government not to interfere with the Liquor License Act. They urged that the time was not opportune in a half-settled province, and supported their plea by a large deputation and a number of telegrams to the Ministers.

On February 2, 1909, Dr. Spencer handed to the Premier, the Hon. Richard McBride, a draft bill, approved by the executive of the League and supported by a deputation of

150 men and petitions of 9,473 electors. The answer of the Government was given in twenty-six days. They decided that, in spite of the great number of petitions, the people as a whole had not expressed their view on such a far-reaching and drastic change as a local option law would involve. They announced that a referendum would be held, free from any complication of issues, on the question of whether or not the people were in favor of legislation putting a local option law on the statute books. The humor of this action does not seem to have appealed to the legislators at that time, nor how ridiculous it was that they should ask the people to vote upon whether they should be allowed to vote or not.

On March 4th, the Premier supported a resolution in favor of the appointment of a Royal Commission to inquire into the question of the liquor traffic and desirable legislation concerning it. The matter was brought up by Mr. Hawthornthwaite, Socialist member for Nanaimo. In the preamble to his resolution Mr. Hawthornthwaite declared that local option was objectionable from certain standpoints, and ineffective, but that the Gothenburg system removed many of the evils complained of. It was desirable to secure full information concerning the working of that system, and the traffic in the province, with a view to the possible adaptation and establishment of the Gothenburg system in British Columbia. An outline of Mr. Hawthornthwaite's speech will illustrate the nature of the liquor party's arguments.

In support of his resolution the honorable member declared that the agitation for a local option law necessitated immediate action being taken by the Legislature, and he thought that the Government's plan of a plebiscite was a wise one. As for the petitions, they represented only ten per cent. of the electorate; personally he put little faith in petitions. The evils of the liquor traffic were recognized, but they did not necessarily constitute an objection to the continuation of the traffic. One of the evils, incidentally, was that the opponents of the trade were little short of fanatical. It was a popular error that medical science had

PROVINCIAL PROHIBITION.

declared against the practice of drinking. It was also a mistake to say that drink caused an enormous waste of money that would otherwise be saved by working-men; since self-denial in luxuries meant, by the iron law of wages, that the rate of remuneration would tend downward. Prohibition was no remedy for the evils complained of; it did not prohibit, as the State of Maine showed. Moreover, prohibition was objectionable from the standpoint of human liberty.

Beyond this speech by the mover of the resolution, there was no discussion of the measure, which was carried by a vote of nineteen to twelve. Four Conservatives voted with all the Liberals against it.

The Local Option League, in a manifesto issued by Rev. Dr. Spencer, expressed indignation at the appointment of the commission to shelve the issue, and blamed the Premier who had asked his followers to support it. Without endorsing either existing party, the manifesto intimated that the Government deserved defeat, and declared: "We think that whatever man or party will make local option and kindred reforms a plank in their platform should command the support of the electors."

The plebiscite was to take place at the time of the election of a new Legislature. The terms of voting were copied from the Ontario Referendum; i.e., no matter how many votes should be polled, the minority should win unless the majority equalled fifty per cent. of the electors who voted for candidates. Thus the Government assumed that all who did not vote were opposed to the temperance legislation, and thus the liquor men did not need to vote at all to secure a victory for their side.

The conditions of the vote seriously hampered the temperance party for the reason that British Columbia has some constituencies which elect four or five representatives to the Legislature, and each elector has as many votes for candidates as there are members to be elected in his constituency, whereas for local option he had but one vote.

PROHIBITION IN CANADA.

The Local Option League condemned the plebiscite as unnecessary, but announced its readiness to accept the challenge and fight out the issue of local option at the polls. Churches, Temperance Societies, Woman's Christian Temperance Unions, and other forces joined the Local Option Leagues in a hard fight. Many difficulties were met with in almost every constituency, but the result of the vote was a great victory.

> For local option.................. 22,779
> Against local option.............. 19,084
>
> Majority for local option........ 3,695

Eleven constituencies secured the necessary fifty per cent. with 753 votes to spare; eight gave good majorities, although they did not reach the fifty per cent.; sixteen recorded an adverse vote. The total vote fell short of the required majority by 563½ votes, and the Government refused to accept it as an instruction.

Defeated in their effort to secure a local option law, temperance workers fell back on the Canada Temperance Act, which was amended by the Dominion Parliament to make it applicable to the subdivisions of British Columbia. In 1910, contests were brought on in the districts of Chilliwack and Prince Rupert. The liquor sellers raised the cry that the movement was one of opposition to the Government, seeking to supersede the license system which the Government favored. Their agitation was successful in defeating the Canada Temperance Act in both constituencies.

In the meantime the Government had introduced and secured the passing of a new license law, which was the most rigid piece of legislation that British Columbia had yet enacted. It increased the license fees, imposed heavy restrictions, and provided severe penalties for law-breaking. The Government was empowered to appoint an inspector for the province to see to law enforcement. Municipalities were to be under the Municipal Clauses Act in relation to the issue

PROVINCIAL PROHIBITION.

of licenses. In unorganized districts, in order to secure a license, a petition was required, signed by two-thirds of the householders within three miles of the premises to be licensed, the signatories to include two-thirds of the wives of the married men signing the petition.

In 1911, Mr. Bowser's Municipal Clauses Act amendment gave municipalities the right to abolish saloon licenses and to license only hotels.

Prior to the general provincial election of March 28, 1912, the Government was again asked to declare itself on the local option issue, and again refused to undertake such legislation as the temperance people desired. The Liberal party, on the other hand, under the leadership of H. C. Brewster, in convention in Vancouver, on February 28th and March 1st, adopted both the planks of Local Option and Woman Suffrage. Mr. Brewster declared that the liquor traffic in British Columbia was under the absolute control of the Provincial Government and was used as a political machine. He was resolved to insist upon the complete removal of the liquor question from party politics, and would advocate a local option law.

Not one Liberal was returned to the Legislature in that election. The liquor men claimed that this was a declaration of the electors against local option, although it is possible that local option had nothing at all to do with the defeat, and although other issues and conditions were such as to make a Conservative victory absolutely certain.

In 1913, the license law was amended but, still, no local option clause was introduced. The new legislation took away from municipalities the authority to allow bar-rooms to remain open indefinitely, and provided for general closing at eleven o'clock on ordinary evenings and ten o'clock on Saturday. Better facilities were provided for law enforcement. The penalty of imprisonment was to be imposed for the first offence of illegal manufacture, with no option of a fine.

PROHIBITION IN CANADA.

On August 14, 1915, a deputation from the Provincial Social Service Commission waited on the Premier, Sir Richard McBride, and earnestly requested the Government to " take steps to bring about the prohibition of the sale of liquor during the period of the war," and to provide that such prohibition should not be repealed without a vote of the electors in favor of such action. The Premier's reply did not convey much definite information concerning the details of the Government policy, but contained the following statement:

" It has been decided, after careful deliberation, to submit the whole question to a plebiscite of the electorate. The date of the taking of the plebiscite will be announced as soon as it has been decided what shall form the basis of the referendum. I may say that it is intended to direct the course of legislation in this regard according to the general result of the vote to be taken."

On August 25th and 26th, there was held in Vancouver a great convention, representing all parts of British Columbia, and commanding more public attention than had ever been conceded to any such gathering. Rev. Principal Lloyd of Saskatchewan, President of the Dominion Alliance Council, Rev. F. W. Patterson, Alberta, and Mrs. Nellie McClung, Manitoba, along with local speakers, stirred great audiences to immense enthusiasm. A public mass meeting, preliminary to the convention, had an attendance of 4,000, while many were unable to obtain admission.

When the convention was opened in Hamilton Hall on August 25th, that auditorium, which seats five hundred, was crowded to the doors, while many delegates were obliged to stand. Mr. John Nelson was chosen to preside, and the communication of the Premier was committed for consideration to a committee appointed for that purpose. The committee reported a policy which was threshed out at some length, remitted for further consideration, and again discussed in detail, the final result being the adoption of the following declaration:

PROVINCIAL PROHIBITION.

Whereas, the evil arising out of the traffic in intoxicating liquors results in an economic waste and loss of efficiency, resulting in social and moral degradation; and

Whereas, it is believed the sentiment in favor of the abolition of this traffic is predominant throughout the Province of British Columbia; and

Whereas, it is the sense of this convention that the time is now ripe for a definite step to be taken in regard to the enactment of a prohibitory measure; and

Whereas, the reply of the Premier of the province to the delegation which waited on him asking for a prohibitory measure did not state upon what the electorate would be asked to vote or the time at which the vote should be taken;

Therefore, be it resolved that the delegation from all parts of the Province of British Columbia, duly assembled in convention, do hereby place themselves on record in favor of the principle of prohibition, and request the Provincial Government that they do on the earliest legal date present to the electorate of the Province of British Columbia a bill to be drawn by a committee of this convention similar in wording and in intent to that endorsed by the electors of Alberta on the 21st day of July, 1915, and entitled "The Liquor Act."

In the event of the said bill being approved by a majority of the electors of the Province of British Columbia voting on the said measure, the same to be enacted as law, to come into force not later than the last day of January, 1917.

And be it further resolved that it is the sense of this convention that the presentation to the electorate of the Province of British Columbia of the aforesaid bill shall not be made at the time of an election, this being an issue separate and distinct from party politics.

A report of an organization committee provided for the formation of a body of one hundred men representing all parts of British Columbia, to be known as "The Committee of One Hundred of the People's Prohibition Movement." This organization was to supervise the formation of committees for aggressive work in every electoral district, and to have its headquarters in the city of Vancouver. Mr. Jonathan Rogers, of Vancouver, President of the Board of

Trade, was elected president of the new movement, and a committee was appointed to carry out organization details. The committee met after the convention had adjourned, and selected convenors to initiate organization in different localities.

On September 14th, a deputation composed of members of the committee, formally submitted to Premier McBride the wishes of the convention. The Premier promised an early reply and the committee went ahead vigorously with campaign organization.

Repeated appeals from the committee to the Premier failed to elicit any definite answer as to the Government's plans for the proposed referendum, the only statement offered being that the matter was receiving the careful consideration of the Government. Finally Sir Richard McBride retired from the premiership and was succeeded by the Hon. W. O. Bowser, former Attorney-General. The new Premier was interviewed and petitioned, with little result, until a by-election gave an opportunity for a clear indication of the strength of temperance public sentiment.

It had been the expressed desire of temperance workers from the start to keep the movement entirely out of the political arena; but the protracted and deliberate inaction of the McBride Government called forth an intimation that if the Government continued to refuse satisfaction, new methods would be pursued. When two members of Mr. Bowser's Cabinet were up for re-election, the temperance organization lent its influence in having them both defeated by overwhelming majorities. When a temperance deputation next waited on Premier Bowser on February 28, 1916, and asked for a definite answer to the request made to the Government in the preceding August, the Premier gave a very satisfactory verbal reply, confirmed in detail by letter on March 10th. On behalf of the Government the Premier promised to bring down a bill drafted in conformity with the views of the People's Prohibition Movement, the bill to be given three readings in the House and then placed before the elec-

PROVINCIAL PROHIBITION.

torate at the next general election, and if carried by a majority, to come into force on January 1, 1917.

The liquor men were not slow in waking up to the need for strenuous counter attacks upon the People's Prohibition Movement. In accordance with a time-worn device for securing popular sympathy and with the possible idea of working under cover, they organized under the name of Merchants' Protective Association. Money was poured out unstintingly and every campaign agency that could be bought was enlisted. Newspaper advertising publicity was used on a more gigantic scale than in any previous campaign fought in Canada. Journalistic opposition was hushed into silence in all the leading dailies of the province with the notable exception of the Vancouver *World,* which not only campaigned vigorously for prohibition, but refused to sell its space for the liquor traffic's advertisements. Certainly the tactics of the anti-prohibitionists were not above reproach. A petition was brought forward, which the liquor men claimed represented the sentiment of the province, but which proved upon investigation to be largely fraudulent, the same names appearing several times, and many names being recorded that were not to be found on any voters' list or directory.

On March 23rd a big deputation of hotelmen waited on the Cabinet to express their strong opposition to the government proposal. "I submit," said A. E. Tulk, leader of the anti-prohibitionist organization, who argued the case of the liquor party, "that the decision come to by the Premier was an ill-advised and hasty action based on the application of a propagandist deputation, and arrived at *ex parte* without hearing all the evidence." In the name of the liquor dealers, he demanded compensation, declaring that without it the prohibition bill was immoral, unjust and undemocratic. The Premier stated that in regard to details of the proposed measure the Government had not yet reached conclusions.

The Committee of One Hundred on April 4th expressed their hearty approval of the government plan, adding a reminder that the policy of the organization was for a clear-cut issue, not qualified by any modifications, and protesting strongly against the compensation suggestion of the liquor dealers.

On May 10th, a deputation representing the British Columbia Pharmaceutical Association urged that the druggists be not required by the Prohibition Act to be the purveyors of liquor in the province. They informed the Premier that a plebiscite of druggists on the question taken by the Association showed that ninety-five per cent. of the members were absolutely opposed to handling liquor. Premier Bowser expressed his sympathy with the members of the profession and promised every consideration for their request.

On May 23rd the Premier presented to the Legislature the Government Bill entitled "The British Columbia Prohibition Act," embodying legislation for the total prohibition of the liquor traffic to the limit of provincial authority. Rumors that the Lieutenant-Governor had refused to sign the bill were evidently unfounded, for the measure came before the House in a message from him. There had been some apprehension lest one or more of the proposals made by the liquor men might have been incorporated in the bill in its final form, as for instance the provision for compensation in the bill itself, or in the form of question submitted in the referendum. But these fears were not realized; the bill was presented in precisely the form agreed upon in caucus and provided for a clear-cut issue to be put to the electorate on the general election day: "Are you in favor of the British Columbia Prohibition Act? Yes or No." If ratified by the referendum, the law was to go into operation on July 1, 1919.

Mr. Bowser, in moving the second reading on May 25, discussed the clauses of the act in detail. Penalties are very severe for the selling or keeping for sale of intoxicating liquor otherwise than as provided by the act. The first offence penalty is imprisonment with hard labor for a term of not less than six months and not more than twelve months. For a second offence the penalty is imprisonment with hard labor for not less than twelve months and not more than

PROVINCIAL PROHIBITION.

twenty-one months. If the offender be a corporation, the penalty is a fine of one thousand dollars.

For other offences, such as the supplying of liquor by vendors or druggists without proper authority, the failure to record and report permitted sales, allowing the consumption of liquor on the premises of a vendor or druggist, and the like, the first offence penalty is a fine of not less than fifty dollars, with imprisonment in default of payment; and for a second offence, imprisonment of from two to four months, or a fine of from two hundred dollars to five hundred dollars; and for any subsequent offence, imprisonment of from three to six months without the option of a fine.

Any constable, police officer, or other official who fails to prosecute for a second or third offence, when he knows of previous convictions, is liable to the severe penalties just mentioned.

The principal officer in charge of the work of enforcement is to be the superintendent of provincial police of the province, and the regulations governing him and the other law-enforcing officers will be orders-in-council passed directly by the Provincial Government. Outside of the foregoing differences, " The Ontario Temperance Act " and the " British Columbia Prohibition Act " are almost identical.

At their special request the druggists had been relieved of handling the liquor sold for permitted purposes, which would be in charge of the Attorney-General's department.

The Premier stated his desire to be fair to both sides in the prohibition controversy, and promised that investigation of the claims of the liquor sellers for compensation would be made by a judicial commission if the prohibition bill were carried by the referendum vote.

Mr. Brewster, the Leader of the Opposition, made the only other speech on the measure. He thought it not quite stringent enough, but said that it evidently satisfied the executive of the People's Prohibition Movement. He thought it should not be handicapped by any party bias, and he would support it. The plan of handling the question by

PROHIBITION IN CANADA.

direct legislation had been conceived by the Liberal party and taken up by the Conservatives, proof that the Liberals did some good although they might take a subordinate place in the House. "As to this bill, it may be necessary to move amendments in committee to make it more drastic, or to make necessary changes, but the bill is certainly called for in this, the last province of Canada, after it has been shown that the world, from one side to the other, has changed in its feeling toward the consumption of liquor."

The bill passed its second reading unanimously.

The British Columbia prohibition law is a very strong measure. It follows largely the lines of the Manitoba Liquor Act, which has also been taken as a model in framing the prohibitory laws of Ontario and New Brunswick.

Headquarters were opened in the Rogers' Building, from which organizers were sent out. The churches and the W.C.T.U. gave loyal co-operation. The temperance people were at the outset badly handicapped by lack of funds, and this enabled the liquor propaganda to gain considerable headway. The Dominion Council of the Alliance came to the assistance of the British Columbia workers, and sent out $2,600, with the Ontario Secretary, Mr. Ben. H. Spence, to help in the struggle.

On September 14, 1916, the poll within the province showed 39,864 votes in favor of the Prohibition Act; 29,334 against; leaving a majority of 10,512 in favor. Provision was made also to submit the question to the soldiers, and on account of the difficulty in getting the votes in England and France, the time for the overseas poll was extended to December 3rd. When the result was finally announced it was claimed that the soldiers' vote had reversed the decision of the province, and had piled up a majority of 800 against prohibition.

Mr. W. D. Bayley, prohibition representative at the overseas voting, at the request of Sir Richard McBride who was entrusted with the administration of the act, was allowed access to certain military rolls, had interviews with

PROVINCIAL PROHIBITION.

a number of soldiers alleged to have voted, and took about fifty affidavits. He reported that the supervision of the balloting had been such as to give every opportunity for improper practices, and that scandalous irregularities took place.

Three officials who gave him no notice of holding poll, as required by the act, secured in December 3,500 votes, whereas in November a thorough comb of the same territory under scrutiny secured less than 500 votes.

At the unscrutineered polls, soldiers were falsely informed that, owing to votes having been torpedoed at sea, the Government had ordered a revote; thus hundreds of men appear to have innocently voted a second time, having voted previous to September 14th in Canada or England. In addition to these repeaters, the poll books of the above three officials show that 300 men voted twice during December, giving the same name or number. At one place liquor was used in connection with the polling so openly that a military investigation resulted in the severe reprimand of the sergeant who conducted the polls, and of six other sergeants. Men openly declared that beer and whiskey were obtained for fraudulent voting. Affidavits from voters indicate that the men were not properly sworn, that they were not allowed to seal up their ballots in an envelope, as required by the law, and many marked their ballots in full view of the presiding official. Many men, indeed, were not even given ballots, but just asked to state verbally their wish. Out of some thirty parcels of votes, averaging 100 each, taken under these conditions, fifteen parcels did not contain a single "dry" vote, and only four parcels contained over ten.

A number of meetings were held in British Columbia to protest against the irregularities reported, and a deputation on March 29th urged the Government to make a prompt investigation, the findings of which would be available either to bring the act into force by July 1st, or to demonstrate that it was fairly defeated. The Premier promised prompt consideration of the matter and a definite answer before the

PROHIBITION IN CANADA.

session closed. After seven weeks, at the close of the session, the Government's policy was announced to be the appointment of a commission to investigate the overseas vote, and the holding of a special session of the Legislature, not later than August 15th, when, if it was found that the irregularities had taken place to such an extent as to defeat the spirit of the referendum, a prohibition bill would be passed, to become effective not later than October 1st. Premier Brewster referred to contradictory statements made by those favoring and opposing prohibition, and intimated that the information received up to date was not sufficient on which to base a decision or take action. Although the plan of the Government met with some opposition, a few of the members believing that the Government ought to bring in prohibition on July 1st, the resolution was passed without a division.

The commission, consisting of Messrs. Whiteside, Pauline and Nelson, reported to the Legislature at its opening on August 14th. Their report substantiated all the charges made by the prohibitionists, and recommended that out of 8,505 votes cast overseas after September 14th, 4,697 be rejected. Granting all the remainder to the anti-prohibitionists, the prohibitionists were left with a majority vote. The report of the commission was accepted unquestioningly and passed the House without a division.

On the 17th of August the Government brought in a new bill giving effect to the old prohibition measure. The Leader of the Opposition, Mr. Bowser, offered his support to the Government measure, as it was merely enacting his own bill. The Legislature, with the exception of one member, voted for the bill, and twenty minutes later the Governor entered the Chamber and gave the act his signature. Its passage was greeted with vigorous applause from the floor of the House and the crowded galleries. The law went into effect on October 1, 1917.

PROVINCIAL PROHIBITION.

X. YUKON TERRITORY.

The Yukon Territory was the last spot in the Dominion to secure a prohibitory regulation. It had in 1916 about seventy bars and between 5,000 and 7,000 white people. The Territory stood in a different position from the provinces in that the Elective Territorial Council, while controlling the licensing and regulation of the liquor traffic, had not power to prohibit the sale of liquor, but could only forward a petition for and recommendation of such prohibition to the Dominion Governor-in-Council.

In 1916 a campaign was conducted by temperance workers with that purpose in view. The movement had its beginning at the meeting of the British Empire Club of Dawson City. The meeting expressed unanimous approval of the action of the committee of representative business men of Ottawa in making an urgent appeal to Canadian Clubs, Boards of Trade, and similar organizations in the Dominion for prompt and vigorous measures to secure the immediate suppression of the liquor traffic in view of the war situation. Following this, a mass meeting was called, committees formed, and "dry" petitions put in circulation. The local temperance organization was the People's Prohibition Movement, with Mr. Henry Dook, of Dawson City, as president, and Mr. J. T. Patton as treasurer. Members of the W.C.T.U. and other helpers made the first canvass of the city of Dawson, and copies of petitions were sent to reliable persons in other parts of the territory. A whirlwind campaign was necessary since the petition was to be presented to the Yukon Council at the session in June. The signatures of a majority of the electors were secured.

The liquor-sellers, to meet the situation, circulated a petition asking for a reduction in the number of licenses, increase in the license fee, and enforcement of the law.

Although the prohibition petition asked for immediate action, the Council decided that before forwarding the petition to Ottawa they would get an expression of public

PROHIBITION IN CANADA.

opinion in regard to it by a plebiscite held on August 30th. The following proposition was presented to be voted upon:

"Are you in favor of prohibiting the sale, importation and manufacture of intoxicating liquor for beverage purposes in the Yukon Territory?"

The ordinance which provided for the plebiscite went on to say:

"If the majority of the votes polled are in favor of prohibiting the sale, importation and manufacture of intoxicating liquor in the Yukon Territory for beverage purposes, the Commissioner shall with all reasonable despatch memorialize the Governor-in-Council on behalf and in the name of the Commissioner-in-Council of the Yukon Territory, for the enactment or passage of legislation or order-in-council prohibiting the sale, importation and manufacture of intoxicating liquors in the Yukon Territory for beverage purposes from and after the 14th day of July, 1917."

Acting on the suggestion of the workers in the West, the Dominion Council of the Alliance sent Mr. Ben. H. Spence, Secretary of the Ontario Branch of the Dominion Alliance, to assist in this campaign.

The conditions of the vote were favorable to election irregularities. There was no voters' list, the only qualifications for voting being that a person go to the polling place on election day, make a declaration that he was a British subject, twenty-one years of age, and had lived in the territory one year, and thirty days in the district in which he was voting. Between the time of the circulation of the petition and the taking of the vote, a large number of citizen-soldiers were sent to outside camps and therefore could not vote. An idea of the sentiment of these men may be gained from the fact that they themselves took a vote in one camp in Sydney, the result showing sixty-four for prohibition, thirty-five against. In one case the polling place was actually switched from a settlement to where there was located a road gang that was working on the winter trail between White Horse and Carmack, and at this poll the vote stood eleven to three against prohibition.

PROVINCIAL PROHIBITION.

Enormous sums of money were spent by the liquor interests to defeat prohibition, and most unscrupulous methods were resorted to. An example of this is a statement that was issued purporting to come from a leading prohibitionist, setting out how it was proposed the revenue should be raised if prohibition carried. This document, which was a pure fabrication, provided that a poll-tax should be levied upon each individual in the territory; then also a head-tax on every dog, on all cattle and horses, a wheel-tax on all vehicles, and a business-tax on all businesses. Another device used is described in a letter, which said:

"The French-Canadians and the Japanese voted 'wet' almost solid. Although Father Lewis worked hard for prohibition, he had no influence with the French because he is a Welshman. The French looked upon it as a Protestant movement. The 'wets' used rather a clever argument with the Japanese. They represented the case to them that if prohibition should carry there would be no work for the Japanese, because the white men would then do the work. There are seventy-odd Japs in the Territory, and they are nearly all cooks. They are sober, industrious little fellows, and they are nearly always preferred to the white men because the white cooks will get drunk, while the Japs, being sober, are always on duty. But if prohibition should carry, the white men would not be able to get drunk and the Japs would not be able to get work."

The poll was held independently and, therefore, was rather small. The result of the voting was as follows:

	For prohibition.	Against prohibition.
North Dawson	134	181
South Dawson	214	234
Bonanza	177	125
Klondike	231	222
White Horse	115—871	112—874

In view of the closeness of the vote, a recount was appealed for, but it made no change in the results. The organized body of workers were not content to accept as

PROHIBITION IN CANADA.

final this decision, and the monster petition originally prepared was sent on to Ottawa with an explanation of the facts.

The order-in-council regarding the Yukon Territory was passed on March 11, 1918, and was as follows

After the first day of May, 1918, the Yukon Territory shall be a prohibited area within the meaning of these regulations, provided that any intoxicating liquor actually shipped before the first day of May, 1918, may be delivered in the Yukon Territory by a common carrier within such period of time as is required for such delivery under the ordinary and usual conditions governing the business of such common carrier, but not later than the first day of June, 1918; provided, further, that nothing in these regulations shall prevent the sale or other disposal within the Yukon Territory of intoxicating liquor by any person under a license issued under the authority of any ordinance of the Governor in Council relating to the Yukon Territory.

This was amended by a further order-in-council passed on April 8th, by which liquor actually shipped before May 1st might be delivered in the Yukon Territory not later than June 1st.

An interesting development during this period was the swinging of the churches into better organized fighting form in connection with prohibition work.

At the Methodist General Conference, held in Winnipeg in 1902, a Temperance and Moral Reform Department was formed, and Rev. Dr. S. D. Chown elected General Secretary. He held office till 1910 when, upon his election as General Superintendent, Rev. Dr. T. Albert Moore, the present Secretary, was appointed. The name of the Department has been changed to that of "Evangelism and Social Service."

Other churches have followed the lead thus set, notably the Presbyterian Church, under the leadership of Rev. Dr. J. G. Shearer. These Departments have meant the lining up of the militant Christianity of Canada as a very definite, powerful aid in all social reform work. They made themselves felt in all recent campaigns for local option, C.T.A., Provincial and Dominion prohibition.

SECTION XII.

DOMINION PROHIBITION.

Society, the community, the state, has an unchallenged right to call its individual members to service for the protection of the lives and liberties and rights of all. It has also the right to demand of those individual citizens the highest mental and physical efficiency of which they are capable. It has the right to say to its young men: You will not be permitted to traitorously injure your country by weakening its powers or aiding its enemies, either in selling military secrets for money or in sacrificing for personal gratification the mental and moral and physical strength which belongs to the whole nation as well as to yourself.

DOMINION PROHIBITION.

In 1913, the Council of the Dominion Alliance met in the city of Toronto and took up again in earnest the matter of Dominion prohibition. The following resolution was unanimously adopted:

"Recognizing that in face of the conditions confronting our Dominion created by the tremendous tide of immigration pouring in amongst us from the countries where the liquor traffic is not so effectually curbed as here, and realizing the importance of cultivating the highest form of sobriety if we are to build a great democracy out of the many races that are now turning to Canada as the land of promise—the land which is to give the world a civilization embodying the best features of older civilizations without their drawbacks, we deem it all-important that every effort should be made to secure at the earliest possible date the enactment of a Dominion prohibition law of the amplest character.

"That we instruct our Executive Committee to take steps to secure the introduction of a declaration in favor of prohibition into the Dominion Parliament during the next session."

During the same year a Dominion-wide organization of the licensed hotel-keepers was formed in the city of Winnipeg. By unanimous vote a declaration containing the following clause was adopted:

This convention however, re-affirms its declarations that it is not a political organization, but that *Our trade our politics* is the motto of the association.

It was not, however, until 1916 that the matter was taken up in Parliament. In the meantime the efforts of the Dominion Council were supplemented by the work of the local committee at Ottawa, for which A. W. Fraser, K.C., was the chairman and Edwin Seybold, the secretary. This special

PROHIBITION IN CANADA.

committee had been pressing an economic view of war-time prohibition upon public attention. As a result of conferences, Mr. H. H. Stevens of British Columbia, and Hon. Charles Marcil of Quebec, introduced the following resolution:

" That at this time when the Empire is at war, the conservation of the wealth and resources of the Dominion and the promotion of the efficiency of our nation would be materially aided by the prohibition of the manufacture, importation, and sale of intoxicating liquors for beverage purposes, and that in the opinion of this House legislation for this purpose ought to be enacted forthwith."

A deputation waited upon the Dominion Government requesting it to: (1) Facilitate the discussion of the resolution and the vote thereon, (2) To introduce prohibitory legislation if the House votes for the resolution.

The deputation was welcomed by Sir Robert Borden, Premier, with whom were associated Sir Geo. Foster, Sir Thos. White, Hon. T. W. Crothers, Hon. Dr. J. D. Reid, Hon. T. C. Casgrain, and R. B. Bennett. Among those who took part in the deputation were Rt. Rev. J. C. Roper, J. R. Booth, E. Seybold, Rev. Dr. A. S. Grant, W. G. Bronson, A. W. Fraser, K.C., Rev. Dr. T. A. Moore, His Hon. Justice Lafontaine, Rev. H. R. Grant, Alderman S. J. Carter, John H. Roberts, Rev. C. Flemmington, F. S. Spence, C. Lawrence, J. Keane, Rev. H. R. Grant, Rev. C. A. Williams. The Government heard the request of the deputation and promised to give it most careful and attentive consideration.

Mr. Stevens moved his resolution in the House of Commons on March 6th, and it was further discussed on March 27th, when Mr. R. B. Bennett moved an amendment, the principal part of which was in the following terms:

That as public opinion varies in the several provinces, it is desirable that such enactments depending for their efficient enforcement upon public opinion should in the first instance be determined by the respective legislatures of the several provinces.

DOMINION PROHIBITION.

That up to the full measure of provincial jurisdiction the subject should in the first instance be dealt with by the respective provincial legislatures.

That this Parliament should at the present session enact legislation to prohibit the transportation or importation of intoxicating liquor into any province for any use or purpose which is or may be forbidden by the law of such province.

The amendment was adopted by a vote of sixty-six ayes against nine nays, and at a later date the amended resolution was adopted by a vote of 103 to 15.

Before Mr. Bennett's amendment was moved, the Minister of Justice had introduced a bill giving effect to the amendment. This bill was debated at length in both the Commons and Senate, and was amended in various ways before being finally passed. Besides being modified in some details, it had embodied in it sections giving effect to the request of the Alliance for legislation requiring full and informing labelling and addressing of packages containing liquor.

The resolution was side-tracked, however, by the introduction of a bill by the Hon. C. J. Doherty, Minister of Justice, who stated:

"After careful consideration the Government has reached the conclusion that, in the absence of Dominion legislation, each province has ample power to secure within its own territory such measure of prohibition as in its judgment is deemed necessary to bring about abatement of evils resulting from intoxicating liquors. It was thought that a provincial law would have behind it more assurance of general public opinion and support, than could be hoped for in relation to Dominion-wide legislation. It has been, therefore, decided to introduce a bill, proposing to enact a law forbidding the sending into any province of intoxicating liquors to be used or dealt with in contravention of the law of the province."

The bill as finally passed was practically useless. The section regarding interprovincial shipment was operative only in regard to provinces wherein the Legislature enacted a law making it an offence for any person to use liquor or keep

PROHIBITION IN CANADA.

it in his private residence, a kind of legislation that no province had or would undertake.

A section of the act, however, provided severe penalties for shipping, carrying, or receiving liquor not plainly labelled or fictitiously addressed.

On November 20, 1916, a meeting of the Dominion Executive of the Dominion Alliance was held in Toronto. This was preceded by a monster public mass meeting in Massey Hall, Toronto, on Sunday, November 19th. The feature of the programme was a roll call of Canadian provinces, responded to by:

British Columbia—Rev. Principal Vance, Vancouver, Vice-President of the People's Prohibition Movement of British Columbia.

Alberta—Rev. A. W. Coone, M.A., Edmonton, General Secretary, Alberta Temperance and Moral Reform League.

Saskatchewan—W. J. Stewart, Regina, General Secretary, Banish the Dispensaries Crusade.

Manitoba—Rev. A. E. Smith, Brandon, President, Manitoba Conference of the Methodist Church.

Ontario—Chas. E. Steele, Port Colborne, President of the Ontario Branch of the Dominion Alliance.

Quebec—John H. Roberts, Montreal, General Secretary, the Quebec Branch of the Dominion Alliance.

New Brunswick—Rev. W. D. Wilson, Fredericton, General Secretary, The New Brunswick Branch of the Dominion Alliance.

Nova Scotia—Rev. Hamilton Wigle, Halifax, President, Nova Scotia Temperance Alliance.

Prince Edward Island—Rev. Geo. Morris, Charlottetown, representing the Prince Edward Island Temperance Alliance.

At the meeting of the Executive Committee the following day, upon consultation with the Executive Committee of the Citizens' Committee of One Hundred, it was decided to call a Dominion prohibition conference to be held at Ottawa on December 14th. One of the main features of this gathering was the unanimous adoption of the following resolution, upon motion of Mr. F. S. Spence:

DOMINION PROHIBITION.

"Resolved, that in view of the necessity for conserving our country's national resources and preventing any impairment of the efficiency of our country's manhood, in the Dominion's present great effort to aid the Empire in her self-sacrificing struggle for the principles of honor and justice and liberty, the Dominion Government and Parliament be earnestly urged to enact as a war measure, a law prohibiting the manufacture of intoxicating liquor for beverage purposes into the Dominion of Canada, and also prohibiting the sending, carrying or bringing of any such liquor for beverage purposes from any place in Canada into any province or area in which the sale of such liquor is prohibited, and also prohibiting the delivering or receiving of any such liquor by any person in any such province or area.

"The question of maintaining or repealing the same to be submitted in a referendum to the electors after the conclusion of the war, but not before the expiry of three years from the time of the act going into force; or

"In the alternative, if the Government and Parliament deem it desirable that a referendum be taken upon such a measure before its coming into force, that such vote be taken before next June, the result of the referendum to be effective on a majority vote, within three months after the voting."

Another important step was the formation of the Dominion Prohibition Committee with an executive consisting of two representatives from each provincial unit and a sub-executive of ten persons to superintend details of the campaign. It was agreed that copies of the resolution should be sent to the Premier and the Leader of the Opposition, and arrangements were made for a personal representation at a later date. The deputation waited upon the Government on January 11th, the speakers being the Hon. Justice Lafontaine, G. A. Warburton, Dr. J. Gauvreau, J. R. Booth and F. S. Spence.

Sir Robert Borden's reply was friendly in tone, but indefinite. Sir Robert alluded to and conceded the high motives of the delegation and assured them that very earnest consideration would be given to their demands. He said it was very desirable that the Government should be made acquainted with every point of view of public opinion.

PROHIBITION IN CANADA.

At a meeting of the sub-executive of the Dominion Prohibition Committee, held in Montreal on January 22, a plan of campaign was adopted. The detail work was to be done by the provincial organization in each province, while the Dominion Committee was to act as a co-ordinating body. It was decided that a standard form of petition to Parliament be prepared, praying for the enactment of legislation; that churches, temperance societies, Boards of Trade, and other organizations be asked to adopt the uniform petition; and that a systematic appeal be made to the electors, asking for support of the measure. Plans were laid for arousing public interest by means of the press, mass meetings, and the pulpit.

In March a notable manifesto was issued by the Dominion Prohibition Committee, asking Parliament to enact war-time prohibition of the importation, manufacture and interprovincial trade in intoxicating liquors.[*]

After the death of Mr. F. S. Spence, who was the moving spirit of the Dominion Prohibition Committee, the committee was reorganized at a meeting held in March, as follows:

President, Judge Eugene Lafontaine.
Vice-President, Mr. Miles Vokes.
General Secretary, Mr. G. A. Warburton.
Recording Secretary, Mr. J. H. Roberts; and an executive of 24 members.

In the Province of Ontario, the petitioning campaign was conducted by the Ontario Branch of the Dominion Alliance. Petitions from organizations were sent in duplicate to the House of Commons and the Senate, in the standard form authorized and approved by the Dominion Committee. Beside those sent direct by the organizations subscribing thereto, nearly three thousand were returned to the Ontario Alliance office and forwarded to members of Parliament. Mass meetings were also held in different centres throughout Canada and arrangements made for delegations to wait upon members of Parliament in many constituencies. Continued and combined pressure produced results.

---

[*] See Appendix XII.

DOMINION PROHIBITION.

The first small beginning was made by the Food Controller, the Hon. W. J. Hanna, on August 9, 1917, when an order-in-council was passed prohibiting the use of wheat in the distillation or manufacture of alcohol unless used for manufacturing or munitions purposes.

In September, 1917, Mr. D. B. Harkness, of Winnipeg, became General Secretary of the Dominion Prohibition Committee. Several of the provinces were visited by Mr. Harkness and a group of influential men and women were enrolled in the Strengthen Canada Movement, which emphasized the need of prohibition as a war measure for the conservation of men, money and food.

Nothing further was done until the Union Government was organized. One of the first actions of the new Government, however, was to pass an order-in-council on the 2nd of November, providing that "after the first of December no grain of any kind, and no substances that can be used for food shall be used in Canada for the distillation of potable liquors."

A Dominion election was close at hand at the time, and further action was postponed until after the election. As soon, however, as the Union Government had received the approval of the people, no time was lost in announcing the Government's policy. On December 22, 1917, the Prime Minister announced·

"On December 17 the people gave to the Government an unmistakable mandate for the vigorous prosecution of the war and for the employment of all the country's energies and resources necessary to achieve victory. It is essential, and indeed vital, for the efficient conduct of the war that wasteful or unnecessary expenditure should be prohibited, and that all articles capable of being utilized as food should be conserved. It is beyond question that the use of liquor affects adversely the realization of this purpose.

"The subject has been under consideration of the War Committee of the Cabinet, and the following conclusions have been reached:

PROHIBITION IN CANADA.

" (1) Any liquor or beverage containing more than 2½ per cent. alcohol shall be regarded as intoxicating liquor.

" (2) The importation of intoxicating liquor into Canada is prohibited on and after December 24, 1917, unless it shall have been actually purchased on or before that date for importation into Canada, and unless, having been so purchased, it is imported into Canada not later than the 31st day of January, 1918. The final determination upon any question respecting such purpose shall rest with the Minister of Customs. This regulation shall not apply to importations for medicinal, sacramental, manufacturing or chemical purposes.

" (3) The transportation of liquor into any part of Canada wherein the sale of intoxicating liquor is illegal will be prohibited on and after April 1, 1918.

" (4) The manufacture of intoxicating liquor within Canada will be prohibited on and after a date to be determined upon further investigation and consideration of the actual conditions of the industry.

"As above mentioned, the prohibition of importation becomes effective on Monday next, December 24.

" The regulations to carry into effect the other provisions above mentioned are being prepared, and as soon as approved, they will be enacted under the provisions of the War Measures Act.

" The foregoing provisions will remain in force during the war and for twelve months after the conclusion of peace."

Following out this statement of the Government's policy an order-in-council was passed the same day prohibiting the importation of liquor as stated by the Premier. This order-in-council recites:

Whereas the War Committee of the Privy Council reports that there is urgent necessity for conserving all the energies and resources of Canada for the vigorous prosecution of the present war;

And whereas the War Committee recommends that for the purpose of preventing waste, and for the promotion of thrift and economy, the conservation of financial resources, and the increase of national efficiency, the importation of intoxicating liquors be prohibited during the continuance of the war, and for one year thereafter.

DOMINION PROHIBITION.

The order-in-council defined liquor as containing more than 2½ per cent. of alcohol. This was not the intention of the Government and on the 26th of December a supplementary order-in-council was passed, to provide that for the purpose of this regulation any beverage containing more than 2½ per cent. of proof spirits shall be deemed to be intoxicating liquor. This was in keeping with the existing legislation in nearly all the provinces of Canada.

Yet another amendment of this order-in-council was rendered necessary in the opinion of the Government by the exceptional difficulties of ocean transportation owing to the submarine menace, and it was accordingly provided by order-in-council of January 19, 1918, that liquor shipped, or in transit on January 31, 1918, and ordered before December 24, 1917, might be imported into Canada upon producing satisfactory evidence to the Minister of Customs of these facts.

These various orders-in-council were afterwards consolidated, and provision for their enforcement was made by an order-in-council issued on Monday, March 11, 1918.*

The immediate objective having been obtained, no further action was taken for some time by the Dominion Prohibition Committee.

The Dominion Council of the Alliance held its Annual Meeting in St. James Parish Hall, on March 1, 1919. There was a large attendance. Fifty-five delegates registered representing twenty-four organizations and six provinces.

The following officers were elected:

Hon. President—J. R. Dougall, Esq.
Fraternal Representative—Ven. Archdeacon George E. Lloyd.
President—Miles Vokes, Esq.
Vice-Presidents—Presidents of provincial branches or analogous organizations, Presidents of provincial W.C.T.U's.
Treasurer—W. H. Orr, Esq.
Corresponding Secretary—Rev. Ben. H. Spence.
Recording Secretary—Rev. R. M. Hamilton.
And an executive committee.

---
* See Appendix XIII.

PROHIBITION IN CANADA.

With the signing of the armistice it was at once seen that it would be necessary for the temperance forces again to become active in the Dominion sphere.

On December 2, a meeting of the Dominion Prohibition Committee was held in the Y.M.C.A., Toronto, at which the following statement of policy was adopted:

In view of the benefits now generally recognized by the people of Canada as having resulted from prohibition, as provided by means of orders-in-council, limiting the trade in intoxicating liquor to sacramental, industrial, artistic, mechanical, scientific, and medicinal purposes, thereby greatly reducing drunkenness, crime, and waste of money and manhood; and

In view of the general desire that every precaution shall be taken to reduce to a minimum the social, industrial, and political unrest incident to the restoration of the affairs of the nation to normal peace conditions; and

In view of the status of the order-in-council of March 11, 1918 (P.C. 589), when the articles of peace shall have been signed; and

In view of the impossibility of submitting at this time the question of making prohibition permanent to a vote of the people of Canada without a manifest disregard of the right of soldiers overseas to a vote thereon;

Therefore, we recommend—

(1) That the Prime Minister and Government of Canada be requested to take the steps necessary to continue in effect the provisions of the orders-in-council of March 11, 1918 (P.C. 589), by having the same embodied in legislation to be enacted by the Parliament of Canada.

(2) That the legislation so enacted be continued in effect until such time as a vote of the electors of the Dominion of Canada shall have been taken on the question of its continuance or discontinuance.

(3) That the vote on this question be taken at a date to be fixed by the Government of Canada at least six months prior to the day of voting, and with due regard to the restoration to civil life in Canada of the Canadian soldiers now overseas.

DOMINION PROHIBITION.

This was presented to the Government on December 6, by a deputation consisting of G. A. Warburton, Dr. J. G. Shearer, Justice Lafontaine, Dr. T. Albert Moore, Rev. D. B. Harkness. The interview was very cordial. Following this, large advertisements were inserted in the daily papers throughout Canada.

At the call of the Dominion Prohibition Committee a conference of workers was held at Château Laurier on March 14, 1919, at which there was a splendid and representative attendance. The convention then adjourned to go as a deputation to the House of Commons and assembled in room 318 at 6 p.m. to meet the Acting Prime Minister, Sir Thomas White, and other members of the Government, of whom Hon. N. W. Rowell, Hon. J. A. Calder, Senator P. E. Blondin, Brig.-Gen. Mewburn, Senator Robertson, and Hon. Frank Carvell were present.

The deputation was introduced by the Hon. Justice Eugene Lafontaine. Mr. D. B. Harkness of Winnipeg, General Secretary of Dominion Prohibition Committee, read the statement of policy. The speakers for the deputation were Rev. Dr. H. R. Grant, Nova Scotia, Secretary; Mrs. W. E. Sandford, President of the National Council of Women; Mr. R. N. Miller, British Columbia; Mr. A. A. Powers, representative of the United Farmers of Ontario; Mr. W. L. Best, Legislative representative of railway organizations; Mrs. Gordon Wright, Dominion President of the W.C.T.U., and Mr. George A. Warburton, Vice-President of the Dominion Prohibition Committee.

In replying to the deputation Sir Thomas White said that he fully appreciated the influence and representative character of the deputation and realized its earnestness. The policy of the Government for the duration of the war was to prohibit the sale and importation into dry provinces, of liquor beyond a certain strength, as a war measure and for the duration of the war and one year thereafter. The official declaration of peace, which has not yet been made, might make ineffective the order-in-council, though he was not certain on this point. The policy of the Government, however, was to enact legislation which would continue the war measure until the end of the war and for one year after the official declaration of peace. The Acting Prime Minister, Sir Thomas White, said that the question of a plebiscite, and all the other representations made by the deputation, would receive the earnest consideration of the Government.

The final chapter of Canada's prohibition history cannot yet be written. But the record of the years points to only one possible outcome—the complete abolition of the legalized liquor traffic. The present opportunity, the result of long, unfaltering faith and effort, is a challenge. Great events are impending. From the heroes of the past, for the citizens of the future, the call comes to Canada to-day to act wisely and with courage.

SECTION XIII.

WORLD PROGRESS.

COMPILED BY
MYRTLE FLUMERFELT.

Lust for power. Determined desire for self-aggrandizement, utterly regardless of all considerations of humanity and humaneness: This is the poisonous root from which Kaiserism has sprung.

Lust for wealth. Selfish, determined desire for self-aggrandizement, utterly regardless of the welfare of others: This is the evil motive which makes it possible for men to carry on the liquor traffic.

Both of the world's greatest curses have the same origin. Both owe their awful power and nature to the same antagonism to the Golden Rule that bids men think of the welfare of others and not solely of their own.

The two great cruel burdens under which humanity groans to-day are the outcome of purposes the very reverse of the gospel of the Great Master who taught the world the grandeur and beneficence of our duty towards our fellow-men.

Both will end in the same way. Kaiserism will be utterly overthrown. The liquor traffic as a legalized institution will be completely destroyed. Righteousness is mighty and will prevail.

WORLD PROGRESS.

THERE is perhaps nothing more marvellous in the history of social progress than the phenomenal growth of temperance sentiment throughout the world during recent years, and the embodiment of that sentiment in legislation for the restriction or suppression of the liquor traffic.

The core about which the temperance movement crystallized in the latter part of the 19th century and the beginning of the 20th, was the biennial International Congresses on Alcoholism. Between 1885 and the outbreak of the European war, fourteen of these great international gatherings were held in European cities, as follows: Antwerp (1185); Zurich (1887); Christiania (1890); The Hague (1893); Basle (1895); Brussels (1897); Paris (1899); Vienna (1901); Bremen (1903); Budapest (1905); Stockholm (1907); London (1909); Scheveningen (The Hague) (1911); and Milan (1913). In 1890, there was founded the official scientific organ of the continental movement, the *Internationale Monatsshrift zur Erforschung des Alkoholismus*, the files of which constitute a leading source for the temperance history of the world. At the congresses, a great body of scientific information was presented by experts and skilled investigators; so that the volumes containing the reports of these meetings, form a veritable treasure trove of knowledge about the alcohol question. After the London conference of 1909, the International Prohibition Confederation was established—an organization in which to-day agencies of forty-three countries are linked up to further the progress of reform.

It would seem as if the increasing knowledge of the nature and effects of alcoholic liquor, and the development of high moral purposes and strong sense of social duty all through Christendom, had been changed from mere existence into active forces, by the outbreak of the great European war.

PROHIBITION IN CANADA.

Certainly since that event, the temperance cause, which before had been moving rapidly, has gone on by leaps and bounds. This is largely, no doubt, due to the overwhelming evidence given by the events of the opening of that campaign, to the mischievous effects of alcoholic indulgence.

In the pages which follow, an attempt has been made to give a few of the interesting facts in connection with the temperance movement in other parts of the world.*

NEWFOUNDLAND.

Newfoundland is not a part of Canada politically, but is independent in its local government under British sovereignty. In 1839 (six years after the granting of representative government) the first local license act was passed, providing that a license fee should be paid, and that the name of the person selling intoxicants should be placed over the door of his shop. Penalties for adulterating liquors were imposed. Subsequently the act was amended and improved many times, so that a very comprehensive licensing law was produced.

Local option, similar to that given by the Scott Act of Canada, came into force in 1873. The law provided that a poll should be taken if petitioned for by one-fifth of the electors of any defined districts. A two-thirds vote was necessary to carry local option. In 1883, the traffic was prohibited by popular vote in Twillingate, Greenspond, Placentia, Grand Bank, Fortune, Lamaline, Catalina, and Random. The local option law was amended in 1887 so that a bare majority vote might prevail.

References: Alliance Year Books; Anti-Saloon League Year Books; Australian Prohibition Year Book; Control of the Drink Trade (Carter); Cyclopædia of Temperance and Prohibition (pub., Funk and Wagnalls); Cyclopædia of Temperance, Prohibition and Public Morals; Proceedings of Anti-Saloon League Convention, Columbus, Ohio, 1918; Prohibition Advance in All Lands (Hayler); Scientific Temperance Journal; Scottish Temperance Annuals; Temperance in All Nations (Stearns); Temperance Year Book of Presbyterian Church in Ireland; World Book of Temperance (Crafts).

WORLD PROGRESS.

By 1915, local prohibition was in force throughout the island except in the City of St. John's. There the hotels were expressly prohibited from having licenses, the sale being confined to public houses, which made no pretence at furnishing any other accommodation to man or beast. The saloons in the city were closed at 6 p.m., but this was not satisfactory, even to the people of the outports. Large numbers of fishermen, gathering in the city during the spring and fall for business purposes, came into contact with the traffic. Moreover, a stream of liquor was continually going out over the whole of the island.

In 1915, the Government decided that the people should be allowed to settle the temperance issue, and submitted to the electors the following question: "Are you in favor of prohibiting the importation, manufacture and sale of spirits, wine, ale, beer, cider, and all alcoholic liquors for use as beverages?" The law provided that to abolish the liquor traffic, not only must there be polled against it a majority of the votes cast on the question, but also that the total number of votes cast must not be less than forty per cent. of the names on the 1913 voters' lists. November 25th was proclaimed as the date for taking the vote.

The following description of the campaign is condensed from an account written by Rev. Arminius Young, of Musgrove Town, Newfoundland, for the *Alliance News*:

"The temperance people of all denominations and all parties threw themselves into the fight. It was certainly inspiring to see how many of the business men of St. John's joined in the struggle for prohibition. Many of these men were not, as they confessed themselves, teetotalers, but they wisely considered that they were their brothers' keepers, and were in duty bound to use their strength and influence in the interests of the victims of the liquor trade. It would be impossible to mention all who took a leading part in the campaign.

"A central committee was formed in St. John's, which took the oversight of the campaign throughout the island. Sub-committees were formed, and committees in all the outports where sufficient interest was found in the cause of temperance; and in

PROHIBITION IN CANADA.

some places every home was canvassed and every man asked to give his vote for prohibition.

"The battle was hard and close. As the various counts of the districts came in, we were sometimes below and sometimes above the required number of votes.

"The following table may be of interest:

	For.	Against.
Port de Grace	820	136
Carbonear	590	49
Bay de Verde	1,464	97
St. John's West	2,158	262
Trinity	2,862	239
Bonavista	2,805	466
Fogo	1,189	249
Burin	1,275	198
Twillingate	3,552	357
Fortune	1,091	110

"Where prohibition failed to carry·

	For.	Against.
Harbor Main	383	236
Harbor Grace	1,176	181
St. John's East	2,291	463
St. George's	549	336
Burgeo	597	251
St. Barbe	1,069	437
Ferryland	305	381
Placentia	789	909
Totals	24,965	5,348

"Total vote required was forty per cent. of 61 451, or 24,581. There were just 384 to spare.

"While these figures show only 384 votes more than the required number, they show a sweeping majority in favor of prohibition."

The law, which came into force January 1, 1917, was a very stringent one. Intoxicating liquors, which were defined to mean all liquors containing 2 per cent. or upwards of alcohol, were allowed in the country only for medicinal and sacramental purposes; and the penalties for violation were severe. The druggists, not wishing to have the reputation of not being strict in the observance of the law, refused to carry any liquor. The Government appointed a public controller to superintend all sales in St. John's; magistrates and doctors were to be in control in other places, and churches were to have an agency of their own for the supplying of wine for sacramental purposes.

THE UNITED STATES OF AMERICA.

The history of the temperance movement in the United States follows a course similar to that of the reform in Canada.

In the 17th and 18th centuries, various measures were enacted which aimed to restrict public drunkenness. A few of these will illustrate the character of the legislation. As early as 1642, the colony of Maryland passed a law, punishing drunkenness by imposing the extraordinary fine of 100 pounds of tobacco. Three years later in Connecticut, the sale of liquors to Indians was made illegal. In 1647, drunkenness was prohibited in Rhode Island under penalty of five shillings, and sale to Indians under penalty of five pounds. A law passed in Connecticut in 1650 forbade tippling above the space of half an hour at one time, or at unreasonable times. In 1654 licensed persons in Massachusetts were forbidden to allow excessive drinking, under fine of twenty shillings, and in 1657 the penalty for selling to Indians was fixed at forty shillings. In 1658 Maryland punished drunkenness by confinement in the stocks for six hours. The Assembly of Virginia in 1664 passed a law prohibiting ministers from excessive drinking, and in 1676 forbade the sale of wines and ardent spirits outside of Jamestown. New Jersey in 1668 forbade persons drinking after 9 o'clock, and in 1677 prohibited the sale of liquor to Indians. By an enactment of 1700, innkeepers in New Hampshire were not permitted to allow townspeople to remain in their houses drinking on Saturday

PROHIBITION IN CANADA.

and Sunday. In 1715, in Maryland, it was made illegal for anyone to sell more than one gallon of liquor a day to any Indian, under penalty of 3,000 pounds of tobacco. In 1733, the governor of Georgia declared against the importation of ardent spirits, and two years later it was forbidden by the English Parliament; the Assembly of Georgia in 1737 forbade the issue of licenses to those capable of getting a livelihood by honest labor.

A pioneer of the temperance movement in the United States was Dr. Benjamin Rush of Philadelphia, who in 1785 published a celebrated essay dealing with the effects of ardent spirits on the body and mind, a document which earnestly urged moderation in the use of spirits.

Recognizing the value of associated effort for inducing individuals to reform and for promoting the cause in the community, advocates of temperance soon began to form organizations. The basis of these unions was the pledge, which in the early days rarely indicated more than moderation or self-restraint, but later was altered to mean abstinence from spirits, and by 1850 generally included malt liquors among the proscribed beverages. In 1789, the first temperance society was organized in Litchfield County, Conn., by two hundred farmers, who pledged themselves not to use spirits on their farms in the ensuing year. In 1808, a temperance society was founded by Dr. B. J. Clark at Moreau, N.Y., the constitution of which contained the following article:

"No member shall drink rum, gin, whiskey, wine, or any distilled spirits or composition of the same, or any of them, except by the advice of a physician or in case of actual disease, excepting also wine at public dinners, under penalty of twenty-five cents, providing this article shall not infringe on any religious ordinance.

Temperance organizations soon sprang up in New Jersey, Maine, Pennsylvania, New York, Rhode Island, and the District of Columbia. The evangelical churches—the United Brethren in Christ, the Presbyterian Church, the Baptist Church, the Methodist Church, the Friends and others—

WORLD PROGRESS.

declared against the traffic in intoxicating liquors. In 1826, Dr. Lyman Beecher preached six famous temperance sermons, of which five editions were published within a year. In the same year the American Society for the Promotion of Temperance was formed in Boston, with a total abstinence pledge. In 1836, at the second national temperance convention held at Saratoga, N.Y., churches and temperance societies reached a conclusion that total abstinence from all alcoholic beverages was the only sure basis for temperance reform. The Sons of Temperance and the Independent Order of Rechabites were organized in 1842 on a total abstinence basis.

About this time, a man very prominent in the temperance movement was John B. Gough, an Englishman by birth, who emigrated to America, where at the age of twenty-four he was described as a "hopeless sot." However, he signed the pledge in 1842, and his fame as an orator gave him an international reputation.

It soon became evident that moral suasion alone could not bring about permanent amelioration of the evils caused by the liquor traffic. A fighting Quaker of Maine, Neal Dow, afterwards Governor, secured in 1842 a prohibition ordinance for Portland; and in 1846 the State Legislature passed a prohibitory law, but adequate enforcing machinery was not provided in either case. In 1851, a bill introduced in the Maine Legislature by Neal Dow was passed, providing for state-wide prohibition. The law was repealed in 1856 by the enactment of a license provision, but became operative again in 1857. It has been in force ever since, and has become a standard for the world.

Prohibition laws similar to the Maine law of 1851 were enacted by the Legislatures of Massachusetts, Rhode Island, Minnesota and Vermont in 1852, by Connecticut in 1854, and by Michigan, New Hampshire, Delaware, Nebraska, Wisconsin and New York in 1855. Then came the Civil War. Temperance workers failed to follow up their victories and most of the state prohibitory laws were either declared unconstitutional or repealed.

PROHIBITION IN CANADA.

In 1867, the National Grand Division of Good Templars in session at Richmond, Indiana, recommended the organization of a national political party, whose platform should contain prohibition. Two years later the National Prohibition Party was organized in Chicago, with five hundred delegates in attendance. The principle upon which it was founded is that the State and Federal Government can be united against the liquor traffic only by the victory at the polls of a political party, pledged to prohibition. At each presidential election and in many states, since 1872, the Prohibition Party has put up candidates but its influence has been larger than its vote, for on several occasions a slight increase in the vote for the Prohibition Party candidates has brought substantial concessions by the old parties to prohibition sentiment.

In 1870, the Royal Templars of Temperance were organized at Buffalo, N.Y. The Catholic Total Abstinence Union of America was formed in 1872. The next year a remarkable woman's temperance crusade was begun against the saloons of Southern Ohio. Its success continued throughout 1874 and on November 19, the first Woman's Christian Temperance Union, "the sober second thought of the woman's crusade," was formed. In 1877 an organization known as the Citizen's League of Chicago was formed to save young men from intemperance.

The period from 1880 to 1896 is marked by attempts to secure constitutional prohibition in various states, by experiments with high license laws, and by the growth of scientific temperance instruction.

During these years the Woman's Christian Temperance Union bore the brunt of the battle against intoxicating liquors. In addition to forming the main army of temperance in the contests for constitutional prohibition, they set about to create sentiment in favor of scientific temperance instruction in the schools. Largely owing to the indefatigable efforts of Mrs. Mary J. Hunt, the Woman's Christian Temperance Union succeeded in getting laws passed in practically every state, providing that all boys and girls

WORLD PROGRESS.

attending the public schools should be taught the facts regarding the nature and effects of alcohol. This early work of instructing the young has been largely responsible for the phenomenal progress of temperance reform in the United States during the last few years.

The first state to write prohibition into its constitution was Kansas, which in 1880 adopted an amendment to this effect by eight thousand votes. By a popular vote in 1881, the people of North Carolina rejected a bill to prohibit the manufacture and sale of alcoholic liquors. A prohibitory amendment was ratified by a majority of nearly 30,000 votes in Iowa in the following year, and became effective in 1884. Twice in 1883 a prohibitory constitutional amendment failed to carry in Ohio, once being defeated by the electors and the second time set aside by technicalities. A clause which may be taken as a fair sample of the constitutional amendments of this period was passed in Maine in 1884. It read:

"The manufacture of intoxicating liquors, not including cider, and the sale and keeping for sale of intoxicating liquors, are and shall be forever prohibited, except, however, that the sale and keeping for sale of such liquors for medicinal and mechanical purposes and the arts, and the sale and keeping for sale of cider may be permitted under such regulations as the Legislature may provide. The Legislature shall enact laws with suitable penalties for the suppression of the manufacture, sale and keeping for sale of intoxicating liquors, with the exceptions herein specified."

Constitutional prohibition was rejected by the following states: Tennessee, Michigan, Oregon, and Texas, in 1887; New Hampshire, Pennsylvania, and Connecticut in 1889; and Nebraska in 1890. It was carried in Rhode Island in 1886, in both North and South Dakota in 1889. It was repealed by Rhode Island and Washington in 1889 and by South Dakota in 1896.

High license originated in Nebraska in 1881 and spread rapidly. It was adopted by Missouri and Illinois in 1882, by Minnesota and Pennsylvania in 1887, by Massachusetts

PROHIBITION IN CANADA.

in 1888, by Rhode Island in 1889, by Maryland in 1890 and by New Mexico in 1891.

In certain states measures granting various kinds of local option were adopted and under these laws the liquor traffic was voted out of parts of Georgia, Dakota, Montana, Missouri, Wisconsin, and Delaware.

The first scientific investigation of the economic aspect of the alcohol question was undertaken by the Century Magazine in 1893. They appointed a body of distinguished men known as the Committee of Fifty, and donated the sum of $30,000, for the work. The report of the committee comprises several books of valuable statistics.

In 1893, an organization was founded at Oberlin, Ohio, which was destined to become the most powerful temperance organization in the world. The founder of the Anti-Saloon League of America was Rev. Howard H. Russell, D.D., who gave up everything to devote himself to this work. In the same year the District of Columbia Anti-Saloon League was organized. The national organization was formed at a meeting in Washington in 1895. The League aims to work in co-operation with the denominational bodies to secure the extermination of the liquor traffic, by legislation. It pledges itself " to avoid affiliation with any political party as such, and to maintain an attitude of strict neutrality on all questions of public policy not directly and immediately concerned with the traffic in strong drink." The Anti-Saloon League has organizations in every state, and at Westerville, Ohio, it maintains the largest prohibition press in the world.

From 1896 to 1906, and later, when campaigns for state-wide prohibition were again inaugurated, the distinctive feature of temperance history was the winning to prohibition of many districts, chiefly in small cities and rural municipalities, by the local option method. Beginning with 1906 there was another wave of state-wide prohibition which has continued till the present time.

WORLD PROGRESS.

Practically every state constitution provides means by which the people may, by vote, make amendments to it. If this be done, the Legislature cannot modify or repeal such amendment without again remitting the matter to the people. A statutory enactment may be amended or repealed by the Legislature at will.

The *Union Signal* published the following list of states and territories which have (to March, 1919) adopted prohibition, and the date of its going into effect:

Maine (Constitutional)	1851
Kansas (Constitutional)	1880
North Dakota (Constitutional)	1889
Oklahoma (Constitutional)	1907
Georgia (Statutory)	1908
North Carolina (Statutory)	1909
Mississippi (Statutory)	1909
Tennessee (Statutory)	1909
West Virginia (Constitutional)	1914
Alabama (Statutory)	1915
Arizona (Constitutional)	1915
Virginia (Statutory)	1916
Colorado (Constitutional)	1916
Oregon (Constitutional)	1916
Washington (Statutory)	1916
Arkansas (Statutory)	1916
Iowa (Statutory)	1916
Idaho (Constitutional)	1916
South Carolina (Statutory)	1916
Nebraska (Constitutional)	1917
South Dakota (Constitutional)	1917
District of Columbia (Statutory)	1917
Alaska (Statutory)	1918
Indiana (Statutory)	1918
Michigan (Constitutional)	1918
New Hampshire (Statutory)	1918
Montana (Constitutional)	1918
New Mexico (Constitutional)	1918
Texas (Statutory)	1918
Florida (Constitutional)	1919

PROHIBITION IN CANADA.

Utah (Constitutional)	1919
Ohio (Constitutional)	1919
Nevada (Statutory)	1919
Wyoming (Constitutional)	1920
Delaware (Statutory)	1920

Porto Rico	1918
Canal Zone	
Island of Guam	1918
Territory of Hawaii	1918
Virgin Islands	1919

PROGRESS IN WAR YEARS.

War conditions accelerated national legislation by increasing the restrictions upon alcoholic drinks. The state laws were greatly strengthened by measures passed by Congress, which prohibited the use of the mails for carrying into prohibition areas any advertisements of such liquors; prohibiting also, except for scientific, sacramental, medicinal, and mechanical purposes, the shipment of alcoholic liquors through the channels of interstate commerce to individuals in states, or portions of states, that now prohibit the manufacture and sale of intoxicating liquors. **The anti-shipping clause caused this legislation to be termed "the bone-dry law,"** and many of the prohibition states hastened to enact corresponding state legislation to secure its full benefits.

During the spring of 1917, tremendous interest was awakened in all parts of the country over the amount of food material that was being used in the manufacture of alcoholic liquors. Demands that the food economy of the nation begin with this enormous leakage, flooded Congress. Many notable organizations and individuals, not before identified with temperance activity, petitioned for prohibition as a war measure to save the needed foodstuffs. The General Federation of Women's Clubs, the Conference of Charities and Corrections, the Daughters of the American Revolution, the

WORLD PROGRESS.

Mothers' Congress, and the Nurses' Association were among the large influential bodies which took this action.

The National House of Representatives included in the Administration Food Control Bill a clause prohibiting the use of food materials in the manufacture of all alcoholic beverages, including beer and wine. But this clause was bitterly contested, especially by the brewing interests. Threats of holding up all war legislation if this were pressed were freely made. The measure, as finally passed, eliminated the clause relating to beer, but prohibited the manufacture or importation of distilled beverages during the war; the President was authorized to limit the alcoholic content of beer and wine, and to commandeer distilled beverages when necessary, including not only those in bond but also those in stock.

The Army Bill, passed in May, made it unlawful to sell or supply any intoxicating liquors, including beer and wine, to men in uniform. As soon as the law went into effect (July 12) the Secretary of War notified commanders of army posts, training camps, and mobilization centres, that the requirements must be faithfully carried out. He also appealed to the governors of the states urging the elimination of all places for the sale of liquor, and of houses of vice in the vicinity of army camps, and later issued an order that a five-mile dry zone be established around all camps unless a city or town came within such limits. In such cases special Government agents were sent to co-operate with the local authorities to make the towns safe for the soldiers.

The representatives of various temperance organizations formed a United Committee on Temperance War Activities, in Army and Navy, which through the Y.M.C.A. promoted educational anti-alcohol work in the camps. Before the end of 1917, this committee and the co-operating organizations had raised nearly $50,000 for the work, had provided for the installation of 23 stereomotorgraphs, and had commenced to distribute a million copies of a manual of facts about alcohol and the same number of a special pamphlet on wine. Lectures and motion pictures dealing with this question were systematically given.

An order issued on November 27, 1917, reduced the amount of grain that might be used in making fermented liquors to 70 per cent. of the quantity previously used, and ordered that these liquors should not exceed 3½ per cent. alcoholic strength. A later order reduced the alcoholic content to 2¾ per cent.

In September, 1918, Congress passed the twelve million dollar emergency Agricultural Appropriation Bill, with its rider for national war-time prohibition. It provided that after May 1, 1919, no more liquor for beverage purposes should be made, and that on June 30, 1919, the sale of such liquors should cease. The President was empowered to create dry zones around industrial and military establishments without limit, as a safeguard to meet immediate or intervening emergencies. On November 21, President Wilson signed the bill, thus making the country absolutely "dry" from July, 1919, until the army should be entirely demobilized.

A contributing factor to the great victory in the United States was the revelation of the close connection between the brewers and the German-American Alliance. Early in 1918, a United States Senate Judiciary Committee was appointed to inquire into the activities of the German-American Alliance, an un-American organization for the propagation of German ideals and culture and for the perpetuation of race cleavage. As a result of the evidence produced, the charter of the German-American Alliance was revoked. Later in the year it became evident that the United States Brewers' Association had been working in close co-operation with the Alliance. The investigation grew out of the exposure made by Mr. Mitchell Palmer, Alien Property Custodian, of the fact that the United States Brewers' Association and many other brewers, most of them of German blood, had put up hundreds of thousands of dollars to secure the *Washington Times,* which was to be used in behalf of the beer trade although the financial interests of the brewers were to be carefully concealed.

The political machine of the United States Brewers' Association was the so-called "National Association of Commerce and Labor," which operated in alliance with German-American and other foreign language interests. The Association tried to shape public thought by financing newspapers, controlling the foreign-language press, subsidizing magazine writers, and operating behind the mask of men with reputation but without honor. The Brewers' Association had a method of coercing men and corporations, which was essentially a boycott system. So close became the alliance between the brewers and German-Americanism that the president of the German-American organization became the supervisor of the beer lobby at Washington. His service to Germany was appreciated by the Kaiser, who declared in a council of high German officers at Potsdam that if ever man was worthy of decoration, it was Dr. Hexamer, President of the National German-American Alliance. The very document stating the position of the German-American Alliance in regard to the European War, and protesting against the manufacture of munitions for the Allies, was prepared by employees of the United States Brewers' Association.

In January, 1918, as the result of a conference between the Legislative Committee of the Anti-Saloon League of America and the Secretaries of the War and Navy, it was decided to send a commission consisting of Dr. James Cannon, Jr., of Virginia, and Dr. E. J. Moore, of Ohio, to visit England and France and report upon the conditions surrounding the American soldiers overseas. The investigations of the Commissioners were facilitated in every possible way by army and navy officials. Their report confirms the situation as it was formerly known to thousands who had made inquiry with a view to protecting their boys who had gone overseas.

Simultaneously with the fight waged in Congress to secure war-time prohibitory legislation, a campaign was brought on to make prohibition the permanent law of the nation. The

PROHIBITION IN CANADA.

Senate passed, by a vote of 65 to 20, a resolution submitting to the states a prohibition amendment to the federal constitution. The resolution with some amendments was passed by the House of Representatives on December 17, 1917, and the amendments were concurred in by the Senate on December 18th.

The text of the proposed amendment was:

"Resolved by the Senate and House of Representatives, that the following amendment to the constitution be, and hereby is, proposed to the States, to become valid as part of the constitution when ratified by the Legislatures of the several States as provided by the constitution:

"Section 1. After one year from the ratification of this article the manufacture, sale or transportation of intoxicating liquors within, or the importation thereof into, or the exportation thereof from the United States and all territory subject to the jurisdiction thereof, for beverage purposes is hereby prohibited.

"Section 2. Congress and the several States shall have concurrent power to enforce this article by appropriate legislation.

"Section 3. This article shall be inoperative unless it shall have been ratified as an amendment to the constitution by the Legislatures of the several States, as provided in the constitution, within seven years from the date of the submission hereof to the States by the Congress."

In order that the prohibition amendment should be incorporated in the national constitution, it had to be ratified by thirty-six states. The organized temperance forces, therefore, inaugurated a vigorous ratification campaign and by January 16, 1919, the necessary thirty-six states had endorsed nation-wide permanent prohibition. Since then, nine more have ratified the constitutional amendment. The three which have not as yet (April, 1919) taken favorable action regarding the amendment, are: Rhode Island, Connecticut, and New Jersey.

The following table showing the order in which the states ratified, and the votes for and against in the Houses

WORLD PROGRESS.

of the Legislature, is taken from *The American Issue* of March 15, 1919:

Total House vote .... 3,737 for to 934 against—80 per cent. dry.
Total Senate vote   1,289 for to 213 against—86 per cent. dry.

HONOR ROLL.

States.	Ratified by Senate.	Ratified by House.
1. Mississippi	Jan. 8, 1918, 28 to 5	Jan. 8, 1918, 93 to 3
2. Virginia	Jan. 10, 1918, 30 to 8	Jan. 11, 1918, 84 to 13
3. Kentucky	Jan. 14, 1918, 28 to 6	Jan. 14, 1918, 66 to 10
4. South Carolina	Jan. 18, 1918, 28 to 6	Jan. 28, 1918, 66 to 29
5. North Dakota	Jan. 25, 1918, 43 to 2	Jan. 25, 1918, 96 to 10
6. Maryland	Feb. 13, 1918, 18 to 7	Feb. 8, 1918, 58 to 36
7. Montana	Feb. 19, 1918, 35 to 2	Feb. 18, 1918, 77 to 8
8. Texas	Feb. 28, 1918, 15 to 7	Mar. 4, 1918, 72 to 30
9. Delaware	Mar. 18, 1918, 13 to 3	Mar. 14, 1918, 27 to 6
10. South Dakota	Mar. 19, 1918, 43 to 0	Mar. 20, 1918, 86 to 0
11. Massachusetts	Apr. 2, 1918, 27 to 12	Mar. 26, 1918, 145 to 91
12. Arizona	May 23, 1918, 17 to 0	May 24, 1918, 29 to 3
13. Georgia	Jun. 26, 1918, 34 to 2	Jun. 26, 1918, 129 to 24
14. Louisiana	Aug. 6, 1918, 21 to 20	Aug. 8, 1918, 69 to 41
15. Florida	Nov. 27, 1918, 25 to 2	Nov. 27, 1918, 61 to 3
16.*Michigan	Jan. 2, 1919, 30 to 0	Jan. 2, 1919, 88 to 3
17. Ohio	Jan. 7, 1919, 20 to 12	Jan. 7, 1919, 85 to 30
18. Oklahoma	Jan. 7, 1919, 43 to 0	Jan. 7, 1919, 90 to 8
19. Maine	Jan. 8, 1919, 30 to 0	Jan. 8, 1919, 120 to 20
20. Idaho	Jan. 7, 1919, 38 to 0	Jan. 8, 1919, 62 to 0
21. West Virginia	Jan. 9, 1919, 26 to 0	Jan. 9, 1919, 78 to 3
22. Washington	Jan. 13, 1919, 42 to 0	Jan. 13, 1919, 90 to 0
23. Tennessee	Jan. 9, 1919, 28 to 2	Jan. 13, 1919, 81 to 2
24. California	Jan. 10, 1919, 24 to 15	Jan. 13, 1919, 48 to 28
25. Indiana	Jan. 13, 1919, 41 to 6	Jan. 14, 1919, 87 to 11
26. Illinois	Jan. 8, 1919, 30 to 15	Jan. 14, 1919, 84 to 66
27. Arkansas	Jan. 14, 1919, 34 to 0	Jan. 13, 1919, 93 to 2
28. North Carolina	Jan. 10, 1919, 49 to 0	Jan. 14, 1919, 93 to 10
29. Alabama	Jan. 14, 1919, 23 to 11	Jan. 14, 1919, 64 to 34
30. Kansas	Jan. 14, 1919, 39 to 0	Jan. 14, 1919, 121 to 0
31. Oregon	Jan. 15, 1919, 30 to 0	Jan. 14, 1919, 53 to 3
32. Iowa	Jan. 15, 1919, 42 to 7	Jan. 15, 1919, 86 to 13
33. Utah	Jan. 15, 1919, 16 to 0	Jan. 14, 1919, 43 to 0
34. Colorado	Jan. 15, 1919, 34 to 1	Jan. 15, 1919, 63 to 2
35. New Hampshire	Jan. 15, 1919, 19 to 4	Jan. 15, 1919, 221 to 131
36. Nebraska	Jan. 13, 1919, 31 to 1	Jan. 16, 1919, 98 to 0
37. Missouri	Jan. 16, 1919, 22 to 10	Jan. 16, 1919, 104 to 36
38. Wyoming	Jan. 16, 1919, 26 to 0	Jan. 16, 1919, 52 to 0
39. Wisconsin	Jan. 16, 1919, 10 to 11	Jan. 17, 1919, 58 to 0
40. Minnesota	Jan. 16, 1919, 49 to 11	Jan. 17, 1919, 93 to 35
41. New Mexico	Jan. 20, 1919, 12 to 4	Jan. 16, 1919, 45 to 1
42. Nevada	Jan. 21, 1919, 14 to 1	Jan. 20, 1919, 33 to 3
43. Vermont	Jan. 16, 1919, 26 to 3	Jan. 29, 1919, 155 to 58
44. New York	Jan. 29, 1919, 27 to 24	Jan. 23, 1919, 81 to 66
45. Pennsylvania	Feb. 25, 1919, 29 to 16	Feb. 4, 1919, 110 to 93

*Repassed in House to correct error, January 23, 1919.

PROHIBITION IN CANADA.

At 11.35 a.m., January 29, 1919, the Secretary of State formally signed the declaration that the amendment to the constitution had been ratified by the required number of states. On January 16, 1920, or five months before the wartime measure expires, national prohibition of the most thorough-going kind becomes a part of the federal constitution. The stupendous and far-reaching character of that victory has hardly yet been grasped by the world.

MEXICO.

The disturbed condition of the nation has prevented the temperance reform from gaining much headway in Mexico. The teaching of scientific temperance in the schools is however, being strongly advocated by the World's Woman's Christian Temperance Union, and a number of Governors have endorsed their policy.

President Carranza was reported by the *Boston Traveller*, November 27, 1917, to have issued a decree "increasing the taxes and import duties on all wines and alcoholic liquors, to take effect January 1st." All alcoholic liquors produced in Mexico were to be subject to a tax of 50 per cent.; native wines were to be taxed 25 per cent.; foreign wines and spirits were to have imposed upon them a stamp tax of 70 per cent. above the import duties, and foreign-made beers a tax of 80 per cent.

For fifteen years, an Anti-Saloon League has existed in the State of Yucatan, and has carried on the war against the traffic so successfully that the state is now "dry." In Sonora State, the Governor, General Plutarco Callas, has prohibited the sale of liquors. He is so strong an enemy of alcohol that he will not hesitate to shoot a bootlegger. The Governor of Chihuahua, one of the leading champions of the temperance cause, recently called a congress to discuss ways and means of freeing Mexico from the traffic.

WORLD PROGRESS.

The liquor forces in Mexico are not yet organized, but temperance workers express some apprehension lest American saloon-keepers, on being driven from the United States, may establish themselves across the border.

CENTRAL AMERICA.

The only region of Central America under prohibition is the canal zone, in all of which, except the two ports, a prohibitory regulation issued by Colonel Gorgas is in force. The sale of liquor in other parts of Panama seriously hampers the effectiveness of this order. The manufacture of spirits is largely a government monopoly, and practically no restrictions are placed upon their sale, except that in San Salvador sale to minors is prohibited.

SOUTH AMERICA.

Attempts to curtail or suppress the traffic have made very little progress on the Continent of South America. In Brazil, Argentina, Venezuela, Ecuador, Colombia, and Paraguay, the manufacture and sale of liquors is unrestricted. In British Guiana, the sale of intoxicants to Indians is forbidden. Peru prohibits the sale of liquor on Saturday and Sunday, and the Congress of Bolivia has recently passed a law closing all saloons on Sunday. In Chili, the sale of liquor to children under sixteen is prohibited, and a system is in vogue by which licenses are put up at auction every three years. Cities and towns have power to grant or refuse licenses. Liquor may not be sold within 200 yards of any church, school, or theatre, or in railway stations, or on trains. Saloons are closed between midnight and 6 a.m.

PROHIBITION IN CANADA.

GREAT BRITAIN.

In spite of the fact that about four thousand acts of Parliament have been passed with a view to regulating the liquor traffic in the British Isles, the problem has not yet reached a final settlement. From the earliest days, the liquor legislation of Great Britain has been regulatory and permissive. Attempts were frequently made to mitigate the evils resulting from the traffic, by imposing heavy taxes and by prohibiting distillation, but such restrictions were regularly removed soon after coming into effect.

In 1818 an act was passed, which provided greater facilities for the manufacture and sale of spirits, and the result was that within five years the national increased consumption of spirits amounted to 120 per cent. In 1828, the Duke of Wellington, arguing that if there were free trade in beer the working classes would use it in preference to spirits, forced through Parliament a bill under which anybody could set up a beer shop by merely paying 7s. 6d. for an excise license, instead of having to procure a license from a magistrate, as had been the rule for centuries. By the Beer Bill of 1830, 30,000 beer shops were opened throughout the country. In 1834, at the request of James Silk Buckingham a Parliamentary Committee on drunkenness was appointed, which recommended a reduction in the number of liquor shops, partial Sunday closing and a national system of education, which should include temperance teaching for all children. No legislative action, however, was taken on this report.

By an act of 1839 all drink shops were to remain closed until one o'clock on Sunday, Good Friday and Christmas Day. The Sale of Intoxicating Liquor on Sunday (regulation) Act of 1848 enacted that no liquor should be sold on Sunday in the United Kingdom before 12.30 p.m. The Sunday Closing Act for Scotland was enacted in 1854. In 1864 Sir George Grey's Public House Closing Act closed all metropolitan public houses from 1 to 4 a.m. and gave town councils in England and Wales power to do the same. In 1869 the ratal qualification of beer houses was raised and the result of this measure was that 300 beer-houses in Liverpool alone were closed. It is recorded that 557 beer houses in Dublin were closed when Meldon's Irish Beer House Act came into operation in Ireland in 1877. In 1878 an act was passed providing for the closing of all public houses in Ireland on Sunday except those in Dublin, Belfast, Cork, Limerick and Waterford. Three years later all the public houses in Wales were closed on Sunday.

In 1872 the payment of wages in public houses to coal and other miners was prohibited. In 1881 the Admiralty announced that spirits would no longer be issued in the navy to officers, or youths under twenty years of age. In 1887 it was made illegal for farmers to supply liquor in part payment for wages. Inebriate reformatories for habitual drunkards were established in 1898. In 1901 Parliament enacted a measure prohibiting the sale of alcoholic liquor in unsealed vessels to children under fourteen years of age.

The first attempt to gain for the people the right of local option was made in 1863 by Sir Wilfrid Lawson, a great parliamentary leader and for many years president of the United Kingdom Alliance, who moved a resolution in Parliament declaring the method under which licenses were granted to be eminently unsatisfactory and therefore requiring alteration. The motion was lost by a vote of 87 to 21. Later he introduced a bill to enable the ratepayers of given districts, to prohibit the issue of liquor licenses in their districts. This measure also was defeated. After the general election of 1880, Sir Wilfrid Lawson's resolution again came before the House and was adopted. Similar motions were carried in 1881 and 1883. In 1893 the Government took the matter up, and Sir William Harcourt proposed a bill to give the people power to forbid by a two-thirds majority the issue and renewal of licenses, but the bill was withdrawn. In 1904, a new License Act was passed, which enunciated the vicious principle that, upon being refused renewal of a liquor license, the trafficker should be compensated by the State.

Four years later, Mr. H. H. Asquith introduced a licensing bill, which was the most advanced piece of liquor legislation ever proposed in Britain. His measure passed the House of Commons by a vote of 351 to 113, but was refused by the Lords; and even after the curtailment of the power of the Lords, no further legislation was proposed by the Government prior to the beginning of the war.

Following the example of Sir Walter Trevelyan, the first president of the United Kingdom Alliance, a number of landowners closed up the public houses on their estates. A government official report, published in 1911, shows that in 3,903 rural parishes in England and Wales, with a population of 575,219, there were no public houses for the sale of liquors on the premises. Similarly many large districts in certain towns and cities are without public houses because of the orders of the landowner.

Temperance Organizations.

The root principle of the temperance reform movement in England is total abstinence. "The Seven Men of Preston" have become famous as the signatories of the first total abstinence pledge in 1832. Temperance organizations, exhibiting a great diversity of opinions upon proposals for the legislative or administrative control of the liquor traffic, nevertheless actively co-operate in promoting total abstinence. Numerous proposals for amalgamation have been entertained by the various temperance societies, but upon investigation it has generally been considered wiser for each organization to work along its own particular line to secure national sobriety. The most powerful of the temperance organizations in Great Britain, the United Kingdom Alliance, founded in 1853, is practically the only one which uses legislative as well as suasional methods.

WORLD PROGRESS.

The following is from its declaration of principles·

"That it is neither right nor politic for the State to afford legal protection or sanction to any traffic or system that tends to increase crime, to waste the national resources, to corrupt the social habits and to destroy the health and lives of the people.

"That the history and results of all past legislation in regard to the liquor traffic abundantly prove it is impossible satisfactorily to regulate a system so essentially mischievous in its tendencies.

"That, rising above class, sectarian or party consideration, all good citizens should combine to procure enactments prohibiting the sale of intoxicating beverages as affording most efficient aid in removing the appalling evils of intemperance."

Moral suasion has been recognized by the temperance organizations as the force behind legal action, and great attention has been paid to education. Definite temperance instruction is given to a very large number of children in the public schools of Great Britain and Ireland. In October, 1917, there was begun an educational campaign which extended through the winter, and in which speakers from Canada, Australia and United States assisted.

BRITISH WAR-TIME REGULATIONS.

In the early days of the war, the temperance question attracted the attention of the nation as never before, and men of widely different views united in deploring the damage caused to the army and navy, by the liquor evil. Eight days after the official declaration of war, two regulations were issued under the Defence of the Realm Act. One gave to the "competent naval or military authority" power to close all licensed premises in or near a defended harbor during such hours as might be specified in the order. The other regulation made it illegal for anyone to give or sell liquor to any member of His Majesty's forces for the purpose of eliciting information likely to be of value to the enemy, and to give or sell liquor to anyone employed in the defence of railways, docks, or harbors when on duty, or when not on duty with intent to make him drunk or inefficient. The powers given by the above regulations were subsequently considerably extended. An order from the competent naval and military authority or from the Minister of Munitions might be made to apply either to the people generally, or to any or all of His Majesty's forces, or to the forces of any of His Majesty's Allies mentioned in the order. The bringing of liquor into any dock, or the possession of liquor within the dock premises, or on any vessel in the dock, might be declared illegal. Intoxicants were not to be supplied to any member of His Majesty's forces when proceeding to a port for embarkation. No soldier undergoing hospital treatment was to be furnished with intoxicating liquor except under a doctor's orders.

In addition to the increased powers for regulating the liquor traffic which the army and navy obtained, the licensing justices were given power in August, 1914, to restrict, upon the recommendation of the chief of police, the sale and consumption of intoxicating liquor in their licensing districts, It was provided, however, that any such order suspending the sale of liquors at an hour earlier than 9 p.m., should not be effective unless approved by the Secretary of State.

Contemporaneously with the attempts to mitigate the evils of drunkenness by conferring unusual powers on the naval and military authorities and on the justices, prominent statesmen made appeals to the nation for abstinence during the period of national peril. On October 24, 1914, Lord Kitchener issued his "Message to the Nation," in which he urged the people to avoid treating the soldiers to drink, and declared that only through hard work and strict sobriety, could the men keep themselves fit. The Archbishop of Canterbury, in a letter to the press, requested all who could do so to become abstainers for the duration of the war. On November 7, Lord Roberts issued an appeal to the people, in which he referred to the havoc being wrought by drink, and added, " I therefore beg most earnestly that publicans in particular, and the public generally, will do their best to prevent our young soldiers from being tempted to drink. My appeal applies equally to the members of the overseas contingents, who have so generously and unselfishly come over here to help us in our hour of need."

On March 29, 1915, an influential deputation from the Shipbuilding Employers' Federation waited upon the Chancellor of the Exchequer to urge " the total prohibition of the sale of excisable liquors." They pointed out that, in spite of Sunday labor and all other time, the total time worked on the average in almost all the yards was below the normal number of hours per week. The deputation was of the opinion that this was principally due to the effects of drink, and stated that, speaking from an experience of from twenty-five to forty years, they believed that 80 per cent. of the present avoidable loss of time could be ascribed to no other cause than drink. In reply to the deputation, Lloyd George made the following famous declaration: " I must say that I have a growing conviction, based on accumulating evidence, that nothing but root and branch methods will be of the slightest avail in dealing with the evil. I believe that to be the general feeling. The feeling is that if we are to settle German militarism, we must first of all settle with drink. We are fighting Germany, Austria and Drink; and, as far as I can see, the greatest of these three deadly foes is Drink."

Shortly afterwards, it was officially announced that the King had issued orders against the consumption of alcoholic liquors in the royal household for the duration of the war. The King's example was voluntarily followed by many of his subjects.

Chiefly through the efforts of the churches and the Y.M.C.A., steps were taken to provide places of non-alcoholic refreshment in the neighborhood of camps as a counter-attraction to the saloon.

There were in England in the early days of 1915, four classes of people actively at work on the liquor problem: the liquor traffic; the prohibitionists; those who, like Lloyd

PROHIBITION IN CANADA.

George, thought that the Government should purchase the traffic; and those who advocated a policy of restriction and regulation. The solution of the problem which was finally offered by the Defence of the Realm (Amendment No. 3) Bill, passed in May, 1915, was in the nature of a compromise. The act provided that:

1. (1) Where it appears to His Majesty that it is expedient for the purpose of the successful prosecution of the present war that the sale and supply of intoxicating liquor in any area should be controlled by the state on the ground that war material is being made or loaded or unloaded or dealt with in transit in the area or that men belonging to His Majesty's naval or military forces are assembled in the area, His Majesty has power, by order-in-council, to define the area and to apply to the area the regulations issued in pursuance of this act under the Defence of the Realm Consolidation Act, 1914, and the regulations so applied shall, subject to any provision of the order or any amending order, take effect in that area during the continuance of the present war and such period not exceeding twelve months thereafter as may be declared by order-in-council to be necessary in view of conditions connected with the termination of the present war.

(2) His Majesty in Council has power to issue regulations under the Defence of the Realm Consolidation Act, 1914, to take effect in any area to which they are applied under this act:

(a) For giving the prescribed government authority to the exclusion of any other persons, the power of selling or supplying or controlling the sale or supply of, intoxicating liquor in the area, subject to any exceptions contained in the regulations; and

(b) For giving the prescribed government authority to acquire, compulsorily or by agreement, and either for the period during which the regulations take effect, or permanently, any licensed or other premises or business in the area, or any interest therein, so far as it appears necessary or expedient to do so for the purpose of giving proper effect to the control of the liquor supply in the area; and

(c) For enabling the prescribed government authority, without any license, to establish and maintain refreshment rooms

WORLD PROGRESS.

for the supply of refreshments (including, if thought fit, the supply of intoxicating liquor) to the general public or to any particular class of persons or to persons employed in any particular industry in the area; and

(d) For making any modification or adjustment of the relations between persons interested in licensed premises in the area which appears necessary or expedient in consequence of the regulations; and

(e) Generally, for giving effect to the transfer of the control of the liquor traffic in the area to the prescribed government authority, and for modifying, so far as it appears necessary or expedient, the provisions of the acts relating to licensing or the sale of intoxicating liquor in their application to the area.

(3) Any regulations made before the passing of this act under the powers conferred by any act dealing with the Defence of the Realm as respects the restriction of the sale of intoxicating liquor, are hereby declared to have been duly made in accordance with those powers.

The following concise summary of the act is given by Rev. Henry Carter, a member of the Board of Control appointed by the Government, to exercise the new powers of the State:*

"Total prohibition and a plan of national state purchase were shut out of the bill. In scheduled areas where drink was shown to be inimical to public interests, the board were to be free to prohibit, to purchase, to regulate, or to restrict. Neither existing agreements—as, for instance, between brewer and tenant —nor even the existing licensing acts, were to impede the board in their onerous task; they could set aside either. These drastic powers were to operate during the war, and for a term not exceeding twelve months after."

At its third annual meeting held in June, 1917, the Control Board reported that 38,000,000 inhabitants of Great Britain were covered by its operations. The typical restrictions imposed by the Board in these areas are explained in *The Control of the Drink Trade* and may be summed up as follows:

---
*See "The Control of the Drink Trade."

PROHIBITION IN CANADA.

(1) The sale or supply of intoxicating liquor, for consumption on the premises, is ordinarily restricted on week-days to two and a half hours in the middle of the day, and to three (or, in some cases, two) hours in the evening; that is to say, it is permitted during the usual times of the principal meals, and is prohibited before the mid-day period, throughout the afternoon and after 9 or 9.30 in the evening. On Sundays, in England, the hours of sale are usually reduced to five or four and a half.

(2) Off-sales* of spirits are made subject to certain additional restrictions, and they are prohibited on Saturdays and Sundays and after the mid-day period on other days. Off-sales of other intoxicating liquors are ordinarily required to cease in the evenings an hour before the closing hour for on-sales.

(3) Payment for intoxicating liquor elsewhere than at the licensed premises, and soliciting or canvassing for orders, are prohibited.

(4) "Treating" and credit sales are, subject to certain minor exceptions, absolutely prohibited.

(5) Clubs, as well as licensed premises, are made subject to the restrictions.

(6) Licensed premises are permitted to open for the purpose of the supply of food and non-intoxicating drink and of solid refreshment, at an early hour in the morning, so as to meet the requirements of men proceeding to their work; and they are allowed to remain open for this purpose during the hours when they are prohibited by the board's order from selling intoxicants on Sundays as well as on week-days.

(7) Permission is given to reduce the strength of spirits by dilution to a much greater extent than is allowed by the general law.

In 1916 a very significant appeal to the British Government, known as the "Strength of Britain Memorial," asking for prohibition during the war, was signed by more than 2,000,000 adult persons in England and Wales, more than 400,000 women in Scotland, and more than 150,000 adults in Ulster. The signers of this remarkable document repudiated any special prejudice in favor of the temperance movement, but based their plea entirely upon the nation's needs,

---

*I.e., Sales for consumption off the premises.

declaring that the liquor traffic hindered the army, hampered the navy, threatened the mercantile marine, destroyed food supplies, wasted financial resources, diverted the energies of the nation and shattered its moral strength.

To these declarations are signed the names of fifteen members of His Majesty's Privy Council, twenty-one Admirals, four Vice-Admirals, nine Generals, twenty-five Major-Generals, four Brigadier-Generals, eight Surgeon-Generals, thirteen Lieut.-Generals, besides a great array of other men high in the Empire's civil, naval and military service and hundreds of thousands of others who are prominent in important departments of social life and duty.

Lord D'Abernon, chairman of the Central Control Board, (Liquor Traffic) in an address in the City Temple, London on May 6, 1918, said in part:

"Immediately before the war, in the year 1913, the average number of convictions per week in scheduled areas in England and Wales was 3,482. At the present time it is 620—a reduction of 82 per cent.

"The decline in drunkenness has been accompanied by a fall in sickness and mortality from alcoholic excess, which is almost precisely what the statisticians among you would have told you to expect.

"Cases of delirium tremens in those large towns, such as Liverpool, for which figures are available, have fallen by 80 per cent.

"The number of deaths from alcoholism in England and Wales, which in 1913 were 1,831, had fallen to 580 in 1917—a decrease of 70 per cent."

It must however, be remembered that in addition to the work of the Central Control Board, other causes militated for increased national sobriety. The fact that so large a number of men were absent from the country is important. Moreover, the output of beer was curtailed, the price of intoxicants was raised and restrictions were placed on the consumption of spirits. The Output of Beer (Restriction) Act fixed the quantity of beer to be brewed in the year

PROHIBITION IN CANADA.

beginning April 1, 1916, at 26,000,000 standard barrels, a reduction of 10,000,000 barrels from the year preceding the war. The next year, by order of the Food Controller, the output of beer for 1917-1918 was reduced to 10,000,000 standard barrels, but this order was relaxed during the summer of 1917 to allow one-third increase for the quarter ending September 30, and in December the barrelage was increased 20 per cent. for the first quarter of 1918 with an additional increase of 13 per cent. in munition areas. The duty on beer which had been 7s. 9d. per standard barrel was raised to 25s. by April, 1917. The Government took over the manufacture of spirits for munitions purposes. The importation of spirits was reduced by three-fourths to save tonnage. The maximum strength of spirits sold for beverage purposes was not to exceed 25 per cent. As a result of the limitation of the supplies of beer and spirits the price of these liquors rose. All these factors made for the restriction of consumption of alcoholic liquors. In spite of all regulations, however, in 1917 in the United Kingdom there was spent for alcoholic beverages £259,000,000, as compared with £203,989,000 in 1916, £181,959,000 in 1915, and £164,463,000 in 1914.

PROHIBITION PLEBISCITES.

During the war a number of plebiscites on prohibition were taken in large industrial centres of England, Scotland and Wales. The results of the voting, as given by the *Western Temperance Herald*, follow·

ENGLAND.

Place.	For.	Against.	Majority.
Batley	9,664	3,827	5,837
Birstall	2,063	776	1,287
Cleckheaton	4,869	1,149	3,720
Dartmoor	467	203	264
Dewsbury	13,801	8,681	5,120
Driglington	1,171	195	976
Gomersal	1,036	418	618
Heckmondwike	3,641	1,828	1,813

WORLD PROGRESS.

Place.	For.	Against.	Majority.
Hull	50,084	38,572	11,512
Liversedge	2,402	1,262	1,140
Mirfield	2,696	1,692	1,004
Morley	6,488	2,482	4,060
Nelson	13,363	4,794	8,569
Osseltt	4,576	979	3,497
Spennymoor	2,765	143	2,622

SCOTLAND.

Place.	For.	Against.	Majority.
Alva	1,332	·47	1,285
Annan	906	257	649
Barrhead	3,343	299	3,044
Carluke	2,595	119	2,476
Clydebank	8,207	1 861	6,346
Cowdenbeath	2,371	576	1,795
Govan	3,607	2,398	1,209
Lesmahagow	1,076	32	1,044
Oban	1,249	80	1,169
Paisley	11,182	1,378	10,004

WALES.

Place.	For.	Against.	Majority.
Blaenau Festiniog	2,685	229	2,456
Llanelly	9,054	4,043	5,011

The total number of votes cast at these places was:

    For war-time prohibition 166,693
    Against war-time prohibition 78,066

    Majority for war-time prohibition........ 88,627

A plebiscite of more than usual interest was taken in Annan, Scotland, a community in which the most approved methods of the Central Control Board (liquor traffic) had been demonstrated. Annan is in the immediate neighborhood of Gretna, which was made by the Minister of Munitions the site of one of the largest of the National Factories.

PROHIBITION IN CANADA.

Annan, like Carlisle and other towns near Gretna, was invaded with navvies and other laborers, with the result that drunkenness and disorder prevailed. With regard to this district, the Central Control Board at once issued a drink-restriction order, according to its customary scheme, involving the reduction of the hours for sale, the abolition of treating, and the dilution of spirits. In spite of these restrictions, scenes of a most nauseating and degrading character became a common occurrence. It was decided to try State Purchase and Direct Control. A number of licenses were suppressed, further restrictions on the sale of spirits were made, sale to children under sixteen was declared unlawful, Sunday closing was ordered, and an extensive scheme for providing good food in up-to-date cafés, and counter-attractions to the public house, was entered upon. Yet, in spite of this trial of State Purchase, the plebiscite vote was 906 for prohibition and 257 against.

SCOTLAND.

Greater progress along prohibition lines has been made in Scotland than in the rest of the British Isles. Prior to the founding of the Scottish Permissive Bill and Temperance Association in 1858, the movement followed moral suasion lines. The Association co-operated with Mr. Peter McLagan, M.P., who introduced session after session a bill to give to Scotland the power of local veto.

The Government which was returned to power in 1910, was pledged to grant a measure of temperance reform for Scotland. Accordingly in 1912 the Temperance (Scotland) Act was introduced and passed in the House of Commons by a majority of 157. In the House of Lords a number of amendments designed to make the bill less effective were inserted. The Commons rejected the amendments, and the Lords refused to allow the measure to become law; but the next session the bill was re-introduced and certain com-

WORLD PROGRESS.

promises were agreed upon. The act as finally passed provides that in September, 1920, a requisition signed by not less than one-tenth of the electors in any area* may demand a poll, such poll to be taken in November or December, 1920. A new poll may be taken every three years. Both men and women are entitled to vote on the issue. There will be three questions submitted:

(1) A no-license resolution, which will be carried if fifty-five per cent. of those voting, and thirty-five per cent. of the voters on the roll, are in favor of no-license.

(2) A limiting resolution—which means a reduction of one-quarter of the licenses—will not be carried unless a majority of those voting, equal to thirty-five per cent. of the voters on the roll, are in favor of it. If no-license is not carried, those in favor of it will have their votes added to the resolution in favor of reduction.

(3) No change—if a majority of the voters are in favor of no change that resolution will be carried.

The following provisions of the act are now in force:

(1) Intoxicating liquors shall not be sold in clubs between 2 a.m. and 10 a.m.

(2) Intoxicating liquors shall not be sold in theatres, except during the same hours as in public-houses. No license-holder in Scotland is now allowed to sell intoxicating liquor before 10 a.m.

(3) A drunken person endeavoring to enter a public-house is liable to fine.

(4) Sheriffs have power to close public-houses during a riot.

(5) Magistrates cannot order any alterations on license premises until 1920.

The Scottish Temperance League, one of the most potent temperance forces in Scotland, through the columns of the *Temperance Leader* disseminates a great deal of temperance

---

*Area.—Towns with less than 25,000 inhabitants will be treated as a single area. Towns with over 25,000 inhabitants will have the wards as areas. Where the ward has less than 4,000 inhabitants, the town council may join it to another ward. In counties the parish is the area.

information. The Independent Order of Good Templars, which was introduced into Scotland in 1869, unites with the Scottish Temperance Bill and Permissive Association, and the Scottish Temperance League, for joint political work. Temperance sentiment among the women is fostered by the British Women's Temperance Association.

IRELAND.

The most important temperance movement in the history of Ireland was that launched in 1838 by Father Matthew, who in five years pledged five million people to total abstinence. The public houses, however, were allowed to remain, and the traffic again gained a strong foothold in the Emerald Isle.

As mentioned above, the Irish Sunday Closing Act of 1878 closed all public houses except those in Dublin, Belfast, Cork, Limerick, and Waterford. Subsequently the hours of Sunday sale in the five exempted cities were reduced, and earlier Saturday closing throughout the country was enacted.

In 1909 a "Catch-my-Pal" campaign, inaugurated at Armagh by Rev. R. J. Patterson, a Presbyterian minister, gave a great impetus to the temperance cause. The force of this movement has now, however, largely spent itself.

No new licenses have been issued since 1902. A great deal of liquor is illegally manufactured in Ireland. The Government returns for 1917 show that during the year there were 1910 seizures of illicit distillation plants in Ireland, two in Scotland, and none in England.

At the instance of the Irish Temperance League, which has done much pioneer work in the line of education, the Board of National Education is giving some attention to the teaching of temperance in the schools. Lecturers have been sent by the League into most of the schools of the island,

and for many years prizes have been given to the pupils and teachers who show highest efficiency in this work.

No part of Ireland comes under the jurisdiction of the Central Control Board (Liquor Traffic).

FRANCE.

Until the outbreak of the war, the wine producers in France, who controlled the Chamber of Deputies, effectively prevented legislation to restrict the traffic in intoxicating liquors. At that time, there was one wine shop in the republic for every forty of the population. In 1910, M. Reinach, leader of the anti-alcohol party in the Chamber of Deputies, made an unsuccessful attempt to secure laws prohibiting absinthe and restricting the number of licensed saloons to one for every 200 persons. Premier Briand, who supported M. Reinach, said:

"The Government views the situation with alarm; it is terrible, and it is a question of national interest, for the life of the nation is at stake."

Early in 1915, an order was issued by the Minister of War, prohibiting the sale of liquor to soldiers, but the supreme court decided that the military power had no right to punish civilian offenders, and the law was declared void. In February, 1915, the Absinthe Prohibition Bill was passed, the vote in both Houses being overwhelmingly favorable. This prohibited for all time the manufacture and sale of absinthe. The sale of distilled liquors to women and children was forbidden in October.

By an act of Parliament, dated June 30, 1916, home distillation was prohibited, except that peasants were permitted to distil as much as ten litres for their own personal consumption. In December, 1916, M. Briand, introduced into the Chamber of Deputies a bill empowering the Government to take over for munition purposes all existing stocks of alcoholic liquors. He also announced his intention of asking for legislation to prohibit all spirituous liquors, but the request was never made. In March, 1917, an act was passed making it an offence for spirits or intoxicated persons to be permitted in work-shops. In the same year, the Minister of War was given power to prohibit the sale of liquor to soldiers, and he issued an order similar to that set aside by the courts in 1915.

The National League against Alcoholism in June, 1917, petitioned Parliament to grant total prohibition of all alcoholic liquors, or if this should be impracticable, war-time prohibition of all liquors containing more than eighteen per cent. alcohol, and reduction of saloons. Parliament, however, contented itself with enacting measures whereby intoxicated persons appearing in public should be punished, sale to children under eighteen was prohibited, and employment in saloons of girls under eighteen years of age was forbidden.

SPAIN AND PORTUGAL.

In these two countries, few temperance organizations and little temperance sentiment exist. There is no special license fee exacted for the privilege of selling intoxicants, and except in a few of the larger cities like Madrid, there are no restrictions in regard to the hours of sale. During the war no special measures to lessen the traffic seem to have been contemplated.

BELGIUM.

The beginning of a serious movement against intemperance was made in 1878 when some philanthropists united in a Belgian Association against the Use of Alcoholic Drinks. They organized the Second International Temperance Congress, which forced the question upon public consideration.

WORLD PROGRESS.

Subsequently, the Association changed its name to the Patriotic League against Alcoholism, which has disseminated temperance literature and endeavored to lessen intemperance by legislation. In 1885, as a result of the International Congress against Abuse of Alcoholic Liquors, held in Antwerp, *The Blue Cross*, the Swiss Total Abstinence Society, was introduced into Belgium, where it has made some progress.

In 1886, because of industrial unrest, a Royal Commission was appointed to investigate workers' conditions. The commission found themselves confronted by the alcohol question and recommended that legislation be passed to arrest the ravages caused by intoxicants. Another measure, enacted in 1889, diminished the number of drink shops. According to the Minister of Finance, under this law the number of drinking places was decreased from 185,000 to 155,000.

In 1912, the Socialists of Belgium determined on a general strike with a view to forcing the Government to grant universal suffrage. Contrary to all expectations, the strike, which lasted for over a week, was not attended by any great disturbances. The Brussels correspondent of the *London Daily Mirror* wrote on April 20, 1913:

"The most wonderful feature of the strike is its teetotalism. Belgium has the unenviable record of heading the consumption per head in Europe of alcohol, both in beer and spirits. Yet the strike organizers have succeeded in inducing the strikers to become, for the time being, teetotalers, and at the various strike headquarters I have only seen coffee and milk drunk."

Shortly before the outbreak of the war, the sale and manufacture of absinthe in Belgium was forbidden. In that part of the country which was not overrun by the Germans, the importation and sale of spirits was prohibited in November, 1914. In this section of Belgium, it is said that there were 2,520 saloons for a civilian population of only 62,500.

The leader of the Social Democratic Party, Dr. Emil Vandervelde, who at the beginning of the German invasion was made Minister of War, is the champion of the temperance forces in the country. He was appointed head of a commission to formulate an alcoholic policy. "It is tolerably certain," says the *Scientific Temperance Journal,* "that the plan to be presented for legislation will prohibit production and sale of spirits for beverage use while promoting their industrial use. It is also expected to reduce the number of retail licenses, for which there was a strong agitation before the war."

HOLLAND.

At Leyden in 1842 the Dutch National Temperance Society against the use of spirits was organized. One of the most zealous of the members of this society was Dr. Adama Van Scheltema, who stated that after years of abstinence from spirits he became convinced that he should take the logical step of adopting total abstinence, which was popularly regarded as folly and fanaticism. However, in 1862, he founded the first total abstinence society in Holland. Largely as a result of this society's efforts, a law was passed in 1881, providing that many of the forty thousand existing spirit licenses should be discontinued. In 1880, the Government of Holland began an annual grant of $3,000 to the temperance cause. By 1887, the aggregate number of dram shops licensed to sell spirits had been decreased to twenty-eight thousand. In 1891 a new law was passed, regulating the sale of spirits and reducing the number of licenses. An amendment to the act of 1881, which came into force in 1910, forbade the sale of whiskey, gin, brandy, and other kinds of spirits at railway stations and on steamers. Parliament also passed an amendment giving to local councils power to prohibit the issue of licenses on certain streets, and enabling them to petition the Crown at the end of every five years for a reduction of licenses in their districts.

A National Local Option League was organized in April, 1916, and secured 600,000 signatures to a petition asking the

Queen to grant local option. Late in the same year, the Government forbade the use of cereals in the manufacture of distilled liquors, the order to be effective for the duration of the war.

DENMARK.

Before the beginning of the twentieth century, practically no prohibitory or restrictive legislation was in force, except that in Copenhagen dram shops were required to close at midnight and barmaids were prohibited. A liquor dealer did not require any special license to sell intoxicating liquors. In 1903 Parliament was asked to appoint a commission to amend the existing license laws. The request was granted, and the commission, consisting of both advocates and opponents of temperance, set to work on the problem. After careful consideration, they brought in their report, which recommended the reduction of public houses in towns and cities to a fixed maximum, the giving to country areas power of local option to prevent by a two-thirds majority the opening of new liquor shops, and to abolish old licenses when the licensee died or sold his property. The committee further recommended that the license laws be revised every five years.

The above recommendations were incorporated in a bill introduced by the Minister for the Interior, in January, 1908, which, however, was not carried. The next year the measure was reintroduced, but the debate on it was adjourned until 1910, when the bill was passed in the Lower House with one amendment providing that in country areas a majority (but not less than twenty-five per cent.) be substituted for the three-fifths majority. The bill was thrown out by the Upper House. Thereupon, the Minister for the Interior, in whom power to grant or refuse liquor licenses is vested, declared that he would arrange for a vote to be taken in the parishes, and in every case he would give his decision in accordance with the wishes of the people.

PROHIBITION IN CANADA.

A number of contests of this kind have been held, which showed that in the great majority of parishes the people were overwhelmingly in favor of license reduction.

Since the Upper House of the Danish Parliament persistently blocked temperance legislation that had been accepted by the Lower House, a committee representing both Houses met to consider the situation. They finally brought in a compromise bill, which was passed. With regard to the new act which came into operation in 1913, Mr. Larsen-Ledet, editor of the daily temperance paper, *Reform,* said:

"We did not get local option. The Upper House said 'no,' and at last we were obliged to take what we could get. The new law refers licensing matters to the town or parish council (both elected by universal suffrage). I feel sure that not many of the councils will give any licenses before a general vote of the people is taken. The law says that the councils can fix a limit of age under which spirits cannot be sold to young men and women. The limit fixed by the majority of the councils is from eighteen to twenty years of age. The councils can also fix the closing hours of public houses, and the majority have decided that the houses must be closed from eight to ten hours during the day and night. The Temperance Party of Denmark say they must be closed the whole twenty-four hours."

In March, 1917, a three weeks' suspension of spirit sales was ordered to enable the nation to take stock. As a result, all manufacture and importation of spirits was forbidden until March, 1918, and subsequently distillation was suspended for the period of the war. The output of beer was reduced to eighty per cent. of the 1916 allowance, and none but imported grain might be used for malting. During the war, the tax on wine and spirituous liquors increased one hundred per cent., and that on beer fifty per cent. on the old retail prices. A petition was widely circulated and signed, asking the Government to continue all the war-time restrictions after the signing of peace, and to submit to a popular vote the question of permanent national prohibition.

WORLD PROGRESS.

ICELAND, GREENLAND, AND FAROE ISLANDS.

The International Order of Good Templars was introduced into Iceland in 1884, and since that time the temperance reform has made great progress in the country. The existing restrictive laws were superseded by an act of 1899, which prohibited the manufacture of intoxicants after January 1, 1900, forbade treating, credit sales, and sales to minors, and introduced a complicated system of local option. In 1905, when a bill providing for total prohibition was introduced into the Parliament, the whole matter was referred to a special committee to investigate. In their report, the committee stated that although much good had been done by the prohibition of 1900, they were of the opinion that the only effective remedy for the extermination of alcohol was to forbid the importation of all intoxicating liquors and to grant no further licenses. They further recommended that a vote on prohibition should be taken in 1907. Parliament changed the date for the vote to 1908, and adopted the report unanimously. The result of the poll was:

For prohibition	4,645
Against prohibition	3,181
Majority for	1,464

A bill was at once passed forbidding the importation of liquors into Iceland after January 1, 1912, and the sale after January 1, 1915. Beer containing two per cent. alcohol was exempted. The act received the approval of the King of Denmark, who said when signing it:

" Few, if any of my actions since I became king, have given me more satisfaction than that of signing the prohibition law for Iceland, and if the Parliament of Denmark will pass a similar law, I shall be more willing yet to approve."

GREENLAND.

The importation of any kind of intoxicating liquor into Greenland has been prohibited and the law is well enforced.

PROHIBITION IN CANADA.

FAROE ISLANDS.

By a vote taken in 1907, the Faroe Islands declared in favor of prohibition. In consequence of this poll, which stood at 1,541 for prohibition and 64 against, all liquor shops were closed on January 1, 1908, so that the Islands are to-day under prohibition.

NORWAY.

Until the middle of the nineteenth century, there was free distillation in Norway, and no special places were set apart for the sale of intoxicating liquor. To check the evils resulting from drunkenness, in 1845 an act was passed providing for the issuance by municipal councils of licenses for the sale of alcoholic liquors. Licenses so granted were to be continued during the lifetime of the licensee, provided the license fee was paid annually. A heavy tax was placed upon all distillers, but beer brewed in Norway could be sold without tax or license. In 1854, power was given to country districts to veto the traffic in intoxicants locally. By 1892, in all of Norway outside of the larger towns and cities, there were only twenty-seven licenses for the sale of spirits. By a law of 1866, new licenses granted were to be for one year only instead of for life.

The first Norwegian total abstinence society was formed in Stavanger in 1859 by Asbjorn Kloster, who has been called the Father Matthew of Norway. When the society was founded, it had thirty members, and during the presidency of Mr. Kloster, who held office until his death in 1876, the membership increased to eight thousand. He travelled, lectured, distributed tracts, and organized societies from Lindesnes to North Cape. The Good Templars, organized nationally in 1878, are very strong in Norway.

By an act of 1871, the so-called " Norwegian System " of dealing with the liquor traffic came into existence. The power of selling spirits was given to Spirit Companies

(Brandevin Samlag), which were joint stock companies. They paid five per cent. to the shareholders and turned over all further surplus profits to the communities in which they existed. Licenses granted for one year only were not to be renewed, so that gradually the spirit companies replaced the private sellers of liquor. The act also contained a clause which stated that drunkards and intoxicated persons might not be served with liquor. In 1904, the sale of beer and wine was given over to beer and wine companies, which were organized similarly to the spirit companies. Town councils could prohibit any private person who did not hold a life liquor license from selling beer and wine; the tax on beer and wine to retailers was increased.

The establishment of liquor companies was not supported by the temperance people of Norway, and did not prove an effective method of dealing with the traffic. In 1893, Consul-General Mitchell, in a report sent from Christiania to the British Government, thus described the work of the system:

"The original philanthropic object of the Associations has been departed from, and the old licensed victualler has been replaced by hundreds of holders of five per cent. shares, politically and otherwise interested in the distribution of larger surpluses from the sale of spirits, and by municipalities well content to improve and embellish their towns without recourse to communal taxation."

In 1894, the power of local veto, which had been enjoyed by country districts, was extended to the towns. The polls were to be held every six years, and every adult over twenty-five was to have a vote. The act of 1894 further provided that all surplus profits of new liquor companies should be used for public utility purposes within the community in which the company operated. In 1913 there were thirty-seven Norwegian towns in which the liquor companies had been prohibited, and twenty-seven where they still remained. In the attempt to vote out the liquor companies, the cause of temperance was handicapped by the necessity of obtain-

PROHIBITION IN CANADA.

ing a majority of the voters on the register, all who failed to cast their ballots being regarded as against prohibition.

In 1910, the French Bourse stipulated, as one of the conditions for granting loans needed by Norway for new railway lines, that the duties on French wines and spirits should be lowered. This was accepted by the Norwegian Parliament, but not without considerable opposition.

When war broke out, Parliament passed an act forbidding anyone to sell alcoholic liquors to soldiers, men of the war-fleet, and railway men on duty. From August 4, 1914, to October 11, 1914, the sale of spirits was prohibited. During the general strike in November, 1916, the sale of all alcoholic liquors was forbidden. Prohibition of the manufacture and sale of intoxicants was enforced from December 18, 1916, until January 8, 1917; and produced such satisfactory results that it was extended to March 1. Legislation passed in 1917, brought to an end life licenses and left communities with absolute power to prohibit the sale of alcoholic beverages. The precarious state of the food supply led the Government to completely prohibit distillation and to reduce beer production. The use of cereals and malt in the manufacture of beer containing over two and one quarter per cent. alcohol was also forbidden.

A new law was passed in July, 1918. It gives to the liquor companies a monopoly over the importation and sale of intoxicants. No company may be established in a town of less than four thousand population, and in towns which have over four thousand no company may be organized, unless a majority of those on the voters' lists declare in favor of the liquor shops.

SWEDEN.

According to C. A. Wenngren, writing in the Cyclopædia of Temperance and Prohibition, there were in the early days of Sweden, periods of prohibition. In the 16th century, Gustavus Vasa forbade the use of spirits. From 1622 to

1632, by a decree of Gustavus Adolphus, whiskey was prohibited. In 1698, Charles XII prohibited the manufacture of whiskey, and in 1756 the party known as the "Hats" again had prohibition enacted. Gustavus III, on his accession to the throne in 1771, proclaimed prohibition of spirituous liquors, but three years later it was revoked and following the Russian plan, crown stills were established. In 1809, the royal monopoly of the production of spirits was abolished, and it was made possible for every householder to manufacture spirits on payment of a small fee. Distilleries multiplied so that by 1834 their number reached approximately 170,000.

About this time Peter Wieselgren, a powerful orator and organizer, started a crusade directed especially against distilled liquors. In 1838, the Swedish Temperance Society was established for the special purpose of securing abolition of home distillation. In 1854, a committee of the Diet reported that:

"The researches of the philosopher and the honest feelings of the ordinary man have led us to the conclusion . . . that the comfort of the ordinary people—even their existence as an enlightened, industrious, and loyal people—is at stake unless means can be found to check the evil."

The next year, a licensing act was passed which abolished domestic stills, and gave to parochial authorities (subject to the approval of the Provincial Governor) the right to fix every year the number of spirits shops and public houses. From 1850 to 1869, the number of distilleries had decreased from 44,000 to 457.

The towns and cities did not share the powers given to rural municipalities, but instead, town councils were empowered to continue or to limit or to control the traffic in spirituous liquors. The town councils put the spirit licenses up to auction, and the bidder who promised to sell the largest number of litres during the period of the license was successful. If he sold more liquor than the quantity he had specified, he escaped paying the sale tax on all liquors in excess of that quantity. To increase sales, the liquor shops were kept open at all hours, clothing and other commodities were accepted in payment for intoxicants, and credit was given. The town council, with a view to obtaining increased revenue at the next auction, paid little attention to the enforcement of the law.

In Gothenburg, the second city of Sweden, in 1864, the council evolved a new method of dealing with the liquor traffic—a method which has become known all over the world as the Gothenburg System. A company (Bolag) was organized which was to operate a limited number of public houses as eating-houses, where spirits would not be served except with meals. The giving of credit was forbidden; and provision was made for further reducing the consumption of distilled liquor by a regulation that the managers were to be paid a fixed salary for spirit sales, but were to receive a bonus on the profits from the sales of food and malt liquors. The shareholders were to receive six per cent. on their investments, and all further net profits were to be paid into the city treasury. Private inspectors were to be appointed to co-operate with the public in supervising the public houses. In 1865, all the public-house licenses in the city of Gothenburg, with the exception of seven held by private persons, were taken over by the Bolag, and in 1875 all the grocery licenses were transferred to it. The Gothenburg system was widely adopted in the cities of Sweden. It has been regarded as the best restrictive license system ever devised. That this method, which makes the traffic highly respectable and important, is inferior to prohibition as a solution of the alcohol problem, may be inferred from a speech made by Hon. Oskar Eklund, a member of the Upper House of the Riksdag in 1908. He said:

"Our Gothenburg Liquor Companies are quite as desirous of getting their liquors sold as ordinary publicans would be. Complaints are repeatedly made that the Bolags are making strenuous efforts in order to push the sale of brandy—sometimes by unlawful means, such as the sending out of agents to canvass for orders in areas where the people have prohibited drink shops. The Liquor Bolags say, 'We are working in the interests of morality and sobriety.' It is false. Whenever any proposition to restrict the sale of spirits has been formulated in Parliament or embodied in memorials to His Majesty, the Bolags have always attempted to hinder them by warning the authorities against their acceptance."

During the great national strike of trade unionists in 1909, which lasted five weeks, all liquor shops throughout the country were closed; only beer and wine could be sold with food. Arrests for drunkenness, disorder, and crime showed a marked decline during the period.

In 1913, a measure was passed which provided that all profits from the Bolag should accrue to the state treasury. A bill to give to towns the power of local veto was defeated in 1916 in the Upper House of the Riksdag by a vote of eighty-five to fifty-two. In 1916, an inventory of existing stocks of spirits was made, and the amount which any person might purchase was limited to two litres per month for the period between November 16, 1916, and October 1, 1917, spirits being defined as any liquor containing over twenty-five per cent. of alcohol.

In August, 1917, there was a temporary cessation of distillation, owing to the need for conserving grain.

In the same year, the Lower House of Parliament went on record in favor of immediate war-time prohibition, and total prohibition to go into force in ten years' time. The Upper House, however, declined to endorse these proposals, so that legislation effecting a compromise was enacted, and became operative in January, 1918. Wine and beer were to be both brought under the Gothenburg system; liquor was not to be served to minors, to any person against whom a conviction for drunkenness had been registered within two years, or to any person who within three years had committed an offence while intoxicated. The Bolags were to come under the supervision of temperance committees established in every community.

The hours for the retail sale of spirits, on Saturdays and the days before holidays, are limited to the period from 2 p.m. to 7 p.m. On Sundays and holidays, spirits may not be sold before 2 p.m. Beer and wine may, however, be served before this time with meals which reach a stipulated price.

The agitation in Sweden for national prohibition is the result of years of general educational propaganda. An ordinance of the Government, issued in 1892, commanded that in both lower and higher schools of the kingdom instruction should be given about the nature and effects of alcoholic liquors, a law from which a great deal of good has resulted.

RUSSIA.

For the eight years from 1819 to 1826, the Government of Russia controlled the liquor traffic. In 1826, the state monopoly was abolished, and a policy was initiated of deriving revenue from the sale of intoxicants by private individuals.

In the decade 1836-1846, there was a great temperance movement among the people of the Baltic Provinces. The formation of temperance societies was, however, forbidden by the Minister of the Interior, and so fifty years later hardly anyone remembered the great movement.

The Holy Greek Orthodox Synod of St. Petersburg sent out in 1899 an order to all Russian priests to work against drunkenness. As a result, great numbers of people pledged themselves, not as in the earlier campaign to abstinence from spirits, but to abstinence from all intoxicating beverages.

The state monopoly of the sale of intoxicants was again put into operation in 1894. The immense importance of the liquor traffic as a producer of revenue proved a tremendous bar to temperance progress; nevertheless some societies were formed, chiefly among the poorer classes, the leaders of which were mostly teachers.

Before the outbreak of the war, protests were voiced in the Duma against the forcing of vodka on unwilling communities in order to increase the Government's revenue. In 1912, the Duma passed a resolution proposing that poison labels, instead of labels bearing the arms of the empire, should be placed on vodka bottles. By order of the Minister of Marine in 1912, issue of spirits to sailors in the Russian navy was to be discontinued. In the following year, a bill restricting the hours of sale was introduced in the Duma, but had not been finally disposed of up to the outbreak of war.

Early in 1914, an edict of the Czar forbade the increase of the state revenue through the vodka monopoly. On January 30, 1914, the Czar sent a letter to M. Barck, the new Finance Minister, in which he said, "It is not meet that the welfare of the exchequer should be dependent upon the ruins of the spiritual and productive energies of numbers of my loyal subjects."

During mobilization, by order of the Czar, all wine shops, beer saloons, and government vodka shops were closed. In September, 1914, another order prohibited the sale of vodka and all other spirits until the end of the war. A month later, in answer to a petition from the Russian people, the Czar declared his intention of making the prohibition of vodka permanent. In June, 1916, a measure was passed by the Duma, prohibiting vodka and beer after the war, and giving to towns and cities power to permit or forbid the sale of wine.

The Provisional Government in April, 1917, prohibited all intoxicating liquors containing over one and a half per cent. alcohol, except in wine-producing districts where the sale of twelve per cent. wine is optional.

In the present chaotic condition of affairs in Russia, the temperance situation is uncertain.

PROHIBITION IN CANADA.

FINLAND.

Temperance reform really began with the abolition of private stills in 1864, although it was not until 1877 that total abstinence societies began to be formed. In 1883 the Government gave to rural districts power of local option, and to towns power to adopt a modification of the Gothenburg system. Under this law the country districts had, by 1900, practically freed themselves of the spirit traffic, 413 out of 422 parishes having abolished it by popular vote.

Twice the Finnish Landtag voted for the prohibition of the liquor traffic before it was granted. In 1907, a stringent measure providing for the total prohibition of the manufacture, importation, and sale of intoxicating liquors, without compensation, was passed by a large majority, but the measure was vetoed by the Czar, the Grand Duke of Finland. Two years later a similar bill met a like fate. Finally in May, 1917, total prohibition of all alcoholic beverages except very weak beer was proclaimed by the Parliament which has since asserted its independence of Russia.

GREECE.

The Greeks have been termed one of the most temperate of Christian nations. Although they make a great deal of strong wine, they drink but little. Neither during the Balkan wars nor the great European conflict were legislative measures taken to restrict the consumption of intoxicating liquors.

SERBIA.

Under the special patronage of the King, and guided by the Neutral Order of Good Templars, the temperance movement has made some progress both among adults and children. Early in the war the Minister of the Interior issued a decree forbidding proprietors of hotels and cafés to sell liquor in any large quantities to soldiers or habitual drunkards. No other steps seem to have been taken to restrict the traffic.

BULGARIA.

During the centuries that Bulgaria was under Mohammedan rule, the faith of Islam prevented the alcoholization of the country. The per capita consumption of alcoholic liquors is to-day smaller than in most European countries. No special liquor legislation has been enacted.

ROUMANIA.

In 1907 public sentiment aroused by the National Temperance League and the Good Templars, pressed the Government to enact a measure to check the spread of alcoholism. A bill was introduced providing for the abolition of credit sales and sales to minors, for the punishing of drunkenness, and for the reduction of saloons. The bill failed to become law in this session, but another measure embodying similar provisions was enacted in 1908.

TURKEY.

Sobriety is enjoined upon the Turks by their religion, so that the country is virtually a prohibition area. The use of intoxicants in Turkey is largely due to other peoples than the natives. Early in the war the Sultan decreed that drunkenness should be regarded as a crime, subject to trial and condemnation by court martial.

GERMANY.

Temperance agitation in Germany has been chiefly directed against over-indulgence in spirituous liquors, very little restriction of any kind having been placed on beer and wine. Before the war, the business of brewing beer ranked second in importance among German industries.

Numerous scientific investigations carried on by German experts have materially aided the progress of the anti-alcohol movement in all countries.

In 1837, under royal auspices, the German Temperance Society, an organization advocating moderation, was founded following the visit of Robert Baird, an American, who succeeded in arousing the people of the large towns in Northern Germany. A number of branches were formed and carried on good work until the revolution of 1848. In 1883, a Society Against the Abuse of Alcoholic Drinks was formed, but neither of these organizations attempted to do anything to diminish the use of beer or wine. Good Templary, established in the same year, spread into Germany from Denmark and made good progress among the spirit-drinkers of Northern Germany. The International Blue Cross Temperance Society and the Woman's Christian Temperance Union also have well-organized sections in the country.

In 1912, a local option petition, which filled nineteen large volumes and contained over half a million signatures, was presented to the Reichstag, but no legislative action was taken regarding it.

During the fall of 1914, while the troops were mobilizing, orders were issued forbidding the sale of alcoholic liquors in German towns. In the following spring, local authorities throughout the empire were empowered to curtail or forbid the sale of intoxicants.

The scarcity of foodstuffs was responsible for an order limiting the beer production for 1917 to twenty-five per cent. of that of normal times, except in Bavaria, where thirty-five per cent. was allowed. The brewers were, however, able to obtain grain for only about fourteen per cent. of the quota allotted them. An Associated Press despatch from Zurich, Switzerland, in January, 1918, reported that the whole brewing industry had been brought to a standstill. The production of spirits as well as the production of malt liquors was greatly reduced during the war

AUSTRIA-HUNGARY.

Before the great war there were few legal prohibitive measures operative in the Dual Monarchy. The forces striving to eliminate drunkenness are concentrated in the Austrian Society for Checking Inebriety, which was founded in 1884, and has secured the allegiance of a number of eminent men. The society seeks to restrain the abuse of alcoholic liquors, especially of ardent spirits, without aiming at the diffusion of total abstinence principles. It did, however, in 1890, forward teetotalism among the Ruthenian peasants of Galicia and Bukowina.

Since 1902, temperance instruction has had a place on the curriculum of the primary schools, and in 1912 the Minister of Education enjoined such teaching for all normal school students.

As war measures, restrictions were placed on the manufacture of beer and distilled beverages, and the hours of sale were considerably shortened.

SWITZERLAND.

Early in the nineteenth century, a number of temperance societies appear to have existed in Switzerland, but none of them seem to have been long-lived or to have accomplished much of permanent value in their work of reclaiming drunkards. About 1875, renewed efforts were made to found societies on the moderation principle, but the first total abstinence organization was the Blue Cross Temperance Society started in Geneva in 1877. At Zurich in 1890, a society was organized of which Dr. Forel and Dr. von Bunge are the leading men. This association, not content with enjoining total abstinence upon its members, aims at prohibition on purely hygienic and economic grounds. Finally in 1892, the Swiss Patriotic League against Alcoholism came into existence with the avowed purpose of fighting the liquor traffic by legal, civil, and educational means.

In 1908, a bill providing for the prohibition of the manufacture, importation, and sale of absinthe, received the approval of both Houses of Parliament and was submitted to the people for ratification. The vote was as follows:

For the prohibition of absinthe.. 241,078
Against   "   "   138,669

Majority for prohibition   102,409

The food shortage in 1917 occasioned the presentation to Parliament of a petition signed by over 340,000 persons, asking that the use of rice for malting be prohibited and that the supply of other food materials be greatly curtailed. No legislative action seems to have followed this request. Switzerland is practically the only country in the world where fermented liquors are not taxed either directly or indirectly by the national Government.

ITALY.

The great problem which confronts the temperance workers of Italy is that of effectively combating the wine-drinking habit, which until recently was almost universal. The nation produces one-third of all the wine used in the world. There are few measures regulating the liquor traffic in Italy. The retail trade in wines and liquors for consumption on the premises has been made subject to municipal license and taxation. Stringent laws are in force against the adulteration of wines. During the war, the sale of absinthe and sale to children under 16 years, were absolutely forbidden.

WORLD PROGRESS.

INDIA.

The largest number of the people of India are Hindus, by whose religious faith the use of intoxicants is strictly forbidden. Moreover, the Moslems, who conquered Northern India about 1000 A.D., and whose religion now numbers 66,000,000 followers in India, are enjoined to total abstinence by the Koran. Among the aboriginal tribes of India, however, drinking is very common, especially at feasts and on religious holidays. As the people of India have come into contact with western civilization and western society, an increasing tolerance of alcoholic indulgence has been noticeable, and social and religious restrictions on drinking have been gradually relaxed.

Intoxicating liquors are divided into two classes by the Excise Department—foreign and native. The foreign liquors are spirits and beer, while the native liquors are tody, made from the juice of the palm, and drinks made from hemp and other plants. In 1889, Lord Crewe, Secretary of State for India, laid down the following principles for the Indian excise·

1. Any extension of the drink habit must be discouraged.
2. Taxation must be as high as possible without encouraging illicit manufacture and sale.
3. Subject to these considerations the maximum revenue must be raised from the minimum consumption of liquor.

Rev. Stephen H. Kearsey, in an article on the "Rise, Progress and Present Condition of the Temperance Cause in India," written in 1892, said:

The Government of India have from time to time passed measures for the regulating of the traffic in intoxicants. The two principal systems being the Sudder Distillery and the Out-still, the former being a central still under the Government, no one else but the officer in charge was allowed to distil spirits in the district, and no one without a special permit was allowed to take more than one quart away at any one time. The latter is more lax, the monopoly being sold by auction to the highest bidder, who farms it out, and, of course, uses all means in his power to push the sale; the natives are often led to believe that it was a government order that the people should drink. Sometimes very sad cases occur from the giving away of surplus liquor just before the auction, in order to show a greater consumption in a given period to run up the price. The out-still system has caused an increase in intemperance. We are glad to note that the out-still system has been replaced by the distillery system with good results.

In 1899, a notable memorial asking for prohibition for Indians was presented to the Government by more than 100 editors and 300 planters. Its provisions were:

1. Prohibition of sale of intoxicating beverages to and by natives.
2. Prohibition of distillation of intoxicating beverages.
3. Permission of the home-brewing of fermented beverages by those long accustomed to their use.
4. Tax on home-brewed fermented liquors if a tax was considered necessary.

The memorial helped to awaken public sentiment but failed to produce any action on the part of the Government.

Repeatedly the Government, which establishes liquor shops where it chooses, announced that its policy was the subordinating of all consideration of revenue to an effort to minimize the temptation of those who do not drink, and the discouraging of excess among those who do. But the Government's revenue from the sale of drink has steadily increased. In 1905, Lord Curzon, Viceroy of India, appointed a commission of officials to inquire into the excise administration. In their report, published in December, 1906, the committee admitted that the consumption of imported liquors was increasing enormously, and recommended higher import duties and limitation of the number of liquor shops.

The agitation for reform was continued by natives and missionaries. In 1912, a deputation from the Anglo-Indian Temperance Association waited upon the Secretary of State.

WORLD PROGRESS.

The speakers, Hon. G. K. Gokhale, C.I.E., and Hon. D. P. Sarvadhikary, M.A., both distinguished statesmen, pointed out that the consumption of liquor was contrary to the sentiment of the majority of people in India; that such consumption was increasing; and that the British Government derived extremely large revenue from the traffic. They urged that the number of liquor shops be reduced, and that the hours for sale be shortened. The Secretary of State admitted the reasonableness of the requests presented to him, and promised to refer the suggestions to the Government of India.

In the same year the Government established "Excise Advisory Committees," composed of "official and non-official members to recommend the withdrawal of licenses." Between 1912 and 1914, 326 such committees were established. In 1916, all municipal boards were made excise advisory committees. They were empowered only to recommend. The excise officers accept or reject the recommendation, and when in April, 1918, Hindu leaders advocated giving these advisory committees power to decide the number and location of liquor shops, the government representative opposed the proposition in the Legislative Council, and it was lost by a close vote. In certain sections, a decided reduction of liquor licenses has resulted. For example, the first year after the creation of local advisory committees in the Bombay presidency, the reduction amounted to 77; in Bengal, the number was decreased by 100; and in Calcutta by 26.

The mightiest force moving for temperance in India is the Christian missionary, who is putting forth strenuous efforts to stem the tide of the drink habit which is rising in the Indian Christian communities through the example of European society in India. Temperance instruction is given in the schools. The Indian and European societies at work in the country for the promotion of temperance are federated in the Anglo-Indian Temperance Association, which issues a well-edited journal called *Abkari* and has the following objective:

PROHIBITION IN CANADA.

1. To save India from the alarming growth of the drinking habits of the population, which is shown by the fact that the revenue derived by the Indian Government from the sale of intoxicants rose from 1,561,000 pounds sterling in 1874-5 to 8,498,000 pounds sterling in 1915-16, the annual yield having been more than quintupled in forty years.

2. To establish societies in every Indian city and town; engage organizing lecturers in every province; circulate suitable literature, and extend in every direction the work which has already been accomplished, until the whole of India is brought under the influence of the temperance movement.

3. To educate public opinion at home as to the evils with which India is threatened in consequence of the rapidly increasing consumption of intoxicants.

4. The great end of the association is the promotion throughout India of total abstinence principles among all classes; a watchful criticism of the excise administration; the encouragement of the principle of local option; and the final extinction of the traffic in alcoholic liquors, opium, and other intoxicating drugs.

CHINA.

As the use of intoxicating liquors is not extensive in China, the alcohol question has been completely overshadowed by the opium menace. An edict was issued by the Emperor of China in 459 B.C., prohibiting the use of intoxicants, and ever since that time China has been under prohibition. Liquor dealers of foreign countries are, however, endeavoring with some success to fasten drinking customs upon the Mongolian race.

JAPAN.

The national drink of the Japanese, "saké" is brewed from rice and varies in alcoholic content from 4 to 50 per cent. The brewing industry was brought from Korea and has existed since the beginning of the Christian era, but it has never, in Japan, reached the importance that attaches

WORLD PROGRESS.

to the manufacture of beer in Europe. A large proportion of the population of Japan are abstainers because of religious conviction, the faiths of Buddha and Confucius both prohibiting the use of alcoholic liquors.

In 1868, when Japan was thrown open to foreigners, European and American traders rushed to the country, introduced their social usages, and allowed the liquor traffic with its attendant evils to enter the Empire. A large number of breweries and distilleries sprang up, and the consumption of these foreign liquors has increased to an alarming extent.

In the Russo-Japanese war (1904-1905), the superiority of the Japanese army was largely due to its sobriety. Between 1907 and 1918, however, several bills to prohibit the sale of alcoholic liquors to all persons under 20 years of age, after passing the Lower House, were thrown out by the Upper House. Official notices to liquor dealers have been issued by the Department of Education, warning them not to sell to young people.

The temperance organizations of Japan, formed for the purpose of combating the growing alcoholization of the country, have amalgamated to form the Japanese National Temperance League, which has over 100 affiliated societies in the nation.

KOREA.

There are practically no restrictions on the liquor traffic in Korea, both drinking and drunkenness being very prevalent.

OTHER ASIATIC COUNTRIES.

The following account of the prohibition situation in other Asiatic countries is given in the Anti-Saloon League Year Book for 1918:

In Arabia, the new ruler, Hussain, established by the revolt against the Sultan, has prohibited all alcoholic liquors throughout his domain. By order of the government, the authorities of Djeddah seized and destroyed thousands of bottles of alcoholic liquors. He also requested the representatives of the various European governments to notify the merchants of their respective countries that from the date of the order the Arabian Government would not permit any intoxicants to enter its borders.

Prior to 1914 no country in Asia was cursed by the liquor traffic more than Siberia. Russian vodka flooded this great section of the Russian Empire and the Government itself did not hesitate to promote the sale of liquor wherever possible. By virtue of the Czar's decree, however, prohibiting the sale of vodka throughout the Empire, a vast change has taken place in Siberia, and the beneficial results of prohibition on the peasantry and Siberian life and institutions are to be seen on every hand.

In Ceylon a temperance pledge-signing movement which swept over the island in 1904, resulted in a total abstinence pledge being signed by 190,000 persons.

Persia has, perhaps, suffered as much or more in proportion to its size, from the liquor traffic than any other country of middle or southern Asia. In spite of the efforts of Mohammedan leaders, the people have become debauched—first through the importation of liquors from Europe and more lately through the production of spirits in the local distilleries which have been established.

Siam is closely following in the footsteps of Persia. The sale and manufacture of alcohol, as well as opium, is in the hands of the government.

In the Philippine Islands the liquor traffic has grown to an alarming extent since those islands have been under the United States Government. With practically every ship taking missionaries, school teachers and physicians from America to the Philippines, there goes a sufficient amount of intoxicating liquors to do more harm in a few months than can be offset by the work of the missionaries, schools and health boards in several years.

Asia, in fact, presents a continent once under absolute prohibition with the exception of Siberia. To-day, however, the Asiatic nations are gradually yielding to Western intoxicants and their sure results.

WORLD PROGRESS.

AFRICA.

In 1889 1890 an International Conference was held in Brussels to consider what measures should be adopted regarding the slave trade and the liquor traffic in Africa. The results of the deliberations of this conference were embodied in the Brussels General Act of 1890, of which the following nations were signatories: Belgium, The Netherlands, France, Great Britain, Norway, Sweden, Germany Austria, Hungary, The Congo, Italy, Portugal, Spain, Russia, Turkey, Persia, the United States of America and Zanzibar. Chapter VI of the act provided for the prohibition of importation and manufacture of spirits in all Central Africa, lying between what is usually known as North and South Africa. The text of Chapter VI is as follows:

Article XC.—Justly anxious about the moral and material consequences which the abuse of spirituous liquors entails on the native population, the Signatory Powers have agreed to apply the provisions of articles XCI, XCII, XCIII, within a zone extending from 20th degree north latitude to the 22nd degree south latitude, and bounded by the Atlantic Ocean on the west and by the Indian Ocean on the east, with its dependencies, comprising the islands adjacent to the mainland, up to 100 sea miles from the shore.

Article XCI.—In the districts of this zone where it shall be ascertained that, either on account of religious beliefs or from other motives, the use of distilled liquors does not exist or has not been developed, the Powers shall prohibit their importation. The manufacture of distilled liquors there shall be equally prohibited.

Each Power shall determine the limits of the zone of prohibition of alcoholic liquors in its possession or protectorates, and shall be bound to notify the limits thereof to the other Powers, within the space of six months. The above prohibition can only be suspended in the case of limited quantities destined for the consumption of the non-native population and imported under the regime and conditions determined by each government.

Article XCII.—The Powers having possessions or exercising protectorates in the region of the zone, which are not placed

PROHIBITION IN CANADA.

under the action of the prohibition, and into which alcoholic liquors are at present either freely imported or pay an import duty of less than 15 francs (12s. 8½d. or $3.55) per hectoliter (nearly 22½ imperial gallons) at 50 degrees Centigrade, undertake to levy on these alcoholic liquors an import duty of 15 francs per hectoliter at 50 degrees Centigrade for three years after the present general act comes into force. At the expiration of this period, the duty may be increased to 25 francs (19s. 9½d., or $5) during a fresh period of three years. At the end of the sixth year, it shall be submitted to revision, taking as a basis the average results produced by these tariffs, for the purpose of then fixing, if possible, a minimum duty throughout the whole extent of the zone when the prohibition referred to in article XCI is not in force.

The Powers have the right of maintaining and increasing the duties beyond the minimum fixed by the present article in those regions where they already possess that right.

Article XCIII.—The distilled liquors manufactured in the regions referred to in article XCII, and intended for inland consumption, shall be subject to an excise duty. This excise duty, the collection of which the Powers undertake to ensure as far as possible, shall not be lower than the minimum import duty fixed by article XCII.

Article XCIV.—Signatory Powers having in Africa possessions contiguous to the zone specified in article XC, undertake to adopt the necessary measures for preventing the introduction of spirituous liquors within the territories of the said zone by their inland frontiers.

Article XCV.—The Powers shall communicate to each other, through the office at Brussels, and according to the terms of chapter V, information relating to the traffic in alcoholic liquors within their respective territories.

The above six articles were ratified by all the Powers and came into force in July, 1901.

In 1910, at the International Missionary Conference, held in Edinburgh, the question of the liquor traffic in Africa was discussed and a memorial to the various nations which had endorsed the Brussels General Act was drawn up and signed by 492 delegates from Europe, 273 from America, 130 from

WORLD PROGRESS.

Asia, 25 from Africa, 12 from Australia, and five others. The petitioners urged that, in view of the fact that new regions of Africa were being brought within the sphere of commercial activity by the opening up of railways, the Great Powers should again meet and take up the alcohol question. In July, 1911, an influential deputation presented the memorial to the Hon. Mr. Harcourt, Secretary of State for the Colonies, who promised that His Majesty's Government would call another meeting of the Brussels Conference, and would reserve the right to take further steps in British Africa, if necessary, than the other Powers were prepared to do.

The International Conference met again in Brussels in 1912, and heard the request of the International Federation for the Protection of the Native Races from the Liquor Traffic. They pointed out that the results obtained from the Act of 1890 were insufficient for several causes, the chief of which were, on the one hand, the diminution in the net cost of spirits and the cost of their transport and, on the other hand, the increasing value of native labor. Under these conditions they urged the extension of the prohibition zone, increase of customs and excise duties, strict supervision over the quality of spirits, reduction of the alcoholic content of liquors, and prohibition of drinks of the absinthe type. No action was taken, however, by the Conference of 1912.

In the Belgian Congo, prohibition, which however does not apply to beer and native wines, was enacted in 1912. In the following year, the rum shops of Angola, the most ancient of Portuguese possessions in Africa, were closed. Madagascar had prohibition by an edict of the Queen issued in 1876; but when, twenty years later, the Queen was deposed and France gained sovereignty over the island, the traffic was restored to increase the market for French wines.

Sir Harry Johnston, the eminent British Administrator of Africa, in April, 1918, described the situation in British Africa in these words:

PROHIBITION IN CANADA.

"The British West African possessions are divided as follows in their relation toward alcohol: Nearly all the territory we know as Sierra Leone, i.e., the protectorate as compared with the tiny coast fringe colony, is prohibition, at the wish of its native chiefs. The Gold Coast Colony and Ashanti are steeped in alcohol, to their grievous detriment, but the larger 'Northern Territories' behind are prohibition, also at the wish of their chiefs and peoples, who are Mohammedan. South Nigeria, with the exception of some districts, is open to alcohol; the much vaster region of Northern Nigeria, with the exception of some districts, is closed to it. As regards other parts of British Africa, the protectorates of Somaliland, British East Africa, Uganda, 'German' East Africa (pro tem), Nyasal and Northern Rhodesia, are all closed to alcohol (so far as the natives are concerned), so also is British Bechuanaland and to some extent Basutoland. The imports into Gambia mainly affect the gin-sodden 'colony' of the Gambia estuary; the strips along the river inland are less injured by alcohol because the population is mainly Mohammedan and abstaining."

AUSTRALIA.

The first Australian temperance society was formed in Sydney in 1838. Since that time most of the American and English total abstinence societies have had their counterparts in Australia. The New South Wales Alliance, following in the footsteps of the United Kingdom Alliance, was founded in 1857. In each state, the Alliance represents the forces at work to dethrone alcohol. The Australian Alliance Prohibition Council, composed of representatives of the various state alliances, sought to obtain prohibition for the period of the war and of repatriation, and aims to secure an amendment to the federal constitution which would prohibit the manufacture, sale and importation of alcoholic beverages.

On January 10, 1918, the Senate appointed a Select Committee to inquire into the extent to which intoxicating liquor was affecting the outgoing and returning soldiers. Evidence was taken in Melbourne, Adelaide, Perth, Hobart,

WORLD PROGRESS.

Launceston, Sydney, and Brisbane, and almost all of the witnesses admitted that drink had been a hindance in prosecuting the war.

Most of the states of the Australian Commonwealth have local option laws, but these require a three-fifths majority to prevail. The following is an outline of the situation in the various states:

NEW SOUTH WALES.

The political party which came into power after the general election of 1903 was pledged to introduce a measure giving to the people veto over the liquor traffic. The bill introduced at the next session, passed the Assembly by a large majority but encountered more strenuous opposition in the Council where an attempt was made to insert a clause providing for compensation of the liquor dealers. It was finally passed, without compensation, by a majority of one and became law on January 1, 1906. By the provisions of the act all liquor saloons were to be closed on Sundays and on parliamentary election days. Persons under 17 years of age were forbidden to enter liquor bars, and barmaids under 21 years could not be employed. Clubs selling liquor were brought under the regulation and the law preventing the sale of intoxicants to aborigines and other colored people, was strengthened. The most important clause contained in the act, however, provided for a vote at each general election, which comes on automatically every three years, on the issues of continuance, reduction, or no-license. Both men and women are entitled to vote. To carry no-license, 60 per cent. of all the votes cast must be in favor of prohibition. If no-license is not carried, the votes for it are added to those recorded for reduction, and if the combined vote constitutes a majority, a reduction of from 12 to 25 per cent. of licenses in electorates may be effected. Four hundred licenses have been wiped out in this way. Owing to the handicap of the three-fifths requirement, no-license has not carried in any of the 90 electorates, although 20 have decided for it by a majority vote.

PROHIBITION IN CANADA.

In 1916, in New South Wales a popular vote was taken to determine at what hours the bars should be closed and the result was, 347,494 votes for six o'clock closing, and 209,404 votes for all later hours.

In addition to co-operating with the prohibition organizations of the other states to obtain Commonwealth prohibitiou, the Alliance of the Mother State is directing its energies through its weekly paper, *Grit,* and by other means, toward securing a vote on state-wide prohibition, the issue to be decided by a straight majority vote.

VICTORIA.

The laws of Victoria forbid the sale of liquor to natives or to children under eighteen. Bars are closed all day Sunday and at 6 p.m. every other day. Victoria has a Licensing Reduction Board empowered to reduce down to the statutory number, which is 1 to 500. The publicans themselves provided a compensation fund so that the Board, in reducing licenses, had to wait until the liquor traffic provided the compensation. From January 1, 1917, except in a few special cases, the number of victuallers', grocers', or wine licenses or club certificates, has not been permitted to exceed the number then in existence.

The first general local option poll on the question of continuance, reduction, and prohibition will be taken in 1920, simultaneously with the next general election, and thereafter a vote will be taken at each general election provided that a period longer than 18 months elapses between polls. The Victorian Alliance, organized in 1881, is making splendid preparations for the vote, and the monthly paper, the *Advance,* is proving of great value.

SOUTH AUSTRALIA.

South Australia has power to secure, by local option, reduction of licenses. Alcoholic liquors must not be sold to natives or children under 18 years; children under 16 are not permitted on licensed premises. The six o'clock closing law became effective on March 27, 1916. The South Australian Alliance reports that literature is being circulated in large quantities and that the circulation of the organization's monthly journal, *The Patriot,* has been doubled.

The Queensland Licensing Act of 1885 provided that no new license could be issued except by a vote of a majority of electors. One-tenth of the ratepayers could demand a poll on reduction of licenses or prohibition. The latter required a three-fifths majority to prevail. By the Denham Act of 1912 amending the act of 1885, local option polls could be held every three years on reduction of licenses by one-fourth of the existing number, the polls to be decided by a majority vote.

Numerous requests for six o'clock closing have been presented to Parliament, urging the Government to take the necessary steps to enact such a measure, but these petitions were consistently refused. In July, 1918, Mr. P. M. Bayley, M.L.A., moved that liquor bars be closed in Queensland, as in the other states of Australia, at six o'clock for the period of the war and six months thereafter; but this motion too was side-tracked, and the bars are still open from 6 a.m. to 11 p.m.

Under the War Precautions Act the Federal Government made it illegal to supply soldiers with liquor after 8 p.m. or to furnish liquor to any invalid soldier while on leave from any hospital. During the passing of troop trains, all bars within a mile of the station were closed.

In 1925, a vote on absolute prohibition for which a three-fifths majority is required, will be taken.

TASMANIA.

It is illegal for a publican to supply liquor to anyone under 21 years of age. Six o'clock closing is in force. A bill to forbid treating was passed by the Legislative Council in 1917, but was summarily rejected by the Assembly. The local option polls which had been provided for by an act of 1908 took place in 1917, but proved abortive, owing to the

PROHIBITION IN CANADA.

improper drafting of the act. The Premier, the Hon. W. H. Lee, in 1918 introduced a bill to remove the objectionable features of the old act and to add the option of prohibition.

WEST AUSTRALIA.

Barmaids, unless registered prior to 1910, are prohibited. Local option will come into force in 1921, when a majority of three-fifths will be required to prohibit the liquor saloon.

NEW ZEALAND.

In 1894, the first local option poll was taken. One of the conditions of the vote was that one-half of the voters on the roll were obliged to vote or the poll would be void. Three questions were to be voted upon: (*a*) continuance; (*b*) reduction; (*c*) no-license. If (*c*) failed to carry, the votes for no-license could be added to (*b*) to secure reduction. In 1894 the vote was: continuance, 41,165; reduction, 15,856; no-license, 48,856.

The New Zealand Parliament in the same year changed the Local Option Act, giving a vote to every adult male and female, and arranging for a poll to be taken at every general Dominion election. A three-fifths majority was required to abolish the liquor traffic. Under the new law, a voter might vote for two out of the three questions, but there was no adding together of votes. The votes taken under this law resulted as follows:

Year.	Continuance.	Reduction.	No-license.
1896	139,580	94,555	98,312
1899	143,962	109,449	120,542
1902	148,449	132,249	151,524
1905	182,884	151,057	198,765
1908	118,140	162,562	221,471

In 1911, the first voting upon national prohibition was held in New Zealand. The result of the poll was: for prohibition, 259,943; for continuance, 205,661. The vote for total prohibition was 55.8 per cent. of the total vote, but 60 per cent. was necessary for prohibition to prevail.

In 1914, in the period of unrest following the outbreak of war, another poll was taken, the figures of the vote being, for prohibition, 247,217; for continuance, 257,442.

During the war, regulations were secured to prohibit treating or "shouting," as it is called, on or about licensed premises. Barmaids were eliminated, six o'clock closing was enacted, and the sale of liquor to persons under 21 was forbidden. Wet canteens in military camps were prohibited by the Minister of Defence.

The Government appointed a National Efficiency Board, consisting of men of wide business knowledge and recognized ability, to take stock of the Dominion and its needs. After the examination of more than 60 witnesses from various classes of the community, the Board in a memorandum dated July 9, 1917 (published as a white paper) stated that, "From a National Efficiency point of view, the Board is convinced that it would be beneficial to the nation and conducive to the well-being of the people that the importation, manufacture, and sale of wines, beer and spirituous liquors (including medicinal preparations containing alcohol) should be prohibited." Under the Dominion law, if national prohibition were carried, the liquor trade would receive four years' notice in lieu of compensation. The Board recommended that compensation be given instead of time.

The New Zealand Alliance decided to accept the recommendations of the National Efficiency Board, and to ask Parliament for a special poll on prohibition instead of having the vote postponed until the next general election, which would not take place until the end of the year. The petition asking for a poll on these prosposals was signed by 240,000 persons. The liquor traffic circulated a counter petition which was padded until it was larger than that of the prohibitionists. The dishonesty in securing and forging signatures was overdone, however, and the fact was too apparent to deceive anyone. The liquor petition asked that "State

PROHIBITION IN CANADA.

Control" be placed upon the ballot paper, along with "Continuance" and "Prohibition."

Parliament fixed the voting date as April 10, 1919, and provided that the ballot should read as follows:

1. I vote for national continuance.
2. I vote for prohibition with compensation.

If prohibition carried, it was to come into effect at an early date; but if continuance carried, the question was to be voted upon in the regular way at the general election, which would probably be in November, when there should be three issues on the voting paper: Continuance, State Control, and Prohibition without Compensation.

The campaign cry of the New Zealand Alliance was "Strike out the top line." A section of the temperance people had such strong objection to the payment of compensation that they either abstained from voting, or voted for continuance, knowing that, provided prohibition did not carry in the pending election, another opportunity for a vote upon the straight issue would be afforded in about six months.

The result of the poll of April 10th was, according to an Associated Press despatch from Wellington, N.Z., dated April 22nd, a majority of 1,800 against prohibition.

INTERNATIONAL CO-OPERATION.

In November, 1918, a great convention of prohibition workers was called by the Anti-Saloon League of America to meet in Columbus, Ohio. Delegates from Great Britian, China, India, Mexico, and Canada were present, and at this assemblage definite plans for co-operative action to secure world-wide prohibition were determined upon.

The conviction repeatedly voiced by the 400 or 500 delegates to this conference was that the present is a psychological moment to launch a world-wide prohibition. The keynote of the addresses delivered in the various sessions

WORLD PROGRESS.

was that no nation can live unto itself, that the welfare of the one is the welfare of all. This idea was embodied in the resolutions adopted by the convention in the following language:

Rejoicing in the widening rule of democracy, we are conscious that the idealism of democracy is not so much structural as it is spiritual, and democracy will endure not fundamentally because the people rule, but to the extent that they rule in righteousness. That the world may be made safe for democracy we need a democracy that is safe for the world, and by every rule of right we must have a democracy here and in all lands that is free from the curse of the traffic in intoxicating liquors.

The League was authorized to formulate and carry into effect plans for an international league of temperance workers, and was empowered to render such assistance, financial and otherwise, as might be deemed advisable in promoting prohibition in other countries.

In April, 1919, the Anti-Saloon League of America and the Council of the Dominion Alliance of Canada united in the following convention call:

WORLD PROHIBITION CONFERENCE.

The Anti-Saloon League of America and the Council of the Dominion Alliance of Canada hereby unite in calling a World Prohibition Conference, to meet in Toronto, Canada, Wednesday and Thursday, May 21st and 22nd, and in Washington, D.C., Thursday, June 3rd, and following days.

The world is astir these days. Mighty reform impulses are moving humanity to higher moral ground. Constructive national reformers are seeking to make democracy safe for the world by casting out those debilitating and disintegrating forces that prevent communities from developing and putting forth their full strength.

In the United States of America and the Dominion of Canada, this great uplift movement has reached such proportions and achieved such success that incalculable benefits have come to many communities, and the ultimate extinction of the beverage drink traffic is in sight.

The lessons from practical experience that have come through the operation of local and state prohibitory laws, we desire to

PROHIBITION IN CANADA.

share with the peoples of the world, and with hearty hospitality invite representatives of all nations to " come and see."

No great problem which has to do with human welfare can be solved fully and permanently by a single nation, regardless of others. Races and nations alike are subject to that high law of international ethics which insists that the solution by any people of a problem which concerns the world carries with it the duty and responsibility of passing on such solution to others.

World conditions present an unparalleled opportunity for the prompt organization and speedy success of such a movement for moral betterment as that represented by the Anti-Liquor Crusade. Hearts have been softened and chastened by the cataclysm through which the nations have passed. Humanity has a larger vision; men are thinking and talking in world terms, and are prepared for a bigger programme of reform. The time is opportune for a great aggressive world drive against the drink traffic.

The last word as to methods in temperance work has not yet been spoken, and no organization or nation holds all the truth or all of the elements of success, but one great objective unites us: we seek a saloonless and drinkless world. We desire to aid the moral regeneration of humanity through the elimination of the curse of intemperance.

Divesting ourselves of all pride of method, we ask only that representative workers and helpers come together in a spirit of cordial comradeship to see and tell what has been and can be done and how; then to plan for a finer and bigger programme than ever yet has been attempted. America and Canada throw open their doors. Neither race, language, color, nor creed is a bar to our desire to serve. An earnest invitation is given. A cordial welcome will be extended to the prohibition workers of the world.

On behalf of the Anti-Saloon League of America,

HOWARD H. RUSSELL,	PURLEY A. BAKER,
Associate Superintendent.	*General Superintendent.*

ERNEST H. CHERRINGTON,
Secretary Executive Committee.

On behalf of the Council of the Dominion Alliance,

MILES VOKES,	WM. H. ORR,	BEN. H. SPENCE,
President.	*Treasurer.*	*Secretary.*

APPENDICES.

CONTENTS.

		PAGE
I.	Constitution of Dominion Alliance	569
II.	Constitution of Ontario Branch	571
III.	Jacob Spence	573
IV.	First Meeting of Dominion Alliance	574
V.	Scott Act Voting	575
VI.	Results of Ontario Plebiscite	579
VII.	Text of Privy Council Decision	581
VIII.	Dominion Alliance Manifesto, 1904	584
IX.	Liquor Licenses in Ontario . .	587
X.	Premier Hearst's Speech . .	588
XI.	Ontario Temperance Act . .	596
XII.	Dominion Prohibition Committee Manifesto, 1917	604
XIII.	Order in Council, 1917 . . .	609
XIV.	Milestones of Temperance . .	612

APPENDIX I.

CONSTITUTION OF THE COUNCIL OF THE ALLIANCE.

Article I.—Name.

The name of this organization shall be the Council of the Dominion Alliance for the total Suppression of the Liquor Traffic.

II.—Object.

The object of this Council of the Dominion Alliance shall be the immediate prohibition of the liquor traffic.

III.—Members.

This Council shall be composed of its officers and representatives of bodies in sympathy with the object of the Alliance as follows:

1. Churches and other bodies having a Dominion organization each to the number of six with one additional for each twenty thousand above twenty thousand members of the body.
2. Churches not having a Dominion organization each to the number of two and one additional for every twenty thousand members of the body.
3. Provincial branches of the Alliance and other analogous bodies to the number in Ontario of twenty, in Quebec of sixteen, in New Brunswick of eight, in Prince Edward Island of five, in Nova Scotia, Manitoba, Saskatchewan, Alberta, and British Columbia of ten each.
4. Synods, Conferences or other similar church organizations, four each.
5. Provincial organizations of the Woman's Christian Temperance Union, Sons of Temperance, Independent Order of Good Templars, Royal Templars of Temperance, or other provincial temperance bodies, four each.

And the General Secretaries of provincial branches of the Alliance and analogous bodies.

IV.—Annual Meeting.

The Council of the Alliance shall meet annually for the transaction of business at such time and place as may have been decided on at the previous annual meeting.

V.—Officers.

The officers of the Council shall be a President, two Vice-Presidents for each province, a Corresponding Secretary, a Recording Secretary, and a Treasurer, who shall be elected at the annual meeting.

VI.—Executive Committee.

The officers named, together with twenty-one members of the Council who shall be elected at the annual meeting, and the General Secretaries of provincial branches of the Alliance and analogous bodies, and the Superintendents for the time being of the several religious denom-

APPENDICES.

inational Departments of Temperance and Moral Reform, shall constitute the General Executive, to carry out the decisions of the Council and to attend to necessary business during the interim of sessions. The General Executive shall also convene and arrange for the annual meetings of the Council. The outgoing Executive shall retain office until the close of the annual meeting. The General Executive shall elect its own chairman, who shall preside at its meetings and sign orders and documents drawn in its name. At all meetings of the General Executive five members shall constitute a quorum for the transaction of business.

VII.—Duties of Corresponding Secretary.

The Corresponding Secretary shall, under the direction of the General Executive, assist, by correspondence and otherwise, in organizing and carrying on the work in the various provinces, endeavor to secure the co-operation of leading workers and societies throughout the Dominion, and report to the General Executive when required. He shall also prepare a report for submission to the Council at its annual meeting.

VIII.—Duties of Recording Secretary.

The Recording Secretary shall take the minutes of the meetings of the Council and prepare the same for publication.

IX.—Duties of the Treasurer.

The Treasurer of the Alliance shall receive such funds as are under the control of the Council, distribute the same as instructed by that body only on the order of the Chairman and the Secretary of the Executive Committee, and present a report to the Council at its annual meeting.

X.—Committee on Legislation.

There shall be appointed at the annual meeting a special standing committee of the Council to be known as the Committee on Legislation, composed of members of both Houses of Parliament, and other members of the Council, which shall hold a special meeting at Ottawa during each session of Parliament, to watch and advise concerning legislation.

XI.—Funds of the Council of the Alliance.

The funds of the Council shall be derived as follows: (1) By assessments upon provincial branches of the Alliance made by the Council at its annual meeting or in the form of grants or subscriptions. (2) Collections at public services in connection with the annual meetings of the Council, or at public meetings held under the auspices of the Council or of the General Executive, and at its expense.

XII.—Change of Constitution.

This constitution may be altered at any annual meeting of the Council, provided there are present when such change is made not less than twenty regularly elected representatives from the bodies entitled to send delegates to such meeting.

APPENDICES.

APPENDIX II.

CONSTITUTION OF THE ONTARIO BRANCH, DOMINION ALLIANCE

(Incorporated under Revised Statutes of Ontario.)

NAME.

The name of this organization is "The Ontario Branch of the Dominion Alliance for the Suppression of the Liquor Traffic."

OBJECTS.

The purposes of the society are as follows: To call forth and direct an enlightened public opinion to procure the total and immediate suppression of the traffic in all intoxicating liquors as beverages, and to unite all churches and temperance and moral reform organizations in judicious effort for the attainment of this end.

METHODS.

With this object in view the Alliance shall work for the enactment and enforcement of all available prohibitions and limitations of the liquor traffic, and the election to all legislative and executive political positions of representatives who are known, avowed and trustworthy supporters of the principles and methods of the Alliance.

MEMBERSHIP.

This branch of the Alliance shall be composed of its Executive Committee, and delegates chosen to represent churches, temperance societies, and other organizations which are in sympathy with the objects and methods of the Alliance, on the basis hereinafter provided.

The plan of representation is as follows: Every church and society to be entitled to two representatives, and each church or society having more than fifty members to be entitled to an additional delegate for each fifty or fractional part of fifty after the first full fifty members.

The following organizations are to be entitled to representation on the basis named: Church congregations, branches of the W.C.T.U., Divisions of the Sons of Temperance, Lodges of the I.O.G.T., Councils of the R. T. of T., branches of the League of the Cross, Prohibition Clubs, and other prohibition or temperance organizations, Young Men's Christian Associations, Salvation Army Corps, Societies of Christian Endeavor, Epworth Leagues, Presbyterian Guilds, Baptist Young People's Unions, Organized Adult Bible classes, branches of St. Andrew's Brotherhood, and other men's organizations and young people's associations in connection with church work.

Ontario members of the Council of the Dominion Alliance, elected from representative ecclesiastical, temperance, and prohibition bodies, Ontario members of Parliament, and members of the Provincial Legislature in favor of the suppression of the liquor traffic shall also be members.

APPENDICES.

THE ALLIANCE COUNCIL.

This branch of the Alliance shall recognize the Council of the Dominion Alliance as the bond of union between the several provincial branches, and shall co-operate with it on questions relating to temperance legislation for the Dominion and interprovincial work; and the political platform of the Dominion Alliance, and the declaration of principles of the same body shall be accepted by this branch of the Alliance, and carried out as far as practicable.

OFFICERS.

The officers of this society shall be an honorary president, a president, vice-presidents, a secretary, and a treasurer. They shall be elected yearly at the annual meeting, and shall hold office for one year and until their successors are elected.

Presidents of county Alliances shall be *ex officio*, vice-presidents of the Alliance.

EXECUTIVE.

The Executive Committee shall consist of the officers named, the presiding officer of each, or some other person appointed by the Presbyterian Synod, Methodist Conference, Provincial Baptist Union, Congregational Union, Anglican Diocese, Roman Catholic Diocese, and of every other Ontario church body having a membership of not less than one thousand; the chairman and permanent secretaries of each organized church department of temperance, and moral and social reform, and seventy-five other persons elected at the annual convention. It shall elect its own chairman, and shall meet at the call of the secretary, who shall be under the direction of the chairman of the committee.

The Executive Committee may appoint a Managing Committee, a Finance Committee, a Campaign Committee, a Literature Committee, and any other committees in their discretion. The powers of the same shall be determined by the by-laws of the Executive Committee.

During the interim between conventions of the Alliance, questions of policy that may arise shall be determined by the Executive Committee in conformity to the constitution and the declaration of the annual conventions.

MEETINGS.

The annual convention of the Alliance shall be held each year at a time and place to be fixed by the Executive Committee. Special conventions may be held at the call of the Executive Committee. Twenty-five delegates shall form a quorum for the transaction of business.

BY-LAWS.

The Executive Committee may enact by-laws for the government of its officers, the control of its proceedings and finances, or for any purpose deemed necessary for the carrying out of its objects or the transaction of its business. Such by-laws before becoming operative must be adopted by at least a two-thirds vote at a regularly called meeting of the Executive Committee.

APPENDICES.

AMENDMENTS.

This constitution shall be amended only by a two-thirds vote of properly accredited delegates present and voting at any session of a convention, provided that notice of such amendment shall have been given at a preceding session of such convention.

APPENDIX III.

JACOB SPENCE.

One of the pioneers of the prohibition movement was Jacob Spence. For years he toiled amidst disheartening difficulties. Many veteran workers will yet remember the earnest, quaint, stirring, logical appeals of this hero of the reform. He went through the country holding meetings, preaching and distributing literature. Here is a facsimile reproduction of an old hand bill:

ONTARIO TEMPERANCE AND PROHIBITORY LEAGUE.

JACOB SPENCE

Secretary, will (D V) Lecture on the Prohibition of the Liquor Traffic,

NOVEMBER, 1875.

Monday, 1st............Chatsworth	Monday, 15th............Sunderland
Tuesday, 2nd........Owen Sound	Tuesday, 16th............Wilfred
Wednesday, 3rd........Markdale	Wednesday, 17th......Cannington
Thursday, 4th............Flesherton	Thursday, 18th............Manella
Friday, 5th............Priceville	Friday, 19th............Hartley
Monday, 8th............Ashburn	Saturday, 20th............Cambray
Tuesday, 9th............Port Perry	Monday, 22nd............Argyle
Wednesday, 10th........Greenbank	Tuesday, 23rd............Kirkfield
Thursday, 11th....Victoria Corner	Wednesday, 24th............Bolsover
Friday, 12th....Valentine Corner	Thursday, 25th, Victoria Road, S.
Saturday, 13th............Wick	Friday, 26th............Beaverton

*See Posters for Place and Time of Meetings. (Collection at each. in aid of League Fund.)

Bell & Co., Printers, 13 Adelaide St. East, Toronto.

He had a hand printing press in his own home and the boys of the house were called to serve the cause in their spare time by printing leaflets, cards, etc., which were sent out in hundreds and thousands, and in these early days of the reform were the seed-sowing from which the harvest was afterward reaped.

APPENDICES.

APPENDIX IV.

FIRST MEETING OF DOMINION ALLIANCE.

The first page of the Minute Book of the Dominion Alliance has a signed statement setting out the purpose and plan of the organization; it is given hereinunder with facsimiles of the signatures attached:

THE DOMINION ALLIANCE.

Constituted, September 18th and 19th, 1877.

In response to a numerously signed circular the Dominion Alliance and the Ontario Prohibitory League held special meetings in the City of Toronto on Tuesday and Wednesday, September 18th and 19th, 1877. There was also held a general conference of both bodies to which all prohibitionists were invited. After a prolonged discussion, during which the freest interchange of opinions took place, it was agreed that the bodies named should dissolve (as the Quebec Prohibitory League had previously done) for the purpose of forming a new organization, to be known as "*The Dominion Alliance for the Total Suppression of the Liquor Traffic.*" In view of the dissimilarity of laws in the several provinces and the extent of territory embraced in the sphere of Alliance operations it was deemed absolutely necessary to have Provincial Councils, whose duties should be to superintend Alliance work in reference to provincial legislation and such other efforts as the state of the movement and the circumstances of the various provinces may require. Provision was also made by which all existing temperance organizations could become affiliated with the Alliance. Members of the Alliance in the several counties may form County Auxiliaries.

Whilst the name and principles of the Alliance fully declare its aim to be the Total Suppression of the Liquor Traffic, the Alliance will countenance and as far as possible assist in procuring any practical legislation, either provincial or Dominion, that will be a step towards securing its great object. It will also be regarded as legitimately within the sphere of the operations of the Alliance to endeavor to procure the adoption of the Dunkin Act or any similar law in localities where it is deemed best to, or to assist in securing the practical suppression of the Liquor Traffic by such laws as the one now in force in Nova Scotia.

It being absolutely necessary that those entrusted with the management of the work should be so situated as to permit of frequent consultations, an Executive was formed, composed principally of gentlemen within easy reach of Toronto, which city was selected as the present centre of operations. The General Secretary will act under the immediate direction and supervision of the Executive Committee. The hearty co-operation of all who have hitherto been connected with the bodies

APPENDICES.

now united is earnestly desired to the end that the Executive may be enabled to carry out such plans as shall result in the organization and efficient working of a strong national prohibitory Alliance whose labors and successes will fully justify the action that has been taken.

Signed

J.C. Aikins, Chairman of the Conference
A. Vidal, President of the Alliance
John Cameron, President of the Ontario League
Robert McLean, Secretary of the Ontario League
Thomas Gales, Secretary of the Alliance

Toronto Sept 25th 1877

APPENDIX V.

SCOTT ACT VOTINGS.

*The Ontario Branch of the Dominion Alliance annual meeting in 1880 advised counties not to take action in Canada Temperance Act till decision of Supreme Court had been given.

QUEBEC.

	Date.		Place.		Votes Polled. For.	Votes Polled. Ag'st.	Majority. For.	Majority. Ag'st.
1879	Sept.	11.	Megantic		372	844		472
1880	June	21.	Stanstead	(1)	760	941	....	181
1884	July	17.	Arthabaska	(1)	1,487	235	1,252	
1884	Oct.	9.	Stanstead	(2)	1,300	975	325	...
1884	Nov.	26.	Compton		1,132	1,620	....	488
1885	Jan.	15.	Brome	(1)	1,224	739	485	
1885	Mar.	5.	Drummond	(1)	1,190	170	1,020	
1885	Mar.	19.	Missisquoi		1,142	1,167		25

APPENDICES.

QUEBEC—Continued.

Date.			Place.		Votes Polled. For.	Votes Polled. Ag'st.	Majority. For.	Majority. Ag'st.
1885	April	9.	Chicoutimi		1,157	529	628	
1885	Dec.	29.	Argenteuil		526	601		75
1886	Jan.	28.	Pontiac		533	935		402
1888	May	30.	Stanstead	(3)	1,187	1,329		142
1888	July	12.	Arthabaska	(2)	230	455	....	225
1888	Nov.	29.	Richmond	(1)	1,231	721	510	
1889	June	27.	Drummond	(2)	739	600	139	...
1892	Nov.	17.	Drummond	(3)	505	1,010		505
1893	June	16.	Brome	(2)	1,207	1,073	134	

ONTARIO.

1879	May	29.	Lambton	(1)	2,567	2,352	215	...
1881	April	13	*Hamilton		1,661	2,811	...	1,150
1881	April	19.	Halton	(1)	1,483	1,402	81	...
1881	April	22.	Wentworth		1,611	2,209		598
1881	Nov.	10.	Welland		1,610	2,378		768
1881	Nov.	29.	Lambton	(2)	2,857	2,962	...	105
1884	Mar.	20.	Oxford	(1)	4,073	3,298	775	
	Sept.	9.	Halton	(2)	1,947	1,767	180	
	Oct.	9.	Simcoe	(1)	5,712	4,529	1,183	
	Oct.	16.	(Stormont, Dundas, Glengarry)	(1)	4,590	2,884	1,706	...
	Oct.	23.	Peel		1,805	1,999	...	194
	Oct.	30.	Bruce	(1)	4,501	3,189	1,312	
	Oct.	30.	Huron	(1)	5,957	4,304	1,653	
	Oct.	30.	Dufferin	(1)	1,904	1,109	795	...
	Oct.	30.	Prince Edward	(1)	1,528	1,653	...	125
	Nov.	7.	Renfrew	(1)	1,748	1,018	730	
	Nov.	11.	Norfolk	(1)	2,781	1,694	1,087	
	Dec.	11.	Brant	(1)	1,690	1,088	602	...
	Dec.	11.	*Brantford		646	812	...	166
	Dec.	18.	Leeds & Grenville	....	5,058	4,384	674	
1885	Jan.	15.	Kent		4,368	1,975	2,393	
	Jan.	15.	Lanark	(1)	2,433	2,027	406	
	Jan.	15.	Lennox & Addington	(1)	2,047	2,011	36	
	Jan.	22.	*Guelph	(1)	694	526	168	
	Jan.	29.	Carleton	(1)	2,440	1,747	693	
	Feb.	26.	Durham & Northumberland	(1)	6,050	3,863	2,187	
	Mar.	19.	Elgin	(1)	3,335	1,479	1,856	
	Mar.	19.	Lambton	(3)	4,465	1,546	2,919	
	Mar.	19.	*St. Thomas	(1)	754	743	11	
	April	2.	Wellington	(1)	4,516	3,086	1,430	
1885	May	21.	*Kingston		785	842	...	57
	May	21.	Frontenac	(1)	1,334	693	641	
	June	18.	Lincoln	(1)	2,060	1,490	570	...
1885	June	18.	Perth		3,368	3,536	...	168
	June	18.	Middlesex	(1)	5,745	2,370	3,375	
	July	2.	Hastings		2,369	2,376		7
	July	16.	Haldimand		1,755	2,063		308

APPENDICES.

ONTARIO—Continued.

Date.			Place.		Votes Polled. For.	Votes Polled. Ag'st.	Majority. For.	Majority. Ag'st.
1885	July	16.	Ontario	(1)	3,412	2,061	1,351	
	July	16.	Victoria	(1)	2,467	1,502	965	
	Sept.	24.	Peterboro	(1)	1,915	1,597	318	
	Nov.	19.	*St. Catharines		478	1,066		588
	Nov.	16.	Prescott & Russell	(1)	1,535	3,131		1,596
1888	Mar.	1.	Halton	(3)	1,853	2,050		197
	April	6.	Dufferin	(2)	1,451	1,664		213
	April	6.	Huron	(2)	4,695	6,005		1,310
	April	6.	Norfolk	(2)	2,082	2,804		722
	April	6.	Renfrew	(2)	1,670	2,580		910
	April	6.	Simcoe	(2)	3,894	6,996		3,102
	April	6.	Stormont & Dundas	(2)	3,155	5,298		2,143
	April	19.	Bruce	(2)	3,693	5,085		1,392
1889	April	4.	Brant	(2)	1,289	1,441		152
	April	4.	Frontenac	(2)	1,177	1,690		513
	April	4.	*Guelph	(2)	480	929		449
	April	4.	Lennox & Addington	(2)	1,462	2,066		604
	April	4.	Northumberland & Durham	(2)	4,305	4,932		627
	April	4.	Victoria	(2)	1,560	2,552		992
	April	4.	Ontario	(2)	2,866	4,787		921
	April	4.	Peterboro	(2)	1,564	1,926		362
	April	4.	Lincoln	(2)	1,493	2,090		597
	April	4.	Lanark	(2)	1,538	2,309		771
	April	4.	St. Thomas	(2)	429	1,001		572
	April	4.	Wellington	(2)	2,084	3,944		1,860
	April	19.	Carleton	(2)	1,682	2,407		725
	May	2.	Leeds & Grenville	(2)	3,660	4,938		1,278
	May	9.	Lambton	(2)	2,044	3,374		1,330
	May	9.	Middlesex	(2)	2,992	5,530		2,538
	May	9.	Oxford	(2)	1,538	3,460		1,922
	July	3.	Elgin	(2)	547	1,770		1,223
	April	4.	Kent	(2)	2,835	4,455		1,620

NEW BRUNSWICK.

Date.			Place.		Votes Polled. For.	Votes Polled. Ag'st.	Majority. For.	Majority. Ag'st.
1878	Oct.	31.	*Fredericton	(1)	403	203	200	
	Dec.	28.	York	(1)	1,229	214	1,015	
1879	Mar.	14.	Charlotte	(1)	867	149	718	
	April	21.	Carleton		1,215	69	1,146	
	April	21.	Albert		718	114	604	
	June	23.	Kings		798	245	553	
	July	3.	Queens		315	181	134	
	Sept.	11.	Westmoreland	(1)	1,082	299	783	
1880	Sept.	2.	Northumberland		875	673	202	
1881	Feb.	17.	Sunbury		176	41	135	
1882	Feb.	23.	*St. John	(1)	1,074	1,076	...	2
	Oct.	26.	*Fredericton	(2)	293	252	41	
1884	Aug.	14.	Westmoreland	(2)	1,774	1,701	73	
1885	Nov.	12.	*Fredericton	(3)	298	285	13	
1886	April	19.	*St. John	(2)	1,610	1,687	...	77
	April	19.	*Portland	(1)	667	520	147	
	April	20.	St. John	(1)	467	424	43	

APPENDICES.

New Brunswick—Continued.

	Date.		Place.		Votes Polled. For.	Votes Polled. Ag'st.	Majority. For.	Majority. Ag'st.
1888	Feb.	16.	Westmoreland	(3)	2,464	1,698	766	
1889	Nov.	28.	*Fredericton	(4)	370	302	68	...
1890	April	17.	*Portland	(2)	124	558	...	434
1891	Nov.	17.	Charlotte	(2)	1,785	855	930	...
1892	Feb.	9.	St. John	(2)	450	595	...	145
	Sept.	29.	Northumberland		1,780	1,561	219	

Manitoba.

1880	Sept.	27.	Marquette	612	195	417
1881	April	7.	Lisgar	247	120	127

Nova Scotia.

1880	Nov.	8.	Digby		944	42	902	
1881	Jan.	3.	Queen's		763	82	681	
	Mar.	17.	Shelburne		807	154	653	
	April	14.	King's		1,478	108	1,370	
	April	19.	Annapolis		1,111	114	997	
	May	13.	Colchester		1,418	184	1,234	
	Aug.	11.	Cape Breton		739	216	523	
	Sept.	15.	Hants		1,082	92	990	
1882	Jan.	6.	Inverness		960	106	854	
	Jan.	9.	Pictou		1,555	453	1,102	
1883	Mar.	25.	Cumberland		1,560	262	1,298	
1884	Mar.	7.	Yarmouth		1,287	96	1,191	
1885	June	26.	Guysboro		463	31	432	...
1889	April	4.	Colchester	(2)	43	1,107		1,064

Prince Edward Island.

1878	Dec.	28.	Prince	(1)	1,762	271	1,491
1879	April	24.	*Charlottetown	(1)	837	253	584
	May	29.	King's		1,076	59	1,017
1880	Sept.	22.	Queen's		1,317	99	1,218
1884	Feb.	7.	Prince	(2)	2,939	1,065	1,874
	Oct.	16.	*Charlottetown	(2)	755	715	40
1887	Nov.	24.	*Charlottetown	(3)	689	669	20
1891	Jan	8.	*Charlottetown	(4)	686	700	14

APPENDICES.

APPENDIX VI.

RESULTS OF ONTARIO PLEBISCITE.

	Total men's vote polled.	Total men on voters' list.	Total women's vote polled.	Total women on voters' list.	Spoiled ballots.
Counties—					
Brant	2,573	4,794	177	510	81
Bruce	9,708	15,002	325	846	317
Carleton	4,109	7,752	110	417	124
Dufferin	3,466	6,019	133	355	54
Elgin	5,360	9,601	208	800	274
Essex	6,226	10,134	218	611	178
Frontenac	3,871	6,733	79	307	119
Grey	10,092	18,396	362	1,066	383
Haldimand	3,880	5,783	150	467	160
Halton	3,056	5,695	165	553	126
Hastings	6,479	11,642	246	716	223
Huron	11,068	16,793	450	1,214	414
Kent	7,749	12,389	272	854	281
Lambton	8,847	15,125	376	1,002	300
Lanark	4,062	8,376	216	719	179
Leeds and Grenville	8,106	13,220	415	1,221	314
Lennox and Addington	4,170	6,815	199	575	159
Lincoln	3,787	5,393	152	526	138
Middlesex	9,805	16,309	460	1,385	430
Norfolk	4,379	7,994	232	702	149
Northumberland and Durham	9,608	15,131	490	1,385	430
Ontario	7,346	10,732	407	1,009	198
Oxford	8,153	12,619	560	1,208	312
Peel	3,966	6,305	194	542	144
Perth	6,395	9,851	211	627	178
Peterborough	3,475	6,580	119	440	119
Prescott and Russell	4,640	8,681	95	355	61
Prince Edward	3,399	5,588	152	463	141
Renfrew	4,845	9,729	139	379	119
Simcoe	10,356	20,728	429	1,360	464
Stormont, Dundas and Glengarry	9,275	16,578	419	1,255	306
Victoria	4,549	8,777	192	616	144
Waterloo	7,329	12,255	436	1,012	235
Welland	4,470	6,916	243	796	162
Wellington	7,137	12,090	393	1,071	220
Wentworth	4,314	7,117	211	768	158
York	7,455	9,052	481	1,391	545
Haliburton (provisional County)	577	1,454	2	31	16
Total	228,082	384,148	10,118	29,554	8,355

APPENDICES.

RESULTS OF ONTARIO PLEBISCITE—*Continued*.

	Total men's vote polled.	Total men on voter's list.	Total women's vote polled.	Total women on voter's list.	Spoiled ballots.
Districts—					
Muskoka	1,925	4,266	59	203	90
Manitoulin	582	1,118	21	41	16
Thunder Bay	798	1,811	37	97	59
Rainy River	560	1,397	6	28	31
Parry Sound	1,855	3,630	65	171	56
Nipissing	1,112	3,059	35	106	18
Algoma	1,255	2,975	28	132	50
Total	8,087	18,256	251	778	320
Cities—					
Belleville	1,367	2,875	179	446	29
Brantford	2,168	3,325	231	503	111
Guelph	1,557	2,790	148	367	96
Hamilton	6,701	10,911	592	1,514	504
Kingston	2,131	3,921	231	604	143
London	4,249	7,616	383	1,066	225
Ottawa	5,121	10,544	332	1,055	115
St. Catharines	970	2,055	100	462	37
St. Thomas	1,446	3,131	108	353	96
Stratford	1,146	2,760	94	323	45
Toronto	20,086	42,163	1,287	5,006	1,213
Windsor	1,322	3,064	130	399	120
Total	48,264	95,155	3,815	12,098	2,734
Separated Towns—					
Aylmer	374	585	50	116	
Chatham	1,387	2,349	155	446	96
Perth	267	669	35	169	10
Prescott	395	735	25	127	21
St. Mary's	542	904	90	192	
Trenton	336	1,029	45	135	9
Toronto Junction	732	1,364	39	202	45
Separated Township—					
Pelee Island	115	175	5	16	8
Total	4,148	7,810	444	1,403	189
Combined Totals	288,581	515,369	14,628	43,833	11,598

APPENDICES.

APPENDIX VII.

TEXT OF PRIVY COUNCIL DECISION IN MANITOBA LIQUOR CASE.

Present—Lord Macnaghten, Lord Shand, Lord Davey, Lord Robertson, and Lord Lindley.

The Attorney-General for the Province of Manitoba v. the Manitoba License Holders' Association.

This was an appeal brought by special leave against the judgment of the Court of King's Bench for the Province of Manitoba, given on February 23 last, in the matter of an act passed by the Legislative Assembly for Manitoba, entitled the Liquor Act (Vict. 63 and 64, c. 22), and certain questions respecting the same referred to the court for hearing and consideration under Chapter 28 of the Revised Statutes of Manitoba.

Mr. Haldane, K.C., the Hon. Colin H. Campbell, K.C., Attorney-General for Manitoba, and Mr. R. O. B. Lane, junior, were counsel for the appellant. The Hon. Edward Blake, K.C., and Mr. F. H. Phippen, both of the Canadian bar, for the respondents. Mr. E. L. Newcombe, K.C., of the Canadian bar, watched the case for the Dominion Government.

The arguments were heard last July before a Board composed of Lord Hobhouse, Lord Macnaghten, Lord Davey, Lord Robertson and Lord Lindley, when judgment was reserved.

Lord Macnaghten, in now delivering their Lordships' judgment, said, in July, 1900, an act was passed by the Legislature of Manitoba for the suppression of the liquor traffic in that province. The act, which was known by its short title of the Liquor Act, was to have come into operation on June 1, 1901. Before that date, on a reference under Chapter 28 of the Revised Statutes of Manitoba, the Court of King's Bench pronounced the whole act to be unconstitutional. From that decision the present appeal has been brought. Although the questions submitted to the Court of King's Bench were eleven in number, the only one considered in the court below and argued before that Board was the first: "Had the Legislative Assembly of Manitoba jurisdiction to enact the Liquor Act, and, if not, in what particular or respect has it exceeded its power?" To that the answer given was: " It exceeded its powers in enacting the Liquor Act as a whole." The other questions were either of an academical character or such as could be material only in the event of the act being declared partially and not wholly unconstitutional. No answer that could be given to any of those questions would be of any practical value. Their Lordships therefore, would confine their attention to the subject to which the judgment of the Court of King's Bench and the arguments at the bar were addressed. The question at issue depended on the meaning and effect of those sections in the British North America Act, 1867, which provide for the distribution of legislative powers between the Dominion and the provinces. The subject had been discussed before the Board very frequently and very fully. Mindful of advice often quoted, but not, perhaps, always followed, their Lordships did not propose to travel beyond the particular case before them. The drink question, to use a common expression, which was convenient, if not altogether accurate, was not to be found specifically mentioned either in the classes of subjects enumerated in section 91, and assigned to the Legislature of the Dominion, or in those enumerated in section 92, and thereby appropriated to Provincial Legislatures. The omission was probably not accidental. The result had been somewhat remarkable. On the

APPENDICES.

one hand, according to "Russell v. Reg." (7 App. Cas. 829), it was competent for the Dominion Legislature to pass an act for the suppression of intemperance, applicable to all parts of the Dominion, and when duly brought into operation in any particular district, deriving its efficacy from the general authority vested in the Dominion Parliament to make laws for the peace, order and good government of Canada. On the other hand, according to the decision in "The Attorney-General for Ontario v. the Attorney-General for the Dominion" (1896, A.C., 348), it was not incompetent for a Provincial Legislature to pass a measure for the repression or even for the total abolition of the liquor traffic within the province, provided the subject was dealt with as a matter "of a merely local nature," in the province, and the act itself was not repugnant to any act of the Parliament of Canada. In delivering the judgment of the Board in the case of "The Attorney-General for Ontario v. the Attorney-General for the Dominion," Lord Watson expressed a decided opinion that provincial legislation for the suppression of the liquor traffic could not be supported under either No. 8 or No. 9 of section 92. His Lordship observed that the only enactments of that section which appeared to have any relation to such legislation were to be found in Nos. 13 and 16, which assigned to the exclusive jurisdiction of Provincial Legislatures (1) "Property and civil rights in the province," and (2) " generally all matters of a merely local or private nature in the province." He added that it was not necessary for the purpose of that appeal to determine whether such legislation was authorized by the one or by the other of those heads. Although that particular question was thus left apparently undecided, a careful perusal of the judgment led to the conclusion that in the opinion of the Board, the case fell under No. 16, rather than under No. 13, and that seemed to their Lordships to be the better opinion. In legislating for the suppression of the liquor traffic, the object in view was the abatement or prevention of a local evil rather than the regulation of property and civil rights—though, of course, no such legislation could be carried into effect without interfering more or less with "property and civil rights in the province." Indeed, if the case were to be regarded as dealing with matters within the class of subjects enumerated in No. 13, it might be questionable whether the Dominion Legislature could have authority to interfere with the exclusive jurisdiction of the province in the matter. The controversy, therefore, seemed to be narrowed to this one point. Is the subject of "the Liquor Act" a matter " of a merely local nature in the province" of Manitoba and does the Liquor Act deal with it as such? The judgment of the Board in the case of "The Attorney-General for Ontario v. the Attorney-General for the Dominion" had relieved the case from some, if not all, of the difficulties which appeared to have presented themselves to the learned judges of the Court of King's Bench. The Board held that a provincial legislature had jurisdiction to restrict the sale within the province of intoxicating liquors so long as its legislation did not conflict with any legislative provision which might be competently made by the Parliament of Canada, and which might be in force within the province or any district thereof. It held, further, that there might be circumstances in which a Provincial Legislature might have jurisdiction to prohibit the manufacture within the province of intoxicating liquors and the importation of such liquors into the province. For the purpose of the present question it was immaterial to enquire what those circumstances might be. The judgment, therefore, as it stood, and the report to her late Majesty consequent thereon, showed that in the opinion of that tribunal, matters which were "substantially of local or of private interest" in a province—matters which were of a local

APPENDICES.

or private nature "from a provincial point of view"—to use expressions to be found in the judgment, were not excluded from the category of "matters of a merely local or private nature," because legislation dealing with them, however carefully it might be framed, might or must have an effect outside the limits of the province, and might or must interfere with the sources of Dominion revenue and the industrial pursuits of persons licensed under Dominion statutes to carry on particular trades. The Liquor Act proceeded upon a recital that "it is expedient to suppress the liquor traffic in Manitoba by prohibiting provincial transactions in liquor." That was the declared object of the Legislature set out at the commencement of the act. Towards the end of the act there occurred this section: "119· While this act is intended to prohibit and shall prohibit transactions in liquor which take place wholly within the Province of Manitoba, except under a license or as otherwise specially provided by this act, and restrict the consumption of liquor within the limits of the Province of Manitoba, it shall not affect *bona fide* transactions in liquor between a person in the Province of Manitoba and a person in another province or in a foreign country, and the provisions of this act shall be construed accordingly." Now that provision was as much part of the act as any other section contained in it. It must have its full effect in exempting from the operation of the act all *bona fide* transactions in liquor which came within its terms. It was not necessary to go through the provisions of the act. It was enough to say that they were extremely stringent—more stringent probably than anything that was to be found in any legislation of a similar kind. Unless the act became a dead letter it must interfere with the revenue of the Dominion, with licensed trades in the Province of Manitoba and indirectly at least with business operations beyond the limits of the province. That seemed clear. And that was substantially the ground on which the Court of King's Bench declared the act unconstitutional. But all objections on that score were, in their Lordships' opinion removed by the judgment of the Board in the case of "The Attorney-General for Ontario v. the Attorney-General for the Dominion." Having attentively considered the very able and elaborate judgments of Chief Justice Killam and Mr. Justice Bain, in which Mr. Justice Richards concurred, and the arguments of counsel in support of their view, their Lordships were not satisfied that the Legislature of Manitoba had transgressed the limits of its jurisdiction in passing the Liquor Act. Their Lordships would, therefore, humbly advise his Majesty that the judgment of the Court of King's Bench of the Province of Manitoba, dated February 23, 1901, ought to be discharged, and that in the lieu thereof there ought to be substituted the following answers to the eleven questions submitted to it: (1) In answer to the first question—that the Legislative Assembly of Manitoba had jurisdiction to enact the Liquor Act; (2) In answer to the questions numbered 2 to 11, both inclusive—That no useful answer could be given to those questions. There would be no costs of the appeal.

APPENDICES.

APPENDIX VIII.

DOMINION ALLIANCE MANIFESTO, 1904.

The Executive Committee of the Ontario Branch of the Dominion Alliance desires to call the attention of the electorate throughout the Province of Ontario to the following facts:

In the year 1893 the Provincial Government undertook to secure a decision of the courts upon the question of the power of a Province to prohibit and restrain the liquor traffic, and the Legislature passed an act providing for a vote of the electors on the question:

"Are you in favor of the immediate prohibition by law of the importation, manufacture and sale of intoxicating liquors as a beverage?"

The votes polled in this plebiscite taken at the municipal elections of 1894 were as follows:

	Men.	Women.	Total
Votes "Yes"	180,087	12,402	192,489
Votes "No"	108,494	2,226	110,720
Majority "Yes"			81,709

Shortly after the taking of this vote, in reply to a deputation, the then Premier and Attorney-General, Sir Oliver Mowat, expressed his deep sense of the importance of the prohibition movement and the strength of public sentiment behind it, as evidenced in the plebiscite, the result of which was eminently satisfactory. He went on to say:

I think the vote a remarkable one, not only because of its size, and not only because of the magnificent majority of 82,000, but because of its wonderful proportion of two to one. It is impossible not to regard the vote as expressing strongly and emphatically the public sentiment of this country. . . . The recent vote removes all difficulty in the way of prohibition being demanded by the people.

At the close of this speech he read to the deputation the following statement:

If the decision of the Privy Council should be that the Province has the jurisdiction to pass a prohibitory liquor law as respects the sale of intoxicating liquor, I will introduce such a bill in the following session, if I am then at the head of the Government.

If the decision of the Privy Council is that the Province has jurisdiction to pass only a partial prohibitory liquor law, I will introduce such a prohibitory bill as the decision will warrant, unless the partial prohibitory power is so limited as to be ineffective from a temperance standpoint.

On the evening of the day on which Sir Oliver Mowat made this statement, Hon. G. W. Ross, at a temperance convention in the Horticultural Pavilion, delivered an address, a part of which was reported by *The Globe* as follows:

The result has exceeded his expectations. He expected a majority, but not such an overwhelming one. "The verdict of the people has been accepted by the Government heartily and by me gladly." He was glad the Government were able to express themselves in a way to satisfy the delegates. "It is what you had a right to expect. It is what it ought to do, and," he added, " it is the only kind of a Government I would be a member of."

APPENDICES.

Hon. A. S. Hardy, who succeeded Hon. Sir Oliver Mowat as Premier of Ontario, declared his policy on the temperance question to be the same as that of his predecessor.

When the Hon. G. W. Ross, the present Premier, succeeded Hon. A. S. Hardy, he accepted the responsibility of carrying out the pledges that had been given by his predecessors. A decision by the Judicial Committee of the Imperial Privy Council of Great Britain sustaining the Manitoba Liquor Act affirmed the right of a province to enact a comprehensive measure of prohibition of the retail sale of intoxicating liquor. Hon. Mr. Ross proposed to carry out the promises that had been made by the enactment of the Liquor Act, 1902, which was substantially the same as the act that had been declared valid.

The proposed measure was not, however, made directly operative, but was submitted to the electors with the condition that its ratification would require a majority of the votes polled on the question, and also that such majority would be equal to a majority of the votes polled in the general election of 1898. Voting took place on December 4, 1902, and resulted as follows:

Votes for the act 199,719
Votes against the act 103,548

Majority for the act 96,201

The arbitrary and unfair requirements for the ratification of the act was not, however, fully met. The number of votes polled in favor of the measure, although actually and relatively very large, was not equal to a majority of the votes cast in the general election of 1898. The promises of advanced legislation, therefore, remained still unfulfilled.

Following up the voting a large and representative conference of temperance workers adopted a resolution which has since been ratified by two large provincial conventions, setting out a programme of legislation which it was unanimously agreed ought to be enacted in view of the great vote polled. The resolution was as follows:

"That in view of the recent expression by the electors of the Province of Ontario in favor of the Liquor Act, 1902, we deem it advisable to appoint a deputation to wait upon the Government and request that effect be given to said vote by the abolition of the public bar, the treating system, and drinking in clubs, and the imposition of such other restrictions on the liquor traffic as shall most effectually curtail its operation and remedy its evils."

In 1903 the Speech from the Throne promised temperance legislation, but up to the present time there has been no legislation in fulfilment of the pledges given.

It was hoped that the Liberal convention, assembled in Massey Hall, on November 23 and 24, would take such advanced steps as would secure the fulfilment of the pledges that had been given. This expectation was justified by the fact that under Liberal leadership in the past the Ontario Legislature had enacted important measures reducing the number of liquor licenses and imposing upon the traffic many useful restrictions of much benefit to the country in the curtailment of the liquor evil.

A request from the Alliance for legislation abolishing bar-rooms as above stated, was referred by the convention to the Committee on

APPENDICES.

Resolutions, but though strongly supported by a number of delegates, was voted down by a majority of the committee. Although this clause fell far short of being a fulfilment of the promises that had been made, it was the most advanced and useful in the committee's report. It was struck out in the convention upon an urgent appeal from two members of the administration, Hon. Messrs. McKay and Graham. The clause was as follows:

"That in each municipality a vote be taken at the municipal elections of 1906 on the two questions of abolition of bar-rooms and of shop licenses, the result to be decisive, and to go into effect at the expiration of the then outstanding licenses and that all necessary legislation be introduced in the meantime to enable this to be done. In municipalities in which licenses are continued, a similar vote may be taken at any time after three years."

This Executive regrets that after careful and serious consideration, it is forced to the conclusion that the rejection by the convention of this resolution dispels all hope that may have been entertained that this administration would endeavor to redeem the pledges quoted.

We regret also that not only did the Premier and Hon. Mr. Gibson take no part in supporting this resolution, but they acquiesced in its defeat, and the Premier stated to the convention that he was "delighted with the convention's decision upon the temperance question."

In view of the promises made, the overwhelming mandate of the electors and the need for effective measures to check the evils of intemperance, the Alliance views the situation as it now exists with the deepest regret and disappointment. The Government has trifled with the great temperance question, has been unfaithful to the pledges and promises of its successive premiers, and has by its record and recent course on this, the most important issue in provincial politics, forfeited all claim to the support of electors who put temperance principle above partisanship in political affairs.

It is manifest that no useful advance in temperance legislation can be hoped for until temperance men determinedly refuse to support any party or candidate that continues to trifle with or ignore this great question, and this Executive Committee respectfully and earnestly requests temperance men in every constituency to take immediate steps to secure the nomination and election of a candidate who can be relied upon to do all in his power to secure effective temperance legislation at the earliest possible opportunity, and who will hold himself absolutely free from party dictation in relation to such legislation, and to secure the defeat of any candidate who does not comply with these requirements.

By effective temperance legislation is meant legislation abolishing the bar and the treating system and drinking in clubs, and imposing upon the liquor traffic such other restrictions as shall most effectually curtail its operation and remedy its evils.

APPENDICES.

APPENDIX IX.

LIQUOR LICENSES IN ONTARIO.

The number of liquor licenses issued in the Province of Ontario during the past thirty-nine years is set out in the following table, which is taken from the "Report on the Operation of the Liquor License Acts, Ontario, for the Year 1913," printed by order of the Legislative Assembly of the Province of Ontario. The list does not include the different kinds of liquor manufacturers' licenses, which for the year 1912-13 were as follows: Distillers', 9; Brewers', 51; Brewers' Warehouse, 49; Sample and Commission, 11; all of which, as well as the wholesale licenses set out in the table, are for different forms of sale by wholesale. The table gives the figures in each case for the license year commencing on May 1st of the year named in the first column, and ending on April 30th of the following year. The figures are striking evidence of the steady growth of public opinion against the liquor traffic.

The great reduction shown for the year 1877 was due to the Crooks Act. The reduction in shop licenses in 1877 was caused by the law prohibiting the sale of liquor in places where any other business is carried on. Vessel licenses, permitting the sale of liquor on boats, were abolished in 1891.

The temporary reduction shown for the years 1885 to 1890 was due to the Canada Temperance Act. It will be noticed that if these years are omitted the number of licenses has been steadily diminishing for twenty-three years, notwithstanding a steady increase in population.

Years.	Tavern.	Shop.	Wholesale.	Vessel.	Total.
1875	4,794	1,307	52	33	6,185
1876	4,459	1,257	78	24	5,818
1877	2,977	787	147	27	3,938
1878	2,845	739	65	27	3,676
1879	2,910	724	52	29	3,715
1880	3,199	757	42	22	4,020
1881	3,227	760	40	22	4,049
1882	3,311	764	34	24	4,133
1883a	3,317	787	35	24	a4,163
1884a	3,363	781	36	21	a4,201
1885a	3,253	675	28	14	a3,970
1886b	2,574	525	24	9	b3,132
1887c	1,567	367	28	12	c1,974
1888c	1,496	325	28	13	c1,862
1889d	2,066	336	26	17	d2,445
1890	3,073	445	27	15	3,560
1891	3,071	428	24		3,523
1892	2,990	403	21		3,414
1893	2,966	378	25		3,369
1894	2,888	357	31		3,276
1895	2,785	337	29		3,151
1896	2,779	327	26		3,132
1897	2,747	323	26		3,096
1898	2,725	317	22		3,064
1899	2,641	312	23		2,976

APPENDICES.

Years.	Tavern.	Shop.	Wholesale.	Vessel.	Total.
1900	2,611	308	21		2,950
1901	2,621	303	24		2,948
1902	2,613	308	26		2,947
1903	2,628	307	22		2,957
1904	2,577	300	22		2,899
1905	2,516	298	22		2,836
1906	2,384	283	24	Club	2,691
1907	2,207	267	23	24	2,521
1908	2,110	262	25	35	2,432
1909	2,010	253	23	42	2,328
1910	1,873	245	32	50	2,200
1911	1,630	226	31	51	1,938
1912	1,537	221	30	52	1,841
1913	1,469	219	29	57	1,774
1914	1,371	218	28	63	1,680
1915	1,285	216	31	61	1,593
1916	1,224	211	30	64	1,529

May 1st, 1916, the Ontario Temperance Act in force.
a. One county under Canada Temperance Act. b. Nine counties under Canada Temperance Act. c. Twenty-five counties under Canada Temperance Act. d. Seventeen counties under Canada Temperance Act.

APPENDIX X.

EXTRACTS FROM THE HON. MR. HEARST'S SPEECH IN APRIL, 1916, ON THE ONTARIO TEMPERANCE ACT.

But it is not enough to justify the legislation before the House, that all admit and none deny the terrible evil that flows from the liquor traffic. There must be some ground for the belief and hope that the legislation proposed will at least to some degree minimize these evils, and it is on this phase of the subject that we find the gravest divergence of opinion.

That this bill will do away with all, or nearly all, the evil of intemperance, no reasonable man will pretend. So long as liquor can be purchased or produced, so long will men drink it and drink it to excess. But I believe that not only will the bill before the House largely reduce temptation to the youth and rising generation of our land, and produce a more sober citizenship in the future, but that it will be a blessing to thousands in our province to-day who are battling manfully against their appetites for strong drink, but are unable to withstand the temptation now openly presented for the purchase of strong drink, while tens of thousands more who drink in moderation will rejoice at the fact that no opportunity or temptation longer remains to waste time, money and energy and efficiency in drinking liquor in hotels, in clubs and elsewhere.

But notwithstanding all this, the bill before the House would not now be before this House, at all events in its present state, but for the war. The war has not only changed, for the time being, at all events, the sentiments of the people on this question, but it has placed obligations and emphasized the duty of economy and efficiency that did not exist

APPENDICES.

before, and my contention is that if the bill would bring no benefit to the province from a moral standpoint, if the results that flow from its enactment would add nothing to the health and happiness of our people, that as a war measure, for the purpose of aiding economy, thrift and efficiency, it is justified—yes, demanded—and made possible by public opinion.

And it is on that basis that I urge the passage of the bill in its present form, and it is on that basis that I will deal with it in the further remarks I desire to make. I want to state frankly and clearly to the House and the country that I would not think of urging the passage of this bill through the House without a vote of the people but for the war and the obligations imposed thereby.

I am of the opinion, and strongly of the opinion, that this question should be eventually decided by the direct vote of the electors of the province by means of a referendum. In a democratic country like this, public opinion is the last supreme arbitrament on every question, and it seems to me a question of this kind so closely affecting our people is particularly one in which public opinion should have an opportunity of reflecting itself in the ballot box as freely and untrammelled as possible. The principle of submitting this question to the direct vote of the electors has been admitted for years in this House, and also in the Federal House, and recognized by the two political parties in connection with the Local Option Act of Ontario and the Canada Temperance Act of the Dominion.

* * * * * * * *

Surely if it is justifiable to submit any question to the direct vote of the people, it is a social and moral question such as this which comes home so closely to every one of us and affects so much the lives, comfort, and happiness of our people. Surely if there ever was a question that should be removed so far as possible from the strife of party politics and upon which temperance people should be united, untrammelled and unprejudiced, it is a question of this kind, the success of which depends so largely upon public opinion and the co-operation of the people in making it a success.

* * * * * * *

I would have much preferred to have taken a vote of the electors on the subject before taking any action, had that course been possible. I think it would have been the most advisable one from every standpoint, but from the first I was determined that when a vote was taken all the electors should have a free and equal opportunity of expressing their views in the ballot box, and that above all, our brave soldier boys, who are fighting in the trenches, would be given the same opportunity as those who remain at home to express by the ballot their wish on such a momentous question. On investigation and enquiry from the military authorities, I found that it would not be practicable to secure by any means a full vote of the soldiers, and for that reason I decided that no vote should be taken now. To me, however, the call for action, and for action now, came clearly, and I determined to answer that call.

The claim that this Government had no mandate to pass even a temporary measure was met by the fact that it was conceded by everyone that if a vote were now taken it would be overwhelmingly in favor of

APPENDICES.

the measure proposed. This was conceded by those opposed to the bill and by representatives of the liquor trade themselves as freely as it was claimed by the temperance workers; and prohibitionists and anti-prohibitionists seemed equally opposed to a vote at the present time. In addition to this, there were, of course, the very strong arguments against the expenditure of any money that could be avoided, both by the Government and by the people under present conditions, and the stronger arguments still that so far as possible nothing should be now introduced that would cause a division among our people or prevent the harmony that should exist among all classes in working together for the end that prohibitionists and anti-prohibitionists alike have in view, the bringing of the present war to a successful conclusion at the earliest possible moment.

The Government, therefore, has decided, as provided by the bill, to bring the Act into force without the direct vote of the people, but after a period of about three years when the people have had an opportunity of judging as to the efficacy or the failure of the Act as a temperance measure, when we hope that the war will be over and our soldiers back from the front and conditions generally have assumed their normal character, then the people of the province will have an opportunity by their free vote to decide this question for themselves. If the war should unfortunately not be over by the time named, the vote would be deferred for a reasonable time after the war.

* * * * * * * *

The question of prohibition and all the evil effects of alcohol has been a burning one for many years in this country. We have tried the license system; we have tried restriction, and every person agrees to-day that the situation is not entirely satisfactory, having regard to the situation that now exists. Then what I say to the prohibitionist and to the anti-prohibitionist, to the man who believes in this legislation and to the man who is dissatisfied with it, it this: We have tried the license system for many years in this country, let us try prohibition.

Let us abstain from intoxicating liquors for two or three years at least, while we have a death struggle on, when our very existence as a nation is at stake, and at the end of that time when the war is over, when the people have had a trial of the Act and know its benefits and its weaknesses, when the people have had time for sober second thought, if they are hysterical on this subject at the present time, above all, when our boys have come back from the front covered with glory and honors and laurels won on the bloody battlefields of France, Flanders and Germany, in maintaining for us the priceless gem of liberty and freedom, if they feel that it is in the best interest of this province to repeal this legislation and return to the present system or some other license system, then we all must and will bow to the judgment and will of the people in this great democratic country, and the people then will be enabled to pass a more intelligent verdict upon this question than they could in any other way.

* * * * * * * *

Some honorable gentlemen point us to England, in this, as in other matters, as an example to follow—and we are glad to look to England for example in many things. To my mind Great Britain to-day gives

APPENDICES.

the greatest object lesson we possibly could have and shows us the course in this matter that we as a young country should shun. Through centuries of liquor traffic during which immense businesses have been built up in distilling and brewing of liquors for home trade as well as a lucrative export traffic, and during which the custom and habit of using intoxicants as a beverage has become almost a part of the life of the people, the trade has become so confirmed and entrenched and the sentiment of the people so firmly set, that notwithstanding the admission of the Government that in this hour of the nation's peril, that strong drink is a greater enemy than the Hun, that efficiency demands prohibition, they are only able to take partial measures, by reason of the anti-prohibition habits and sentiments of the people.

Surely we, as a young country in the making, must so shape our legislation and educate our people that no Government of this country will have to make the admission the Government of Great Britain has had to make, and be, like that Government, impotent to remove the evil. If it should ever be in years to come, when Canada has a population, as she is destined yet to have, as great as Great Britain, when she perhaps has become the centre of wealth and influence of the British Empire and she is threatened with some foe from without as England is to-day, that her statesmen will have to admit, as England's have had to on the present occasion, that great as the danger was from the enemy from without, that we had a greater danger from within, from something we had licensed, tolerated, and cultivated—if so it will stand as a reproach to us and to this generation, and public men of the future will curse us for our cowardice and weak-heartedness.

The situation in the Old Land to-day speaks to us in this new land in tones of thunder to avoid the path that land has taken, and to shake off that which hampers progress in times of peace, and may destroy entirely in times of war.

We all know the great difference in the habits and sentiments on this question between the people of the Old Country and the people of this country. We know the strength of the liquor trade in all its branches built up in that country through centuries. We know the settled customs and habits of the people of the Old Land on this question, but notwithstanding these adverse factors very strong measures have been taken enforcing non-treating, limiting the hours of sale and otherwise curtailing the drink traffic, and notwithstanding what has been done, leaders like Lloyd George and others feel how much the drink traffic is still handicapping them in the great struggle in which they are engaged, and I am sure no honorable gentleman in this House, and I do not believe any honorable gentleman in this country, would, for one minute, suggest that if public sentiment in favor of prohibition was as strong in Great Britain as it is in Canada, that the British Government would not long ago have enacted as far-reaching a prohibitory measure as the bill now before this House.

In other words, the British Government recognizes to the full the necessity of action from the standpoint of economy and efficiency, and the only thing that prevents further and more drastic action by that Government is the lack of strong enough public opinion to warrant such legislation.

Is it asking too much? Is the sacrifice too great for Canadians, and particularly for citizens of this loyal Province of Ontario, whose hearts are as true to the old flag and whose loyalty and patriotism are as great as those in any section of our far-flung Empire, to abstain at

APPENDICES.

this time when not only that Empire but freedom itself is at stake, from the reckless waste of money that is now incurred for intoxicants that could be so well used for the purchase of munitions, for the aid of the wounded and for other purposes in connection with the cause for which we are now fighting.

* * * * * * * *

When we as public men are preaching economy to the people and urging our boys to enlist and risk their lives in this great war, surely it would be the height of inconsistency on our part if we did not refrain from a luxury that costs the people of Canada one hundred million or one hundred and twenty-five million dollars a year; and if we did not place upon the Statute Book every measure that will assist in enforcing the saving of this amount or as much of it as possible.

Surely those of us who are too old or too infirm or not courageous enough to enlist for the present contest should at least give up the pleasure of our beer and our whisky, give up even what we may consider our personal liberties and personal rights so that we can save every dollar and conserve every ounce of energy for a cause in which our sons, our brothers and the best men of our land are freely shedding their blood.

* * * * * * * *

It cannot be denied that many individuals and corporations and a number of lines of trade will be disturbed by this bill and that readjustment will be required, but I am convinced that the net economic result from this bill will be a vast gain to the community.

True, there will be some dislocation of trade, and many cases of hardship through parties interested in this trade that I wish with all my heart could be avoided, but ultimately, and that in the near future, I believe the capital and labor used will be turned to more productive service, where that capital will bring substantial and permanent returns to the men who own it, where it will give employment to thousands more men and women than it does to-day, and where, instead of waste, and worse still, sorrow and suffering, it will bring comfort and happiness and strength and stability to the State. We regret the loss and suffering it may entail, but the public good must be supreme.

Will any man pretend that if we can reduce, even to a substantial extent, the annual expenditure in this province for strong drink, we will not have accomplished much towards the conservation of our financial strength and resources and immensely added to our ability to do our part, and our full part, in the present great struggle?

The cost to consumers of strong drink in Ontario has been estimated at thirty million to forty million dollars annually. If we can by our legislation but cut this bill in two we have saved from expenditure in luxury a sum equal to ten times the amount raised and disbursed by this province, with no small source of satisfaction and pride to all of us, for war purposes.

But when we charge up the amount of money actually expended for strong drink, we are by no means at the end of the bill chargeable to the traffic. For while much of the money spent in traffic may harm to a slight degree, if at all, those making such expenditure, we all must undoubtedly recognize it is the cause of a serious loss in the working

APPENDICES.

and earning power of our people, a cause—and a very substantial cause—of inefficiency in men in every walk of life. This is emphasized by the ever-increasing number of employers of labor who demand not only sobriety, but in many cases total abstinence on the part of their employees. But we have not only loss in money, loss in work, loss in efficiency, by those who indulge in strong drink, but we have loss of labor as well.

Bartenders, brewery workers, cigarmakers, etc., say you will deprive us of our work by the passage of this bill, and it is a serious thing to interfere with any industry, and more serious still to interfere with the means by which a workman earns his livelihood. But what are the facts to-day? Our recruiting sergeants are pleading on every street corner for recruits for our overseas contingents, and leading men allege that it will be impossible to reach our quota of one-half million already promised by this country, and urgent requests come from all sections for further organization in order to secure the necessary number of men for enlistment; our agriculturists are calling, and calling in vain, for men to till their ground, sow their seed, and reap the harvest so essential to not only the prosperity of this country but to the success of Great Britain and her Allies; our munition factories and factories of almost every kind are crying for help and more help; our banks, our trust companies and other institutions are calling for men to take the place of those going to the front, or who ought to go to the front. Never in the history of this country were there so many avenues open for the worker of all classes and conditions to find employment as there is to-day. Never was there such necessity for every citizen being employed at some constructive and productive work as there is to-day. Never was there a time when there could be such a readjustment as the proposed act may entail with so little loss, so little suffering to the men employed in the trade. And under the conditions I have named might we not well ask why should hundreds and thousands of men be employed in providing and administering a luxury, to put the case as mildly as possible. The call comes to-day in this province and throughout the Empire with greater insistence than ever for men and more men, not only for the battlefield but for productive work that is equally essential for the winning of this war.

The soil of France and Flanders is red to-day with the blood of Canada's best and bravest. The flower of our young manhood is marching out daily in thousands. How long can this fair young province stand the strain? Before our 500,000 men from Canada that we have promised have been secured, at the present ratio of recruiting, Ontario will be depleted of the very pick and best of her citizenship; and it will take us generations to make good in man-power what this war is costing us. In the name of high Heaven then what is the duty of this House and this country? Surely it is to bend every energy, to use every effort, to enact every law that we may believe will bring to an end, and 'that as soon as possible, the terrible war tragedy now being enacted.

Is this a time to talk of personal liberty, to think of our pleasures, our appetites, our enjoyments, when the civilization of the world is hanging in the balance and the very foundations of liberty are tottering and dependent upon the strength of Great Britain and her Allies in the field and on the high seas?

Are we who are staying at home and comfortable and safe around our firesides going to cavil about our rights, our privileges and our pleasures, while the stream of our richest and best life's blood continues to flow unstanched for the cause of liberty?

APPENDICES.

I may be wrong in the judgment I have formed. The Act before the House may not accomplish what I hope for it, but I would a thousand times sooner be guilty of an error of judgment in taking an action of this kind with the object of conserving our strength and mobilizing our resources to the utmost so that this war may be brought to an end and the life of our young manhood saved, as far as possible, and the grief and suffering and woe minimized to the greatest extent we can, than to sit with folded arms free from criticism and censure.

Let me repeat the language of His Gracious Majesty, our beloved King, when he said: "I rejoice in my Empire's efforts. I feel pride in the voluntary response from my subjects all over the world who have sacrificed home and fortune and life itself, in order that another may not inherit the free Empire which their ancestors and mine have built. I ask you to make good these sacrifices." And in that spirit I ask the Members of this House, the people of this province, yes the men engaged in the trade themselves who will suffer financial loss, but who are as patriotic and loyal as anybody, let the cost be what it may, to make good the sacrifice. I appeal with the greatest earnestness of soul that I have ever appealed to this House or to any body of men before for a united support of this measure. Let us pass this measure without opposition, without division. Let us show an example to the Empire and the world, of how the men of this province far off from the seat of war, are willing to rise above party and prejudice, are willing to sacrifice personal pleasure and habits, are willing to forfeit business interests and investments themselves; are willing to sink, if need be, into political oblivion, if by so doing they can the better play their part in the greatest war of the ages, and if by so doing they can the sooner bring to an end the bloodshed, sorrow and suffering being caused by this war.

* * * * * * * *

I recognize, and recognize to the full, the necessity of public opinion to enforce a prohibitory law. Everyone now, however, recognizes that there is an immense wave of public opinion in favor of prohibition. Temperance workers, those engaged in the liquor trade, and those opposed to prohibition all agree as to this. Some say it is simply a wave that will recede, that it is hysteria, fanatical. However, that may be, none can deny that there is greater earnestness to-day on the part of our people on this subject and on other moral and important subjects than ever before. There never has come to us such a call before to live sober, thoughtful and sacrificing lives. There has never been such a call to us to forget self and act for the general good of humanity. In fact, we are going through the most tragic days the world has ever seen, when the foundations of civilization and liberty are tottering and when we as a people are being tested to the very foundation of our national life.

I believe a prohibitory law by the common consent of the people can be enforced to-day and will be observed as it never was before in this or in any other country in the world.

You say the wave in favor of temperance will ebb. It possibly may. Very well then; when the war is over and the necessity for thrift and economy is not so great, if the people by their free vote want to undo what we have to-day done they will be given a full opportunity so to do. In a country with free institutions such as we enjoy, the will of the

APPENDICES.

people must in this as in everything else be supreme. In a democratic country like this we must all bow to the sovereign will of the people.

* * * * * * * *

Some men as honest and as sincere as I am have said that this measure will not make for temperance or the real welfare of the province. Some have said that by this measure I have sealed the political doom of my Government and signed my death warrant as a public man. But I would rather ten thousand times go down to political oblivion and disappear forever from view as a public man than to fail in what I believe to be my duty at the present time. The man who chooses the path of political expediency as against the path of duty is not worthy of the support of the splendid body of men that sit to the right of the Speaker in this House, or of the great body of citizens that belong to the grand old Conservative party, and above all is not worthy to stand in the shoes of the great Whitney who was ever bold enough to be honest and honest enough to be bold.

In this day of national peril, in this day when the future of the British Empire, the freedom of the world, and the blessings of democratic government hang in the balance, if I should fail to listen to what I believe to be the call of duty, if I should neglect to take every action that in my judgment will help to conserve the financial strength and power and manhood of this province for the great struggle in which we are engaged, I would be a traitor to my country, a traitor to my own conscience and unworthy of the brave sons of Canada that are fighting, bleeding and dying for freedom and for us.

Since I have been honored with the leadership of this House and of the great Conservative party in this province I have earnestly struggled to keep an undimmed eye on the goal of what is best for this province and its people, and I trust that so long as I may be honored with such leadership I may be able to keep a clear and unclouded eye upon that goal and to follow the path of duty as I see it, with feeble, perhaps, but nevertheless with unfaltering step and with unswerving determination.

Personally it matters little to me whether my career as Prime Minister of this province is long or short, but it does matter much that I discharge my duty to the best of my ability while I retain that high position. It matters much to this province that its Prime Minister, whoever he may be, should be guided, and guided solely by a sense of duty, and while I am not unconscious of the fact that many of my best and warmest personal and political friends feel that I have made a mistake, even some may feel that they cannot continue further to give their allegiance to the party while I am its leader, if such should be the case I regret it very much. I have, however, personally, faith without a doubt that not only the public of to-day, but the public of to-morrow and the public of years to come will say that the Government did what was right under conditions as they existed at the time, and I fear not the verdict of this day or of future generations, and I am content to await, and will await with confidence the verdict of the people when the right time comes for them to render their verdict. And I am satisfied that the Conservative who in years to come reads the record of his party we are writing to-day will have no cause to blush as he reads that record. And whatever comes, approval or condemnation, I will always have the witness of a clear conscience that in the hour of my country's greatest peril I hesitated not to do what to me seemed right, and waited not to count the cost.

APPENDICES.

APPENDIX XI.

THE ONTARIO TEMPERANCE ACT.

The most important provisions of The Ontario Temperance Act are embodied in the following summary:

THE RIGHT TO HAVE, KEEP, AND GIVE LIQUOR IN ONTARIO.

No person shall have, keep or give any liquor in Ontario except in the private dwelling house in which he resides or except as expressly permitted by this act. (Sec. 41.)

This clause, read together with section 88 of the Ontario Temperance Act, it has been stated by Mr. Justice Middleton, means "that possession of liquor in Ontario is *prima facie* unlawful. Once possession is proved, conviction may follow if the accused is unable to satisfy the magistrate that he was legally entitled to have or keep the liquor found in his possession. He may satisfy the magistrate by proving that he comes within one of the following exceptions:

Possession of Liquor in a Private Dwelling House.

It is an absolute defence to such a charge if the liquor is had or kept in the private dwelling house in which the accused person resides. What is meant by "private dwelling house" is consequently very important, and is elaborately defined. Generally speaking, it means, "a separate dwelling with a separate door for ingress and egress, and actually and exclusively occupied and used as a private residence." (Sec. 2.)

A private dwelling house, however, does not mean:

(1) Any house or building (with certain exceptions) occupied or used or partially occupied or used as an office, shop, or other place of business. (Sec. 2, (i),).

(2) Any house or building occupied or used or partially occupied or used as a club house or club room, public hall, or hall of any society or order.

(3) Any house or building, occupied or used or partially occupied or used as a boarding house or lodging house, where there are more than three lodgers or boarders other than the members of the family, or as a livery stable or garage or as an inn, tavern, hotel, or other house or place of public entertainment.

In none of the places above enumerated may liquor be had, kept or given.

The right to give liquor is also confined to one's private residence. The law permits a person to consume liquor in the house in which he lives and to give it to anyone in the house either for consumption on the premises or to be taken to a place where it can be legally kept.

No restriction is placed on the quantity of liquor which a person may keep in his private residence.

Possession of Liquor Under Special Circumstances.

In addition to the right above discussed, to have, keep and give liquor in the house in which one lives, the law of necessity permits liquor to be had, kept and given under certain special circumstances and by special persons, where it is being kept for permitted purposes.

APPENDICES.

Thus, any person may have or keep liquor anywhere in the province if it has been lawfully furnished to him upon the prescription of a legally qualified physician, but only in such quantities as may be so prescribed. (Sec. 51.)

So also, any person may carry or convey liquor from a place where it may be lawfully kept and delivered in Ontario to another place in or out of Ontario where it may be lawfully kept, "but no person, during the time such liquor is being carried or conveyed shall open or break any package or vessel containing the same. (Sec. 43.) Thus a person moving his residence from one place to another may take liquor with him. (Sec. 30 (a).)

Persons authorized by law to keep or sell liquor for permitted purposes may only have or keep quantity of liquor which the statute provides for. The quantity which government sales agencies authorized by the 1919 statute may keep is of course controlled directly by the Board. Retail druggists may only have ten gallons of liquor at one time, exclusive of alcohol and sacramental wine. (Sec. 130 (2).) A dentist may keep in his office six ounces of liquor for medicinal use only, and a veterinary surgeon may keep one quart of liquor for use in his practice. (Sec. 51.) Subject to the approval of the Board a physician may have in his private dwelling house or in his office or dispensary, 10 gallons of liquor, and may have one quart in his possession when visiting patients. (Sec. 51 a.) Persons engaged in mechanical business or scientific pursuits may have four gallons of alcohol at one time, in addition to alcohol used in the preservation of specimens for scientific purposes. (Section 41 (3).) A minister of the gospel may have in his possession wine for sacramental purposes. A hospital or institution for the care of old people may keep liquor to be administered to patients or inmates upon doctor's prescription. Any manufacturing or industrial establishment may keep on the premises one pint of liquor for use in case of accident, upon permit by the Board.

Drinking Liquor.

" Any person who drinks liquor in a place where such liquor cannot lawfully be kept shall be deemed to have liquor" contrary to the law. (Sec. 41, (1) a.) But liquor cannot lawfully be drunk in all places where it may be lawfully kept, for example it cannot be drunk upon the premises of a manufacturer (secs. 50 and 44) or druggist. Nor can it be used for beverage purposes when supplied for use in mechanical or scientific pursuits or for medicinal or sacramental purposes. In short, the only place where liquor may lawfully be consumed for beverage purposes is in a private dwelling house, and the penalty for drinking it anywhere else is the same as for illegally having or keeping liquor.

THE RIGHT TO SELL LIQUOR IN ONTARIO.

No person shall either directly or indirectly sell or agree to sell any intoxicating liquor unless authorized by the law of Ontario to sell liquor within the province. (Sec. 40.)

The law of Ontario permits the sale of liquor within the province for sacramental, industrial, artistic, mechanical, scientific and medicinal purposes. Liquor can only be sold in Ontario by the following persons under the circumstances stated and not otherwise.

1. A distiller, brewer or other person duly licensed by the Government of Canada may sell liquor to a person in another province or in a foreign country (section 45), but such licenses will only be granted to manu-

APPENDICES.

facturers of liquor for permitted purposes, and such liquor may only be sold or shipped to persons authorized to sell for permitted purposes, whether in this province or elsewhere.

Under the amending statute adopted at the 1919 session of the Legislature, distillers and brewers can only sell to the Board hereafter and the Board distributes its liquor to those entitled to dispose of it under the act.

2. A manufacturer of native wine may sell such wine to any person in Ontario in quantities of not less than five gallons in each cask or vessel at any one time, and when sold in bottles, not less than one dozen bottles of at least three half-pints each at any one time. (Sec. 44.)

3. Government sales agencies may sell alcohol and other liquor for permitted purposes to such persons as are entitled to purchase the same. They cannot, however, sell liquor in greater quantities, in any other place to other persons, for other purposes or otherwise than as provided by the law. (Sec.34.) No liquor may be sold for consumption on the licensed premises nor during prohibited hours. (Sec. 37.) An accurate record of sales must be kept. Special provision is made for auditing the agencies' accounts and safe-guard against fraud. Government sales agencies may sell liquor to the following persons and for the purposes stated only:

(a) To any person engaged in mechanical business or in scientific pursuits for mechanical or scientific purposes.

(b) To any minister of the gospel, or to a druggist for resale for sacramental purposes (sacramental wine only).

(c) For medicinal uses as follows:

1. To wholesale druggist, alcohol; to any duly registered pharmaceutical chemist, alcohol and sacramental wine; to any duly qualified physician, to any duly qualified dentist, to any duly qualified veterinary surgeon, to any public or private hospital, institution devoted exclusively to the care of old people, sanitarium for consumptives, or private sanitarium, liquor, and to any person upon the prescription of a duly qualified medical practitioner. The following quantities of liquor may be sold by a government sales agency on a physician's prescription:

(1) Ale, beer and porter in quantities not exceeding one dozen bottles, containing not more than three half-pints each, at one time.

(2) Wines and distilled liquor not exceeding one quart at one time.

(3) Alcohol or liquor mixed with any other drug not exceeding one pint.

4. A duly registered pharmaceutical chemist or druggist may, upon the written or printed prescription of a physician, sell liquor for medicinal purposes, not exceeding six ounces, except in the case of alcohol for bathing or other necessary purpose, or liquor mixed with any drug, when a quantity not exceeding one pint may be sold. (Sec. 128.)

5. While the prescription of liquor by a duly qualified physician may not, strictly speaking, be a sale of liquor, yet it may with advantage be discussed here.

Any physician may prescribe liquor who is lawfully and regularly engaged in the practice of his profession.

Before such a physician may prescribe intoxicating liquor, however, he must deem it necessary for the health of his patient. "No such prescription shall be given except in cases of actual need, and when in the judgment of such physician the use of liquor is necessary." (Sec. 51).

Prescriptions for liquor must be written or printed, according to statutory form, or in words to the like effect. Only one sale may be made upon one prescription. Every prescription must contain a certificate

APPENDICES.

that the quantity therein mentioned is the minimum quantity necessary for the patient for whom it is ordered.

A real duty is cast upon a physician to obtain sufficient evidence to satisfy him that the patient is in need of liquor.

In addition to the right to prescribe for liquor, a physician may also administer liquor himself to his patients and for that purpose may have liquor in his office or dispensary and one quart of liquor in his possession when visiting his patients.

PENALTIES.

The penalties for unlawfully having, keeping, or selling liquor are as follows:

1. A manufacturer of native wine who sells wine contrary to the law is liable for the first offence, to a penalty of not less than $10 and not more than $100, and in default of immediate payment, to imprisonment for not less than ten days nor more than two months.

2. A druggist who sells liquor contrary to the act is liable, for the first offence, to a fine of not less than $50 and not more than $300, and in default of immediate payment, to imprisonment for not less than two months nor more than four months, and for a second or subsequent offence, to a penalty of not less than $100 nor more than $500, and in default of immediate payment to imprisonment for a term of not less than four months nor more than eight months, and his certificate as a chemist shall *ipso facto* be void for a period of two years from the date of his conviction. (Sec. 132.)

3. Any other person, including a distiller, brewer, etc., who unlawfully has, keeps or sells liquor is liable to the following penalties:

For the first offence, a fine of not less than $200 nor more than $1,000 or in default of immediate payment, imprisonment for not less than three nor more than six months, and if the offence is committed by a licensee or by any person with his privity or consent, he may have his license forfeited. For the second offence, imprisonment for not less than six nor more than twelve months without the option of a fine. If the offence is committed by a licensee or by any person with his privity or consent, his license shall be forfeited and he shall be incapable of becoming a licensee under this Act for a period of three years thereafter. (Sec. 58.)

4. A physician who prescribes liquor in evasion or violation of the act is liable to the same penalties as a druggist who sells liquor contrary to the law (except of course as to certificate).

SPECIAL PROVISIONS.

The Ontario Temperance Act, also contains several special provisions designed to strengthen the main prohibitory features of the law already dealt with, by first, preventing their evasion, and secondly meeting special difficulties not adequately covered by the general prohibitions stated.

To Prevent Evasion.

1. *Medicated Wines.*—All such compounds, mixtures and preparations must contain sufficient medication to prevent their use as alcoholic beverages. (Sec. 125.) This is a question of fact, to be determined by the magistrate whose decision is final in this regard.

2. *Patent Medicines.*—Patent medicines are subject to the same rule as medicated wines, some of which, of course are registered as patent medicines. The fact that a preparation is registered as a patent medicine does not

APPENDICES.

authorize its sale contrary to the Ontario Temperance Act. Penalties incurred for breach of the Patent Medicines Act are deemed to be in addition to penalties recoverable under the O.T.A. The Provincial Board of Health, may on complaint, cause an analysis to be made of any such preparation, and if the medication found therein is not sufficient to prevent its use as an alcoholic beverage, the Board shall certify accordingly. If the Board finds that the medication contained, if taken in quantities, would be injurious to health, the sale of such patent medicine may be prohibited. (Sec. 126, 1918.)

3. *Essences.*—Flavoring extracts, tinctures and essences containing more than two and one-half per centum of proof spirits may only be sold by retail in bottles containing not more than two and one-half ounces. A record of sales must be kept by the druggist, merchant, or manufacturer. No pedlar or transient trader may sell such tinctures. The sale of essence of ginger is specially restricted. It may only be sold by retail by a druggist, and then only (1) upon the order of a physician or (2) to a person having a permanent residence in the community, upon an affidavit that such essence is required for legitimate purposes and in a quantity not exceeding two ounces.

To Meet Special Difficulties.

1. *Canvassing.*—It is unlawful for a person, whether licensee or not, or whether by himself, his servant or agent, to canvass for or receive or solicit orders for liquor for beverage purposes in Ontario. It is immaterial that orders are not received in consequence. The real substance of the transaction will be looked to in deciding whether an offence has been committed or not.

2. *Minors.*—Liquor shall not be given, sold, or otherwise supplied to any person apparently under the age of twenty-one years, except (a) by the parent or guardian of such person for medicinal purposes only, or (b) by a druggist or vendor upon the prescription of a duly qualified medical practitioner. (Sec. 52.) Thus, liquor may not be given to a minor, even in the private dwelling in which he resides, by anyone except his parent or guardian, and then for medicinal purposes only.

3. *Habitual Drunkards.*—" Any person who has the habit of drinking liquor to excess may be prohibited from having liquor in his possession, except under the order of a duly qualified medical practitioner, or from purchasing or procuring, or attempting to purchase or procure liquor." Any Justice of the Peace having jurisdiction may, upon proof either in open court or by affidavit, issue such a prohibitory order. So also the license inspector for the county may, of his own motion, or at the request of any near relative, or the employer of such person, give a similar notice to the person to be prohibited. Notice may also be given to express companies not to deliver liquor to the prohibited person. Such a person is not permitted to have liquor even in his private residence while the prohibitory order is in force. Procedure is provided by the act for the repeal of the order in proper cases. The penalty for breach of these provisions is the same as for the illegal sale of liquor. (Sec. 55a.)

4. *Prohibited Areas.*—In any case of emergency the Lieutenant Governor in Council may issue a proclamation forbidding any person from having liquor in his possession within the area mentioned in such a proclamation except under a special permit.

5. *Near Beer.*—" The keeper of a standard hotel (licensed under the Ontario Temperance Act) shall be entitled to sell non-intoxicating drinks and beverages, cigars, cigarettes and tobacco, and to conduct an ice cream

APPENDICES.

or general restaurant or cafe, without further or other license." (Sec. 146 (5).) The keeper of any hotel, inn, or house of public entertainment not so licensed as aforesaid shall not sell or traffic in any of the articles above mentioned.

PROSECUTIONS.

1. *Information and Complaint.*

Any person may lay an information or prosecute for an offence against the Ontario Temperance Act.

All information or complaints must be made in writing (but not necessarily on oath) within three months after the commission of the offence.

Complaint may be made before any Justice of the Peace for the County in which the offence is alleged to have been committed, but the trial, except in the case of a licensee, must take place before two Justices or a Police Magistrate. (Sec. 61.)

The description of any offence in the words of the act or in words of like effect is sufficient. (Sec. 76.) Any time before judgment a magistrate may amend any information and substitute for the offence charged therein any other offence against the provisions of the act, but if it appears that the defendant has been materially misled by such amendment, the magistrate must adjourn the hearing unless the defendant consents to immediate trial. (Sec. 78.)

2. *Procedure at Trial.*

Offences against the Ontario Temperance Act are dealt with by magistrates under the ordinary procedure governing the trial of criminal offences over which magistrates have summary jurisdiction. (Sec. 72.) It is important to note, however, that no conviction or proceeding is held insufficient or invalid by reason of any defect in form or substance, provided it can be understood that the conviction or proceeding was made for an offence against some provision of the act within the jurisidction of the magistrate and provided there be evidence to prove some offence under that act. (Sec. 101.)

3. *Evidence.*

Generally speaking the burden of proving innocence is put upon the person accused of violating the act. If a person is accused of selling, giving or having liquor contrary to the law, and is shown to have had the liquor in his possession, concerning which he is prosecuted, then, unless he can prove that he did not commit the offence charged, he may be convicted accordingly.

In keeping with this general rule as to the burden of proof, the occupant of any house in which it is proved there exists a beer pump or other appliance usually found in hotels, may be convicted of illegally selling liquor unless he proves that the appliance in question was for legitimate purposes. (Sec. 82.) The occupant of any house or other place in which liquor is kept or sold illegally is personally responsible for the offence, but the "actual offender" and the occupant cannot both be convicted for the same offence. (Sec. 84.) The fact that there is on any premises not licensed under the Ontario Temperance Act "more liquor than is reasonably required for persons residing therein shall be deemed *prima facie* evidence of the unlawful sale and keeping for sale, and having and keeping of liquor by the occupant of the

APPENDICES.

premises." (Sec. 89.) This last section loses its chief virtue because it does not specify any time limit. The certificate of a government analyst as to the analysis of liquor is conclusive evidence of the facts stated in such certificate. (Sec. 90.)

If liquor seized in transit is consigned to a person in a fictitious name or is shipped as other goods, or concealed in any way, that is *prima facie* evidence that it was intended to be sold or kept contrary to the law.

4. *Penalties and Disposition of Penalties.*

The penalties applicable to the various offences have been stated in the chapters dealing with such offences. It may be pointed out, however, that the discretion of a magistrate as to the proper penalty to be imposed within the limit of the minimum and maximum penalties laid down, is final except where an appeal is allowed to the County Judge.

"No magistrate, justice of the peace or municipal council shall have any power or authority to remit, suspend or compromise any penalty or punishment inflicted under this act." (Sec. 114.) This section apparently overrides the usual procedure in cases where summary conviction may be made, by which time for payment may be given. A fine or penalty may be remitted, however, upon an application to the Attorney-General of Ontario under The Fines and Forfeitures Act, in cases of hardship, as for example, where there has been a technical breach of the law with no intent to commit an unlawful act.

Where a fine is imposed, the magistrate may, in his discretion, order that in defaut of immediate payment distress shall issue for its recovery, or he may, if he sees fit, commit the accused to bail. (Sec. 109.) Where the license inspector prosecutes, fines are paid over by the magistrate to him and remitted to the Board at Toronto. Where, however, a municipality has appointed an officer to enforce the act, fines are paid to the treasurer of that municipality.

5. *Appeals, Applications to Quash Convictions, Etc.*

The general rule is that a decision by a magistrate under the act is final. (Sec. 92.) To this there are two important exceptions.

Firstly, where the person convicted is a druggist, licensed vendor or the holder of a standard hotel license, an appeal may be taken by him to the County Judge from the magistrate's decision; also where any person accused of an offence against the act is acquitted, and the Attorney-General of Ontario so directs, an appeal may be taken to the County Judge. On such appeals the County Judge may hear the entire evidence over again, may affirm or reverse the decision of the magistrate and increase or decrease the penalty. (Sec. 92.)

Secondly, although these are the only cases in which appeals may be taken, yet the magistrate's decision may also be reviewed where the accused complains that the magistrate had no jurisdiction to try him, or that there was no evidence at all upon which a conviction could be made. Such applications are usually made by a motion to quash the conviction before a Judge of the Supreme Court of Ontario. Where the question of jurisdiction is raised, the usual objection is that the acts of the accused did not constitute an offence under the statute. All such applications are required to be disposed of on their merits, and if it is apparent that the merits have been tried, and there was evidence to support the conviction, it will not be interfered with.

APPENDICES.

RIGHTS AND DUTIES OF THE LICENSE BOARD, INSPECTORS AND OFFICERS.

1. *Responsibility for Enforcement.*

The Ontario Temperance Act originally provided for the appointment by the Lieutenant-Governor in Council of a Board of License Commissioners for Ontario, to be composed of five persons. The number of members composing the Board was subsequently reduced to three, and may be still further reduced if that is deemed necessary. The members of the Board hold office during pleasure. (Sec. 118.)

The duty of seeing that the Ontario Temperance Act is enforced throughout the whole province and of prosecuting persons offending against is provisions, devolves upon the Board and the License Inspectors, and other officers appointed pursuant to the act. (Secs. 61, 63, 64.) Every policeman and constable, however, is deemed to be within the provisions of the act, and it is his duty to carry out and enforce it. Where information is furnished to any inspector, policeman or constable, it is his duty to inquire into the truth of such information, and to enter complaint in his own name, without communicating the name of the person giving him such information. Every inspector and provincial officer is, for the purpose of enforcing the Ontario Temperance Act, a constable for every county and district in Ontario, and is required to take an oath of office and to furnish security. (Sec. 119.)

The Council of any municipality may by by-law appoint an officer whose duty it shall be to enforce the Ontario Temperance Act within the limits of that municipality. (Sec. 120.) Where such an officer is appointed, fines recovered are paid to the municipal treasurer.

"Every inspector, policeman, or constable, neglecting or refusing to carry out and enforce this act shall incur a penalty of $10.00 and may be summarily dismissed from office."

2. *Duties.*

(a) *Right of Search and Seizure.*—To assist officers to enforce the law, they are given wide powers of search and seizure. Any officer may, for the purpose of preventing or detecting the contravention of the act, at any time enter and search any place of public entertainment, shop, warehouse or other place wherein refreshments or liquors are sold or reputed to be sold or kept contrary to the act. (Sec. 66.)

Liquor discovered may be seized, and if the occupant of the premises, or any other person, is convicted of having or selling liquor contrary to the act, it may be forfeited to the Crown. (Sec. 68.)

Where any officer finds liquor in course of delivery in any railway or express office, or other place, and believes that such liquor is to be sold or dealt with contrary to the law, he may seize the liquor. So, also, where any officer believes that liquor is contained in any vehicle upon a public highway or elsewhere, or is concealed upon any land, or is contained in any trunk, box, bag or other receptacle on a public highway or elsewhere, and believes that liquor is intended for sale, or to be kept for sale, or otherwise contrary to the act, he may seize such liquor, whether in the custody or under the control of any person or not. (Sec. 70 (2).) No person but the consignee, or his duly authorized agent, can lawfully take delivery of liquor from a common carrier. The records of railway and express companies must show every consignment of liquor, and these records are open to the inspection of any license inspector or provincial officer. (Sec. 70a.)

APPENDICES.

(b) *Arrest.*—"Any intoxicated person and any person found committing the offence of selling, giving or drinking liquor upon a street, highway, or in any public place, may be arrested without warrant." (Sec. 68 (2).) These are the only cases in which arrest without warrant is permitted for breach of the Ontario Temperance Act. In all other cases, where power to arrest is required, a warrant must first be obtained from a magistrate or justice. A magistrate may, also, of course, issue a summons if he sees fit.

APPENDIX XII.

MANIFESTO OF DOMINION PROHIBITION COMMITTEE, APRIL, 1917.

This memorandum has been prepared for the purpose of explaining the proposal agreed to at the conference held in Ottawa on December 14th last, at which there were present representatives chosen by the active organizations of all the provinces of the Dominion that are seeking legislation to remedy the evils of intemperance. It is believed that such legislation is specially desirable and necessary because of the war emergency. The proposal will be presented to the Dominion Parliament when it reassembles in April, by petitions which are now being signed in every part of the Dominion, and which are in the following form:

It is earnestly desired that your Honorable Body will forthwith pass, as a war measure, an Act prohibiting

1. The manufacture in, and the importation into, the Dominion of Canada, of intoxicating liquors, for beverage purposes; and,
2. The sending or carrying of any such liquors into, and the delivering or receiving of any such liquors in any province or area in which the sale of such liquors for beverage purposes is prohibited.

Or in the alternative, if it is deemed desirable to have a vote of the electors on the question, that your Honorable Body will pass such an Act, to come into operation within three months of the voting thereon, if it is approved by a majority of the electors voting, such voting to be at the earliest possible date and in any case before June 1st, 1917.

The Call of the King.

This appeal is to the Dominion Government and Parliament. They have shown their high patriotism and their loyalty to the great principles and interests for which the Empire is making such unstinted sacrifices of the treasure which the toil of centuries has won, and of the flower of the manhood that has been the pride and joy of her hearts and homes. Mighty has been the response to the call of our King:

I rejoice in my Empire's efforts. I feel pride in the voluntary response from my subjects all over the world who have sacrificed home and fortune and life itself, in order that another may not inherit the free Empire which their ancestors and mine have built. I ask you to make good these sacrifices.

Now the needs of the war situation make another demand upon Canada's statesmanship and citizenship, and tens of thousands of citizens

APPENDICES.

are hoping and praying that the demand will be met with wisdom and courage that will make the answer prompt and complete.

WASTE AND HARM.

The resources of the Dominion are being squandered to a serious extent, and the efficiency of our man-power is impaired, by the liquor traffic. That traffic is absorbing millions of dollars, millions of bushels of grain, the labor of thousands of men, and badly needed transportation facilities; to which immense loss must be added the weakening of mental and physical power and skill, and the misery, disaster and crime that the traffic entails. All this keeps our country from taking the full part she ought to take in the fierce struggle of which the British Premier said: " We are fighting Germany, Austria and Drink, and, so far as I can see, the greatest of these deadly foes is Drink."

A GREAT ADVANCE.

In practically every country in the world, the question of temperance is now receiving special attention, and in nearly all cases efforts to improve conditions are taking the form of legislation to restrain or suppress the traffic of intoxicating beverages. This legislation is not aimed at traffic in intoxicating liquors for industrial, medicinal and sacramental purposes, but only against the traffic for beverage purposes.

The Legislatures of eight out of nine Canadian provinces have already passed Acts suppressing the sale of intoxicating beverages as far as it is believed a province can constitutionally go; that is, to the extent of prohibiting transactions in liquor that begin and are completed within the limits of the province; it cannot prohibit the sending in of liquor from outside places. These laws have already gone into force in six provinces, and in every case there has been the most gratifying reduction in drinking, drunkenness and all the evils resulting from drinking. At the same time there still exist in all these provinces sufficient drunkenness and other evils resulting from drinking, to call for further action, specially when war conditions make desirable the conserving of all our national resources and the attainment of the highest possible efficiency on the part of our citizens.

PROVINCIAL PROHIBITION A SUCCESS.

Attention is called to the following figures concerning two of these prohibition provinces, as evidence of the great good that has been accomplished, and as evidence of the need there is for further and more thoroughgoing action:

Here is a table showing the arrests for the offence of drunkenness in the five largest cities of Ontario during the first full three months of prohibition, ending December 31st, 1916, as compared with the arrests for the corresponding three months of 1915 under license:

	1915.	1916.
Toronto	2,908	953
Ottawa	286	234
Hamilton	498	61
London	367	144
Brantford	152	16

The situation in Ottawa is, of course, readily understood, being caused by the operation of licenses in the City of Hull across the river, result-

APPENDICES.

ing in the arrests in Ottawa of not only residents, but men who have come from other places and have to be taken charge of by the police after coming back drunk from Hull.

The following table of arrests for drunkenness in the principal cities of the Province of Alberta for the first six months of prohibition, compared with the corresponding six months of the preceding year under license, conveys the same lesson as do the Ontario figures:

City.	1915.	1916.
Edmonton	247	64
Calgary	476	47
Lethbridge	325	21
Medicine Hat	70	18
Wetaskiwin	35	4
Red Deer	6	1
Total	1,159	155

A Reasonable Request.

These facts show not only the good done, but the great evil that remains, and that would be vastly lessened, if not practically abolished, by legislation that prohibited the manufacture and importation of, and interprovincial traffic in, alcoholic beverages; which legislation the Dominion Parliament alone has power to enact, and which the Federal Government is now earnestly urged to initiate and promote.

As the petition shows, the request made by the Dominion Prohibition Committee is for the immediate enactment of such legislation, to remain in force till after the war, and then to be subject to a vote of the electors;

Or in the alternative, the passing of such an Act, to come into operation only if ratified by the people at the polls, the voting on the question of ratification to be at the earliest possible date.

The Present Law Insufficient.

At its 1916 session the Dominion Parliament passed an Act making it unlawful for any person to send, ship, take, bring or carry into any province any intoxicating liquor, knowing or intending that such liquor will be thereafter dealt with in violation of the law of that province. It has been argued that the Dominion Parliament does not need to go any further, that this legislation would prevent the sending of liquor into a province in which it was unlawful for any person to have or use liquor, because in such a case the sending of intoxicating beverages into the province would be contrary to the Dominion law.

Of course, to make the sending unlawful, it would be necessary for the Provincial Legislature to pass an Act making it an offence for anyone to have in his private home, or to use under any circumstances, any intoxicating liquor for beverage purposes. It is further stated that a Provincial Legislature has authority to pass such a law.

It must be borne in mind, however, that the provincial legislation thus suggested would be something entirely new, and would mean a complete alteration of the legislative method hitherto used in dealing with the evils of intemperance. All Canadian temperance legislation, so far, has been aimed at the traffic in liquor, without directly undertaking to dictate the personal conduct of private citizens.

APPENDICES.

THE BETTER WAY.

Legislation against the *liquor traffic* has not only done immense good, but has had the support of many citizens who would not favor a law that punished private parties for having or using liquor. It has been thought wise to lessen drinking and drunkenness by making it difficult or impossible to procure liquor, instead of by imposing punishment upon a person who has or uses it. There is no doubt that there are very many citizens who will support Dominion and provincial laws prohibiting liquor-selling, who would not favor laws imposing fines or imprisonment upon every person who had or kept a bottle of liquor in his home. It is also clear that the great good desired could be attained by wise Dominion legislation against the liquor traffic, without the adoption of the other drastic method.

SLOW AND UNCERTAIN.

Let it be assumed, for the sake of argument, that the opinion stated concerning provincial power is correct, and that the Dominion law already passed would prohibit the sending of liquor into a province which enacted the new kind of legislation, which, it must be remembered, has not yet been tested, either judicially or practically, and which would involve an invasion of domestic life that legislators have hitherto endeavored to avoid. There still remains the facts that the result sought can be more readily attained by the Dominion legislation asked for, that this legislation may be more quickly secured, that it will certainly be less harsh in appearance, that different provinces have practically approved of it in many votings, and that Parliament's power to pass it is not only unquestioned, but has been affirmed by Privy Council decisions.

Furthermore, to attain the object aimed at, under the legislation of last session, would require the passing of laws against the having and using of liquor in private homes, by the Legislatures of eight different provinces, while the desired result could be attained by one Act passed by the Dominion Parliament, much less stringent in its form but equally effective.

A HEAVY HANDICAP.

Every loyal, well-informed citizen will agree that "The Strength of Canada," our ability to help the Empire, ought not to be handicapped, as it is, by the interprovincial liquor traffic which the Dominion Parliament has full power to suppress.

Belgium is starving for bread. Even in Britain a Food Controller has power to regulate the diet of the people. A year ago Canada promised the Empire 500,000 soldiers, and has not yet been able to make good her word.

Yet, during the last fiscal year, Canada destroyed 150,000,000 lbs. of foodstuffs in the making of intoxicating liquor, which drink in turn made Canadian manhood less efficient. Transportation facilities, badly needed because of war conditions, were clogged and hindered by carrying the grain to destruction and carrying the destructive product back to those who consumed it. For this hurtful product, the people of this country paid many millions of dollars. In the last ten years, Canada has spent for liquor far more money than she has yet contributed in every form for war purposes and for every form of patriotic service growing out of the war conditions.

Our long promise of half a million men would long ago have been met had all who offered themselves as recruits been able to pass the necessary medical inspection. While high respect and gratitude is due

APPENDICES.

every man who has shown himself willing to serve his country in this grave emergency, it is a sad fact that in many cases the disqualifying weakness was the result of habits of dissipation, or of habits of dissipation on the part of ancestors, or of home privations in childhood days, which privations were caused by drink indulgence. The liquor traffic that Canada has fostered holds Canada back to-day from doing her duty at this terrible crisis in the history of humanity and civilization, when the British bulwark of that civilization is so sorely tried.

Must We Fall Behind?

Is not the demand that the Dominion Parliament should prohibit the liquor traffic during the war a demand that should have the support of every high-purposed patriotic citizen?

Heretofore Canada has had the high honor of leadership in the march of social progress and reform. For many years her per capita consumption of alcohol has been lowest among civilized nations. Recently the spread of knowledge and self-sacrificing patriotism has been very marked in other communities also. The Russian Empire has prohibited the whole traffic in vodka, the national intoxicant, in a population of 170,-000,000 people. In the United States, where individual states have even more prohibitory power than Canadian provinces, the Federal Legislature has come to their aid. Twenty-five of them have enacted prohibitory laws, and a few days ago, by overwhelming majorities in both Houses of Congress, an Act was passed containing the following clause:

"Whoever shall order, purchase or cause intoxicating liquors to be transported in interstate commerce (except for scientific, mechanical, or medical purposes), into any state or territory, the laws of which state or territory prohibit the manufacture or sale therein for beverage purposes, shall be punished by a fine of not more than $1,000, or imprisonment for not more than six months, or both; and for any subsequent offence shall be imprisoned not more than one year."

That is just the kind of protection that is now asked for prohibition provinces. Canada needs it more than does the United States because of the war emergency, and Canadians are just as willing as are the citizens of the United States to make any needful sacrifice for the common good.

The Soldiers' Vote.

If it is said that the soldiers at the front ought to have a voice in such legislation and that the taking of their votes would involve difficulty or delay, it may be answered that the proposal is for the legislation requested "as a war measure," to be voted upon after the war is over. Then the soldiers will have a share in the decision of whether or not it will continue in this country after their return. This fact makes immediate action as absolutely fair as it is manifestly right.

Canada's Purpose.

Loyal Canadians in Parliament and out of it earnestly desire to do what they can to help the Empire to win the war and destroy the terrible menace of German militarism, to defeat which such awful sacrifices have already been made.

Is there a well-informed citizen who will not admit that the complete suppression of the traffic in intoxicating beverages would make Canada

APPENDICES.

and the Empire stronger in money and manhood, and therefore better able to discharge the great duty that has been laid upon them?

It is earnestly hoped that the movement will have the support of all patriotic journals and citizens in every part of the Dominion, and this statement is made for the purpose of giving full information to those who, regardless of all minor considerations, will unite in support of a movement to put Canada in the position she ought to occupy.

On behalf of the Dominion Prohibition Committee.

EUGENE LAFONTAINE,　　　　　　　　　　MILES VOKES,
　　　Chairman.　　　　　　　　　　Sub-Executive Chairman.
　　　　　　　　　JOHN H. ROBERTS,
　　　　　　　　　　　Secretary.

APPENDIX XIII.

ORDER IN COUNCIL.

AT THE GOVERNMENT HOUSE AT OTTAWA,

Monday, the 11th day of March, 1918.
Present:

His Excellency the Governor-General in Council.

Whereas the War Committee of the Cabinet, after review of the existing conditions due to the war, is of the opinion that it is urgently necessary to concentrate to the fullest extent the energy and resources of Canada upon work of national importance in the present emergency;

Whereas in consequence of such necessity and in the interest of national economy certain regulations were made and enacted as follows:

By Order in Council of November 2nd, 1917 (P.C. 3116), it was forbidden to use grain, or any substance that can be used for food, for the distillation of potable liquors in Canada, on and after the first day of December, 1917;

By Order in Council of the 27th of November, 1917 (P.C. 3203), the quantity of malt manufactured in Canada, and the quantity of barley used in the manufacture of malt in Canada, were limited to the quantity of malt manufactured and barley used for the manufacture of malt during the year ended the 31st of March, 1916, except under a license to increase such quantities of malt or barley to be issued by the Minister of Inland Revenue;

By Orders in Council of the 22nd of December, 1917 (P.C. 3473), of the 26th December, 1917 (P.C. 3484), of the 19th of January, 1918 (P.C. 134), of the 26th of January, 1918 (P.C. 224), the importation of liquors containing more than two and one-half per centum of proof spirits was prohibited on or after the 24th of December, 1917, save under license for certain permitted purposes, unless actually purchased for importation into Canada before the 24th of December, 1917, and actually shipped on or before the 31st of January, 1918;

Whereas laws have been passed in every province of Canada prohibiting the sale of intoxicating liquor, and such laws are now in force save in the Province of Quebec, where the prohibitory law is to go into force on May 1st, 1919, and in order to make such legislation more effective it is desirable to enact regulations supplementing these provincial laws;

APPENDICES.

Whereas on the said 22nd day of December, 1917, the Prime Minister announced that the transportation of liquor into any part of Canada wherein the sale of intoxicating liquor is illegal would be prohibited on and after April 1st, 1918, and that the manufacture of intoxicating liquor within Canada would be prohibited on and after a date to be determined upon further investigation and consideration of the actual conditions of the industry;

And whereas the War Committee, in order to give full effect to such declaration of policy, and in order still further to prevent waste, to promote thrift, to conserve resources, and thus to increase national efficiency, is of the opinion that regulations should be enacted prohibiting the manufacture of intoxicating liquor in Canada, and forbidding the transportation of such liquor into any part of Canada wherein the sale of such liquor is by law prohibited, and the sale of such liquor for delivery in any such part of Canada, and the delivery in any such part of Canada of liquor sold in any other part of Canada;

Therefore His Excellency the Governor-General in Council, on the recommendation of the Prime Minister, and under and by virtue of the provisions of The War Measures Act, 1914, is pleased to make the following recommendations, and the same are hereby made and enacted accordingly:

REGULATIONS:

1. In these regulations:

(a) "Person" includes any body, corporate and politic.

(b) "Province" means any province of Canada and also includes the North-West Territories and the Yukon Territory.

(c) "Prohibited area" means any province, territory, municipality, district, county, or other area wherein the sale of intoxicating liquor is under or by any law, federal or provincial, prohibited.

(d) "Licensee" means a person authorized by the law of a province to sell within that province intoxicating liquor for use within that province.

(e) "Manufacturer" means a person licensed by the Minister of Inland Revenue of Canada to manufacture intoxicating liquor for sacramental, industrial, mechanical, artistic, scientific or medicinal purposes.

(f) "Intoxicating liquor" means and includes any liquor or beverage which contains more than two and one-half per centum of proof spirits.

2. No person shall make or manufacture intoxicating liquor or cause intoxicating liquor to be made or manufactured within the Dominion of Canada after the first day of April, 1918: Provided that in case the sale of intoxicating liquor of any class for beverage purposes is permitted in any province, this regulation shall not apply to the manufacture of such intoxicating liquor in such province until the thirty-first day of December, 1918: Provided further, that the provisions of the above recited Orders in Council of November 2nd, 1917 (P.C. 3116), and November 27th, 1917 (P.C. 3203), shall continue to apply to any such manufacture.

3. Nothing in these regulations shall prevent a manufacturer from making or manufacturing intoxicating liquor for sacramental, industrial, artistic, mechanical, scientific, and medicinal purposes, in accordance with the terms of his license.

4. No person after the first day of April, 1918, shall send, take, transport into, or deliver in any prohibited area any intoxicating liquor or cause any intoxicating liquor to be so sent, transported or delivered.

APPENDICES.

5. No person after the first day of April, 1918, shall either directly or indirectly sell or contract or agree to sell any intoxicating liquor which is in, or which is to be delivered within any prohibited area.

6. Nothing in these regulations contained shall prevent a licensee or manufacturer from selling, sending, taking or transporting intoxicating liquor to a licensee in any prohibited area, or prevent a common carrier by water, or by railway, from transporting or carrying intoxicating liquor from any licensee or manufacturer to a licensee in a prohibited area, or prevent any intoxicating liquor from being so carried through a prohibited area, nor prevent a licensee in a prohibited area, from selling and delivering intoxicating liquor, for sacramental, industrial, artistic, mechanical, scientific and medicinal purposes, in accordance with the terms of his license.

7. If in any prohibited area there should be no licensee authorized to receive and sell intoxicating liquor for sacramental, industrial, artistic, mechanical, scientific and medicinal purposes, the Governor in Council may authorize one or more persons in such prohibited area to receive and sell intoxicating liquors for such purposes, and any person so authorized shall be deemed a licensee within the meaning of these regulations.

8. The carriage of intoxicating liquor from a licensee or manufacturer to a licensee in a prohibited area, and carriage through any prohibited area shall be only by means of a common carrier by water or by railway, and not otherwise.

9. During the time any intoxicating liquor is being transported or carried into or through a prohibited area as aforesaid, no person shall open, or break, or allow to be opened or broken, any package or vessel containing it, or drink or use, or allow to be drunk or used any intoxicating liquor therefrom.

10. The burdens of proving the right to make or manufacture intoxicating liquor, or cause intoxicating liquor to be made or manufactured, or to send, carry, or deliver intoxicating liquor or cause intoxicating liquor to be sent, carried or delivered into or in a prohibited area, shall be on the person accused.

11. Every person who violates any of the provisions of these regulations shall be guilty of an offence, and shall be liable on summary conviction to a penalty for the first offence of not less than $200, and not more than $1,000, and in default of immediate payment to imprisonment for not less than three, nor more than six months, and for a second offence to imprisonment for not less than six months nor more than twelve months.

12. If it is proved upon oath before any judge of the sessions of the peace, recorder, police magistrate, stipendiary magistrate, two justices of the peace, or any magistrate having the power of authority of two or more justices of the peace, that there is reasonable cause to suspect that any intoxicating liquor is being taken, transported or carried in violation of these regulations, or is in any premises or place, and that such intoxicating liquor has been manufactured or dealt with contrary to the provisions of these regulations, such officer may grant a warrant to search premises, or place, including any government railway, vehicle or steamship, for such intoxicating liquor, and if the same or any part thereof is there found, to seize and bring the same before him; and when any person is convicted of any offence against any of the provisions of these regulations, the officer or officers so convicting shall adjudge and

APPENDICES.

order, in addition to any other penalty, that the intoxicating liquor in respect of which the offence was committed, and which has been seized under a search warrant as aforesaid, and all kegs, barrels, cases, boxes, bottles, packages, and other receptacles of any kind whatsoever, found containing the same, be forfeited to the Crown, and such order shall thereupon be carried out by the constable or peace officer who executed the said search warrant or by such other person as may be thereunto authorized by the officer, or officers who have made such conviction.

13. These regulations shall be construed as supplementary to the prohibitory laws now in force or that may be hereafter in force in any province or territory, and shall continue in force during the continuance of the present war, and for twelve months thereafter.

RODOLPHE BOUDREAU,
Clerk of the Privy Council

APPENDIX XIV.

MILESTONES OF TEMPERANCE.

1855—New Brunswick Prohibition Law—repealed 1856.
1864—Dunkin Act.
1875—Dominion Royal Commission.
1876—Formation of Dominion Alliance.
1876—Crook's Act (Ontario License Law).
1878—Canada TemperanceAct. SCOTT ACT
1883—Formation of Dominion W.C.T.U.
1883—McCarthy Act—declared invalid 1885.
1892—Dominion Royal Commission appointed.
1892—Manitoba Plebiscite.
1893—Prince Edward Island Plebiscite.
1894—Nova Scotia Plebiscite.   ONTARIO PLEBISCITE
1895—Report of Royal Commission.
1898—Dominion Plebiscite.
264 - 1900—Prince Edward Island Prohibition Law.
261 - 1902—Manitoba Referendum.
278 - 1902—Ontario Referendum.
212 - 1906—Ontario Local Option—Three-fifths Requirement.
329   1910—Nova Scotia Temperance Act.
        1915—Saskatchewan Prohibition Law.
400 - 1916—Ontario Temperance Act,
454   1916—Alberta Prohibition Law.
1916—Nova Scotia Prohibition Law.
426 1916—Manitoba Prohibition Law.
349 1916—New Brunswick Prohibition Law.
470 1916—British Columbia Prohibition Law.
371 1918—Quebec Prohibition Law.
489 1918—Dominion Prohibition Orders in Council.
1919—Quebec Beer and Wine Referendum.

INDEX.

INDEX.

Abraham, Dr. R. H. 308
Advanced Prohibitionists ...193, 202
Africa 555
Aikins, Sir J. A. M.264, 269, 409, 424
Alabama 505, 511
Alaska 505
Alberta .... 446, ff
  Government Control .. 454
  License Law Amendments.... 450
  Local Option Campaigns..... 452
  Prohibition Act .... 454, ff
  Prohibition vote in... 457
  Prohibiton amended .. 459
  Temperance and Moral Reform
    Committee .... 448, ff
  Woman Suffrage 70
  W.C.T.U. organized 63
Anglo-Indian Temperance Association 550, 551
Anti-Alcoholic League of Quebec 378
Anti-Alcoholic League, Montreal.
                  363, 365, 370
Anti-Alcoholic League 504
Anti-Saloon League of America—
  Unites with Dominion Alliance of Canada in calling
    World Convention 565
Anti-Saloon League Convention
  at Columbus, Ohio, in 1918 564
Arabia 553
Arizona 505, 511
Arkansas 505, 511
Armstrong, E. H............. 336
Assessment Act, N.S., amended.. 332
Austria-Hungary 547
Australia 558
  See also New South Wales.
    Victoria.
    South Australia.
    Tasmania.
    West Australia.
Ayearst, J. A.................. 407

Baird, J. H................... 415
Baxter, Hon. J. B. M.......... 350
Bayley, W. D................. 472
Bazin, Dr. J. A............... 356

Beaver River — First Canadian
  Temperance Society..... 38-40
Beecher, Dr. Lyman........... 501
Belgium 530
Bengough, J. W............... 243
Bennett Amendment 483
Blake, Hon. Edward........... 261
Bond, Major E. L..........245, 356
Borden, Sir Robert..........482, 485
Bourinot, Sir John............. 284
Bowles, Rev. R. P............. 273
Bowser, Hon. W. O............ 468
Brewster, Hon. H. C........465, 474
British American Order of Good
  Templars, The.. .51, 53, 54
British Columbia .459, ff
  C. T. A. made applicable to... 138
  Dominion Plebiscite Campaign 246
  Local Option League........ 460
  New License Law passed..... 464
  People's Prohibition Movement 467
  Plebiscite on Local Option.... 464
  Prohibition Law . 470
  Royal Commission appointed.. 462
  Soldiers' Vote 472
  W.C.T.U. organized 63
  Woman Suffrage 70
Brown, Edward 409
Bruchesi, Mgr. 357, 358, 363
Buchanan, W. W...195, 201, 277, 411
Bulgaria 545
Bulmer, J. T.................. 148
Bustin, S. B.................. 350

Calder, Hon. J. A............. 440
Cameron, Hon. Malcolm.86, 89, 91, 106
Campbell, Hon. Colin H.....266, 269
Campbell, C. A............337, 339
Camp Fire, The................ 297
Canada Casket 41, 99
Canada's New Party..........141, ff
Canada Temperance Act..107, 122, ff
  Amendments 133
  Made applicable to B.C...... 138
  Ontario campaign ....131, ff
  New Brunswick 343

INDEX.

Canada Temperance Act—*Con.*
  Quebec 370
  Quebec City 373
  Repealed in
    New Brunswick 352
    Nova Scotia 341
    Prince Edward Island...... 329
  Validity established ....125, *ff*
  Voting upon 127
Canada Temperance Advocate... 41
Canada Temperance Union..... 106
Canada West—
  Prohibition Bill for 1859..... 90
  Sunday Closing Act passed... 91
  Temperance missionaries organize societies .... .44, 45
Canadian Prohibitory Liquor Law
  League 88
Canadian Temperance League..59, 60
Canadian Temperance League organized 1853 (London).. 87
Carman, Rev. Dr...244, 281, 290, 386
Carson, J. H................171, 356
Carter, Rev. Henry............ 521
Carter, S. J.................. 365
Casey, T. W...............37, 41, 149
Catch-My-Pal Campaign in Ireland.528
Catholic Total Abstinence Union
  of America 502
Central America 513
Central Control Board, typical restrictions of 521
Ceylon 554
Charlottetown—
  Enforcement of Prohibition Act 327
  Period of "Free Rum"...... 323
China 552
Chiniquy, Father, work of.42, 43, 353
Chown, Rev. Dr. S. D..287, 292, 410, 447
Christie, Dr. Thos.......175, 254, 256
Christmas, Rev. Mr., organized Montreal Society.........38, 39
Citizens' Committee of One Hundred ....400, *ff*
Clark, Dr. B. J...... 500
Club Licenses, Manitoba 416
Coatsworth, Emerson, M.P...... 209
Colbert favors—
  Sale of fire-water 23
  Talon's Brewery 24
Colorado 505, 511
Committee of Fifty in U. S..... 504
Connecticut 501, 503, 510
Coone, A. W................... 455

Cooper, Rev. C. F............. 337
Courtice, Dr. A. C............ 223
Crawford, Hon. Thos.......279, 291
Crooks' Act 100, 284
Czerwinski, C. F............411, 414

D'Abernon, Lord 523
d'Avaugour, Baron—
  Enforced prohibition 22
  Annulled the law.. 22
Delaware 501, 506, 511
Denmark 533
Deputation to Ontario Legislature after the Plebiscite. 215
Dewart, Rev. Dr. E. H......... 202
Dickie, R. 241
Dispensaries—
  Established in Saskatchewan.. 437
  Voted out in Saskatchewan..441, *ff*
District of Columbia........505, 511
Dodds, E. King................ 96
Doherty Bill 483
Dominion—
  Royal Commission of 1874...112, *ff*
  Elections of 1891............ 157
  Election Campaign of 1896..237, *ff*
Dominion Alliance—
  Attitude to Third Party Movement 141
  Council of 72, 481
  Declaration of Principles. 72
  Formed 115
  Legislative Committee, 1891.. 161
  Manitoba Branch opposes referendum 272
  New Brunswick 349
  Ontario Branch of 73
  Ontario Branch Department of Work 73
  Ontario Branch Manifesto, 1904 318
  Ontario Convention, 1902..... 286
  Ontario Plebiscite Campaign.197, *ff*
  Political Action 150
  Provincial Branches formed.. 118
  Quebec 354, 357
  Unites with Anti-Saloon League to call World Convention. 565
Dominion Order-in-Council—
  War-Time Prohibition 489
  Yukon Territory 478
Dominion Plebiscite ....229, *ff*
  Bill 247
  Campaign ....240, *ff*
  Campaign in B. C............ 246
  Campaign in Ontario......... 244

INDEX.

Dominion Plebiscite—*Con.*
  Ontario W.C.T.U. in......... 247
  Campaign, N.-W. Territories.. 246
  Campaign, Quebec 245
  Vote ....248, *ff*
Dominion Prohibition ....481, *ff*
  Conference, 1874 .. 110
  Government policy announced. 487
Dominion Prohibition Committee
  formed 485
  Manifesto 486
Dougall, John 42
Dougall, J. R.................. 155
Douglas, Rev. Dr., M.P......... 258
Dow, General Neal. 77, 91
Dunkin Act ....91, *ff*
  Campaign in Prince Edward
    County 95
  Provisions of ....92, *ff*
  Quebec 355
  Still in force in Ontario...... 100
  Votings in Ontario and Quebec 99
  Voted on in Toronto... 97
  Voted on in York County..... 97
Dunkin, Christopher . 92

Early closing, Ontario......... 399
  Quebec 367, 371
Eby, Rev. Dr.................. 246
Electoral action in Saskatchewan 436

Facts of the Case.............. 176
Faroe Islands 536
Field Day 73
Finland 544
Fisher, Hon. S. A..138, 154, 155, 233,
    241, 253
Flavelle, J. D................. 407
Flemmington, Rev. C.......... 349
Flint, Senator Bill............38, 39
Flint, Hon. T. B. 161, 165, 236, 254, 256
Florida 505, 511
Foster, Hon. Geo. E..135, *ff*, 151, 163,
    164, 252
Fortune, Rev. W. G. W......... 450
France 529
Franciscan Crusade ......357, 359, *ff*
Francolin, J. N................ 373
Fraser, Donald . 349, 350
French Monarchs, Edict of—
  1657 21
  1664 24
  1669 26
  1705 26

Frontenac opposed temperance
  work 26
Gales, Rev. Thos............... 117
Georgia 505, 511
German-American Alliance 508
German Bill 279
Germany 545
Gibbs, Malcolm 201
Gibson, Joseph 96
Gold, W. F.................... 455
Goodhue, Mr. 357
Gough, John B................ 501
Gothenburg System—
  Discussed in N. S 332
  Sweden 540
Gouin, Sir Lomer......363, 371, 373,
    374, 376
Government Control in Alberta...454
Grant, Rev. H. R...333, 334, 340, 341
Great Britain ....514, *ff*
  Carlisle experiment with state
    purchase 526
  Central Control Board (Liquor
    Traffic) 521
  Defence of the Realm (Amend-
    ment No. 3) Bill 520
  Prohibition plebiscite in. 524
  Strength of Britain movement 522
  War-time regulations 517
Greece 544
Greenland 535
Greenway, Hon. Thos.......261, 265
Greenwood, Mr. T. E........... 262

Halifax—
  Campaign for Prohibition Law 341
  Licenses in 330
  Made prohibition city........ 342
  Special License Law for...... 333
Hamilton Temperance Federation 391
Hanna, Hon. W. J..382, 386, 396, 487
Harcourt Bill ....222, *ff*
Harcourt, Hon. R.............. 226
Hardy, Premier 222, 227
Harkness, D. B................. 487
Haverson, Jas., K.C........224, 241
Hawaii 506
Hazen, Hon. J. D............. 346
Hearst, Hon. Wm..397, 401, 403, 405
Henry, Rev. E. A.............. 293
Hickson, Sir Joseph........166, 172
Holland 532
Hotel problem, Saskatchewan... 438
House of Commons Committee,
  1873 107

617

INDEX.

House of Commons, bar abolished 135
Howland, W. H.................. 152
Hudson Bay Co................ 263
Hull 372
Hundred Thousand Voters' Movement 255
Hunt, Mrs. Mary J............. 502
Huxtable, Rev. G. D........... 239

Iceland 535
Illinois 503
Independent Order of Good Templars, The 49, 51
India 549
Indiana 505, 511
Indians—
  Letter from 456
  Liquor first given to......... 19
  Peculiarly susceptible to liquor.19,20
  North-West 183, 189
  Ordinance of 1777 forbids sale of liquor to............. 28
International Congresses 495
International Co-operation 564
Interprovincial Conference 107
Iowa 503, 505, 511
Ireland 515, 528
Italy 548

Jamieson, Hon. J......137, 154, 155, 161-163
Japan 552
Jesuits, Temperance of........19-21
Johnston, Sir Harry........... 558
Jurisdiction—
  Decision concerning Ontario Local Option Law 212
  Difficulty, 1876 .. 119
  Manitoba Liquor Act submitted to the courts. 266
  Privy Council Decision, 1896.. 237
  Privy Council Decision on Manitoba Liquor Act.... 282
  Manitoba Liquor Law declared invalid by King's Bench.. 326
  P.E.I. Prohibition Act declared valid 327
  Provincial Privy Council decision 219
  Questions submitted by Ontario Government 206
  Question 190
  Severn vs. Queen............ 121
  Validity of C.T.A. established.125, *ff*

Kansas 503, 505, 511
Ketchum, Jesse—
  Donated site for Temperance Hall 56

Ketchum, Jesse—*Con.*
  Helped to found first Temperance Society in Toronto.. 43
Kettlewell, Rev. Wm........203, 288
Korea 553
Kribs, Louis P... 170, 171, 178

Labelling Bill, N.S.........330, 332
Ladies' Total Abstinence Society. 61
Lafontaine, Judge E...363, 366, 371, 378, 486
La Ligue Anti-Alcoolique, Quebec 363
Laurier, Sir Wilfrid....232, 239, 240, 242, 245, 250, 257
Lawson, Sir Wilfrid....... 515
Laval, Bishop, opposes liquor traffic 19, 21-23
Law and Order League, Montreal 152
Legislative Committee of Dominion Alliance, 1891....... 161
Lemieux, Sir François.......... 363
Liberal Convention, 1893......231, *ff*
Liberal platform, Quebec, 1919.. 373
License Commission in Ontario.397, *ff*
License Commissioners 383
License Law—
  British Columbia 464
  Lower Canada 28, 31
  New Brunswick 343
  Nova Scotia 329
  Ontario 100
  Quebec :.................... 355
  Manitoba 414
License Law Amendments—
  Alberta 450
  New Brunswick 344, 347
  Ontario ....382, 385, 391, *ff*, 398
  Quebec 363, 372
  Saskatchewan 428
Licenses in Montreal........... 354
License Reduction in Ontario... 390
License system first established under British rule....... 27
Liquor licenses in Manitoba..... 420
Lloyd George, Hon. David...... 519
Lloyd, Principal 430, 455, 466
Local Option—
  Advocated by F. S. Spence after the Ontario Plebiscite 212
  Campaigns, Alberta 452
  League formed in Alberta.... 460
  Law of Ontario appealed to the Courts 212
  Law in Ontario 212

INDEX.

Local Option—*Con.*
  Manitoba   262, 412, *ff*, 423
  Ontario .   384, *ff*, 388, 389
    Three-Fifths Clause 385
  St. John, N.B............... 348
  Saskatchewan .... 427, 428, *ff*
  United States 504
Lower Canada—
  License Law of............ 28, 31
  Organization of Temperance Societies in 40, 42
Louis XIV refers prohibition question to the Sorbonne.. 23

Macdonald Act in Prince Edward Island 326
Macdonald Bill 425
Macdonald, Hon. Hugh J. 262, 263, 266
Macdonald, Sir John A......... 107
MacKenzie, Hon. Alexander. 117, 123
Mackenzie, William Lyon, on the first temperance society in Toronto 43
Maclaren, J. J., Q.C.... 119, 209, 213
McBride, Sir Richard... 461, 466, 468
McCarthy Act .... 135, *ff*, 190
McClung, Mrs. Nellie...... 422, 466
McGregor Bill, N.S............ 336
McKay, Rev. Dr. W. A...... 280, 282
McKinney, Mrs. L. C...... 456, 458
McLennan, J. K................ 272
McLeod, Rev. Dr. Joseph... 166, 170, 176, 177
Maine   .77, 503, 505, 511
  Law secured 501
Maine Law agitation, United Canada   ....85, *ff*
Malcolm, S. J. H... 415
Manitoba ....408, *ff*
  Branch of the Dominion Alliance opposes referendum. 272
  Club license question......... 416
  Elections of 1914............ 422
  Elections of 1915............ 424
  Liberal platform 409, 419
  Liquor Act, Privy Council decision on 282
  Liquor Act submitted to courts 266
  Liquor License Law........ 412, *ff*
  Liquor license in...... 420
  Local Option 262
  Local Option campaign in.. 412, *ff*, 423
  Moral and Social Reform Council .... 411, 412, 414, *ff*

Manitoba—*Con.*
  Plebiscite .... 190, *ff*
  Prohibitory League 191
  Prohibition Party in......... 146
  Prohibition Act Referendum in 1916 426
  Referendum ....261, *ff*
  Referendum Bill passed...... 271
  Referendum Campaign ..... 268, *ff*
  Referendum vote .... 274, *ff*
  Royal Commission 417
  Royal Templars of Temperance in 412
  Women enfranchised 69
Manners-Sutton 80
Maps, Wet and Dry......... 447, 448
Marcil, Hon. C. H............. 482
Maritime Provinces W.C.T.U. organized 63
Marter Bill .... 199, *ff*
Marter, George F.. 199, 202, 227, 291, 296, 305
Martin, Premier 443
Maryland 504
Massachusetts 501
Matthew, Father 528
Mathieu, Bishop 430
Meredith, Hon. W. K.......... 205
Methodist Church, General Conference 156, 281
Mézy, Governor 23
Mexico 512
Michigan 501, 503, 505, 511
Mills, Mr. Alexander........... 300
Minnesota 501
Missouri 503
Mississippi 505, 511
Mitchell, Hon. Walker......... 374
Moderate drinking first step in temperance reform 37
Montana 505, 511
Montreal Convention—
  1875 115
  1888 150
Montreal—
  Early closing by-law in....... 364
  Law Enforcement Campaign.. 366
  Law and Order League....... 152
  Licenses in 354
  Temperance Society .. 38, 40, 41, 44, 45, 107
Moore, Rev. Dr. T. Albert...... 478
Moral and Social Reform Council, Manitoba ....411, 414, *ff*

619

INDEX.

Moral and Social Reform Council, New Brunswick..... 346
Morley, A. I................... 459
Mormons 446
Mowat, Sir Oliver..203, 205, 215, 240
Mulock, W. R., Q.C........191, 277
Murray, Hon. G. H.336, 338, 339, 342

Nebraska . 501, 503, 505, 511
Nelson, John 466
Nevada 506, 511
New Brunswick ....343, ff
  C.T.A. in 343
  C.T.A. repealed in.......... 352
  Dominion Alliance 349
  License Law amended...344, 347
  Liquor License Law........ 343
  Moral and Social R'f'm C'n'l 347
  Passes prohibition ....77, ff
  Plebiscite 192
  Pledge-signing movement ... 77
  Prohibition Act 349
  Royal Commission in.....77, 345
  Repeal Prohibition Law..... 79
  Sons of Temperance in...343, 344
  Temperance Act 351
  Temperance Federation in.. 346
  Temperance and Prohibitory League 107
Newfoundland ....496, ff
New Hampshire ..501, 503, 505, 511
New Jersey 510
New Mexico . 503, 505, 511
Newnham, Bishop 435
New Party, Canada's....141, ff, 153
New South Wales............ 559
New York 501
New Zealand 562
Norris, T. C. 417, 419, 422, 424
North Carolina 503, 505, 511
North Dakota 505, 511, 503
North-West Experiment in Prohibition Law ....183, ff
North-West Territories—
  Campaign for Prohibition .. 188
  License System Introduced.. 189
  Dom. Plebiscite Territories.. 246
Norway—
  Norwegian System 536
Nova Scotia ....329, ff
  Assessment Act Amended... 332
  C.T.A. Repealed 341
  Conservative Platform, 1905. 335
  Convention, 1905 333
  Early History .. 82

Nova Scotia—*Con.*
  Early Prohibition Agitation. 83
  Labelling Bill 330, 332
  Legislature Aids Temperance Lectures 83
  Legislature, Petitioned for Prohibition in 1835 40
  Liberal Platform, 1905...... 335
  License Law 329
  McGregor Bill 336
  Organization of Temperance Societies in 40
  Pearson's Bill 332
  Plebiscite ....216, ff
  Picton Co. Temperance Association 334
  Prohibition Bill of 1856 Rejected 85
  Prohibition Convention, 1902 330
  Prohibition Party 148
  Sons of Temperance........ 82
  Temperance Act ....339, ff
  Temperance Alliance 334

Ohio 503, 506, 511
  Woman's Crusade 502
Oklahoma 505, 511
Ontario Branch of the Dominion Alliance. *See* Dominion Alliance, Ontario Branch.
Ontario Temperance Act ....400, ff
Ontario Temperance and Prohibitory League 105
Oregon 503, 505, 511
Owen Sound, First W.C.T.U. in Canada 60
Ontario .... .381, ff
  C.T.A. Campaign .131, ff
  Conservative Platform, 1911. 395
  License Commission 397
  Dominion Plebiscite Campaign 244
  Dunkin Act, Votings on..... 99
  Early Closing 399
  Election Campaign, 1904.... 313
  Liberal Convention, 1904.... 314
  Liberal Platform, 1911...... 394
  Liquor License Act, Amended 398
  License Commissioners 383
  License Law 100
  License Law Amended...382, 385
  License Law Amendments.. 391
  License Reduction in 390
  Local Option Law.......... 212

INDEX.

Ontario—*Con.*
  Local Option Law—Decision
    of Privy Council 219
  Local Option Campaign...384, *ff*
  Plebiscite ....193, *ff*
    Bill 199, 206
    Campaign of Dominion Alliance ....197, *ff*
    Campaign ....207, *ff*
    Results, Appendix No. 7... 211
    Provincial Elections, 1905... 320
    Referendum ....278, *ff*
    Referendum Bill ......284, *ff*, 290
    Referendum Campaign.....292, *ff*
    Referendum Vote 299
    W.C.T.U. in Referendum Campaign 290
  Three-Fifths Clause ......385, *ff*

Palmer, Mitchell 508
Parmelee 257
Parsons, J. F. L. 171
Patrick, Rev. Principal 273
Pearson's Bill, N.S. 332
Pennsylvania 503
Persia 554
Petitioning Campaign, 1891.... 157
Petitions for Ontario Plebiscite 199
People's Prohibition Movement, B.C. 467
Philippine Islands 554
Picton County Temperance Association 334
Pioneer, The 73, 297, 410
Pledge Signing Movement in N.B. 77
Plebiscite, Dominion ....229, *ff*
  Dominion Bill 247
  Dominion Campaign ......240, *ff*
  Dominion Vote ....248, *ff*
  Provincial ....180, *ff*
  Manitoba ....190, *ff*
  New Brunswick 192
  Nova Scotia ....216, *ff*
  Ontario ....193, *ff*
  Ontario Bill Passed 206
  Ontario, Results 211
  Prince Edward Island.... 192
  Saskatchewan, 1914 432
  Local Option, B.C. 464
Political Action Policy, Dominion Alliance 150
Porto Rico 506
Portugal 530
Potts, Rev. D. 215

Presbyterian Church, General Assembly 157
Prince Edward Co., Dunkin Act Campaign in ... 95
Prince Edward Island ......323, *ff*
  Alliance 325
  Canada Temperance Act Repealed 329
  Law Violation ... 130
  Liquor Regulation Act 323
  Plebiscite 192
Prince Edward Prohibition Act 326
  Prohibition Act Amended... 328
  Prohibition Act Declared Valid 327
Prince Edward Island Prohibition Law 264
Prince Edward Island Tax Act 324
Privy Council Decision—
  Upon McCarthy Act 190
  Upon Canada Temperance Act 190
  On Provincial Jurisdiction.. 219
  Of 1896 237
Prohibition Act, Alberta.....454, *ff*
  Manitoba Referendum on... 426
  New Brunswick ....349, *ff*
  Quebec ....371, *ff*
Prohibition Becomes Law in Saskatchewan 442
Prohibition Law, in B.C. 470
Prohibition Law Amended, Alberta 458
Prohibitory Legislation Announced in Saskatchewan... 457
Prohibition Vote in Alberta... 457
Prohibition Party, Nova Scotia 148
  In United States . 502
Prohibition Resolution, 1875.. 114
Prohibitory League, Manitoba. 191
Proudfoot, Wm. 393, 396
Provincial Action ....259, *ff*
Provincial Plebiscite Period. 180, *ff*

Quebec ....353, *ff*
  Anti-Alcoholic League 363
  Canada Temperance Act in.. 370
  Committee of Moderation....381
  Dominion Alliance 354, 357
  Dominion Plebiscite Campaign 245
  Dunkin Act in 355
  Dunkin Act, Votings in 99
  Early Closing Bill 367
  Early Closing Law 371

INDEX.

Quebec—*Con.*
License Law in 355
License Law Amendments.. 363
License Law Amendments.. 372
Prohibition Act .... 371, *ff*
R.C. Church in 353, 354, 357
R.C. Total Abstinence 364
Revenue Act of 1774......... 27
Roman Catholic Church..... 357
Royal Commission 368
Temperance and Prohibitory League 107
Quebec W.C.T.U. Organized. 65
Quebec City, Votes on C.T.A... 373

Raney, W. E., K.C. ...., ... 391
Rechabites, Independent Order of 501
Referendum, Manitoba ...... 261, *ff*
Manitoba Campaign ...... 268, *ff*
Manitoba Bill Passed....... 271
Referendum, Manitoba Vote 274, *ff*
Referendum Method, Discussed by Sir John Bourinot... 284
Referendum, Ontario ..:.... 278, *ff*
Referendum, Ont. Bill 284, *ff*, 290
Referendum Campaign, Ontario .... 292, *ff*
Referendum, Ontario Vote.. 299
Rhode Island 501, 503, 510
Roblin, Rodmond P...266, 269, 271, 413, 414, 420, 422
Roblin-Rogers Riffyrandum.... 276
Roberts, John H. 367, 368
Rochemontaix, Perede........ 19, 20
Rogers, Hon. Robert 266, 276
Rogers, Jonathan 467
Roman Catholic Church in Quebec ... 353, 354, 357
Roman Catholic Total Abstinence Union 364
Ross, Hon. G. W. ..111, 114, 204, *ff*, 216, 278, 284, 301, *ff*, 312, 318
Roumania 545
Rowell, Hon. N. W. ...317, 394, 396, 398, 404, 406, 441, 455
Royal Commission, for Dominion, 1874 .... 107, 112, *ff*
Of 1892...159, *ff*, 175, 176, 177, 183, 187, 189
Royal Commission Appointed, B.C. 462
Royal Commission, Manitoba.. 417
Royal Commission, New Brunswick 77, 345

Royal Commission in Quebec. 368
Royal Commission, Saskatchewan .. ..439, *ff*
Royal Templars of Temperance, The 54, 56, 193
Royal Templars of Temperance, Manitoba...263, 271, 412
Royal Templars of Temperance, Organized in United States 502
Rush, Dr. Benjamin.......... 500
Russia 542
Rutherford, Mrs. A. O......... 281
Rutherford, Hon. H. C. 447

St. John, N.B., Disturbances in 79
Local Option Campaign in... 348
Salvation Army 209
Saskatchewan .... 427, *ff*
Dispensary Established 437
Dispensaries Voted Out....441, *ff*
Electoral Action 436
Hotel Problem 438
License Law Amendments... 428
Local Option Granted 427
Local Option Contests ....428, *ff*
Plebiscite, 1914 432
Prohibition Convention of 1913 430
Prohibitory Legislation Announced 437
Prohibition Becomes Law... 442
Royal Commission .439, *ff*
W.C.T.U. Organized 63
Woman Suffrage 70
Schools, Temperance Teaching in U.S., in.............. 502
Scotland, Temperance Act..... 526
Sunday Closing Act 514
Temperance Organization 527, 528
Scott Act, see Canada Temperance Act
Scott, Premier 430, 431, 437
Searchlight, The 452
Serbia 544
Sillery, First Temperance Meeting at 20
Shearer, Rev. J. G. 410
Sifton, Hon. A. L. 455
Sifton, Hon. Clifford 262
Siam 554
Siberia 554
Soldiers' Vote, B.C. 472

INDEX.

Sons of Temperance, The.... 46, 48
  In New Brunswick 343, 344
  In Nova Scotia 82, 216
  Organized in U.S. 501
South America 513
South Australia 560
South Carolina 505, 511
South Dakota 503, 505, 511
Spain 530
Sparling, Rev. Dr. 273
Spence, Ben H   74, 276, 455
Spence, F. S., Advocates Local
  Option 212
  Connection with Royal Commission, 1892 .   170
  Dominion Prohibition Resolution   484
  Interviews Premier Ross.... 280
  Municipal Career .. 5, 6, 11, 14, 78
  Official Positions in Temperance Work 12, 14
  Political Principles 9
  Published Facts of the Case. 176
  Resolution at Dominion Liberal Convention ..   232
  Trip to North-West Territories 187
  Work in Dunkin Act Campaign 96
Spence, F. S., Quoted on—
  Advanced Prohibitionists ... 196
  Election Campaigning 7
  Compromising 6
  Liberal Convention 235
  License Reduction 6
  Local Option 213
  Marter Bill 200
  Measuring Progress 10, 11
  Ontario Liberal Party Platform 315
  Ontario Referendum 301
  Plebiscite 195, 201, 203
  Procrastination 10
  Regulation of Evils 18
  Revenue Question 241
  Ross Letter 312
  Royal Commission 172
  Temperance Movement and Prohibitory Legislation. 45
  Third Party Movement. 145, 146, 155
  Value of Conservation...... 9, 10
  Value of Educational Work in Temperance 36
  W.C.T.U. 71

Spence, Mr. Jacob   573
Spencer, Rev. Dr. D. 461
State Purchase, in Britain.... 526
Stevens-Marcil Resolution..... 482
Stevens, H. H. 482
Stavert, Rev. R. H. 345
Stewart, W. J. 443
Stipendiaries Act, N.S.   See Assessment Act
Supreme Court Decision on Provincial Jurisdiction.. 190
Sutherland, Dr. Alexander.. 142, 143, 153
Switzerland 547
Sweden 538
  Gothenburg System 540

Talon, Intendant 24, 25
Tanner, C. E.   335, 336, 337
Tasmania 561
Temperance Act, Ontario...... 399
  New Brunswick 351
  Nova Scotia .... 339, ff
Temperance Alliance, N.S. 334
Temperance Federation in New Brunswick 346
Temperance Legislation League 277, 293, 297, 301
Temperance & Moral Reform Committee, Alberta.... 448, ff
Tennessee .   503, 505, 511
Texas 503, 505, 511
Third Party Movement. See Canada's New Party and Nova Scotia Prohibition Party.
Thornley, Mrs. May. R. ..70, 215
Tilley, Sir Leonard   77, 78, 80
Total Abstinence, Early Opposition to 37, 38
  Adopted by Montreal Temperance Society .   41
  First Society in Upper Canada 44
  Toronto, First Temperance Society in 43
  Temperance Reformation Society 56, 58
  District W.C.T.U. organized. 62
  Headquarters 62, 63
  Young Men's Pro'b't'n Club 58, 59
Trueman, G. J. 377
Turkey 545

INDEX.

Union Committee—
  Ontario Plebiscite Campaign 207
  Report of Plebiscite Campaign 214
United Canada—
  First Temp. Measure Introduced 86
  License Laws of 31, 33
  Maine Law Agitation in.... 85, ff
United Canadian Alliance . 91
  Organized at Montreal; Merged in the O.T.P.L.. 106
United Kingdom Alliance. 515, 516
United States of America.... 499, ff
  Anti-Saloon League 504
  Anti-Saloon League's Investigation of Overseas Conditions 509
  Army Bill 507
  Committee of Fifty 504
  Constitutional Amendment, Honor Roll 511
  Constitutional Prohibition in 502, 505
  Early Legislation .. 499
  Effect of Civil War on Temperance Movement 501
  German-American Alliance.. 508
  High License in ... 503
  Independent Order of Rechabites Organized in 501
  Local Option in 504
  Liquor Advertisements Forbidden in Prohibition Areas. 506
  Prohibition Party in 502
  Prohibition Amendment to Federal Constitution— Text of 510
  Progress in War Years.... 506, ff
  Royal Templars of Temperance Organized in 502
  Sons of Temperance Organized in 501
  Statutory Prohibition 505
  Temperance Teaching in Schools 502
  United Committee on War Activities 507
  War-time Prohibition Bill.. 508
  W.C.T.U. Formed in .. 502
  See also Maine, Massachusetts, New York, Ohio, etc.
Upper Canada—
  Organization of Temperance Societies in 43

Upper Canada—*Con*.
  License Laws of 31
Utah 506, 511
Vandervelde, Dr. Emil 531
Vermont 501
Victoria 560
Vidal, Hon. Alex.... 92, 115, 120, 123, 134, 154, 163, 201
Virginia 505, 511
Vodka, Prohibited 543
Voters' Leagues 308
Warburton, G. A. 400, 485
War-time Prohibition for Canada 487
  Campaign to Make Permanent 490
Washington 503, 505, 511
West Australia 562
West Virginia 505, 511
Wet Canteen, Removed From Camps 70
Whitney, Hon. J. P... 228, 290, 310, 317, 382, 395
Wilson, Rev. W. D. 350, 353
Wisconsin 501
Woman's Christian Temperance Union
  Dominion Union Organized. 64
  Dominion Plebiscite Campaign in Ontario.....244, 247
  Franchise Dept. Organized.. 69
  On Ontario Plebiscite 201
  Principles of 64, 65
  Pledge of 65
  Departments of 65, 66
  Scientific Temperance 66, 68
  Woman's Franchise 68
  Formed in U.S. 502
  Ontario in Referendum Campaign 290, 292
  War Work 70, 71
Woman Suffrage 69, 70
  British Columbia 70
  Alberta 70
  Saskatchewan 70
World Progress ....493, ff
Wyoming 505, 511
Yukon Territory ....475, ff
  Order-in-Council for 478
York County Dunkin Act Advocate 97
  Dunkin Act Voted on 97
Youmans, Mrs. Letitia....62, 64, 95

CPSIA information can be obtained
at www.ICGtesting.com
Printed in the USA
LVHW01s1444180318
570245LV00023B/575/P